Cultures of Scholarship

Cultures of Scholarship

S. C. HUMPHREYS, EDITOR

Ann Arbor

THE UNIVERSITY OF MICHIGAN PRESS

2000   1999   1998   1997   4   3   2   1

A CIP catalog record for this book is available from the British Library.

Library of Congress Cataloging-in-Publication Data

Cultures of scholarship / S.C. Humphreys, editor.
        p.   cm. — (The comparative studies in society and history
   book series)
      Includes bibliographical references and index.
      ISBN 0-472-09654-0 (hardcover). — ISBN 0-472-06654-4 (pbk.)
      1. Ethnology.   2. Culture.   3. Learning and scholarship—Social
   aspects.   4. Intellectual life—Social aspects.   I. Humphreys, S.
   C. (Sarah C.)   II. Series.
   GN357.C87   1997
   306—dc21   97-9816
                                                                   CIP

Contents

Foreword

For nearly forty years the quarterly issues of *Comparative Studies in Society and History* have published articles about human society in any time or place written by scholars in any discipline and from any country. Those articles, inevitably reflecting the changing methods and interests within the specialized fields of research from which they grew, have presented new evidence and new techniques, challenged established assumptions, and raised fresh questions. Now this series of books extends and refocuses the comparisons begun in some of the most stimulating of those essays.

The editors of each volume identify a field of comparative study and then determine which essays from among all the articles that have appeared in *CSSH* best exemplify the range and excitement of their topic. In making their selection they consider everything published from the first issue of *CSSH* in October 1958 to the present (including scores of new manuscripts currently under consideration). The book thus builds on a group of articles that are part of a continuing dialogue among scholars formed in different disciplines, traditions, and generations. To this core, the editors add essays never before published, essays they have commissioned in order to round out the book and illustrate more fully the potential range of their topic and the new directions it is taking. The authors of the published articles are given the opportunity to revise their essays in the light of this project, and each volume is therefore a new work in the specific sense that its chapters are abreast of current scholarship but also in its broader purpose, a cooperative enterprise reconsidering (and thereby reconstructing) a common topic.

Having established the theme to be addressed and identified the scholars to do it, the editors then invite these colleagues to join in exploring the ramifications of their common interest. In most instances this includes a conference in Ann Arbor, attended by contributors and by many other scholars, where issues of conceptualization, interpretation, and method can be debated. Sometimes the volume's topic is made the basis of a graduate course, with contributors giving a series of lectures in a seminar lasting a term or more and attended by a variety of interested specialists. Thus the books in this series, which in each case started from an indirect dialogue in the pages of *CSSH,* took form through direct exchanges. Individual manuscripts were criticized and new suggestions tried out through open-ended and lively discussions that identified common concerns and reflected on each particular study in light of different disciplines and the experience of different societies. Reshaped by the community it had created, each volume becomes a statement of where scholarship currently stands and of questions that need to be pursued. Through the process in which individual chapters are reconsidered and revised, general problems can be better identified and usefully reformulated.

In this way this series extends the tradition that *CSSH* represents. A scholarly quarterly is a peculiar kind of institution, its core permanently fixed in print, its rhythmic appearance in familiar covers an assurance of some central continuity, its contents influenced by its past yet pointing in new directions. *CSSH* seeks to create a community without formal boundaries, a community whose membership is only loosely determined by subject, space, or time. Just as footnotes and references embed each article in particular intellectual traditions while stretching beyond them, so the journal itself reaches beyond editors, contributors, and subscribers, speaking in whatever voice unknown readers respond to, whenever and wherever they turn its pages. The resulting dialogues are not limited to any single forum, and the journal itself changes from within while balancing between venturesomeness and rigor as old debates are refined and new problems posed.

The books in this series further in another form aspirations acknowledged in the opening editorial of the first issue of *CSSH,* in which Sylvia Thrupp declared her belief that "there is a definite set of problems common to the humanities, to history, and to the various social sciences." Changes in the way these problems are conceived and in the vocabulary for expressing them have not lessened the determination to reject "the false dilemma" between "error through insularity and probable superficiality." Insistence upon thorough, original research has been the principal defense against superficiality, emphasis upon comparison the means for overcoming insularity. Many of the articles published in *CSSH* are systematically comparative, across time and between societies, and that is always welcome; but many are not. Each published article was independently chosen for its qualities of scholarship and imagination as well as for its broader implications. For the contributors to and readers of that journal, comparison has come to mean more a way of thinking than the merely mechanical listing of parallels among separate cases. Articles designed to speak to scholars in many disciplines and to students of different societies are recognized as intrinsically comparative by the nature of the problems they pose, the structure of their argument, and the effect of their conclusions.

Every piece of research deserves to be seen in many contexts: the problems and concerns of a particular society, the immediately relevant scholarly literature with its own vocabulary and evidence, the methods and goals of a given discipline, a body of theory and hypotheses, and sets of questions (established, currently in vogue, or new). Nor can any prescription delimit in advance how far subsequent comparisons of similar problems in different contexts may reach. After its first decade, *CSSH* began placing articles within rubrics that call attention to a central comparative theme among adjacent essays. In addition an editorial foreword in each issue notes other sets of connections between current articles and earlier ones, inviting further comparisons of broad themes, specific topics, and particular problems or methods. A variety of potential discourses is thus identified, and that open-ended process has culminated in this series of books. Some of the volumes in the series are built around established themes of comparative study, subjects known to require comparison; some address topics not always recognized as a field of study, creating a new perspective through fresh questions. Each volume is thus an autonomous undertaking, a discussion with its own purposes and focus, the work of many authors and its editors' vision of the topic, establishing a field of knowledge, assessing its present state, and suggesting some future directions.

The goal, in the quarterly issues of *CSSH* and in these books, is to break out of received categories and to cross barriers of convention that, like the residual silt from streams that once flowed faster, have channeled inquiry into patterns convenient for familiar ideas, academic disciplines, and established specialties. Contemporary intellectual trends encourage, indeed demand, this rethinking and provide some powerful tools for accomplishing it. In fact such ambitious goals have become unnervingly fashionable, for it no longer requires original daring nor theoretical independence to attack the hegemony of paradigms— positivism, scientism, Orientalism, modernization, Marxism, behavioralism, and so forth—that once shaped the discourse of social science. Scholars, however, must hope that the effort to think anew can also allow some cumulative element in our understanding of how human societies work; and so these books begin their projects by recognizing and building upon the lasting qualities of solid scholarship.

The title of this volume expresses its theme, that scholarship is a special kind of culture—one that selectively but formally carries with it the culture from which it emerged and that does so explicitly in values proclaimed, implicitly in methods used. At the same time, scholarship is also a process for creating culture which, once created, it protectively wraps in a carapace of truth, certified by God or science. Postcolonial perception has made it easy to recognize how the culture of scholarship may serve other ends, but these essays carry the discussion further. Many show how the cultures studied, often vibrant and local, reciprocally reconstrue the culture of scholarship; and collectively they support Sally Humphreys' call for the cooperation of many disciplines in order to comprehend the intellectual process by which the assumptions and habits of one culture are used to construct the scholarly understanding of another.

Perhaps her experience as a scholar of ancient Greece made it easier for Professor Humphreys to recognize that the culture of scholarship was a topic needing investigation, one in which the meanings of text and tradition raise issues more general (and significantly subtler) than the relationship of knowledge and power within European imperialism. The essays she has selected employ anthropological sensibilities and ideas from literary studies to give history to traditional culture and culture to scholarship. These are studies of formal knowledge as living encounter that do not settle for facile relativism, for they are constructed in ways that respect the canons of argument and evidence associated with nineteenth-century European learning, even while exposing and challenging many of the assumptions on which it rested.

Taken together, these essays stimulate new questions by inviting comparisons that move back and forth between present and past, local and central, cultural encounters and cultures of knowledge. They probe the peculiarities of authority unattached to office and of discourse that is, more than anything else, about the possibility of discourse. They use theory to explore how in practice scholarship works. The first three articles explore examples of learning as the codification of culture. Stefan Tanaka demonstrates how childhood in Japan could be conceived as a metaphor of development that required a common ideology. Patrick Wolfe tracks the anthropology of selective appropriation that categorized Austrialian aborigines as children, and Uli Linke reveals that systematic collection of folklore and statistics in Germany was part of the process of state making.

Constructing identity and strengthening the state are, in fact, recurrent motifs throughout the volume. That does not mean that knowledge is always subservient to power, as the next several essays illustrate by revealing how frameworks of knowledge adapt to and co-opt change. In the erudition of south China's chrysanthemum festivals, Helen Siu finds the astute application of genealogy, economics, and tradition on behalf of local interests; and Nancy Florida underscores the durable creativity of Islamic religious culture in Java despite a high culture that refused to see it. Even a kind of mistranslation can institutionalize social change, as in India, where Lloyd and Susanne Rudolph identify the difficulty the British had in recognizing a legal system that rested on oral tradition, with the resulting irony that the codes they then created were neither native nor English but new.

Such forms of knowledge could, then, have effects like Orientalism; but they were rooted in a textual tradition as well as the ambitions of imperial power. Anthony Grafton reminds us of that in his essay on humanist scholarship, which built on classical and Islamic learning to define a sense of history that distanced both. The familiar theme of cultural encounters (and European misperception of the other) takes on new complexity and significance when considered in terms of the culture of scholarship. That very concept, Sabine MacCormack adds, is a modern one that in the sixteenth century would not have been fully comprehensible. Then, Spaniards' sense of erudition led learned men to see the Inca as Romans, in the process overriding their own good intentions and calls for tolerance. Grammar and culture-bound conceptions of the book could have a similar effect, and Walter Mignolo's sensitive account exposes the destructiveness of that inadvertent imperialism.

The problematic relationship of knowledge and authority leads naturally back to questions raised by the opening essay about how knowledge is legitimated and passed on from generation to generation. F. Niyi Akinnaso inquires into the differences between literate and nonliterate societies in this regard, establishing similarities that invite a fresh look at the very idea of schooling; and that in effect is what Brinkley Messick provides in writing on Islamic learning in modern Yemen.

Every chapter of this book intersects with all the others, for each relates formal learning and those who sustain it to the society that produces it and gives scholars a distinctive status. By examining the culture codified in the texts that scholars honor and create, each invites some rethinking of the connections between culture and identity, religion, and the state. These essays help to explain the transcultural seriousness of the holders of knowledge who in every society are simultaneously the embodiment of tradition and agents of change. Self-reflexiveness is now in fashion, but the authors of the essays in this book had larger reasons to see scholarship about the cultures of scholarship as a way to better understand society and history.

Raymond Grew

Acknowledgments

My first debt is to Raymond Grew, who enthusiastically accepted the idea of a conference on the comparative study of scholarly cultures and has done much to help me put both conference and book together. I was also immensely helped in organizing the conference, held in March 1995, by Setrak Manoukian and Anne Waters, both students of the University of Michigan Ph.D. program in History and Anthropology. I owe to Setrak also my knowledge of a book no scholar in any culture should be without, Gaetano Volpi's *Del furore d'aver libri* (1756), an encyclopedic guide for bibliophiles running from *A* for *Acqua* ("see Rain") to *U* for *Unguenti,* equally damaging.

Five of the papers in this volume were originally published in *CSSH:* Uli Linke, Walter Mignolo, Helen Siu, and Patrick Wolfe have all made changes and additions for this publication. Lloyd and Susanne Rudolph's paper "Barristers and Brahmans" (*CSSH* 1965) was circulated to conference participants; we publish here their thoughts on the topic after thirty years. The other papers here are new: those by Tony Grafton and Brinkley Messick have been substantially revised since the conference.

I am grateful to all the contributors for their remarks at the conference as well as their papers; also to Bruce Mannheim, Rudolf Mrázek, and David W. Cohen, who kindly agreed to act as discussants at the conference. We all learned from their comments, and none of us is likely to forget Mrázek's description of the employment of foreign scholars considered unfit to teach, in communist Prague, in the depot to which newspapers were brought for recycling, where they held their own seminars amid growing piles of never-recycled historical documentation.

Comparative Studies in Society and History has graciously given permission to reproduce the following articles in this volume (in some cases under new titles):

F. Niyi Akinnaso, "Schooling, Language, and Knowledge in Literate and Nonliterate Societies," *CSSH* 34 (1992): 68–109.

Uli Linke, "Folklore, Anthropology, and the Government of Social Life," *CSSH* 32 (1990): 117–48.

Walter Mignolo, "On the Colonization of Amerindian Languages and Memories: Renaissance Theories of Writing and the Discontinuity of the Classical Tradition," *CSSH* 34 (1992): 301–30.

Helen F. Siu, "Recycling Tradition: Culture, History, and Political Economy in the Chrysanthemum Festivals of South China," *CSSH* 32 (1990): 765–94.

Patrick Wolfe, "Should the Subaltern Dream? 'Australian Aborigines' and the Problem of Ethnographic Ventriloquism," *CSSH* 33 (1991): 197–224.

Introduction:
Let's Hear It for the Magpies

S. C. Humphreys

Our concern with the cultural dimensions of scholarship in this volume has two principal foci. One is the role of cultural presuppositions and frameworks in making sense of the accumulation and transmission of information and theory. What appears from within a culture or discipline as purposeful, beaver-like, scholarly activity may well from the outside look like the random accumulation of a miscellany of useful and useless data by magpies.[1] The West has too often regarded not only the scholars of other cultures but also those of its own premodern past as magpies. In this volume we try to go beyond merely pointing out the blind spots in modernism to probe deeper into the ambiguities in its rejection of traditional knowledge and scholarly traditions, and analyse the problems that scholars all around the world now face as a result.

Our second focus is on cultural variations in scholarship—loosely defined as the production and transmission of culturally valued, specialized knowledge—as a practice. How does one become a learned person? Where scholars learn partly from books, how are oral instruction and book-learning combined and what relations between writer and reader are imagined or institutionalized? In what practices do scholars demonstrate their expertise? What communities, actual and imagined, do they serve, and how is this service manifested? What are the sources of their authority? What images of the permanence, certainty, fixity, or progress of knowledge obscure the processes of drift, elaboration, reinterpretation, and modification through which scholarship is adapted to changing interests and circumstances?

As a classical scholar, I work in a tradition in which the contradictory gestures of rebellion against tradition and the canonization of "classic" texts have been prominent almost from the start. By the sixth century presocratic philosophers were starting to reject traditional myths and conceptions about the gods,[2] while the Athenians were (allegedly) standardizing the text of Homer recited by rhapsodes at their new Panathenaic festival.

Rationalism and classicism are not diametrically opposed. Though the one denies value to earlier thought and the other canonizes it, both draw a line between past and present. The processes of commentary and interpretation deployed around the boundaries of canonized texts were also used to revalue myth, poetry, ritual, and representations of the gods, through historicizing rationalization of legends and rituals, allegorical interpretations of poetry and symbols, and the development of discourses of literary criticism and art history. Moreover, the line between the past and present did not, before the modern period, inhibit thinkers from taking up and developing ideas that they found in ancient texts.

The modern period's interpretation of the classical tradition in terms of evolution from mythical to rational thought and subsequent decline after the fourth century B.C. into decadence (with various exceptions recognized according to the interpreter's interests) has a peculiar and very limiting perspective. It dogmatically excludes theology, and with it the development of Plato's thought from the Hellenistic period to late antiquity and beyond. It operates with a sharp dichotomy between art and positive knowledge which rides roughshod over the complex dialogues between poets and prose writers that began when prose genres emerged, and remained as a constitutive feature of a genre-based writing practice.[3]

It may be interesting here to push further the comparison between theologians and humanists sketched in Grafton's paper in this volume. Both reified their texts, made a sharp distinction between texts inherited from the past and their own interpretive practices. Theologians had a more extreme respect for the integrity of their sacred text, but were also free to develop their own interpretive speculations over a broad though not unlimited range of possible positions. Humanists felt free to emend texts but tended to represent much of their own interpretive practice as merely exegetic and ancillary. Or at least this is how their practice has come to be interpreted. But we need more critical studies of domain variation, both in terms of the forms in which additions and comments were attached to texts[4] and in terms of oral practices in which text and interpretation were mingled: sermons, university lectures, legal argument.[5] Recent anthropological work has given us the impression of more living, permeable relations between text and interpretive community in Islam and Judaism than in the humanist or Christian traditions. To what extent is this an illusion based on lack of research?

For a more differentiated assessment of the assumptions with which western scholars, administrators, and missionaries confronted the scholars and texts of other cultures, it is important to develop a clearer idea of the history of scholarly practices in the west. In this volume three papers address this problem by looking at intercultural encounters in the early modern period. Grafton studies humanists' relations with Jewish rabbis and a Syrian patriarch, while MacCormack and Mignolo analyse European encounters with the scholars and texts of Mexico and Peru. I shall return to these papers. For the moment I will only stress the repeated insistence of all contributors on the importance of problematizing assumptions that have a long history but hardened in the modern period: that "texts" have an existence independent of interpretive communities, and thus interpretation and commentary do not change texts; and that the function of texts is to provide (in varying combinations) information, aesthetic pleasure, or dogma.[6]

We start, in Stefan Tanaka's article, with a phenomenon that takes the separation of scholarship from everyday knowledge, and text from community, to its limit: the modern idea of the child as a blank slate on which schooling will inscribe the information and dogmas valued by the state. The idea of the writable, moldable child[7] is related to concepts of individual identity, of class, and of the opposition between progressive urban society and "backward" village (cf. Linke, this volume). The education process, through its stress on the child's success in passing through a series of tests and texts, is represented as a journey that takes him or her through the education process and "out" into national society as a citizen, rather than one that takes the apprentice from a peripheral position on the edge of a scholarly community toward its center. The segregated, quasi-monastic schooling that, Akinnaso argues here, characterizes the training of specialists in knowledge even where this training is entirely oral, becomes in the modern period the process by which every child is socialized. The child subjected to this process can then be seen as a natural being who has to be acculturated, and as that part of the self which escapes the roles and positions in which it is interpellated by society. Childhood becomes a focus of nostalgia, of desire for a lost harmony; the site of a "repressive authenticity" (Wolfe, this volume) which postulates a space of personal autonomy only to insist on its elimination.

The metaphor of childhood, in turn, becomes available for thinking about adult others who have not been socialized into modernity and are seen as *Naturvölker,* "nature-people". Patrick Wolfe's article brilliantly analyses the appeal to ethnologists and their imperial-colonial public of the term *Dreamtime* applied to the scholarship of the Koori.[8] In a gesture repeated over and over again by modernizers, handed-down knowledge and the authority of its specialists are bracketed off by association with values that turn them into museum objects, unchanging, beautiful, but irrelevant.[9] In the long run, it is perhaps the contagion of desire in this process that may have the most lasting effects, through the opposition set up between modernity and ethnic identity, which pretends that modernity is not a culture and that ethnic identity is "primordial" and not the result of historical processes.

More light is shed on the ambiguities of the modern opposition between modernity and "folk" knowledge by Uli Linke's comparison of the history of research on "folklore" in Germany, Britain, and China.[10] Like colonial regimes (Dirks 1993a, 1993b), governments at the beginning of the modern period wanted to survey their territory and reorganize production in order to increase revenues. Surveyors, administrators, and travelers had the sense that they were observing a vanishing world inhabited by living relics of the past, walking, talking fragments of a lost reality. Many of them had spent at least parts of their childhood in rural villages;[11] folklore represented the childishness of the peasant which had to be overcome, but also nostalgia for remembered beliefs and, increasingly, for a new complex of "traditional" rituals and literary genres to be shared by adults with children.

As in the Dreamtime case, the devaluation-through-revaluing of local knowledge now labeled "traditional" offered scholars some new opportunities and cultural niches, clustered around the role of "informant." Schoolmasters and antiquarians collected stories, texts, artefacts, and "customs"; they were Janus-headed, maintaining their role as local scholars while at the same time presenting themselves, often in print, as conforming to the scholarly standards of a wider audience.

The figure of the "antiquarian" is an interesting and problematic one;[12] the term is often loosely and derogatively used of provincial "magpies." At best antiquarians were seen, until recently, as precursors of the modern social-cultural historian and of the museum curator; they collected material that would be used by the former, and helped develop some of the connoisseur skills of the latter. Antiquarian history was considered to be sharply separated from political history, an example of the pursuit of scholarship for its own sake.[13]

Recent research has attacked this view. Though the local Indian histories collected and constructed by Brahmans that made their way into the Mackenzie archive were later dismissively characterized as "miscellaneous and embellished by mythological distortion" (Dirks 1989:46, cf. 1993a), they were part of a colonial sociology of knowledge, seeking to legitimate claims to rights and status, and categorizations of persons and communities, within new configurations of power. It is equally clear that in antiquity interest in relics of the past played an important role in cultural politics at all times and in all areas: it was not connected with a sense of collective identity only in the case of colonized nations or religious movements. Some of the earliest antiquarian travel books came from Hellenistic Troy, one of the most famous sites of pagan pilgrimage; accounts of picturesque rituals began with Callimachus' *Aitiai* ('origin-stories') in the third century B.C. Small communities made the most of attractions they had to offer the visitor; temples became home to an accumulation of relics, pickled monsters, and works of art. Local historians' accounts of past events, marvels, and customs were directed toward an external reading public, were attempts to put the local community on a regional or worldwide map.[14]

Helen Siu's and Nancy Florida's papers study local scholars engaged in the same dialogue with a wider world in China and Java. The beginning of the Javanese poem *Babad Jaka Tingkir,* recently translated and edited by Florida (1995), is exemplary:

2   It was Sunday when this writing of history began
     The twenty-second of Safar
     At the strike of eleven
     The reigning star was
     Jupiter at that time
     The year was Jimawal
     In Sancaya's eight-year term
     In the third month of the solar year
     On the sixteenth, in chronogram: "The Excellent sage
     Orders the Enormity of the world" [1757]

3   In the year of the Prophet's Hijrah
     Chronogrammed: "The Sage Magical
     Is reverenced by all the world" [1237]
     In the Dutch month of August
     On the twenty-third rendered
     In chronogram: "Ever Reverenced
     Is the Person of the King" [1829]

The author situates himself or herself in Javanese solar, Javanese lunar, Islamic, and colonial times, and reads each date as a chronogram.[15] Chronography, scholarship, and writing are all skills that allow the scholar to transcend limits of time and place.

Helen Siu's paper focuses especially on the way in which provincial leaders strive to attach themselves and their families to the central tradition of scholarship by composing family histories and organizing local festivals. Genealogy is a mapping device even more widely distributed in cultures of scholarship than chronography and calendar-making.

Siu's view of Confucianism from the periphery is fresh and carries an implied challenge to ask how far our stereotype of a center-dominated Confucian elite culture corresponded to local understandings. Levenson's classic study (1968) of the revisions of Confucianism in reaction to western influence and political change remains an important model for analysis of the transformation of a stratum of scholars into an intelligentsia, but it assumes a baseline in which Confucianism was the habitus of the literati, without asking how their culture was structured by social experience. Siu gives us a new view, focused on the ongoing construction through the system of examinations and offices of a centripetal system in which institutionalized career patterns shaped the desires and aspirations of provincial gentry. She shows that the Xiaolan chrysanthemum festival provided a stage both for the claims of landowning lineages to literati status and for the local ambitions of the town and its merchant and military leaders. The festival thus continued to serve as a resource for the ambitious despite changes in the local power distribution and in the structure of relations between periphery and center. However, tradition now has to be reinvented; ex-scholars educated in traditional arts of civilization such as the arrangement of floral displays are hard to find. The popular explanation of the collapse of the parade bleachers at the 1994 festival—that they had been erected on ground where infants and the dying had been abandoned during the war to die unburied—suggests that the grave of literati culture is an unquiet one.

The Chinese case is interesting from a comparative perspective because the construction of a classical canon and pressures toward cultural orthodoxy came from internal sources rather than colonialism.[16] But we lack serious comparative studies of canon-formation and traditionalism; current discussions of the invention of tradition rest on detailed local analyses that do not provide a general framework in which to locate and discuss the varying social sites to which inventions and revivals are attached.

Whereas Siu's paper deals with local scholars who identify with a wider system of cultural symbols while using them to enhance the reputation of their own town and province, Nancy Florida deals with the intersection of three scholarly cultures: those of Javanese court poets writing in an archaizing dialect according to traditional conventions of genre, of the Islamic study-centers from which they received much of their education, and of the Dutch colonial establishment's program of detaching ancient Javanese "classics" from the interpretive dialogue carried on with ancient stories and contemporary ideas by the Javanese scholars whom they used as informants.

There are clearly important parallels between the Javanese and Indian situations[17] in the colonial effort both to detach "classics" from the interpretive tradition that connected them with modern times and to separate Hinduism from Islam. Florida's study, however, together with her recent book (1995), give us an exceptionally detailed picture of local scholars at work. Florida's analyses are based on the experience of cataloguing three archives of Javanese scholarship in manuscript, from two palace libraries and one museum collection, and on her edition, translation, and commentary of *Babad Jaka Tingkir,* an unfinished poetic "prophetic history" of the sixteenth century written ca. 1829.

This poem has characteristics that I find also in local histories from the ancient world, which are presumably widely distributed in such works: genealogies, topography, and political relations are mapped onto each other;[18] local landmarks are prominent, both sites to which oral traditions are anchored (the "spring of the suicide maid," II.21)[19] and major monuments (the Grand Mosque of Demak); miraculous stories are "grounded" by touches of rationalization (in IV–VI, Jaka Prabankara is magically carried to China by a kite-balloon, but in VI.41–43 his knowledge of Chinese is rationally explained); local rituals are described (XVIII, XXXI.3–5); origins of texts are recounted (XXIV). It addresses the political situation of the author and his contemporaries implicitly, through a selective renarration of past history that has prophetic implications; the local historian writes with the "intention of touching his readers' presents and futures through commemorations of their pasts in writing."[20]

Postcolonial scholarship, Florida urges, needs to "interpret and decenter the fabulous project of universalizing history itself" (1995:394) by studying third world histories in their relation to cultural traditions and historical circumstances. This is, indeed, what it means to study cultures of scholarship. *Babad Jaka Tingkir* is not only a history; it is also a great poem (a delight to read in Florida's translation) which skillfully blends tradition, mysticism, and sophisticated linguistic play, and is accompanied by a rich commentary on its poetics, cultural presuppositions, and intertextual allusions. The commentary brings out the tension between center and margins in the poem. Although it ostensibly traces the genealogy of the first Islamic ruler in central Java, its main episodes almost all focus on marginal figures: the exiled painter Prabangkara, the transgressive invisible herd-boy Karèwèd, the mystics Siti Jenar, Malang Sumirang, and Ki Ageng Pengging. Even the story of the construction of the Grand Mosque of Demak is centered on the marginal: the miraculous production of a pillar made of discarded wood-chips by the maverick *wali* Sunan Kalijaga, who in his youth had been a highwayman, and the completion of the structure with a roof made by "everyone." The mosque also has an external reference; it can only be set in place by another miracle, which reveals the true orientation to Mecca.[21]

Florida's paper in the present volume explores two topics more briefly treated in her book: the political background of the reluctance of colonial scholars to recognize the role of Islam in Javanese thought and literature, and the role of the scholar as court poet, historian, prophetic thinker, and expert/informant to colonial philologists in Java in the eighteenth and nineteenth centuries. Both Florida's paper and that by Lloyd and Susanne Rudolph, which follows it, raise major questions for historians of western imperialism, especially on two fronts: the conceptions of text that colonial scholars brought to their work on early texts in oriental languages, and their conceptions of Islam. The two questions are connected, in ways that reveal fault-lines both within the "orientalism" complex and within the range of assumptions with which colonial scholars and administrators, educated in traditions that offered a variety of models for the use of texts as "authorities," approached the texts they encountered in the orient. Islam was still at the beginning of the nineteenth century the religion of an extensive empire; Europeans worked hard at persuading themselves of its weakness but were evidently aware that it could become a focus of anticolonial hopes.[22] The Koran and the legal and theological commentary by which it was accompanied could no more be treated merely as "dead" material for scholarly analysis than could the Bible—or Justinian's *Digest.* It is not a simple matter to draw the distinction between a philological approach that reifies texts and considers them all equally subject to critical emendation and a sacralizing attitude in which texts are protected from emendation but embedded in a coral-like growth of living commentary and interpretation.

Colonial scholars took with them, as they set out to study Sanskrit and *Kekawin* texts, a complex baggage of ideas about early poetic texts as repositories of cultural lore; sacred texts and their relations to religious law; legal and cultural evolution; and the oppositions between ritual, mysticism, and rationalism, as well as conceptions of the discipline of philology. We need some cooperation between historians of classical studies, Bible studies, law, and orientalist philology in studying these episodes. As the Rudolphs note in their paper, we not only need to deconstruct stereotypes of "the orient" but also to take a critical and more differentiated view of the colonizing cultures, one which uncovers peculiarities in our own assumptions and categories.

Florida's paper, in addition to sketching the "philological romance" in which a textual canon of High Javanese literature was constructed,[23] provides a detailed analysis of the ambiguous relations between the colonial power and the scholar-informants who personally represented this imaginary past culture, the court poets of the Kraton Surakarta. Dutch philologists ignored these poets' Islamic education, interests, and writings, and criticized their philological competence; the colonial authorities, on the other hand, arrested at least one member of the family on suspicion of treason and exiled him. The poem *Babad Jaka Tingkir* may also have been written in exile. Native scholars in colonized societies, although their authority was in theory, and within limits, respected, were operating under pressures specific to the colonial situation (cf. Dirks 1989).

Lloyd and Susanne Rudolph's article "Barristers and Brahmans in India: Legal Cultures and Social Change" (1965) was for me and, I suspect, many other readers a revelation in its analysis of the selectivity and blind spots of British "recognition" of Indian law,[24] its definition of the problem as an encounter of "legal cultures," and its sharp characterization of the "myths" of British legal thought. Since its publication, as the Rudolphs remark in the new paper published here, in which they "revisit" their 1965 article, there has been a massive explosion of postcolonial studies, given special impetus by Edward Said's *Orientalism* (1978).[25] Much remains to be done, however, both in deepening our understanding and critique of the cultural bases and dynamics of the orientalism complex and in studying the impact on Indian scholarly and intellectual culture of the new conceptions of textuality, the authority of legal texts, "Hindu religion," and the role of scholars, in dialogue with which Indian intellectuals had to negotiate their identity.

The Rudolphs' emphasis on diversity in the presuppositions and interests of colonial scholars, and on the gradualness of the process by which colonial stereotypes crystallized, parallels that of recent work by Nicholas Dirks (1989, 1993a). Dirks contrasts the catholic interest in historical texts and monuments of the survey officer Colin Mackenzie with later disregard of material that did not fit disciplinary categories; philologists and historians focused on "classic" texts rather than local histories produced by scholars in the eighteenth and nineteenth centuries.[26] The Rudolphs suggest that the idea that Hindus and Muslims each had their own law, legal texts, and legal experts led only gradually to a view of the population, history, and culture of India as divided into two basic categories defined by religion.[27] The neglect of materials like those collected by Mackenzie, and the growing colonial tendency to categorize Indian scholarship as irrational, have left a gap in Indian intellectual history. Western scholars were not interested in Indian editions, revisions, and commentary on Hindu legal texts (see now L. Rocher 1986) or in the Islamic legal tradition in India; studies of relations between barristers and brahmans still tend to tell us more about the former than the latter (R. Rocher 1993). It is difficult to form a detailed and concrete idea of the activities of Mackenzie's "learned Brahmans" or Warren Hastings' "maulvies and pundits," and of the continuities and dislocations that lie between their scholarship and that of the modern Indian intellectual elite—or rather elites. Anthropologists have been more attracted to kings than to brahmans (Dirks 1987; Appadurai 1981); contemporary Indian academic historians, although they are now beginning to study the construction of new images of Indianness, in dialogue with western categories and disciplinary models, by scholars such as Rabindranath and Abanindranath Tagore,[28] seem to imagine an absolute caesura between the local scholarship of the early colonial period and the modern Indian intellectual. There are certainly examples of very striking discontinuity.[29] On the other hand, there seem to be clear lines of continuity from the discourse of colonial religious controversy—defenses of Hinduism and Islam against Christian pressure to convert (Jones 1992)—through modern Hindu movements to nationalism. What seems noteworthy at present, in academic discourse, is the almost total lack of overlap, in terms both of study of Indian sources and citation of secondary literature in English, between postcolonial historical anthropology and sociocultural history, on the one hand, and postcolonial studies of religious history, theology, and philosophy on the other. Powerful undercurrents of rationalizing prejudice still seem to be exerting an influence here on historians and anthropologists.

Grafton's paper supplies some of the background to the history of concepts of culture and civilization called for by the Rudolphs, and to the history of western concepts of the text—the two sets of concepts intersecting at the point where a scholar steeped in knowledge of the culture from which "his" text comes focuses that knowledge on a problematic word, reading, or passage in order to emend or annotate it. How much difference is there between the western humanist's conception of a diffuse yet still text-based knowledge, produced in the form of references cited as "evidence," and the cultural knowledge of Jewish informants that impressed Scaliger?[30] How much did schooling techniques differ? Presumably the late Renaissance university—in which lecturers might well be engaged in reediting the texts they were teaching, and books were not easy to come by—was much closer to the traditional Islamic schools described by Eickelman (1985) and Messick (1993) than to the modern university.[31] The difference was surely one of perspective rather than techniques of transmission. Humanists, as Panofsky argued, taught classical texts as the products of a past world. As in single-point perspective, the viewer was definitely located outside the picture.

Grafton's paper shows, however, that a history of Renaissance humanism written—as has been the case until recently—from the point of view of the modern discipline of philology screens out two important facets of humanist thought. One—only hinted at by Grafton—is the role of Jewish-Christian polemics and disputations in introducing humanist ideas into discussions of the text and textual transmission of the Bible, both in Jewish and in Christian circles. The theological dispute begins to emerge as one of the oldest and longest-lived genres of cultural contact between scholars, one that would clearly repay further study both in European and in colonial settings.[32] Scaliger himself—the first classical scholar to form an idea of the colonial culture (as we may now call it) of Hellenistic Judaism—had engaged in such disputations as a young man when studying Hebrew. In sixteenth-century Italy they were a court diversion.[33]

The second aspect of humanist thought occluded by Whig histories of philology is its fascination with semiotic forms of occult wisdom—Egyptian hieroglyphs, gnostic pseudepigrapha,[34] and Cabala. Trained to be sensitive to nuances of language, humanists could understandably be drawn into the desire to deploy elaborate techniques of translation and decipherment in order to discover hidden meanings behind the surface of texts.[35] As Mignolo emphasizes here, there is much work to be done on the history and ethnohistories of writing.

Spanish missionaries and administrators thus traveled to the New World to encounter Inca and Mayan scholars and records with a mixed cultural baggage of ideas and expectations. The papers by Sabine MacCormack and Walter Mignolo deal with the results of this encounter. MacCormack shows the achievements and limitations of the Spanish attempt to understand the Inca empire by using Roman history as a model. As in Grafton's paper, the effect of studying culture contact (for us) is to highlight distinctions in European models that were taken for granted and contradictions that were displaced.[36] The Spanish used Roman roads, bridges, aqueducts, and laws; they read Roman history but also had a cultural model of their own, in a different form (verse); they had ambiguous feelings about the reliability of the early history of Livy and about the suppression by the Romans of native Iberian culture. Similarly, they intended to make use of the Inca infrastructure of communications and law, but relegated Inca history to the past and projected onto it some of the ambiguities of their own feelings about the distinction between the history of Livy's later books and the less reliable but still in some way valuable legends of early Rome and epics and ballads in which their own medieval history was celebrated. They failed to see, in studying Quechua texts, semiotic practices that were part of their own cultural habitus but were not the focus of conscious attention: the language of cloth and clothing, the subtle use of linguistic codes to create bonds with readers/hearers of the author's choice and exclude others, and the parallel transmission of (in the Inca case, lineage-owned) histories, which nevertheless entered into dialogue with each other through the use of shared images of achievement and good government. They brought across the Atlantic not only models of empire, government, and history derived from Europe but also theories of language and meaning and powerful categoric structures: the distinctions between present and past, writing and speech, the law of persons and the law of things, sexual intercourse and parenthood. We see them momentarily glimpsing the possibility of alternative structures, but we see this only because we ourselves are now seriously starting to imagine such alternatives.[37]

Walter Mignolo's article explores in more detail the difficulties Europeans faced in trying to understand Mexican *amoxtli* and *vuh* and Peruvian *quipus* as books. What was at issue was not merely a question of technology, as the Spanish perhaps tended to think, but different ways of thinking about the relation between signs and speech and about the framing and accessing of knowledge. Writing, in the western alphabetic tradition, has been defined as "a coded system of visible marks . . . whereby a writer could determine the exact words that the reader would generate from the text" (Diringer 1962:82). This definition contains problematic assumptions about authorial concern with form, about the possibility of gaps in time and space between writer and reader, and about the degree of shared culture required to decipher the marks and the practices through which this culture is acquired (specific or diffuse, oral or written). Even the concept of "word" is neither self-evident nor independent of grammatical structures and ethnolinguistic theories. The authority of a book may derive from its association with a named author, from being copied in a school recognized as a legitimate milieu for the transmission of valued texts and commentary on them,[38] from remaining in the possession of the man who compiled or commissioned it, or from rules of storage and access that stress its status as repository of the shared knowledge of a group.

Mignolo's story seems to suggest that European conceptions of writing and the book privileged the function of message-communication over those of mnemonic (storage of knowledge) and standard (inventory, model). The prominence in the sources of missionary texts, with their conception of holy writ as the message of god, and the importance in the early colonization period of communication with the Spanish authorities and a Spanish reading public may partly account for this bias, but it is also present in Greek sources.[39] Comparing the activities of Mexican and Peruvian scholars with those of European humanists, I am struck by the extreme individualism of the latter. Although they must all have passed through practices of collective schooling, their image of scholarly activity seems to pit the solitary reader against the text of which he has acquired possession (which he will understand or misunderstand, accept or emend, believe or disbelieve) and against the page on which he will shape his own message. The relation between scholar and text in humanist hero-tales is antagonistic: he corrects error, exposes forgeries.

One has to wonder, however, whether this individualistic interpretation is not influenced by later ideas. In fact the idea of the (modern) book was perhaps not so very clear-cut in humanist scholarship; humanists read texts cluttered with commentary from a variety of sources and quite often published their own ideas in loosely organized collections of *Adversaria* and *Variae lectiones.* They relied on networks of colleagues and friends to supply information about readings, lend manuscripts, and help them get jobs; they savagely criticized each other's work. Rather than working in isolation in their private studies, they were conscious of addressing an imaginary public of scattered colleagues whose common interests supported what might otherwise seem magpie-like collections of opinions and information.

F. Niyi Akinnaso rightly reminds us that we should neither overstress the context-free character of book learning nor assume that societies without writing (as we understand it) have no institutions in which specialized learning is formally transmitted, no "organized training or systematic transfer of advanced knowledge."[40] In some of Akinnaso's cases we might wonder whether the society can really be said to be without writing since, for example, elaborate systems of man-made signs are taught and material mnemonic devices are used in the Luba Bumbudye secret society. On what basis could we decide that the Luba *nkasa* are "mnemonic devices" used in a nonliterate culture whereas Peruvian *quipus* are books? We need to think more about the relation between scholarship and sign-systems, without reifying distinctions between alphabetic or syllabic writing and other uses of signs as supports or substitutes for speech.[41] But Akinnaso is surely right to argue that these methods of specialized instruction can usefully be classed as "schools."

Our last paper, by Brinkley Messick, brings us back to the question of the modern school and alternatives to it. This is a text that looks at contemporary Islamic scholarship and scholarly education in the context of historical and ethnographic questions about practices of reading.

As Messick shows, studies of Islamic schooling have played a key role in recent attempts to break down the sharp dichotomy between "oral" and "literate" societies into a more nuanced appreciation of interrelations between text and speech. The Islamic study circle provides a material example of the "interpretive community" of readers, whose choice of books can be listed and used as a basis for questions about shifts in scholarly categories and interests— modern readings cross earlier boundaries of discipline and school, introduce Sufi interpretations of legal literature, and mingle "scientific" and religious categories ("psychology of revelation").

Scholarship is a discursive activity, building and sustaining, as Messick says, a "textual habitus" in which texts are as real as houses. The attempt to map the habitus of scholars in other cultures can help us to see past the walls of our own. Rather than imagining that we approach the scholarship of other cultures, like the modern child going to school, with blank minds, we try in this book to enter into dialogues with scholars and texts in other cultures that respect the specificity and appreciate the art and ingenuity of their conversations with contemporaries, and at the same time force us to recognize the equally culture-specific and context-shaped character of our own assumptions and perceptions. As scholars, we can hardly help believing that the way to escape from the constricting dichotomies of the Enlightenment and reconfigure the categories with which we discuss scholarship is to read more texts and listen to a wider range of voices.

A recent book about Thatcher's Britain (Wright 1985) is called *On Living in an Old Country.* Perhaps that is the scholar's habitat. But scholarly practice does not consist only of polishing, repairing, and cataloguing the furniture. The past is constantly reconfigured in acts of dialogic bricolage directed toward new interlocutors and audiences. Philologists who forget that do indeed take an objective, or rather objectifying, stance, treat authors and texts they canonize as dead.

NOTES

1. The image is taken from Grafton's paper in this volume.

2. Hero-myths of the victory of light over darkness occur repeatedly in this tradition; see Grafton's paper, below, on the victory of humanism over scholasticism, and Feldhay 1995 on the Galileo story.

3. Bakhtin 1981; genres are defined in dialogue with each other.

4. Krevans (forthcoming) provides some information for antiquity.

5. Medical teaching, in which the book has never eliminated the need for the presence of the human body, both dead and alive, is an interesting case.

6. Dogma is often represented as "values," moral instruction.

7. Steedman 1994, cf. 1990. It is disconcerting to realize that as a child, compelled to take part in massed school gymnastic displays, I was acting out a modern image of education.

8. I do not discuss or try to pin down definitions of *scholarship* here, both because definitions are always context-dependent and because we are deliberately stretching the conventional use of the term in paradoxical directions in order to make the point that the accumulation, creation, and transmission of specialized knowledge does not depend on writing or academic institutions.

9. I use *museum* here in a broad sense, to include reservations, national parks, and so on. See Pemberton 1994.

10. Cf. Herzfeld 1982 on Greece.

11. Cf. Lukács 1962 [1937] on Scott's novels, and Buchan 1932 on his childhood.

12. Bravo 1971; Humphreys 1997a.

13. Momigliano 1950, 1966. The latter article hints at religious motives for Maurist research but does not investigate (cf. Momigliano 1990, 72–75, 132–37).

14. Demetrius of Scepsis in the Troad (second century B.C.) wrote a topographical work in thirty books on the catalogue of Trojan forces in the *Iliad;* Polemon of Ilium (late second century B.C.) was perhaps the most comprehensive and serious antiquarian traveler of antiquity. Callimachus' work on rituals was followed by Ovid's *Fasti* (cf. Miller 1992a, 1992b) and Plutarch's *Greek Questions.* For Pausanius and nationalism, see Elsner 1995, and Alcock 1994; for relics of saints, see Brown 1981.

15. See the commentary in Florida 1995. There are problems in reconciling the dates. The combination of dates is uncharacteristic, but palace libraries contained a wealth of chronographic materials. See Grafton, this volume and 1993, for the popularity of chronography in sixteenth-century Europe; and Chatterjee 1993:78–80 for a parallel form of dating.

16. For a comparison between Chinese and European philology with respect to the collection and edition of fragments of noncanonical works and authors, see the paper by Rudolf Wagner in Most 1997.

17. Cf. the Rudolphs' paper in this volume.

18. The local system of offices is also mapped onto the construction of the Demak mosque.

19. Cf. references to sacred sites in XX.31–XXI.2; see also Humphreys 1997a for classical parallels.

20. Florida 1995:393. I would not see this as *only* "characteristically Javanese"; cf. Adorno 1986:5–6 on Guaman Poma.

21. The standard of analysis of both local and colonial historical cultures in contem-

porary Indonesian studies is exceptional and is making this a central field for the comparative study of historiography: see, for example, Siegel 1979; Maier 1988; and Pemberton 1994.

22. Cf. the role of Turkey in the ninteenth-century Javanese Jayabaya prophecy, discussed in Florida's paper here (202); and Chatterjee 1993:87.

23. For other aspects of this imagined past, see Pemberton 1994.

24. Humphreys 1985. Cf. also Derrett 1961; and papers collected in Cohn 1987.

25. *Pace* the Rudolphs' paper here, I do not think it can be maintained that Said was unaware of the nuances in Schwab's history of orientalism (1950; cf. Said 1978:252–54). Whereas Bernal 1987 is a crude and simplistic example of the stereotyping of western research (cf. Humphreys 1993), Said's book demands and repays careful reading; it is a serious attempt to trace the life-history of a stereotype.

26. On the history of archaeology in India, see Guha-Thakurta 1994.

27. A comparison with the history of Ireland might be interesting. Cf. Metcalf 1992; Chatterjee 1993: chap. 5; and Dirks 1989 on the gradual increase in the importance of caste.

28. Nandy 1983, 1994; Guha-Thakurta 1992a, 1992b; Chatterjee 1993. For earlier dismissal of such intellectual activities, see the review of Tagore's novel *The Home and the World* in 1922 by Georg Lukács (quoted by Nandy 1994:15–17), and Prakash (1990) on Marxist historians in India.

29. See Nandy 1983:87–96 on the life of Aurobindo Ghose. Bakker 1993:195–201, though hagiographic in genre, is also interesting. See Chatterjee 1993:26–34 on the sources of resistance to narratives of continuity. What we perhaps need—and Chatterjee's book goes some way in providing it—is, as Messick suggests in this volume, closer attention to the dislocations imposed by colonialism and modernization.

30. Scaliger 1627:594, quoted in Grafton, this volume (265–66).

31. Cf. Makdisi 1981; and Pfeiffer 1976:106 on the importance of oral teaching and transmission.

32. See Ruderman 1981; Jones 1992; Adorno 1986; and Mignolo's paper in this volume.

33. Grafton 1993; Ruderman 1981.

34. See Grafton 1990 on Hermes Trismegistus.

35. Cf. Humphreys (1997b) on the mechanisms of desire in scholarship.

36. See MacCormack 1994 on contradictions in theology.

37. As noted by the Rudolphs, in this volume, and Dirks 1993a, perceptions of the colonized culture became progressively simpler over time.

38. Cf. Messick 1993: chap. 6, on Islamic resistance to printing.

39. I am here using an analogy with the functions of money. Writing was used as a standard in early Greece in the publication of laws; storage functions were perhaps less prominent (before Thucydides) since poems that preserved the memory of past deeds were intended for performance. See Humphreys (1997b); and Thomas 1989.

40. I have some quibbles about the idea that Melanesian and Polynesian naviga-

tional knowledge is "all in the head"; it seems to me that forms of body-knowledge, feeling the shape of waves, etc., are involved. But the importance of knowledge of stars and calendars is significant.

41. Bruce Mannheim made the important point in discussion that cultural variations in metalinguistic awareness might be more significant than the presence or absence of writing.

REFERENCES

Adorno, R. 1986. *Guaman Poma: Writing and Resistance in Colonial Peru.* Austin: University of Texas Press.

Alcock, S. E. 1993. *Graecia Capta: The Landscapes of Roman Greece.* Cambridge: Cambridge University Press.

———. 1994. "Landscapes of Memory and the Authority of Pausanias," in *Pausanias historien,* J. Bingen, ed., 241–67. *Entretiens de la Fondation Hardt* 41 (Geneva).

Appadurai, A. 1981. *Worship and Conflict under Colonial Rule. A South Indian Case.* Cambridge: Cambridge University Press.

Bakhtin, M. 1981. *The Dialogic Imagination.* Austin: University of Texas Press.

Bakker, F. L. 1993. *The Struggle of the Hindu Balinese Intellectuals: Developments in Modern Hindu Thinking in Independent Indonesia.* Amsterdam: Vreie Universiteit Press.

Bernal, M. 1987. *Black Athena.* Vol. 1. New Brunswick: Rutgers University Press.

Bravo, B. 1971. "Remarques sur l'érudition dans l'antiquité," in *Acta Conventus XI Eirene,* 325–35. Wroclaw: Ossolineum.

Brown, P. R. L. 1981. *The Cult of the Saints: Its Rise and Function in Latin Christianity.* Chicago: University of Chicago Press.

Buchan, J. 1932. *Sir Walter Scott.* London: Cassell.

Chatterjee, P. 1993. *The Nation and Its Fragments: Colonial and Postcolonial Histories.* Princeton: Princeton University Press.

Cohn, B. S. 1987. *An Anthropologist among the Historians and Other Essays.* Delhi: Oxford University Press.

Derrett, J. D. M. 1961. "The Administration of Hindu Law by the British," *CSSH,* vol. 4, 10–52.

Diringer, D. 1962. *Writing.* New York: Praeger.

Dirks, N. B. 1987. *The Hollow Crown.* Cambridge: Cambridge University Press (2d ed. 1993, University of Michigan Press).

———. 1989. "The Invention of Caste: Civil Society in Colonial India," *Social Analysis,* vol. 25, 42–52.

———. 1993a. "Colonial History and Native Informants: Biography of an Archive," in *Orientalism and the Postcolonial Predicament: Perspectives on South Asia,* C. A. Breckenridge and P. van der Veer, eds., 279–313. Philadelphia: University of Pennsylvania Press.

————. 1993b. "The Policing of Tradition." Manuscript.

Eickelman, D. 1985. *Knowledge and Power in Morocco.* Princeton: Princeton University Press.

Elsner, J. 1995. *Art and the Roman Viewer.* Cambridge: Cambridge University Press.

Feldhay, R. 1995. *Galileo and the Church: Political Inquisition or Critical Dialogue?* Cambridge: Cambridge University Press.

Florida, N. K. 1995. *Writing the Past, Inscribing the Future: History as Prophecy in Colonial Java.* Durham, N.C.: Duke University Press.

Fowden, G. 1993. *Empire to Commonwealth: Consequences of Monotheism in Late Antiquity.* Princeton: Princeton University Press.

Grafton, A. 1990. *Forgers and Critics: Creativity and Duplicity in Western Scholarship.* Princeton: Princeton University Press.

————. 1993. Joseph Scaliger. *A Study in the History of Classical Scholarship.* Vol. 2: *Historical Chronology.* Oxford: Clarendon Press.

Guha-Thakurta, T. 1992a. *The Making of a New "Indian" Art: Artists, Aesthetics, and Nationalism in Bengal.* Cambridge: Cambridge University Press.

————. 1992b. "The ideology of the 'Aesthetic': The Purging of Visual Tastes and the Campaign for a New Indian Art in Late Nineteenth/Early Twentieth Century Bengal," *Studies in History,* vol. 8, 237–81.

————. [1994]. "Monuments and Lost Histories: The Study of 'Antiquities' in Colonial India." Manuscript.

Herzfeld, M. 1982. *Ours Once More: Folklore, Ideology, and the Making of Modern Greece.* Austin: University of Texas Press.

Humphreys, S. C., ed. 1985. *Law as Discourse. History and Anthropology,* I.2.

————. 1993. "Diffusion, Comparison, Criticism," in *Anfänge politischen Denkens in der Antike,* K. Raaflaub, ed., 1–11. Munich: Oldenbourg.

————. 1997a. "Fragments, fetishes, and philosophies," in Most 1997, 207–24.

————. 1997b. "From Riddle to Rigour," in *Proof and Persuasion,* E. Lunbeck and S. Marchand, eds. Turnhout: Brepols.

Jones, K. W. ed. 1992. *Religious Controversy in British India: Dialogues in South Asian Languages.* Albany: SUNY Press.

Krevans, N., ed. (forthcoming). *The Book in Antiquity.*

Levenson, J. 1968. *Confucian China and Its Modern Fate: A Trilogy.* Berkeley: University of California Press.

Lukaćs, G. 1962 [1947]. *The Historical Novel.* London: Merlin Press.

MacCormack, S. 1994. "Ubi Ecclesia? Perceptions of Medieval Europe in Spanish America," *Speculum,* vol. 69, 74–100.

Maier, H. M. J. 1988. *In the Center of Authority.* Ithaca: Cornell University, Southeast Asia Program.

Makdisi, G. 1981. *The Rise of Colleges: Institutions of Learning in Islam and the West.* Edinburgh: Edinburgh University Press.

Messick, B. 1993. *The Calligraphic State: Textual Domination and History in a Muslim Society.* Berkeley: University of California Press.

Metcalf, B. D. 1992. "Imaginary Community: Polemical Debates in Colonial India," in Jones 1992:229–40.

Miller, J. 1992a. "Introduction: Research on Ovid's *Fasti,*" *Arethusa,* vol. 25, 1–7.

———. 1992b. "The Fasti and Hellenistic Didactic: Ovid's Variant Aetiologies," *Arethusa,* vol. 25, 11–31.

Momigliano, A. D. 1950. "Ancient History and the Antiquarian," *Journal of the Warburg and Courtauld Institutes,* vol. 13, 285–315.

———. 1966. "Mabillon's Italian Disciples," in *Terzo contributo alla storia degli studi classici e del mondo antico,* 135–52. Rome: Storia e Letteratura.

———. 1990. *The Classical Foundations of Modern Historiography.* Berkeley: University of California Press.

Most, G. W., ed. 1997. *Collecting Fragments. Aporemata.* Vol. 1. Göttingen: Vandenhoeck and Ruprecht.

Nandy, A. 1983. *The Intimate Enemy: Loss and Recovery of Self under Colonialism.* Delhi: Oxford University Press.

———. 1994. *The Illegitimacy of Nationalism: Rabindranath Tagore and the Politics of Self.* Delhi: Oxford University Press.

Pemberton, J. 1994. *On the Subject of "Java".* Ithaca: Cornell University Press.

Pfeiffer, R. 1976. *History of Classical Scholarship from 1300 to 1850.* Oxford: Clarendon Press.

Prakash, G. 1990. "Writing Post-Orientalist Histories of the Third World: Indian Historiography is Good to Think," *CSSH,* vol. 32, 383–408 (revised version in *Colonialism and Culture,* N. B. Dirks, ed., 353–88. Ann Arbor: University of Michigan Press, 1992).

Rocher, L. ed. 1986. *The Dharmasindhu.* Delhi: Sri Satguru Publications.

Rocher, R. 1993. "British Orientalism in the Eighteenth Century: The Dialectics of Knowledge and Government," in *Orientalism and the Postcolonial Predicament,* C. A. Breckenridge and P. van der Veer, eds., 215–49. Philadelphia: University of Pennsylvania Press.

Ruderman, D. B. 1981. *The World of a Renaissance Jew: The Life and Thought of Abraham ben Mordecai Farissol.* Cincinnati: Hebrew Union College Press.

Rudolph, L. I. and S. H. Rudolph. 1965. "Barristers and Brahmans in India: Legal Cultures and Social Change," *CSSH,* vol. 8, 24–49.

Said, E. 1978. *Orientalism.* New York: Pantheon.

———. 1993. *Culture and Imperialism.* New York: Knopf.

Scaliger, J. 1627. *Epistolae omnes quae reperiri potuerunt,* D. Heinsius, ed. Leiden.

Schwab, R. 1950. *La renaissance orientale.* Paris: Payot.

Siegel, J. T. 1979. *Shadow and Sound: The Historical Thought of a Sumatran Kingdom.* Chicago: University of Chicago Press.

Steedman, C. 1990. *Childhood, Culture, and Class in Britain: Margaret McMillan, 1860–1931.* London: Virago.

———. 1994. *Strange Dislocations: Childhood and the Idea of Human Interiority, 1780–1930.* Cambridge, Mass.: Harvard University Press.

Thomas, R. 1989. *Oral Tradition and Written Record in Classical Athens.* Cambridge: Cambrige University Press.

Wright, P. 1985. *On Living in an Old Country.* London: Verso.

Childhood: Naturalization of Development into a Japanese Space

Stefan Tanaka

In this sense, to experience necessarily means to re-accede to infancy as history's transcendental place of origin. The enigma which infancy ushered in for man can be dissolved only in history, just as experience, being infancy and human place of origin, is something he is always in the act of falling from, into language and into speech.

—Giorgio Agamben

A common symbol and metaphor in modern society is childhood (Ariès 1962; Kessen 1979). It has penetrated to the level of everyday life, a part of our common sense and residing in our memories. Yet it is an ambiguous category, "a concept [that] binds a variety of historical experience and a collection of theoretical and practical references into a relation that is, as such, only given and actually ascertainable through the concept" (Koselleck 1985:84). Despite (or because of) this tautology, it possesses clarity, the certainty of an early or originary stage—a separable site—within a developmental process. It is a site where the ambiguities and contradictions of modernity are ameliorated into a coherent whole personified through the child. That is, the human body serves as an object that makes the abstractions of modernity seem natural.

Childhood as we think of it today is inextricably linked to the modern, liberal-capitalist society, the "West" (Edelstein 1983). Even though the transformation of childhood occurred over centuries since the sixteenth century, it was not until the nineteenth century that children became "children," a separated category of purity, innocence, protection, nurturance, and formal education. This does not mean that the child is Western, but that the way we understand the process of development is tied to the Industrial Revolution and the Enlightenment (see, for example, Polanyi 1944). Franco Moretti writes:

21

But when status society starts to collapse, the countryside is abandoned for the city, and the world of work changes at an incredible and incessant pace, the colourless and uneventful socialization of "old" youth becomes increasingly implausible: it becomes a *problem,* one that makes youth itself problematic. . . . [Youth] is a necessary exploration: in dismantling the continuity between generations, as is well known, the new and destabilizing forces of capitalism impose a hitherto unknown *mobility.* But it is also a yearned-for exploration, since the selfsame process gives rise to unexpected hopes, thereby generating an *interiority* not only fuller than before, but also—as Hegel clearly saw, even though he deplored it—perennially dissatisfied and restless. (1987:4, original emphasis)

Childhood has become a symbol for several aspects of modernity: of a new progressive society, one looking forward to a seemingly better future; of temporariness, that idealized past or originary state that must be guided and transformed; and of immanence, the constant regeneration of that pure originary state. In these modern meanings, the child becomes what Viviana Zelizer has called sacralized into a priceless asset (1985), but it is an asset of a culture of modernity circumscribed by the nation-state.

The transformation of childhood also parallels the emergence of the nation-state. This connection between childhood and the nation was recently brought to the surface in Japan's public dismay when Oe Kenzaburo declined to receive the Imperial Order of Culture, that nation-state's highest cultural honor; he was hastily added to the list of recipients after the announcement that he would receive the 1994 Nobel Prize in literature.[1] Kazuo Aichi, one of the more reform-minded members of the Diet, stated: "My own feeling was that he hadn't changed at all over the years. I would have expected that he would have matured, so to speak, and accepted the award" (Sterngold 1994). The word *mature* is juxtaposed to the child; it suggests that those who do not conform to social norms of the nation-state are still childish. The child, in this case, is the origin of a progressive developmental scheme that embodies the interiority and hopes of the nation. But when the child does not develop that full interiority, childhood becomes an exteriority that threatens (while simultaneously reinforcing) that same interiority.

Such criticism of Oe illustrates the extent to which childhood has become a common metaphor that orients behaviors and expectations without calling attention to itself. Drawing on Vico's discussion of the conceit of scholars, John Shotter points to the entrapments that are possible within "closed, harmonious *systems* of thought" (1993:62, original emphasis). A limitation in our understanding of nation-states and nationalism is the focus on modern institutions and ideologies, the very categories of modern society and nation-states. Historiography on Japan has been dominated by Enlightenment, Whiggish, Marxist, or Modernization theory approaches that explicate institutions of the state, both structural—constitutional systems, governments and policies, corporations, and social institutions—and concepts and ideologies that facilitate them—individualism, rationality, and science. One problem of this focus on the objects of modern society is the categorical dichotomy that it encourages— good/bad, mature/immature, modern/traditional, Western/indigenous, and adult/child. Discussion of the Japanese nation-state remains within those "closed, harmonious *systems* of thought," the categories that were created to maintain the socio-political unit (for a recent example of an attempt to critique modern Japanese historiography, without problematizing the discourse of modernity, see Garon 1994).

A part of the difficulty in extricating oneself from such closed systems of thought is the convergence of nature and thought in the construction of the nation-state.[2] The notion of the child is a good example of this convergence. Even though it is now treated as a self-evident, natural form, childhood is a historical idea that has played a central role in the reorientation of locales into the nation and was central in intellectuals' efforts to make sense of and bring order to their societies in the nineteenth century. In Japan as well as in other societies it emerged as part of a process that involves a transition "from concrete to abstract relationships, from modalities of life dominated by particulars of experience to modalities of life dominated by abstract and universal regulations, by computational experiences, or . . . by bureaucratic rationality" (Edelstein 1983:56). Modern societies are organized around categorical hierarchies of learning, growth, development, and civility (self-control), a corollary of which is the notion of maturation (See Karatani 1993:123–25). Like progress, childhood incorporates notions of change, measured and described through stages, and presupposes some origin or purity. As an originary point of a developmental sense of time, childhood is a conceptual category that reinforces this linear time—progress and maturation. It becomes a temporal abstraction in this transformation from a cyclical to progressive time, which all modern societies have experienced (Elias 1990; Koselleck 1985). Childhood provides experience by establishing the primacy of a national culture as the experience of all individuals. In other words, childhood is one of those sites where the interiority of the nation-state is naturalized. Here, childhood becomes a political tool; it is part of the effort of a nation-state to monopolize those mnemonic devices that reinforce its vision of what society should be—in the case of Japan, the marginalization of dissatisfaction and restlessness in favor of obedience and loyalty. The child comes to personify sensate boundaries of national similarity and difference, thereby blurring the difference between knowledge and the sensate in the logic of the nation.

A result of this transition is the separation of experience from knowledge, or perhaps more accurately the compartmentalization of experience. Experience is determined not by what is around the individual, but how that environment connects with abstract criteria—knowledge, be it objectified by science or a national common sense. This raises the question of whether (or in what way) experience is possible outside the norms established to maintain a national unity. One might argue that the criticism leveled against Oe is peculiar to a society like Japan, one that places a premium on an ideology of conformity. But Giorgio Agamben, in the epigraph above, suggests otherwise, that the *problem* of childhood is embedded in modern society itself. Infancy[3] is a mediating site that informs different roles according to social needs. But in today's societies those needs, "language and speech," are circumscribed within national sites—geographic and ideational.

This blurring of the distinction between ontogeny and phylogeny turns a certain kind of social time into a natural progress in which individuals and nations are used interchangeably. As a metaphor for development it is something temporal and temporary, being transformed "into language and into speech." When applied to national society it reorients social organization toward translocal (such as national and class) categories that re-produce an ideal national society. These criteria are institutionalized and projected in educational places that make criteria that fragment seem natural. Success is measured by the extent to which one distances oneself from childhood and moves toward socially objectified ideals—notions of civility, ethics, and morals. Distinctions occur by measuring the extent to which one improves from that pure state. Moreover, while childhood is useful in constituting the nation-state, it is also a metaphor used among nation-states. Here, it is especially problematic for nonmodern places that must confront their position as a child. Descriptions of nonmodern places and people as childlike—always connoting a lack or inferiority—are common within scholarly discourse. In this sense, the child naturalizes an asymmetry—in human development, in society, in the nation-state, and globally. The word *maturation* suggests norms that are separate from the child; what is natural is in those norms, not in its actions.

By focusing on the historicity of the child—the processes, the reorientation of a sociocultural matrix that is at the core of this transformation and a part of the constant negotiations of modernity—I hope to limit (or avoid) my entrapment within those "closed, harmonious *systems* of thought" that often inadvertently return us to the very concepts we try to write against. Although they seem "natural" today, we need to bring out those moments when thought and nature, nation and universalistic categories, merged. Only after we do so can we make an attempt (no matter how preliminary and inadequate) to understand some of the conditions under which we "experience" and believe within the nation-state.

Premodern Children

It would be ludicrous to assert that the "invention" of childhood suggests that the human child did not exist prior to that conceptualization (as some critics of notions of invention, such as deMause [1974], have claimed).[4] Physiologically, children have obviously existed as long as humans have; but the roles and treatment of children differ throughout the past, as well as in different cultures. Those familiar with recent work on the concept of childhood would find numerous similarities with the transformation of childhood in Japan (Ariès 1962; Kessen 1979; Steedman 1992, 1995; Zelizer 1985). In fact, childhood in early Meiji Japan bore more similarity to Wolfgang Edelstein's description of the child in premodern rural Europe than to childhood in modern Japan: "the bond of meaning and mutual responsibility [is] in a world of work that does not know childhood as an age of play but, rather, an age of transient functional imperfection" (1983:59). Isabella Bird's description in 1878 of Japanese children as "little men and women rather than children" (1984 [1880]:80) indicates a similar world of transient functional imperfection. For Bird, as well as other foreign travelers,[5] difference was described as an unfamiliar culture, but it also shows quite different conceptions of time. Bird writes: "At three [years old] they put on the *kimono* and girdle, which are as inconvenient to them as to their parents, and childish play in this garb is grotesque. I have, however, never seen what we call child's play—that general abandonment to miscellaneous impulses, which consists in struggling, slapping, rolling, jumping, kicking, shouting, laughing, and quarrelling!" (199). Bird's comment is reminiscent of Lévi-Strauss' complaint that Nambikwara children, who constantly imitate adult behavior, are not familiar with games (1971:272–85, esp. 275). This does not mean that children did not play, but that the visual codes that give hints to these cultures' notions of the child and child's play were not attached to a clearly marked temporal stage, as those ethnographers expected.

Children in premodern or early modern Japanese society did not exist as future citizens but as members of their locale. Childhood was not a unifying category that represented children as some empty vessel, a metaphor for some romantic period, or an early stage of linear growth. Moreover, abstractions, such as nation, emperor, and race, were not yet defining concepts. Instead, a "space of experience" (Koselleck 1985), rather than time, established the parameters for social organization of the world of children (Kuroda 1994:10–11; Yanagita 1942:28–29); children differed by environment—locale, class, family occupation, and so on—where learning, play, and child-rearing occurred simultaneously. Bird observed of a remote farm village in Tochigi: "Old women were spinning, and young and old usually pursued their avocations with wise-looking babies tucked into the backs of their dresses, and peering cunningly over their shoulders. Even little girls of seven and eight were playing at children's games with babies on their backs, and those who were too small to carry real ones had big dolls strapped on in similar fashion" (1984 [1880]:51). Socialization occurred within the social codes of the adults of their specific environs. Children of samurai learned the techniques of that bureaucratic/warrior class, while in villages children participated in the work and rituals of farm life.[6]

Symbols of age and life-course changes were not absent, but marked different notions of the human being. *Kodomo-gumi* (children's groups) of rural, commoner, and samurai classes were the clearest form of age-based segmentation in the pre-Meiji period. Yet, where they existed, *kodomo-gumi* were usually temporary and informal groupings that facilitated the participation of children (from six or seven to fourteen or fifteen years of age) in special events or rituals. For example, the bonfires and bird-chasing on the fifteenth day of the first lunar month combined play with instruction in the relation between production and one's cosmic world (Yanagita 1942; Kami 1989:174–82). Formal schooling was more indicative of the notion of functional imperfection than of developmental growth stratified by age. For example, at a private academy (usually attended by commoners such as priests, poets, doctors, merchants, and wealthy farmers) in Kyushu, the age at admittance between 1801 and 1871 ranged from seven to fifty-nine, with most entering between sixteen and twenty-one years of age (Rubinger 1982:89–90).

A ritual that today is symbolic of childhood, the 7–5–3 ceremony, in which parents dress their children in elaborate kimonos (sons at ages three and five, daughters at three and seven) and take them to a temple or shrine, is a good example of the transformation of developmental stages from practices tied to immediate exigencies to rather commercialized observations of abstract (age-based) categories. Prior to the Meiji period children were considered godlike and not yet subject to the rules of human society. Seven, as reflected in a proverb that children are "among the gods until seven," was a watershed year, marked by recognition paid to the gods. This observance was conducted in the home (Kuroda 1994:10).[7] But these observances were not uniform throughout the archipelago; for example, in Kansai, the region around Osaka and Kyoto, the end of childhood was marked by a ceremony at the age of thirteen. The early observances suggest a different connection between society, nature, idea of children, child-rearing, and so on.

I must emphasize that childhood prior to the nineteenth century was not static; indeed, a narrative of transformation can plausibly begin this discussion in the urban culture (especially Edo) of the Tokugawa period. The transformation of the 7–5–3 ceremony into a quite prevalent ritual today suggests a gradual change in the concept of the child that is tied to the rise of the commercial economy. During the Tokugawa period, some of the rituals marking the survival of the infant spread to wealthier merchants and peasants, and the visits to the shrines and temples began in the prosperous quarters of Edo. But what is evident is the lack of homogeneity; it is evidence of different, coexisting temporalities depending on immediate environment.

The Child as Originary Stage

The transformation of the child accelerated after the Meiji Restoration (1868) as Japanese intellectual and political leaders sought to redefine society into a national culture. Whereas the communities of Tokugawa Japan were based on a cyclical notion of change in which the ideal was to be found in some eschatological realm, post-Restoration Japan was characterized by a directional shift in the concept of time. The rational, abstract norms, conceived of through a linear temporal framework—progress—transformed and unified the "space of experience" into a "horizon of expectations." Koselleck describes this transition:

> It will become apparent that it is with History experienced as a new temporality that specific dispositions and ways of assimilating experience emerge. Our modern concept of history is the outcome of Enlightenment reflection on the growing complexity of "history in general," in which the determinations of experience are increasingly removed from experience itself. (1985 [1979]:xxiv)

In the reorientation of the social into a nation-state, the social is altered according to abstract categories that symbolize this new temporality, such as childhood, mechanical time, and ethnicity, which define specific experiences. History becomes the idea that gives meaning to these categories in a way that coincides with the nation-state and brings the idea of the nation to the level of all individuals.

The early Meiji period (indeed, any period of transition toward a modern society) was a period of the reconceptualization of time and space. For example, the Gregorian calendar replaced the lunar calendar, the clock became the keeper of a time that facilitated the operation of factories and the railways, the administrative reorganization in 1871 reduced the approximately three hundred semiautonomous regional units into seventy-two prefectures (*ken*) and three cities (*fu*), and new technologies such as the railway and telegraph altered the conceptual landscape. A common point of these changes is centralization; each example, ordered around an abstraction, provided greater precision for the unification of disparate parts. Past knowledge was no longer a guide to the present, and language did not correspond to the new epistemology; this led to disorientation and dissatisfaction. For example, a critique in the *Tokyo nichi nichi shimbun* just after the announcement expresses the disorientation created by the shift from the lunar to the Gregorian calendar:

> Now, we will carry out your august will announced in the imperial edict to abolish the old calendar and disseminate the solar calendar. However, there is one matter that will most likely shock the unenlightened and ignorant; . . . it is certainly difficult to anticipate the new moon on the first day of the month and the full moon on the 15th night. When the moon rises at the end of the month no longer corresponding to the word *tsugomori* (end of the month) and when the fifteenth night seems like *yamiyo* (moonless night), how can one not lose the certainty that we have come to expect? This brings up an amusing anecdote that compares the reality of the geisha to the corner of an egg; this is a parable for the new moon at the end of the month. Should we transform these proverbs? . . . In this way, yesterday's masquerade becomes today's truth, how can this be? (Okada, 1994:236)

In a sense, this disorientation of everyday life, natural rhythms, and beliefs was planned. Intellectuals during the early part of the Meiji period debated the extent of the change necessary within the archipelago. Most agreed that the masses had to replace old habits with new ideas. In the *Meiroku zasshi*, the premier journal expounding enlightenment, Nakamura Masanao wrote in 1875: "Rather than changing the political structure, therefore, we should aspire instead to change the character of the people, more and more rooting out the old habits and achieving 'renewal' with each new day. . . . Should you ask how to change the character of the people, there are but two approaches—through religious and moral education and through education in the arts and sciences" (Braisted 1976:373). That renewal was the imposition of a totally new system in which rationality and knowledge would further the objects of modern society while ethical codes would produce the social responsibility and "civil" deportment of a liberal-capitalist society. Historical (or social and political) time was now separated from and prior to individual time, the time of the body and seasonal rhythms.

Such a rupture brings to the surface a fundamental issue in human apprehension of time. Sociologist Thomas Luckmann describes this as the interplay between an inner time of the individual and the intersubjective time of social interaction. Inner time is embedded in the body; it is a "natural" time of everyday habits and bodily rhythms. It is also tied to the social, for our awareness of time is through socially objectified norms. Luckmann states: "The rhythms of inner time are the basis of experience, and all other structures of time in human life are erected upon it. The latter, however, do not *originate* in the (pre-predicative) inner time of a solitary self. They originate in social interaction" (1989:155, original emphasis). During the Meiji period the transformation that the archipelago underwent was in this inversion of social interaction into an inner time of a Japan that spoke for experience.

Luckmann is warning against a common problem in modern scholarship, the use of the social as an ahistorical narrative device, thereby leading scholars into those traps of which Shotter warns. Childhood becomes one of those sites of social interaction that is apprehended as something natural and experiential, thus prior to the social. Because children have always existed, childhood also comes to stand for something timeless, that pure state before learning (of good and bad) occurs. Childhood becomes a socially objectified site, one of those mediating layers that gives procedure and meaning to social interaction. The socially constituted is then naturalized (or turned into inner time) by our everyday experience. It becomes a temporal category with specific meanings, a category that cuts across spatial divisions and experiential categories and facilitates the unity of previously disparate categories into a whole. It is seemingly universal because it is tied to the body and "experienced" by everybody (i.e., it is a period through which all adults pass).

The notion of the child in modern society was described, albeit rather obliquely when abstracted from his essay, by Agamben:

Within this perspective, ghosts and children, belonging neither to the signifiers of diachrony nor to those of synchrony, appear as the signifiers of the same signifying opposition between the two worlds which constitutes the potential for a social system. *They are, therefore, the signifiers of the signifying function,* without which there would be neither human time nor history. Playland and the land of ghosts set out a utopian topology of historyland, which has no site except in a signifying difference between diachrony and synchrony, between *aiōn* and *chrónos,* between living and dead, between nature and culture (1993:84–85, original italics).

The combination of child and ghosts as unstable signifiers is fascinating. Agamben reminds us of what was eliminated through history—the ghosts, spirits, and superstitions that pervaded communities on the archipelago (see for example Hearn 1971). They indicate the eschatological, cyclical world characteristic of premodern societies. Even the child, as discussed above, was treated more like a spirit, akin to the gods, than a "child." This is the inversion that Luckmann exposes. The reconstitution of society as progressive, rather than cyclical, requires a readjustment of the relationship of signifiers from the spiritual—ghosts—to the natural—children.

Indeed, intellectuals and bureaucrats sought to eradicate this past filled with superstitions, the myriad and omnipresent beliefs that guided everyday life. The spread of scientific knowledge relegated other apprehensions of the unknown to the level of superstition. Inoue Tetsujirō, professor of philosophy at Tokyo Imperial University, states: "When one doesn't develop knowledge, evils—all superstitions and the bewitching of people's hearts—spread. When one develops knowledge the principle of things [*jibutsu no dōri*] become clear and superstitions naturally [*onozukara*] disappear" (1974 [1891]:170). The change is profound; past knowledge, if not authorized by the nation-state through its institutions (in particular the Imperial University), becomes anachronistic or superstitious. The ghosts and spirits of the past are virtually reduced to some form of absence—of education, of knowledge, of common sense (newly defined).[8] Mnemonic sites of this past were also reduced. In 1906 thousands of shrines that protected hamlets, communities, and villages throughout the archipelago and symbolized many of those superstitions were destroyed, and their spirits ranked in the hierarchical order of what is known today as Shinto (Fridell 1973). Only ancestors remain, now elevated to a stable relationship that connects a past with the present.

In this sense, the child becomes that "potential for a social system" that sets out a "utopian topology of historyland [Japan] . . . between nature and culture." As a universalized stage, childhood cuts across regions, making possible different forms of social organization that facilitate unification. Nature is now abstract, no longer locally based, while the child becomes juxtaposed to the putative complexity of the modern factory. For a place attempting to establish its unity from a mass of local communities to a developmental whole, childhood also provided a language for the naturalization of a national space where nature, industry, and society occupy discrete places in the whole.

This transformation was signaled in number of tracts by Japanese intellectuals and policymakers throughout the early Meiji period (See for example Lincicome 1995). But the centrality of the child to the character of the new nation-state—the utopian topology of historyland—was most evident in the Imperial Rescript on Education (1890), one of the most important decrees of the Meiji government. The Rescript, on the one hand, has been characterized as a conservative document that keyed the reaction against the westernization of Japan. If one's goal is to exalt modernity, this is true. It is a document that uses the emperor to establish filiality and loyalty as the foundation of a communal patriotism that, in Inoue's words, "return[s] the dignity of the Japanese people [*nihon kokumin*] before decades pass" (1974 [1891]:156). But that dignity can also be seen as an attempt to bring back some of the synchrony that Agamben discusses. To label this as traditionalistic and anti-Western denies the possibility that these are conditions inherent to the process of modernity. First, the very idea of a Japanese people as a nation is new.[9] Second, no nation-state can exist as a purely a diachronic place. Enlightenment, at least as it is proposed in its ideal form, is close to pure diachrony. Throughout the nineteenth and twentieth centuries one can find numerous intellectuals in Europe trying to revive a synchrony of place, to reestablish the primacy of experience (see, e.g. Nietzsche 1983 [1874]; and Eagleton 1990).

To establish the unity of a Japanese nation, some kind of connection to a past was necessary—but to pasts that do not counter the formation of a rational society. From the nineteenth century on, historians have been preoccupied with origins.[10] In counterpoint to Patrick Wolfe's discussion of the concept of *dreamtime* as the originary site for a narrative of settlement, I argue that children filled that signifying function for the idea of a Japanese people (*kokumin*). The child became that originary point (mythic) that unifies all Japanese as the same; it is simultaneously one's own past, the present (through contemporary children), and a hope and prescription for a better future.

But, in contrast to the role of the aborigines, the internal and external are marked differently. The externality of the child is a temporary position, not a fixed category in a temporal hierarchy. It embodies the physiology of a group of people, and it cuts across other divisive categories that had once existed, such as class (hereditary), wealth, or region, as well as new categories, such as class (economic), knowledge, or putative ability. Difference is now altered into temporal hierarchies of the Same—that is, through the diachrony of human growth and progress—and childhood signifies the synchrony of ethnicity or race. While orienting society around a diachronic epistemology, the child is also a visible form (body and images), the "like us" that facilitates the construction and maintenance of a national "we." Inoue describes such a role of the child in the *"chokugo engi,"* the official commentary to the Rescript: "If all children receive this national education [*kokuminteki kyōiku*], there is no doubt that our land will coalesce into one country" (1974 [1891]:156). The combination of learning and children turns the latter into an experiential site for the nation-state. Children become that past (synchrony) and future (diachrony) that bring the interiority of the nation into being. In this sense, the Rescript is also a quite modern document, one that envisions the unity of a nation-state. But such a function is only possible with the presence of Western nation-states, an alter that validates the national idea in conjunction with geographic boundaries.

This developmental notion of the human body appeared earlier in the *Meiroku zasshi;* Mitsukuri Shūhei foresaw the changing role of the child. "From infancy until they are six or seven, children's minds are clean and without the slightest blemish while their characters are as pure and unadulterated as a perfect pearl. Since what then touches their eyes and ears, whether good or bad, makes a deep impression that will not be wiped out until death, this age provides the best opportunity for disciplining their natures and training them in deportment" (Braisted 106). A key age (seven) that signifies a lifecourse change remains the same, but the child has been transformed from the godlike, or "among the gods until seven," to an infant as an empty vessel to be trained as a proper citizen. In other words, the child changes from an uncertain being—poised between death and life—to the preparatory stage in which its externality is molded into sameness, the interiority of the nation-state.

Now the child, still temporary, becomes a temporal category for a future good. Whereas in the past initiation rites, the ritual at seven years of age, recognized the child as a member of the world, whereupon he/she would go off and work/learn, the modern child should go to school. Inoue writes, "In the first place, human life is like climbing a mountain: the climb is remembered as long, but we know the second half, the descent, to be very fast. In this way, people need to study hard during their youth. Actually, one's life is determined by one's diligence in the first half, just as the organization of a day is determined in the morning" (1974 [1891]:169). Inoue is describing the space of childhood, a temporal site in which deferred work, the acquisition of knowledge, is not considered wasted time, but an asset more important than material resources. He states quite emphatically: "time, in other words, is an asset" [*kazai*] (1974 [1891]:169).[11] By placing a value on time, Inoue is sacralizing the child, who, divorced from its immediate relations, becomes, in Zelizer's words (1985), "useless" that is, childhood is a time when the individual is nonproductive. This similarity to the process described by Zelizer indicates that the issue, despite the rhetoric, is not one of western rationality versus indigenous (non-western) tradition. Inoue, who is considered a conservative ideologue, is working within a progressive linear concept. The child who goes to school does not represent uselessness but deferred gratification, improvement, functionalization, and rationality.

Inoue is codifying, as a national character, a notion of the child that gained popularity when early Japanese educational policymakers turned to western experts, such as Pestalozzi and Froebel, to rebuild the educational system. Early educators, such as Morokuzu Nobuzumi, the first principal of the Tokyo Normal School, and Isawa Shūji, one of the first students to study educational systems in the United States and an important functionary in the Ministry of Education, advocated an idea of the child as a pure, naïve being who should be educated according to levels that correspond with its developing intellect. This contrasts with early modern education, the rote memorization of the Confucian classics (Lincicome 1995). The educational structure that emerged after the Fundamental Code of Education of 1872 included compulsory education through six grades and textbooks that emphasized gradual, developmental learning. Subsequent debates focused on content; while early curriculum focused on knowledge acquisition and cognitive development, later reforms emphasized morals to cultivate social character. A revision in 1890, corresponding with the Rescript, went one step further, emphasizing "education for citizenship" (Lincicome 1995:90–91). By 1912, the end of the Meiji period, the Ministry of Education boasted of an attendance rate of 98.2 percent of Japanese children in compulsory education (Kami 1989:497–507).

Yet, as Zelizer's account suggests, the transformation of the child was not easy, nor was it as thorough as the Ministry of Education's figure suggests. As late as 1938 a teacher in a remote farm village in Yamagata (northern Japan) recalls an encounter with a small farmer while riding home on his bicycle. He describes the child's appearance, commenting that he looks just like an adult: "He wore straw sandals quite skillfully. Even his way of walking was that of an adult. . . . It was the image of a laborer, a small peasant" (Kokubun 1972:220).

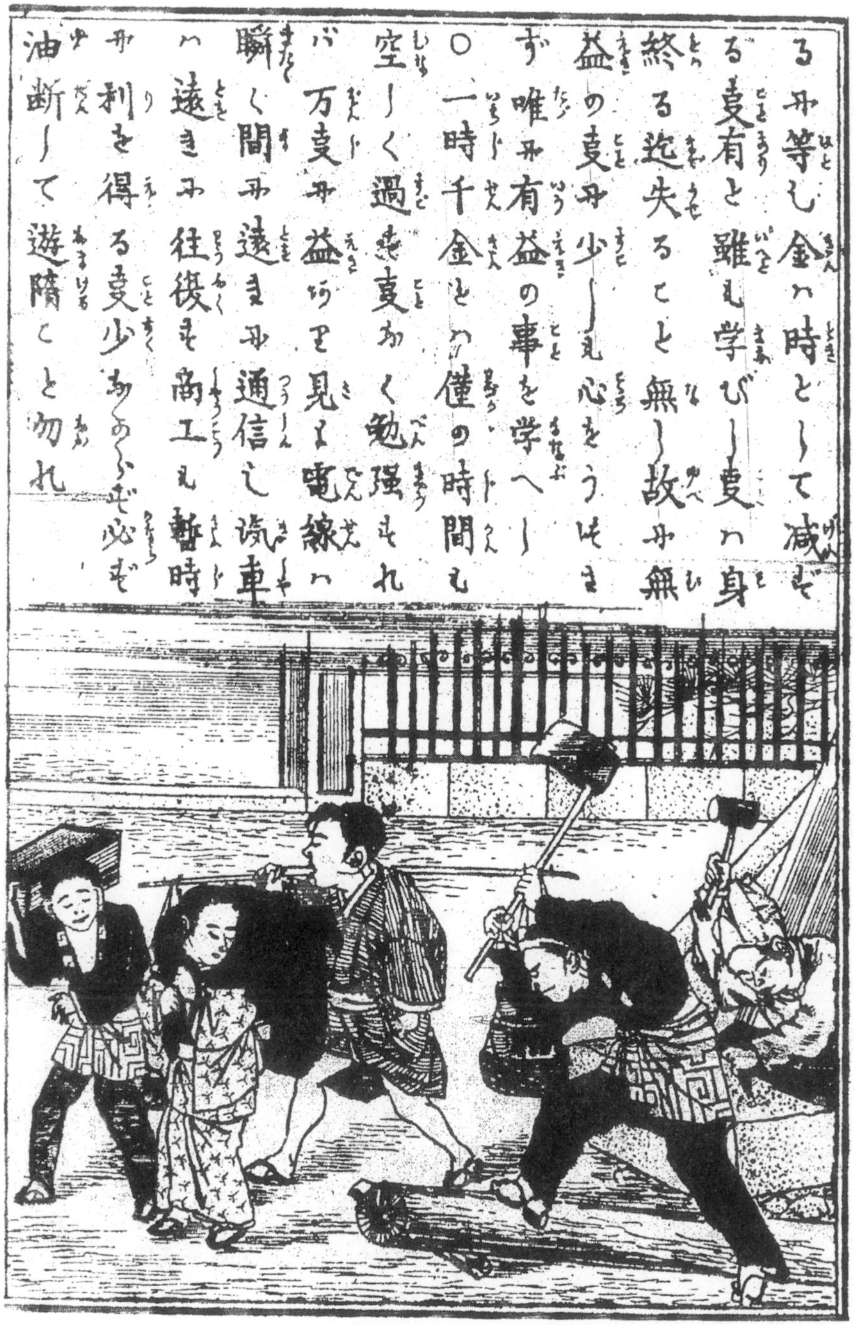

油断して遊惰ことと切れ　刈を得る愛少あるぞ必ぞ　瞬く間に遠きみ往復を商工も暫時　バ万愛も益可を見よ電線に　空しく過愛かく勉強れ　〇一時千金との僅の時間も　ず唯丑有益の事を学へし　益の愛丑少し見心をうひま　終る迄失ること無し故丑無　る愛有と雖も学び丑度丑身　る丑等し金ハ時とーて減ぞ

Fig. 1.   A primary school text exhorting students on the value of study. (From Kido 1886.)

○古語中一字千金ニ當る
と曰文字の徳の廣大成ハ數
千里の海陸を隔つ地形モ坐し
て音信を通じ數百年の古
への支を知る自今後子年を
歴て支を知らん人も悉皆文
字の有が父然ズ人トして學
び知らむ人ハ殆ど貧人のと

○一事千金と云るが總て有
益の事ハ一度たり共是を學
び得る時ハ千圓の金を得た

古語三
一字千金
一事千金
一時千金

But beyond the lack of distinction between child and farmer/laborer, the conversation raised questions of utility and the category of the child.

> I asked suspiciously, aren't you Shunichi who, even though now in the fourth grade, was scolded for not knowing your multiplication tables? Well, wonderful. I had to reconsider that I scolded, again today, such a useful fellow for not being able to read. He laughed, 'Sensei [honorific for teacher], today I've tilled three fields. Heh, I've even developed blisters.' . . . Then whenever I saw him I wondered, what am I doing when he is working in the fields? I'm recording detailed lesson plans and buried among countless, worthless reports. (Kokubun 1972:220)

Such doubts notwithstanding, society did change, but differentially depending on region, population density, and wealth. American and European travelers noticed the progress (i.e., growing signs of civilization as they understood it) and rejoiced. Mabel Alice Bacon proudly exclaims: "But in spite of its hard work, the new school life is cheerful and healthful, and the children enjoy it. It helps them to be really children . . ." (1891:51). But to be "really children" means to be restricted to an orderly system in which children had a clearly demarcated realm. She observed: "Now, every morning, the streets of the cities and villages are alive with boys and girls clattering along, with their books and lunch boxes in their hands, to the kindergarten, primary, grammar, high, or normal school. Every rank in life, every grade in learning, may find its proper place in the new school system, and the girls eagerly grasp their opportunities" (1891:50).

These observations encapsulate many of the problems of a facile overlay of modern cultural norms over a non-western one. The description ends with the celebration of the transformation. Any failure to complete the transition is a problem in adaptation, that is, of the indigenous people and culture, not the system itself. It ignores Agamben's sage observations on the interaction and dependence of both stable and unstable signifiers and the presence of diachrony and synchrony, while one is pretending to obliterate the other. Like so many of the mediating categories of the modern world, the reconstitution of childhood as an abstract temporal category both separates experience and knowledge and simultaneously mediates the schism. Edelstein states this differently: "The progression of rationality towards the transformation of the objective structure of social relations . . . increasingly incorporates the whole person under its iron sway. The rational planning of the conduct of life, which liberated the individual from the bondage of opaque traditions, in the end totally and irrevocably determines his subjective lifespace and dispossesses him of the very freedom that rationality had earned him" (1983:70). This is well depicted in figure 1. The students on the right are freed from the world of adults to be children, that is, to occupy a defined realm that is orderly, uniform, and attentive. They are taught a modern curriculum; the writing on the board, *ichiji senkin,* uses different characters to denote the rationality of the new world. It reads, "literacy is wealth, material is wealth, time is wealth" (see for example, Kinmonth 1981). Childhood, as an association based on common interests—age-based categories of various early levels of intellectual development—becomes a temporal category that reinforces the social rationalization and fragmentation that is part of modern society.

Childhood and Nation

These quotations suggest that the transformation of the child was not serendipitous but inextricably tied to the idea of a modern society, in particular, the Japanese nation-state. But this metaphor or signifier has become an abstraction, a temporary and impermanent stage in the progress and development of individuals and nation-states. It suggests constant change, an image of mobility and inner restlessness: "Modernity as a bewitching and risky process full of 'great expectations' and 'lost illusions.' Modernity as—in Marx's words—a 'permanent revolution' that perceives the experience piled up in tradition as a useless dead-weight, and therefore can no longer feel represented by maturity, and still less by old age" (Moretti 1987:5). Moretti brings out one of the paradoxes within the idea of the nation-state: it is built upon an idea of perpetual change (progress), but its rationale is dependent upon the very past that is being jettisoned.

The individualism that the modern child enables—the space to act autonomously no matter how circumscribed—calls into question the way that a nation will become and remain unified, whether it is a solidarity built up through alliances based on common interests (imposed or willful) or whether "individuals are enjoined to act within a collectivity because, it is believed, bonds of solidarity that tie them together already exist" (Chatterjee 1993:163). The child embodies certain concepts and characteristics that mediate this paradox by allowing "children to be children." Such freedom occurs within a narrowly bounded, homogenized category that facilitates notions of what society should be. The transition in the curriculum from knowledge to morals and ethics throughout the 1880s suggests that Japanese intellectuals and leaders opted for the latter, the "principle of community" adapted to the nation-state.

Here the idea of the child is part of the resolution of a moral and political problem of the new nation-state—how the national "we" *should* relate to one another (Shotter 1993:87). For children this *should* had not been natural to their everyday lives; they had to be taught to conform to this "natural" state.

While childhood has the potential to reorient society from local communities—sites of experience—to universalistic categories of development—horizons of expectations—it did not become the antithesis of community. Childhood simultaneously facilitates a "principle of community," now of the nation rather than the locale. One of the powerful aspects of the temporality of childhood is that it is a temporary condition that depends on a prior knowledge. The child has become what Carolyn Steedman calls a "first metaphor for all people . . . a mapping of analogy and meaning for the self, always in shape and form *like us,* the visual connection plain to see" (1992:141). The child represents both past and future, romance and hope. Even though it has become the origin of human development, it also relies upon and reinforces a synchrony that occults such diachronic time. Maeda Ai describes childhood in modern Japan: "Struggling back to the time of the child, combined with the inclination toward a natural cycle, is the illusory axis that stimulates our escape from modern industrial society, and at the same time it is that irreplaceable horizon through which we can see beyond the barrenness of life that is hidden in the everyday" (1982:279; see also Karatani 1993). Childhood provides that illusion of idealized pasts that facilitate a unified conceptual space yet remain separate from the present. This nature is both a pristine site of longing and rescuer of a corrupt world (Steedman 1992:130).

This transformation of the individual and national body into categories of experience is made possible by an inversion where the socially constituted child becomes everyday experience; but it is an experience that is only meaningful in connection with nationally constituted norms. A principal goal of any new nation-state is to convince all people to accept and participate in, actively or through a lack of resistance, the parameters and goals established by the state—to paraphrase Chatterjee, to act as a collectivity because of previously and always existing bonds of solidarity. As suggested above, this reorientation necessitates the dissolution of regional or local ties, or, more accurately, the superimposition of national over individual relations. In early Meiji Japan, few commoners were concerned with Tokyo; most identified with their immediate community, not some distant idea like the nation or nation-state. For example, less than half the population knew about the emperor (Irokawa 1973:487; Fujitani 1993). Social and political policy during the early Meiji period was characterized by much experimentation and seemed to follow social disorder.

Rebellions and protests continued throughout the early period; new movements, such as the Freedom and Popular Rights Movements (1874–89), involved greater numbers of people in the political arena; and counterrevolution, especially the *Seinan sensō* (literally the Southwestern War, but commonly translated as the Satsuma Rebellion), threatened the new government. These events offered competing visions of citizenship and constitutional government that questioned the vision and knowledge of the oligarchy of leaders. This perceived disorder formed the background to Inoue's commentary on the Rescript.

To foster ties between the individual and the nation, leaders turned to the family, or more broadly, to affect.[12] The idea of the family, as Philippe Ariès has pointed out, rose in tandem with the concept of the child; indeed, it is difficult if not impossible for the idealized family to exist without the child (1962:353). Again, we must be careful not to conflate the reproductive system with the conceptual family.[13] The family of course existed in pre-Meiji Japan, and many travelers commented on the affection parents had for their children. My attention will focus only on the family as it facilitated the reconceptualization of space, from an immediate, experiential environment to a delineation of ideal roles guided by the emperor.

The newly defined modern family replaced intermediary organizations— village, city, prefecture—now emplotted into secondary categories. Inoue describes the linkage between family and nation:

> The relation between the ruler [*kokkun*] and subjects is like that between parents and offspring [*shison*]. In other words, a country is an expanded family, and there is no difference between the leader of a country who commands his subjects and parents of a family who benevolently direct their offspring. Thus, today, when our emperor calls upon all throughout the land, these subjects must listen attentively and reverently as do all offspring to their honored father and affectionate mother. (1974 [1891]:159)

Inoue employs the metaphor of the organism to obscure the tenuous connection of family and nation (see also Inoue 1911). Ideas of growth, development, and nurturing suggest an inner time of the nation, but one that while connected to, indeed formed by, the historical, is also timeless. The appeal to the nation as an organism blurs the distinction between the past and the future, or experience and expectation. As in childhood, there is an inversion of the historical process—the historicity of the modern nation is elided. Even though the nation is created through history, those diachronic narratives that provide and order details of the national experience are now conflated with the nation-state; they exist prior to history. Past, present, and future are merged: "Subjects should possess a spirit of cooperation, assist and defend the imperial lineage, preserve the age-old *kokutai,* and prepare for the safety and prosperity of future generations" (1974 [1891]:179). This is the inversion of which Luckmann warns: that, despite narratives that naturalize, structures like the nation do not originate in some inner time that is natural, but through a social interaction. To ignore this inversion returns the historian to an ahistorical position where past, present, and future are connected (as they are today) as the common sense of the nation-state.

The notion of nation as an organism turns an idea, the ethnos, into a natural, pre-predictive category. It allows claims to a new experience despite conceptual gaps. Inoue does not claim a logical relation: "Those who exist in one country are all interconnected. Why? Because the interests [*rigai*] of one person become the interests of the nation-state, and its influence extends to all nationals" (1974 [1891]:177). Inoue recasts the notion of interests, crucial to bourgeois society, within a national, not individual, unit, orienting it toward the collective singular of the nation. In his argument for unity, Inoue mentions the variation, diversity, and disagreement within the archipelago. Yet difference is blurred in this appeal to the ethnos, a leap of faith (the "because") in the nation as the origin. While this is evident in the 1891 text, Inoue is much more explicit on the relation between individual and nation in an 1899 revision:[14] "Each individual [*kakuji*] is one element of the nation [*kokumin*] and the nation is produced from each individual. There is no individual outside the nation; there is no nation outside of each individual. For this reason, the fortunes of the nation influence each individual and the fortune of each influences the nation. Individuals and the nation are indivisibly bound together. In other words, the individual is the small ego and the nation is the big ego" (1899:509). Here the word *kakuji* for 'individual' refers to the person of the nation but also connotes an abstract thing. Importantly, it depicts the growing abstraction of individuals as nationals. While individuals become abstract units, their conceptual bodies naturalize the nation. "The Japanese ethnos continues the lineage from the same ancient texts, has resided on the same territory for thousands of years, and possesses the same language, habits, customs, history, etc. . . . Thus those who are part of the Japanese ethnos, just like a member of a family, are related by blood" (1899:509).

The child validates this social notion of organic community, one of growth, continuity, and posterity. It serves as a mnemonic object for the codes that define nationness. Inoue writes: "In the first place, the special kind of affection the child feels for its parents originally emerges from a relation of flesh and bones and is a thoroughly natural [*shizen*] feeling. . . . Thus, even though parents and child are completely different, they are not at all different. One has to say that the filiality of the child toward its parents is this inevitable force [*hitsuzen no ikioi*]" (1974 [1891]:159). Inoue conflates the biological and the social—birth and filiality are the same. The blood family becomes the primary social unit (itself problematic, since many families used adoption to perpetuate their line), and the child, now interchangeable with the citizen, is a reminder of continuity and the future. But the experience of the past that is to be continued is not that of the child but of an ideal society, in history.

Inoue hints at this new notion of experience in his analogy of child and parent to citizen and emperor. The social idea that makes this experience seem natural is the conflation of filiality and loyalty, combining the family with the national past: "Our Japanese nation-state long ago formed the family system: the country is an expanded family, and the family is a contracted country. . . . Thus in the family children obey the head, and in the country, through the spirit of obedience toward this family head, they obey the monarch. In other words, it is the extension of filiality directly to loyalty" (1899:513). Such passages make clear that he understands that part of the transformation of society is changing the way people think and the way their lives are oriented, from the local to the nation. To do so it is necessary to create different reasons, an ideology, apprehended through everyday experience to tie them to the whole. The family becomes a caricature of the various units that were part of a local economy; it is now the primary site that specifies, on an everyday level, the roles of good citizens.

The analogy between filiality and loyalty further binds citizens to the nation by locating childhood as the moment when citizens become indebted to the nation-state. Inoue writes: "People receive protection from the country [*honkoku*], develop in safety, and receive education in the schools of the country, thereby refining their abilities, developing their knowledge, and acquiring skills. Because of these the great obligation [*daion*] to the country, being profound and superior to all other obligations [*onkei*], must obviously be requited, and more important, the peace and prosperity of the whole country must not be damaged for one or a few persons" (1974 [1891]:168). Here the child mediates the interaction of the individual with the nation-state. By receiving something from superiors—protection, knowledge, guidance, and so on— it incurs an obligation that should be returned in the future. The horizon of expectations shifts attention from the individual and family to the nation.

Like the nation, the concepts of child and family become synchronic forms, separate from history (see Murakami 1984 for a recent example). The seduction is that the individual child and human family become the sites of experience, obfuscating the historicity of the particular meanings that are objectified. Everyday life—indeed, the body—is turned into a mnemonic device for the nation-state. Inner time, while believed to be "natural" time embedded in everyday habits or bodily rhythms, is only meaningful as socially objectified norms. This is a powerful source for ideological construction. Social constructs of interpersonal interaction are described in naturalized forms of development. The child becomes that origin, not of an experience prior to knowledge, but of a mythical origin, the empty vessel or dependent being, always in need of some guidance. The power of this ideology is that such a placement in the body of the child eradicates the artificiality of a social time, the origination in social interaction against which Luckmann warns.[15]

This public discourse was codified in two ways, through law and ethical education. In law, the Old Civil Code (1889) and the Civil Code (1898) legalized a patriarchical system that connected the hierarchy of the family to the nation (Kawashima 1957; Hastings and Nolte 1989). From the 1880s on, educators became increasingly concerned with social harmony and national unity. Motoda Eifu, the tutor to the Meiji Emperor, writes in his *Yōgaku kōyō*, a guidebook for elementary education published in 1882 by the Imperial Household Agency:

> Between heaven and earth no person is without a mother and father. One begins in the womb, is born, and grows. Their love and nurturance are profound; the mother and father have no equal. We must remember this benevolence and constantly strive to be reverent. Such love and respect is the Way of children. Filial piety is the highest principle of humanity. (quoted in Kawashima 1957:37)

Motoda is combining an idealized past—the extraction of filiality from Confucianism—with the modern—the concept of the child—in a way that elides the historicity of his idea. It is presented as a natural idea, the "Way of children," a combination of timeless forms: ethical norms suggesting the Confucian ideal and scientific knowledge shown through the human body. These ideas were taught in ways that did not eliminate the local but relocated it to a temporal category as a romanticized past. As early as 1881 Isawa, believing that affect was an important tool in conveying information to children, published a book of songs through the Ministry of Education for primary school students. These songs (many of which are remembered today) celebrate the village, a romanticized place of nature, "tradition," and family (Matsunaga 1975:83–90; Isawa 1881). For example, the song, "Kokyō no sora" ("The Skies of Home")[16] celebrates the ancestral village as a peaceful natural site while suggesting the importance of forbearance: "A clear night sky and autumn breeze / The moonlight dims, the *suzumushi* sings / Oh, how distant, the skies of home / Aah, how our mother and father have endured" (Matsunaga 1975:84). As Matsunaga points out, this song, which appeared just before the promulgation of the Constitution (1889), is connected to bourgeois society; one can easily imagine the migrant daughter in the textile mills or the son who ventured to the city looking for work (and fortune) remembering their home and parents at points of particular hardship. Using an aesthetic language of natural beauty, the song celebrates the nation-state, that is, the ancestors of the land. Individuality of and within each village is absent, and instead the village—described in terms of nature—becomes an abstract notion of a place of origin. The rural village takes on some of the transitory character of the child.

This naturalization of the nation could not have been possible apart from the imperialist nineteenth-century world. Both the similarity to Western discourse and the otherness of the West reinforced the redefinition of space, as Japan. The metaphor of the child, while useful in constructing the sameness of the nation, was also useful in constructing comparative frameworks that explained the asynchrony of nation-states. Here, we return to the diachrony of the child metaphor. Miyake Setsurei states: "Thus emulation is actually an effective form when, like a child [*shōni*], intellectual abilities are not yet developed; there are aspects [of the West] one should fervently recommend because it fosters development of knowledge, virtue, talent, and skills." The child becomes a metaphor for national development; the nation is assumed. But the child also gives hope. Miyake criticizes government policy of the 1890s for Japan's lack of cultural autonomy: "But one is already older and has reached the twenties. . . . Truly it turns into the absurd, as with the bewitching goblin and autonomous samurai" (1931 [1891]:257). In other words, intercultural comparisons now alter the horizon of expectations; the nation-state, too, must leave the temporary condition of childhood, in this case, mimetic ways, for an unknown but better future.

The Japanese nation-state was able to complete this development around the turn of the century. The Sino-Japanese War (1894–95) and Russo-Japanese War (1904–5) provided evidence of its new position in the linear hierarchy as an adult. China and Korea were emplotted on the lower end, becoming children to Japan's maturity.[17] Naitō Konan, the professor of Sinology at Kyoto Imperial University, used the metaphor of the child in a discourse commonly found among imperialists. He states: "The kindest thing the Japanese can do for the Koreans is to implement an austere government and remake their human natures which have fallen into decay over the past few centuries. . . . [A child] must first submit to disciplined training. Even if you provoke the child's resentment for a time, such treatment will bring true happiness in its future growth" (quoted in Fogel 1984:238). This conviction, common within Japan during the twentieth century, allowed Japanese to act in good faith as friends of their colonies while justifying their imperialistic rule (see also Nitobe 1920). The identification of others as children confirms that Japan has left that temporary site, and authorizes it to lead/dominate/punish others.

Ambiguity and Functionalization

The child as an abstract category brought a certainty to society that united a "plentitude of meanings." As in the idea of Dreamtime in Wolfe's essay in this volume, the definition of childhood as a temporal category is useful in facilitating the synchronization of different temporalities, what Ernst Bloch calls nonsynchronism, that "not all people exist in the same Now" (1977), into an orderly, usually hierarchical form. But an ambiguity also resides in this nonsynchrony, which allows childhood to be used in numerous ways. The variable and temporary nature of the concept of the child facilitates a variable reflexivity in which childhood serves as a site to fix and order things: problems are addressed as immature, romantic, hope, or in need of correction through education.

In his discussion of the pre–World War II Japan, Kuno Osamu, for example, has described society as containing exoteric and esoteric ideologies. The exoteric (*kenkyō*) was the public ideology proffered to most citizens in which the authority of the emperor, and thus of the state that governed for him, was absolute. In other words, it was a system based on belief. In contrast, the esoteric (*mikkyō*) served as the canon of the ruling elite, which recognized the limitations of the emperor within a constitutional system predicated on rationality—the mechanism and rationale for (and against) rule (Kuno [1956] 1978). This system could easily be described through the metaphor of childhood, in which citizens are infantilized and the state apparatus becomes the adult, the possessor of the knowledge required to rule. The child is the antithesis—an other located in a prior time—that confirms the process of socialization as knowledge acquisition. As an empty vessel in need of edification and discipline, children are those in need of direction (in little bits and pieces) before becoming participating members. Successful internalization of the proper codes—learning—allows the child to leave that temporary site for the "mature" condition of citizen. In Inoue's discussion of ethics, he uses the ambiguous word *shōnin* ('small person') for child; it suggests both the child and the uneducated.[18] Through edification (the context of his discussion is the efficacy of humiliation), "even the child changes, becomes a man of character [*kunshi*], and this man of character has an ethical conscience [*ryōshin*]" (1899:493). In other words, all people are first childlike; citizens must learn to behave and act in an appropriate way.

The metamorphosis of the child out of childhood overlays the alterity of childhood with another temporality, that of an idealized past. The child also serves as the embodied site for the future of the nation; it reminds adults of what is wrong with the present and provides the possibility for reform. In this case it is a hope for improvement—progress—but improvement based on an imagined experience. Steedman states: "In this way, childhood as it has been culturally described is always about that which is temporary and impermanent, always describes a loss in adult life, a state that is recognised too late" (1992:140). Here, the child plays an interesting role; it is to be something that does not exist and is based on an idealization of past experience. Education becomes the hope to correct what is "recognized too late." Inokuma Yōko's criticism of Ogawa Mimei, an author of children's books such as *Akai fune,* which is often considered to be the beginning of modern children's literature, illustrates this use of past and future to verify the present. She writes: "Mimei needed the imaginary world of children's stories in order to describe his own inner world, and once he gave up 'my unique form of poetry' in order to try writing 'for the sake of' children, he instructed them, from the viewpoint of adults, on how to live harmoniously in the real world" (quoted in Karatani 1993:115). The imaginary world of Mimei's children—näiveté, sensitivity, gentleness, and honesty—is conceptually similar to the pristine world of Japan's mythical origin in Inoue's commentary on the Rescript. He writes: "The virtues that were established when our imperial founder and ancestors founded the country are very deep. Thus, the unification of past beliefs [*jūrai kokoro*] of the commoners and adherence to the path of loyalty and filiality is for the prestige of our country and its preeminence over all others. To achieve this, education of our country must serve as the foundation" (1974 [1891]:158). The world of the child is a mirror leading to the future, a desire in the guise of guidance, which imposes restrictions on actions based on the present. For Inoue, the purpose of education was to provide all citizens with an understanding of "public affairs" (*seimu*). But his notion of *seimu* was quite specific:

attentiveness, obedience to law, and punctuality (the latter, he laments, is particularly lacking among common Japanese) (1899:500). The historical, *seimu,* and the real world of Mimei are ideals that people must internalize, even as far as bodily habits, which have become inherent national characteristics.

These restrictions, however, are not the draconian policies of a totalitarian government but the bounding of experience as the proper behavior of good citizens. Mimei's imaginary child's world hints of an antithetical time, a romance or escape to a lost time. But this picture of innocence and näiveté is the imagination of an adult world (Maeda 1982:284–85). The child rescues one from the present, the problems, corruption, and alienation of modern society (Steedman 1992:139). It is an escape to a past, both a past of exploration and restlessness, where one can vicariously escape the limits of "mature" behavior, and a past where corrections could have been made. On an individual level, it places responsibility for not being higher in the social hierarchy on oneself and one's childhood. And for the nation-state it is a constant reminder of the failings of past forms in teaching its members how the national "we" should relate to one another (Shotter 1993:87). The rise of children's literature around 1890 reflects this longing that is tied to the future of the nation-state. The magazine *Shōkokumin* ("Young [lit: small] Citizen") and the series *Shōnen bungaku* ("Children's Literature") were filled with historical stories of exemplary figures and rarely included folk stories (such as *Kogane maru,* often considered the first children's story). The main themes were effort and proper moral and ethical behavior. The child linked an idealized past and future, now history; it became the idealized site for hard work, study, obedience, and filiality.

As was evident above, the transformation of childhood elevated the family into a public institution that mediates between individual desires and national prescriptions. Inoue writes: "However, a family, as in the organism of a cell, actually, is the pillar of a country; when families are reconciled there is tranquility within the country. But because one cannot unify the hearts [*kokoro*] of millions when there is strife among families, the power of the country will consequently collapse" (1974 [1891]:162). But the formalization of the family weakened rather than strengthened its influence. Importantly, the chief role of parents is to provide a nurturing environment, not the transmission of social knowledge. Education, formerly a process of socialization by members of the community, regardless of age, now became the obligation of the state. Public schools took on the role of education, shifting learning from integration into the local economy to becoming a good citizen. Indeed, here, too, parents were considered as children. Elites were convinced that the state, through the educational system, knew what was best for children. Aoki Sukekiyo's 1876 manual for primary school teachers displays a distrust of parents that has characterized modern educational systems. He states: "What determines whether habits of good behavior and diligence, or bad behavior and indolence will form are the standards and models provided by the conduct of parents and teachers. Especially in Japan, whose culture is shallow, parents lack the know-how to educate their children, so it is the teacher who bears the greatest responsibility" (quoted in Lincicome 1995:37). Others, such as Mitsukuri, were more direct in lamenting the lack of parental attention, regardless of wealth (Braisted 1976:107). Zelizer finds a similar distrust in the United States (1985:84); it is a distrust reflecting the authority invested in the possessor of knowledge—the rationality of modernity—rather than a cultural trait. The establishment of compulsory primary education in Japan institutionalized this shift of power; education— the teaching of morals, ethics, history, writing, and so on—was removed from the home to the school, allowing parents to concentrate on work or housekeeping.

The decline of family influence was furthered in this functionalization of daily habits. Each part of the unit was to act within proper, or assigned, roles and rules. Tasks that had been shared were increasingly assigned to specific people (Edelstein 1983; Liljestrom 1983). Inoue was quite aware of this change: "When they form a family unit, it leads, without fail, to the separation of work between husband and wife. In other words, the husband exists outside and works, while the wife remains and tends to the house; by planning together and helping each other, in hopes for future prosperity, they must work for their mutual development and progress" (1974 [1891]:163). Prior to the Meiji period roles of individual family members, especially among the nonsamurai, were not as restrictive (see for example Uno 1991). Implicit in the deferred gratification, "hopes for future prosperity," is the child, the one who will perpetuate the family line. The description of an ideal working family not only separates work as a male endeavor from the household and en-genders the now devalued housework, but also ties labor to abstract gratification, some nonexperiential "reward" in the future. The child as rescuer encourages resignation to one's present conditions.

The reorientation of the archipelago into a nation-state during the early Meiji period can be described as an effort by intellectuals and the political elite to create a rational order that, through synchronization, could account for the great diversity that existed. This synchronization occurred in history, the constitution of a social time of the nation-state. The child was central to this transformation; in Meiji Japan, childhood provided a centripetal force, always being drawn on to structure a national society. By turning the child into the focus of a developmental notion of human life, intellectuals merged ontogeny and phylogeny as if they were an "underlying essence," the mysterious and hidden, now placed in the realm of science rather than that of the supernatural (ghosts).

But the child only existed through the body of "the Japanese." Far from being universalistic, the constant birth of children provided that synchrony of nation, the same passage of all Japanese since the beginning of time. The preoccupation of the elite in early Meiji Japan was the formation of an idea of nation that created a sense of unity and thus, occasionally by design, eradicated existing differences in favor of variations that could be rendered within that orderly system. The chosen characteristics were part of a coherent image that reoriented society around those abstract forms of knowledge, something seemingly common that could give a point of sameness to all people of the archipelago, despite the considerable differences of region, class, occupation, and so on. This synchrony fostered a different form of interaction in which certain past codes could be retained as something inherent. The child became a site of that new temporality, which established "specific dispositions" and demonstrated "ways of assimilating experience."[19]

In this constitution of history, knowledge was separated from experience: first, the previous understanding of the world was no longer valid, eliminated willingly by some or forcefully by others (or retained in some capacity by many willing to remain on the margins); and second, it was replaced by new forms, now abstract and still separated from the immediate. Childhood filled the void created by this separation; it is a natural being, clear for everyone (with the proper knowledge) to see, that becomes the metonym for a historical construction that seeks monopoly over experience itself. As the specific idea of childhood became increasingly common, the artificiality of this new ethical system faded and it became "natural."[20] It is the replacement of the historical with the natural that imbues ideas of the nation-state with the tenacity of belief, despite empirical information to the contrary, and it is here that scholars have often been blind to the entrapments of our discourses. This returns us to the troubling statement that begins Agamben's chapter on infancy and history: "The question of experience can be approached nowadays only with an acknowledgement that it is no longer accessible to us" (1993:13).

Epilogue

Even though the Japanese philosophers, educators, and political leaders mentioned in this essay mapped out what citizens/children should experience, it does not mean that the latter actually did so. If experience is socially constituted—which I believe it is—then on one level Agamben's warning harks back to an Enlightenment ideal, that there can be a pure experience. When we recognize the historicity of the social, then we can also recognize the various socials that constitute experiences. The monological claims of science and the nation-state are one, albeit predominant, of those socials. In the case of Japan, the common sense of the nation is that "orderly or coherent mental representation—the urge in reflection to *command a clear view*—[that] in fact *prevents* us from achieving a proper grasp of the pluralistic, nonorderly nature of our circumstances" (Shotter 1993:19).

This leads to a problem that has no singular answer but must be confronted if we are to better understand questions of nation and identity: what is the relation between knowledge and belief? While a nation-state like Japan suggests a rather thorough internalization of codes that evoke a common belief, our archives today are rich with evidence of a great variety of experiences beyond what has been described through history. Indeed, there are many socials that guide individual experiences, and the ambiguity of categories such as childhood also creates spaces, albeit rather narrow, in which individuals can act autonomously (Herzfeld, 1992). One can find many different types of experience throughout pre–World War II Japan. For example, a year after the law establishing compulsory education (1872), riots erupted in Tsuruga, Okayama, Tottori, Kagawa, and Fukuoka, and in some cases schools were burned. To be sure, these riots were not directed solely against education, but the educational system was seen as a part and symbol of the new government (Karatani 204). Even by the 1930s, while the child as symbol of the hope of the nation-state was pervasive, the process of incorporation varied considerably and did not necessarily lead to betterment for children/citizens (see also Steedman 1992:134–36). For example, villagers in Takagami village in Chiba rose up in 1930 against those who symbolized the nation-state, the police, teachers, and the wealthy.[21] Children who participated in the riots indicate the presence of multiple temporalities, the presence of a different social knowledge, that of a local, participatory form which, in this case, resisted the homogenization to a national, abstract form. These children were not innocents, nor were they uninformed about changes brought about by the new government: "By yelling at the bushy-faced thugs [police] who tried to drive us off and by showing resistance as much as we, the smallest, could, we wanted to show again and again that we knew. It was they who oppressed our fathers; they squeezed everyone for as many as twenty years" (Seki 1972:473–74). The children obviously did not directly experience the twenty years of embezzlement, but they were part of a community that transmitted what it considered to be knowledge necessary to function within the village. Indeed, this socialization for village life conflicted with the socialization for the nation-state: "At school the teacher taught us: it was bad to create such trouble, etc. etc. But that? No one is that tight: those who made our fathers suffer so; those thugs who oppressed those who have endured in silence. How can we remain silent at the bidding of the government teacher? To eyes that still only see this as proper? That's why we yelled and threw rocks; we wanted to attack again and again" (Seki 1972:474). To the teachers, the children were innocents who should not know about such troubling things: "No matter how much those thugs told us that we could not watch and tried to chase us away, we always returned, yelling" (Seki 1972:473). This incident suggests the presence of many experiences; while the event is described as local versus national, these are not dialectical categories but varied, coexisting, and conflicting forms of knowledge. The children possessed several voices. On the one hand, they were only heard by authorities through the monological codes of the nation-state—they were unruly and uneducated. But, on the other hand, they also had a different knowledge (more sophisticated than the authorities believed) about the relation between power and individuals. While learning (but differentially internalizing) the codes of the nation-state, they were also defending their world, a space of experience, which included, but was not incorporated by, the hierarchical horizons of the nation-state.

NOTES

1. The award given to Oe is often construed within (and outside) Japan as Japan's Nobel Prize. Indeed, after Oe's award, the *New York Times Book Review* listed Mishima as a Nobel laureate, conflating the two authors into a single category, Japanese.

2. This convergence of nature and thought in the scientific discourses of the late nineteenth century was described by Heinrich Hertz, the physicist who discovered radio waves: "In endeavouring . . . to draw inferences as to the future from the past, we always adopt the following process. We form for ourselves images or symbols of external objects; and the form that we give them is such that the necessary consequents of the images in thought are always the images of the necessary consequents in nature of the things pictured. In order that this requirement may be satisfied, there must be a certain conformity between nature and our thought" (quoted in Shotter 1993:74).

3. While today we use several categories to mark stages of human development—infant, toddler, adolescent, and so on—I use the child as a concept for this early period that historically was not precisely defined.

4. For an account of the controversy provoked by Philippe Ariès' *Centuries of Childhood,* see Schultz 1995.

5. Such comments on Japanese children were common among foreign travelers in the nineteenth century. See, for example, Mitford 1966 [1871]; Griffiths 1901; and Bacon 1891.

6. Child-rearing practices differed by class: infants of commoners and peasants were carried about on the backs of older children, in the middle classes babies rode the backs of nurses, while the offspring of the elite were carried about in the arms of attendants (Bacon 1891:7).

7. Children were generally naked, keeping warm within the clothes of the caregiver, until the age of three (Kuroda 1989:89–94). Although not rigidly codified, samurai marked changes at the third year by no longer shaving children's hair; at five, boys received a *hakama,* the traditional skirtlike pants, and at seven the girls began wearing the *obi* (the girdlelike sash).

8. For an example of this transformation in which ghosts and spirits become the imagined world of children—that is, the unlearned—see Tanizaki 1988:68–69.

9. Like the concept of the child, the physiological Japanese is conflated with the idea of "the Japanese." For a recent study that examines this construction of the nation, see Fujitani 1993, and 1996.

10. Foucault writes: "It is no longer origin that gives rise to historicity; it is historicity that, in its very fabric, makes possible the necessity of an origin which must be both internal and foreign to it: like the virtual tip of a cone in which all differences, all dispersions, all discontinuities would be knitted together so as to form no more than a single point of identity, the impalpable figure of the Same, yet possessing the power, nevertheless, to burst open upon itself and become Other" (1973:329–30).

11. Interestingly, Inoue's and Mitsukuri's division of childhood has not changed significantly today: infants are dependent upon parents and society for basic needs, then at the age of six or seven the child goes to school, and by age twenty he or she is generally capable of becoming autonomous (Inoue 1974 [1891]:160; Braisted 106). Again, this is less something that was introduced from the West than a process that was catalysed. For example, Kaibara Ekiken described a somewhat developmental educational structure, beginning at six, that bears some resemblance to the ideas Japanese in the Meiji period were to pick up from Pestalozzi and other educational reformers. For the latter, see Lincicome 1995 (esp. chaps. 1 and 2).

12. Much has been written about the family and its connection to the emperor system. See, for example, Irokawa 1985; Kawashima 1957; Bernstein 1991; and Gluck 1986.

13. For a study that argues that the family system has been the defining unit of Japanese society throughout history, see Murakami 1984.

14. Inoue more clearly articulates the position of the individual in the nation-state in this revised and enlarged version than in the original. I have used passages from the revised version (which is often not differentiated from the original) where different. The

difference, I believe, indicates a greater concern for articulating the contemporary indigenous sites for unity, rather than arguing for unity to avoid the atomization of modern/Western society.

15. For a criticism of this conflation of loyalty and filiality as a strategy that occults the historicity of Japan, see Tsuda 1938.

16. It was written by Owada Takeki in 1888 using the melody of the Scottish tune "Comin' through the Rye." The *suzumushi* is a type of cricket.

17. The position of China was ambiguous, at times being the child and on other occasions the old, decrepit man. Shiratori Kurakichi, professor of Oriental History at Tokyo Imperial University, compared Chinese and Japanese families to assert Japan's distinctiveness and superiority (1920).

18. From the latter context, it is clear that he is discussing the uneducated, a category extending well beyond that of children.

19. Steedman describes this role: [D]evelopments in scientific thought in the 19th century showed that childhood was both a stage of growth and development common to all of us, abandoned and left behind, but at the same time, a core of the individual's psychic life, always immanent, waiting there be drawn on in various ways" (1992:129).

20. This naturalization is made painfully evident in Norma Field's essay (1995), which points to the further reduction of this temporal category in Japan to that of laborer and consumer of the educational system that must give them the knowledge to become good citizens.

21. Takagami was a combined farming and fishing village not far from Tokyo. It was not impoverished. The riot was precipitated by the discovery of embezzlement of public funds by the mayor and an increase in local taxes.

REFERENCES

Agamben, Giorgio. 1993 [1978]. *Infancy and History: Essays on the Destruction of Experience.* Liz Heron, trans. London: Verso.

Anderson, Benedict. 1983. *Imagined Communities.* London: Verso.

Ariès, Philippe. 1962. *Centuries of Childhood: A Social History of Family Life.* Robert Baldick, trans. New York: Vintage.

Bacon, Alice Mabel. 1891. *Japanese Girls and Women.* Boston: Houghton Mifflin.

Berlin, Isaiah. 1980. "Nationalism: Past Neglect and Present Power." In *Against the Current,* 333–55. New York: Viking.

Bernstein, Gail L., ed. 1991. *Recreating Japanese Women, 1600–1945.* Berkeley: University of California Press.

Bird, Isabella. 1984 [1880]. *Unbeaten Tracks in Japan.* Boston: Beacon Press.

Bloch, Ernst. 1977. "Nonsynchronism and the Obligation to Its Dialectics." *New German Critique* vol. 11, 22–38.

Braisted, William, trans. 1976. *Meiroku zasshi: Journal of the Japanese Enlightenment.* Cambridge: Harvard University Press.

Chatterjee, Partha. 1993. *The Nation and Its Fragments: Colonial and Postcolonial Histories.* Princeton: Princeton University Press.

deMause, Lloyd. 1974. "The Evolution of Childhood," in *The History of Childhood,* Lloyd deMause, ed., 1–74. New York: Psychohistory Press.

Eagleton, Terry. 1990. *The Ideology of the Aesthetic.* Oxford: Basil Blackwell.

Edelstein, Wolfgang. 1983. "Cultural Constraints on Development and the Vicissitudes of Progress," in *The Child and Other Cultural Inventions,* Frank S. Kessel and Alexander W. Siegel, eds., 48–88. New York: Praeger.

Elias, Norbert. 1992. *Time: An Essay.* Oxford: Blackwell.

Field, Norma. 1995. "The Child as Laborer and Consumer: The Disappearance of Childhood in Contemporary Japan," in *Children and the Politics of Culture,* Sharon Stephens, ed., 51–78. Princeton: Princeton University Press.

Fogel, Joshua. 1984. *Politics and Sinology: The Case of Naitō Konan, 1866–1934.* Cambridge: Council on East Asian Studies, Harvard University.

Foucault, Michel. 1973. *The Order of Things: An Archeology of the Human Sciences.* New York: Vintage.

Fridell, Wilbur M. 1973. *Japanese Shrine Mergers, 1906–1912: State Shinto Moves to the Grassroots.* Tokyo: Sophia University.

Fujitani, Takashi. 1993. "Inventing, Forgetting, Remembering: Toward a Historical Ethnography of the Nation-State," in *Cultural Nationalism in East Asia: Representation and Identity,* Harumi Befu, ed., 77–106. Berkeley: Institute of East Asian Studies, University of California.

———. 1996. *Emperor, Nation, Pageantry: A Historical Ethnography of Modern Japan.* Berkeley: University of California Press.

Garon, Sheldon. 1994. "Rethinking Modernization and Modernity in Japanese History: A Focus on State-Society Relations." *Journal of Asian Studies,* vol. 53 (May), 346–66.

Gluck, Carol. 1986. *Japan's Modern Myths: Ideology in the Late Meiji Period.* Princeton: Princeton University Press.

Griffis, William Eliot. 1901. "The Games and Sports of Japanese Children," in Matilda Chaplin Ayrton, *Child-life in Japan and Japanese Child Stories.* Boston: D. C. Heath.

Hearn, Lafcadio. 1971. *Kwaidan: Stories and Studies of Strange Things.* Rutland, Vt.: Charles E. Tuttle.

Herzfeld, Michael. 1992. *The Social Production of Indifference: Exploring the Symbolic Roots of Western Bureaucracy.* Chicago: University of Chicago Press.

Higuchi Ichiyō. 1981. "Child's Play," in *In the Shade of Spring Leaves: The Life and Writings of Higuchi Ichiyo, a Woman of Letters in Meiji Japan,* trans. Robert Danly. New Haven: Yale University Press.

Hobsbawm, Eric, and Terence Ranger, eds. 1983. *The Invention of Tradition.* Cambridge: Cambridge University Press.

Inoue Tetsujirō. 1974 [1891]. "Chokugo engi," in *Shiryō, chokugo engi: kappatsuji oyobi kanrensho shiryō,* Katayama Seiichi, ed. Tokyo: Kōryōsha shoten.

———. 1974 [1899]. "Zōtei chokugo engi," in *Kyōiku chokugo kankei shiryō,* Furuta Shōkin, ed., 457–520. Tokyo: Nihon daigaku seishin bunka kenkyūjō.

———. 1911. "Waga kokutai to kazoku seido." *Tōa no hikari,* 6–9 (September), 1–18.

Irokawa Daikichi. 1973. *Meiji seishinshi (shinpen).* Tokyo: Chūō kōronsha.

———. 1985. *The Culture of the Meiji Period,* Marius Jansen, ed. and trans. Princeton: Princeton University Press.

Isawa Shūji. 1881. *Shōgaku shōkashū shohen.* Tokyo: Monbusho.

Kami Shōichirō. 1989. *Nihon jidōshi no kaitaku.* Tokyo: Komine shoten.

———. 1994. "Jidō bungaku: edo kara Meiji e," in *Ukiyoe no kodomotachi,* Inagaki Shinichi, Kami Shōichirō, and Kuroda Hideo, eds., 7–9. Tokyo: Tōbu bijutsukan.

Karatani Kōjin. 1993 [1980]. *Origins of Modern Japanese Literature,* Brett de Bary, ed. and trans. Durham: Duke University Press.

Kawashima Takeyoshi. 1957. *Ideorogii to shite no kazoku seido.* Tokyo: Iwanami shoten.

Kern, Stephen. 1983. *The Culture of Time and Space: 1880–1918.* Cambridge: Harvard University Press.

Kessen, William. 1979. "The American Child and Other Cultural Inventions." *American Psychologist,* 34:(10), 815–20.

Kido Shōsaburō. 1886. *Kodomo no chie mashi.* Osaka: Akashi chūsadō.

Kinmonth, Earl. 1981. *The Self-Made Man in Meiji Japanese Thought: From Samurai to Salaryman.* Berkeley: University of California Press.

Kokubun Ichitarō. 1972. "Kodomo zuihitsu: mura no kodomo." In Matsunaga Goichi, *Kindai minshū no kiroku: nōmin,* 205–27. Tokyo: Shinjinbutsu ōraisha.

Koselleck, Reinhart. 1985 [1979]. *Futures Past: On the Semantics of Historical Time,* Keith Tribe, trans. Boston: MIT Press.

Kuno Osamu. 1978. "The Meiji State, Minponshugi, and Ultranationalism," in *Authority and the Individual: Citizen Protest in Historical Perspective,* J. Victor Koschmann, ed., 60–80. Tokyo: University of Tokyo Press.

Kuroda Hideo. 1989. *"Emaki" kodomo no tōjō: chūsei shakai no kodomozō.* Tokyo: Kawade shobō shinsha.

———. 1994. "Edoki no kodomo o shakai shiteki ni miru," in *Ukiyoe no kodomotachi,* Inagaki Shinichi, Kami Shōichirō, and Kuroda Hideo, eds., 10–12. Tokyo: Tōbu bijutsukan.

Lévi-Strauss, Claude. 1971. *Tristes Tropiques: An Anthropological Study of Primitive Societies in Brazil,* John Russell, trans. New York: Atheneum.

Liljestrom, Rita. 1983. "The Public Child, the Commercial Child, and Our Child," in *The Child and Other Cultural Inventions,* Frank S. Kessel and Alexander W. Siegel, eds., 124–57. New York: Praeger.

Lincicome, Mark. 1995. *Principle, Praxis, and the Politics of Educational Reform in Meiji Japan.* Honolulu: University of Hawaii Press.

Luckmann, Thomas. 1991. "The Constitution of Human Life in Time," in *Chronotypes: The Construction of Time,* John Bender and David E. Wellbery, eds., 151–66. Stanford: Stanford University Press.

Maeda Ai. 1982. *Toshi kukan no naka no bungaku.* Tokyo: Chikuma shobō.

Matsunaga Goichi. 1975. "Morbusho shōka no giman." *Furusato kō,* 83–90. Tokyo: Kōdansha.

Mitford, A. B. 1966 [1871]. *Tales of Old Japan.* Rutland, Vt.: Charles E. Tuttle.

Miyake Setsurei. 1931 [1891]. "Giakushu nihonjin," in *Gendai nihon bungaku zenshū,* vol. 5, 239–57. Tokyo: Kaizōsha.

Moretti, Franco. 1987. *The Way of the World: The* Bildungsroman *in European Culture.* London: Verso.

Murakami Yasusuke. 1984. "Ie Society as a Pattern of Civilization." *Journal of Japanese Studies,* vol. 10, 281–363.

Nagatsuka Takashi. 1990. *The Soil: A Portrait of Rural Life in Meiji Japan.* Anne Waswo, trans. Berkeley: University of California Press.

Nietzsche, Friedrich. 1983 [1874]. "The Uses and Disadvantages of History for Life," in *Untimely Meditations,* 57–123. R. J. Hollingdale, trans. Cambridge: Cambridge University Press.

Nitobe Inazō. 1920. "Japanese Colonization." *Asiatic Review,* vol. 16, 113–21.

Nolte, Sharon H., and Sally Hastings. 1991. "The Meiji State's Policy toward Women, 1890–1910," in *Recreating Japanese Women, 1600–1945,* Gail L. Bernstein, ed., 151–74. Berkeley: University of California Press.

Okada Yoshirō. 1994. *Meiji kaireki: "toki" no bunmei kaika.* Tokyo: Dashūkan shoten.

Polanyi, Karl. 1944. *The Great Transformation.* Boston: Little, Brown.

Rubinger, Richard. 1982. *Private Academies of Tokugawa Japan.* Princeton: Princeton University Press.

Schultz, James A. 1995. *The Knowledge of Childhood in the German Middle Ages, 1100–1350.* Philadelphia: University of Pennsylvania Press.

Seki Genkichi. 1972. "Kodomotachi," in Matsunaga Goichi, *Kindai minshū no kiroku: nōmin,* 473–74. Tokyo: Shinjinbutsu ōraisha.

Shiratori Kurakichi. 1920. "Kōdō no konpongi ni tsuite." *Kōdō,* 344 (November), 2–17.

Shotter, John. 1993. *The Cultural Politics of Everyday Life.* Toronto: University of Toronto Press.

Steedman, Carolyn. 1992. *Past Tenses: Essays on Writing, Autobiography and History.* London: Rivers Oram Press.

———. 1995. *Strange Dislocations: Childhood and the Idea of Human Interiority, 1780–1930.* Cambridge: Harvard University Press.

Sterngold, James. 1994. "Japan Asks Why a Prophet Bothers." *New York Times,* November 6, 1994, 4,5.

Tanizaki Junichiro. 1988. *Childhood Years: A Memoir,* Paul McCarthy, trans. Tokyo and New York: Kodansha International.

Tsuda Sōkichi. 1938. *Shina shisō to nihon.* Tokyo: Iwanami shinsho.

Uno, Kathleen S. 1991. "Women and Change in the Household Division of Labor," in *Recreating Japanese Women, 1600–1945,* Gail L. Bernstein, ed., 17–41. Berkeley: University of California Press.

Yanagita Kunio. 1942. *Kodomo fudoki.* Osaka: Asahi shinbunsha.

Zelizer, Viviana A. 1985. *Pricing the Priceless Child: The Changing Social Value of Children.* New York: Basic Books.

Should the Subaltern Dream?
"Australian Aborigines" and the
Problem of Ethnographic Ventriloquism

Patrick Wolfe

Introduction

For all the homage paid to heterogeneity and difference, the bulk of "post"-colonial theorizing is disabled by an oddly monolithic, and generally unexamined, notion of colonialism. This would seem to spring from two distinct sources. The first is a pervasive Eurocentrism—or, as we might better term it, Occidocentrism—on the part of academic theorists, for whom colonialism figures, narcissistically, as a projection (the western will to power, etc.). The second consists in the historical accident (or is it?) that the native founders of the "post"colonial canon came from franchise or dependent—as opposed to settler or creole—colonies. This gave these guerrilla theoreticians the advantage of speaking to an oppressed majority on the supply of whose labor a colonizing minority was utterly dependent. For Amil Cabral (1967:47), therefore, genocide of the natives could only be counterproductive, creating "a void which empties foreign domination of its content and its object: the dominated people." Analogously (in this regard at least), when Frantz Fanon asserted (1967:47) that "colonization and decolonization are simply a question of relative strength," he was referring to relative capacities for violence, on which basis the colonizer was ultimately superfluous. Given certain African contexts, especially in the 1960s, the material grounds for such optimism can reasonably be credited. But what if the colonizers are not dependent on native labor?—indeed, what if the natives themselves have been reduced to a small minority whose survival can hardly be seen to furnish the colonizing society with more than a remission from ideological embarrassment?

In contrast to the kind of colonial formation that Cabral or Fanon confronted, settler colonies were not primarily established to extract surplus value from indigenous labor.[1] Rather, they are premised upon displacing indigenes from (or *re*placing them on) the land. The relationship between Native and African Americans provides the clearest illustration. In the main, Native North Americans were cleared from their land rather than exploited for their labor, their place being taken by displaced Africans who provided the labor to be mixed with the expropriated land. In the Australian case, the labor that was imported to add value to the land was primarily that of British and Irish convicts. In such a situation, it is difficult to speak of an articulation between colonizer and native, since the determinate articulation is not to a society but directly to the land, a precondition of social organization. Since it is incoherent to talk of an articulation between humans and things, this social relationship can be conceived of as a negative articulation. Settler colonies were (are) premised upon the elimination of native societies.

The split tensing reflects a determinate feature of settler colonization. The colonizers come to stay—invasion is a structure rather than an event. In contrast, for all the hollow formality of decolonization, at least the legislators change color. Such distinctions ramify throughout the different colonial formations. They are particularly apparent at the level of ideology—the romance of extinction, for instance (the dying race, the last of his tribe, etc.), encodes a settler-colonial imperative that would be confounded by the hyperfecundity, natural sense of rhythm, etc. that are typically attributed to slave races. In the analysis to come, I shall argue that the Australian "Aboriginal Dreamtime" constitutes a settler-colonial discourse[2] par excellence, an ideological elaboration of the doctrine of *terra nullius* which emptied the scene of invasion so that settler and landscape comprised a primal duality. To the invaders of Australia, who sought to replace indigenous society, pastoral settlement was seen as a zero-sum conflict. It could be settlers or it could be natives: as the graziers' aphorism had it, "niggers and cattle don't mix" (Reynolds 1982:129). For this culture of settlement, dreaming had a particular ideological resonance on account of its conformity with the idea that colonial intrusion was a form of awakenment. Though the narrative of awakenment was a commonplace of the doctrine of progress, legitimizing conquest right across the colonized world, the settlement of land belonging to "nomads" gave it a special twist. For what was to be aroused there was not the people but the land itself, which, having never felt the improving iron of cultivation, had yet to become property.[3] In reducing the land to productive order, then, colonial settlement was rescuing it from nature as reason rescues consciousness from the chaos of dreaming. Whereas the colonization of surplus-generating civilizations that had had golden ages was depicted as renaissance, dreaming Aborigines had merely occupied the land, so settlement was not occupation. Like the morning mist, therefore, the Dreamtime evaporated with the dawning of settlement, leaving behind only land as the other party to the colonial encounter.

This argument will be elaborated below. First, though, some of the implications of the foregoing need to be spelled out. In particular, if we are to take the heterogeneity of different colonial formations seriously, we cannot use morphological generalizations such as "the level of ideology" without qualification. Since any given colonial formation at any given time constitutes a specific configuration of elements and relations, we should expect that distinctions as to the workings of different ideologies will not be confined to their representational contents. Rather, the mechanics, location, and relative efficacy of ideology itself—regardless of its specific contents—will vary between different colonial formations, whose "levels" will not necessarily be commensurable.[4] In this respect, settler colonies' relative immunity to the withdrawal of native labor is highly significant. As noted, this immunity contrasts sharply with the master-slave structuring of Fanon's schema, in which the colonist "owes the fact of his very existence, that is to say his property, to the colonial system" (1967:28). In the settler-colonial economy, it is not the colonist but the native who is superfluous. This means that the sanctions practically available to the native are ideological ones. In settler-colonial formations, in other words, ideology *has a higher systemic weightage* —it looms larger, as it were—than in other colonial formations. In the purest of instances, this means that ideology is all there is: that the zero-sum conflict between native and settler is entirely constituted at the level of ideology, and is waged around the issue of assimilation.

Where survival is a matter of not being assimilated, positionality is not just central to the issue—it *is* the issue. In a settler-colonial context, therefore, the question of who speaks goes way beyond liberal concerns with equity, dialogue, or access to the academy. Claims to knowledge about indigenous discourse made from within the settler-colonial academy necessarily participate in the continuing usurpation of indigenous space (invasion is a structure rather than an event). This theoretical conclusion is abundantly borne out by the Australian academy's deep involvement in successive modalities of settler-colonial oppression. Whether by accident or design, whether by measuring, quantifying, pathologizing, expunging, or essentializing, a comprehensive range of authorities—anthropologists, biologists, archaeologists, psychologists, criminologists, the whole Foucauldian line-up—have produced an incessant flow of knowledge about Aborigines that has become available for selective appropriation to warrant, to rationalize, and to authenticate official definitions, policies, and programs for dealing with "the Aboriginal problem."[5] The following analysis documents a single, anthropological instance of this generalized institutional practice.

Anthropology is analysed here, in a manner adapted from Marcel Mauss, as a total cultural practice: in this case, one that expresses and sustains the hegemonic process of colonial settlement.[6] In other words, my tribe is the anthropologists. Anthropological debates are my primary data, rather than a means to a shared end. Thus I am neither attempting to answer the questions that anthropologists have asked themselves nor arbitrating in their disputes, since to do so would be to analyse indigenous, as opposed to anthropological, discourse. Indigenous discourse only intrudes into the analysis when it submits to anthropological language, at which point it acquires new significance in relation to oppositions and associations that have developed within the colonizing culture. The object of the following analysis is, therefore, an anthropological construct called the Dreamtime, and not any presumptive Koori precedent. It should by now be clear that any attempt on my part to recuperate an originary Koori trace from behind the textual surface of the Dreamtime—any slippage, as Gayatri Spivak (1988:288) puts it, "from rendering visible the mechanism to rendering vocal the individual"—would not only be an appropriation. By the same token, it would be empirically self-defeating. Thus the insistence on discourse analysis is not merely some moral or political scruple that can be distinguished from scholarly investigation. While it may be such a thing, it is also a necessary outcome of methodological rigor.

In Australia, then, the Dreamtime discourse signifies everything that was or remains Aboriginal. Its currency encompasses scholarly and popular culture. Though introduced into the Australian settler vocabulary through the writings of White anthropologists, the Dreamtime has become one of the central symbols of Koori cultural revivalism. In the context of the Australian cultural field as a whole, however, the concept encodes and sustains the subjugation and expropriation of the Koori population. This discursive irony is my object of analysis.

This paper traces the origin and historical development of the Dreamtime concept, showing how its affinity with the theoretical environment of late-nineteenth-century anthropology followed from an ideological legacy that linked the concept to themes fundamental to European colonial expansion. These themes penetrate cultural reaches that would otherwise appear to be historically and geographically distinct. Thus, from situating the Dreamtime in relation to broad post-Enlightenment generalities, the paper traces the concept's genealogy through more specifically anthropological theorizing to the local ideologies of a frontier culture, where it provides a rationale for territorial expropriation. The local ideology is not simply a reflection of macrohistorical determinations but a culturally specific formulation which undergoes transformations as settler-colonial society develops.

The discussion therefore covers a number of historical and cultural registers, between which there is some terminological variation, but in which a reference to dreaming is constant. To express this continuity, the term "Dreaming complex" will be adopted. This term has the further significance that, as a focus of intersection, a complex reflects the paper's holistic approach. The Dreaming complex is, in short, a total cultural practice, the special term being necessitated by the variety of names that its referent has borne.

Beginnings

That the Dreaming complex was an invention of the anthropologists' own culture[7] can be seen from the extraordinary success that it enjoyed once it had been coined in the ethnography of Frank Gillen. Indeed, before Gillen's phrase was even introduced, it had been advertised in advance by an Englishman, Baldwin Spencer, who spoke no Koori language, as "aptly" and "appropriately" rendered from the (Ab)original (Spencer 1896b:50, 111). The phrase subsequently acquired such a peerless hegemony over Australian Aboriginal anthropology that the discipline's foremost practitioners mutually misrepresented the phrase's history in order to associate themselves with its discovery. The sequence of events was as follows.

Spencer, professor of biology at the University of Melbourne, met Gillen, postmaster at Alice Springs, in 1894, while Spencer was on the Horn Scientific Expedition to central Australia.[8] The ensuing partnership between the biologist and the local man harnessed scientific credentials to an otherwise incompatible familiarity with savagery.

"The dream-times" was one of the first fruits of this partnership. Spencer (1896a) edited the report of the Horn Expedition. At his instigation, Gillen (1896) contributed a memoir on some manners and customs of the Arunta. This memoir was appended to the fourth volume of the report, an arrangement that enabled Gillen's phrase to have been explicitly corroborated on two occasions by Spencer, in his sections of the report, before the reader had even encountered it.

In the first volume of the report, Spencer condemned the Hermannsburg Mission, near Alice Springs, emphasizing the wretched condition of the remnants of its Aboriginal population and maintaining that there was no evidence of the mission ever having done them any good. He contended that the missionaries should give up the attempt to improve the moral order of the Arunta, which, though it could not compare with White morality, was unequivocally preferable to the degeneracy that followed acculturation. This undisturbed order was the Dream times:

> The morality of the black is not that of the white man, but his life so long as he remains uncontaminated by contact with the latter, is governed by rules of conduct which have been recognised amongst his tribe from what they speak of as the "alcheringa," which Mr. Gillen has aptly called the "Dream times." (Spencer 1896b:111)

From the outset, therefore, the Dream times were fatally susceptible to contact. According to Spencer's Social Darwinist rationale, Aborigines confronted their far-distant future in the form of the Whites, a strain whose superiority exemplified the cumulative operation of selection in a whole range of ways, from cranial enlargement to the attainment of abstract thought. Thus the ensuing doom of the Aborigines was a result inscribed in the natural order of things and bound to follow once others had reached a level of progress that enabled the crossing of barriers that were at once both geographic and phylogenetic.[9]

Gillen's actual translation, which followed in the fourth part of the report, was a nondescript debut. It occurred during an exposition of Arunta explanations for the origin of fire, which ancestors were held to have acquired "in the distant past (*ŭlchurringa*), which really means in the dream-times" (Gillen 1896:185). Yet the anticlimax is immaterial, since what matters is not Gillen's coinage of the term but the cultural logic whereby Spencer, who gave Alcheringa its new spelling, should have found Gillen's rendering so apt.[10] This was the moment when a mere aside—one of many, which could otherwise only have been regarded as equally random and inconsequential[11]—was first appropriated into discourse. Spencer's selection was not unmotivated. Nor did it cause the term's success. Rather, it was but the first in a cognate series of such selections whose aggregation consolidated the Dreaming complex.

Once coined, Gillen's phrase took off immediately. By 1900, it had found its way into the writings of European theorists who had not been to the ethnographic field but who had encountered it in a number of articles published jointly by Spencer and Gillen after 1896:

> I dislike offering a theory about what occurred in the "Dream-time" (*Alcheringa*) behind our historical knowledge of mankind. (Lang 1900:9)

Though the Alcheringa featured prominently in Spencer and Gillen's classic 1899 book on the Arunta, the term *dream-times* did not appear in it. But in her book *The Euahlayi Tribe,* which went to press around the time that Spencer and Gillen's 1904 book (in which the phrase did appear) was published, Kath Langloh Parker (1905:2) was already referring to "the Arunta myth of the Dream Time, the age of pristine evolution" without further explanation. The phrase would seem to have traveled by way of Oxford, since Andrew Lang, who wrote the introduction to Langloh Parker's book, had corresponded with her over its preliminary drafts.[12] In any event, the Euahlayi were not from central Australia but from the east coast, so the equivalence asserted between their ideology and that of Spencer and Gillen's Arunta constituted an enormous geographical diffusion of the dream-times—one that was soon to extend to all Aborigines.[13]

Yet one needs to go no further than the initial move from the Arunta to the Euahlayi for clear evidence that the extension of the term *Dream Time* was not ethnographically motivated. Not only was there no suggestion that the Euahlayi equivalent had anything to do with dreaming, but the doctrine to which the term was reapplied differed fundamentally from its original Arunta referent. For although, as will be seen, Spencer and Gillen went to considerable lengths to refute Carl Strehlow's claim that the Aranda (as he called them) had a monotheistic All-Father, insisting instead that the Alcheringa referred to an age of mythical but non-theistic ancestors, Langloh Parker's Euahlayi had a monotheistic supreme being in Byamee. Yet it was this Byamee who "in the first place, is to the Euahlayi what the 'Alcheringa' or 'Dream Time' is to the Arunta" (Parker 1905:6). Thus no claim about Koori discourse is necessary to invalidate the extension of the Dreaming complex from the Arunta to the Euahlayi.

The diffusion of the Dreaming complex through anthropological writing will be considered in greater detail below. For the moment, the point is that this diffusion was not prompted by ethnographic observation. The Dream Time was appropriate to the Euahlayi because they were Aborigines, rather than because of any particular beliefs that they may have espoused. The meaning of the term resided not in the doctrinal content of Alcheringa but in a thematic affinity between the two signs "dream" and "aborigine," an affinity that obtained within the anthropologists' culture rather than within that—or those— of their subjects. Thus the success of Gillen's translation did not simply result from Spencer's having approved it in advance. Rather, that approval was itself culturally prefigured.

To set the subsequent demonstration of the Dreaming complex's prefiguration into context, it should first be noted that the concept's very opportuneness encouraged a mystification of its origins. This was because its success gave it high value in anthropological discourse: the Dreaming complex was something to be associated with. Thus two of the three most eminent figures in Australian Aboriginal anthropology misrepresented its origins in order to attach it to their own respective names, while the third (Radcliffe-Brown) left the field to the first two by ignoring the concept altogether.[14] It is, therefore, little wonder that its true origins should have become obscured. This explains the otherwise puzzling fact that, even though the occurrence of the Horn Expedition was well-known, none of the major figures in Australian Aboriginal anthropology could correctly locate the concept's introduction.[15]

The obscurity surrounding the origins of the Dreaming complex enhanced its ethnographic credibility by virtue of its marginalizing the role of anthropologists. Indeed, it was appropriate that the Aboriginal category par excellence should have no beginning, since Aborigines were a people without a history. Even if its original authorship had been recognized, therefore, the concept's universal distribution within Aboriginal culture would mean that Gillen's happening to be the first to place it on record could hardly be accounted a discovery, much less an invention. Thus a circle is closed: the very cultural appeal that first commended the concept to anthropologists subsequently effaces itself, in the process reinforcing the hold of the concept.

The two who muddied the water were Spencer himself and, later, A. P. Elkin. Although Gillen's memoir was published in 1896, the Horn Expedition had actually taken place in 1894. Writing in 1926, however, Spencer was to trace the term back to fieldwork among the Arunta that he and Gillen had undertaken together two years after the Horn Expedition, and that had formed the basis for their first major work, *The Native Tribes of Central Australia,* which had appeared in 1899:

> It was during our work amongst the Arunta in 1896, when we were able to watch and study in its entirety the long and great Engwura ceremony that we first became acquainted with the terms *Alchera* and *Alcheringa.* . . . As indicating a past period of a very vague and, it seemed to us, "Dreamy" nature, we adopted, to express as nearly as possible the meaning of the word *alcheringa* (*alchera,* a dream, and *ringa,* a suffix meaning "of" or "belonging to") the term "dream times." (Spencer and Gillen 1927:592)

Though this account leaves no room for doubt as to the year 1896, Elkin was later to use it to claim that Spencer had not discerned the dreaming connotation of Alcheringa until 1926. This then enabled Elkin to suggest that *he* had discovered the term at around the same time as Spencer, but over a much wider ethnographic range:

> The concept "Dream-time" arose out of Spencer and Gillen's use of the Aranda word Alcheringa (*Altjiranga*) in their classic *The Native Tribes of Central Australia* (1899) to denote the mythic times of the ancestors of the totemic groups. However, when revising that book in Alice Springs in 1926, Professor Spencer found that "past mythic time" was only part of the meaning of Altjira; it also meant dream and, moreover, those Aborigines who were becoming familiar with English referred to the ancestral heroes, their past times and to everything associated with them as their Dreaming. And, in my own field-work from 1927 onwards in southern, central, north-western and northern regions of Australia, whatever the term, it was the "dreaming." *Altjira* in the Aranda tribe, *Djugur* in the vast western region of South Australia and neighbouring areas of Western and Central Australia, *Bugari* around La Grange and Broome, *Ungud* on the north of the King Leopold Range, Northern Kimberley, *Wongar* in North-Eastern Arnhem Land, and so on. (1964:210)

Three points anticipated in this version of events will figure prominently below. First, the fact of a single English word being interchangeable for all these different words derived from separate cultural regions has the effect of smothering multiplicity under a single undifferentiated category— "Aboriginal"—defined in contradistinction to settler-colonial society. Second, Elkin represents Aborigines as proffering the English word *dreaming* as if they had been the authors of its translation. The third point is the terminological shift from dream-times to Dreaming, especially insofar as a reference (or lack of it) to time is concerned.

Before developing these points, however, the cultural background to the Dreaming complex needs to be sketched in. Since it is not my intention to account for Eurohistorical watersheds, socially-contexted analysis will be restricted to the local level, where it is possible to show the cultural selection and specification of a general post-Enlightenment theme.

Discursive Background

Dreaming has long signified the subordinate aspect of a lopsided ambivalence between scientific empiricism and various forms of subjective or romantic idealism in European discourse. Needless to say, this ambivalence also extends to dichotomous representations of nature and of the female, as well as to the enduring alternation of base and noble savagery (*D'Alembert's Dream* was, after all, the Noble Savage's finest hour). This double-edgedness endows the romantic aspect with a contrary subtext, so that when, say, Andrew Lang (1898:xviii) placed Aborigines among the "most distinguished" of the world's dreamers, he was bestowing the distinction to satirical ends. This ambivalence continues to the present day in the common settler quip equating the Dreamtime with alcoholic stupor. As will be shown, this ambivalence, which is an aspect of the cultural irony to which this paper is addressed, has substantial implications for settler-colonial ideologies concerning rights to land.

Being both subjective and impervious to logic, dreaming was bound to invite scientific antipathy (which was, indeed, expressed at least as early as Descartes' first *Meditation*[16]). In particular, dreaming's notorious disregard for sequential regularity ran counter to the whole discourse of time, discipline, and order that Foucault (1967, 1977) famously analysed. A century after Descartes, Buffon, one of the greatest of the Enlightenment systematizers, made the capacity to distinguish between dreams and reality a threshold that separated humans from animals. For Buffon, the reason that animals were incapable of distinguishing between dreams and reality was that they lacked a sense of time:

> We remember dreams for the same reason that we remember former sensations: the only difference between us and the brutes is, that we can distinguish dreams from ideas or real sensations; and this capacity of distinguishing is a result of comparison, an operation of memory, which includes the idea of time. But the brutes, who are deprived of memory and of the faculty of comparing past and present time, cannot distinguish their dreams from their actual sensations. (1812 [1749]:530–31)

By the second half of the nineteenth century, within the emergent discipline of anthropology, aspirations to scientific status ruled out any romantic reverence for dreaming's creative freedoms. Rather, the abasement and promiscuity that characterized dreaming in the private realm were transferred to a scientifically constructed realm of savagery. From within the heartland of romanticism, for instance, the German anthropologist Adolf Bastian, whose international standing was yet to be rivaled by that of the Englishman Tylor, could hardly have expressed the construction more clearly:

> Tribes in the state of nature surrender passively to the all too overwhelming impressions of the external world. For them, hallucinations and illusions

maintain a half-conscious oscillation between dreaming and waking as a normal condition. Their entire mental condition enables them to create supernatural agencies or to believe in these unconditionally, with an intensity and to an extent, to the direct understanding of which luckily our logical thinking has long ago destroyed the bridge, or at least should have done so. (1868:118)[17]

The difference between this statement and Buffon's is that, whereas Buffon had distinguished between people and animals, Bastian, though citing essentially the same criteria, was distinguishing between types of people. The theoretical watershed separating the two approaches was Darwinism, which both relativized Buffon's hiatus and enabled the opening up of comparable divisions within *genus homo*. Indeed, a quarter of a century before the emergence of the dream-times, Darwin himself, who had been to Australia, had compared the consciousness of Australian Aborigines, who had "hardly any abstract words" and could not count above four, to the twitching of a sleeping dog reliving the chase in its dreams (1871:i, 62).

Aborigines' unquestioned proximity to the animal state entailed in advance that they, like animals, should be held to confuse dreaming with everyday experience. An anthropological preoccupation with ritual encouraged such a conclusion, since ritual added to the input of the irrational. In this regard, scientific rationalism sustained discursive continuities that encompassed centuries. Thus, by way of Spencer and Gillen's account of totemic announcements among the Arunta, Frazer attributed precisely the same role to Aboriginal ritual as, over a hundred and fifty years earlier, Buffon had attributed to animals' lack of a sense of time:

These announcements perhaps sometimes originate in dreams, for what a savage sees in a dream is just as real to him as what he sees in his waking hours. The thoughts of the natives are at times so much taken up with the performance of sacred ceremonies that it is quite natural that they should dream of them and take the visionary images of sleep for revelations of those spirits with whom their own spirit has been communing during the lethargy of the body. (Frazer 1910:1, 212)

To turn more specifically to anthropology, Frazer's estimate of the importance of dreaming in savage life was not simply a general reflection of European rationalism. Within that overall tradition,[18] it was specifically predicated upon Tylor's theory of animism, which assigned a key role to dreaming, and which dominated late-nineteenth-century anthropological thought. According to this theory, paradigmatically formulated in Tylor's landmark (1871) *Primitive Culture,* the first abstract conception was the notion of a soul, or of a spiritual double detachable from the body, which occurred to savages as an explanation for the sensation of moving about in their dreams. Animism had both cognitive and religious significance since, once spirit doubles had been conceptualized, they could be attributed to a whole range of objects—hence fetishism, totemism, and other forms of idolatry.

In keeping with the conventional evolutionary conflation of ontogeny and phylogeny, or individual and species development, Tylor (1871:1, 431) deemed animism a childish doctrine, "the infant philosophy of mankind," which was no different from the nursery belief that sticks or toys were alive. It was not that the conclusions that savages drew from their experiences were invalid. Rather, an incapacity to distinguish between dreams and veridical sense data[19] rendered their reliance upon experience a mockery of the sensory foundations of scientific empiricism:

> Everyone who has seen visions while light-headed in fever, everyone who has ever dreamt a dream, has seen the phantoms of objects as well as of persons. How then can we charge the savage with far-fetched absurdity for taking into his philosophy and religion an opinion which rests on the very evidence of his senses? (Tylor 1871:1, 431).

In sum, then, savages' impartial crediting of all sensation made them the hapless dupes of somatic caprice. It is in this connection that the singular value of dreaming for evolutionary anthropology can be most clearly seen, for, emanating from within the private constitution of the sleeper, dreams afforded a nexus that linked the physical and the mental. Thus they provided a bridge between the animal and the human, the concrete and the abstract, craniology and culture. Aborigines thought with their bodies: their brute senses were geared to tracking game, they counted on their fingers, and so on. Thus their sign language testified to their still having failed to abandon direct tactile reference in favor of the relative abstraction of vocal representation (hence they needed to stay within the light of their campfires in order to converse at night).[20] It was this combination of the somatic and the semiotic that had made Aborigines into dreamers long before the Dreamtime.

The contention that the Dreaming complex constituted the culmination of a historical discourse that subordinated dreaming savages to the level of animal nature shares some ground with Ortner's (1974) claim that the category "female" is universally subordinated in an analogous manner. Thus it is no accident that the dream-times should have emerged at the same time as psycho-analysis, which brought together a similar assemblage of themes—women, savagery, childhood, irrationality, instinct, ritual, and so forth—within a scientific discourse on dreaming.[21]

A further consequence of the theory of animism was theological, for the idea of a world populated by a multitude of vitalized objects did not entail their being worshipped. The issue was of some moment, as religious sentiment had also been proposed as a feature distinguishing people from animals.[22] In contrast, Tylor's theory eliminated moral and theological criteria from a scientific definition of humanity. Though not jeopardizing the human status of its practitioners, however, the lowest, dream-related form of animism was categorically pretheistic in Tylor's scheme, merely furnishing the ground upon which gods would later develop (Tylor 1871:1, 1).

This clear distinction between animism and theism illuminates one of the transformations of the Dreaming complex. For, whereas the Dreaming was later to be adduced by Stanner (1965:213–21) as evidence of Aboriginal religiosity, Spencer and Gillen not only avoided the term *religion* in relation to the dream-times but actually resisted its use. Following Turgot and Comte, Frazer had ranked religion as an evolutionary advance upon magic, with science subsequently developing out of religion. On this basis, Spencer (1904:404) explicitly proscribed the use of the word *religious* in relation to the Arunta, for whom the term *magical* was appropriate.

This exclusion of the dream-times from religion underlay the long-running dispute between Spencer and the Lutheran missionary Carl Strehlow, whose Hermannsburg Mission had been the subject of Spencer's disparaging remarks. For, though they were in total opposition over the question of Aboriginal religiosity, neither doubted that the dream-times and religion were incompatible. Thus the dispute was over whether or not blacks had a dream-time, rather than over what it would mean if they had.

Strehlow repudiated Gillen's translation, contending that "a 'dream-time' is unknown to the blacks."[23] While Strehlow's rare proficiency in Aranda might seem to have made him a more credible authority than Spencer and Gillen,[24] the concept of the dream-times brought the protagonists' professional interests into direct conflict. Spencer's interest in the primitiveness of his ethnographic discovery encouraged a denial of the very faculty—a religious sentiment—that was prerequisite to the success of Strehlow's evangelical enterprise. Thus Strehlow alleged that the word *Altjira* (the "alchera" in Alcheringa) referred to an Aranda good god, to which Spencer responded (Spencer and Gillen

1927:596) with the claim that, in translating the Lutheran canon into Arunta, the Hermannsburg missionaries had rendered *Gott* as Altjira and had inculcated the usage in daily prayers, which accounted for Strehlow now finding that the word had a monotheistic import.[25]

Beyond the particular issue of theology, however, a more general transformation took place between Spencer's and Stanner's approaches. Though Stanner is not to blame for the New Age caricature that enveloped Aborigines in the wake of the 1960s, his celebrated 1956 article, "The Dreaming," which remains the definitive expression of the concept, represents a distinct shift toward the romantic pole:

> The truth of it [The Dreaming] seems to be that man, society, and nature and past, present, and future are at one together within a unitary system of such a kind that its ontology cannot illumine minds too much under the influence of humanism, rationalism, and science. (1956:54)

Though cautioning against a European tendency to view all Aboriginal thought as ruled by mysticism, Stanner depicts his blackfellow as a stock transcendental other to the order and efficiency of settlement:

> What defeats the blackfellow in the modern world, fundamentally, is his transcendentalism. (61)

Defeat, here, has serious implications, since it is equated—in a manner at first sight reminiscent of Spencer's Social Darwinism—with "extinction" (Stanner 1956:61). Yet Stanner's rhetoric is very different from Spencer's evolutionist resignation. When Spencer asserted (1896b:111) that "in contact with the white man the aborigine is doomed to disappear," he meant that the people would die out. For Stanner, on the other hand, extinction has the quality of a literary event:

> A good analogy is with the process in Chinese poetry by which, according to Arthur Waley, its talent for classical allusion became a vice which finally destroyed it altogether. (1956:61)

The bizarre levity of Stanner's own allusion is inexplicable until one decodes what he means by extinction. In the overall context, this judgment does not refer to the lives of the erstwhile inhabitants of the Dreaming (by 1956, their physical extinction was no longer a feasible prospect), but to their transcendental mentality.

The difference between Spencer and Stanner is symptomatic of a much more general process. On the ideational level, this process can be characterized as the extension of the scientific realm. On the local level, it has a material correlate in the extension of colonial settlement. The two are cognate. Moreover, in addition to thematic continuity through the shared imperatives of order, regularity, and control, they have a common developmental structure.

To deal with this common structure first: when Tylor coined his theory of animism, he was, as observed, engaged in establishing anthropology's credentials as a science.[26] In the process, he not only had to carve out a space between established sciences (archaeology, philology, and so forth). He also took it upon himself to discredit the dissenting "pseudo-sciences" of spiritualism, astrology, divination, and the like, which he stigmatized as anomalous modern survivals of the savage germ of animism.[27] Animism's association with dreaming was part of the stigma. There was nothing unusual about Tylor's attitude, which Frazer and Spencer shared. It simply represented a continuation of the long-standing scientific opprobrium that attached to dreaming as a signifier for subjectivity and disorder. As Freud observed (1976 [1900]:212): "The phrase 'Dreams are froth' seems intended to support the scientific estimate of dreams." This estimate is the contemporary context in which Spencer's selection of Gillen's phrase should be understood. By contrast, when Stanner was writing, over half a century later, anthropology was well established and no longer had grounds for anxiety over its possible lack of disciplinary status.[28] Stanner had no need to prove that he was on the side of science.

This academic consolidation echoed the consolidation of settlement in Australia. In the 1890s, when Spencer was among the Arunta, the frontier remained a reality to the north and to the west.[29] Hostile natives were still being "dispersed," as the official euphemism put it, to make way for settlement.[30] By the time of Stanner's article, however, colonial settlement had been effectively completed. On both academic and political counts, therefore, natives and their dreaming had become detoxified by the 1950s.

Besides the common developmental structure, there are certain thematic continuities. So far, we have only considered ideas and theories in isolation from the social forces that bore them. We have also remained within the realm of learned discourse. When we move from the level of metropolitan theories to consider their appropriation into local culture, however, it becomes possible to suggest the diversity of the discourses that the Dreaming complex combined. In the next section, ideologies that are distinctive of a particular frontier culture will be shown to be reformulations of the general post-Enlightenment themes outlined earlier, which are further modified as the local situation develops.

Thus, though the imperative of order is an obvious common denominator between science and colonization, it takes on idiosyncratic forms in the Australian context.

The addition of a local dimension allows the concept of total cultural practice to be clarified. As will be seen, the Dreaming complex tied different levels of discourse (epistemic, local, political, poetic, etc.) into a culturally distinctive knot. Similarly, though expressed in language, it was language that operated synecdochically, both encapsulating and contributing to the historical development of settler society. Thus the cultural appropriation of the Dreaming complex was not a passive process. Rather, the concept was taken into use as an active representation within Australian settler-colonial culture, where it took on new contextual meanings that shifted its original significance.

Local Appropriations

We have already noted that the common colonial theme of awakenment became specifically nuanced in the Australian context, where the idea of banishing the sleep of reason had a peculiar affinity with the doctrine of *terra nullius*, which lifted the natives out of the dual interaction between settler and landscape. This ideological bracketing-off—whereby Aborigines were either effaced from the land or assimilated to it, leaving "a blank page on which the white man could write his will and his hopes"[31]—is of such cultural depth that journalists, popularizers, schoolbooks and children's stories have repeated it tirelessly:

> The unique aspect of the Australian colonial experience was that there were two great protagonists, the settlers and the very land itself. (Harris 1967:1–2)

The theme of precolonial somnambulance, a blend of dreaming and the aimless Walkabout, suffuses Australian liberal culture, as evidenced by its coffee-table literature *(Time Before Morning, The Dawn of Time,* and so on). Walkabout could only be aimless, as there was nowhere to go in a signless void unorganized by pioneering purpose. For settlers, the wilderness was void because its contents had no use; a random assemblage of protean forms, they were to be replaced rather than domesticated or employed. Thus land was but a spatial condition, rather than one of the forces, of production. Hence Aborigines' assimilation to the landscape amounted to the same thing as their effacement from it. According to this ideology, they were part of its useless original contents rather than acknowledged sources of labor, as witnessed by their legendary unsuitability for work.[32] In what might be called its hard version, this formula implied that Aborigines needed clearing along with everything else on the land. While it is relatively rare to find modern examples of this version, it was predicated upon a narrative structure that remains abundantly alive in the softer trappings of liberal romanticism:

> What a fascinating place Australia is! When one thinks of the centuries of civilisation that have passed over China, India, and Europe and here you have a situation—still—in 1982 that most Australians are entirely ignorant of some parts of the continent, be it structure, wildlife, or the heart and soul of this beautiful old bronze raft that severed itself from the rest of the world, and slumbered in a "dream time" with its bizarre marsupials and its gentle Aboriginal people who believed that the landscape itself was the creation of their known world. (Olsen 1984:12)

This theme is not dependent upon Gillen's particular verbal formula, having been recognizably, albeit unromantically, expressed before the appearance of the dream-times:

> [T]he weird savages, birds without wings, mysterious animals of land and water in this weird and "Strange Land of Dawning." (Purcell 1893:289)

Even on a strictly local level, the general theme was clearly present to the minds of colonists who were responsible for dealing with the Arunta. Thus Gillen's superior, a mounted policeman named W. H. Willshire who was local Protector of Aborigines, wrote a number of books recounting his homicidal exploits in the outback, one of which—published in the same year as the report of the Horn Expedition—was entitled *The Land of the Dawning* (1896).

Despite its thematic compatibility, however, *The Land of the Dawning* does not mention the dream-times.[33] For the purposes of cultural selection, the verbal difference is critical. As the earlier outline of the significance of dreaming in European thought should suggest, it was simply not open to the Dawning, or to other local analogues, to acquire the same purchase upon anthropological theory. The different levels of discourse that were conjoined by the Dreaming complex gave it a wide range of possible meanings, so that no synonym could substitute for it through all its uses. A further consequence of this versatility, to which discussion now turns, is that it enabled the Dreaming complex to become transformed in use.

Ignored thus far has been the fact that the phrase "dream-times" seems to involve a paradox, the sense of time being conventionally excluded from dreams.[34] Indeed, controversy over whether or not the concept had a time reference accompanied the formulation of alternative nomenclatures such as the Dreaming, the eternal dream-time, and so forth. In its infancy, however, as Spencer and Gillen's 1904 "Glossary" illustrates, the dream times unequivocally referred to the past:

> *Alcheringa.* Name applied by the Arunta, Kaitish and Unmatjera tribes to the far past, or dream times, in which their mythic ancestors lived. The word "alcheri" means dream. (Spencer and Gillen 1904:745)

Yet this temporality contrasts with later characterizations of the Dreaming complex:

> We realise that Spencer and Gillen's translation of Alcheringa and similar words as Dreamtime and Radcliffe-Brown's reference to World-Dawn, both meaning a past time, are not wrong, but are inadequate. The Aboriginal word includes the idea of "belonging to the dream" and my early translation of *djugur* as "eternal dreamtime," with which Roheim agreed, at least suggests that the Dreaming is an ever-present condition of existence. (Elkin 1961:203)

The reason why Elkin deemed it not wrong, but merely inadequate, to represent the concept as applying to a past time is that it did refer to such a time. It was inadequate, however, so to limit it, since the concept also expressed a continuing or eternal reality, persisting, as Stanner (1956:52) put it, "everywhen." The discursive structure is, therefore, twofold, juxtaposing past origin and continuing present. For the argument to come, the fact that the two are juxtaposed (and thus coexistent), rather than amalgamated or collapsed, is central. Though ultimately encompassed, the two aspects are categorically distinct. A beginning did actually take place, while the ever-present evades location in time—or, as Berndt (1974:8) expressed it:

> Generally, the concept of the Dreaming refers to a mythological period which had a beginning but has no foreseeable end . . . these beings are believed to be just as much *alive* today as they ever were and as they will continue to be. They are eternal.

The juxtaposition of origin and presence is echoed in Australian nationalist ideology, where the two are divided by a notional moment of settlement. Here the retrospective aspect, which is the counterpart of origin—"back in the Dreamtime"—refers to the inscrutable (but occasionally glimpsed) era before Captain Cook, the First Fleet, or whatever might serve to summarize the origin of the nation.[35] Lacking a history, precontact Australia was unimaginable and, accordingly, unreal. Though it may seem to be laboring the obvious to state that the Dreamtime maps on to nationalist constructions of Australian prehistory, it is in its second aspect, that of the timeless ever-present, that the ideological consequence of the juxtaposition can best be appreciated. For the corollary to this unreal past became an unreal present, which was the outcome of anthropological representations in which Aborigines figured as ritually constituted entities.

The preponderance of ritual in anthropological representations of Aborigines has already been noted with reference to Frazer, who saw habituation to ritual as encouraging savage credulity with regard to their dreams. There are further reasons for the attractiveness of ritual, quite apart from a certain prurience discernible in the literature. Ritual presented condensed expressions of aspects of social structure, especially details of kinship systems, that might otherwise have escaped notice. In the case of small groups traversing large expanses of territory, even the people themselves, let alone the details of their social organization, were liable to escape notice—a problem that was alleviated by the relative conspicuousness of large-scale ritual gatherings (which, given appropriate inducement, could usually be arranged).[36] Furthermore, ritual, with its exotica, together with the alien collectivism of classificatory kinship systems, constituted well-defined social-anthropological subject matter at a time when the discipline was in its institutional infancy.

In addition to these considerations, however, there was an overwhelming economic reason for the preponderance of ritual and kinship in anthropological discourse, which was that the great majority of anthropological data was collected from people who were dependent upon the settler economy. This does not mean that they were necessarily residents of missions, stations, prisons, or other settler institutions, although most were. Pastoralism had such far-reaching ecological effects upon water, vegetation, and game that people could lose control over the reproduction of their traditional mode of production even though they might be at a considerable distance from settlement, hence the cumulative pattern of unincorporated groups "coming in" off their land.[37] Thus anthropological photographs that depicted functioning precontact social systems were usually misleading—as, of course, were representations of kinship as a conceptual diagram that systematized reproduction as if it required no terrestrial support. Similarly, though ritual practices could be adapted to meet changed conditions, anthropological analyses that presented ritual data as if they were embedded within viably functioning precontact societies had the effect of obscuring the expropriation of those societies.

In its second, ever-present aspect, the Dreaming complex was a quintessentially ritual concept. Thus it is significant that Spencer's misrepresentation of the history of the first, originary version of the concept should have derived it from the *Engwura* ceremony. In immortalizing this three-month-long series of rituals as a kind of precontact swan-song, Spencer and Gillen's 1899 book froze the Arunta in a present poised at the parting of the ways, when their empirical substrates passed on to acculturation or beyond. Moreover, the ritual Aborigine that transpired conduced to the ideological bracketing-off whereby Aborigines were excluded from the dual encounter between settlers and the land. To make this last observation clear, it is necessary to develop the twofold structure of the Dreaming complex more fully.

The twin aspects, origin and presence, have in common the feature of being discontinuous with the economic realities of settlement. Thus the Dreamtime as precontact idyll is lost, while, in the potentially more controversial realm of the present, dreaming Aborigines hover in a mystically supported ritual space that does not conflict with the practical exigencies of settlement. The two coexist without meeting. Thus the timelessness of the ever-present Dreaming is actually a spacelessness.[38]

The primary ideological significance of the Dreaming complex was that it established ideal versions of settlers and Aborigines that excluded shared features. Since the feature most crucially shared between the two was an economic interest in the same land,[39] it is consistent that the aspects of Aboriginal life most stressed by the Dreaming complex should be precisely those that had least connection to economic existence. In other words, the scheme was the simplest of binary oppositions, substituting an ideal horizontal relationship—"encounter"—for the vertical reality of incorporation. Hence ambiguity was rendered repugnant. This feature received its most public expression where "miscegenation" was concerned, to the extent that "mongrel" remains one of the most potent insults in the settler repertoire. In a more general sense, however, mediation of the pure opposition was not adaptation but aberration. The cultural hybrid, even though "full-blooded," could only be ridiculous, grotesque, or nefarious. Thus the incorporation of Blacks into White society split into two the ambivalent post-Enlightenment image of savagery, attaching its negative side to the acculturated, leaving the good savage (or "bush black") as a completely good residue, but always somewhere else. The ideal was a formula for imposing liability upon its empirical counterparts. Thus the romantic ideal and the repugnant hybrid represent opposite sides of the single message that bad savages don't deserve the land while good savages don't use it.

As a denial of the disruptive presence of those who bear the marks of history, the Dreaming complex produces a wholesome Aboriginality with which the Australian state can negotiate absolution from its foundational illegitimacy. Thus the ideal constitutes a formula for imposing liability upon its fallen empirical counterparts. Moreover, being both demographically marginal and definitionally brittle, it represents a minimal concession to the continuity of Aboriginal entitlement. The return on this concession is a depoliticization of dispossession. In disqualifying those whose dreaming has been brutalized by conquest, the Dreaming complex converts invadedness into a welfare problem. In other words, the Dreaming complex is a prime instance of the discursive structure that, with a nod to Herbert Marcuse, I have elsewhere termed repressive authenticity. Repressive authenticity "cannot be understood by studying the symbols that it promulgates. Rather, the reverse is the case, since attracting attention to its symbols is the whole point of the strategy, a diversionary ruse that works by pointing away from its practical effects. To understand repressive authenticity, we have to attend to the consequences for those whom it renders *in*authentic" (Wolfe 1994:110–11).

As a critique of racial romanticism, repressive authenticity invests settler-colonial nostalgia with a historical motive.[40] Ironically, this oppressive motive is strengthened rather than undermined by its dependence upon public goodwill. The new romantics do not, as Kropotkin thought, have to tamper with their consciences in order to live comfortably with their complicity in dispossession (in James Baldwin's terser idiom, we can forgive them anything but their innocence). This is not to deny that Kooris can exploit the manifest contradictions in the Dreaming complex or reappropriate it to their own advantage. That, however, is their business. Inescapably, speaking as I do from within the settler-colonial academy, my positionality is such that my progressing from diagnosis to prescription could only aggravate the affliction. At the risk of repetition, therefore, in analysing the Dreaming complex, I am analysing the fabrication of a colonizing discourse.

The two modes of the Dreaming complex emerged at separate stages in the history of Australian settlement. The originary, dream-times version was a frontier concept—to cross the frontier was to go back into the deep time preceding history. The emergence of the ever-present Dreaming, on the other hand, did not commence until over a quarter of a century later, in the late 1920s. Thus it coincided both with the statistical turning-point at which Aboriginal numbers began to rise from their lowest level, recorded in 1921 (Lancaster Jones 1970:3–6), and with the formal disappearance of a frontier. These two developments concurred in placing Aborigines within settler society. It is, therefore, consistent that Bates, who devoted a whole book (1938) to the contention that Aborigines were "passing," should have referred in it to the Dreamtime, while Elkin, who opposed the claim that Aborigines were dying out (1952:244), should have been closely associated with the ever-present mode of the Dreaming complex.

With the emergence of the ever-present Dreaming, then, Aborigines came in from behind the frontier and were finally assimilated into the nation-state, only on terms of their economic invisibility. So far as this second mode is concerned, therefore, Elkin's eternal dream-times might perhaps be entitled to the priority that he claimed for it (1932:128–29; 1933:11–12). As already observed, however, the classic statement of the ever-present version was to be Stanner's (1956) article, "The Dreaming," which exemplifies many of the preceding observations.

Stanner's article places blackfellows in a dimension quite separate from serial European time:

> A central meaning of The Dreaming *is* that of a sacred, heroic time long long ago when man and nature came to be as they are; but neither "time" nor "history" as we understand them is involved in this meaning. I have never been able to discover any aboriginal word for *time* as an abstract concept. And the sense of "history" is wholly alien here. . . . Although, as I have said, The Dreaming conjures up the notion of a sacred, heroic time of the indefinitely remote past, such a time is also, in a sense, still part of the present. One cannot "fix" The Dreaming *in* time: it was, and is, everywhen. (1956:51–52)

The gulf between linear and blackfellow "time" is augmented by Stanner's discussion of territorial subsistence, represented as an aetherially flimsy contrast to the established solidity of settlement. Blackfellows "stay nowhere long":

> They make almost no physical mark on the environment. Even in areas which are still inhabited, it takes a knowledgeable eye to detect their recent presence. Within a matter of weeks, the roughly cleared campsites may be erased by sun, rain, and wind. After a year or two there may be nothing to suggest that the country was ever inhabited. (1956:58)

A transparence on the part of its inhabitants thus has the effect of emptying the land. But the illusion that nomads "stay nowhere long" can only be maintained on the basis that "somewhere" means a fixed point without dimensions. For, in the following lines, it becomes clear that, far from staying nowhere, Stanner's subjects inhabited their own defined territory throughout their lives. Indeed, his account of their cyclical routine renders them visible to an extent that, though admittedly not abstract, rests at least awkwardly with the notion of their timelessness:

> One can almost plot a year of their life in terms of movements towards the places where honey, yams, grass seeds, eggs, or some other food staple, is in bearing and ready for eating. (1956:58)[41]

Significantly, the conditions under which they exhibit such chronological acumen obtain between rituals, when the tribe has split up into subsistence bands following events such as "a feast, a corroboree, a hunt, an initiation, or a formal duel" (58).

A significant feature of Stanner's article is the way in which he refers to blackfellows as a unity, rather than to distinct groups. Thus the diffusion of the Dreaming complex has become complete.[42] Stanner's article is suggestive in this regard, since, after crediting Spencer and Gillen with immortalizing the term, he goes on to make the striking observation that it is not, after all, a translation of corresponding blackfellow words:

> In their own dialects they use terms like *Alcheringa, mipuramibirina, boaradja*—often almost untranslatable, or meaning literally something like "men of old." (Stanner, 1956:51)

A little lower, however, we find Stanner wondering:

> Why the blackfellow thinks of "Dreaming" as the nearest equivalent in English is a puzzle. (52)

Expressed thus, Stanner's puzzlement may seem curiously naive. It becomes understandable once it is set against the paradox of a precontact anthropology. For, just as the Dreaming complex had no place for the economics of incorporation, so, by the same token, did it preclude the consequences of a colonial *lingua franca*. Operating within the working assumptions of his discipline, Stanner did not have access to a range of possible reasons why blackfellows should so mistranslate.

Dreaming and Speaking

Reports of Aborigines referring to their Dreaming raise a question not so far considered. The cultural affinities that commended the term to a predominantly

European imagination could hardly have appealed to such Kooris as had come to appreciate them.

Kooris' submission to anthropological language was the result of invasion rather than of cultural selection. With the spread of settlement, settler and Koori discourses intertwined. It follows that the isolation of anthropology for discrete analysis can only be a heuristic device. For, as part of the discourse of colonial power, anthropology becomes an object of contestation for the colonized, who may seek to appropriate it to their own advantage, turning it back upon their expropriators. In the process, however, the colonized acquiesce in the terms encoded within that discourse, whereby collective self-assertion on their part finds expression as a species of nationalism, which, in turn, encodes the progress-based rationale for colonization. Thus the collective unity underlying Koori (or "pan-Aboriginal") identity is itself the product of colonial conquest, which installed the prerequisite of a generalized other. More specifically, however, insofar as it adopts the twofold discursive structure of the Dreaming complex, Koori rhetoric recapitulates the familiar mythology of the nation-state, which has an origin but is eternal. The irony of Kooris' adoption of the Dreaming complex is, accordingly, a symptom of the containment, or relative powerlessness, of their discourse.

Tracing the diffusion of the Dreaming complex does not, therefore, explain why Kooris came to submit to anthropological language. It merely accounts for the particular form taken by that language. In this regard, as the earlier example of Byamee suggests, the term's dissemination was a text-effect of anthropology.

After their initial fieldwork, Spencer and Gillen mounted an expedition from Arunta country up to the shores of the Gulf of Carpentaria. This resulted in their second (1904) major book, which contained the above-mentioned "Glossary." Though the actual term *dream-times* only appeared once in the text of that book, they liberally allocated synonyms for Alcheringa, which thus entailed that the words concerned meant dream-times. Hence they opened their account of Urabunna cosmology with the brief statement that

the Urabunna belief is as follows:—in the Alcheringa (the Urabunna term for this is Ularaka) . . . (1904:145)

and then dispensed with Ularaka. Thus, transmitted within the Alcheringa, the dream-times can be followed across huge tracts of country within the space of a sentence:

Thus the Arunta term for the far past, during which their ancestors lived, is *alcheringa,* so also is that of the Kaitish and Unmatjera. In the Warramunga, Walpari, and Wulmara it is *wingara;* in the Tjingilli it is *mungai;* and in the Umbaia and Gnanji it is *poaradju.* (1904:12)

It would seem, therefore, that the well-known overture "What is your Dreaming?" (Elkin 1933:11–12) was not, after all, a Koori invention, but an English lesson. Thus established, the concept could travel full circle, even back to the Arunta themselves. Hence Spencer achieved a poker-faced reversal, whereby the dream times became prior to the Alcheringa:

According to the Arunta ideas, their ancestors who lived in the dream times, or, as they call it, the Alcheringa. . . . (Spencer 1904:392)

The fact that Alcheringa was synonymous with the dream-times enabled a syllogistic contagion whereby any number of other Aboriginal words could become dream-times by virtue of their being equated with "Alcheringa" within the mystifying confines of Aboriginal language. The singular is significant here, since linguistic diversity—along with Aboriginal heterogeneity in general—was minimized, notably by the use of the term *dialect* rather than *language.* Thus Alcheringa became a linguistic double agent, a conduit whereby an equivalence established within anthropological discourse could be projected back onto Aboriginal cosmologies.[43]

This process can be observed particularly clearly in Langloh Parker's presentation of the Euahlayi Dream Time. On the first occasion that she used it, the term referred to a local spirit doctrine on which her Euahlayi agreed with Spencer and Gillen's Arunta. This agreement was expressed in English:

There is a belief in spirit-haunted trees, as among the Arunta, and there is a form of the Arunta myth of the "Dream Time," the age of pristine evolution. (1905:2)

As noted, however, the Euahlayi creator-god Byamee conflicted directly with beliefs that the Arunta had been reported to hold. In his case, an equivalence was asserted behind the screen of savage language. Thus, rather than the Dream Time, Byamee was first equated with Alcheringa—which, though coming from a far distant language, was still an Aboriginal word—whereupon, back in English, he automatically became Alcheringa's established synonym:

Byamee, in the first place, is to the Euahlayi what the "Alcheringa" or "Dream Time" is to the Arunta. (1905:6)

Anthropologists' reluctance to concede the extent of their reliance upon the pidgin *lingua franca* produced a linguistic leveling. On the one hand, the differences between Koori languages are minimized, while, on the other, the general use of English is largely ignored. Yet a measure of the consequences of the settler elaborated code can be gauged from the conspicuous decline of Aboriginal sign language in the literature after the generation of Howitt, Roth, and Spencer. Once translated into the overarching idiom of English, terms could be exchanged outside the contexts of their customary use without local differences becoming apparent.[44] Referential heterogeneity is reinforced in the case of secret-sacred knowledge, where access to a range of different meanings varies according to ritual status. Since an externally imposed universal code was necessarily the least esoteric medium, interlocutors using it to exchange terms such as *Dreaming* (or *totem, tribe, clan,* and the like) could successfully conduct parallel conversations without the code occasioning their mutual interruption.[45]

The hegemony of an English-language formulation for an Aboriginal construction of the sacred is multiply ironic. For, though ethnographers were generally loath to confess their reliance upon pidgin, in other contexts they regularly furnished evidence of a thoroughgoing exclusion from sacred affairs of anything associated with settlers.[46] Thus the claim that the Dreaming expressed the sacred was a contradiction in terms: rather than a way of talking about the sacred, the Dreaming provided a way of *not* talking about it.[47]

Whether or not a particular term that a speaker intended to render by the word *Dreaming* had any coincidental connection with ordinary dreaming in the speaker's local language is, therefore, quite irrelevant, since *Dreaming* was a word in English,[48] with a semantic root system that, as I have tried to show, was a historical product of that fact.[49] As a single alien word, introduced through conquest, it bore no such roots. Thus there is no puzzle attaching to Kooris' use of the word *Dreaming*. They were simply speaking English.

Afterword

In so speaking, however, they were also bespeaking their irrevocable participation in history—or, more accurately, in a shared and unequal history. Since the first version of this article (Wolfe 1991) was published, some have suggested that such conclusions violate my own injunction to stick to discourse analysis and refrain from attempting to mimic a Koori voice.[50] But this is to presume that nothing lies beyond colonial discourse; that there is but a single monosemic "English." I was not, and am not, suggesting that, in speaking English (which I intend to be read synecdochically), Koori subjects become mutely interpellated in some Althusserian sense. It is rather that, insofar as they ratify subject-positions that settler-colonial discourse holds out for them, they will already be spoken for in that discourse. Other discursive domains are a different matter. Moreover, there are many ways of speaking English (with varying degrees of potency), so even in English mimicry is not the only option.

With the question of indigenous alternatives to settler-colonial discourse, my positionality becomes inescapable. The relationship between academic and Koori knowledges is structured by a political version of the uncertainty principle. Writing two buildings down from where Baldwin Spencer wrote (though anywhere within the Australian academy would be enough), I have no grounds for claiming a personal exemption from the effects of an invasive discourse which, not satisfied with territory, hurries on into the inner being. Academic knowledge about Aboriginal knowledge can never be innocent. It is too deeply enmeshed in a historical relationship through which one's power is the other's disempowerment.[51] From the outset, authoritative pronouncements on Aboriginal mentalities have been central to the invasion and expropriation of Koori people—*terra nullius* was, after all, a discourse on rationality.[52] Good intentions cannot absolve me from this legacy. The road to oppression has consistently been paved with good intentions (read, for instance, Spencer's fateful statement [1913:21] advocating the Australian state's abduction of Aboriginal children, which evidences a definite concern for the children's welfare). Nor could I seek amnesty on methodological grounds (e.g., that mine is a semiotic/interpretivist—as opposed to a positivist or evolutionist—project) since the issue is a relationship rather than its modes. A refusal to acknowledge this relationship underlies an emergent academic industry devoted to the analysis of Aboriginal cultural production. The fluidity of the category "cultural production" is particularly insidious in this regard since, by means of the self-righteous posture of not privileging literate discourse, it enables the academy to claim the deepest recesses of Aboriginal life for its unblinking gaze. In this way, the linguistic turn becomes a key invasive strategy. Semiotics is often held to run counter to the invasive scientism of the Enlightenment, both because it is not humanist (in Foucault's sense) and because it is seen as ideographic rather than as nomothetic. But this is to overlook the semiotician's octopodean ambitions. For inherent in Saussure's dream of a unified field of communication lies the totalizing possibility of claiming the whole world of human practice for signification. This is not to rehearse the old charge of idealism. The point is, rather, the thoroughgoing penetration to which semiotics aspires, that panopticism whereby nothing can escape being turned into communication for the analyst to appropriate, interrogate, and reconstruct. In this hegemonic communicational economy, all use-values become exchange-values. Silence constitutes consent. The outcome is a dialogic frogmarch in which invaded subjects are refused the option of not speaking. Worse—they are even made to speak unawares, in contexts in which they could well believe that they were doing something else. A cigar is never just a cigar for semiotics.

My position has clear implications for the current liberal preoccupation with writing in the agency of the subaltern. A question that generally goes resound-ingly unasked in this connection is: writing into what? In the settler-colonial context, the question answers itself: the ideal of writing in agency is a con-tradiction in terms. To write in is to contain within discourse. This is a function of the relationships involved and obtains irrespective of content. It follows, therefore, that what needs to be written in is not the agency of the colonized but the historical genealogy that produces the scene of writing. Historian heal thyself.

None of this means that non-Koori scholars should feign deafness when Koori people address us within settler-colonial discourse, particularly when they turn its contradictions to our own discomfort. Thus I am not free to ignore critiques such as that recently voiced by Philip Morrissey, one of the scan-dalously few Koori scholars in the Australian academy:

> *The invasion of Australia:* I realise something is happening when I read these words again, offered without qualification, in another postcolonial essay. An intellectual—two steps ahead of the [Koori] community—at least in the area of naming. Australia wasn't settled—it was invaded. "Not by me" is the epistemological ground of this statement. (1995:1)

Hmmm. Whatever else might be said about this comment, it is an invitation to dialogue (incitement to discourse?), which challenges, rather than reproduces, the Australian academy's invasion of Koori space. With specific reference to the Dreamtime, much the same could be said of ironic strategies such as Koori author Bill Rosser's decision to entitle his (1985) book on Kooris in the Queensland cattle industry *Dreamtime Nightmares*. Rosser's title works by forcing history back into a space set aside for myth. Even strategic essentialism (Spivak 1985:342) can acquire enhanced impact from an insistence on history. For instance, when the Ramingining people of northern Australia were invited to contribute an installation to the National Gallery of New South Wales' exhibition to mark two hundred years of White settlement in Australia, they contributed a large number of upright poles, which were decorated in canonically "traditional Aboriginal" style—the catch being that these were funeral poles, and there were two hundred of them.

Thus I am not seeking to prevent non-Koori academics from engaging with Kooris in the public domain of Australian settler-colonial discourse. When the "dialogue" cuts across domains, however, all that speaks is the power imbalance between the domains. The Dreamtime provides an example of this general condition, one whose salience derives from the crucial ideological role that temporalities play in settler-colonial—and, beyond it, nation-state—discourse. The Dreamtime functions as an alter ego to the homogeneous space-time of Benedict Anderson's (1983) imagined national community. As Stefan Tanaka notes in this volume (his example is Japanese, but the point is general), the production of the nation-state required a separation of this homogeneous civic time from the particular—and categorically subordinate—temporalities of seasonal and bodily cycles. In like manner, since the Australian nation-state has been constructed as the "not-Dreamtime," to promote the Dreamtime in opposition to it can only promote the Australian state.

NOTES

For their advice and criticism of the first version of this chapter, I would again like to thank Maurice Bloch, Dipesh Chakrabarty, Raymond Grew, Michael Muetzelfeldt, Linda Williams, and Aram Yengoyan. For her pointed editorial comments on the revised version, I have come round to feeling grateful to Sally Humphreys. Thanks to Philip Morrissey for showing me his paper before it appeared on the Internet.

1. Not all "colonies of settlement" are settler colonies in the strict sense that I am specifying here. In the case of Rhodesia, for instance, though the settlers went to stay, they also went to exploit the surpluses to be derived from mixing native labor with the land. No two situations are identical. Thus, when I refer to "settler colonization," I mean the social structure that is associated with Australia and whose primary characteristics are shared by colonial regimes such as those that were imposed upon the majority of Native North Americans, Ainu, Palestinians, Guanches, and others. Colonial regimes in Ireland, Rhodesia, Kenya, and elsewhere share some but fewer such characteristics, and so on. Even within Australia, a number of subsidiary articulations (as in the case of the north Australian cattle industry, the Torres Strait pearling industry, or sealing in the Bass Strait) have coexisted with the primary one at various times.

2. The object of analysis is anthropological discourse. Accordingly, "Aborigines," "aborigines," "savages," "blackfellows," etc., are figures of discourse, here reproduced as they appear in the primary textual data. I have spelled and capitalized these terms in conformity with the usages of texts under discussion. To avoid offense, however—and bearing in mind that others can legitimately quote from this chapter without reference to

this note—I have used a capital *A* for Aborigines/Aboriginal except in the case of direct quotations. When it is necessary to distinguish the generality of indigenous people in Australia from the figures of discourse, I use the name Koori, since that is the appropriate name in Melbourne, which is the place of writing. "Settler-colonial culture" is shorthand for a dominant (as opposed to unitary) set of Australian popular discourses with which anthropological concepts are here held to be continuous. Nevertheless, the following discussion exemplifies both anthropological opposition to the prevailing disciplinary consensus (the Strehlows) and divisions within settler-colonial society at large (Gillen vs. Willshire). Such controversies do not, however, detract from the manifest generality of the Dreaming complex as here analysed.

3. The reference is to the concept of *terra nullius.* Though a legal doctrine (see, e.g., Frost 1990, Reynolds 1987), *terra nullius*—roughly, the principle that proprietary rights to land only accrue to settled agricultural societies that have "improved" the land and made its ownership subject to a regular system of law—has been manifest throughout Australian culture, as in the case of the Land Reform League's usage of the following passage from Herbert Spencer's influential *Social Statics,* which they republished in pamphlet form in Melbourne in 1870: "Cultivation is commonly considered to give a legitimate title. He who has reclaimed a tract of ground from its primitive wildness, is supposed to have thereby made it his own" (H. Spencer 1870:7).

4. "[T]here *cannot* be a general theory of ideology, a theory which will specify the universal preconditions, significances and effects of discourse" (Asad 1979:620).

5. I cannot do justice to this very large topic here. I am currently completing a monograph, to be entitled *White Man's Flour,* which goes some way toward analysing the social relations of anthropology in this regard.

6. "In these *total* social phenomena, as we propose to call them, all kinds of institutions find simultaneous expression: religious, legal, moral, and economic. In addition, the phenomena have their aesthetic aspect and they reveal morphological types" (Mauss 1970 [1925]:1). Apart from the obvious differences of application, I have supplemented Mauss' formula with a Marxist emphasis on sustaining (i.e., contributing to the reproduction of) social processes.

7. Cf. Urry 1979:15.

8. Mulvaney and Calaby 1985:chap. 9.

9. He maintained this outlook until the end of his career: "The greater the difference between the cultural levels of two associated races, the more rapidly does the lower one succumb; there is no such thing as grafting the higher upon the lower" (Spencer 1921:29).

10. Cf. Mountford 1976:53, n. 12.

11. For instance, in the same Memorandum, Gillen had referred on various occasions (1896:177, 181, 185) to "the long, long ago."

12. As early as 1898, E. B. Tylor, with whom Spencer had worked on the Pitt Rivers Museum in Oxford, had referred to "the old alcheringa or dream times" (Tylor 1898:148).

13. Exceptions such as "The Law," "History" or "Stories," though used locally by Kooris, have not affected the Dreaming complex's monopoly in settler discourse.

14. Radcliffe-Brown (1913:169) referred early to "the times long ago," a formula consistent with Gillen's initial (1896:177) "the long, long ago." Later, when the Dreaming complex was firmly established, Radcliffe-Brown claimed (1952 [1945]:166) for his term "World Dawn" the preposterous ethnographic warrant that it "corresponds to certain ideas that I have found amongst the aborigines of some tribes."

15. Apart from Spencer's and Elkin's versions, the principal accounts of the textual origins of the Dreamtime and the Alcheringa are as follows: Stanner (1956:51) stated merely that Spencer and Gillen "immortalized" the concept, without further reference. Ronald Berndt (1974:7) found that the moment of its introduction was "not clear from the literature," but later (Berndt 1987:480) settled on the probability of a "Glossary of Native Terms" appended to Spencer and Gillen's (1904:745) *The Northern Tribes of Central Australia,* the source cited previously by Ralph Piddington (1932:374) and Carl Strehlow (1907:2). The dream-times had actually been mentioned in the text of the 1904 book, but in a passing reference to the Walpari rather than to the three groups (Arunta, Kaitish, Unmatjera) mentioned in the Glossary (Spencer and Gillen 1904:576). More recently, Mulvaney (1989:116; cf. Mulvaney and Calaby 1985:124) alluded to Spencer's earliest reference to the term (Spencer 1896b:50) as "the first published general application of the concept of the 'Dreamtime', although precedence in its use belongs to a German missionary at Hermannsburg." It is not clear either what Mulvaney meant by "general" or which German missionary he had in mind. In any event, there had been no preceding reference to the Dreamtime, only to *altjira* and the like (in Krichauff 1890 [1887]:77, "*altgiva*").

16. Descartes 1945 [1642]:61–63. Even earlier, dream divination and the dream-books had been attacked by elements of the medieval Church establishment on the basis of canon law (Kruger 1992:11–13).

17. Bastian 1868, trans. F. Goodman, 118.

18. For a classical precedent opposing dreams and science in a manner closely anticipating Tylor's theory of animism, see Lucretius 1886:iv, ll. 29–39. Voltaire (1967 [1770]:425) anticipated the theory by a century, while Hobbes (1909 [1651]:17, 83) had anticipated it a century before Voltaire.

19. This was a common theme. Herbert Spencer (1871:150), for instance, claimed that savage languages were incapable of distinguishing between "I saw" and "I dreamed that I saw." Thus it was conventional that Howitt (1884:187; 1904:411) should attribute Aboriginal beliefs to a failure to distinguish between dreaming and reality. Spencer and Gillen's (1904:451) version repeated Tylor and Herbert Spencer word for word.

20. For a model statement of the whole formula from a follower of Tylor, see Clodd 1885:223–24 (cf. H. Spencer 1871:142–97).

21. The first, German edition of Freud's *The Interpretation of Dreams* was published in 1899, though its title page was postdated to 1900 (Freud 1976:34).

22. This was proposed in Australia, and with reference to Aborigines, by J. Dunmore Lang (1861:374). Cf. Schmidt 1931:58.

23. Strehlow, quoted in Thomas 1905:430.

24. In an article on the Jindyworobak poets, the Australian poet Les Murray reported (1977:555) that: "In a private discussion, Emeritus Professor A. P. Elkin of Sydney University told me that [T. G. H.] Strehlow was really the *only* white man who had ever really learned an Aboriginal language. Spencer and Gillen, on the other hand, had to rely on native informants speaking a limited pidgin English, because they spoke no Aranda at all." See also Hocart 1938.

25. For full details of the textual background to the Alcheringa/Altjiranga, see Wolfe 1991:219–20 (app. B). Though this appendix corrected his misrepresentation of this background, Tony Swain subsequently chose to repeat the error, making it an important prop to the argument of his book (1993:21).

26. Burrow 1968:234–41. Cf. (re Tylor) Marett 1941:308; Stocking 1987:267.

27. Tylor 1867:91.

28. See Markus 1990:144–45.

29. In practice, there was, obviously, no simple demarcation between two monolithic societies, but a range of articulations, which developed in the aftermath of the first encounter. Thus the term *frontier* is used here to signify a settler construct for the continuing existence of unincorporated Aboriginal social units. It is, therefore, equivalent to the term *bush black.*

30. Mulvaney 1989:100.

31. The quotation comes from the jacket notes to Fisher 1968—a widely used school textbook. Examples of this point could be multiplied indefinitely.

32. Aboriginal resistance to the discipline of labor imposed by the settlers is encapsulated in another English-language signifier for Aborigines, Walkabout. By 1925, the cohegemony of the two signifiers had become such that Strehlow's anthropologist friend Basedow (1925:279) asserted, in relation to the Aranda, that "Altjerringa is the 'walk-about' of the spirit ancestors."

33. Nor does Willshire's (1888) vocabulary of the Alice Springs natives, published eight years earlier. The first ever exhibition of Aboriginal art (as "art"), held in the late 1880s in Adelaide, was entitled "Dawn of Art" (Jones 1988:165).

34. Hence Sydney Hartland objected (1909:238) that alcheringa was "not very happily rendered by 'Dream-time', seeing that the Aranda believe the events to have actually occurred in an indefinite but far past period."

35. Scholarly examples include Flood's (1983) *Archaeology of the Dreamtime* and Fitzgerald's (1982) *From the Dreaming to 1915—A History of Queensland.* As the Australian ambassador to the United States put it in a speech delivered in New York in 1962: "And so January 1788 [the landing of the First Fleet] was the ending of one time and the beginning of another—a new era 'After the Dreaming Time'" (Beale 1962:10).

36. See T.G.H. Strehlow 1947a:190, 1947b:9, 1969:48–49, 1978:7. Cf. Howitt 1904:517–18, 624; Stirling 1896:28.

37. See Reynolds 1982:chap. 6; Rowley 1972:206–11; cf. Elkin 1951.

38. A settler-colonial elaboration of what Andrew Lang, in a different context, referred to (1897:8) as "the dream's usual power of crumpling up time and space." Relatedly, perhaps, Hans Peter Duerr has more recently intoned (1985:121) that "The 'dream place' is everywhere and nowhere, just like the 'dream-time' is always and never. You might say that the term 'dream place' does not refer to any particular place and the way to get to it is to get *nowhere*."

39. My reason for asserting that this was more crucial than the men's sexual interest in the same women is that the initial motivation for settlement was land rather than women.

40. This element is unfortunately missing from Renato Rosaldo's suggestive description of what he terms imperialist nostalgia: "Imperialist nostalgia revolves around a paradox: A person kills someone and then mourns the victim" (1989:69).

41. The paradox is only apparent, since by "time" Stanner means, of course, the abstract, homogeneous, empty, lifted-out "clock-time" of European instrumental-rational thinking (cf. Bourdieu 1964; Thompson 1967; Thrift 1990). The point is that, though an anthropologist, Stanner does not relativize his own sense of time, still less situate it in relation to settler colonization and his own ethnographic practice (cf. Fabian 1983).

42. Though not, admittedly, as complete as in Micha's (1970:291) turnabout: "Thanks to Carl Strehlow, we have numerous examples of migrations of "dream-time" groups in Central Australia."

43. Thus Howitt (1904:482, 658) equated the Dieri *mura mura*s with the Alcheringa (cf. Parker 1905:6). By 1908, "Alcheringa" had secured a heading to itself in Hastings' *Encyclopaedia of Religion and Ethics* (1908). Under this heading, which was translated as "Dream Times," Urabunna and Warramunga beliefs were classified together despite their being acknowledged to be "widely different" (Thomas 1908). In Oxford, then, Alcheringa and Dream Times had become interchangeable terms for Aboriginal beliefs, without reference to doctrinal content. Across the Channel, van Gennep (1906:xlvii) reversed Spencer and Gillen's procedure, assimilating Alcheringa to Ularaka.

44. Cf. Urry 1980:71.

45. Thus, e.g., Howitt's (1904:513) report of the last intertribal *Kuringal* initiation ceremony: "It was, in fact, the great intermarrying group which met at this ceremony, and the component parts of it differed so much in language, that the most distant could not understand each other without making use of the broken English which passes current all over Australia in those native tribes which have been brought under the white man's influence."

46. Hence a reported alleviation of the rigors of initiation, since white food was not a scheduled proscribed category (Howitt 1904:637). Similarly, "medicine men" were reported to lose their power after drinking white man's tea (Spencer and Gillen 1904:481), a consequence extending to alcohol and to hot liquids generally (Langloh Parker 1898:14).

47. Elkin himself acknowledged (1951:170) the occurrence of code-switching between indigenous and settler spheres: "Among themselves too, the native men and women usually employ pidgin when talking about their work [i.e., for Europeans]. If, however, the subject be tribal [he meant secret-sacred], the native language is used."

48. In an extended critical response to the original version of this article, Howard Morphy (1996) oddly fails to address this central point. Morphy ducks the associations and significations that attach to, or are connoted by, the word *dreaming* in English in favor of a generalized defense of the Australian anthropological tradition as he represents it.

49. With the exception of the Berndts (and, of course, of the Strehlows and Spencer) the question of the term's relationship to "ordinary" dreaming was hardly ever addressed directly (Berndt and Berndt 1946:68; cf. Elkin 1933:11, 1937:51–52). More recently, Sutton (1988b:15) has distinguished the Dreaming from ordinary dreaming: "The use of the English word *Dreaming* is more a matter of analogy than of translation."

50. Frederick Buell (1994:252–54) makes it easy for himself to raise this objection by misrepresenting my original argument: "Wolfe's critical description of Australian ethnography seeks to show how primordial connections in the colonial world were severed by colonialism, then utterly reconstructed in the anthropology colonialism brought with it." I hope that I do not need further to labor the point that I have had nothing to say about "primordial connections in the colonial [by which I take Buell to mean the indigenous] world." On the contrary, I have confined myself as rigorously as I can to analysing a settler-colonial fantasy about that world/those worlds.

51. Much of the remainder of this paragraph is culled from a review article ("Reluctant Invaders") that I contributed to the Australian literary journal *Meanjin* (1992:333–38).

52. The familiar bourgeois criterion for rationality—a capacity to maximize the means-end calculus—was presupposed in the doctrine's requirement for efficiency, whereby land became property as a result of labor being mixed with it so that it could support a higher population than it could in its natural state. As a discourse on rationality (or on Aborigines' lack of it), *terra nullius* became practically cognate with skull-measuring, intelligence-testing and other discourses on Aboriginal cognition, together with associated practices such as the grave-robbing whereby the bulk of craniometric specimens were obtained.

REFERENCES

Allen, L. 1975. *Time Before Morning. Art and Myth of the Australian Aborigines.* New York: Crowell.

Anderson, B. 1983. *Imagined Communities: Reflections on the Origin and Spread of Nationalism.* London: Verso.

Asad, T. 1979. "Anthropology and the Analysis of Ideology." *Man* (n.s.), vol. 14, 607–27.

Bascdow, H. 1925. *The Australian Aboriginal.* Adelaide: F. W. Preece and Sons.

Bastian, A. 1868. *Beiträge zur vergleichenden Psychologie: Die Seele und ihre Erscheinungsweisen in der Ethnographie.* Berlin: Ferd. Dümmler.

Bates, D. 1966 [1938]. *The Passing of the Aborigines. A Lifetime Spent among the Natives of Australia.* London: John Murray.

Beale, H. 1962. *"After the Dreaming Time". The Story of the Economic Development of Australia.* New York: Newcomer Society. Pamphlet.

Berndt, R. M. 1974. *Australian Aboriginal Religion.* Leiden: Brill.

———. 1987. "The Dreaming," in *Encyclopedia of Religion,* M. Eliade, ed., 4:479–81. New York: Macmillan.

Berndt, R. M., and C. H. Berndt 1946. Review of G. Roheim, *Eternal Ones of the Dream. Oceania,* vol. 17, 67–68.

———. 1987. *End of an Era. Aboriginal Labour in the Northern Territory.* Canberra: Australian Institute of Aboriginal Studies.

Bourdieu, P. 1964. "The Attitude of the Algerian Peasant Towards Time." In *Mediterranean Countrymen,* J. Pitt Rivers, ed., 55–72. Paris, Hague: Mouton.

Buell, F. 1994. *National Culture and the New Global System.* Baltimore: Johns Hopkins University Press.

Buffon, George Louis Leclerc, Comte de. 1812. *Natural History, General and Particular.* Vol. 3: *The History of Man and Quadrupeds,* W. Smellie, trans., W. Wood, ed. London: Cadell and Davies.

Burrow, J. W. 1966. *Evolution and Society: A Study in Victorian Social Theory.* Cambridge: Cambridge University Press.

Cabral, A. 1973. *Return to the Source: Selected Writings of Amil Cabral.* New York: Monthly Review Press.

Clodd, E. 1885. *Myths and Dreams.* London: Chatto and Windus.

Darwin, C. 1871. *The Descent of Man, and Selection in Relation to Sex.* 2 vols. London: John Murray.

Descartes, R. 1954 [1642]. *Philosophical Writings,* E. Anscombe and P. T. Geach, ed. and trans. London: Nelson.

Dixon, R. M. W., W. S. Ramson, and M. Thomas. 1990. *Australian Aboriginal Words in English: Their Origin and Meaning.* Oxford: Oxford University Press.

Duerr, H. P. 1985. *Dreamtime: Concerning the Boundary between Wilderness and Civilization,* F. Goodman, trans. Oxford: Basil Blackwell.

Durkheim, E. 1912. *Les Formes élémentaires de la vie religieuse. Le système totémique en Australie.* Paris: Alcan.

Elkin, A. P. 1932. "The Secret Life of the Australian Aborigines." *Oceania,* vol. 3, 119–38.

———. 1933. *Studies in Australian Totemism. Oceania* (Monographs, no. 2). Sydney: Oceania.

———. 1937. "Notes on the Psychic Life of the Australian Aborigines." *Mankind,* 2:3, 49–56.

————. 1951. "Reaction and Interaction: A Food Gathering People and European Settlement in Australia." *American Anthropologist,* vol. 53, 164–86.

————. 1952. Review of C. Simpson, *Adam in Ochre. Oceania,* vol. 23, 243–44.

————. 1961. "The Yabuduruwa." *Oceania,* vol. 31, 166–209.

————. 1964. *The Australian Aborigines: How to Understand Them.* 4th ed. Sydney: Angus and Robertson.

Fabian, J. 1983. *Time and the Other: How Anthropology Makes Its Object.* New York: Columbia University Press.

Fanon, F. 1967. *The Wretched of the Earth.* Harmondsworth: Penguin U.K.

Fisher, J. 1968. *The Australians: From 1788 to Modern Times.* Adelaide: Rigby.

Fitzgerald, R. 1982. *From the Dreaming to 1915—A History of Queensland.* St. Lucia: University of Queensland Press.

Flood, J. 1983. *Archaeology of the Dreamtime.* Sydney: Collins.

Foucault, M. 1967. *Madness and Civilization,* R. Howard, trans. London: Tavistock.

————. 1977. *Discipline and Punish,* A Sheridan, trans. Harmondsworth: Penguin U.K.

Frazer, J. G. 1910. *Totemism and Exogamy. A Treatise on Certain Early Forms of Superstition and Society.* 4 vols. London: Macmillan.

Freud, S. 1976 [1900]. *The Interpretation of Dreams.* Penguin Freud Library, vol. 4. Harmondsworth: Penguin U.K.

————. 1976 [1901]. *The Psychopathology of Everyday Life.* Pelican Freud Library, vol. 5. Harmondsworth: Penguin U.K.

Frost, A. 1990. "New South Wales as *terra nullius:* The British Denial of Aboriginal Land Rights," in *Through White Eyes,* S. Janson and S. Macintyre, eds., 65–76. Sydney: Allen & Unwin.

Gennep, A. van 1906. *Mythes et légendes d'Australie. Études d'ethnographie et de sociologie.* Paris: Guilmoto, Librairie Orientale et Américaine.

Gillen, F. J. 1896. "Notes on Some Manners and Customs of the Aborigines of the McDonnell Ranges Belonging to the Arunta Tribe," in Spencer 1896a:4, 159–96.

Harris, M. 1967. "Introduction," in M. Harris and A. Forbes, *The Land That Waited,* 1–2. Melbourne: Lansdowne.

Hartland, E. S. 1909. *Primitive Paternity.* Vol. 1. London: Folk-Lore Society.

Hastings, J., ed. 1908. *Encyclopaedia of Religion and Ethics.* Vol. 1. Edinburgh: T. and T. Clark.

Hobbes, T. 1909 [1651]. *Leviathan.* Oxford: Clarendon.

Hocart, A. M. 1933. "Arunta Language: Strehlow vs. Spencer and Gillen" (letter), *Man* (o.s.), 33: 92 (no. 96).

Howitt, A. W. 1884. "On Some Australian Beliefs." *Journal of the Anthropological Institute,* vol. 13, 185–98.

————. 1904. *The Native Tribes of South-East Australia.* London: Macmillan.

Jones, P. 1988. "Perceptions of Aboriginal Art: A History," in *Dreamings: The Art of Aboriginal Australia,* P. Sutton, ed., 143–79. London: Viking.

Kempe, H. 1883. "Zur Sittenkunde der Centralaustralischen Schwarzen." *Mittheilungen des Vereins für Erdkunde zu Halle*, 52–56.

Krichauff, F. E. H. 1887 [1890]. "Further Notes on the 'Aldolinga' or 'Mbenderinga' Tribe of Aborigines," *Proceedings of the Royal Geographical Society of Australasia, South Australian Branch*, vol. 2, (1886–88): 77–80.

Kruger, S. F. 1992. *Dreaming in the Middle Ages*. Cambridge: Cambridge University Press.

Lancaster Jones, F. 1970. *The Structure and Growth of Australia's Aboriginal Population*. Canberra: Australian National University Press.

Lang, A. 1897. *The Book of Myths and Dreams*. London: David Nutt.

———. 1898. Introduction to Parker 1898:xvii–xxiii.

———. 1900. "Australian Gods. A Reply." *Folk-lore*, vol. 10, 1–46.

Lang, J. D. 1861. *Queensland, Australia*. London: Edward Stanford.

Leonhardi, M. Freiherr von. 1907. "Über einige religiöse und totemistische Vorstellungen der Aranda und Loritja in Zentralaustralien." *Globus*, vol. 91, 285–90.

Lucretius. 1886. *De Rerum Natura libri sex*, H. A. J. Munro, trans. 4th ed. Cambridge: Deighton, Bell.

Marcuse, H. 1965. "Repressive Tolerance," in R. P. Wolff, B. Moore, and H. Marcuse, *A Critique of Pure Tolerance*, 95–137. London: Jonathan Cape.

Marett, R. R. 1941. *A Jerseyman at Oxford*. Oxford: Oxford University Press.

Markus, A. 1990. *Governing Savages*. Sydney: Allen and Unwin.

Mauss, M. 1970 [1925]. *The Gift*, I. Cunnison, trans. London: Routledge and Kegan Paul.

Micha, F. J. 1970. "Trade and Change in Aboriginal Australian Cultures: Australian Aboriginal Trade as an Expression of Close Culture Contact and as a Mediator of Culture Change," in *Diprotodon to Detribalization: Studies of Change among Australian Aborigines*, A. R. Pilling and R. A. Waterman, eds., 285–313. East Lansing: Michigan State University Press.

Morphy, H. 1996. "Empiricism to Metaphysics: In Defence of the Concept of the Dreamtime," in *Prehistory to Politics. John Mulvaney, the Humanities and the Public Intellectual*, T. Bonyhady and T. Griffiths, eds., 163–89. Melbourne: Melbourne University Press.

Morrissey, P. 1995. "Lines in the Sand." <http://werple.mira.net.au>

Mountford, C. P. 1976. *Nomads of the Australian Desert*. Adelaide: Rigby.

Mulvaney, D. J. 1989. *Encounters in Place: Outsiders and Aboriginal Australians, 1606–1985*. St. Lucia: University of Queensland Press.

Mulvaney, D. J., and J. H. Calaby. 1985. *"So Much That Is New": Baldwin Spencer, 1860–1929. A Biography*. Melbourne: Melbourne University Press.

Murray, L. A. 1977. "The Human-Hair Thread." *Meanjin Quarterly*, vol. 36, 550–71.

Olsen, J., M. Durack, G. Dutton, V. Serventy, and A. Bortignon. 1984. *The Land Beyond Time: A Modern Exploration of Australia's North-West Frontier*. South Melbourne: Macmillan Australia.

Ortner, S. B. 1974. "Is Female to Male as Nature Is to Culture?" in *Woman, Culture, and Society,* M. Z. Rosaldo and L. Lamphere, eds., 67–87. Stanford: Stanford University Press.

Parker, K. Langloh 1898. *More Australian Legendary Tales.* London: David Nutt.

———. 1905. *The Euahlayi Tribe. A Study of Aboriginal Life in Australia.* London: Archibald Constable.

Piddington, R. 1932. "Totemic System of the Karadjeri Tribe." *Oceania,* vol. 2, 373– 400.

Purcell, B. H. 1893. "Rites and Customs of Australian Aborigines,' in *Verhandlungen der Berliner Gesellschaft für Anthropologie, Ethnologie und Urgeschichte,* 286– 89. Berlin: Verlag von A. Asher.

Radcliffe-Brown, A. R. [A. R. Brown]. 1913. "Three Tribes of Western Australia." *Journal of the Royal Anthropological Institute,* vol. 43, 143–95.

———. 1952. *Structure and Function in Primitive Society.* London: Routledge and Kegan Paul.

Reynolds, H. 1982. *The Other Side of the Frontier: Aboriginal Resistance to the European Invasion of Australia.* Melbourne: Penguin Australia.

———. 1987. *The Law of the Land.* Melbourne: Penguin Australia.

———. 1989. *Dispossession: Black Australians and White Invaders.* (The Australian Experience Series) Sydney: Allen and Unwin.

Roberts, A., and C. P. Mountford. 1969. *The Dawn of Time: Australian Aboriginal Myths in Paintings.* Adelaide: Rigby.

Rosaldo, R. 1989. "Imperialist Nostalgia," in id., *Culture and Truth. The Remaking of Social Analysis,* 68–87. Boston: Beacon.

Rowley, C. D. 1970. *The Destruction of Aboriginal Society.* Canberra: Australian National University Press.

Schmidt, W. 1931. *The Origin and Growth of Religion: Facts and Theories,* H. J. Rose, trans. London: Methuen.

Schulze, L. (Rev.) 1891. "The Aborigines of the Upper and Middle Finke River: Their Habits and Customs with Introductory Notes on the Physical and Natural-History Features of the Country," J. G. O. Tepper, trans. *Transactions and Proceedings and Report of the Royal Society of South Australia,* 14:2, 210–46.

Spencer, H. 1870. *The Right to the Use of the Earth.* Land Reform League Tract no. 1. Melbourne: Robert Bell.

———. 1871. *The Principles of Sociology.* Vol. 1 (vol. 6 of his *A System of Synthetic Philosophy).* London: Williams and Norgate.

Spencer, [W.] B. (Baldwin) ed. 1896a. *Report on the Work of the Horn Scientific Expedition to Central Australia.* London: Dulan.

———. 1896b. *Through Larapinta Land: A Narrative of the Horn Expedition to Central Australia,* in Pt. I of Spencer 1896a:1–136.

———. 1904. "Totemism in Australia," in *Report of the Tenth Meeting of the AAAS,* 376–423. Dunedin: New Zealand.

————. 1921. *Presidential Address to the Fifteenth (Hobart-Melbourne) Meeting of ANZAAS, January 10, 1921.* Melbourne: Mullett (Government Printer).

Spencer, W. B., and F. J. Gillen. 1899. *The Native Tribes of Central Australia.* London: Macmillan.

————. 1904. *The Northern Tribes of Central Australia.* London: Macmillan.

————. 1927. *The Arunta.* 2 vols. London: Macmillan.

Spivak, G. C. 1985. "Subaltern Studies: Deconstructing Historiography," in *Subaltern Studies, IV.* R. Guha, ed., 330–63. New Delhi: Oxford University Press.

————. 1988. "Can the Subaltern Speak?" in *Marxism and the Interpretation of Culture,* C. Nelson and L. Grossberg, eds., 271–313. Basingstoke: Macmillan Education.

Stanner, W. E. H. 1956. "The Dreaming," in *Australian Signpost: An Anthology,* T. A. G. Hungerford, ed., 51–65. Melbourne: Cheshire.

————. 1965. "Religion, Totemism and Symbolism," in *Aboriginal Man in Australia: Essays in Honour of Emeritus Professor A. P. Elkin,* R. M. Berndt and C. H. Berndt, eds., 207–37. Sydney: Angus and Robertson.

Stirling, E. C. 1896. "Anthropology," in Spencer 1896a: Part IV:1–158.

Stocking, G. W., Jr. 1987. *Victorian Anthropology.* New York: Macmillan Free Press.

Strehlow, C. 1907. *Die Aranda- und Loritja-Stämme in Zentral-Australien.* Vol. 1: *Mythen, Sagen, und Märchen des Aranda Stammes in Zentral Australien.* Frankfurt: Joseph Baer.

Strehlow, T. G. H. 1947. *Aranda Traditions.* Melbourne: Melbourne University Press.

————. 1969. *Journey to Horseshoe Bend.* Sydney: Angus and Robertson.

————. 1971. *Songs of Central Australia.* Sydney: Angus and Robertson.

————. 1978. *Central Australian Religion: Personal Monototemism in a Polytotemic Community.* Australian Association for the Study of Religions, Special Studies in Religions, vol. 2. Adelaide: AASR.

Sutton, P. 1988. "Dreamings," in *Dreamings: The Art of Aboriginal Australia,* P. Sutton, ed., 13–32. London: Viking.

Swain, T. 1993. *A Place for Strangers: Towards a History of Australian Aboriginal Being.* Sydney: Cambridge University Press.

Thomas, N. W. 1905. "The Religious Ideas of the Arunta," *Folk-Lore,* vol. 16, 428–33.

————. 1908. "Alcheringa," in *Encyclopaedia of Religion and Ethics,* J. Hastings, ed., vol. 1, 298. Edinburgh: T. and T. Clark.

Thompson, E. P. 1967. "Time, Work-Discipline, and Industrial Capitalism." *Past and Present,* no. 38, 56–97.

Thrift, N. 1990. "The Making of a Capitalist Time Consciousness," in *The Sociology of Time,* J. Hassard, ed., 105–29. London: Macmillan.

Tylor, E. B. 1867. "On Traces of the Early Mental Condition of Man," in *Notices of the Proceedings at the Meetings of the Members of the Royal Institution of Great Britain with Abstracts of the Discourses Delivered at the Evening Meetings.* Vol. 5, *1866–69,* 83–93.

————. 1871. *Primitive Culture: Researches Into the Development of Mythology, Philosophy, Religion, Art and Custom.* 2 vols. London: John Murray.

————. 1898. "Remarks on Totemism, with Especial Reference to Some Modern Theories Respecting It." *Journal of the Anthropological Institute,* vol. 28, 138–48.

Urry, J. 1979. "Beyond the Frontier: European Influences, Aborigines, and the Concept of 'Traditional' Culture." *Journal of Australian Studies,* vol. 5, 1–16.

————. 1980. "Aborigines, History, and Semantics—A Reply." *Journal of Australian Studies,* vol. 6, 68–72.

Voltaire, F. M. A. de. 1967 [1770]. *Dictionnaire Philosophique.* Paris: Garnière Frères.

Willshire, W. H. 1888. *The Aborigines of Central Australia, with a vocabulary of the dialect of the Alice Springs natives.* Port Augusta: Dugsdale.

————. 1896. *The Land of the Dawning. Being Facts Gleaned from Cannibals in the Australian Stone Age.* Adelaide: W. K. Thomas.

Wolfe, P. 1991. "On Being Woken Up: The Dreamtime in Anthropology and in Australian Settler Culture." *Comparative Studies in Society and History,* vol. 33, 197–224.

————. 1992. "Reluctant Invaders," *Meanjin,* vol. 51:2, 333–38.

————. 1994. "Nation and MiscegeNation: Discursive Continuity in the Post-Mabo Era." *Social Analysis,* no. 36, 93–152.

Colonizing the National Imaginary: Folklore, Anthropology, and the Making of the Modern State

Uli Linke

Despite the enormous diversity of research within the anthropological tradition, a common unifying theme has been the "reach into otherness" (Burridge 1973:6), the venture of discovering humanity through the exploration of other cultures. From the inception of anthropology as a distinct domain of knowledge, this ethnographic curiosity has been staged within a comparative frame of reference (Hymes 1974). Early inquiries into different customs and social forms were based on the writings of European travelers, whose observations about people in distant lands provided the narrative material for constructing a plausible vision of their own world.[1] As Jean-Jacques Rousseau sarcastically remarked in his *Discourse on the Origin of Inequality* (1978 [1755]:130):

> For the past three or four centuries, during which the inhabitants of Europe have flooded other continents and continuously published new collections with descriptions of their travel and commerce, in my opinion, of all peoples, we have come to know only the Europeans well; for it seems that, in light of the ludicrous stereotypes which have not died out even among writers, no one produces anything but studies about the peoples of their own nation, under the pompous pretense of investigating humanity.

Initially, insights into the workings of society remained implicit, hidden beneath the projected images of "otherness." By the second half of the eighteenth century, these encounters with the unfamiliar through travel and commerce had begun to generate among Europeans a conscious desire for societal self-knowledge. The haphazard collection of ethnographic information was gradually transformed into a reflective methodology.

In Germany, attempts to systematize the acquisition of social data led, in the decade of Rousseau's death, to the creation of a new field of inquiry. The principal research methods and aims were introduced under the heading *Ethnography* in 1772 by the German scholar A. F. Schlözer, professor of history at Göttingen (Stagl 1974). The terms *Völkerkunde* (anthropology) and *Volkskunde* (folklore) first appeared at this time—the former in the *Treatise of Geography*[2] (1775) by Johann Christian Gatterer, the latter seven years later in the Hamburg weekly *The Traveler* (Lutz 1982:34–37; Weber-Kellermann and Bimmer 1985:3). The German fascination with otherness was thus from the beginning directed *inward* as much as *outward: Volkskunde* (the science of a single people) was applied to the study of European peasants, particularly the rural population within one's own nation or state. By contrast, *Völkerkunde* (the science of multiple peoples) dealt with more distant cultures and the inhabitants of other continents.

Such terminological distinctions had little ideological significance at first. The ethnographic representations of otherness, although divided along regional or geographic lines, were tenaciously linked and covertly complicit— the one feeding off the other. Such a merging of perceptions is evident, for instance, in the work of Christian Garve, professor of history at the University of Breslau, who noted in 1786:

> The character of the peasant approximates the mentality of the untamed man-in-nature [*Naturmensch*] . . . [like] the Iroquois or the Hottentot . . . [who] can sit part of the day in one spot, or cower, rolled up like a hedgehog, without movement, without emitting a sound. The same human being, if hunger or air drives him to hunt, will roam through the woods without tiring. . . . This description seems to be nothing other than a caricature of the image of many of our peasants. Their laziness always stands in relation to their coarseness and stupidity. (1786a:24)

The typification of the "peasant" at home and the "wild man" abroad in similar ethnographic terms served a common purpose: it permitted the creation of a new vision of truth by objectifying the social imagination in the discourse of otherness.

By the late 1700s, popular fantasies of exotic primitivism revealed a growing sense of discontent with European civilization. Such feelings were framed by a longing to return to a state of *wilderness* within the natural world, accompanied by a romanticization of the "simple" life among country peasants and wild aborigines (Kohl 1987; Taussig 1987). Images of *absence* came to dominate the European concept of otherness: the perceived lack of such social institutions as law, government, or religion was seen as the essence of "primitive" or "uncivilized" existence. These perceptions were reinforced by the selective focus of early ethnographic reports on nudity, cannibalism, witchcraft, and violence among both aborigines and peasants (Kohl 1986). The symbolic construction of such an antithetical world, the formulation of a counterreality through metaphors of otherness, conveyed an implicit critique of European society.

During the same period, the symbolic concern with otherness assumed overt political dimensions. Social knowledge was transformed into an agent of power (Elias 1978–82) appropriated as an instrument of domination in the "civilizing" and "domesticating" efforts of the state. In England, the orientation of social inquiry was directed *outward,* influenced by the colonial encounter with distant peoples in the overseas empire. In other parts of Europe, such as Scotland or Germany, the quest for social knowledge was directed *inward,* motivated by problems of national identity and political disunity. Therefore, by participating in the tasks of "empire-building" and "nation-building" (Stocking 1982:172), anthropology (*Völkerkunde*) and folklore (*Volkskunde*) became distinct academic fields.

Given the common origins of the two disciplines, the concepts and methods that enter into the interpretation of people abroad cannot be treated as unique: folklore research is an important, although much neglected, component of the anthropological tradition. Any attempt to investigate the history of anthropology is thus seriously incomplete without some attention to the ways in which Europeans dealt with cultural diversity in their own part of the world.

The present work is a contribution to the history of folklore as part of the broader history of anthropology. It is an attempt to show that the emergence of folklore scholarship in eighteenth-century Germany can be linked to two distinct political movements: romantic nationalism and administrative particularism. The romantic folklorists aimed toward a politically unified nation based on a common cultural and historical heritage that was reconstructed from relics of the ancient traditions in German folk customs and narratives. The administrative folklorists, in contrast, sought to enhance the governing power of single German states by introducing novel procedures—such as comprehensive statistical surveys of local folk culture—for "knowing" the population. While the romantic school was committed to the interpretation of single texts in an attempt to rediscover a lost national heritage, the administrative/statistical school was primarily concerned with the pragmatic and practical problems of national development. As a result, this type of scholarship tended to produce detailed ethnographic studies of whole communities rather than collections of isolated narratives. These approaches to the study of folklore reveal two basic principles by which knowledge of local peoples was appropriated to become an integral part of the political sphere.

The relation between romantic and administrative/statistical folklore in eighteenth-century Germany comprises the first part of this essay. Since the influence of the romantic movement on folklore scholarship has been exhaustively dealt with elsewhere (cf. Ergang 1966; Hobsbawm 1990; Lukaćs 1963; Stocking 1989; Wilson 1976), the current paper focuses on the statistical approach, its scholarly significance, and its participation in the political process through the complicity of power and knowledge. The history of folklore in Germany will then be placed in a larger, comparative context by examining the beginnings of folklore research in England, Scotland, and China. As we shall see, the dualism that characterized the origin of German folklore is also apparent in the various forms that the quest for social knowledge has assumed at different times and in different national traditions.

The Romantic and Administrative Traditions in German Folklore

The origins of folklore research in Germany have generally been traced to the romantic movement and its fascination with narrative genres. Inspired by the works of Johann Gottfried Herder (1773, 1778–79), German romantics saw the oral traditions of the common or rural population as a repository of ancient customs and beliefs. It was Herder's conviction that folk poetry, like the lyrics of songs, contained the essence of a nation's creative heritage. The collection of such traditional forms of verbal art was therefore seen by the romantics as a means for Germans to uncover traces of a more glorious era in history.

This quest for national lore coincided with the beginnings of a movement toward German unification. The romantic search for common cultural traditions was thus motivated in part by concrete political concerns (Ergang 1966; Weber-Kellermann 1969:12–19; Wilson 1973). Early romantics were distressed to see that large segments of the German population had abandoned their native heritage in favor of foreign models of refinement: common German was considered vulgar, and French became the principal medium of expression in literature and education (Bendix 1978:391–96). The growing resentment toward the external appropriation of culture was exacerbated by the French annexation of German territories during the Napoleonic wars of 1803–

15. Thus, the perhaps subtle sense of loss in the realm of culture was dramatically affirmed by the more tangible loss in land. In response to these feelings of absence and loss, German romantics turned toward the excavation of peasant lore. Framed by the experience of cultural estrangement and military defeat, the study of narrative folklore was gradually transposed into an instrument of popular resistance.

Romantic nationalism in Germany came into being as a revolutionary force. Initially a literary movement of cultural protest, German romanticism promoted the collection of folk narratives as a means for transforming basic social attitudes. The movement's nationalistic concerns, like its quest for a collective folk heritage, were directed at changing the *internal* realities of German political rule. In the late eighteenth century, imperial Germany consisted of a loosely organized confederation of some 250 sovereign territories. Austria, Bavaria, Prussia, and Saxony were the most important of the eight electoral states. Additional territories belonged to twenty-seven spiritual members of the College of Princes, thirty-seven lay princes, ninety-five imperial counts, forty-two imperial founders, and fifty free or imperial towns (Bendix 1978:379). The constituent units of the German empire were composed of scattered territories. Every region, even if governed by the same sovereign, possessed its own administration and judiciary. The many territorial and administrative divisions not only inhibited attempts to standardize commercial or religious practices, but also hindered any efforts toward national unification. Under these circumstances, the study of folklore was perceived by the romantics as a means to forge a sense of unity among the German population and thereby supersede all existing (sociopolitical) boundaries.

Herder's philosophy of history inspired other talented writers, poets, and dramatists of his period to begin an extensive search for the remains of German folk traditions. In their investigations, the romantics sought to unlock the experiences of the Germans, which were encased not only in words, grammatical forms, and poetic verses but also in the narrative genres of folklore. By the early nineteenth century, large collections of folk songs, epic poems, ballads, popular legends, and tales had appeared in print (e.g., Tieck 1803; Arnim and Brentano 1806–8; Görres 1807; Grimm 1812; Grimm and Grimm 1816; Jahn 1810). These collections were more than simple reproductions of existing lore. In many cases, oral folk narratives were deliberately rewritten and transformed into a type of literary discourse about German values, manners, and virtues (Snyder 1951; Zipes 1979). Early romantics thus acted ideologically by presenting through folklore their notions regarding society and the state. As a result of their educational and moralizing efforts, the collections of romantic folklore were politicized: narrative genres became pedagogical tools in a process of "national" socialization.

Despite the enormous following of the romantic folklorists, there were opposing voices. Among the many critics was the German poet and dramatist Friedrich von Schiller, who delivered as early as 1791 a "sociological" explication of contemporary poetry collections in which he called into question the romantic assertion that such oral traditions expressed collective or national German sentiments (Weber-Kellermann 1969:13). The process of reconstructing history through the interpretation of folk culture thereby became a principal target of contemporary disbelief. By the turn of the century, even poets like August Wilhelm Schlegel began sharply to oppose what they saw as a "futile" search for the "scattered traces and rubble of antiquity" (Weber-Kellerman and Bimmer 1985:29). Others, like Johann Heinrich Voss (1808), initiated debates about the authenticity of so-called traditional narratives that had been intentionally changed or composed from several fragmented texts. The romantics' attempt to uncover a common German heritage was thus consistently rejected on scholastic grounds. Such methodological concerns were coupled with objections to the source materials themselves: traditional narratives—dismissed by many critics as nonsensical, irrational, and trivial—were designated as inferior forms of German culture because of their supposed vulgarity and lack of morals (Zipes 1979:26). Opponents of the romantic approach therefore took issue not only with the opportunistic application of research methods but also with the use of folk narratives as a primary source of social knowledge.

These scattered references to what appears to be a literary debate about the basic aims and principles of folklore scholarship point toward the presence of an important countertradition. Indeed, the works of the scholar and political pragmatist Wilhelm Heinrich Riehl (1823–97), most of which had appeared by the middle of the nineteenth century, represent the culmination of a major alternative to the focus and methods of the romantic folklorists (Bausinger 1969:54–61; Köstlin 1979:81–94). Riehl, a social conservative, began his career as a student of theology at Marburg. Upon completing his academic commitments, he worked for several years as a journalist. Soon after the publication of his first series of books (*Civil Society* [1851]; *Land and People* [1854]; *The Family* [1855]; and *Cultural Studies from Three Centuries* [1859a]), Riehl accepted a chair in political science, law, and cultural history at the University of Munich. He was later appointed director of the Bavarian National Museum.

Perhaps in part as a result of his broad training, Riehl looked upon the nineteenth-century obsession with collecting and classifying isolated narratives as a futile enterprise. In his descriptive monograph, *The Inhabitants of the Palatinate* (1857), he sarcastically compared the philological zeal of the romantics to that of botanists and butterfly collectors, "who set out with a tin can to . . . gather superficial folk antiquities . . . in order to place them, properly pressed, dried, and classified, into a Germanic herbarium . . . [and] who try to catch unknown folk song specimens, in order to pin them in categories, well spread out, in a collection" (Wiegelmann and Bimmer 1977:18). It was Riehl who argued that German folklore was not simply an expression of an abstract poetic force; rather, it was the product of particular social conditions and realities. As such, folk traditions could only be studied effectively "in context" through comprehensive population surveys. Consequently, throughout his works, Riehl tended to emphasize the importance of field research, outlining those methods of investigation that later were to be known as "anthropological." Thus, in his *Travel Book* of 1869, he promoted the idea of the encyclopedic traveler and ethnographer, the scholarly "observer," who gathered reliable facts about the inhabitants of specific regions and territories.

The study of German folklore was, in Riehl's view, primarily a *political* tool: as a relevant source of social information, folkloristic knowledge was essential to the formulation of cultural and administrative policies. In fact, Riehl repeatedly emphasized that "knowledge of a territory and its people" (geography and folklore) was essential to the art of governing (Weber-Kellermann and Bimmer 1985:43). The administration of state power, Riehl (1869) argued, had to be framed by an ethnographic understanding of the population: the regulation of society depended on systematic inventories of folk culture. Thus, in contrast to the German romantics, who used folklore as an ideological discourse in their quest for national unification, Riehl saw an explicit political application of folklore to the management of populations. In *Civil Society* (1851), Riehl declared:

Political folklore is . . . the guarantee for our political future (p. 5) . . . [because] a liberal and popular administrative policy is unthinkable without regard for all the natural characteristics of folk life. (p. 10) . . . I would like to show . . . that a social policy, that is, the art of state administration, . . . is based on the scientific study of the population through all its groups and estates. (p. 11)

Riehl further elaborated these ideas eight years later in a lecture entitled "Folklore as Science" (1859b):

The study of folklore will be most beneficial to the whole sphere of administrative discipline. . . . For if the policing of culture [*Culturpolizei*] is merely conditioned by the practical needs of the population, then it can and must be able to organize itself according to the ethnographic laws on which these needs are based. . . . The highest triumph of the internal art of administration would then consist of the assimilation of every police action to the inner life [*Natur*] of the folk such that the population would come to believe that even in troublesome and aggravating matters, the police acted only in their own interest and on behalf of their sentiments. (225)

The "policing" of culture was in Riehl's work equated with the administrative efforts of the state: the art of governing required comprehensive ethnographic surveys for the political management of social life. The study of the population was defined as the task of "political" folklore, a sociological discourse designed for the subtle and perhaps even cunning application of bureaucratic power.

The political pragmatism of scholars like Riehl found little resonance among nineteenth-century German romantics, who saw the study of folklore primarily as a powerful *ideological* tool: through the reconstruction of a common Germanic heritage, folklore research was to inspire a desire for national unification in the population. Riehl's social conservatism thus stood in striking contrast to the revolutionary goals of the romantics. According to Riehl, the task of folklore was not to initiate political change but rather to enhance the administrative control of the state. This explicit link of Riehl's scholarly contributions to the tactics of governing power significantly decreased his popularity in contemporary academic circles. As a result, his work had little impact on the subsequent development of folklore theory (Linke 1995a, 1995b; Dow and Lixfeld 1986).

Despite this rejection by his romantic contemporaries, Riehl was to become one of the most important figures in the German tradition of *political* folklore (Wiegelmann 1979). His ideas on the collusion of "social knowledge" and "power" were put into effect, in rather different ways, both by the hegemonic rule of the Prussian state and, later, by German fascism (Lixfeld 1994). By facilitating the administrative implementation of educational and welfare reforms under Bismarck, Riehl's work promoted the constitution of folklore research as a political practice. The potential of German folk traditions as (in Riehl's words) a "lever for political agitation" was rediscovered in the 1930s by the National Socialists, who incorporated Riehl's scholarship into the fascist procedures of population management and "adjustment." Here the appropriation of cultural knowledge assumed legitimating functions: societal contradictions and political brutalities were hidden from public consciousness through the construction of elaborate "mythologies" (Kamenetsky 1972; Lidtke 1982; Linke 1988:130–31; Mieder 1982). Such an overt ideological manipulation of folklore was coupled with attempts to create a "science of populations" (*Volksthumskunde*) modeled after Riehl's conception of political folklore. In the words of one contemporary, this science was concerned primarily with "the societal coexistence of different peoples" (Weber-Kellermann 1969:22). In fascist Germany, the concept of "populations" was, however, defined in terms of "race." Consequently, the focus of research shifted from the original study of social relations to concerns with reproductive "purity." The ethnographic inventories of culture, as previously outlined by Riehl, were similarly transformed into inventories of human physiognomy. Statistical or political folklore and its methods of information management (examining, measuring, ordering) had thus become aligned with political procedures of genetic surveillance (cf. Linke 1995c). While Riehl could not possibly have foreseen this particular application of his ideas, he nevertheless laid the groundwork for the appropriation of folklore as a tool of the state. As we shall see, however, the roots of this tradition lie even further back in history.

German Folklore and the Science of the State

One of the earliest uses of the German term for "folklore" has been documented in 1787 in the work of Joseph Mader (1754–1815), a professor of imperial history and political science at Prague (Möller 1964:220–21). The word initially appeared in the title of a short essay, "Register of a Few Printed Aids for a Pragmatic Geography, Folklore, and Science of the State in Bohemia" (1787:23). While the text itself contained little explanatory information about the meaning of the term, Mader's later publications provided a definition that explicated the aims of the discipline: "Anthropology [*Menschenkunde und Völkerkunde*] . . . attempts to describe the size, characteristics, and customs of human beings, their domestic and societal life" (1793:6); by contrast, folklore (*Volkskunde*) seeks to investigate "the finer shades and differences in the customs, manners, principles—which make up the individual, characteristic elements [of a people]" (1793:14). Here, Mader defined folklore with reference to anthropology, and he presented the two human sciences as complementary fields. Somewhat broader in scope, anthropology was concerned with the study of humanity in a general sense, while folklore was focused more narrowly on a population's distinctive cultural traits. Mader further suggested that the acquisition of social knowledge was an integral part of what he called "statistics": "Statistics, when understood in a narrow sense, has as its object only the study of the [population's] political disposition. Yet this is closely tied . . . to the thinking, the way of life of the people, their religious sentiments, trades, customs, habits, etc. One cannot separate these subjects, since they are intertwined" (1793:51). Mader thereby implied that the political or legal administration of people could not be divorced from information obtained about their way of life and culture. He asserted that a governing bureaucracy was functionally dependent upon the acquisition of such knowledge.

In Germany, the collection of folkloristic information for administrative purposes began in the middle of the eighteenth century. At that time, folklore emerged as a field of investigation—a department of knowledge within the "science of the state" (*Staatswissenschaft* or *Staatskunde*), then also called "statistics" (*Statistik*), which denoted "statesmanship" and referred to the art of governing (Lauffer 1931:135; Lutz 1982:30–37; Narr and Bausinger 1964:238). Through its link with statistics and political science, German folklore came into being as a pragmatic, administrative science. The adviser to the royal court Gottfried von Achenwall, who presented a series of lectures on statistics in 1748, is generally regarded as the founder of this discipline. When he published his *Digest of the Newest Science of the State* in 1749, he had laid the foundation for a new technology of power. Achenwall asserted that "the ability to understand how every state gradually evolved into its present form, that is, the acquisition of insight into the cause and reasons behind the current political constitution" was the subject matter of statistics; such investigations, however, required knowledge of religious institutions, principles of justice and order, matters of finance, commerce, and war (1754:4–5). Thus, to administer its affairs, a state required not only knowledge of a terrain and its geography but also information about the social characteristics of a population as revealed "through sickness, thoughts, customs, virtues, and vices" (1752:35–36). In this sense, Achenwall's work marked the beginnings of a scholarly discipline that was characterized by the production of systematic surveys and extremely detailed ethnographic studies of ordinary social life.

What prompted such a sudden quest for social knowledge? This question has been addressed at some length in the context of other human sciences. For instance, the beginnings of social anthropology in Great Britain have been linked to the information requirements of the colonial administration during its encounters with distant peoples in the overseas empire (Asad 1973). Similarly, the emergence of European history as a professional discipline, based on archival study and rigorous methodological training, can be traced to the nineteenth century, when historians were primarily concerned with the rise of nation-states in the West, their political/administrative development, and their military and cultural expansion (Himmelfarb 1987; Stone 1987). Likewise, the beginnings of history as an academic field of inquiry in early twentieth-century Japan can be traced to political efforts to build a modern nation-state and promote its growth in wealth and power: in Japan, early historians facilitated their country's colonial expansion by conducting the kind of intelligence research needed for the political/economic administration of China, southern Manchuria, and Korea (Tanaka 1993).[3] The implications of power in this field of knowledge are clear. Likewise, the origins of German sociology in the seventeenth and eighteenth centuries can be traced to attempts by fiscal administrators (i.e., cameralists) to tighten state controls over the collection of public revenues (Small 1967:110–31; Zielenziger 1966). This would suggest that a bureaucratic government of social life is dependent upon local knowledge. The administration of people by political means, in contrast to military domination or control by force, inevitably leads to the sponsorship of some form of ethnographic research.

Unfortunately, very few scholars of German folklore have attempted to investigate the bond between social knowledge and political power in the history of their own field. As a result, only some scattered references, mere allusions, exist about the expansion of administrative power and its link to folklore research in eighteenth-century Germany. Much of the data indicate that the beginnings of political or statistical folklore can be attributed to the intelligence requirements of the German states attempting to increase their control over the economy and population (Narr and Bausinger 1964:238; Weber-Kellermann et al. 1985:7). This idea was expressed perhaps most clearly by Hermann Bausinger, who suggested that "folklore and statistics provided the conceptual framework for a systematic description of social conditions that was to serve the state administration" (1969:30). The apparent link between the early acquisition of ethnographic information and the exercise of power, however, demands further analysis.

Imperial Germany in the eighteenth century was characterized by enormous divisions in political territory, which promoted a continuous struggle for sovereignty and governing power among neighboring states (Small 1967:110–18). Within this context of political fragmentation, every German state saw a need to promote the economy and increase its military strength. To achieve these goals, it became necessary to obtain productive service from individuals and to coordinate their activities with the economic apparatus (Foucault

1980:125). Consequently, the governing bodies began to tighten their hold on the population by controlling it with finer, subtler, power mechanisms. Power was to be "incorporated" into the bodies of individuals; it had to gain access to their acts, attitudes, and learning processes in order to ensure not only their submission but also a constant increase in their productivity. Such concerns with the effective regulation of society—the complete *government of social life*—produced an enormous effort to adjust the mechanisms of power and to create a machinery that placed the everyday behavior and identity of individuals under examination.

Under these circumstances, the "population" emerged as an object of scientific investigation. Inquiries began into issues of demography, public health, marriage, fertility, and religious practices, and people began to say for the first time that it was impossible to govern a state without *knowing* its population (see Foucault 1980:124). The understanding of the phenomenon of population became the domain of folklore, a discipline appropriately called *Volkskunde* in German, a term that meant literally 'knowledge of the common folk' or 'population science'.[4] The study of folklore in Germany produced an effective instrument for the accumulation of social knowledge by developing methods of observation, techniques of registration, and procedures of investigation and research. The emergence of the population as a target of folklore research thus finds its early beginnings in the pragmatic concerns of the German states and not, as is generally assumed, in the ideological concerns of the German romantics. In fact, neither Herder nor the Grimms ever used the term *Volkskunde* (Lutz 1982:38); "population science" remained the verbal emblem of the administrative tradition until the second half of the nineteenth century, when the name acquired romantic connotations by association with the English term *folklore,* newly coined at that time.

Throughout the eighteenth century, folklore research remained a prerogative of the German state and its administration. Information gathering and effective management of social knowledge depended above all on a sizable bureaucracy, which was in place at this time. Indeed, every sovereign territory, down to the smallest imperial knight, relied on the services of a corps of officials. For instance, in the electoral state of Mainz, some nine hundred officials were employed for a population of less than a quarter of a million, not counting court personnel and clergy; there was one official for every 250 inhabitants (Bendix 1978:386). The enormous size of the administrative apparatus can be attributed to attempts to enhance the governing power of imperial rule: effective control over a multiplicity of sovereign territories necessitated a large number of officials. The need for records of agreement and the administration of allegiances, capital, and materials all resulted in the explosion of a bureaucratic social class trained in the description and translation of information (Bendix 1978:386). The stage was thus set for the beginnings of a new discourse aimed at the acquisition of social knowledge. Statistical folklore, as a human science, came into being at the moment when the procedures of surveillance and the taking of records were being established (e.g., Foucault 1980:74–75). Inquiry and examination emerged as a model, an administrative and political schema, which was to become a matrix for the population surveys of the late eighteenth century. Not surprisingly, folkloristic information was gathered primarily by civil servants, who in contemporary Germany included not only government and administrative officials but also protestant clergymen, teachers, and physicians. As employees of the state, these were hardly in a position to refrain from exercising those tactics of power that sustained their own role in society.

Some of the most comprehensive ethnographic surveys, however, were furnished independently by German travelers, poets, journalists, and geographers who either explored their own districts or ventured into neighboring territories (Schmidt 1966:21; Bausinger 1969:28–29; Güntz 1897–1902). Among these very detailed records of regional folk culture is the *Description of a Journey through Germany and Switzerland,* a twelve-volume work by Friedrich Nicolai (1783–96). Other similar works include *A Kurlander's Travels through Swabia* (Gaum 1784); *Travels through Southern Germany* (Röder 1789–91); *A Livonian's Journey from Riga to Warsaw* (Schulz 1795–96). A comprehensive bibliographic collection of such ethnographic travelogues, compiled in 1784 by the novelist Gottlieb Heinrich Stuck, lists a total of 3,452 published titles. The immense production of such ethnographic travel guides in the eighteenth century is one of the signs marking the ascent of the bourgeoisie to new social and political privileges (Rupp-Eisenreich 1984:91); it points to a reevaluation of geographical mobility and the prestige attached to travel.

The observations made by German travelers were sometimes conveyed in the form of fictive letters (such as *Briefe eines Reisenden*). These narratives, perhaps as dictated by the literary style, began to typify the customs and manners of the inhabitants from different territories. Examples include such titles as *Letters from a Journey to Cassel* (Ackermann 1780); *Letters by a Traveler about Pyrmont, Cassel, Marburg, Würzburg, and Wilhelmsbad* (Hassencamp 1783); and *Letters about Bavarian Mentality and Customs* (Westenrieder 1778). Such personalized travel reports contributed to a growing body of satirical literature that appeared regularly in the weekly papers and journals, providing lengthy descriptions of country life, the strange customs of the rural folk, and the curiosities of the landscape. Here, folklore came to be equated with the "art of travel" (Rupp-Eisenreich 1984:100): ethnographic publications provided descriptive guides for voyagers, offered them information about an unknown terrain, and thereby helped them to focus their inquiries.

Interestingly, the earliest formulation of the German term for "folklore" can be traced to one of these guides for voyagers. The word *Volks-Kunde* appeared in 1782 in the first publication of the Hamburg weekly *The Traveler: A Periodical for the Dissemination of Commonly Useful Knowledge.* According to the preface in the first issue (Weber-Kellermann and Bimmer 1985:7), the aim of this journal was to describe human beings in all rural settings, because knowledge of peasant life had been neglected. Such knowledge was, however, especially important for poets, for it revealed

the most genuine simplicity in thought and language, in folksongs, entertainment, and sociabilities, of which urban dwellers have few notions. . . . We also take this occasion to appeal to all those who are as concerned with knowledge-about-the-common-folk [*Volks-Kunde*] as with knowledge about the courts and noble estates, so that they may not neglect to gather information about popular festivals.

Interestingly, the journal's quest for social information was framed by romantic ideas: "folklorists" were to investigate the simple life of country peasants, thereby providing the urban elite with long "forgotten" knowledge. By idealizing these aims, the journal encouraged its readers not only to collect but also to report and publicize previously unknown cultural facts. While the political importance of this type of ethnographic research remained implicit, its empirical requirements (direct observation and the ordering of information) were integrated for the first time by these guides for travelers.

The information thus gathered and systematized by German travelers also furnished the material for statistics—information that was useful in an administrative sense. The work of the Swabian theologian Friedrich August Köhler provides a typical example. During his university studies, which he began in 1786, Köhler undertook several journeys through the southern parts of Germany. He kept a diary of his observations and later published this information in a travel report (Bausinger 1963:357–58). Köhler acquired a wide range of knowledge in the fields of topography, statistics, and economy—including information about occupation, dress code, language, religious belief, and architecture. In the early nineteenth century, Köhler applied his ethnographic experience to the compilation of a systematic population survey of Württemberg at the request of the local administration.

While much of this type of work was sincere in its attempt to document the life and behavior of a given German population, there exists some evidence that such eighteenth-century travelers acted as "intelligence" gatherers by collecting and mapping information of immediate interest to German government administrators. French historians have noted that many such narratives, subsequently repeated as travelers' tales about all sorts of marvels and curiosities, were actually coded reports (Foucault 1980:75). Although ascribed to the persistent naïveté of certain eighteenth-century naturalists and geographers, they were in reality extraordinarily precise accounts of the military situation of the territories traversed as well as their economic resources, markets, wealth, and possible diplomatic relations.

Of course, most eighteenth-century travel descriptions and surveys were not explicitly designed to be politically exploited. Nevertheless, it is noteworthy that, since the state traditionally had the prerogative to possess such information, its collection necessarily became a matter of power and politics. German travelers came to acquire social knowledge that previously had been the monopoly of rulers. According to "the biography of the 'founder of the political-statistical method of geography,' Anton Friedrich Büsching (1724–93), he was the first to publish information about the different German territories, which until then was guarded like a state secret" (Rupp-Eisenreich 1984:100). With the appearance of the journals and guides for voyagers, as well as the many personalized travel reports, the previously "secret" knowledge about life in different regions came to be openly organized. Such a dramatic change in the control of social information had several important consequences.

Most significantly, with the shift in information management from state control to public accessibility, new possibilities for organizing and using knowledge became apparent to governing authorities. The "opening" of social knowledge generated a heightened awareness of its potential usefulness for politics. Recognition of the administrative value of such information was prompted by the works of the early statistical folklorists, who encouraged the politicization of societal knowledge. Thus, travel and the firsthand collection of folk customs were methods of inquiry advocated earlier by Gottfried von Achenwall (1754), who had also stressed the political need for this type of research: knowledge of the factories, agriculture, finances, and commerce in other territories allowed one to better manage one's own affairs and better defend oneself when menaced by others. Several years later, the geographer Büsching likewise declared that travel and the empirical study of populations was a matter of "rendering service to the politicians for the greater good of all" (Rupp-Eisenreich 1984:100–101). The science of folklore was thus perceived as an indispensable tool for the effective management of the state. Influenced by these perceptions, German government administrators sought to intervene in the opening of social knowledge, thereby attempting to tighten their political control over the procedures of internal order and defense.

The political concern with population management resulted in the merger of folklore, statistics, and geography into a single discourse. This is reflected in part by the descriptive titles of various works from the late eighteenth and early nineteenth centuries. Some examples include *A Topographical Excursion . . . with Particular Consideration for Geology, Forestry, Geography, and Folklore* (Behlen 1823); *An Ethnography of Salzburg and Berchtesgaden through Contributions from History, Statistics, Geography, and Political Economy* (Koch-Sternfeld 1810); *Ethnography; or, Geography and Statistics . . .* (Memminger 1820); and *A Geographic, Statistical, Topographic Dictionary of Swabia* (Röder 1791–92). Such studies usually contained a topographical section, which mapped the given "domains" of political control in the territory that it set out to describe. The administration of knowledge, through such spatial demarcations, was transposed into an element of power that came to inscribe itself on the soil. A novel dynamic of power thereby emerged: statistics provided the science of folklore with the means to conceptually reduce the population to quantifiable elements for administrative purposes; geography acted on the dispersion of power through the mapping of political territories.

Furthermore, the link between geography, folklore, and statistics had a direct effect on matters of practical administration. Within the context of geography, topographical studies tended to describe the climatic and geological conditions of particular territories. As these conditions were outside human control, the analysis could only recommend measures of correction or compensation in order to obtain, for instance, better results in agricultural production. In contrast, statistical folklore was embedded in urban and rural topographies that not only described the culture of a given population but also began to outline the general principles of a concerted social policy.

An exemplary expression of this approach may be found in the works of Christoph Heinrich Niemann (1761–1832), professor of culture, customs, and morality at the University of Kiel, who continued the statistical and ethnographic orientation of German folklore scholarship (Bausinger 1969:29; Weber-Kellermann and Bimmer 1985:8–9). Among Niemann's many publications are several important works about the life of northern German population groups. His *Handbook of Schleswig-Holstein's Lore of the Land* (1799) is characteristic of the studies carried out by eighteenth-century state employees in its meticulous observation of detail, the set of techniques—the whole corpus of methods, descriptions, plans, and data. Niemann's *Handbook* also points to the growing political awareness that such knowledge of small matters could be used for purposes of social control. In the preface, Niemann introduces the work as a "collection for the perfection of the societal condition" (1799:v). This expression of a desire for a political utopia was coupled with an inventory of communal life in which a technology of population begins to be sketched in statistical terms: records of births and deaths; the growth of urban populations; the number of villages and towns; data on schools, churches, and hospitals; figures on taxation, personal property, and the distribution of wealth; records of roads, types of transportation, and the flow of information. Such an anatomy of society continues in Niemann's later work, such as his *Outline for the Description of a Provincial District,* which consists of a brief essay and a forty-page sample questionnaire designed to evaluate geographic, cultural, and administrative topics. The publication appears to be an actual manual for research; it attempts to instruct the reader in the efficient collection of social information and the strategies of power deployed through the demarcation of territories. The construction of rational classifications, methods of observation and administration of the population are the dominant themes of this work.

In *Digest of Statistics and Political Science* (1807), Niemann constructed a model for the collection of social information in the form of a "statistical" or organizational table. In this chart, folklore appears below the general heading "Science of the State" (as opposed to "Geography") and below the subheadings "Administrative/Judicial Discipline" and "National Lore." Folklore research is divided into broad categories of "Commerce and Trade" and "Customs and Culture." Below these are listed various topics of research, including descriptions of the attitudes and psychological disposition of a population, as well as data relating to general forms of existence such as work and leisure, folk festivals, marriage, clothing, the layout of living space, poverty and wealth, aging, illness, and death. The construction of such "tables" was, of course, one of the problems of the scientific and political technology of the eighteenth century, for the procedures of administrative discipline had their place among these contemporary techniques of classification and tabulation.

The Political Uses of Administrative Folklore

The beginnings of folklore research in Germany can be traced to a time when a network of new forms of political control was set in place. It was an era marked by the installation of state control over public institutions, including hospitals, establishments of correction, education, and commerce. Such a novel exercise of power required a different knowledge of society. Various fields of inquiry came into being, and new bodies of information were produced to accommodate the tactics of power with its procedures of administrative management, the strategies of police surveillance and inspection, tabulations of economic growth, and the task of encouraging obedience and work. The science of folklore, as an instrument of social knowledge, provided a practical solution to this search for a new technology of power.

One manifestation of increased state control in imperial Germany during the eighteenth century was the growth in importance of the army. In Prussia, for example, the army increased from 40,000 soldiers in 1713 to over a quarter of a million men in 1806. It then comprised some 16 percent of the eligible male population. By 1740, the army included every twenty-fifth person in the population, in contrast to France, where the army included one of every 150 (Bendix 1978:164). Along with this growth of dynastic militarism came an increasing emphasis on the health and strength of the men who would make up the army. The physical fitness of the recruits and the ability of the soldiers to endure the disciplinary training with its long exercises and maneuvers was directly equated with the success of military victory. This new emphasis on the constitution of the body was reflected in the work of German folklorists. Thus the historian and folklore scholar Christian Garve observed in 1786:

> The instruction and moral education of the peasants, whether or not it can be supported by the landowner, is primarily the task of the government (1786a:119). . . . [And yet] the landowner cannot be indifferent to the conditions in which the peasant finds himself since his youth: because whether he eats to satisfy half or all his hunger, whether he eats good bread, healthy food, or whether he eats completely indigestible, weak meals, on this depends not only the growth and beauty of his body, but also the firmness of his limbs and their strength—two things which he [the landowner] must desire in those who will replenish his army. (1786a:152)

While these ideas of health and physical strength originated in the context of the army, they were no less important to the early industrial economy. The military imperative of combat with fit soldiers was deemed equivalent to the economic requirements for healthy and productive workers. Therefore, once the population had been defined as an essential labor force, its well-being became one of the basic objectives of political power. The maintenance of public health was enforced by a multitude of regulations and institutions, which in the eighteenth century took the generic name of "police." The term *police* did not exclusively signify the institution of police in the modern sense. It referred to an ensemble of mechanisms serving to ensure order, the properly channeled growth of wealth, and the preservation of public welfare in general (Foucault 1980:170; Small 1909:436–58, 505–25). Such a policing of society required an elaborate system of information management. Again, the acquisition of knowledge fell into the domain of statistical folklore. Sometimes local administrative districts established special offices for such purposes of consultation and information. State employees, in their role as "population scientists," were ordered to inspect regional differences in the quality of housing and food (Wiegelmann et al. 1977:15; Brandlmeier 1942). Folklorists thus began to collect quantifiable information about the possible relation between illness, nutrition, and living conditions. They also provided data on work-related prospects of survival and even commented on regional measures of incitement to marriage and procreation. The last such sociomedical topography was compiled in 1860 by Wilhelm Heinrich Riehl, whose five-volume publication *Bavaria* analysed correlations between levels of income and health.

The political concern for economic growth and productivity further extended the scope of folklore scholarship toward the implementation of cultural reforms: population management in contemporary Germany was aimed at the shaping of public attitudes toward the construction of a "rational" society. Included in this concern for the correction of people's worldview was the abolishment of folk belief and superstition. The secularization of traditions was promoted by religious and educational policies (Bausinger 1963; Dümminger 1957; Kramer 1972; Lohoff 1934; Narr 1959; Schmidt 1938). The attitude of the folklorists toward such matters may be illustrated by the following anecdote from 1801, which appeared in the description of a journey through Austria:

> Across from the memorials of Josephine's land surveyance, at some distance away, stands a curiously shaped tree with a flat top. It is marked on the maps and for this reason may not be cut down. The peasants, however, tell the following: the devil once rode by this tree and his horse ate the top. Therefore everyone who touches it becomes unlucky. [The authors then remarked] But for how much longer must this superstition remain an incentive for action or inaction? (Schmidt 1966:23)

Although eighteenth-century folklorists recorded such legends, they reported them with an appeal to the reeducation of the population. Exemplary is

Friedrich Arends' three-volume account of *Eastern Frisia* from the early nineteenth century. The work by Arends consists of a topographical study, which provides details about Frisian settlements, including population size, commerce and general industry, law enforcement, education, agriculture, geography, and climate. The last volume contains details about Frisian "mentality," "way of life," and "customs and rituals" (1820:409–40). Guided by an attitude of enlightened pragmatism, the author devotes special attention to the persistent belief in the supernatural:

> Frisians are superstitious, especially the marshland peasants. Among these are otherwise very rational people, who still believe in hunches, premonitions, witches, and more of the same; who, as soon as a cow stops producing milk, [or] if the butter does not set, etc., begin to scream about witchcraft and rush to the devil's spellbinder, who gives them potions against the evil eye. . . . Among the common folk, in the marsh as well as the cities, the belief in ghosts and their consorts is, however, still widespread. . . . The evil starts in early youth; goal-oriented education would counter such things effectively. (Arends 1820:415–16)

The aims of folklore research were thereby defined in terms of social administration: the systematic acquisition of ethnographic knowledge and the subsequent representation of society in statistical form to promote a process of cultural reformation. Typical of this approach is the work of the Westphalian lawyer, bureaucrat, and politician Justus Möser. With the publication of his comprehensive ethnographic survey of the city of Osnabrück in 1768, Möser became one of the leading political folklorists of the late eighteenth century (see Bausinger 1969:25–27). The first volume of his *Patriotic Fantasies,* a collection of short essays compiled from weekly editorials that reflect an extraordinary spectrum of folkloristic observations about German culture and customs, appeared in 1774. Each essay carried a descriptive title, as, for example: "May a Master Craftsman Employ as Many Apprentices as He Likes?" (vol. 1); "Reflections about the Elimination of Holidays," "About the Education of Children in Rural Areas," "About Public Credit and Its Great Advantages" (vol. 2); "Should One Give Every Town Its Particular Political Constitution?", "A Certain Method for Eliminating the All Too Frequent Drinking of Coffee" (vol. 3); and "A Contribution for the Rural Population about the Policing of Pleasure" (vol. 4). Predominantly moralistic and didactic in tone, the essays made an effort to instill certain ethical standards in the population. The message of virtue included the demand for obedience toward established authority and willingness to contribute toward the common welfare by "staying within one's proper sphere" and meeting one's obligations. Here the author made effective use of folklore in establishing the legitimacy of traditional authority and the state.

Almost identical in style is Christian Garve's *Inquiry into the Population* (1786b). The book contains chapters on such diverse issues as "The Tendency to Sensual Enjoyment," "Begging and Poverty," and "Public Education." One section is devoted to a "Survey of the Causes for the Population's Moral Decadence" (chap. 2, sec. 2); it includes discussions on brothels, prostitutes, buffoons, idlers, servants, celibacy, family quarrels, the lottery, a moral handbook for the population, the elevation of the lowly image of the authorities, and methods to combat heresy. These essays, which contain detailed observations of folk culture, were addressed primarily to questions of reproduction, raising children, economic competition, the observance of traditional values, and a person's proper conduct. The chapter is followed by another on the "Administration of Poverty" (chap. 2, sec. 3), in which the author advocates the establishment of special institutions for pregnant women, children, adults who do not want to work or never learned a useful trade, the impoverished, the sick and decrepit. Implicit in these essays is the assumption that the state can and should work actively to administer people's attitudes and actions.

The German folklorist of the eighteenth century became the great adviser and expert in the art of governing, in correcting and improving the social "body," as well as maintaining it in a permanent state of order, health, and productivity. The education of the population was to be aided by the presence of the folklorists in the academies and learned societies, acting as counselors to representatives of power, and their participation in the production of pedagogical textbooks (see Becker 1788) and encyclopedias, which were distributed throughout the German empire in "an effort to fill the mind of the youth with the correct knowledge of these things" (Krünitz 1786:xiv).

By the end of the eighteenth century, the procedures of power and administrative discipline had been integrated into a single mechanism. The practice of folklore—with its methods of surveillance, research, and gathering information—became fused with teaching and education. It was in this context that folklorists were able to transmit disciplinary norms into the very heart of the population. Although no state of the eighteenth century could ever achieve the complete regulation of society required by the German ideology of a "well-ordered police state," the technology of power became so refined and subtle that in the 1850s Professor Riehl could claim: "Today, the state is the most powerful [machinery], through which the authority of the laws—and the authority of customs—are most deeply and naïvely engrained in the consciousness of the population" (1854:1, 276).

According to Riehl, the science of folklore assumed an essential role in German political rule. This assertion was triggered in part by the realization that the study of traditional culture in Germany had become an effective instrument of patriotic agitation, capable of arousing nationalistic sentiments. As Riehl observed, the romantic belief in the individuality or uniqueness of German society could easily be transformed into an ideological tool of the state. Therefore attempts for tighter control of the population through administrative procedures did not require a rejection of the romantic ideal, even though such attempts put this ideal to a different purpose. It is probably no coincidence that these tactics of power were implemented by the Prussian state just twenty years after the appearance of Riehl's major works. Bismarck's social reforms and welfare programs were based on an intricate knowledge of the population and—together with the idealization of military discipline, government service, and education—procured the hegemonic supremacy of the German state.

Contrasting Cases: Great Britain and China

The history of folklore scholarship in Germany, marked by the simultaneous formation of two competing traditions, is probably unique. Nevertheless, the romantic and statistical approaches to folklore have coexisted elsewhere and at different times. The emergence of folklore research in Great Britain and China, where such knowledge acquired very different political dimensions, provide instructive contrasts.

Throughout the British Isles, the collection of folk traditions had been subsumed under the name of *popular antiquities* since Elizabethan times (Dorson 1968:1–2). The earliest use of the term in the seventeenth century signified a search for the physical remains of the past: social research was initially equated with the excavation of material artefacts. "Antiquarians" were primarily interested in reconstructing how people had lived during an earlier historical era from the records and relics of ancient practices. It was probably no coincidence that such a quest for history began with the rise of the British empire: in a country aspiring to greatness, evidence of ancient monuments or other traces of a civilized past stimulated a nationalistic pride in a shared cultural heritage.[5]

By the eighteenth century, the historical insights drawn from material artefacts were combined with other sources of information, such as descriptions of "natural history," "scenery," and "curiosities" of custom in the British Isles. In this context, English antiquarians began to investigate the traditional culture of the common folk and peasants (Dorson 1968:2–90). The value of gathering such information was emphasized by the Rev. John Brand, a fellow and secretary of the Society of Antiquaries. In the introduction to his influential work *Observations on Popular Antiquities* (1777), he declared that "nothing can be foreign to our enquiry, much less beneath our notice, that concerns the smallest of the vulgar: of those little ones who occupy the lowest place in the political arrangement of human beings" (p. ix).

The study of popular antiquities in the British Isles was essentially an outgrowth of an archaeology of history: the primary goal of antiquarians was to salvage the remnants of a distant past, whether through the excavation of Roman ruins and Celtic burial mounds or the unearthing of peasant culture. Folklore research in Britain was thereby perceived as a means of reconstructing an ancient national heritage—a concept later adopted by the German romantics. The ideological orientation of the British antiquarians was subsequently expressed in their choice of names for the discipline. The expression "popular antiquities" was replaced in 1846 with the term *folk-lore,* coined by William John Thoms (Bausinger 1969:50), possibly derived from an approximate translation of the older German term *Volks-kunde* (initially spelled with a hyphen), the verbal "emblem" of the administrative school of folklore in Germany. Despite this terminological appropriation, the connotations of the two terms were to be substantially different: German *Volkskunde* meant "knowledge acquired *about* a people"; English *folklore* came to refer to the "teachings or doctrines *of* (generated by) a people." These semantic differences also reflected basic differences in methodology. German statistical folklorists accumulated social information about local populations through comprehensive ethnographic surveys. Within Great Britain, folklore research was directed toward the recreation of the nation's ancient heritage through the study of such cultural antiquities as magic, superstitions, proverbs, legends, songs, and so forth. It was from this antiquarian tradition in Britain (and its romantic offshoot in Germany) that the field of cultural anthropology emerged. This transformation from romantic folklore to anthropology was initiated in England by scholars such as Sir Edward B. Tylor (1871) and his investigations of the development of religion, language, and art, as well as his search (in the British antiquarian tradition) for cultural relics and "survivals" of a more "primitive" past.

The beginnings of folklore scholarship in Great Britain were based to a large extent on the research of Scottish antiquarians during the eighteenth century. Interestingly, the romantic quest for folk traditions in Scotland was prompted by political circumstances comparable to those in Germany: romantic nationalism, and its articulation through folklore research, emerged in response to the threat of foreign domination. The kingdom of Scotland was dissolved in 1707 when it entered into the Union of Parliaments with England. Although this event ended Scottish sovereignty, the country retained some independence, notably in law, administration, and religion (Hobsbawm 1969:300). The central government intervened relatively little in local affairs, and population management, such as relief and welfare for the poor, remained in communal hands until the nineteenth century. Folklore research in Scotland therefore did not fall into the domain of the state. The quest for popular knowledge was triggered by other concerns.

English political control of Scotland was gradually tightened not only by economic tactics but also by a process of cultural domination: standard English was to replace the spoken national language of Gaelic. Moreover, under English rule, the Scots, especially the Highlanders, came to be perceived by their neighbors and their own elite as "disorderly savages" who were in need of a firm government. Thus the philosopher David Hume, himself a Scot, described his countrymen in 1776 as "the rudest, perhaps of all European Nations; the most necessitous, the most turbulent, and the most unsettled" (1932:2, 310). Under these circumstances, Scottish antiquarians began to redirect their research efforts toward a search for special national qualities in the history and oral traditions of their country. As a result, the concept of the common folk underwent a drastic change. In the writings of the Scottish folklorists (Dorson 1968:107–59), the image of the rural population was transformed from a superstitious, backward peasantry to a civil people attuned to the simple life and glowing with natural morality. Among the first to cultivate such notions was Sir Walter Scott (1771–1832), a novelist and dedicated antiquarian. For instance, when investigating the relation between historical romance, popular fiction, and local legends, he claimed that he was struck by the "ancient traditions and high spirit of a people, who, living in a civilized age and country, retained so strong a tincture of manners belonging to an earlier period of society" (1833:1, 10). The central theme of Scottish works was the *national* tradition as it unfolded in local history, scenery, and folklore.

The romantic exaltation of national characteristics was also an important element of Scottish parish studies. Particularly noteworthy are the twenty-one volumes of Sir John Sinclair's *Statistical Account of Scotland* (1791–99). In this collection of detailed descriptions, histories, and folk traditions from over a hundred parishes (gathered from "communications with the clergy"), the

Scottish population is characterized repeatedly as "a sober, regular and industrious people, . . . generous and humane"; "generally active and spirited, . . .
ready to engage in labor of any kind"; "the happiest of mortals"; who "enjoy
. . . the comforts and advantages of society"; and are "contented with their
situation and circumstances" (1791: vol. I, 24–25, 39, 76, 68, 87–88, 306).
Industry, civility, complacency, and happiness rank first among the many
national traits repeatedly emphasized. The prominence of such positive attributes in Scotland, argued Sir John, resulted from the country's political
stability and progress:

> Crimes are becoming every day more rare. . . . It is, indeed, one of the most
> striking evidences of the progress of civilization, and one of the most
> pleasing effects of regular government, that in a country, formerly the scene
> of depredating violence, fewer instances of crimes, or of punishment, have
> occurred during the last 50 years. (vol. I, 16)

The detailed accounts of Scottish parish life were thus clearly rooted in
nationalistic sentiments and not in attempts at population management or
social reconstruction. Curiously, it was this romantic ethnography that was
publicized and sold as a "statistical" documentation. The study, explained Sir
John, was to describe the "political state of the kingdom" (vol. I, v), "by
analysing . . . and examining, with anatomical accuracy and minuteness, the
internal structure of society" (vol. III, xii). While such an approach to folklore
is reminiscent of the German political quest for "knowing the population," it
was intended in this case to provide an empirical gloss to the research results.
The principal aim of the work was to document "the progress of human
society" for other countries (vol. III, x, xi), and to thereby make certain that the
"example of Scotland in this respect [would] soon be imitated by other nations"
(vol. III, ix). Consequently, Sir John Sinclair's work can be interpreted as an
attempt to put the country on the cultural map, so that it would be recognized
throughout Europe as a civilized nation of "exquisite refinement" and "sensibility" (Trevor-Roper 1983:18), based on the elaborate descriptions of Scottish communal life and folklore.

Despite the incidental publication of such "statistical" works among Scottish folklore studies (e.g., Mitchell and Cash 1917:2, 514–33), none of those
publications is comparable to the German population surveys of the eighteenth
century. Interestingly, Sir John himself explicitly dissociates his elaborate
research project from those inquiries conducted in imperial Germany, as in the
kingdoms of Prussia or Saxony, which, he observed, "have uniformly been

instituted, with a view of ascertaining the state of the country, for the purposes of taxation and of war, and not of national improvement, . . . but to fill the exchequer, or the armies of the state" (1791: vol. III, xiii and note). In contrast to the German case, folklore research in Scotland was instigated not by the state and its bureaucracy but rather by individuals outside administrative or government circles. The study of "popular antiquities" in Scotland began as a leisure-time activity of wealthy gentlemen scholars, who saw folklore as a vehicle for promoting their country's political autonomy.

A very different example of the relation between folklore and power can be discerned in the origins of the discipline in China. There, folklore research was initially not an administrative tool of the state but rather an ideological tool for legitimating movements of popular rebellion. Unlike the case of Scotland or Germany, scholars in China were able to unite a romantic search for cultural antiquities with a pragmatic interest in empirical surveys, seeing both as means to the same political end: the reformation of society and the destruction of the imperial state.

As a field of study, folklore was introduced at National Beijing University in 1918, where it assumed the name *min su xue: min* means 'people', 'nation', or 'population'; *su* refers to 'popular customs'; *xue* denotes 'study' or 'science' (Yen 1967:38). Chinese folklore was thus defined as "the study of a people and their customs." The discipline was broadly perceived as a science that aimed to investigate both Chinese folk culture *and* society (see, e.g., Chao 1942:59). This point was made explicit in 1926 by Professor Cai Yuanpei, the chancellor of Beijing University, who actively promoted the establishment of the field: "Folklore [*min su xue*] is a branch of learning that examines the cultures of peoples . . . [and the] behavioral patterns of ethnological groups" (1962:1, 4– 5). Early research efforts were thus devoted not only to cataloging the different types of folk narrative but also to analysing the information that folklore could provide about the organization of society.

As in eighteenth-century Europe, the Chinese population became a novel source of knowledge during a period of political instability and change. Folklore research began in the early twentieth century, a time when the sovereignty of China was threatened by European imperialism, the military loss of territories, and the less tangible domination of culture through Western literature, religion, and education. The persistence of foreign hegemonic rule resulted in a series of internal upheavals, terminating the era of feudalism in China and bringing about a permanent change in the country's political regime. The traditional system of government was abolished in 1911 by a successful revolution: the Manchu dynasty came to an end with the establishment of the

Republic of China. This transformation in the political order was accompanied by a popular movement directed both at social reform *and* national unification (Yen 1967:5–6; Eminov 1978; Huang 1985). Folklorists in China (in contrast to those in Scotland or Germany) worked actively to promote this dual orientation. The twofold aim of the early folklorists was described by Gu Jiegang, one of the founding members of the discipline at Beijing University: "The political school wishes to glorify the national spirit; the educational school wishes to transform customs" (1928:20). However, these approaches to the science of folklore (nationalism and socialism) were not at first mutually opposed. Scholarly writers, like Pei Wenzhong in 1925, emphasized that folklore research was to be used both "to reconstruct society" and "to save [the] nation" (1925:139). The promotion of China's political sovereignty through the nationalization of folklore was inseparably linked to the simultaneous quest for societal change.

Folklorists began to reconstitute the concept of China as a nation through a process of reordering society. After the dissolution of the old political system, scholars attempted to reform the structure of hierarchy and power; traditional class distinctions were eliminated in order to improve the conditions of the peasants. Effective control over the reproduction of culture was to shift from an aristocratic class of bureaucrats and literary scribes to the common laborers in the countryside. In China, this shift marked the beginning of an unprecedented fascination with the everyday life of the peasants. The expressive culture of the rural population, perceived as the primary source of China's ancient heritage, was romanticized (Hung 1985). Thus the critic and scholar, Hu Shih, concluded, upon analysing the historical relationship between aristocratic and folk literature:

> Every new form, every innovation in literature, had come never from the imitative classical writers of the upper classes, but always from the unlettered class of the countryside, the village inn, and the market-place. I found that it was always these new forms and patterns of the common people that, from time to time, furnished new blood and fresh vigor to the literature of the literati, and rescued it from the perpetual danger of fossilization. (1934:52)

Like the romantics in eighteenth-century Scotland and Germany, folklorists in China believed that the rural population had preserved the unique virtues of the nation in their folklore. Therefore, as early as 1922, scholarly politicians like Chen Duxiu began the search for the "plain, simple, and expressive literature of the people" (Huang 1959:13). Folklorists likewise aimed to uncover the genuine qualities of Chinese culture in folk art and poetry. By the 1930s, literary scholars like Chen Guangyao had assembled large collections of peasant lore, narrative traditions he regarded as "fresh, simple, natural, and sincere" (Hung 1985:6). In contrast to the artistic and literary creations of the elite, folklore was defined as more "authentically" Chinese. Such a romanticized and nationalistic interpretation of oral traditions stimulated the collection of a vast number of texts: songs about far-off soldiers, longing girls and sorrowful women, proverbial phrases, children's rhymes, riddles, tales and legends about emperors, scribes, and immortals (Chao 1942:59; Yen 1967:42; Eminov 1978:165–72; Hung 1985:58–157). Given the great enthusiasm for collecting new materials, the original intent of searching for Chinese national characteristics was sometimes buried in the organizational tasks of motif–indexing and classification.

From its inception as a discipline at Beijing University, the romantic search for a national folk culture was systematically coordinated with comprehensive ethnographic studies. Such a holistic approach to social research was advocated, for instance, by Chang Hui, one of the early folklore journal editors. He noted that a proper analysis of verbal narratives required not only an appreciation of folk art or literature but also an understanding of people's psychology and customs (1925:350–51). This apparent emphasis in Chinese folklore research on acquiring complete social knowledge about the common population was reflected in subsequent surveys (Chao 1942:65–68; Eminov 1978:167), which sought to gather facts about local topography, demography, and regional differences in language, education, and employment patterns, as well as religious beliefs and practices. In China, these new forms of social knowledge were not, however, initially an administrative tool of the state; rather, folklore research furnished a means for generating movements of popular resistance.

As Wolfram Eberhard observed, "the study of folklore, even at its inception in China, was a tool for other movements, and not an independent scholarly field" (1970:15). Chinese folklorists, intent on changing their society, promoted political programs concerned with literary and cultural reforms. Literary critics, led by historical scholars like Hu Shih, tended to idealize the language and traditions of China's peasants as the genuine source of the country's national heritage. These reformers adopted non-Confucian methods of analysis in the hope of finding validation for a revised, nonaristocratic interpretation of China's cultural history (Hung 1985:161–73). The romantic orientation of Chinese historians and linguists was complemented by the pragmatic realism of other folklorists, who were concerned with the immediate problems of modernization. Whereas Chinese nationalists attempted selectively to retrieve those peasant traditions thought worthy of emulation, political pragmatists investigated "backward" customs and "reactionary" institutions that were to be swept away by the reform movement: "idolatrous processions and performances," "concubines and slave girls," "brothel frequenting," and "abandoned children" (Eminov 1978:167). The most extreme expression of this approach to folklore appeared in the 1930s in publications on mass education. The authors of these articles espoused a functional method that aimed only to discover the sociological role of a custom or art form so that reformers might better know how to implement their programs (Schneider 1971:147). By inviting the formulation of such "scientific" strategies of social planning and intervention, the investigation of folk traditions was transformed into a political discourse.

At least until the 1940s, Chinese folklore research furnished an ideology of popular resistance and not a mechanism of administrative control. Even after the founding of the nationalist government in 1928, the work of folklorists remained antiestablishment in the eyes of the state. Under the leadership of Chiang Kai-shek, the nationalist regime, with the support of the urban classes, launched a campaign designed to modernize China by attempting to eradicate superstitions and traditional customs (Eberhard 1965:xxxiv) and abolish "vulgar, unclean, and obscene ideas" that could endanger public morals (Hung 1985:159–60). The movement, aimed at modernization, was government-sponsored. Ironically, folklorists were excluded from this campaign. Romantic folklorists were accused of keeping alive the irrational beliefs and attitudes of the past, and pragmatic folklorists were criticized for emphasizing local differences in Chinese culture. Perceived as threats to the country's national unity and modernity, both types of folklorist reformers were proscribed by the state. In China, folklore scholars thus turned for support to the socialist resistance movement and began to participate actively in revolutionary politics.

Ethnography and Folklore: Fields of Power/Forms of Knowledge

Folklore research in Germany, Great Britain, and China came into being as a logical extension of "nation–building," a process in which knowledge of the various populations was deemed essential to the formation of the new state. While the science of folklore was thus closely linked to the rise of nationalist ideologies, it was also rooted, at least in the German case, in the pragmatic rationality of a bureaucratic state. These dual origins suggest the two basic avenues through which societal self-knowledge could be incorporated into the political sphere.

In eighteenth-century Germany, the study of folklore was associated with two separate political movements: romantic nationalism, which constituted a form of popular resistance; and administrative particularism, a mechanism of governmental domination. Romantic folklorists were engaged in the construction of a German nation, whose political unity was to be based on a common cultural and historical tradition. Administrative folklorists attempted to enhance the power of the existing German states by devising novel procedures for "knowing" the population. The distinction between these movements reflected differences in ideas about the relation between the population and the state. The romantics idealized folk culture as the foundation of the country's national heritage. Administrative folklorists, who were opposed to popular sovereignty, adhered to a belief in the state as a rational instrument of human progress. In spite of these ideological differences, however, both movements were directed toward the concentration of power in a central state.

In Scotland, the historical assertion of a unique cultural tradition served to promote a different political aim: the desire for regional and communal self-government. By romanticizing the industrious, law-abiding citizen, who had preserved the ancient customs, and by minimizing accounts of deviancy and criminality, folklore research (with its "statistical" surveys and collection of antiquities) was designed to deflect attempts by the central state to intervene in Scottish affairs. The science of folklore in Scotland thus became an ideological tool for obtaining political autonomy from imperial England. This endeavor of the Scottish antiquarians for national sovereignty had its analog in the struggle of the German romantics against French cultural and political hegemony. Despite these ideological similarities, there were, however, striking differences in the political effects of the respective movements. In imperial Germany, the acquisition of folkloristic knowledge contributed effectively to the *enhancement* of power by the state: through political centralization and national unification, as promoted by the romantic folklorists; or through the extension of government control and administrative tactics into the population, as advocated by the statistical folklorists. In contrast, folklore scholarship in Scotland, both in its romantic and statistical manifestations, worked toward political decentralization and communal self-government, thereby promoting the *disempowerment* of the state.

Folklore scholarship in China had its origins not only in nationalism or the pragmatism of a newly emerging state, but also in the exigencies of class struggle. Chinese folklorists sought both political autonomy and cultural sovereignty—that is, control by the population over the mechanisms of cultural reproduction. In part an ideological tool, the folklore movement was at the same time a strategy—a set of practices—aimed at regulating social behavior. In China, the birth of "sociological" thought, with its multiple forms of social intervention and planning, set the stage for political revolution and the reformation of the state.

These examples of the historical emergence of folklore reveal that the political quest for social knowledge is not only an instrument or an effect of power but can also serve as a point of resistance and a basis for an opposing political strategy. Such contestation of the dominant discourse may begin with the assertion of a distinctive national identity and culminate in the formulation of contesting realities through folklore. The beginnings of folklore scholarship are therefore linked to the politics of both domination and resistance.

Folklore, Cultural Historicism, and the Modern State

Folklore research came into being as a political strategy. In Europe and East Asia, the academic investigation of peasant culture was implicated in nation-building: folklore research was deeply enmeshed in the development of the modern state. The promulgation of a national consciousness, through the exposure of antiquities and cultural artefacts, was probably contingent upon the growth of historicism in Germany and elsewhere. As suggested by Georg Lukács: "The appeal to national independence and national character is necessarily connected with a re-awakening of national history, with memories of the past, of past greatness, of moments of national dishonour, whether this results in a progressive or reactionary ideology" (1963:25). The political importance of folklore research in the late eighteenth century was accelerated by this growth of historical consciousness. According to Lukács, the sense and experience of history, "the feeling that there [was] such a thing as history, that it [was] an uninterrupted process of changes and finally, that it [had] a direct effect upon the life of every individual" (1963:23), created the necessary conceptual foundation upon which folklorists relied for their visions of political reform. As Stefan Tanaka explains:

> In Europe, the neoclassical conception of historical time (chronologies and stories) was disturbed by the Enlightenment—the epistemological change from a finite world to a probable world. A history that amplified the finite world of states, major events, or persons was superseded by a new history that sought meaning. . . . This it did in two ways: by separating the present from the immediate past and by searching for origins. (1993:13–14)

The establishment of folklore as an academic discipline in both Europe and China reflected this transformation of historical attitudes. Folklore scholarship emerged in response to the perception that society was changeable and changing. The growing awareness of societal change generated romantic folklore as nostalgia for a disappearing rural culture and statistical/ethnographic folklore as a tool for the modernization and development of backward areas. The relation of these two forms of knowledge to history was not, however, antithetical.

In Europe, romantic imaginings of the eighteenth and nineteenth centuries encouraged a dismantling of local identities and languages and advocated their subsumption into unitary form. This process of cultural nationalization was driven "by the scholarly activities of lexicographers, grammarians, folklorists, and philologists, who standardized language forms, produced dictionaries, and published folklore collections in the so-called national languages" (Badone 1992:812). These texts, read by the literate bourgeoisie, enabled that class to imagine itself as part of a larger national community (Anderson 1983). The emergent questions of cultural allegiance were in part resolved by attempts at symbolic recovery of the past. During this era of nation-building, the romanticized life-world of peasants served as a template for the political identity of an emerging modern state. In Germany and Scotland, and later in China, romantic folklorists tended to equate peasant traditions with the unchanging customs of the past: peasant lore was presented as a pristine and authentic repertoire for building a common national culture.

This process of "regressive modernization"—the political journey into the future by way of a detour through the past—was not exclusively engendered by romantic scholars. The pragmatic folklorists, who promoted statistical/ethnographic research to effect radical social change, relied upon similar notions of history for implementing modernizing reforms. In Europe, as in China, statistical folklorists rejected what they perceived as the corruption of foreign influences and promoted the restoration of independent nations. As Lionel Gossman states:

> The Enlightenment attack on tradition, the attempt to cut the present adrift from the past was by no means incompatible with the idea that being cured of what was perceived as an alienated and weary traditional culture might involve a journey back to origins. (1986:29)

Both romantic and statistical folklorists mobilized the symbolic repertoire of the past. Folk culture and peasant traditions were appropriated as meaningful symbols in the romantics' attempts to preserve an authentic national history; likewise, statistical scholars, with their population surveys and contextual ethnographies, legitimated their rejection of present circumstances by reference to the logic of historical progress. Both nationalist and revolutionary movements backed their purported innovations by invoking history: the "people's past," "revolutionary traditions," or "fallen heroes and martyrs," in the struggle for ethno-national autonomy (Hobsbawm 1983). The symbolic appeal of the past transformed the concept of "regressive modernization" into an attribute of nation-building in the nineteenth and early twentieth centuries. Political processes of change, whether driven by romantic or administrative/ statistical interests, sought to legitimate the modern nation through appeal to folklore and cultural history. As Eric Hobsbawm observed:

> We should not be misled by a curious, but understandable, paradox: modern nations and all their impedimenta generally claim to be the opposite of novel, namely rooted in the remotest antiquity, and the opposite of constructed, namely human communities so "natural" as to require no definition other than self-assertion. (1983:14)

Nations are clearly "imagined" political communities, in which sentiments of common membership and culture are constructed (Anderson 1983). The divergent "conceptions of peoplehood" that we have encountered in Germany, Great Britain, and China were cultural constructions of public identities that contained images of what the nation was or should be (cf. Fox 1990:3). As suggested by the different examples of the politicization of folklore, modern nation-building was shaped by a process of internal cultural colonialism: an imagined political reality had to gain public meaning and legitimacy and this process was facilitated by an emergent political/scholarly elite.

Benedict Anderson (1983) has argued that the popular acceptance of a nationalist consciousness in modern societies was dependent upon the emergence of newspapers and novels: through new print technologies, a nationalist identity became mechanically reproducible. The primary aim of a nationalist agenda—as suggested by this broad comparison of folklore movements—was to instill in the population a sense of history and historical situatedness, from which new possibilities for change could be envisioned. While not exclusively dependent on written texts, this kind of political agitation facilitated the large-scale transformation of society: the effective mobilization of masses of people, whether for the military buildup of the army (Germany) or the revolutionary struggle (Scotland, China), was always dependent upon propaganda.

> Such propaganda . . . [had] to reveal the social content, the historical presuppositions and circumstances of the struggle, to connect up the war [or

revolution] with the entire life and possibilities of the nation's development. (Lukács 1963:23–24)

The making of the modern state, in Europe and in China, required that total populations be inducted into political and military service. The resultant immediacy and proximity of power, and the growing pervasiveness of institutions, which tangibly affected the life-world of common people, demanded comprehensible justification. So the wars of nation-building had to be "waged as conscious propaganda wars" (Lukács 1963:24), facilitating both the rise of historicism and the corresponding enthusiasm for folklore research. Folklore scholars, with their commitment to "regressive modernization," thereby implanted in popular consciousness a novel sense of nationhood.

Acknowledgments

Different versions of this paper were presented at the Eighty-fifth Annual Meeting of the American Anthropological Association, Philadelphia, Pennsylvania, December 3–7, 1986; at the Faculty Seminar of the Department of Anthropology at the University of Toronto, March 1987; and at the Sixth International Conference of Europeanists, Washington, D.C., October 30–November 1, 1987. I would like to thank the members of the respective audiences for their critical suggestions. Its conception was inspired by discussions with Jacqueline Urla. I am grateful to Alan Dundes for introducing me to the essential source materials, and to Regina Bendix, Ivan Kalmar, Andrew Lass, Paul Rabinow, and Susan Carol Rogers, who provided helpful comments. I am especially indebted to George Stocking and Dell Hymes for their careful reading of several versions of this manuscript. I thank Jim Schaefer for his untiring pursuit of narrative excellence. Research support from the Department of Anthropology at the University of Toronto and from the Research Council at Rutgers University are gratefully acknowledged.

A final reading of the essay took place at the CSSH Conference, Cultures of Scholarship, at the University of Michigan, Ann Arbor, March 17–19, 1995. I am grateful to Sally Humphreys, who took the time to organize this stimulating and exciting event (with the administrative assistance of Anne B. Waters). As always, Raymond Grew offered much appreciated intellectual inspiration. I thank Helen Siu and Louisa Schein for their helpful assistance with revisions of my work on Chinese scholarship. Additional revisions of the essay are based on the discussions and the commentaries I received at the conference. Critical suggestions from David W. Cohen are gratefully acknowledged.

NOTES

1. See, for instance, the work of Anthony Pagden in *European Encounters with the New World* (1993).

2. Throughout the essay, the titles of foreign books and articles have been translated into English by the author. This was done not only out of courtesy to the reader but also because the headings themselves are often an important source of information.

3. In *Japan's Orient,* Stefan Tanaka (1993) provides a superb analysis of the linkages between history and colonialism, science and national interest. When history was formulated as an independent discipline at Tokyo Imperial University at the turn of the twentieth century, it became the training ground for bureaucratic elites. In the course of several years, the founder of the field, Shiratori Kurakichi, broadened the area of "historical inquiry to include language, mythology, and ethnology, and he actively participated in and founded numerous institutions dedicated to the development of the field" (Tanaka 1993:26). Shiratori forged alliances with the South Manchurian Railway Company, which controlled major transportation, industrial, and urban centers in Manchuria and which would become an aggressive arm of Japan's expansion onto the continent (ibid.:240). Research, designed to enhance Japan's colonial mission, began in 1907, drawing on historical, anthropological, and geographic knowledge to explicate the social and economic customs of the Chinese. Research on "the land and customs" was considered the essential precondition for Japan's administration of the continent. "Knowing especially the legal and economic habits of the people [*minzoku*] is the fundamental secret to a successful colonial policy" (ibid.:242). As Tanaka points out, the connection between such research on customs and imperial policy is clear: "Researchers paid particular attention to matters concerning land for the railroad, the purchase of adjacent land, and land connected to company operations. . . . The work was heavily historical, centering on land use and the formation of landholdings during the Ch'ing dynasty" (ibid.:242). Historical and geographic research merged, both contributing to colonial policy-making. According to one practitioner: "The purpose of the Center for Historical and Geographic Research on Manchuria and Korea was academic, and in this way it had a political purpose" (ibid.:245). Despite their complicity with Japanese imperialism, historical scholars were sometimes critical of the national policy. Yet, when the founder of the field of history retired in 1925, he was replaced by specialists of China, Mongolia, Korea, and Manchuria, the very areas into which Japan directed its imperial mission. In fact, Tanaka argues throughout his book, history was indispensible to the centralization of the nation-state: "Without history, the elite could not have created the new Japan" (ibid.:265).

4. The term *Volkskunde* is a typical example of how the German language accommodates semantic and conceptual innovations by linguistic means, that is, by creating compound expressions that join together two (previously unrelated) base morphemes or nouns: *Volk* and *Kunde.* The second element, *Kunde,* was introduced in the seventeenth century and became a verbal commonplace for "systematic study" or "knowledge" a

hundred years later. The term appeared in many of the novel references for "science," such as *Erdkunde* 'geography', *Naturkunde* 'natural science', *Staatskunde* 'political science', *Landeskunde* 'topography', *Menschenkunde* 'human science', *Wirtschaftskunde* 'economy', and so on. The word *Kunde* was used almost interchangeably with the German synonym *Wissenschaft* 'science', 'truth', 'knowledge', dating from the fourteenth century.

5. A fascinating comparison could be drawn with the Japanese case, that is, the emergence of the discipline of history in Japan and Japan's quest for national identity at the turn of the twentieth century: becoming modern while simultaneously shedding the western category of a backward Orient. Stefan Tanaka (1993) has brilliantly analysed this process. Much of East Asia (*toyo* 'the eastern seas') became the archives—the pasts—from which Japanese history could be constructed. In Japan's nationalist historiography, China (*shina*) was transformed into a geophysical space that signified a troubled place mired in its past, in contrast to Japan, a modern Asian nation. Twentieth-century Japanese historians "discovered" the beginnings of Japan's historical narrative in Asia, thereby locating its origins and relation to China. As Tanaka (1993:20) points out: "these Japanese historians were formulating a unitary notion of a Japan that existed from the beginning of time. They were using artifacts—the pasts of China, Korea, Inner Asia, Japan itself—to create a history that . . . fostered a belief in the nation."

REFERENCES

Achenwall, Gottfried von. 1749. *Abriss der neuesten Staatswissenschaft der vornehmsten europäischen Reiche und Republicken zum Gebrauch in seinen academischen Vorlesungen.* Göttingen: J. W. Schmidt.

Achenwall, Gottfried von. 1752. *Staatsverfassung der europäischen Reiche im Grundrisse.* 2d ed. Göttingen: J. W. Schmidt.

Achenwall, Gottfried von. 1754. *Geschichte der heutigen europäischen Staaten im Grundrisse.* Göttingen: Verlag der Witwe Vandenhoek.

Ackermann, Johann Anton. 1780. *Briefe auf einer Reise nach Cassel.* Leipzig: n.p.

Anderson, Benedict. 1992. *Imagined Communities: Reflections on the Origin and Spread of Nationalism.* London: Verso.

Arends, Fridrich. 1818–20. *Ostfriesland und Jever in geographischer, statistischer und besonders landwirtschaftlicher Hinsicht.* 3 vols. Emden: Wittwe Hymer und Sohn.

Arnim, Ludwig Achim von, and Clemens Brentano. 1806–08. *Des Knaben Wunderhorn: alte deutsche Lieder.* 3 vols. Berlin: Deutsche Bibliothek.

Asad, Talal, ed. 1973. *Anthropology and the Colonial Encounter.* London: Ithaca.

Badone, Ellen. 1992. "The Construction of National Identity in Brittany and Quebec." *American Ethnologist,* 19:4, 809–17.

Bausinger, Hermann. 1963. "Aufklärung und Aberglaube." *Deutsche Vierteljahresschrift für Literaturwissenschaft und Geistesgeschichte,* vol. 37, 345–62.

Bausinger, Hermann. 1969. *Volkskunde: von der Altertumsforschung zur Kulturanalyse.* Berlin: Carl Habel Verlagsbuchhandlung.

Becker, Rudolf Zacharias. 1788. *Noth- und Hülfs-Büchlein für Bauersleute, oder, lehrreiche Freuden- und Trauergeschichte des Dorfes Mildheim.* Gotha: In der Beckerischen Buchhandlung.

Behlen, Stephan. 1823. *Versuch einer Topographie dieser Waldgegend, mit besonderer Rücksicht auf Gebirgs-, Forst-, Erd- und Volkskunde.* Leipzig: F. A. Brockhaus.

Bendix, Reinhard. 1978. *Kings or People: Power and the Mandate to Rule.* Berkeley: University of California Press.

Brand, John. 1777. *Observations on Popular Antiquities: Including the Whole of Mr. Bourne's Antiquitates Vulgares.* Newcastle-upon-Tyne, London: J. Johnson.

Brandlmeier, Paul. 1942. *Medizinische Ortsbeschreibungen des 19. Jahrhunderts im deutschen Sprachgebiet.* Abhandlungen zur Geschichte der Medizin und der Naturwissenschaften, no. 38. Berlin: Ebering.

Burridge, Kenelm L. 1973. *Encountering Aborigines.* New York: Pergamon.

Cai Yuanpei. 1962. *Cai Yuanpei minsu xue lunzhu,* Zhongguo minsu xuehui, ed. Taipei: Zhonghua Shuju.

Chang Hui. 1925. "Tan Beijing de geyao." *Hushi wencun,* 4:2, 342–60.

Chao Wei-pang. 1942. "Modern Chinese Folklore Investigation." [*Asian*] *Folklore Studies,* vol. 1, 55–76; vol. 2, 79–88.

Dorson, Richard M. 1968. *The British Folklorists: A History.* London: Routledge and Kegan Paul.

Dow, James R., and Hannjost Lixfeld, eds. 1986. *German Volkskunde: A Decade of Theoretical Confrontation, Debate, and Reorientation (1967–1977).* Bloomington: Indiana University Press.

Dünninger, Josef. 1957. "Volkstum und Aufklärung in Franken." *Bayerisches Jahrbuch für Volkskunde,* vol. 8, 29–42.

Eberhard, Wolfram, ed. 1965. *Folktales of China.* London: Routledge and Kegan Paul.

Eberhard, Wolfram. 1970. "The Use of Folklore in China," in *Studies in Chinese Folklore and Related Essays,* W. Eberhard, ed., 1–16. Folklore Institute Monographs, no. 23. Bloomington: Indiana University Research Center for the Language Sciences.

Elias, Norbert. 1978, 1982. *The Civilizing Process.* 2 vols. New York: Pantheon.

Eminov, Sandra. 1978. "Folklore and Nationalism in Modern China," in *Folklore, Nationalism, and Politics,* Felix J. Oinas, ed., 163–83. Columbus, Ohio: Slavic.

Ergang, Robert R. 1966. *Herder and the Foundations of German Nationalism.* New York: Octagon.

Foucault, Michel. 1980. *Power/Knowledge: Selected Interviews and Other Writings, 1972–1977,* C. Gordon, ed.; C. Gordon et al., trans. New York: Pantheon.

Fox, Richard G., ed. 1990. *Nationalist Ideologies and the Production of National Cultures.* American Ethnological Society Monographs, no. 2. Washington, D.C.: American Anthropological Association.

Garve, Christian. 1786a. *Ueber den Character der Bauern und ihr Verhältniss gegen die Gutsherrn und gegen die Regierung.* Breslau: Wilhelm Gottlieb Korn.

Garve, Christian. 1786b. *Versuch über das Volk.* Berlin: In Kommission bey G. J. Decker, Königlicher Hofbuchdrucker.

Gatterer, Johann Christian. 1778. *Abris der Geographie.* Göttingen: Vandenhoeck.

Gaum, Johann Ferdinand. 1784. *Reisen eines Curländers durch Schwaben.* n.p.

Görres, Joseph. 1807. *Die teutschen Volksbücher.* Heidelberg: Mohr and Zimmer.

Grimm, Jacob. 1816–18. *Deutsche Sagen.* 2 vols. Berlin: Nicolaische Buchhandlung.

Grimm, Jacob, and Wilhelm Grimm. 1812, 1815. *Kinder- und Haus-Märchen.* 2 vols. Berlin: Realschulbuchhandlung.

Gu Jiegang. 1928. "Guanyu mishi." *Zhongshan daxue minsu zhoukan* 4:2, 15–29.

Güntz, Max Heinrich Edmund. 1897–1902. *Handbuch der landwirtschaftlichen Litteratur* . . . Leipzig: H. Voigt.

Hassencamp, Johann Matthäus. 1783. *Briefe eines Reisenden über Pyrmont, Cassel, Marburg, Würzburg, und Wilhelmsbad.* Frankfurt: n.p.

Herder, Johann Gottfried. 1773. *Auszug aus einem Briefwechsel über Ossian und die Lieder alter Völker.* Paderborn: Schöningh.

Herder, Johann Gottfried. 1778–79. *Volkslieder.* 2 vols. Leipzig: In der Weygandschen Buchhandlung.

Himmelfarb, Gertrude. 1987. *The New History and the Old.* Cambridge, Mass.: Belknap Press of Harvard University.

Hobsbawm, Eric J. 1969. *Industry and Empire.* Harmondsworth: Penguin.

Hobsbawm, Eric. 1983. "Inventing Traditions," in *The Invention of Tradition,* Eric Hobsbawm and Terence Ranger, eds., 1–14. Cambridge: Cambridge University Press.

Hobsbawm, Eric J. 1990. *Nations and Nationalism since 1780: Programme, Myth, Reality.* Cambridge: Cambridge University Press.

Hu Shih. 1934. *The Chinese Renaissance.* Chicago: University of Chicago Press.

Huang Sung-kang. 1959. *Lu Hsun and the New Culture Movement of Modern China.* Amsterdam: Djambatan.

Hume, David. 1932. *The Letters of David Hume,* J. Y. T. Greig, ed., 2 vols. London: Clarendon Press.

Hung Chang-tai. 1985. *Going to the People: Chinese Intellectuals and Folk Literature, 1918–1937.* Cambridge, Mass.: Harvard University Press.

Hymes, Dell. 1974. "The Use of Anthropology: Critical, Political, Personal." In *Reinventing Anthropology,* Dell Hymes, ed., 3–79. New York: Pantheon.

Jahn, Friedrich Ludwig. 1810. *Deutsches Volkstum.* Frankfurt: C. Naumann.

Kamenetsky, Christa. 1972. "Folklore as a Political Tool in Nazi Germany." *Journal of American Folklore,* 85:4, 21–37.

Koch-Sternfeld, Joseph Ernst (Ritter) von. 1810. *Salzburg und Berchtesgaden in historisch-statistisch-geographisch- und staats-ökonomischen Beyträgen.* Salzburg: Mayr.

Kohl, Karl-Heinz. 1986. *Exotik als Beruf: Erfahrung und Trauma der Ethnographie.* Frankfurt: Campus Verlag.

Kohl, Karl-Heinz. 1987. *Abwehr und Verlangen: zur Geschichte der Ethnologie.* Frankfurt: Campus Verlag.

Köstlin, Konrad. 1979. "Anmerkungen zu Riehl." *Jahrbuch für Volkskunde,* vol. 2, 81–94.

Kramer, Karl.-S. 1972. "Einige Nachrichten zum Kampf der Aufklärung gegen volksreligiöse Formen in Bayern," in *Fakten und Analysen: Festgabe für Leopold Schmidt zum 60. Geburtstag,* K. Beitl, ed., 296–303. Vienna: Verein für Volkskunde.

Krünitz, D. Johann Georg. 1786–1811. *Auszug aus des Herrn D. Johann Georg Krünitz ökonomisch-technologischen Encyklopädie oder allgemeinen System der Staats- Stadt- Haus- und Land-Wirtschaft, und der Kunst-Geschichte in alphabetischer Ordnung,* M. C. von Schütz, ed., 31 vols. Berlin: Joachim Paul.

Lauffer, Otto. 1931. "Besprechung von Gustav Jungbauers *Geschichte der deutschen Volkskunde.*" *Zeitschrift für Volkskunde,* vol. 41 (neue Folge, no. 3), 183–87.

Lidtke, Vernon L. 1982. "Songs and Nazis: Political Music and Social Change in the Twentieth Century," in *Essays on Culture and Society in Modern Germany,* King et al., eds., 167–200. College Station: Texas A&M University Press.

Linke, Uli. 1988. "The Language of Resistance: Rhetorical Tactics and Symbols of Popular Protest in Germany." *City and Society,* 2:2, 127–33.

Linke, Uli. 1995a. "Power Matters: The Politics of Culture in German Folklore Scholarship." *History and Anthropology,* 9:1, 1–26.

Linke, Uli. 1995b. "Power and Culture Theory: Problematizing the Focus of Research in German Folklore Scholarship," in *Folklore Interpreted,* Regina Bendix and Rosemary Levy Zumwalt, eds., 417–47. New York: Garland.

Linke, Uli. 1995c. "Murderous Fantasies: Violence, Memory, and Selfhood in Germany." *New German Critique,* 64 (Winter), 37–59.

Lixfeld, Hannjost. 1994. *Folklore and Fascism: The Reich Institute for German Volkskunde,* James R. Dow, ed. and trans. Bloomington: Indiana University Press.

Lohoff, H. 1934. *Ursprung und Entwicklung der religiösen Volkskunde.* Greifswald: Universitätsverlag L. Bamberg.

Lukács, Georg. [1937] 1963. *The Historical Novel.* Boston: Beacon.

Lutz, Gerhard. 1982. "Die Entstehung der Ethnologie und das spätere Nebeneinander der Fächer Volkskunde und Völkerkunde in Deutschland," in *Europäische Ethnologie,* H. Nixdorff and T. Hauschild, eds., 29–46. Berlin: Dietrich Reimer.

Mader, J. A. Ritter von Riegger. 1787–93. "Verzeichnis einiger gedruckter Hilfsmittel zu einer pragmatischen Landes- Volks- und Staatenkunde Böhmens," in *Materialien zur alten und neuen Statistik von Böhmen,* Ritter J. A. von Riegger, ed., vol. 1, 23–24. 12 vols. Leipzig: K. Widtmann.

Mader, J. A. Ritter von Riegger. 1793. *Über Begriff und Lehrart der Statistik.* Prague: Albrecht.

Memminger, Johann Daniel Georg. 1820. *Beschreibung oder Geographie und Statistik, nebst einer Übersicht der Geschichte von Würtemberg.* Stuttgart: J. G. Cotta.

Mieder, Wolfgang. 1982. "Proverbs in Nazi Germany: The Promulgation of Anti-Semitism and Stereotypes through Folklore." *Journal of American Folklore,* 95:4, 233–64.

Mitchell, Sir Arthur, and C. G. Cash. 1917. *A Contribution to the Bibliography of Scottish Topography.* 2 vols. Edinburgh: Scottish History Society.

Möller, Helmut. 1964. "A. Volkskunde, Statistik, Völkerkunde 1787. Aus den Anfängen der Volkskunde als Wissenschaft." *Zeitschrift für Volkskunde,* 60 (neue Folge), 218–33.

Moser, Hans. 1959. "Wege zur Volkskunde als Wissenschaft." *Bayerisches Jahrbuch für Volkskunde,* vol. 10, 124–58.

Möser, Justus. 1774–86. *Patriotische Phantasien,* J. W. J. von Voights, ed. 4 vols. Berlin: Friedrich Nicolai.

Möser, Justus. 1768. *Osnabrückische Geschichte: allgemeine Einleitung.* Osnabrück: Schmidische Buchhandlung.

Narr, Dieter. 1959. "Fragen der Volksbildung in der späteren Aufklärung." *Württembergisches Jahrbuch für Volkskunde,* vol. 60, 38–67.

Narr, Dieter, and Hermann Bausinger. 1964. "B. Volkskunde 1788: aus den Anfängen der Volkskunde als Wissenschaft." *Zeitschrift für Volkskunde,* 60 (neue Folge), 233–41.

Nicolai, Friedrich. 1783–96. *Beschreibung einer Reise durch Deutschland und die Schweiz im Jahre 1781. Nebst Bemerkungen über Gelehrsamkeit, Industrie, Religion und Sitten.* 12 vols. Berlin: n.p.

Niemann, August Christoph Heinrich. 1799. *Handbuch der Schleswig-Holsteinischen Landeskunde: zur leichtern Berichtigung und Ergänzung der bisher vorhandenen Nachrichten: topographischer Teil.* Vol. 1: *Herzogthum Schleswig.* Schleswig: Im Kommission bei J. G. Röhss.

Niemann, August Christoph Heinrich. 1802. "Skize zur Beschreibung eines Landdistrikts." *Schleswig-Holsteinsche Vaterlandskunde,* vol. 1, 9–52.

Niemann, August Christoph Heinrich. 1807. *Abris der Statistik und der Statenkunde, nebst Fragmenten zur Geschichte derselben. Mit einer statistischen Tafel.* Altona: J. F. Hammetich.

Pagden Anthony. 1993. *European Encounters with the New World: From Renaissance to Romanticism.* New Haven: Yale University Press.

Pei Wenzhong. 1925. "Pingmin wenxue de shili." *Chenbao fukan,* September 24, 139.

Riehl, Wilhelm Heinrich. 1851. *Die bürgerliche Gesellschaft.* Stuttgart: J. G. Cotta'scher Verlag.

Riehl, Wilhelm Heinrich. 1854. *Land und Leute.* Stuttgart: J. G. Cotta'scher Verlag.

Riehl, Wilhelm Heinrich. 1855. *Die Familie.* Stuttgart: J. G. Cotta'scher Verlag.

Riehl, Wilhelm Heinrich. 1857. *Die Pfälzer: ein rheinisches Volksbild.* Stuttgart: J. G. Cotta'scher Verlag.

Riehl, Wilhelm Heinrich. 1859a. *Culturstudien aus drei Jahrhunderten.* Stuttgart: J. G. Cotta'scher Verlag.

Riehl, Wilhelm Heinrich. 1859b. "Die Volkskunde als Wissenschaft." In 1859a, *Culturstudien aus drei Jahrhunderten,* 205–29. Stuttgart: J. G. Cotta'scher Verlag. Reprinted in G. Lutz, *Volkskunde* (1958), Berlin: Erich Schmidt Verlag, 23–37.

Riehl, Wilhelm Heinrich. 1860–68. *Bavaria: Landes- und Volkskunde des Königreichs Bayern, bearbeitet von einem Kreise bayerischer Gelehrter,* 5 vols. Munich: Cotta.

Riehl, Wilhelm Heinrich. 1869. *Wanderbuch.* Stuttgart: J. G. Cotta'scher Verlag.

Röder, Philipp Ludwig Hermann. 1789–91. *Reisen durch das südliche Teutschland.* Leipzig: G. L. Crusius and F. C. Walliser.

Röder, Philipp Ludwig Hermann. 1791–92. *Geographisches-statistisch-topographisches Lexikon von Schwaben.* Ulm: Stettin.

Rousseau, Jean-Jacques. 1978 [1755]. Über den Ursprung der Ungleichheit unter den Menschen, V. H. Weigand, ed. Hamburg: n.p.

Rupp-Eisenreich, Britta. 1984. "Aux 'origines' de la Völkerkunde allemande: de la statistik à l'anthropologie de George Forster," in ead., *Histoires de l'anthropologie.* Paris: Klincksieck, 89–115.

Schmidt, Leopold. 1938. "Volkskunde, Gegenreformation, Aufklärung." *Deutsche Vierteljahrsschrift für Literaturwissenschaft und Geistesgeschichte,* vol. 16, 75–94.

Schmidt, Leopold. 1966. *Volkskunde von Niederösterreich.* Vol. 1. Horn: Ferdinand Berger.

Schneider, Laurence A. 1971. *Ku Chieh-kang and China's New History: Nationalism and the Quest for Alternative Traditions.* Berkeley: University of California Press.

Schulz, Joachim Christoph Friedrich. [1795–96] 1982. *Reise eines Liefländers von Riga nach Warschau . . . ,* 6 vols. Berlin: Friedrich Viewegdemaltern. Rev. ed. by Klaus Zernack. 1982. Frankfurt: Suhrkamp Verlag.

Scott, Sir Walter. 1833. *Introductions and Notes and Illustrations to the Novels, Tales, and Romances of the Author of Waverley.* Vol. 1. Edinburgh: Robert Cadell.

Sinclair, Sir John. 1791–99. *A Statistical Account of Scotland. Drawn up from the Communications of the Ministers of the Different Parishes.* 21 vols. Edinburgh: William Creech.

Small, Albion W. 1909. *The Cameralists: The Pioneers of German Social Polity.* Chicago: University of Chicago Press.

Small, Albion W. 1967. *The Origins of Sociology.* New York: Russel and Russel.

Snyder, Louis L. 1951. "Nationalistic Aspects of the Grimm Brothers' Fairy Tales." *The Journal of Social Psychology,* vol. 33, 209–23.

Stagl, Justin. 1974. "August Ludwig Schlözers Entwurf einer 'Völkerkunde' oder 'Ethnographie' seit 1772." *Ethnologische Zeitschrift,* vol. 2, 73–91.

Stocking, George W., Jr. 1982. "Afterword: A View from the Center." *Ethnos,* 1:2, 172–86.

Stocking, George W., Jr., ed. 1989. *Romantic Motives: Essays on Anthropological Sensibility.* Madison: University of Wisconsin Press.

Stone, Lawrence. 1987. Review of *The New History and the Old,* by Gertrude Himmelfarb. *New York Review of Books,* December 17, 59–62.

Stuck, Gottlieb Heinrich. 1784, 1787. *Verzeichnis von aeltern und neuern Land- und Reisebeschreibungen. Ein Versuch eines Hauptstücks der geographischen Litteratur mit einem vollständigen Realregister.* 2 vols. Halle: J. C. Hendel.

Tanaka, Stefan. 1993. *Japan's Orient: Rendering Pasts into History.* Berkeley: University of California Press.

Taussig, Michael T. 1987. *Shamanism, Colonialism, and the Wild Man: A Study in Terror and Healing.* Chicago: University of Chicago Press.

Tieck, Ludwig. 1803. *Minnelieder aus dem schwäbischen Zeitalter.* Berlin: Realschulbuchhandlung.

Trevor-Roper, Hugh. 1983. "The Invention of Tradition: The Highland Tradition of Scotland," in *The Invention of Tradition,* Eric Hobsbawm and Terence Ranger, eds., 15–41. Cambridge: Cambridge University Press.

Tylor, Sir Edward Burnett. 1871. *Primitive Culture: Researches into the Development of Mythology, Philosophy, Religion, Language, Art and Custom.* 2 vols. London: J. Murray.

Voss, Johann Heinrich. 1808. (Stuttgarter) *Morgenblatt,* nos. 283–84, 25–26.

Weber-Kellermann, Ingeborg. 1969. *Deutsche Volkskunde: zwischen Germanistik und Sozialwissenschaften.* Stuttgart: J. B. Metzlersche Verlagsbuchhandlung.

Weber-Kellermann, Ingeborg, and Andreas C. Bimmer. 1985. *Einführung in die Volkskunde/europäische Ethnologie: eine Wissenschaftsgeschichte.* 2d rev. ed. Stuttgart: J. B. Metzlersche Verlagsbuchhandlung.

Westenrieder, L. 1778. *Briefe bayrischer Denkungsart und Sitten.* Munich: Fleischmann.

Wiegelmann, Günter. 1979. "Riehls Stellung in der Wissenschaftsgeschichte der Volkskunde." *Jahrbuch für Volkskunde,* vol. 2, 89–100.

Wiegelmann, Günter, Matthias Zender, and Gerhard Heilfurth. 1977. *Volkskunde: eine Einführung.* Grundlagen der Germanistik, no. 12, Hugo Moser and Hartmut Steinecke, eds. Berlin: Erich Schmidt Verlag.

Wilson, William A. 1973. "Herder, Folklore, and Romantic Nationalism." *Journal of Popular Culture,* 6:4, 819–35.

Yen Chun-chiang. 1967. "Folklore Research in Communist China." *Asian Folklore Studies,* 26:2, 1–62.

Zielenziger, Kurt. 1966. *Die alten deutschen Kameralisten: ein Beitrag zur Geschichte der Nationalökonomie und zum Problem des Merkantilismus.* Jena: Verlag von Gustav Fischer.

Zipes, Jack. 1979. *Breaking the Magic Spell: Radical Theories of Folk and Fairy Tales.* Austin: University of Texas Press.

Recycling Tradition: Culture, History, and Political Economy in the Chrysanthemum Festivals of South China

Helen F. Siu

In the mid–nineteenth century, a gentleman in Xiaolan having the Mai surname wrote in his memoir:

> Age eighteen, the forty-seventh year of Qianlong's reign [1782], there was a chrysanthemum festival. Each major surname group put on floral displays, and six platforms were set up throughout the town. There were scores of theatrical troupes whose performance brought together kinsmen and friends. The tradition of the festival started that year.[1]

The narrative continued.

> Age twenty-seven, the fifty-sixth year of Qianlong's reign [1791], the chrysanthemum festival of that year was more elaborate than before.

> Age fifty, the nineteenth year of the reign of Jiaqing [1814], the town held another community-wide celebration. The staging of chrysanthemum operas the year before prompted the lineages to conduct a third festival. It has been twenty-four years since the last gathering. The He surname group provided two sets [of floral displays], the Li surname one set, all at their focal ancestral halls. Our own lineage mounted a display at the hall for an ancestor of the sixth generation. The *weisuo* [military colony] set up its own in front of the Guandi temple.[2] The Xiao surname mounted their display at the hall for their focal ancestor. The Situ [a neighborhood division] gave a

display at the Zhong ancestral hall. A Li lineage also had its own display, as did the Liang of Luoyong and the Shifu temple.

In Xiaolan, a market town in the heart of the Pearl River delta of south China, the chrysanthemum has historically informed popular consciousness in crucial ways. It was believed that original settlers were attracted to the area by the yellow flower seven centuries ago.[3] The local scholars used it in their writings, as had members of the literati[4] in the cities. Documents of major lineages in town also proudly described the role of their prominent members in the staging of the chrysanthemum festivals, where, amid drink, poetry, and operas, they mimicked the imperial examinations by competing with elegant floral displays.[5]

The town's aspiring scholars initiated the major chrysanthemum festival in the late eighteenth century. It continued to be held in the twentieth century, although the power of military adventurers associated with the warlords in the Republican period had replaced the authority of the literati. Surprisingly, under the leadership of the Chinese Communist Party after the Revolution of 1949, the town government continued what it branded as a "feudal" custom. Between 1959 and 1979, the town staged the festival three times, the last one involving the elaborate feasting of overseas compatriots targeted as potential investors in an age of economic reform. Today, local residents take for granted that the officials have given Xiaolan the alias of "Chrysanthemum Town." A hotel and the major state department store also carry the name. Town bakeries advertise their chrysanthemum-flavored egg rolls for export. Party officials—the very same cadres who have denounced the cultivation of chrysanthemums as a decadent pursuit of the leisure class—seek out former landlords and their descendants to revive the art.

That the community-wide chrysanthemum festivals continue to be actively pursued over 200 years, despite dramatic changes in their environment, triggers analytical questions. One can assume that, as with other rituals practised over long periods, an active, continuous, cultural tradition is at work that is improvised in response to diverse needs. But why has the chrysanthemum festival assumed such significance in the popular understanding about history and social identity in Xiaolan? During the last five centuries, the sands of the Pearl River delta developed into an elaborate social landscape with prosperous villages and towns. Had the staging of the festivals in Xiaolan played an integral part in the building of lineage and community, and of the regional political economy? In other words, did the local inhabitants, elites and commoners, actively use symbolic and instrumental means to become part of the

Chinese culture and polity? If they did, how was this cultural symbol recycled and diffused in everyday social living to create new meanings and to reinforce new political interests when the imperial order disintegrated in the twentieth century? By examining the ways the festival's various expressions form a unifying thread in the transformation of the relationship between local society and the centers of power, I hope to highlight the process allowing the development of a region that was autonomous and diverse, but bore the unifying imprint of the larger state culture as well.

The evolution of the Chinese civilization is composed of an infinite differentiation into local cultures and economies, and an intense identification with the larger state system. This characteristic of Chinese culture has long been recognized by scholars, although few offer full accounts of the acculturation process. For the past twenty years, three paradigms in Chinese anthropology have addressed the issue from different angles. G. William Skinner argues that Chinese history is structured by cycles of regional growth and decline (1985). He divides China into macroregions linked to the central polity, each having its hierarchy of marketing systems. The component parts of this hierarchy, the marketing communities, are discrete, culturally homogeneous units at one level but interactive at the next higher level (1964). He emphasizes the rhythms in the opening and closure of these communities in relation to dynastic changes (1971). The unfolding of these functionally differentiated but structurally integrated systems rests on the logic of market exchange and calculations of cost-distance. The Chinese peasant is a rational maximiser responding to changing administrative environments. Skinner's analysis of the marketing hierarchy gives a conceptual coherence to social life in time and space, but politics, culture, and social institutions are given analytical weight only after the economic skeleton is in place.

The seminal works of the late Maurice Freedman (1958, 1966) on lineage, a dominant social organization in south China, became enduring influences on sinological anthropology. Coming from the structural-functionalist tradition in British Social Anthropology, he highlighted certain principles of kinship as unifying features of Chinese culture and examined how these principles found their niches in the river deltas of southeastern China. The wondrous range of lineage communities, made explicit by collective properties and elaborate public rituals, give their members a shared consciousness about cultural identity.

Arthur Wolf (1974) examines the relationship between state and society through popular religion and ritual. He characterizes the major interactive categories in peasant folk religion—gods, ghosts, and ancestors—as projections of peasant perceptions of the imperial bureaucracy, the village stranger, and kin in the material world. The tension between collective representations and differentiated social structure can be traced to a Durkheimian tradition.

Since the 1960s, the theoretical constructs on which these sinological paradigms are based have been scrutinized by a new generation of scholars.[6] Formalist notions of marginal utility serving as the dynamic force in human behavior have long been confronted by political economic approaches emphasizing limits in choice due to dependence and unequal access to power.[7] Sensitivity to rapid and drastic social change after the postwar era has forced scholars to acknowledge process in social systems formerly conceptualized as a state of functional, timeless equilibrium. Moreover, the examination of social structure incorporating cumulative changes has been strengthened by attempts to see how the past informs the present through a subjective, selective use of history.[8] Critical theorists on ideological domination debate about inversion, subversion, and containment in cultural discourse.[9] Rituals are increasingly seen not only as exerting symbolic meaning to reflect society, but also as cultural performances that create new meanings.[10] Their symbolic and instrumental aspects encompass multiple, dialogical, and often contradictory voices. Many of the new theoretical constructs assume that human actors are neither totally programmed by cultural rules nor compelled by economic forces. In the creation of cultural meaning, the concepts of agency and structuring become central.[11]

These theoretical developments are reflected in recent studies in Chinese anthropology. Emily Ahern (1981) analyses ritual as a means to learn about politics and power. Using French structuralist theory as a starting point, Steven Sangren (1987) offers new views on the reproduction of social structure and cultural meaning in a Taiwanese community. James Watson adopts a historical approach to lineage institutions (1982; with Ebrey 1986). He also examines how the standardization of rituals through time has allowed the creation of a unifying cultural identity that gives room for diverse beliefs (1985; with Rawski 1988). Myron L. Cohen argues that cultural discourse in China, dependent on rituals as much as a shared consciousness, arises from the flux of social life and is subject to the state's manipulation (1989).

This article is in line with the spirit of the above scholars in bringing studies of Chinese culture, society, and history closer to the mainstream of contemporary social theory. By analysing the community-wide festivals in Xiaolan from the late eighteenth century to the present and by explicating how the nature, meaning, and dynamics of these cultural expressions intertwined with the evolution of the regional political economy, this essay suggests how one may build upon the rich body of historical materials and rethink the analytical tools.

Xiaolan and the Sands

Xiaolan was situated on the dividing line between the old and the new alluvial plains of the Pearl River delta (see figure 1). Since the Ming dynasty, managers of ancestral trusts, commercial enterprises, and parapolitical associations based in the towns and cities in the older part of the delta had financed and organized the reclamation of river marshes. Known locally as *sha,* or sands, they were formed as the Pearl River continued its southeastward flow into the sea. Similar to other deltas and marshes around China's lakes, the sands reclaimed in the late imperial period were not ordinary frontiers.[12] From the very start, their projects had involved large-scale capital investment and planning. Using the informal political networks of members who had acquired academic degrees and official posts in the imperial bureaucracy, lineage trusts and guilds in the cities secured vast areas from the county magistrates and negotiated tax exemptions for a long period by promising to turn the river marshes into productive fields. They hired functionaries to organize local laborers for these reclamation projects. Referred to as *Dan,* the boat-dwelling laborers have been considered as a subethnic group by the land-based agriculturalists. The two maintained different social customs and seldom intermarried.[13] There were also hardly any villages, except for the temporary straw huts on the dikes built by the laborers who later became tenants. This was partly due to the vast scale of reclamation,[14] but it was also because the landlords explicitly forbade the construction of permanent houses in order to claim the area as "unsettled," a way to avoid taxes. Each outpost the functionaries set up consisted of a granary, a house for the overseers, quarters for the laborers and crop-watching forces, and a fleet of boats for grain transportation.

Xiaolan was probably one such outpost. Local strongmen arose to become the area's tenant-contractors. Known as *baodian,* they paid a cash rent to the landlords in the cities and collected the harvest in kind from their own tenants. To secure the grain was an event in itself. It was not uncommon for the farmers to "cut the green ears" of their crops (*geheqing*) and then flee the area in their boats. A seventeenth-century observer (Qu 1700) recorded that local strongmen countered these acts by blatant force. They organized boatloads of armed men, brandishing flags and weapons, and descended upon the fields to "force harvest" (*qiangge*). Many used the occasion to encroach upon the land and crops of those whose property boundaries were unclear because of the unpredictable flow of the river. The grain was temporarily stored at the outpost and then transported directly to the wholesale merchants in county capitals and cities such as Shiqi, Shunde, Foshan, and Guangzhou.

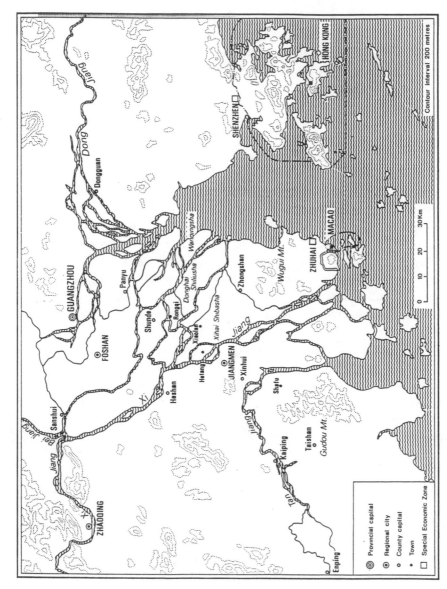

Fig. 1. The Pearl River delta. From Helen Siu, *Agents and Victims in South China: Accomplices in Rural Revolution* (1989a). (Courtesy of Yale University Press.)

The open "frontier," however, allowed multiple ways of accumulating wealth for the local population because there was a limit as to how far the managers of the city-based ancestral trusts and guilds could reach. In time, the local functionaries of these estates established their own bases of operations in the outposts. The upwardly mobile acquired academic degrees, built ancestral halls, and used similar cultural claims embodied in the lineage organizations to challenge the rights of their former patrons. From the east to the west of the delta, one can see a line of such outposts that have grown into supercenters of wealth and power in the last three centuries, separating the older part of the delta from the sands that continued to be reclaimed.

Although the sands were economically an integral part of the town's operations, the two were distinctly different worlds, socially and culturally. The people of the sands have been, up to the recent decade, considered poor, migrant, ethnically inferior, and lacking in social grace.[15] This system of domination was made up of two nexuses. Between the laborers-tenants and the local strongmen there existed a relationship based on a blatant display of force. The tenants were viewed as socially and culturally marginal, whereas there was an arena for dialogue and negotiation based on some common cultural vocabulary between the landlords in town and their functionaries, who could be powerful tenant-contractors. When disputes arose over land rights or when protection was sought against encroachment, patrons and kin in the county capitals and towns were called upon to arbitrate.

Xiaolan had grown from an outpost in the sands in the Ming dynasty (1348–1644) to a prosperous market town in the late nineteenth century. Although nominally administered by the Xiangshan county magistrate, the lowest seat of the imperial government, based in Shiqi some twenty-seven kilometers distant, Xiaolan's social life and politics were dominated by the three major lineages of He, Li, and Mai, whose leading members controlled grain production, trade, and the reclamation of the sands. These lineages had elaborate genealogies showing a dazzling array of academic degree holders and imperial officials from centuries past.[16] Their focal ancestral halls, often dedicated to an original founder of the lineage, were built at the end of the Ming dynasty in the seventeenth century and renovated through the Qing dynasty. Numerous halls for subsequent ancestors were built in the nineteenth century. Extensive in size (consisting of three rows of halls and two courtyards), supported by hardwood beams from Indochina, with curved roofs and carved stone slabs indicating honor and upward mobility in the imperial bureaucracy, these halls served as centers for kinship rituals performed at least biannually. The activities helped the lineages to exert an imposing collective presence on the rural landscape.

The 393 ancestral halls in the town, which in the mid–twentieth century had fewer than 20,000 residents (including those in a district ajoining the town known as Dalan), represented a phenomenal proliferation of wealth under the shadow of ancestors.[17]

The lineage ideal might have originated from the cultural centers of north China and adapted to the "frontiers" of south China, as Freedman envisioned, but local concerns in Xiaolan also worked themselves into the features of the larger society. The extreme proliferation of small ancestral trusts and the un-characteristic importance of the focal ancestral halls of the He, Li, and Mai lineages are cases in point. The multiple sources of income in the sands had allowed individual families to accumulate substantial wealth in order to set up their own ancestral trusts. In a sense, the process of rapid fission of lineage branches can be viewed as a "devolution" of the lineage ideal; however, the scale of the reclamation and the need to flex political muscle against encroach-ment led to constant appeals for consolidation and alliance under the shadow of focal ancestors, an organizational means culturally accepted and politically tolerated by the imperial state.

The focal ancestor halls of the He, Li, and Mai lineages in Xiaolan were moderately endowed with estates.[18] More important, they had served as useful political umbrellas. Centers of lineage and other ritual activities, they operated schools and granaries; collected rent from the sands and particular neighbor-hoods in town; contributed to community temples, local defense, and flood control; and dealt with the tax assessors and collectors for the estates of their lineage branches when settlement rights were involved. In fact, each operated as a community as much as a kinship institution.[19]

As with lineages in other parts of China, those in Xiaolan actively sought connections to the imperial bureaucracy. The focal ancestral halls were named after particular members of the respective lineages who had acquired the highest academic or official ranks. For example, the Li lineage named theirs *Li Shangshu Da Zongci* (The Senior Focal Ancestor Hall of Li the Minister). One of the two major He lineages named their hall *He Neige Da Zongci* (The Senior Focal Ancestral Hall of He in the Imperial Cabinet). The other He lineage named theirs *He Taiqing Da Zongci* (The Senior Focal Ancestral Hall of He the Chief Minister). During the height of their power in the 1873, these two lineages jointly built an ancestral hall for the "grandfather" of their focal ancestors, a high-ranking imperial official in the Song court, and named it after his title. Connections between lineage power and the literati culture were also made by funding scholars aspiring to sit for the imperial examinations, being patrons to local academies, compiling genealogies to show an impressive record of literati pedigree, establishing their voice in the town covenant, and, last but not least, by actively organizing community rituals.[20]

This affluent town was the focus for an intense ritual complex of which the ancestral halls and their wealth formed an integral part.[21] Managers of the ancestral trusts, patrons of the town's 139 temples, monasteries, and many neighborhood shrines (known as *she*), contributed to their festivals and renovations. The rituals created religious, social, and political meanings for participants. To be entitled to a portion of the ritual pork at lineage ceremonies meant having rights to tenure on ancestral estates and free education in lineage schools, settlement in particular villages and neighborhoods, and protection by the elite members of the lineages against encroachment—official and otherwise.

Two temples for the city god (*Chenghuang*) were set up by local elites, and these established linkages to the larger political environment. Such temples were unusual for a place like Xiaolan, whose administrative status was below that of a county capital. Their existence obliged visiting imperial officials to go there to pay their respects. In so doing, the officials acknowledged that they interacted in a common political–moral arena with the local notables who built them.

Based on an annual cosmic cycle, the ancestral rites and local temple festivals mobilized overlapping groups of patrons and participants. The high point of this ritual complex occurred in midyear. Known as the *jiao,* communal exorcism took place on the seventh month of the lunar year. Platforms for operas were erected in front of the biggest community temple. Monks and Daoist priests were hired to perform services for several days in order to cleanse the community of evil spirits. For three days, deities from the five major temples of the town and adjacent neighborhoods were paraded along the small river encircling the town, forming a line of a dozen or so boats. Each day, the deities of one temple led the parade.[22] Rice would be thrown into the river to feed the "hungry ghosts." In return for the annual cleansing and bestowing of fortune, households in these neighborhoods prepared offerings to the deities when the images were paraded past their doors. Amid fireworks, the deities were followed by sets of decorations depicting well-known historical episodes and tales, and children dressed in costumes of legendary figures and skillfully propped up by metal and wooden stands. The displays were known as *se ban.* Whether the sponsors were lineages, neighborhoods centering on an earth shrine, or trade guilds, there was a degree of competition to put on the most elaborate displays.[23] In Durkheimian terms, one could say that together they conveyed the atmosphere of rejoicing in unison. They also confirmed certain epistemological notions about the cosmic forces of harmony and conflict, the *yin* and *yang,* and the spiritual essences that have become long-standing features of the Chinese cultural repertoire.

At the same time, the ceremonies differentiated social status according to gender, age, kin, wealth, and territorial boundaries in the changeable world of human affairs. The rituals reinforced positions of power shrewdly pursued by the locally wealthy at its apex. Despite the patronage of the lineages, the jiao ceremonies were constructed along non–kin lines. The organizational units were temples that accepted donations from ancestral halls, guilds, and neighborhoods.[24] Furthermore, the town residents who were active participants of the parades, making offers and feasting at the conclusion of the jiao, distinguished themselves from the inhabitants of the sands who were onlookers at most. The terms "us over here" and "those out there" continued to be used, the latter referring to the farmers and fishermen outside the town, who were considered poor and uncultured, living on embankments where no sizable community, lineage, or temple existed. Exclusion continued well into the mid–twentieth century. When local bosses in the village of Jiuzhouji three kilometers west of Xiaolan rose to power in the late 1940s and decided to hold a jiao ceremony of their own, the inhabitants of Xiaolan were delighted that a storm washed out the festivities, thus "putting the usurpers in their place."[25] The significance of the ceremonies as a dynamic part of local cultural and political discourses seemed clear to all.

The Chrysanthemum Festivals

Since the beginning of the Qing dynasty (A.D. 1644), the activities of the local scholars took a very visible form. Unlike the jiao ritual, the center of activities rotated around the major ancestral halls and the headquarters of the township covenant (*Lanxiang Gongyue*), poetry associations, and private academies (such as the Congwen and the Lanshan academies).[26]

The first event related to chrysanthemums, recorded in 1736, was not in the form of a community-wide festival. *Jushi,* as the event was named, took place in front of the ancestral hall of a member of the Li lineage who had once acquired the position of minister of rites at the Ming court in Nanjing.[27] Five years later, it was followed by another ceremony in front of the ancestral hall of a member of the He lineage, who was also a senior member of the imperial academy and a minister at the southern Ming court.[28] According to He Lizai, who wrote *Lanxie,* a book of the 1870s about local customs and history, the center of the display ground in both cases was taken up by a platform for operas, with stands on both sides for potted chrysanthemums. The participants followed specific requirements for floral entries based on type, color, and title, as if they were essays presented for the imperial examinations. Then professional opera troupes from Guangzhou performed for several days in front of the ancestral halls, paralleling temple festivals in which operas were performed for the gods.

Although these early displays seem to have disappeared, another form of chrysanthemum-related activities flourished in later years. Identified as *jushe,* these events were organized by literary associations and involved floral displays, but their main purpose was to have aspiring scholars gather from far and near to drink, and recite poetry in connection with the flowers. These events were often held once a year, depending on the resources of the patrons.

The diffusion of this scholarly event into the wider community started with a chrysanthemum festival called *juhua hui* in 1782—the one the gentleman named Mai recorded. Unlike popular religious festivals, with their regular and predictable schedules and forms, the chrysanthemum events were staged in an ad hoc manner. Nine years lapsed between the first and the second festival. The third festival, which took place twenty-four years later, was prompted by a political event the previous year. A dispute had arisen between a certain Liang Chiyu and the township notables over contributions to the local work on flood control. The magistrate intervened and arrested Liang. The major lineages therefore arranged for operas to be staged in front of a temple as a way of acknowledging the supernatural forces behind the magistrate's judgment. It was autumn, and the chrysanthemums were blossoming. As a consequence the theatrical performances were named the chrysanthemum operas. Because the event triggered off complaints that it had been a long time since the festivals themselves had been staged, the major lineages planned one the following year, the year of Jiashu (1814). According to an essay written by a local scholar on that occasion, the festival was conducted in a grand style unmatched by any other. The deliberate purpose was explicit—to revive a historical happening that Xiaolan residents could claim as their own. As Lu Yun Shanfang Jushi wrote (1814):

> In Landu [Xiaolan and Dalan] . . . local residents are experts in the art of cultivating chrysanthemums; . . . Occasionally they have organized events for them . . . named *huanghua hui.* For an area of many miles, the golden colors shine, the air is filled with the songs of operas, the music of stringed instruments, and the chanting of poetry. . . . Yet the occasions have been infrequent; from the xinhai year of Qianlong to now, there were only two, so

that the events become nothing but hearsay in people's minds, or are be-lieved to be an occasional act of the flower deity. Recently, friends and kinsmen from the provincial capital and the neighboring counties would enquire about the event whenever they meet natives of Landu, who are at a loss as to what to say. . . . But they find that in the gardens, the flowers are just about to blossom. This has led to the idea of another festival.

It is worth noting that the focal ancestral halls where operas were performed were the centers of the festival. Moreover, the opera troupes were specialized in a style connected with the *kun qu*. Popular among the higher literati in the metropolitan centers, the style was an extra status symbol for the organizers.[29] That the festival was held in the year of Jiashu was not insignificant. A similar year of Jiashu eight centuries ago was identified by the lineages as the time when their founding ancestors initiated the move from northern Guangdong to the delta. It was suggested that the festival be put on a regular basis, to take place every sixty years, in order to link the initial migration with the cycle of cosmic time. In so doing, the historical and cultural consciousness of the mortals projected the significance of their arrival to the realm of divine forces.[30]

Why was the initial arrival of settlers so important to the local elite? It is useful to examine this issue with relation to other activities around the time of the 1814 festival. Large lineages in the older part of the delta, particularly in the county capitals where the seat of the imperial government was located, had claimed vast areas of the sands. Original claimants who petitioned for their reclamation were entitled to tax exemptions and to a fee paid by the cultivators known as the "skeletal fee" (*sha gu*). In addition, they received rents in kind that formed the bulk of a prosperous grain trade in the area. If these rights were contested, establishing the timing of the initial migration and settlement of the lineages in Xiaolan would have been very important. It seems logical to as-sume that the festival was shrewdly used by their elites at the time to give a historical depth to their presence, even though the legitimacy of their claim was questionable.

Amid the floral displays and drink, there were poetry competitions. The winning pieces were hung in front of the local ancestral halls of the lineages hosting the events. These poetry couplets centered on Tao Yuanming, a fourth-century official who retired to the life of a hermit in his chrysanthemum gardens because he refused to serve another master at a time of rapid dynastic transition. The idea of retirement from official life seemed to go against the general interest of a period when the local elites were just about to reach the height of their achievements as literati in the Qing court and when loyalist feelings for the former Ming dynasty, if they had ever existed at all, were long abandoned as a result of the new social mobilities. Granted that there was a history of anti-Manchu sentiments among individual scholars connected with the southern Ming court, their descendants in Xiaolan in the late eighteenth and early nineteenth centuries were entrenched in the bureaucracy.[31] The genealogies of the major lineages, compiled and revised during these centuries, were showing off their literati members. The play on the symbolisms of the chrysanthemum and Tao Yuanming obviously had other references that only became clear in the context of the larger state culture and the developing regional economy.

The chrysanthemum, together with the plum, orchid, and bamboo, was a popular topic of artistic representation among scholars in Xiaolan and elsewhere. Since the Song period, the flower was seen as expressing the ideals of the hermit, the elevated distance of the scholar from mundane political affairs. However, retreat continued to affirm attachment to the imperial order. Participation in the literati culture, even at a distance from the court, was an important asset in local politics, where the authority of the imperial bureaucracy was often brought to bear. In fact, conflicting parties have striven to attach themselves to lineage and community members who had attained the highest academic degrees or political rank in order to influence the local magistrate's decisions.

Furthermore, notions of retreat from the Manchu court of the Qing dynasty carried with them a benign nostalgia toward the imperial lines in the previous dynasties of the Song and the Ming, both overrun by non-Han groups. Such a connection with the past in the early nineteenth century was no longer politically threatening enough to incur official wrath from the Qing court, but the literati pedigree suggested by such sentiments alluded to a long history of settlement and growth of the major lineages. All this might very well come up against similar claims by competitors in the neighboring counties for the rights in the sands.

The fragmented historical materials do not allow us to conjecture about the expansionist motives of the elites in Xiaolan at the time, and it is also difficult to link the festivals directly with the subsequent economic gains by the lineages. However, one at least notes that the festivities provided the setting in which a long history of settlement, lineage power, and literati pretensions were explicitly interlocked. The created nexus was important. Having collectively appropriated the status symbols of a state culture and thus its political connections, the aspiring elites in Xiaolan aggressively claimed the sands from the county magistrates in the name of their lineages and developed them into productive fields. The economic bases of these elites diversified. Some were managers of estates, native bankers, and merchants; but their wealth continued to be firmly tied to the reclamation of the sands, the rent collected from lineage and private estates, and the control of the grain trade, and to be legitimized by their active participation in the cultural discourse of the imperial state.

The history of the He lineage in the nineteenth century shows this trend. He Yanggao (1964), who documents in detail the accelerated pace by which the He lineage acquired land, academic and official titles, and built ancestral halls during that century, concludes that the lineage reached the height of its power at that time. The community as a whole was also gaining attention. The 1827 edition of the Xiangshan county gazetteer recorded that the number of literati in Landu matched that of the rest of the county. It also had one of the two community academies in Xiangshan. In a charitable donation recorded in the same gazetteer, the major lineages (He, Li, Mai), the military colonies (San weisuo), and the Situ (six lesser surnames) each held shares in the endeavor.[32]

The collective ambitions of the local elites in Xiaolan appeared less subtle to their neighbors and to officials sixty years later, when another generation staged the chrysanthemum festival. As before, the centers of activities were the focal ancestral halls. It is not coincidental that the most senior focal ancestral hall of the He lineage, commemorating the grandfather of the two He brothers who settled in Xiaolan, was built the year before. This time, the festivities of the halls were coordinated with those of the major temples patronized by merchants, guilds, and neighborhoods. They unified the participants under a large communal umbrella. The documents recording this festival repeatedly stressed the territorial identity of the town as made up of the major lineages and community temples. Furthermore, local notables congregated in the Lanshan Academy for a town-wide poetry competition and feast. The theme of the poetry competition centered on Zhang Jiuling, a native of northern Guangdong, a prime minister in the Tang dynasty (618–907). He was remembered for his efforts to upgrade a route through the mountain pass separating Guangdong from the central plains that all the major lineages in Guangdong claimed their ancestors had later used to migrate.[33] By insisting that their ancestors belonged to prominent families in the central plains who had migrated southward with the Song court, the local elites in Xiaolan made every pretense on the one hand to dissociate themselves from aboriginal roots and, on the other, to predate their literati pedigree by a few additional centuries.[34]

There were nevertheless a few setbacks to the 1874 festival. A storm destroyed many of the flowers displayed, but more important than that were the issues brought into the open by the festival from the political storm that had been brewing for some time. The former governor-general of Fujian and Zhejiang, a native by the name of He Jing, who happened to be in the area that year, had specifically warned against theatrical performances. His stated reasons were that Emperor Tongzhi's death earlier in the year made such festivities inappropriate and that the entire country, racked by peasant revolts for over a decade, should have time for recuperation, not extravagance.[35] He Jing seemed to attempt to temper parochial interests by a moral dialogue in which the local elites were obliged to engage, but he had a hidden agenda. The opera troupes in Foshan, a regional city to the northeast, had a wide appeal in the Pearl River delta. Organized under a guild and managed by the Jiqing Gongsuo (the guild's contractor office), the troupes traveled in large red boats to various towns and villages in order to perform in temple festivals. Working under harsh conditions and officially discriminated against (they were barred from taking the imperial examinations), the actors congregated with other low-status groups. A few members of the theatrical troupes in Foshan had become leaders in the Red Turban rebellion.[36] From 1854, when the rebellion began, to 1861, when it was stamped out by the government troops, the local society was militarized as well as polarized. The government's general policy of dealing with the widespread peasant rebellions in the mid–nineteenth century by militarizing local society was led by the gentry for self-defense.[37] Sometimes the lineages and their leaders took sides either with the government or with the rebels, and feuded among themselves over land and property. In Xiaolan, for example, those who sided with the rebels (who were stationed in the center of town for months) perished under the government troops, who recovered control. The Xiao lineage of Dalan, whose influence had been dwarfed by the rise of the He lineage in Xiaolan, seized the opportunity provided by the political turnover to acquire the estates of the Mai lineage.[38]

The theatrical troupes in the rebellion lost their guild; the Qinhua Huiguan in Foshan was razed to the ground. Performances in the Pearl River delta were also forbidden until 1867. By the time the Xiaolan elites proposed a new festival, seven years had passed since the prohibition order had been lifted. Local officials appear to have been apprehensive, because the chrysanthemum festival might very well have turned into a subversive platform against the imperial order if lineages feuding over land rights had risen to the occasion. From the official point of view, it was probably a political situation too volatile to allow taking chances. The Xiaolan elites supposedly complied with the prohibition on the operas, though allegorical statements about the difficulties faced by Zhang Jiuling in the Tang court were loudly expressed in the poems chosen as winners in the poetry competition.[39] Moreover, documents recorded that couplets were hung in front of theatrical platforms, indicating that performances were planned and probably given.[40]

The fears of the officials were not entirely ungrounded. From the mid–nineteenth century on, an alliance of local elites in the county capital Shiqi was known to have disputed fiercely with established lineages in the older parts of the delta, such as the Luo and the Long of Shunde County, over the sands bordering the two counties.[41] The position of the elites in Xiaolan was ambiguous. The town was situated next to the disputed area. Administratively, the elites of Shiqi operated in the social and political circles of the provincial capital (Guangzhou) quite unfamiliar to the elites of Xiaolan, who nonetheless identified with the county. Socially, they were closer to the inhabitants of Shunde. Apart from being business and marriage partners, they also shared the same local dialect. There is little documentary evidence that the elites in Xiaolan took sides, but one may assume that any official sensitive to the issue might think twice about encouraging a community-wide festival with invited guests from both areas.

Although lineages continued to be component parts in the chrysanthemum festival in Xiaolan, elite organizations based on territorial bonds were emerging as a vital force, as highlighted by the festival in 1874. The festival marked a phase of new development in the regional economy centering on the sands of southern Shunde and northern Xiangshan, where Xiaolan established itself as a major cultural and marketing center. The second half of the nineteenth century saw an accelerated accumulation of wealth by merchants based on mechanized grain milling, wine making, pig rearing, and cloth and silk trading. Farmers converted the rice fields surrounding the town to mulberry dikes in order to feed an expanding silk-cocoon industry. The leaves and cocoons were sold in specialized markets in Xiaolan and in Rongqi of Shunde.[42] Lineage trusts gradually shifted their rent collection in kind to cash rents, and reinvested them in commercial enterprises in both counties. In cultural tastes and lifestyles, the Xiaolan elites moved closer to those of Shunde and the older part of the delta, although their economic base required continual control over the sands. A well-known example of cultural affinity between Xiaolan and Shunde is the custom of delayed transfer marriage and later of the "marriage resistance" (*zishunu*). In fact, as early as in the 1827 edition of the Xiangshan county gazetteer, the compiler reported that the northern part of the county had acquired the custom of Shunde and that women who married often remained in their natal home for years. Large dowries, often in the form of land or large provisions of grain, were also given by elite families in both areas.[43]

However, the economy became vulnerable to the volatile world market and the political crisis in the early decades of the twentieth century. The imperial order was crumbling. The Qing government was defeated by the Japanese in 1894 and again by an alliance of eight foreign countries during the Boxer rebellion in 1898. In 1905, the imperial examination system was abolished, meaning that the normal channels of mobility for the literati were truncated. In 1911, a group of civil and military strongmen overthrew the dynasty. A republic was set up under Sun Yat-sen, but the country was immediately fragmented by warlords supported by foreign powers. It was not until 1927 that the Nationalist government under Chiang Kai-shek maintained a shaky unity based in Nanjing. However, the Japanese invaded Manchuria in 1931 and by the late 1930s overran most of the country. The major cities of Guangdong were occupied by the Japanese military from 1938 to 1945.[44] Locked into long-term cash rent agreements with their tenant-contractors, who were often local strongmen in the sands, the managers of the lineage estates were ruined by the monetary crises arising from the disintegration of the imperial order.[45] Many ancestral trusts were unable to finance the elaborate lineage ceremonies and stopped the distribution of ritual pork to their members. Local newspapers reported numerous disputes among kinsmen over ancestral land being parceled out and sold.[46] In the areas away from the coast and major cities, local military bosses carved out their own territories and ruled with their guns.[47]

The linkages among those controlling the vast sands, lineage power, and the authority of state culture, built up in the last few centuries and expressed in and reinforced by the previous chrysanthemum festivals, were broken in crucial ways. Under such circumstances, one may wonder why another chrysanthemum festival was proposed in the early 1930s. In fact, the heads of the major lineages were ambivalent about the idea. To use a metaphor, theatrical performances became meaningless when the stage had fallen into disrepair and the actors were unsure of their roles. Nevertheless, the festival was staged in 1934. There was a clear shift not only in the content of the festival, but also in the centers of activities and in the social bases of the leading organizers. Under the directorship of a committee, the town was divided into several neighborhood districts in which festivities were organized. The defining units were no longer the focal ancestral halls. Instead, community temples, which served as public security offices of neighborhoods and were heavily patronized by local military bosses, overshadowed the ancestral halls. They put on the elaborate display of flowers, hired operas from Foshan and Guangzhou, sponsored community exorcism ceremonies, and paraded images of deities along the canal encircling Xiaolan. The latter two activities carried the religious overtone of temple festivals absent in the previous chrysanthemum festivals.

According to the accounts of local newspapers and from interviews of participants in this festival, the opening ceremonies were officially conducted under the auspices of the native place associations in Guangzhou and Hong Kong[48] at two unusual locations. In the morning, the entire organizing committee and their guests met at the Kentang Shushi, a private memorial hall of a Liu family. Events in the afternoon were held at an open ground on the western edge of town, where the largest platform for operas was constructed. The opera troupes were no longer performing the traditional kun qu. Instead, the more parochial Cantonese versions catering to popular taste were given. The head of the organizing committee, He Fangtan, was a former degree holder and a merchant who had also served in the government of the provincial warlords.[49] Prominent overseas merchants and the head of the administrative district that encompassed Xiaolan (a certain Liang Bingyun) made their respective speeches, followed by a selection of the town's senior residents. Those chosen, 240 in all, were later feasted by a merchant of the Li surname, who had returned from Hong Kong. There was also an exhibition, sponsored by the merchants and town government, of modern machinery for silk and grain production. The troops of the military bosses, whose normal duty was to collect fees from tenants in the sands, were stationed in town supposedly to maintain order. During the half-month of activities, thousands of visitors came, some from as far as Guangzhou and Hong Kong. They were easy prey to the troops, who extracted protection fees from them as they had from opera troupes, temples, opium dens, and peddlers of all kinds conducting business at the festival.[50] The three major lineages also displayed floral sets at their focal ancestral halls, but the talk of the town were the independently rich households, which joined in with their own lavishness. One such notable site was Rong Yuan, a garden jointly owned by a certain Liu Rongjie and a Gan Hanchen, both speculators in gold and commodities with financial bases in Guangzhou and Shanghai. An interview with a former gardener of Liu Rongjie reveals that Liu sold a shop in Guangzhou in order to finance his floral displays and his feasting of over a hundred friends and relatives who came from different parts of the delta.

On the whole, the festival in 1934 reflected the disintegration of a core leadership in town, which used to be bolstered by lineage power based on landed wealth and literati prestige. It nevertheless pointed to the rise of a heterogeneous group of local strongmen and overseas merchants who had linked up with provincial warlords and whose organizational bases were community temples and neighborhood associations. These emergent interest groups imposed their own preferences in the 1934 festival. It was their idea to stage the festival. Activities were organized around their power bases and not those of the ancestral halls. From the selection of the operas and exhibitions to the collection of fees and profits, it was clear to all that the carriers of the state literati culture had been replaced by a commercial and militaristic elite whose tastes were shaped by a regional popular culture. This elite had emerged during the early 1930s, when military bosses carved out their spheres of control from the contenders after the fall of the Qing dynasty and when, for the ensuing two decades, what remained of a central government disintegrated in face of the Japanese advances. The local bosses in Xiaolan also reached the height of their power during this period, using the community temples and public security offices that had been the centers of activities in the 1934 festival as their tax-collection and military headquarters.[51]

The socialist revolution brought drastic changes to Xiaolan and its rural hinterland. The Land Reform conducted in 1951 confiscated all the ancestral estates and divided them among the tenant-farmers in the sands. Many of the landlords, estate managers, merchants, and local bosses were killed or severely persecuted. In the 1950s, collectivization and the imposition of state control over prices and marketing shrank the social and economic world of the local residents.[52] Despite its protestations against feudal customs, and actual prohibitions of lineage and temple activities, the town government set up by the Communists did not wait another sixty years to conduct a chrysanthemum festival. In fact, the festival was given three times under very different political circumstances. The first took place in 1959 in commemoration of the tenth anniversary of the founding of the People's Republic. The second one was quietly put on during an ebb in the radicalism of the Cultural Revolution period. The latest and the grandest festival, given in 1979 in an era of economic reform and political liberalization, attracted national and overseas attention.

The schedule of the festival in 1959 was obviously accelerated to fit an important political event of the new government. The festival in 1973 took place in a time of political uncertainty. In the wake of the Cultural Revolution, the Communist Party remained extremely factionalized. People had hardly recovered from the nationwide political witch-hunt when a group of Taiwanese merchants decided to organize an exhibition of chrysanthemums in Hong Kong. In response, the town government hurriedly staged its own in an attempt to reclaim its community symbol. However, a floral display in the shape of "the fairy maiden showering flowers" (*xiannu sanhua*), a symbol of traditional culture, led to a heated debate between factions in the party concerning the proper "political line" (*luxian*). Although the provincial chairman, Chen Yu, who happened to be traveling in the area, gave the go-ahead to the fairy maiden, a floral design in the form of the revolutionary soldier Lei Feng was finally erected to appease the Maoists.

The festival in 1979 was organized by the town government with a different order of magnitude. The decision of the national party to reverse the Maoist politics of the previous decades was confirmed only the year before. The cadres in Xiaolan felt that staging the chrysanthemum festival was useful and appropriate as an event to show the overseas Chinese, potential investors in the new era of economic reforms, that the government was liberalizing in earnest. Addressing the festival largely to the regional and lineage associations overseas, the organizers shrewdly played the "politics of native roots." The festival was unmistakably a government event, organized by an ad hoc committee set up by the town's Party committee. Assignments for cultivating the flowers, coordinating the boat races, and inviting opera troupes from Guangzhou and Foshan were given to various branches of the government, factories, neighborhood committees, and schools. As mentioned earlier, the party leaders sought out former landlords and "literati types" who had known the art of cultivating chrysanthemums and made them train apprentices. National and provincial broadcasting networks were invited to cover the events, emphasizing the intentions for reform among the party leaders. The town government also invited merchants and the heads of native place associations from Hong Kong and Macao to a feast. Forty thousand visitors came for the opening ceremonies. Another hundred thousand followed. The town ran out of food on the first day in spite of the fact that it had mobilized every individual food peddler it could round up. Traffic blocked the badly paved roads for days. However, the trouble seemed to have paid off for most of the residents. Numerous business contracts poured in afterward. The town received enough donations from overseas compatriots to build, for example, a modern hospital, a secondary school, two Hong Kong-style restaurant-discos, and a six-storey hotel named Chrysanthemum Town, an identity Xiaolan and its residents have quickly assumed.[53]

Rethinking Chinese Anthropology

The fact that little justification is needed to adopt a regional analysis in Chinese history and society is largely due to Skinner. His regional systems approach proposes that the political history of dynastic events must be seen as mediated by the rhythms of human interaction deriving from economic transactions on the ground. The regional systems are functionally integrated by exchange relationships. Their growth and decline depend on how people make use of the material environment, with a given technology based on cost-distance calculations and a government providing different degrees of administrative efficiency. At the subcounty level, which the formal state apparatus has not reached, the dynamics of local society are governed by the strategies of rural marketing. It is upon this economic skeleton that the social communities, the parapolitical and culture-bearing units, are built.

In examining the evolution of a region in which Xiaolan is a part, community building seems to involve more than what is suggested by Skinner. The initial settlement of the sands was shaped by the operational logic of the social institutions already well entrenched in the regional core. Local society in the making undoubtedly had involved shrewd economic calculations, but only in the context of social differentiation, unequal access to power, and cultural exclusion. The development of Xiaolan into a supercenter of wealth and culture and a major marketing center was based on how much its local strongmen were able to maneuver with resources in the larger society in order to exploit and sustain these relationships. The ritual complex, in which the chrysanthemum festivals were an integral part, reflected and advanced these motivations.

Skinner may have provided an economic skeleton for viewing the formation of regional marketing systems, but if we are to understand the dynamic aspects of the body politic, the social cells, and the cultural tissues representing power and domination as much as providing room for maneuver, must be seen not as colorful frills decorating the description of a historical process, but as an integral part of the analysis of its unfolding. To debate whether a Skinnerian analysis can be applied to other parts of China, if not the sands of Guangdong, or whether the macroregions were discrete or integrative misses the point.[54] A history structured by the cycles of regional development should take into account the cultural dynamics underlying the very construction of the regional systems themselves.[55]

At a level of society where the formal apparatus of the state was largely absent, it is useful to examine Xiaolan's social organizations in order to understand the nature of the nucleus of power the elites in the town represented and exerted over the sands. Domination is seldom based on direct coercion. The question is how power has been institutionalized in the everyday social living in Xiaolan.[56]

Because the major actors in Xiaolan's ritual complex were the powerful lineages, Maurice Freedman's lineage model may be used to supply the missing element in Skinner's analysis. He focused on the lineage community, a nucleated settlement of agnates tracing unilineal descent from a focal ancestor, tied together by ancestral trusts, and expressing their solidarities through periodic rituals at the ancestral graves and halls. The imposing presence of the lineage communities was reinforced by their educated members, who compiled genealogies that claimed descent from imperial officials from centuries past and showed off numerous literati among the ranks of their contemporaries. Freedman also observed that asymmetrical segmentation took place in the development of these lineages. Lines without descendants or estates eventually dropped out of sight in the records. His basic assumptions were that lineage formation in south China depended on several factors: a frontier with a need for protection, a river delta requiring organization of large-scale irrigation projects, and rice cultivation offering substantial accumulation of wealth for selected members. This functionalist assumption has taken for granted the a priori existence of such a cultural ideal. It has also led some later scholars to suggest the extreme—that a lineage without corporate property is no lineage at all.[57]

Initially, it may be difficult to doubt that the three major lineages in Xiaolan constituted dominant communities whose focal ancestors had carried with them the Chinese cultural ideals that found favorable niches in the sands. Almost as a corollary, the realization of the kinship ideal was a useful means for aggressive expansion on the rural landscape, but the process is historically specific. David Faure argues that the political privileges of shared status with the literati during the Ming dynasty concurred with the flourishing of elaborate estates and ancestral halls, their founders tracing origin to leading scholar-officials (Faure 1989). Moreover, the open and rapid accumulation of wealth through the reclamation of the sands around Xiaolan, unlike the environment for lineage building of the more recognized kind in the older parts of the Pearl River delta, allowed a proliferation of ancestral estates and halls. The streets of Xiaolan were lined with ancestral halls of the study–chamber kind, built by wealthy individuals to commemorate immediate family members. While in theory every lineage member began a new descent line and every estate started a lineage organization in which descendants claimed a share in the property, the proliferation of these estates led to an actual "devolution" of the lineage structure in Xiaolan. This ran counter to the need for a collective umbrella with official blessings in order to maintain control of the sands.

The structural tension was relieved by a rich ritual complex. The wealthy in Xiaolan did not lack rituals to make their presence felt in the local environment. There were the community rituals based on local temples and the kinship rituals of the focal ancestral and private memorial halls. By late imperial times, literati input was prominent in local cultural dialogue. The activities surrounding the chrysanthemum could very well have been the crucial integrating factor for the various local interests and concerns. In other words, the festivals presented a visible public culture and a coordinated theater of power.

If lineage building on the sands was fraught with internal contradictions and required extra cultural inputs in the form of the festivals, one should reexamine the functionalist assumption in Freedman's process of lineage formation. To approach the problem historically, Freedman's lineage model is useful for understanding the materials of Xiaolan if one assumes that the inhabitants in south China took the Han culture tradition for granted. All the genealogies of the major lineages in Xiaolan (and also in the delta) claimed that their ancestors had migrated from the central plains, where the Chinese civilization was well established, but it is known that historically native populations were inhabiting the area long before any massive land migrations. A recent paper written by David Faure (1989) triggers my suspicions of the origin of the culture-bearers in Xiaolan. He argues that it was in response to a certain tax in the Ming dynasty that the local populations of Guangdong differentiated themselves into the Yao and the Han Chinese, depending on whether they paid the tax or not. Subsequently, the sedentary agriculturalists acquired the cultural priorities of the expanding Chinese state in the plains, whereas the Yao retained the tribal organizations in the hills of northern Guangdong. It also seems more than coincidental that the major lineages in Xiaolan practised the delayed transfer marriage (*buluojia*), with its close parallels to the marriage customs of the hill tribes from southwest to southeastern China.[58] They also insisted that they were Han precisely because of the marriage custom, whereas the Dan, referred to as an inferior group, did not practise it. The question is: did the powerful lineages in Xiaolan originate in the upwardly mobile strata of the native populations who had separated themselves from a marginalized population they referred to as the "Dan out there in the sands"? If that was the case, can one interpret the unusually aggressive institutions of lineage and the rich ritual complex in Xiaolan not entirely as established cultural ends that the economy of the sands had made possible, but as a means through which the local populations excluded others in the process of incorporating themselves into the larger Chinese polity? One does not have to deny Freedman's assumption that lineage building has arisen from functional human propensities, but one should allow room for the history of cultural fusion in which the moral prerogatives of the imperial state were improvised by various social strata to shape the unfolding of the local society.[59] In sum, the language of the Chinese lineage should be historically contextualized.

By stressing cultural discourse as central to state–society relationships in Xiaolan, I can build upon the vast literature on Chinese rituals. Wolf has described the supernatural categories of gods, ghosts, and ancestors in Chinese popular religion as replicating the imperial bureaucracy, the village vagabond, and the senior members of one's line of descent. Underlying these categories and their associated rituals are the peasants' view of the relationships of power, social distance, and affinity. If one accepts the notion that societies are seldom in a state of timeless equilibrium, then how are the meanings embodied in rituals created, maintained, and changed to inform a shared cultural consciousness? To appreciate the nuances embodied in the inherent complexities of any social situation, it is important to ground the ritual activities in the cultural histories of local communities. If power is at stake, who competes for it? On what bases do the participants put forth their claims? For what purposes do they attempt to seize or contest power? How do they make their hidden agendas understood, and what are the means of containment and subversion? By sensitizing oneself to these questions, one may improve on a mechanical "culture as reflection of society" approach on the one hand and, on the other, avoid the danger of improvising on seemingly eternal epistemological and symbolic categories. Instead, one can conceptually integrate cultural dialogue with the evolution of the regional political economy and ask: at the end of the long acculturation process from which a complex state agrarian society emerges, when is a local society most able, on its own terms, to adopt and penetrate an encroaching state culture?

The festivals in Xiaolan did form a unifying thread in the transformation of the relationship between local society and the centers of power. The festivals had created for the participants specific social identities and historical consciousness to which successive generations have attached their own self-interested readings. Strongmen ascending onto the local political stage in the Ming and Qing dynasties actively appropriated the cultural symbols of the larger polity to anchor themselves. When the imperial order became shaky in its foundations in the early twentieth century, a new stratum of local elites rose to the occasion. They too formed groups and recycled the available cultural resources. Competition became multifaceted, with authority and its material gains "up for grabs." Local initiative was given full reign. In the postrevolutionary period, the relationship has been reversed. A powerful socialist state recycled what had become a local tradition of festivals to serve its political goals. In sum, the three sets of local elites contributed to a continuing tradition and a process of change. In establishing themselves, they facilitated the downward percolation of a state culture to make local society.

In an effort to understand how and why the chrysanthemum has informed cultural identity in Xiaolan, past and present, I supplement Skinner's structured history with notions of culture and power. I put Freedman's language of lineage in the context of a history of acculturation and add political nuances to Wolf's ritual representations. I have tried to present a meaning-centered and historically grounded account of cultural change that captures the breadth of lived experience in rural south China. In complex agrarian societies, where hierarchies of power and diverse bases of authority exist and are often contested, stability rests on the ways local elites anchor themselves in relation to the community and to the larger state order. In late imperial China, the literati culture, lineage and community institutions, popular religion, all served to legitimize the state and the peoples' respective places in relation to it. The percolation of these values to everyday life was an important aspect of state making; through the centuries, the state became an administrative machinery as much as a cultural idea. Elites and commoners engaged themselves in numerous arenas and discourses to shape this process. The chrysanthemum festivals of Xiaolan are such arenas. Using them to highlight the junctures of meaning, interest, and power, I stress the point that historical processes are constructed by culturally creative human agents. Together, their actions form the flux of social life that continues to inform and structure experience.

NOTES

This paper is based on research conducted in South China in 1986, funded by the Committee on Scholarly Communication with the People's Republic of China. The author would like to thank the following: Jack Goody, Raymond Grew, William Kelly, Frederic Wakeman, the anonymous reader, colleagues in the Anthropology Department at Yale University, and members of the Ethnohistory Seminar at the University of Pennsylvania, for their thoughtful comments.

1. Mai 1948; this author's translation quoted from a diary of his great-grandfather, Mai Pingde, who lived from the end of the eighteenth century to the mid–nineteenth century.

2. During the early Ming period, soldiers were discharged and assigned with their families to settle in frontier areas. They held military household registrations (*jun ji*) and formed colonies with headquarters often at Guandi temples (the god of war). In Xiaolan and vicinity, there were eighteen colonies, each centered at a Guandi temple. In 1986, I

discovered a stone tablet at the site of a former Beidi temple (the headquarters of all these colonies) listing them.

3. The color yellow symbolizes prosperity, longevity, and imperial mandate.

4. I define literati as scholars who acquired academic degrees in the state examination system in imperial China.

5. After the Song dynasty (A.D. 960–1279), administrators of the empire were mostly recruited through a system of civil service examinations. Candidates were required to submit essays which were judged by the education administrators. Based on these evaluations, the candidates were given academic degrees. Examinations were conducted every two or three years at the levels of county, province, and the imperial capital. Graduates of the metropolitan examinations, who acquired the degree of *jinshi,* were eligible for official assignments. Those who gained academic titles or official posts were listed prominently in lineage genealogies and county gazetteers.

6. See Ortner (1984) for a summary of anthropology theories since the 1960s.

7. See Wolf (1982) and Seddon (1978) for a summary of the works of the French Marxists; for a critical summary, see Donham (1990).

8. See Rosaldo (1980), Hobsbawm and Ranger (1983).

9. See the works of Foucault on power (for example, 1977) and Gramsci (1971) on hegemony, Evans et al. (1985) on the crucial role of the state. For voices of subversion and their containment, see the works of Davis (1975), Thompson (1978), Le Roy Ladurie (1979), and Stallybrass and White (1986) on Bakhtin.

10. See Moore and Myerhoff (1977), Geertz (1983).

11. See Abrams (1982), Bourdieu (1977); see also Ortner (1984) on the theory of practice.

12. See Perdue (1982) on the building of polders around Lake Dongting.

13. For studies of the Dan fishermen in south China, see Ward (1985b), Chen (1946), and Murray (1987).

14. The basic unit for the measurement of land in the sands was *qing,* a hundred *mu.* One mu is approximately one-sixth of an acre.

15. The houses in the sands were made of straw and mud. During the land reform in the early 1950s, the households identified as landlords had nothing more than a tiled roof over their straw huts. Cadres reported to me in 1986 that they were not able to make the peasants in the sands build brick houses and form more nucleated settlements until the 1970s.

16. According to He (1946, 1964), the major lineages in Xiaolan started gaining titles in the Ming dynasty, but the majority were acquired after mid-Qing, reaching a height in the mid–nineteenth century. He actually compiled the biographies of everyone who, to his knowledge, gained a title. The most notable ones, Li Sunchen and He Wuzhou, whose biographies can also be found in the county gazetteers of Xiangshan, attained the post of ministers near the end of the Ming dynasty.

17. The local historian, He Yanggao, traces his origin to Xiwan Tang, the focal ancestral hall of a He lineage in Xiaolan. The He supposedly descended from two

brothers who settled in Xiaolan. Xiwan Tang is the hall for the younger brother. The lineage is larger than the one descended from the older brother, whose hall was named Liuqing Tang. He Yanggao is able to count eleven other ancestral halls built by different generations under the Xiwan Tang from which he can claim direct descent and benefits.

18. The Liuqing Tang had only about three qing of land. The Xiwan Tang had over ten qing.

19. There is a vast literature on how lineage ideals find their expressions in southern China and their relationship with corporate property. See the works of Maurice Freedman (1958, 1966) and scholars who more or less use his paradigm, such as James Watson (1977, 1982), Rubie Watson (1985), Potter (1970), Baker (1966, 1968), Strauch (1983). Faure (1986) on the other hand stresses the issues of community and settlement rights intertwined with the lineage ideal, and offers a revision of the Freedman paradigm.

20. Studies of such connections in other parts of China and in other periods of history are numerous. See Dennerline (1981), Ebrey and Watson (1986), Beattie (1979), Rowe (1984), and Hymes (1986). However, they should be contrasted with the area of the Pearl River delta where lineage and literati power were built literally "on the sands" and reached their peak in the late nineteenth century. Their development should also be contrasted with the shifting of control to more fluid local power bases in the early twentieth century as described by Rankin (1986), Duara (1988), and Huang (1985).

21. As will be shown later, the extremely prominent role of these lineages in community affairs should be contrasted with those in north China, as analysed by Duara (1988) and Cohen (1989), and in the older parts of the Pearl River delta and Hong Kong, as described by Freedman (1958, 1966).

22. The five major temples as identified by the residents are the Guanyin temple of Situ neighborhood in the southwest, the Beidi temple of Jiaokou neighborhood in the east, the Miaoling Gong of Dalan District in the northwest, the Beidi temple of Jitou village in the southeast, and Shifu temple in the northeastern part of town.

23. *Chu se,* as the processions are generally termed, is a common festivity among communities in the Pearl River delta. Among the famous ones are the *Qiu se* (Autumn Varieties) of Foshan, the *Piao se* (Floating Varieties) of Shawan, and the *Shui se* (Water Varieties) of Xiaolan.

24. Many neighborhoods were often made up of a single surname, but the Situ neighborhood was inhabited by six surnames centering on the Guanyin temple. The Beidi temple of Jiaokou, once the headquarters of the military colonies in the Ming dynasties, and the Guandi temples in town were patronized by residents registered as military households.

25. Older residents of Xiaolan can recite the rhymes used to ridicule the jiao at Jiuzhouji.

26. Lanxiang Gongyue was established by the town's three major lineages in the reign of Qianlong (A.D. 1736–1796) for the purpose of civil and political arbitrations. A detailed description can be found in a manuscript by a local historian, He Yanggao (He

1964). The Lanshan Academy, established by the county magistrate in 1740 to promote local education, was financed by the three major lineages and the military colonies in 1749. In 1756 and 1815, the county magistrate assigned to it additional river marshes in the southeast. The academy was supervised by imperial degree holders. See He (1984). See also the genealogies of the He, Li, and Mai lineages for their degree holders. There were only a few for the Ming dynasty, but by the mid-Qing there were many who were graduates of the metropolitan examinations.

27. See He (1946). Li Sunchen was a member of the eleventh generation of the Li Guang military colony. After he became a member of the imperial academy (*Hanlin*) and later assumed the post of minister in Nanjing, the status of the colony was converted to a civil one. The focal ancestral hall of the Li lineage, built during the reign of Qianlong in the eighteenth century, was named after him as Li Shangshu Da Zongci. The Taining Daoguo Tang, a temple exclusively used by the Li lineage members who traced their place of origin from Taining, was another center of activity for the Li lineage in Xiaolan.

28. See He Wuzhou in Xu Xu (1984). See also the He lineage genealogies of Xiaolan (1907). He Wuzhou belonged to the thirteenth generation of the lineage of the younger brother (Xiwan Tang) and was a contemporary of Li Sunchen and Wu Ruilong, both high-ranking officials of late Ming. They were members of a literary club in Xiaolan known as the Wenhong She. The reason for He's death was not known, but it was believed that he was killed in Guangzhou when the Qing army overwhelmed the last of the southern Ming emperors. His ancestral hall was named He Neige Da Zongci.

29. See *Lingnan gujinshi* (Xu Xu 1984) for the different types of Cantonese operas. See also the works of Tanaka Issei (1981, 1985) and Ward (1985a) on the religious operas in Guangdong.

30. In Chinese culture, the sixty years signifies the completion of a full circle of human affairs in accordance with cosmic forces.

31. He Yuechao, a local poet and son of He Wuzhou, was murdered by his own kinsmen for expressing anti-Manchu sentiments in his poetry.

32. I thank Dr. Choi Chi-cheung for sharing historical insights on Xiaolan and Dalan with me; and Anthony Siu for a family division document of the Xiao in Dalan, dated 1877.

33. A rare manuscript map drawn by a European missionary in the 1860s on the Bei River of northern Guangdong actually located the sites through which Zhang Jiuling had supposedly traveled. See Eberhart (1962) on the myths of settlement; see also the lineage genealogies from He (1907, 1925), Li (1914), Mai (1893), among others which reported similar myths. Such a claim was not limited to the lineages in Xiaolan, but common to many others in the Pearl River delta.

34. It is a common practice of the compilers of lineage genealogies to search backward in time to locate relationships with prominent "ancestors," however tenuously linked, in order to boost lineage status. Claims before the Song dynasty are not reliable. Historical documents since the Tang had described the residents of Lingnan, that is,

most of Guangdong and Guanxi, as Yao, Zhuang, Dan fishermen, and Han migrants. Also there are descriptions of political brokers known as the *haoli* (local bosses). See Tsang (1973), Wang (1981), and Qu Dajun (1700).

35. He was referring to the Taipings and the Red Turbans in the 1850s. See He (1964) on He Jing. See "Xiaolan zhenzhi" (1984) on the occupation of the town by the Red Turbans.

36. See articles on Cantonese operas and Li Wenmu in *Foshan wenshi ziliao,* volumes 2, 3, and 4.

37. See Kuhn (1971) on the formation of local defense corps led by the gentry. See also Wakeman (1966).

38. See a nineteenth-century collection of the land deeds of the Xiao lineage of Dalan being compiled by Anthony Siu (n.d.).

39. The allegorical style is a convention in Chinese literati writing.

40. See *Zhongshang Lanzheng juhuahui wenyi gailan* (1936).

41. See Siu (1989a, chap. 2) on the disputes on Donghai Shiliusha. The dispute lasted fifty years and cumulated in the government making a decision in favor of the Shunde elites who organized the region's bureau for the protection of the sands (a tax and surcharge collection agency). See also Nishigawa (1985), Matsuda (1981), Katayama (1982) on gentry power in the sands. See *Dongguan xianzhi* (1922) on disputes involving Wanqingsha to the east of Xiaolan.

42. There were two mulberry markets (*sangshi*) in Xiaolan and a cocoon market (*jianshi*) in Rongqi.

43. See analyses of this custom in Topley (1975), Stockard (1989), Siu (1990b).

44. See Qin (1983) on the financial crisis of Guangdong from 1911 to 1949.

45. In the Republican period, many of the local strongmen were tenant-contractors and tax farmers. They secured the rental of land from the ancestral estates by paying advanced cash rent and sizable rent deposits and then extracted rent and surcharges in kind from their own tenants.

46. Traditionally, ancestral estates were forbidden to be sold. For reports of these legal disputes, see *Zhongshan guomin ribao* in the 1930s and 1940s.

47. For a general description of the local bosses, see Alitto (1979). For north China in the 1930s, see Duara (1988), Huang (1985). For the Pearl River delta, see Siu (1989a, chap. 5).

48. These associations were formed by emigrants overseas who used a surname or a place of origin as organizational bases. Their functions are generally social, such as mutual help and charity. They can also become political in terms of defending the interests of their members against the pressures from the host society, and supporting particular regimes in China.

49. See a short biography of him written by He Yanggao (1987).

50. The local bosses reached the height of their power during the Japanese occupation in the late 1930s and the early 1940s. Yuan Dai and Qu Renze were two such local bosses linked to the provincial warlords.

51. In some cases, they stationed troops in the smaller ancestral halls. They could have forcibly acquired the halls from the owners, but they could also be members of a lineage who colluded with hall managers. I could not find out how many ancestral halls were taken apart and building materials sold, but in Shawan, a similar town in the sands of the neighboring Panyu County, many halls were dismantled by local bosses during the Japanese occupation (Siu 1990a).

52. For a history of the transformation of the town, see Siu (1989b); for the restrictions on popular rituals, see Siu (1989c). For a longer study of the western part of the Pearl River delta, see Siu (1989a).

53. The name was invented by the media during the 1959 festival.

54. See the debate between Sands and Myers (1986) and Little and Esherick (1989) in the *Journal of Asian Studies.*

55. As previously shown by the study of Prasenjit Duara for north China (1988), one needs to rethink the logic of rural marketing and community organization if we argue that culture and power have significant roles to play.

56. For comparative purposes, see Steven Lukes (1978) for a summary of the concepts of power and authority. See Clifford Geertz (1983) and Michael Gilsenan (1986) for Weberian applications. While Geertz takes off in a culturalist direction to examine the symbolic processes of making authority, Gilsenan points to their political/economic bases. In Skinner's construction of the regional systems, these conceptual elements are missing.

57. See Potter (1970) and a counterargument by Strauch (1983); see a summary of different views by Watson (1982).

58. In the delayed transfer marriage, the marrying couples are often very young. After the first night, the women return to their natal homes and only visit the husbands' household periodically. Not until they are about to give birth to their first child do they settle permanently in their husbands' home. See Topley (1975), Stockard (1989), and Siu (1990b) on issues for debate.

59. See Siu (1989a, chap. 3; 1990b) for a full treatment of this issue.

REFERENCES

Abrams, Philip. 1982. *Historical Sociology.* Ithaca: Cornell University Press.

Ahern, Emily. 1981. *Chinese Rituals and Politics.* Cambridge: Cambridge University Press.

Alitto, Guy. 1979. "Rural Elites in Transition: China's Cultural Crisis and the Problem of Legitimacy," in *Select Papers from the Center for Far Eastern Studies,* Susan Jones, ed., 218–75. Chicago: Center for Far Eastern Studies, University of Chicago.

Baker, Hugh. 1966. "The Five Great Clans of the New Territories." *Journal of the Hong Kong Branch of the Royal Asiatic Society,* vol. 6, 25–47.

————. 1968. *A Chinese Lineage: Sheung Shui.* London: Frank Cass.

Beattie, Hilary. 1979. *Land and Lineage in China: A Study of T'ung Ch'eng County, Anhwei, in the Ming and Ch'ing Dynasties.* Cambridge: Cambridge University Press.

Bourdieu, P. 1977. *Outline of a Theory of Practice.* R. Nice, trans. Cambridge: Cambridge University Press.

Chen, Lu. 1981. *Lingnan xinyu* (New Items on Lingnan). Hong Kong: Shanghai Books.

Chen Xujing. 1946. *Danjia yanjiu.* Canton.

Choi, Chi-Cheung. 1987. "Descent Group Unification and Segmentation in the Coastal Area of Southern China." Vols. 1, 2. Ph.D. Disser., Department of Oriental Studies, Tokyo University.

Cohen, Myron L. 1989. "Cultural Identity and National Identity in China." Paper presented to the Workshop on the Construction of Chinese Cultural Identity, Institute of Culture and Communication, East-West Center, Honolulu, Hawaii, August 25–29.

Davis, N. Z. 1975. *Society and Culture in Early Modern France.* Stanford: Stanford University Press.

Dennerline, Jerry. 1981. *The Chia-ting Loyalists: Confucian Leadership and Social Change in Seventeenth-Century China.* New Haven: Yale University Press.

Dongguan xianzhi (Dongguan County Gazetteer). 1922.

Donham, Donald. 1990. *History, Power, and Ideology: Central Issues in Marxist Anthropology.* Cambridge: Cambridge University Press.

Duara, Prasenjit. 1988. *Culture, Power, and the State: Rural North China, 1900–1942.* Stanford: Stanford University Press.

Eberhard, Wolfram. 1962. *Social Mobility in Traditional China.* Leiden: E. Brill.

Ebrey, Patricia; and James Watson, ed. 1986. *Kinship Organization in Late Imperial China, 1000–1960.* Berkeley: University of California Press.

Evans, Peter; Dietrich Rueschemeyer; Theda Skocpol, ed. 1985. *Bringing the State Back In.* Cambridge: Cambridge University Press.

Faure, David. 1986. *The Structure of Chinese Rural Society.* Hong Kong: Oxford University Press.

————. 1989. "The Lineage as a Cultural Invention: The Case of the Pearl River Delta." *Modern China,* 15:1, 4–36.

Foshan wenshi ziliao (The Cultural History of Foshan), n.d. Vols. 2, 3, and 4.

Foucault, Michel. 1977. *Discipline and Punish: The Birth of the Prison.* London: Penguin.

Freedman, Maurice. 1958. *Lineage Organization in Southeastern China.* London: Athlone Press.

————. 1966. *Chinese Lineage and Society: Fukien and Kwangtung.* London: Athlone Press.

Geertz, Clifford. 1983. "Centers, Kings, and Charisma: Reflections on the Symbolics of Power," in Geertz, *Local Knowledge,* 121–46. New York: Basic.

Gilsenan, Michael. 1986. "Domination as Social Practice: Patrimonialism in North Lebanon: Arbitrary Power, Desecration, and the Aesthetics of Violence." *Critique of Anthropology,* 6:1, 17–37.

Gramsci, Antonio. 1971. *Selections from the Prison Notebooks (1929–35).* Quentin Hoare and Geoffrey Nowell Smith, ed. and trans. New York: International.

He, Lizai. 1870s. "Lanxie" (Slivers of Xiaolan). Manuscript.

He Shi Jiulang zupu (The He "Jiulang" Lineage Genealogy). 1925. Reprinted in Hong Kong.

He Xiwan Tang chongxiu zupu (A Renewed Lineage Genealogy of the He Xiwan Trust). 1907.

He Yanggao. 1946. "Lanxi zaji" (Recollections of Lanxi). Manuscript.

———. 1964. "Ju wuo suo zhi Zhongshan Xiaolan zhen He zu lidai de fajia shi ji qita youguan ziliao" (What I Know of the History of the Growth of the He Lineage of Xiaolan, and Other Materials). Manuscript.

———. 1984. "Lanshan shuyuan xingge shilüe" (A Brief History of the Lanshan Academy). *Zhongshan wenshi,* vol. 4, 96–98.

———. 1987. "He Naizhong xiaozhuan" (A Brief Biography of He Naizhong). *Zhongshan wenshi,* vol. 11, 71–72.

He Yuechao. n.d. "Yuechao shiji" (Poetry Collection of Yuechao). Manuscript.

Hobsbawm, Eric; and Terence Ranger. 1983. *The Invention of Tradition.* Cambridge: Cambridge University Press.

Huang, Philip. 1985. *The Peasant Economy and Social Change in North China.* Stanford: Stanford University Press.

Hymes, Robert. 1986. *Statesmen and Gentlemen: The Elites of Fu-chou, Chiang-hsi, in Northern and Southern Sung.* Cambridge: Cambridge University Press.

Katayama, Tsuyoshi. 1982. "Shinmatsu Kōtōshō Shukō deruta no zukōsei ni tsuite—zeiro, koseki, dōzoku" (The Subcounty Administrative Divisions, Tax Accounts, and Lineages in the Pearl River Delta). *Tōyō gakuhō,* 63:3–4, 1–34.

Kuhn, Philip. 1971. *Rebellion and Its Enemies in Late Imperial China.* Cambridge, Mass.: Harvard University Press.

Le Roy Ladurie, Emmanuel. 1979. *Carnival in Romans.* New York: G. Braziller.

Little, Daniel; and Joseph Esherick. 1989. "Testing the Testers: A Reply to Barbara Sands and Ramon Myers's Critique of G. William Skinner's Regional Systems Approach to China." *Journal of Asian Studies,* 48:1 (February), 91–99.

Lukes, Steven. 1978. "Power and Authority," in *A History of Sociological Analysis.* Tom Bottomore and Robert Nisbet, eds., 633–76. New York: Basic Books.

Lu Yun Shanfang Jushi. [1814] 1936. "Jujing huiji" (Recollections along the Chrysanthemum Path), in *Zhongshan Lanzheng juhuahui wenyi gailan.* Guangzhou.

Mai, Yingyang. 1948. "Lanxiang juhua dahui yuanliu kao" (The Origin of the Chrysanthemum Festivals in Lanxiang). *Kaiming bao,* February 2, p. 5.

Matsuda, Yoshiro. 1981. "Minatsu Shinsho Kanton deruta no shatan kaihatsu to kyōshin shihai no kesei katei" (Rural Gentry Control and the Development of the Sands in the Pearl River Delta in the late Ming and the early Qing). *Shakai keizai shigaku,* 46:6, 55–81.

Moore, Sally F.; and Barbara Myerhoff. 1977. *Secular Ritual.* Amsterdam: Van Gorcum.

Murray, Dian. 1987. *Pirates of the South China Coast, 1790–1810.* Stanford: Stanford University Press.

Nishigawa, Kikuko. [1981] 1985. "Qingdai Zhujiang sanjiaozhou shatian kao" (A Study of the Sands of the Pearl River Delta). Cao Lei, trans. *Lingnan wenshi,* vol. 2, 11–22. Reprint of *Tōyō gakuhō,* 63:1–2, 93–136.

Ortner, Sherry. 1984. "Theory in Anthropology since the Sixties." *Comparative Studies in Society and History,* 26:1, 126–66.

Perdue, Peter. 1982. "Official Goals and Local Interests: Water Control in the Dongting Lake Region during the Ming and Qing Periods." *Journal of Asian Studies,* vol. 4, 747–66.

Potter, Jack. 1970. "Land and Lineage in Traditional China," in *Family and Kinship in Chinese Society.* Maurice Freedman, ed. Stanford: Stanford University Press.

Qin, Qingjun. 1983. "Minguo shiqi Guangdong caizheng shiliao 1911–1949" (A History of the Finance Administration of Guangdong, 1911–1949), in *Guangzhou wenshi ziliao,* vol. 29, 1–115. Guangzhou: Guangdong Sheng Zhengxie.

Qu Dajun. [1700] 1985. *Guangdong xinyu* (New Items on Guangdong). Reprint. Beijing: Zhonghua Shuju.

Rankin, Mary. 1986. *Elite Activism and Political Transformation in China: Zhejiang Province, 1865–1911.* Stanford: Stanford University Press.

Rosaldo, Renato. 1980. *Ilongot Headhunting 1883–1974.* Stanford: Stanford University Press.

Rowe, William. 1984. *Hankow: Commerce and Society in a Chinese City, 1796–1889.* Stanford: Stanford University Press.

Sands, Barbara; and Ramon Myers. 1986. "The Spatial Approach to History: A Test." *Journal of Asian Studies,* vol. 4, 721–44.

Sangren, Steven. 1987. *History and Magical Power in a Taiwanese Community.* Stanford: Stanford University Press.

Seddon, David, ed. 1978. *Relations of Production: Marxist Approaches to Economic Anthropology.* Helen Lackner, trans. London: Frank Cass.

Siu, Anthony. n.d. "Nineteenth-Century Collection of the Land Deeds of the Xiao Lineage in Dalan." Compilation work in progress.

Siu, Helen. 1989a. *Agents and Victims in South China: Accomplices in Rural Revolution.* New Haven: Yale University Press.

———. 1989b. "Socialist Peddlers and Princes in a Chinese Market Town." *American Ethnologist,* 16:2, 195–212.

———. 1989c. "Reforming Tradition: Politics and Popular Rituals in Contemporary Rural China," in *Unofficial China: Popular Culture and Thought in the People's Republic.* Perry Link, Richard Madsen, Paul Pickowicz, eds. Boulder: Westview.

————. 1990. "Where Were the Women? Rethinking Marriage Resistance and Regional Culture in South China." *Late Imperial China,* 11:2, 32–62.

————. 1995. "Subverting Lineage, Power: Local Bosses and Territorial Control in the 1940s," in *Down to Earth: The Territorial Bond in South China,* David Faure and Helen F. Siu, eds. 188–208. Stanford: Stanford University Press.

Skinner, G. William. 1964. "Marketing and Social Structure in Rural China." *Journal of Asian Studies,* 24:1, 3–43; 24:2, 195–228; 24:3, 363–99.

————. 1971. "Chinese Peasants and the Closed Community: An Open and Shut Case." *Comparative Studies in Society and History,* 13:3, 270–81.

————. 1985. "Presidential Address: The Structure of Chinese History." *Journal of Asian Studies,* 104:2, 271–92.

Stallybrass, Peter; and Allon White. 1986. *The Politics and Poetics of Transgression.* Ithaca: Cornell University Press.

Stockard, Janice. 1989. *Daughters of the Canton Delta: Marriage Patterns and Economic Strategies in South China, 1860–1931.* Stanford: Stanford University Press.

Strauch, Judith. 1983. "Community and Kinship in Southeastern China: The View of the Multi-lineage Village of Hong Kong." *Journal of Asian Studies,* 103:1, 21–50.

Tanaka, Issei. 1981. *Chūgoku saishi engeki kenkyū* (A Study of Chinese Ritual and Theater). Tokyo: Institute of Oriental Culture, University of Tokyo.

————. 1985. "The Social and Historical Context of Ming-China Chinese Local Drama," in *Popular Culture in Late Imperial China,* David Johnson, Andrew Nathan, and Evelyn Rawski, eds. Berkeley: University of California Press.

Thompson, E. P. 1978. "Eighteenth-Century English Society: Class Struggle without Class." *Social History,* 3:2, 133–65.

Topley, Marjorie. 1975. "Marriage Resistance in Rural Kwangtung," in *Women in Chinese Society,* Margery Wolf and Roxanne Witke, eds., 67–88. Stanford: Stanford University Press.

Tsang, Wah-moon. 1973. *The Centrality of Development of Lingnan in T'ang Dynasty.* Hong Kong: Chinese University Press.

Wakeman, Frederic. 1966. *Strangers at the Gate: Social Disorder in South China, 1839–1861.* Berkeley: University of California Press.

Wang, Shixing. [Ming Dynasty] 1981. *Guang zhiyi* (A Gazetteer of Guangdong). Reprint. Beijing: Zhonghua Shuju.

Ward, Barbara. 1985a. "Regional Operas and Their Audiences: Evidence from Hong Kong," in *Popular Culture in Late Imperial China,* David Johnson, Andrew Nathan, and Evelyn Rawski, eds. Berkeley: University of California Press.

————. 1985b. "Varieties of the Conscious Model: The Fishermen of South China," in *Through Other Eyes,* Barbara Ward, ed., 41–60. Hong Kong: Chinese University of Hong Kong. Reprinted from *The Relevance of Models for Social Anthropology,* Michael Benton, ed. London: Tavistock, 1965.

Watson, James. 1977. "Hereditary Tenancy and Corporate Landlordism in Traditional China." *Modern Asian Studies,* vol. 11, 161–82.

———. 1982. "Chinese Kinship Reconsidered: Anthropological Perspectives on Historical Research." *China Quarterly,* vol. 92, 589–627.

———. 1985. "Standardizing the Gods: The Promotion of T'ien Hou (Empress of Heaven) along the South China Coast 960–1960," in *Popular Culture in Late Imperial China,* David Johnson, Andrew Nathan, and Evelyn Rawski, eds. Berkeley: University of California Press.

Watson, James; and Evelyn Rawski, ed. 1988. *Death Rituals in Late Imperial and Modern China.* Berkeley: University of California Press.

Watson, Rubie. 1985. *Inequality among Brothers: Class and Kinship in South China.* Cambridge: Cambridge University Press.

Wolf, Arthur. 1974. "Gods, Ghosts, and Ancestors," in *Religion and Ritual in Chinese Society,* Arthur Wolf, ed., 131–82. Stanford: Stanford University Press.

Wolf, Eric. 1982. *Europe and the People without History.* Berkeley: University of California Press.

Xiaolan zhenzhi (Xiaolan Town Gazetteer). 1984.

Xinxiu Xiangshan Xianzhi. (Revised Local Gazetteer of Xiangshan). 1827. Compiler: Huang Peifang et al.

Xu, Xu. 1984. *Lingnan gujin shi* (A History of Lingnan). Hong Kong: Shanghai Books.

Zhongshan guomin ribao (Zhongshan Daily). 1930s and 1940s.

Zhongshan Lanzheng juhuahui wenyi gailan (A Survey of the Chrysanthemum Festivals of Zhongshan). 1936. Guangzhou.

Zhongshan Wenshi Bianji Weiyuanhui. n.d. [1960s–1980s]. *Zhongshan wenshi* (Zhongshan Cultural History), vols. 1–11. Shiqi: Guangdong Zhongshang Shi Zhengxie.

Zhongshan wenxian (Zhongshan Documents). 1964. Vols. 1–8. Taipei: Xuesheng Shudian.

An Afterword

My earlier paper has two objectives. First, it is a study of how a scholarly tradition in China and its associated rituals intertwined with the authority of the late imperial state to make regional society and identity. The chrysanthemum festivals are spectacular points of entry into a complex process of self-fashioning by local elites and commoners. The process over the centuries came to define not only the language of lineage and community and an ethnic hierarchy, but also the political-economic space of the Chinese (Han) state and the literati tradition itself.

Second, I use my interpretation of the process to critically evaluate three major frameworks in Chinese anthropology, those of G. William Skinner, Maurice Freedman, and Arthur Wolf. All three scholars have consciously tried to avoid the totalizing biases of Chinese official historiography by guiding our attention to the regional and the popular in understanding Chinese culture and society. However, their theoretical assumptions pose problems that can subvert their very intentions. Without addressing the *complicity* of *local* agents in specific *historical* transformations of a regional *political economy,* it would be difficult for these scholars to evaluate the discourse on the state as well. To explain change, these scholars ultimately fall back on the centrality of a dynastic paradigm, its "civilizing" impact, which local society could at best accommodate and improvise.

Benefiting from recent theories in anthropology and history, I emphasize the polyvocal, negotiated aspect of culture and identity to delineate crucial historical transformations in the *simultaneous* making of state and local society.[1] If the imperial order—all under heaven—is an imagined community, and the state is constructed over time and space, who has been responsible for their real and imagined presences? I argue that the power of the written word, associated with an evolving scholarly tradition that spread over the vast span of history and region to define "Chineseness," lies precisely in it being a symbolic repertoire within which local populations can maneuver. In other words, the idea of the imperial order was hegemonic and totalizing, but the state as a political machinery was not organizationally powerful. Local agents, while eagerly grappling onto what they considered to be legitimate symbols of state power, nonetheless enjoyed more creative room than official historiography had allowed. By "deconstructing" established notions of culture, power, and history in Chinese texts as well as in our own conceptual frameworks, we may better understand the distinguishing character of Chinese civilization—infinite variations in local cultures juxtaposed with an intensely unifying identity. It is the result of individual creativity, historical contingencies, and a degree of structural patterning.

Traditional Chinese Scholarship

Chinese scholarly traditions have had a long history. The literati in China, the brightest minds who passed civil service examinations organized by the state and were then recruited into officialdom, totally captured the imagination of generations of scholars in both China and the West. Until recent years, scholars have generally argued that literacy is intimately linked to the tyranny of history as recorded and interpreted by a bureaucracy of scholar-officials.[2] Confucian philosophy, distinguished by centuries of scholarly interpretation and practice, became synonymous with the civilizing enterprise of the imperial state.

In a state-centered approach, cultural images promoted by this literati elite were seen as essential components of social and political reproduction.[3] Major revisions of the ruling political philosophies are credited with inducing new social developments, even in times of dynastic collapse and a turn to Daoist mysticism in the fourth century, or in the poetic and religious explorations of the tenth century. During the centuries that followed, the neo-Confucian revival, the commercial revolution, the rise of territorial lineages, the establishment of official academies and the extension of ideological control, only reinforced our scholarly preoccupation with the literati.[4] The fortunes of dynasties and those of scholar-officials are assumed to intertwine with the ways social experiences and cultural identity unfolded in late imperial China. Commenting on the impact of the Chinese narrative tradition, the literary scholar Cyril Birch makes a poignant observation:

> Chinese stories and novels no doubt belonged to a minor tradition rather than to the central elite culture of historiography, philosophical prose, and lyric verse. But the divergence can easily be exaggerated. The long early cycles that seem to have grown like coral reefs by processes of accretion ended by enshrining the moral values and philosophical bases of an entire civilization. The insights of the fifteenth-century philosopher Wang Yangming and his school are imprinted on the stories of the following century. Read by children or by the semi-educated, orally presented by storytellers or transferred to the dramatic stage, the great masterpieces of fiction confirmed cultural identity as surely as the dazzling beauty of the cathedral told the European peasant he was a Christian.[5]

Regional History and the Culture of Scholarship in South China

In this larger schema of becoming culturally Chinese, can we envision a distinctly regional culture of scholarship?[6] The late imperial period saw rapid economic development, which linked the region of Lingnan in south China to the political center, on the one hand, and to the cosmopolitan world of foreign trade on the other.[7] Large-scale reclamation projects were financed by merchant capital under the auspices of lineage and other organizations. They turned river marshes into productive farmland, attracting migrants from far and near.[8] Market towns mushroomed on the expanding edge of the sands. They became centers of wealth and power, flaunting unique configurations of cultural resources. Xiaolan zhen of Xiangshan County, where the chrysanthemum festivals were staged, was one such market town.

Instead of being a refuge for exiled bureaucrats who had incurred the wrath of emperors, south China saw prominent scholar-officials emerging in the fifteenth and sixteenth centuries. Chen Xianzhang (1428–1500) of Xinhui county in Guangdong was the neo-Confucian of metropolitan acclaim in the Ming. His writings became the source of inspiration for generations of scholars in Guangdong.[9] Although Chen declined official appointment in order to devote his energies to teaching, one of his most outstanding students, Zhang Ruoshui of Zhengcheng county, was a teacher/philosopher as well as imperial official.[10] Their scholarly efforts made a name for learning in Guangdong and created a sizable generation of scholar-officials. Huang Zuo of Xiangshan county was the first to compile a complete provincial gazetteer of Guangdong (*Guangdong tongzhi*). Commissioned by the governor of Guangdong and Guangxi, he took three years and finished the seventy volumes in 1560.[11] In the early Qing dynasty, Qu Dajun of Panyu county, poet and historian, compiled twenty-eight volumes of local happenings in the province, his topics of interest ranging from flowers to birds, personalities, and events. He entitled the work *Guangdong xinyu* (New Items Relating to Guangdong).[12] The images of these and other literati figures had long been woven into local folklore and the social fabric of everyday life to reinforce a remarkable repertoire of regional culture and history—myths of genealogical origins and settlement, poetry, theater, and song styles, unique marriage customs and merchant practices, and a pantheon of popular deities.[13]

Although the region developed a material presence in its own right, identity with it as a conscious cultural construct was ambiguous. The native roots of these notable figures were not highlighted. Instead, they were proudly presented by local elites and popular folklore alike as having empire-wide impact, in the ranks of the imperial literati. Their contributions to regional culture and society were appreciated only if they helped the region claim a legitimate place in the metropolitan political hierarchy.[14] In fact, Qu Dajun's work captured that ambivalence well. He was eager to promote a knowledge of local observations and histories, as evidenced by his book *Guangdong xinyu*. He also observed the marriage practice of *buluojia* (delayed transfer marriage) of his native Panyu county.[15] However, he was relentless in blaming Zhao Tuo, the Qin dynasty general who set up a capital in Panyu (present day Guangzhou) and declared himself prince of Nanyue in 206 B.C., for having embraced indigenous customs and thus delayed the Han civilizing enterprise for centuries.[16]

Until the twentieth century, the Lingnan region maintained only a marginal place in literate discourse. This was partly due to the fact that nationally recognized figures from the region were few and far between and thus could not form a visible critical mass. More importantly, the upwardly mobile at different levels of society were eagerly grappling onto what they imagined to be symbols of prestige and power from the political center, in order to become legitimately "Han," and shed their local roots.

The purpose of this afterword is to highlight the distinctive characteristics of a scholarly culture that was local in its roots but remarkably drawn toward the political center. It will be too simplistic to assume a top-down percolation of the impact of literati elites to local society via a much studied civil service examination system out of which arose the Chinese bureaucratic tradition. I wrote the paper on the chrysanthemum festivals in Xiaolan because I believe that the history of how the literati tradition was emulated and transformed by local agents deserves to be highlighted. The number of the literati had always been small, but through the emulating process its impact extended far beyond scholarly imagination. The chrysanthemum festivals illuminate a process of cultural interpenetration between center and locality, literati and popular sentiments, state and society.

The Culture of Scholarship in Xiaolan

Despite claims by local genealogies, which dated scholarly connections for residents of Xiaolan back to the southern Song dynasty, the earliest record of writing by a scholar of Xiaolan origin is a book on geomancy entitled *Pijing ji,* written by Li Zhi (Mozhai) and prefaced in the twenty-seventh year of the Jiajing reign in the Ming (1549). Geomancy seldom gained respect in elite scholarly circles, as it was often associated with popular religious beliefs and magical practices. Furthermore, Li Zhi held neither academic titles nor office. It is therefore interesting that his biography was recorded in official historiography, the *Xiangshan xianzhi* (County Gazetteer of Xiangshan, 1827), and again in the postscript to an edition of *Pijing ji* printed in 1834 after a lapse of over two hundred years. According to the text written by Li Guanzhang, a descendant of the seventeenth generation of the Li lineage, Li Zhi was to be credited for having located auspicious grave sites in Xinhui and Heshan counties so that within a few generations the lineage was blessed with literati achievements. From the perspective of a later historical period in Guangdong when lineage pedigree and academic honors were naturally linked, Li's humble efforts in geomancy earned enough respectability for his works to be printed and disseminated.[17]

At the end of the Ming dynasty there was also a surge of local scholarship centering around poetry clubs. Poetry writing was a symbol both of scholarly leisure and of intense involvement with dynastic fortunes, although the poets hardly needed to have earned academic degrees or official appointments. Members of the clubs might also be literati, as in the "Wenhong shishe" organized by the late Ming official Wu Ruilong (1585–1666) and local friends from the Xiaolan area. The clubs provided an arena where aspiring local poets and scholars, degree-holders, and retired officials mingled. The volumes published by Wu, for example, contained numerous exchanges of poetry between him and colleagues. Among them was He Wuzhou, his cousin in Xiaolan, a member of the imperial Grand Council and later minister of a southern Ming court. Although their poetry centered on personal sentiments and intuitive reflections on insignificant occasions in daily life, they were treasured and collected. According to one biographer, Li Guang, their maternal grandfather and tutor, Liu Shiteng (1513–88) of Dalan, who himself was a provincial graduate and county magistrate, was awakened one night by mysterious lights shining from the sleeping quarters of the two boys. He was then convinced that his grandsons were destined for bureaucratic office.[18] Wu Ruilong rose to assume the office of Defence and Surveillance Circuit in Henan Province, but retired into the life of a hermit after capture by the Qing troops in Guangzhou. He Wuzhou was supposedly killed in the chaotic circumstances of dynastic transition. Their poetry and essays, together with their paintings and calligraphy, came to be possessed by private collectors.[19] He Wuzhou's epitaph, set up in 1607 at a grave site in Xiangshan county that purportedly contained only his clothes and belongings, was recovered in the twentieth century and extensively quoted by later scholars.[20]

But immediately following the fall of the Ming dynasty, southern China was far from pacified by the Manchu court. The surge of poetry by those who claimed to be their descendants in Xiaolan centered on protest against alien rule. These sentiments were often hidden in the exchange of poems between parting friends, in the symbolism of flowers and birds. He Yuechao (1642–76), the sixth son of He Wuzhou, was known for his melancholic poetic sentiments. Risking official wrath, he wrote blatant laments on his futile attempts to retrieve his father's body.[21] He was killed by local foes at the age of thirty-six. Contemporaries of his, themselves minor degree-holders, were brave enough to write poems to mourn his untimely death.[22]

By the eighteenth century, however, such fears and sentiments were totally overshadowed by the eagerness to affiliate with the Manchu state, however alien it might have been. Writings and art objects left by those with academic titles or bureaucratic posts were preserved with care and made into symbols of lineage pedigree. He Wuzhou's own biography was entered in the Qing version of Ming official history, and again in the Xiangshan county gazetteer compiled in 1751 during the Qianlong reign.[23] Apart from biographies in official texts, lineage genealogies were compiled by local groups whose members claimed territorial rights in the region. The genealogies of the He, Li, and Mai lineages, which claimed settlement rights in Xiaolan, displayed a dazzling array of members who were officials. The outstanding literati member for the Li lineage was Li Sunchen, a minister of rites in Nanjing during the Ming. The most prominent member of the He lineage was none other than He Wuzhou himself. As described in my earlier paper, these documents became testimonies to as well as tools for upward mobility. The language of lineage was buttressed by artistic documents such as the nine volumes of *Heshi shizheng* (Collected Works of Poetry by Members of the He Lineage) compiled by He Tianqu, local poet and holder of a low-level academic degree, during the late eighteenth and early nineteenth centuries.

The lineage genealogies, revised and printed in the early twentieth century, were written with particular themes and styles. They started with a narrative about origins, claiming ancestral links to prominent officials in the central plains (Zhongyuan, where Han Chinese civilization supposedly prospered). A myth about migration to the south followed, based on particular turns of fortune of the Song dynasty. Rights to settlement in particular localities were attributed to imperial decree or divine power. Eventual legitimation of the "settlers" was linked to scholarly achievements and officialdom. How many of these lineages originated from "migrants from the central plains" remains a question for historians to ponder.[24]

Unofficial histories and biographies, family rules, account books, poetry collections, travel observations, and gazetteers continued to be written by local notables. Some, like the county gazetteers, were commissioned by officials. Others were initiated by local scholars. These documents reinforced literati values and were sensitive to dynastic fortunes while reflecting the peculiarities of the changing local political economy. The "Lanxie" (Slivers of Xiaolan) belonged to this genre of writing. The author, He Dazuo (Lizai), was a provincial graduate (*juren*) in the sixth year of Emperor Qianlong's reign. Apart from writing poetry and essays, he recorded an extraordinary range of events and local observations. Some touched on local figures who performed magical acts, very much in the tradition of popular religious beliefs. Some were accounts of local banditry and family feuds. However, there were tales of what Confucian tradition would consider "virtuous women" (*lienu*) who performed exemplary acts of filial piety, and records of loyal officials defending the empire against rebels and pirates.[25]

The county gazetteers of Xiangshan, of which Xiaolan is a part, revealed the prevalence of local cultural practices while literati values representing the political center were being asserted.[26] The section on "local custom" is particularly illuminating. Editions of the gazetteer recorded local marriage practices in the Xiaolan area (together with the neighboring Panyu and Shunde counties) where married women stayed with their natal family for years. This was generally termed *buluojia*. In the section on exemplary women, local women were praised and remembered for their filial piety and "virtuous" deeds in accordance with Confucian teaching. However, one can read between the lines to detect how local marriage customs were in fact the norm.[27]

Even into the decades of the Republican era, efforts were made by local scholars to compile another version of the region's gazetteer. Li Guang (1904–43) was a graduate of the Zhongshan University, a scholar and poet. In the 1920s, he collected and published the work of local scholars, including his own poetry and that of Wu Ruilong, which he retrieved from private collectors over the years.[28] He began a gazetteer of his home town, Xiaolan, but the project was aborted by his premature death. It was, however, continued by He Yang-gao, a member of the He lineage and the largest landlord in town before the Communist revolution. In the 1940s, he was persuaded by the military boss of the region, Commander Yuan Dai, to compile a gazetteer for fund-raising purposes. He wrote the "Lanxi zaji," one of the few remaining documents of the arts, significant historical sites, and cultural achievements of the town before they were destroyed by the Communists.

Scholarly interests survived after 1949 in unexpected guises. After the wealthy landlords, merchants, local bosses, and scholars were hounded out by Communist Party officials, their properties were either redistributed or destroyed. There were individuals, not necessarily from scholarly families, who, for peculiar reasons, collected and hid many of their works and art collections. Among these individuals in Xiaolan were one who was engaged in the metal molding business and one who was an accountant in a town enterprise. Hardly considered scholars by traditional standards, they by sheer interest and circumstance kept the appreciation of scholarly tradition alive in the local area. Because they belonged to the "good" classes by revolutionary criteria, their homes were not searched during numerous political campaigns after 1949. In the post-Mao era, when the market town government finally decided to promote the town's history in order to appeal to the sentiments of native place of overseas investors, these collectors have become core members of the group charged with the responsibility of compiling a new local gazetteer.[29] The town government also commissioned the group to collect poetic works written by residents of Xiaolan over the centuries. These efforts resulted in the publication in 1994 of *Lanxiang lidai shichui* (The Poetic Essences of Xiaolan over the Generations). The initiative of He Yanggao, local historian and former landlord, produced a new version of *Heshi shizheng* (Poetry Selections of the He Lineage), also in 1994.

Over the centuries, the pretensions to join the literati ranks extended beyond written works. The cultivation of flowers, the forming of poetry and reading clubs, and the collection of art objects were symbols of scholarly leisure eagerly pursued by scholars who wished to distinguish themselves from the popular masses. The activities leading to the chrysanthemum festivals from the early nineteenth century on have been described in my paper. A few observations are worth highlighting. While lineage wealth and power continued to be based on the control of the sands, individual household fortunes were increasingly dependent on commercial developments centering on the town. The various social classes and groups contributed to the formation of a local scholarly culture by participating in the community festivals. In so doing, they changed the meaning of being literati and their relationship with the Republican state. The 1934 chrysanthemum festival, which signaled the rise of nonlocal business and military interests and the demise of the landowning lineages, was a case in point.

The engagement in a scholarly culture and the underlying political agenda could not have been more obvious in the 1994 chrysanthemum festival sixty years later. The imperial literati culture had long since disappeared with the dynastic order. Even the Republican and Maoist revolutions that replaced it for nearly a century became something of the past. In an age of brash materialism in which no ideology can provide the guiding principle for social mobility, local resources are pursued with the shrewdest manipulation of what have been perceived as state policies. In a decade of striving for modernization and prosperity, the politics of native roots has been played up in community festivals by party officials at every level.[30] The array of published documents in support of the recent festival illuminates the multiple bases of power and status, a shrewd reinvention of tradition when few understand what tradition is. The older town residents and their guests who came for the flowers and the exhibition of the arts went to the old section of the town centering on the park. However, many were thoroughly disappointed, as hardly any old members of the elite who know and appreciate the art of cultivating chrysanthemums are left. The only events that gave the appearance of engaging in the arts and culture were an exhibition of calligraphy and paintings by local artists, and another of stones collected by Liang the retired accountant. A poetry volume was compiled. There were contributions from old-time local historians and aspiring poets recommended by various regional poetry clubs. There were also less than polished pieces by party officials.[31]

In a recently developed part of town where the new town government offices stand, exhibitions of another kind greeted the invited guests, while curious migrant workers looked on outside the restricted areas. Promotional brochures for joint ventures were elaborately printed by the town government and disseminated in the exhibition halls during the festival. While children marveled at the neon lights, older viewers were reminded of the beautifully handcrafted lanterns and floral displays of the previous era, which few had seen. The town leadership was satisfied with the presence of overseas guests and officials who added legitimacy to the town's efforts. It looked forward to the prospect of future overseas investments in real estate and factories.

Popular memory, however, continues to linger upon the ultimate sign from the heavens—the fact that the bleachers collapsed during the parade indicated that some natural forces were not pleased.[32] Fortunately there were no serious injuries, and the town officials were able to plead with television crews on site not to broadcast the embarrassing episodes. But in the popular mind it might still be a matter of legitimacy: the town officials, ignorant of local history and sentiments, had chosen the wrong site for the occasion, and had forgotten to perform the proper rituals to appease the spirits before the festival. As party members who rose through the political ranks from poor peasant backgrounds, they are, after all, only pretending to be scholars.

NOTES

1. See the works of Natalie Davis as summarized by Barbara Diefendorf and Carla Hesse, *Culture and Identity* (Ann Arbor: The University of Michigan Press, 1993); Roger Chartier, *Cultural History: Between Practices and Representations* (translated by Lydia Cochrane) (Cambridge: Polity Press, 1988); Philip Abrams, *Historical Sociology* (Ithaca: Cornell University Press, 1982); a recent collection of essays edited by Nicholas Dirks, Geoff Eley, and Sherry Ortner, *Culture/Power/History: A Reader in Contemporary Social Theory* (Princeton: Princeton University Press, 1994); Partha Chatterjee, *The Nation and Its Fragments* (Princeton: Princeton University Press, 1993); and David Faure and Helen Siu, eds., *Down to Earth: The Territorial Bond in South China* (Stanford: Stanford University Press, 1995).

2. See Etienne Balazs, *Chinese Civilization and Bureaucracy* (New Haven: Yale University Press, 1964).

3. On the imperial bureaucracy and the civil service examinations in relation to

social reproduction, see Ho Ping-ti, *The Ladder of Success in Imperial China: Aspects of Social Mobility, 1368–1911* (New York: Columbia University Press, 1962); Chang Chung-li, *The Chinese Gentry* (Seattle: University of Washington Press, 1955); and Benjamin Elman, "The Civil Service Examination: Social, Cultural, and Political Reproduction," *Journal of Asian Studies,* 50:1 (1991), 7–28.

4. See the works of Yu Ying-shih, Ch'ien Mu, Dennis Twitchett, William De Bary, Benjamin Schwartz, Hsiao Kung-chuan, and, among the younger generation, Tu Weiming and Chow Kai-wing.

5. Cyril Birch, foreword to *Chinese Narrative: Critical and Theoretical Essays,* Andrew Plaks, ed. (Princeton: Princeton University Press, 1977), x–xi.

6. In writing this section, I have consulted Liu Zhiwei and Ching Maybo, with whom I went to the field and collected historical records on Guangdong. I also thank Chan Wing-hoi for his insights on local culture and historiography.

7. *Lingnan* is a term referring to a prosperous part of Guangdong and Guangxi provinces. The term literally means "south of the mountain ridges," and had been used in administrative history for centuries.

8. On the reclamation of the sands in Guangdong and the commercialization of agriculture, see Ye Xianen and Tan Dihua, "Lun Guangdong Zhujiang san jiaozhou de zutian" (On the Ancestral Estates of the Pearl River Delta), in *Ming Qing Guangdong shehui jingji xingtai yanjiu* (A Study of the Socioeconomic Conditions of Guangdong during the Ming and Qing Dynasties), Guangdong Lishi Xuehui, ed. (Guangzhou: Guangdong Renmin Chubanshe, 1985) 22–64.

9. His students collected many of his works. See *Chen Xianzhang ji,* vols. 1 and 2 (*The Collected Works of Chen Xianzhang*), Sun Tonghai, ed. Beijing: Zhonghua shuju, 1987.

10. Zhang Ruoshui's achievements were given a great deal of independent attention in the official records on Ming scholars. One such document is the *Ming ru xuean.*

11. See Jiang Zuyuan and Fang Jiqin, eds. *Jianming Guangdong shi* (Shenzhen: Guangdong renmin chubanshe, 1993), chap. 7, sec. 9, on cultural achievements during the Ming. See also *Guangdong wenzheng* by Wu Daorong [late Qing], published in Hong Kong by Zhuhai shuyuan 1973.

12. In his own preface, Qu argued for a record of local observations such as the one he compiled as a complement to official histories.

13. See David Faure, "Guangdong Province: A Brief History," a paper delivered at the British Association of Chinese Studies conference at Oxford University, September 1993.

14. See Faure, "Guangdong Province."

15. See *Qu Wengshan Xiansheng nianpu* (The Biographical chronology of Qu Wengshan) by Wang Zongyan [n.p., n.d.]. On pp. 62 and 76, the text indicates that Qu's first wife Liu practiced the delayed transfer marriage. He married his second wife Wang in the third year of the reign of Kangxi (1664).

16. See Qu Dajun, *Guangdong xinyu* ([1700] 1985), 32.

17. See the postscript to *Pijing ji* by Li Guanzhang, printed in the fourteenth year of the reign of Daoguang (1834).

18. See Li Guang, *Jiu'ai shanren yiji* ([1928]; rpt. Taipei: Li Cheng'en, 1990), 309–35.

19. See Ma Chujian "Ming muo He Wuzhou shangguo zhi shengping yu zhijie" (The Life and Deeds of Prime Minister He Wuzhou at the End of the Ming), *Mingshi yanjiu,* vol. 4 (1981). See also Li Guang *Jiu'ai shanren yiji,* on the collection of Wu Ruilong's poems entitled "Jiu'ai shanren yiji" (A Collection of Essays by Wu Ruilong), reprinted in Taipei in 1990.

20. See Ma Chujian, "Ming muo He Wuzhou."

21. See his poem "Qiusi" (Autumn Thoughts), in Liang Zhijun, *Lanxiang lidai shicui* (Xiaolan, 1986).

22. See Liang Zhijun, *Lanxiang lidai shicui,* 2d ed. (Xiaolan, 1993) on the biography of the poets and their poems. Several poems by Li Hang relate directly to He Yuechao. See Li Hang, "Du Yuechao xiansheng yiji yougan" (On Reading the Poetry Collection of Mr. He Yuechao) and "Jiuri guo He Yuechao xiansheng mu" (Passing Mr. He Yuechao's Grave on the Ninth Day), 37–38.

23. See Ma Chujian, "Ming muo He Wuzhou." Ma was trying to clear He Wuzhou's name, for, according to some historians, He had surrendered to the Qing troops.

24. See the genealogies of the He, Li, and Mai lineages in Xiaolan. See also Tan Dihua, "Cong Zhujixiang shishi lianshang dao de wenti," in *Guangdong lishi wenti lunwenji* (A Collection of Essays on Historical Issues of Guangdong). Tan compares the genealogical myths with those of other lineages in Guangdong. For a case study of how a prominent lineage in the neighboring county of Panyu "constructed" its history, see Liu Zhiwei, "Lineage on the sands," in *Down to Earth: The Territorial Bond in South China,* David Faure and Helen Siu, eds. (Stanford University Press, 1995).

25. This is in the tradition of *Guangdong xinyu,* though of a much less comprehensive nature.

26. See *Zhongshan wenxian* on the various editions of the local gazetteer. The earliest one was compiled in 1751; subsequent editions were compiled in 1827, 1880, and 1923.

27. See Helen Siu, "Where Were the Women? Rethinking Marriage and Regional Culture in South China," *Late Imperial China,* 2:2 (1990), 32–64.

28. See Li Guang, *Chui wan liu shiji* ([1944]; rpt. Taipei, 1988); and Li Guang, *Jiu'ai shanren yiji.*

29. See *Xiaolan zhenzhi* (draft, 1984).

30. In another essay, I have described similar efforts to stage community festivals in the Pearl River delta (Helen Siu, "Economic Transformation and Cultural Improvisation: Community Festivals in Post-Mao South China," in *China Review* [Hong Kong: Chinese University Press, 1995], Chap. 16, 1–17).

31. See *Jiashu Xiaolan juhui shixuan* (Selected Poems for the Chrysanthemum

Festival of Xiaolan in the Jiashu Year), Xiaolan disijie juhua dahui and Lingnan shishe, eds. (Guangzhou, 1994).

32. I was at the site of the parade when the bleachers collapsed. The incident became the talk of the town and also was widely discussed in Hong Kong because some news footage was broadcast. The popular belief became so strong that the town government eventually hired a group of daoist priests to perform some exorcism rituals. Local residents described the site of the parade as an area where unwanted babies and the dying had been abandoned during the war. Some local nuns went to the site and performed cleansing rituals on their own initiative shortly after the festival in 1994.

Writing Traditions in Colonial Java: The Question of Islam

Nancy Florida

The category of "native Islam" posed a problem for the colonial Europeans who ruled Java in the latter part of the nineteenth century. Islam, as an alternative center of authority for those millions of colonial subjects who professed it, was, not surprisingly, apprehended as a potential threat to the continued European domination of the island. In the face of this perceived threat, a conventional colonial defense was to refuse, that is, to deny and divert, the reality of the Islamic professions that issued from the mouths and actions of the Javanese faithful. Although "the Javanese" might believe themselves Moslems, and although their public, external practices often appeared to confirm these professions of faith, colonial authorities wished to disaffirm this apparent truth.

Colonial scholarship on "the Javanese" was thus often propelled by a desire to penetrate the private, inner recesses of native subjects in order to observe the presupposed falsity of these subjects' Moslem claims and professions. The quality of their Islam thought to be diluted by a continuing adherence to older indigenous and Hindu-Buddhist belief complexes, syncretic Javanese Moslems were seen as somehow different from other (truer) Moslems. "No, these are not real Mohammedans," claimed those wishful colonial overlords, who asserted that, underneath and inside, the docile (Hindu-Buddhist) Javanese essences of their subjects remained untouched by the thin Islamic veneer that sometimes seemed to embody them.[1] And nowhere did this non-Islamic essential Javaneseness appear more evident to imperial eyes than in the royal palaces, or *kraton*s, of the Central Javanese heartland. This paper examines both the colonial interest in establishing the palaces as exemplary centers of non-Islamic essential Javaneseness and the literary activities in one of those palaces that quietly circumvented that interest.

Islam Observed in Colonial Java

In 1886 the colonial Resident of the royal city of Surakarta[2] wrote in his annual report to his Batavian superiors: "As far as religion is concerned, the population of this district has only a thin varnish of Mohammadanism over a base of Buddhism and Saivism, and it is only to lament that owing to their gullibility and ignorance, they are such easy prey for those who, under the mask of religion, hide sinister intents."[3] By the 1880s, as a series of (apparently unconnected) self-consciously Islamic uprisings swept the island,[4] the colonial authorities had become increasingly alarmed by the subversive potential of Islam in Java. But, at the same time, their imperial eyes could not, or would not, see the political Islam that these uprisings appeared to represent as truly belonging to the indigenous subjects who participated in them. Instead, they saw this political Islam as pollution from outside, an alien import brought home to Java by returning hajis who themselves had been infected in Mecca with these sinister strains of anti-imperial fanaticism.[5] The radical political Islam that these hajis brought home with them, it was thought, comprised an arid, foreign (Arabic-Turkish) form that was by nature alien to the compliant tropical essences of their Javanese subjects.[6] And yet there remained the threat of real contagion: there was always a danger that the souls inside these only apparently Islamic native bodies might actually succumb to these foreign strains of desert fanaticism. For colonial authority, such Islam constituted a hidden force that threatened to insinuate itself into Javanese subjects, an invisible force that meant to turn "docile natives" into "dangerous revolutionaries."

Perhaps nowhere are these colonial anxieties more artfully disclosed than in Louis Couperus's haunting turn-of-the-century Indies novel, *The Hidden Force.*[7] This novel, which effectively inscribes the impossibility of the colonial project on Java, narrates the inevitable downfall of a "good" Dutch colonial civil servant before the inexplicable "hidden force" that pulses silently through the dark recesses of native culture. In a manner notably counter to the conventional wisdom on Javanese cultural essences, however, Couperus's writing effects an unstable identification of these "mystical" Javanese essences with the dangerous force of political Islam. Suggestively representing, *as* Javanese, the ghastly specter of political Islam in the figure of a ghostly haji whose inexplicable appearances sporadically punctuate the narrative, Couperus indicates the very reality that colonial eyes would refuse to see.

In the final paragraphs of *The Hidden Force,* the unstable identification of dark native mystery and Islam that punctuates the narrative is repeated and centered in a beautifully wrought and horrible scene that dramatically represents the colonial nightmare of "fanatic" Islam come home to Java. The scene is set in a train station, and depicts—to the weary imperial eyes of both Couperus's protagonist and his audience—a humming crowd of frenzied Javanese natives pressing forward in a crush to kiss the hands and hems of a party of new hajis just returned from Mecca. These new hajis are natives, natives who appear—to the colonial witnesses who observe them—too remote, too dignified, and too proud. In a troubled voice, the narrator reflects on the scene:

> And in this land of profound, secret, slumbering mystery, in these people of Java, which, as always, hid itself in the secrecy of its impenetrable soul, suppressed indeed but visible, it was strange to see rising to the surface an ecstasy, to see an intoxicated fanaticism, to see a part of that impenetrable soul revealed in its deification of those who had beheld the Prophet's tomb, to hear the soft humming of a religious rapture, to hear, suddenly, unexpectedly, a shout of glory, not to be suppressed, quavering on high, a cry that instantly sank again, drowned in the hum, as though fearful itself, because the sacred era had not yet arrived . . . (229–30, ellipsis in the original)

And then, quite suddenly, the novel's protagonist, together with his friend (a perfect, and also perfectly disillusioned, colonial woman), come to sense "in the midst of this fanatical multitude" the uncanny, ineffable force that has defeated them. They sense it, but its truth remains unseen by them. *The Hidden Force* closes without closure, setting loose the horrible *unseen* image that had loomed, invisible, behind the novel's pages. Indeed it is an image of the very thing that these colonial witnesses, the novel's tragically undone hero and heroine, could or would not see:

> And in feeling [that ineffable force], together with the sadness of their leave-taking, which was so near at hand *they failed to see* amid the waving, billowing, buzzing multitude that reverently hustled the yellow and purple dignity of the *hadjis* returned from Mecca, *they failed to see* that one tall white *hadji* rising above the crowd and peering with a grin at the man who, no matter how he had lived his life in Java, had been weaker than That . . . (230, emphasis added, ellipsis in original)

This image of the spectral grinning haji whose power rises out of, and above, the "fanatical multitude" portrays, I think, the potential force of popular Islam in Java. It is a highly visible image, and yet one that remains unseen. With this image, Couperus discloses the highly ambivalent position Javanese

Islam occupied in nineteenth-century colonial consciousness. On the one hand, it inspired suspicion as a dangerous reality that, it was feared, could and perhaps would appear anywhere and everywhere. On the other hand, Islam remained a phantom whose presence was denied, in a nearly exorcistic gesture, to genuinely Javanese realities. Islam represented danger, but a danger that a spectrum of colonial authorities needed to understand, and hence saw, as foreign, alien, and intrinsically un-Javanese. And it was because Islam belonged somewhere else, not properly to "their" Java, that so many colonials were wont to call the notoriously "syncretic" Javanese "Moslems in name only." Colonial authority apparently needed to deny the possibility of a truly Javanese Islam or truly Islamic Java. Thus, in spite of the fact that colonial officials obsessively watched for and observed Islam's specter at the margins and in the cracks of the Javanese society that they ruled, it remained in their interest to fail to see indigenous Islam rising out of the very midst of the multitude. Even more to the point: it was in the colonial interest to project and advance that "not seeing" among their Javanese subjects—especially among the elite of those subjects.

The horror for the late-nineteenth-century colonials of a possible coalescence of political Islam and the native elite was born out of collective traumatic memories and disturbing contemporary reminders. Remembered was the Dipanegara War (or, as the Dutch would have it, the Java War). Led by a Javanese prince and supported by a network of rural Islamic masters (or *kyai*), this concerted rebellion against colonial authority raged from 1825 to 1830. Those five years of warfare, in which over 200,000 Javanese and 15,000 colonials (7,000 of whom were "Indonesians") died,[8] demonstrated to the colonial rulers, and to their Javanese subjects, the fury that could be unleashed by the natives when mobilized by their elite under the banner of Islam.[9] Colonial authorities were forcibly reminded of this truth in the late nineteenth century during their decades-long struggle to pacify the Moslem freedom fighters of Aceh on the neighboring island of Sumatra. The Aceh War, which began in 1873, continued into the early twentieth century. The tide was finally turned in favor of the Dutch when, upon the advice of the acclaimed Islamicist Snouck Hurgronje, the colonial authorities moved to co-opt the native aristocracy and to separate them from the "more fanatic" religious leaders. Allowing their more moderate Moslem subjects ritual religious freedom, while vigorously suppressing any signs of political Islam, the policy meant to domesticate the "Mohammedan peril."[10]

This turn-of-the-century Islamic policy played out in Aceh repeated, with a difference, colonial cultural policies that had been earlier deployed on Java.

With the close of the Dipanegara War in 1830, the Dutch had found themselves in a position of power they had hitherto never enjoyed in the Javanese heartland. From this new position, they began to consolidate what was becoming for the first time their real colonial authority over the island. The victorious Dutch were to seal the final subjugation of the Javanese with strategies of domestication that would turn on the cultural isolation and co-optation of the indigenous elite. Insofar as the native elite could be held in colonial service, while at the same time held away, in a kind of honored cultural reserve, both from the masses whom they would govern (for the Dutch) and from the sinister forces of "fanatical" Islam which might threaten that compromised governance, Dutch authority, it was hoped, would reign supreme.

And yet local pockets of resistance to the colonial status quo persisted. Revolts, almost always in the idiom of Islam, continued to break out across the rural Javanese countryside with increasing frequency and violence as the century progressed. To forestall the possiblility that these small-scale revolts might escalate into another full-fledged insurrection, it was useful for Dutch power to see and to publish these disturbances as alien, fanatic intrusions that belonged to the deviant margins of society, intrusions that never penetrated the true Javanese heart that was embodied in docile masses and agreeable elites. It is in this light that we can read the upbeat annual report that the Dutch Resident of the royal Javanese city of Surakarta submitted to the Governor General in 1839. In this report, the Resident boasts of the "surprising" success of the then still new postwar colonial policy for control of the native elites and, through them, the Javanese masses. He tells of a rural "religious revolt" in his district and of the ease with which it was put down. The Resident explains that when the rebels, a man and wife whom he calls "saints," disturbed the state of law and order in rural Surakarta that year, they found no allies among the native elite and little support from "the people."[11] Their revolt was easily crushed, and the two saints were packed off to a Batavian insane asylum. The Resident proudly reports to his superiors that this disturbance, unlike the earlier Dipanegara troubles, was of absolutely "no political import." The Resident offers his analysis of the incident's insignificance: "It seems to me that as long as no prince of name stands at the head of a said endeavor to disturb the peace, that endeavor shall be quickly and easily frustrated." He goes on to caution that, in spite of the policy's success to date, this incident again "shows us how very important it is to keep the native elites comfortable, while at the same time keeping an ever vigilant eye on their conduct and moods."[12]

Keeping an eye on elite "conduct and moods" in colonial Surakarta continued throughout the nineteenth century—as did "religious revolts." And when a wave of Islamic revivalism swept over the island in the closing decades of the century, the anxieties of the colonial officials posted to the Central Javanese Principalities increased; accordingly, surveillance was, it seems, intensified. By the 1880s, significant portions of the Surakarta Residents' annual reports were devoted to the dangers the hajis and other "fanatical Moslem priests" were thought to pose to colonial authority, and to the sinister "religious movements" into which these shrewd villains allegedly "tricked their indolent and ignorant native followers."[13] At the same time, ever more paranoid colonial eyes fearfully surveyed the native elite for dreaded traces of religious fervor. The Surakarta Residents' reports of the latter nineteenth century display a persistent preoccupation with aristocratic trips to the mosque, princely friendships with Arabs, and royal tuition in Arabic language.[14] And although they continued to affirm that "their" elites were essentially "good Javanese," free of fanatic Islam's taint, the Residents' Political Reports of the latter part of the century lack the confident tone of the General Reports of the 1830s and 1840s.[15]

Colonial Oversights and the Renaissance of Javanese Culture in Nineteenth-Century Surakarta

It was, however, during those earlier, more confident, post-Dipanegaran years that the colonial cultural policy I mentioned above, a policy that would define "high Javanese culture" as the non-Islamic preserve of agreeable aristocrats, began to take form. Some aspects of this policy, for instance the preservation and inflation of "traditional" Javanese sumptuary practices to shore up sagging elite status and dignity, were studied and deliberate. Indeed, the post-Dipanegaran Principalities were quite literally founded upon the principle of preserving indigenous elite privilege in the name and service of Dutch colonial governance.[16] Other aspects of this nascent cultural policy were, however, less considered: theirs was a reality that was more implicit to the colonial project. These other aspects were, in part, the result of unconscious assumptions and wishful thinking, the implicit conceptual background, or logic, that was to generate among colonial observers of Javanese subjects the particular form of "not seeing" that Couperus's novel would dramatize at the beginning of the next century.

This peculiar form of conceptual denial was cultivated in the new academic field of Javanology, a field that came into being just after the Dipanegara War along with the Cultuur Stelsel (or forced cultivation system) and the ensuing high colonial age of Dutch rule on Java.[17] Javanology, the colonial science of

Javanese subjects and their culture, worked in the interest of the authorities to frame "traditional Java" through a delineation of that tradition's genuine high culture. And Javanology would understand that culture as standing in opposition to Islam and as the more or less exclusive property of a hyper-refined elite, or *priyayi,* class.

The palaces of Central Java were seen (and to some extent are still seen) as the proper locus and preserve of that true Javanese high culture, a culture portrayed as an (almost) purely indigenous (Hindu-Buddhist) remainder, essentially untouched by the alien accretions of either Islam or the West. Indeed, the image has stuck so firmly that in 1959 Clifford Geertz—no doubt faithful to the professions of his *priyayi* Javanese informants—could still write, in *The Religion of Java,* that "in the court circles of Djokjakarta and, especially, Surakarta, it is possible, if one ignores the furniture and electric lights, to imagine one is in a pre-Dutch Hindu-Buddhist court."[18] Geertz's doubly hypothetical image of the courts, predicated as it is on ignoring realities before one's eyes (that is, electric lights and furniture), repeats the colonial gesture of interested "not-seeing." And by pointing especially to Surakarta, his image also repeats, and thereby reinforces, the privileged status post-1830 Indies scholarship afforded the Palace (or *Kraton*) of the King (or *Susuhunan*) of Surakarta as the truest exemplar of pure Javanese high culture. For it was to the Kraton Surakarta that the nineteenth-century colonial scholars first turned to indulge, and enforce, a wishful image of essential "Javaneseness."

Nineteenth-century colonial scholarship was dominated by the discipline of philology. Language and literature, philology's proper objects, came to enjoy a favored position in the emerging image of Javanese high culture. Because of the paired privileging of literature and of the Kraton Surakarta, what was *imagined* to be the literature of that court was an important factor in the framing of Javanese culture. The implications of that frame are particularly evident in the history of Javanese literature produced by colonial (and also postcolonial) philology.[19]

Philology teaches us that Javanese literature attained the zenith of its sophistication and aesthetic value in the distant pre-Islamic past with classical Hindu-Buddhist Kawi literary culture. This culture, which produced the classical *kekawin* masterpieces, was a culture that belonged to the successive glorious courts of the Old Javanese heartland. We are taught that the robust florescence of Old Java's literary culture was crushed by the coming of Islam in the latter fifteenth century. Philology implies that what followed the conquest was a long period of darkness, characterized by an Islamic literary culture that came out of the *pasisir* area (the northern littoral of Java). It is said that the *pasisir* authors of the middle period produced derivative, and sometimes corrupt, texts on "foreign" Islamic topics.

Only in the late eighteenth century, the philological canon teaches us, was Javanese literature to experience a kind of rebirth at the Surakarta Palace, a rebirth that would effect a partial recuperation of the lost greatness of Old Java's literary culture. The renaissance is conventionally thought to have expressed itself most perfectly in the court poets' translations of the Old Javanese *kekawin* classics into modern Javanese verse. In his immensely influential *Literature of Java,* the renowned Dutch philologist Theodore Pigeaud epitomizes this classical rebirth: "The turning of the attention of Javanese scholars from Islamic texts to Old Javanese *kekawins,* and the ensuing development of Surakarta Court literature in the eighteenth and nineteenth centuries, were tantamount to a renaissance of classical Javanese literature."[20] In effect: because the poets finally turned away from foreign Islam toward their native Javanese Hindu-Buddhist origins, Javanese poetry was reborn.

It was to be, however, a short-lived rebirth (or perhaps but a stillbirth). For by the latter nineteenth century, colonial philology had decided that the famed productions of the Surakarta renaissance were "bad," as it were, translations.[21] Moreover, the discipline had come to categorize much of the newer literature produced at court as degenerate and involuted. The renaissance was declared over, and with it traditional Javanese literature as a serious art form.

It was, however, before the disillusionment, during the early florescence of colonial philological scholarship from about 1830 to 1860, that the image of Javanese high culture was first sketched out. And this image—the one that stuck—belongs to the philological romance of the Surakarta renaissance. The image is a wishful one, one with which colonial scholarship thought to envision and enthrone behind the high walls surrounding the Kraton Surakarta (away, it was imagined, from grinning hajis and from the multitude) a safe renaissance in literature, of the great Hindu-Buddhist kingdoms. Colonial philology happily saw there a return, via texts, of the Javanese to their timeless (read: docile) selves away from the interruption of Islam's sinister (read: political) messages. And it was Dutch power that really delivered this return. For this putative renaissance of Javanese letters in the Kraton Surakarta, colonial scholarship likes to remind us, was a rebirth born of the "peace" afforded by the new colonial order.

The post-1830 philological romance projects the beginnings of the renaissance back into the latter years of the eighteenth century with the founding of Surakarta and the new order division of the old realm of Mataram. The Surakarta court poet Yasadipura I is hailed as the father of that renaissance. And in addition to fathering a rebirth of presumably dead Javanese letters from the grave in which the Moslem conquest had cast them, the elder Yasadipura is also famed as the progenitor of a veritable clan of reborn Javanese literati. His son, and later his great-grandson, succeeded him in the office of palace *pujongga* (roughly, a divinely invested court poet and royal adviser).[22] Among Yasadipura's many literary accomplishments, pride of place is always given to his renderings into modern Javanese verse of the ancient Kawi classics of Old Java (notably, he translated the Old Javanese *Bharatayuda, Ramayana,* and *Niti Sastra,* as well as the Middle Javanese *Bima Suci*). He is conventionally seen as *the* Javanese writer who did the most, through translation, to provide for the diminished latter-day Javanese a glimpse back and partial return to their noble (pre-Islamic) origins.[23]

In this essay, through a reconsideration of the activities of Yasadipura I and his progeny in the literary culture of the Surakarta court, I wish to invite a rethinking of the position of Islam in the body of writing that has come to be known as traditional Javanese literature, a body of writing conventionally exemplified by the works of the so-called Surakarta renaissance and conventionally pictured as un-Islamic. Through a reexamination of these works and their writers, I will demonstrate that much of what is considered the exclusive court literature of Surakarta extends well beyond the palace walls and is thoroughly Islamic in character. And I will suggest that this is at least in part owing to the circumstance that much of this literature and many of the men who wrote it were nurtured in the rural Islamic educational institutions, or *pesantrèn,* of Java.[24] For it is a little discussed fact that *all* the most renowned of the Surakarta *pujonggas,* or "court poets," were products of, among other things, Islamic *pesantrèn* educations.[25]

A Santri Family: The Pujonggas of the Kraton Surakarta

The elder Yasadipura, acclaimed father of the Surakarta renaissance, was born at dawn on September 9, 1729, in the Central Javanese village of Pengging, in the vicinity of the royal palace of Kartasura.[26] Both his parents were devout Moslems. His mother Maryam was the daughter of a learned Islamic religious scholar, or *ulama,* whose name was Kalipah Caripu. His father Kyai Tumenggung Padmanagara, a seventh-generation descendant of the sixteenth-century Sultan of Pajang and a great-grandson of King Mangkurat I (r. Mataram 1645–77), is said to have been a far-ranging *santri,* or "student of Islam."[27] As a youth, Padmanagara reputedly ventured off Java to study in Palembang, in southern Sumatra, under the Sufi master Jenal Ngabidin. When Padmanagara returned to Java, he went into royal service at the Central Javanese Kartasura Palace. Padmanagara held high office (*bupati jaksa*) under Pakubuwana I (r. 1704–19), Amangkurat IV (r. 1719–26), and Pakubuwana II (r. 1726–49). To him is attributed the authorship of the *Serat Tékawardi,* a well-known Sufi song that also concerns matters of Javanese statecraft and of Javanese writing.[28]

Yasadipura, like his father before him, was a *santri* in the original sense of the word: for he, too, was a "wandering student of Islamic religion." In 1737, when he was only eight years old, Yasadipura was sent off to the hinterlands of rural Bagelèn-Kedhu to take his education in Arabic *and* Javanese letters at the *pesantrèn* of Kyai Honggamaya, an associate of his maternal grandfather. While the young Yasadipura was pursuing his course of literary and religious study in the countryside, intrigue and rebellion were brewing in the court at Kartasura. In 1742, when, following a series of complicated turns and reverses, Chinese rebels overran the palace, Kartasura's king, Pakubuwana II, was forced to flee his court. The fugitive king made for Panaraga in East Java, where he took shelter with the Islamic teacher Kyai Ageng Imam Besari.[29] Meanwhile, Yasadipura had completed his course of study with Honggamaya; but instead of returning home to Pengging the young *santri* traced the path of his king to Panaraga and was there accepted into royal service. In 1743, after Madurese allies of the Dutch had retaken the old court city from the Chinese rebels, Yasadipura returned with his king and that king's Dutch supporters to Kartasura.

It was in the shadow of the ruins of the old palace that Yasadipura continued his education in Javanese and Islamic letters. The young *santri*'s teacher was now the old court poet Pangéran (Prince) Wijil Kadilangu, a descendant of the legendary Javano-Islamic saint Sunan Kalijaga.[30] Prince Wijil authored many texts, among which are a number of *suluk,* or Sufi songs.[31] In 1744, when the restored Pakubuwana II decided to abandon Kartasura and move his *kraton* several kilometers to the east, Yasadipura, along with his mentor, is said to have played an important role. As representatives of the spiritual corps of palace literati, Prince Wijil and Yasadipura worked to select and prepare the site of the new palace. The site they chose was the riverside village of Solo. It was also they who discovered this swampy site's connections with the spirit realm of the South Sea and who worked to control that connection, thus making possible the transformation in 1745 of village Solo into the kingdom of Surakarta.[32] Having literally laid the foundations for the kingdom, the young Yasadipura then went on to shine as a literary and political star in the new Surakarta Palace.[33] Over the course of the following decade, the young courtier was a firsthand witness to the Giyanti War (1746–57) that led to the division of Mataram in 1755. He was also a close confidant of the young (literary)

Pakubuwana III (r. 1749–88).[34] He later served as elder statesman and adviser to Pakubuwana III's son and successor, Pakubuwana IV (r. 1788–1820).[35] When Yasadipura died in 1803, he was the senior *Pujongga* of the Surakarta Palace. He had served three generations of Surakarta kings, writing prolifically and reputedly advising wisely for over sixty years.

Yasadipura I's writings, all composed in verse, are wide-ranging. In addition to his famous translations of the Hindu-Buddhist Kawi classics, Yasadipura authored a number of other texts. He wrote several important histories: notably of Kartasura and of the Giyanti War, in which he had participated, as well as of the political and marital intrigues that colored the early years of the new court in Surakarta.[36] *And* he composed an extensive version of the epic *Ménak Amir Hamza,* a lengthy historical romance relating the heroic and amorous adventures of Amir Hamza, the Prophet Mohammad's uncle, as he spread Islam by warfare through a number of Near Eastern kingdoms. Adapted from the Persian, and then the Malay, Yasadipura's *Ménak* remained a favorite at the Surakarta Palace, especially among the ladies of the court, up through the early years of the twentieth century. And it is certainly worth noting that when the colonial Balai Pustaka published Yasadipura's *Ménak* in the 1930s, the editors still felt it necessary to censor from Yasadipura's text what they considered its excessive "Islamic propaganda."[37] Another work traditionally attributed to this father of the Surakarta renaissance is the *Serat Tajusalatin,* a rendering into Javanese of the Malay *Mahkota Segala Raja-Raja* ("Crown of All the Kings").[38] The *Tajusalatin* is a weighty didactic text on the ethics of Moslem kingship; and, according to Surakartan dynastic traditions, it is the single text whose reading is *still* obligatory for all Javanese kings.[39] Also among Yasadipura's compositions are several Sufi songs, or *suluk,* including *Suluk Makmunuradi Salikin* and the renowned *Suluk Déwaruci.*[40]

The elder Yasadipura also wrote the remarkable *Serat Cabolèk,* a profoundly intertextual poem, which comments on, as it reinscribes, other of the author's writings.[41] The *Cabolèk,* a history set in Pakubuwana II's Java, self-consciously treats issues of Javanese kingship, Islamic orthodoxy, Sufi mysticism, *and* classical Kawi literature. At one point in the narrative, the poem's orthodox Moslem protagonist, a decidedly literate *santri* from provincial Kudus, prefaces his reading of an extended portion of the *Déwaruci,* one of Yasadipura's classic translations, with an explanation of what it meant, in the context of eighteenth-century Islamic Java, to read the old Kawi classics:

Moreover the sense [*rasa*] of the Kawi
Bima Suci and *Arjuna Wiwaha*

Emerges through many subtle signs [*sasmita*]
The sense [*rasa*] of its Knowledge [*ngèlmu*] is Ultimate
If s/he who interprets is precise and penetrating
For like the Kawi *Ramayana*
These too are Sufi works[42]

The capacity for penetrating interpretation, Yasadipura goes on to emphasize in this poem and elsewhere, is predicated on the serious and careful
reading of other texts.[43] Foremost among the texts read by Yasadipura to
inform his writing—perhaps especially his necessarily interpretive writing of
the Kawi translations—were apparently works of mystical Islam. In 1815, one
of Yasadipura I's literary grandsons included, in the *suluk* that he was composing, a remembrance of his famous grandfather reading:

I saw him on those nights
When he had no guests
Once resting from his writing
Nothing else was seen by him

Save *suluk* and other Sufi texts[44]

Around 1756, Yasadipura I fathered a son who was to follow in his
footsteps. This son was Yasadipura II (d. 1844); a man of many names, this
Yasadipura was also known as R.Ng. Ronggawarsita I and as R.T.
Sastranagara.[45] Like his father before him, the younger Yasadipura also took
his education in a *pesantrèn*. In fact, he apparently studied in the newly established East Javanese *pesantrèn* of Tegalsari in Panaraga under the same *kyai*
from whom the fugitive king Pakubuwana II, attended by a youthful
Yasadipura I, had once sought spiritual solace.[46] Upon returning to Surakarta,
Yasadipura II went into court service and, by the turn of the nineteenth century,
had become a prominent star in the Palace's lively literary circle. After the
death of his father in 1803, he succeeded to the office of Palace *Pujongga.*
Yasadipura II wrote prolifically through the 1810s and 1820s. In 1826, he was
appointed to the high ministerial position of *Bupati Carik Kadipatèn,* a post he
occupied until his death in 1844.

Yasadipura II's literary productions were perhaps even wider ranging than
those of his father. Like the elder Yasadipura, he too was involved in the
translation of Kawi classics. He produced two literary translations of the

classic *Lokapala,* an epilogue and prehistory to the Indic *Ramayana.* The first of these translations was rendered in Modern Javanese language, but in pseudo–Old Javanese Kawi Miring, or "Crooked Kawi," verse; the second was a translation from the Crooked Kawi into modern Javanese verse.[47] Another text that he rendered in translation was the *Bima Suci Kawi Miring,* a translation "back," as it were, into Crooked Kawi of his father's celebrated classic translation of this work into modern Javanese verse.[48] He compiled Kawi-Javanese lexicons and produced an allusive reading of a cryptic commentary on Java's past.[49] He composed a number of didactic texts, including his biting *Wicara Keras* ("Strong Words"), a work that includes historical commentary on and criticism of his contemporary Surakarta sociopolitical milieu.[50]

The younger Yasadipura also authored historical texts. His *Babad Pakepung* ("History of the Encirclement"), a text surprisingly critical of his royal patron Pakubuwana IV, chronicles a political crisis in 1790s Surakarta that involved the young and headstrong king, contending political meanings of Islamic orthodoxy, and the pressure of consolidating Dutch power on indigenous authority.[51] But Yasadipura II also wrote histories of events that were not set in his native Surakarta: his *Serat Ambiya* ("The Book of Prophets") is an extensive sacred history of Islam, from the Creation through the life of the Prophet Yusup (Joseph), and his *Serat Musa* ("The Book of Moses") is a lengthy history of the Prophet Musa (Moses).[52] This prolific palace *pujongga* also composed several didactic poems whose lessons often turn on issues of Islamic ethics and practices of virtuous Moslem statecraft.[53] And, like his father, the younger Yasadipura also wrote texts of *suluk,* including his *Suluk Burung* ("Song of the Birds"), an allusive mystical discourse upon the grades of perfection (material and spiritual) that the human soul may attain through divine agency. The *suluk* presents a debate among three birds, each of which represents a different ideal body-soul relationship and hence a different strain of Javanese, and Javano-Islamic, mysticism.[54]

But perhaps Yasadipura II's most significant contribution to Javanese letters was his work on the celebrated *Centhini,* an immense and masterful text of which he was one of the three principal authors.[55] Framed by a story that is set in villages and rural *pesantrèn* across an imagined seventeenth-century Javanese landscape, the *Centhini* composes an elegant verbal fabric woven of myriad strands of Javanese and Islamic thought, lore, history, and literature. Emerging out of the Sufi literary genre of *suluk,* the *Centhini* extended that genre to become something that had never before been known in Javanese literary culture: called by many "a Javanese encyclopedia," the *Centhini* is an artful compilation of *ngèlmu* ('knowledge') from the extended *pesantrèn* world of early-nineteenth-century Java.[56]

Two of Yasadipura II's sons had promising, though unfortunately abbreviated, careers as court literati. Ronggawarsita II, his eldest son, had attained the high office of chief of the palace scribes (*Lurah Carik*), when, in 1828, at the height of the Dipanegara War, his career was all too suddenly cut short. Suspected of treason by the colonial authorities (the Surakarta Palace was ostensibly allied with the Dutch against the rebellious Dipanegara), Ronggawarsita II was arrested and exiled. It is worth lingering a moment on his capture. Ronggawarsita was arrested at the home of his Javanese language and literature student. That student, C. F. Winter, Sr. (who is, by the way, widely acclaimed the father of Javanological philology), had set his teacher up for capture. While the Resident and his guard overpowered the hapless literature teacher, other troops were searching Ronggawarsita's home. "All his papers," along with several "military drums" and a banner inscribed in Arabic script, were confiscated. The captive Ronggawarsita, called by his captors "the most intelligent Javanese alive," was incarcerated in the Residency House where he confessed under torture.[57] This Ronggawarsita was forthwith exiled to Batavia, where he died under mysterious circumstances.[58] Reputedly a brilliant writer, none of his works are extant.[59]

Another of Yasadipura II's sons, Mas Haji Ronggasasmita, having studied under a Javanese Shattariyah Sufi master, made the haj with one of his uncles around 1815. It was on his return trip from Mecca that this son wrote his renowned *Suluk Acih,* a widely circulated compilation of Sufi songs.[60] Haji Ronggasasmita is also said to have composed a version of the *Serat Walisana,* a seminal history of the Islamic saints in fifteenth-century Java.[61] Apparently the haji was exiled along with his elder brother in 1828.[62]

R.Ng. Ronggawarsita III (1802–73),[63] far and away the most famous of traditional Javanese writers, the renowned "seal (hence last) of the *pujongga,*" was the son of the exiled elder Ronggawarsita II. Born in Surakarta in 1802, the younger Ronggawarsita also took his education in Javanese and Arabic letters in a *pesantrèn* and, in fact, studied at the East Javanese Tegalsari *pesantrèn* under Imam Besari II, his grandfather's former classmate.[64] Two things are remembered about this Ronggawarsita's *pesantrèn* days: how unruly and poor a student he proved to be, and how it was in the *pesantrèn* that he was struck by the *wahyu,* or "divine light," of *pujongga*ship. Popular tradition also tells us that the first thing the newly enlightened young *pujongga* did upon receipt of his *wahyu* was to perform an exquisite reading of the Qur'ân in Arabic along with an illuminating interpretation of it in Javanese.[65] Several years after finishing his studies at Tegalsari, Ronggawarsita enjoyed a period of less formal *santri* education, traveling from *pesantrèn* to *pesantrèn* across East Java and then on to the hermitage of a Hindu sage in Bali.[66] Like the rest of his family, in 1819 Ronggawarsita joined the corps of court scribes in the Kraton Surakarta. In 1845, he succeeded his grandfather, Yasadipura II, to the office of *Pujongga,* an office he held until his death in 1873.

The *pujongga* Ronggawarsita also had a variety of professional ties outside the *Kraton.* He worked particularly closely with his father's old student C. F. Winter, Sr., the same father of colonial philology who had set up the elder Ronggawarsita for arrest and exile. The younger Ronggawarsita was a well-known "native informant" to a number of other colonial philologists as well, including Cohen Stuart, who in the 1860s "discovered," as it were, that our *pujongga* didn't really know what he was talking about.[67] In the last decades of his life, this last of the Kraton *pujonggas* bridged the transition to what is now thought of as the *moderen* period by serving as an editor of the first indigenous-language newspaper published in the Indies.[68]

An unbelievably prolific writer, Ronggawarsita III is said to have written as many as fifty nine books, several among them tomes thousands of pages long.[69] Like his predecessors, Ronggawarsita also produced translations of classic texts, his most notable contribution evidently a new prose translation and explication of the old *Kekawin Bharatayuda.*[70] His most ambitious work, however, was another prose text. This is, of course, his truly massive *Pustaka Raja* ("Book of Kings") series, a chronological, dynastic history of Java from the Creation, through the Hindu heroes of the *wayang* ("shadow puppet") world and the old Hindu-Buddhist courts, up to the mid-eighteenth-century Surakarta Palace in which his great-grandfather had served.[71] Ronggawarsita also wrote several poetic histories that were set in legendary pre-Islamic Central Java.[72] But he wrote other histories as well: his prose *Tapel Adam* traces an Islamic past from the Creation through the Prophet Mohammad, while his *Kaol saking Kitab Musarar* writes Java's history, backward and forward, in an Islamic frame: back to the time of its first human population (which, as it turns out, was the result of Turkish colonization) and forward to the Qur'anic Day of Judgment.[73] Ronggawarsita also authored poetic *suluk* texts,[74] an immensely popular prose textbook of Islamic mystical practice,[75] treatises on Javanese, European, and Islamic time–reckoning,[76] *and,* perhaps, an interpretive translation of the Qur'ân.[77]

This Ronggawarsita is most famous, however, for his prophecies. His prophetic *Serat Kalatidha* ("Time of Darkness") is, for example, still his most read work, if not the most read of all traditional Javanese literary works.[78] But I wish to close this section on the last of the Kraton *pujonggas* with a word on another of his prophetic texts, that is, the widely read version of the Jayabaya prophecy that he incorporated into his massive *Pustaka Raja*.[79] Like his famous *Kalatidha,* Ronggawarsita's Jayabaya prophecy is actually a work of intralinguistic "translation," a work, in other words, that was composed by means of transposition from, and commentary on, other textual works. Ronggawarsita's primary source for both these texts appears to have been prophetic passages in the encyclopedic *Centhini,* the very text upon which his distinguished grandfather, Yasadipura II, had worked.[80]

Ronggawarsita's Jayabaya prophecy, as did the *Centhini*'s, cryptically charts the entire course of Javanese history: from the Javanese year 1, when colonizers from Rum (Turkey) displaced the demonic forces that had held dominion over prehistoric Java, until the year 2100 when Javanese history, again under Turkish dominion, ends on the Day of Judgment. It is a prophecy that was, in the latter years of the nineteenth century, often associated with messianic movements and Islamic revolts. And it was a prophecy that colonial authority sought to control: the "misuse" of the Jayabaya prophecy was punishable by law, in extreme cases with political exile.[81]

In the version associated with the *pujongga* Ronggawarsita and his *santri* family, the prophecy is attributed to King Jayabaya, a ninth-century (*sic*) king of the Old Javanese realm of Kediri, and a king who was believed to be an incarnation of the Hindu god Visnu. This Jayabaya was—and this is certainly not by chance—the same king for whom was written (in 1157) the *kekawin Bharatayuda,* the classic text that both the elder Yasadipura and his great-grandson Ronggawarsita would translate.[82] According to these palace *pujonggas,* however, the source of King Jayabaya's prophetic foresight was not the Hindu deities celebrated in the epic *Mahabharata* but instead a wandering Sufi saint from Turkey. And Ronggawarsita's distinctive version of the Jayabaya prophecy even tells how this Javanese Vishnu-in-the-flesh was (secretly) converted to Islam by this same saint, a certain Sèh Maolana Ngali Samsujèn. The text goes on to disclose how the Sufi master then revealed to the classical king the past and future (Islamic) history of Java: from its beginning, with the prehistoric colonization by the Sultan of Turkey, to its end, again under a Turkish sultan, with the Day of Judgment. By enclosing Javanese history in a supra-Javanese Islamic frame, and by disclosing that the foremost literary patron of Old Java (Vishnu's incarnation on classical Javanese soil) was "really" a closet Moslem, the last of the Surakarta *pujonggas* thus provides a novel context in which to reread the classical Javanese past and the texts of that past. Reversing the colonial cliché, the Surakarta *pujongga* apparently attests that beneath a thin veneer of Hindu-Buddhist words and stories, the classical Javanese and their texts belong(ed) to the world of Sufi Islam. Like his great-grandfather before him, then, Ronggawarsita realized, and was inviting his readers to realize, the paradoxical truth that the Old Javanese classics had, in postclassical Islamic Java, become Sufi works. In other words, by locating "Java" as such within a supra-Javanese Islamic framework, the neoclassical court poets entered a discursive space in which they might understand *as* Islamic the same classical texts that wishful colonial Javanologists celebrated as un-Islamic bulwarks of essential Javanism.

This brief survey of lives lived and works produced by Surakarta's *pujongga* family suggests, I think, the vital and productive involvement of Surakarta's most prized literati within a larger Javanese-Islamic intellectual world extending well beyond the Kraton walls of the latter eighteenth and the nineteenth centuries—precisely the period when court poets and poetry had supposedly turned away from Islam. My point in reporting all this has not been to pretend that these *pujonggas* were "really" a nest of Moslem radicals. Such a conclusion would, in fact, only reinforce the colonial bias that to be actively engaged in Islamic teachings and texts is to be immediately suspect—that is to reproduce the colonial nightmare of fanatical Islam. Rather, by considering the curiously overlooked Islamic side of the literary culture of "Renaissance Surakarta," I have attempted to complicate the picture of Javanese tradition, to chip away at the very solid fiction of kraton walls imagined as un-Islamic bulwarks preserving behind them an originary Hindu-Javanese high culture. For, when those cultural walls were supposedly being built, the intellectual worlds of the Kraton and the Islamic *pesantrèn* did not stand in simple binary opposition. This is particularly evident if one bears in mind that the bulk of manuscripts housed in the Kraton's scriptorium were not produced by the famed *pujongga* but by a great variety of authors—local royals (both male and female), lowly court servants (often with deep roots in the countryside), regional nobles, village puppeteers, *and* rural *kyai*. Many, though not all, of these *other* traditional writers of texts stored in the Kraton would have come out of, or through, the Islamic *pesantrèn* world, the same world in which the Yasadipura lineage grew.

I will conclude with a few statistics concerning this larger body of Kraton-housed texts. In the early 1980s I had the happy job of examining and describing the contents of all the manuscripts in the Kraton Surakarta scriptorium. Prepared by my reading of the colonial philogical canon, I had arrived on the job ready to see the "belletristic Indic classics" for which this palace is famed. What I found was this: of the 1,450 titles in the collection, there were only 17 of the renowned renaissance renderings of the old Kawi classics into modern Javanese verse. That is just a shade over 1 percent. In contrast to these 17, there were nearly 500 titles belonging to varieties of (more obviously) Islamic literature—that is, a solid third of the entire collection. In short, for every supposed "Indic classic," there were 30 texts of more obviously Islamic content. That colonial scholarship failed to see the significance of such an abundance of Islamic inscription is no doubt testimony to the power the "Indic classic" apparently represents.

Glossary

kawi (kekawin)   Old Javanese classical poetic text, language, metrical form.

kraton   Javanese court or palace.

kyai   "master, venerable gentleman"; a title often used to refer to a teacher/master of Islamic knowledge; the master of a *pesantrèn.*

ngèlmu   (from the Arabic *'ilm*) 'knowledge'; often "divine knowledge."

pesantrèn   place of *santri;* institution of Islamic learning.

priyayi   the administrative and/or bureaucratic elite of the realm.

pujongga   divinely invested court poet and royal adviser.

santri   "wandering student of Islamic religion"; in the twentieth century, the term has come to mean "devout Moslem."

suluk   (from the Arabic *sulûk* 'traversing the Sufi way'), Sufi poem in Javanese sung *macapat* meters.

wahyu   (from the Arabic *wahy* 'revelation', as in Koranic revelation), a divine and manifest light, which, when it falls upon the favored person, supernaturally invests that person with the power of, say, kingship or *pujongga*ship.

The Yasadipura Pujongga Family

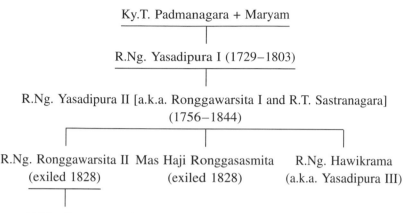

Ky.T. Padmanagara + Maryam

R.Ng. Yasadipura I (1729–1803)

R.Ng. Yasadipura II [a.k.a. Ronggawarsita I and R.T. Sastranagara]
(1756–1844)

R.Ng. Ronggawarsita II   Mas Haji Ronggasasmita   R.Ng. Hawikrama
(exiled 1828)   (exiled 1828)   (a.k.a. Yasadipura III)

R.Ng. Ronggawarsita III (1802–73)
(The Seal of the Pujongga)

NOTES

1. C. Poensen, *Brieven over den Islâm* (Leiden: Brill, 1886), 6–8, and passim; R. A. Kern, "De Javaan als Moslim," in J. Poortenaar and W. Ch. Coolhaas, eds., *Onder Palmen en Waringins: Geest en godsdienst van Insulinde* (Naarden, [1945]), 156–73. These evaluations were not new to the latter nineteenth century. In his influential *History of Java,* Sir Thomas Stamford Raffles (Lieutenant Governor General of Java in 1811–16) quotes the memoir of a Dutch colonial official (Dirk Hogendorp, Governor of Java's North Coast) on the difference of Javanese Islam: "The religion of the Javans is in general Mahometan, but mingled with many superstitious doctrines derived from the ancient Pagan worship. The Javans, however, are far from bigots to their religion, as other Mahometans generally are. They are mild and tractable by nature . . ." (*Hogendorp's Memoir on Java* [1800], in Raffles, *The History of Java,* vol. 2 [London: Black, Parbury, and Allen, 1817]; reprint, London: Oxford University Press, 1965), 2.

I do not mean to claim that the colonial picture or apprehension of native Islam in Java was a unitary or monolithic one, however. There were colonial voices that contested this conventional representation. Indeed, in both his scholarly and his administrative writings, the renowned colonial Islamicist Snouck Hurgronje frequently countered the conventional misconception that Indonesian Islam was somehow essentially different from other Islams. See, for example, *The Achehnese,* vol. 2 (Leiden: Brill, 1906), 279–81. Snouck does not deny the syncretism of Indonesian Moslems; instead he notes the also syncretic nature of the Islam practised by other Moslem peoples (i.e., in Arabia, Egypt, Syria, and Turkey).

2. The Resident was the chief colonial official in any district, or Residency. In the Principalities, or *Vorstenlanden,* the Resident was considered the "older brother" of the ruling indigenous Prince.

3. Algemeen Verslag der Residentie Soerakarta over het jaar 1886, Solo Bundel 4/O, Arsip Nasional Republik Indonesia.

4. See, for example, Sartono Kartodirdjo, *The Peasants' Revolt of Banten in 1888* (The Hague: Martinus Nijhoff, 1966); and id., *Protest Movements in Rural Java* (Kuala Lumpur: Oxford University Press, 1973); and Ann Kumar, *The Diary of a Javanese Muslim: Religion, Politics, and the Pesantren, 1883–1886* (Canberra: Australian National University Press, 1985).

5. On the late-nineteenth-century anti-imperial discourse of Pan-Islamism, and on the significance of the hajj to religious revivalism in Java *and* in the rest of the Moslem world at that time, see Sartono, *Peasants' Revolt of Banten in 1888,* 140–54.

6. There were, of course, indigenous Javanistic texts that shared this disdain for foreign, "desert" Islam. See, for example, the nineteenth-century text *Serat Darmagandhul* (composed [Kedhiri, late nineteenth century]; inscribed Surakarta, 1921) MS. Sasana Pustaka, Karaton Surakarta [henceforth SP] 132 Ca; Surakarta Manuscript Project [henceforth SMP] Karaton Surakarta [henceforth KS] 517; and G. W. J. Drewes's discussion of this text in "The Struggle between Javanism and Islam as Illustrated by the *Serat Dermogandul,*" *Bijdragen tot de Taal-, Land en Volkenkunde* [*BKI*] 122, no. 3: 309–65. See also Benedict Anderson's translation of the *Serat Gatholoco* ("The *Suluk Gatoloco:* Parts One and Two," *Indonesia* 32 (October 1981): 109–50; 33 (April 1982): 31–88.

7. Louis Couperus, *The Hidden Force,* trans. Alexander Teixeira de Mattos, rev. and ed. E. M. Beekman (Amherst: University of Massachusetts Press, 1985); originally published in Dutch by L. J. Veen (Amsterdam, 1900) under the title *De Stille Kracht.*

8. M. C. Ricklefs, *A History of Modern Indonesia* (London and Basingstoke: Macmillan, 1981), 113.

9. Also remembered would have been the fierce Padri War of West Sumatra, in which colonial forces were engaged from 1821 to 1838.

10. See H. J. Benda, "Christian Snouck Hurgronje and the Foundations of Dutch Islamic Policy in Indonesia," *Journal of Modern History* 30, no. 4 (1958): 338–47.

11. Contesting this wishful colonial report to the Governor General, however, are the comments of Pakubuwana IX (ruler of the Kraton Surakarta, 1861–93). In 1876 the King noted, in a didactic poem addressed to his son and heir, that "a multitude of people were carried away" by the teachings of this saint (Mas Jedhig) and that some members of the elite (*pyayi*) were implicated in his movement (*Wulang Putra* [composed 1876], in *Serat Wira Iswara* [Jakarta: Balai Pustaka, 1979], 103).

12. Algemeen Verslag der Residentie Soerakarta over het jaar 1839, Solo Bundel 2/8, Arsip Nasional Republik Indonesia.

13. See especially the note on the subversive potential of religious teachers from the

Panaraga area in Algemeen Verslag der Residentie Soerakarta over het jaar 1885, Solo Bundel 4/N, Arsip Nasional Republik Indonesia.

14. See, for example, Politiek Verslag der Residentie Soerakarta 1856, Solo Bundel 1/1; Algemeen Verslag der Residentie Soerakarta 1885, 1886, 1887, 1888, Solo Bundel 4/N–Q. In royal Surakarta of the latter nineteenth century, the suspects belonged to Kraton Surakarta circles. By then the scions of the minor Mangkunagaran principality were considered model colonial vassals. For a considered discussion of the differences between these two royal establishments, see John Pemberton, *On the Subject of "Java"* (Ithaca: Cornell University Press, 1994), 105–12.

15. The same Resident of Surakarta who continued to send relatively upbeat yearly reports that assured his superiors of the docility of Surakarta's king (Pakubuwana IX) and his Islam apparently confided a rather less sanguine view to an English guest he entertained at the Residency House in 1889. Compare, for example, the official notes of Resident Spaan (served 1884–90) on the tolerant nature of the king's Javanese Islam (Algemeen Verslag der Residentie Soerakarta 1886, Solo Bundel 4/O) with the following notes by Spaan's English visitor: "The city [of Surakarta] is dominated by a fortress almost opposite the Residency, and this would be quite sufficient to quell any disturbances likely to arise in a place rather given to discontent of the Dutch Protectorate, kept alive by the hatred existing in the Emperor's Kraton (or Palace confines) towards the Government, and the constant preaching of the Hadjis, either real or sham ones, who, knowing it will please the Emperor, do what they can to foment sedition. Mr. Spaan is, however, not a man to be trifled with, and the soldiers are ordered out on the slightest provocation, which has a most salutary effect" (Arthur Earle, "A Month in Java in 1889," typescript, 29).

16. See V. J. H. Houben, "Afstand van Gebied met Behoud van Aanzien," M.A. thesis, Leiden University, 1976.

17. Under the Cultuur Stelsel, Javanese peasants were forced to plant a certain proportion of their fields with export crops for delivery to the colonial government. This exploitation of native agricultural labor brought enormous amounts of money into the Dutch treasury over the next half century. The net profits from 1831–77 were 832 million guilders. These remittances accounted for 32 percent of Dutch state revenues in the years 1851–60 (Ricklefs, *A History of Modern Indonesia*, 117).

For more on the colonial project of Javanology, see Kenji Tsuchiya, "Javanology and the Age of Ranggawarsita: An Introduction to Nineteenth-Century Javanese Culture," in *Reading Southeast Asia* (Ithaca: Cornell University, Southeast Asia Program, 1990). See also C. Fasseur, "The French Scare: Taco Roorda and the Origins of Javanese Studies in the Netherlands," in *Looking in Odd Mirrors: the Java Sea,* ed. V. J. H. Houben et al. (Leiden: Vakgroep Talen en Culturen van Zuidoost-Azië en Oceanië Rijksuniversiteit te Leiden, 1992); my *Javanese Literature in Surakarta Manuscripts,* vol. 1, *Introduction and Manuscripts of the Karaton Surakarta* (Ithaca: Cornell University, Southeast Asia Program, 1993), 12–14; and the introduction to my *Writing the*

Past, Inscribing the Future: History as Prophecy in Colonial Java (Durham: Duke University Press, 1995).

18. Clifford Geertz, *The Religion of Java* (Glencoe: Free Press, 1960), 237.

19. For a fuller, and somewhat more complicated, outline of the postcolonial Dutch philological history of Javanese literature, see Theodore G. Th. Pigeaud, *Literature of Java,* 4 vols. (The Hague: Nijhoff, 1967–80), 1:4–9.

20. Pigeaud, *Literature of Java,* 1:236.

21. See, for example, the preface to A. B. Cohen Stuart's philological edition and annotated Dutch translation of Yasadipura I's *Serat Bratayuda.* Yasadipura's text is a Modern Javanese rendering of a twelfth-century Old Javanese classic *kekawin* which was itself a translation of the climax of the Sanskrit *Mahabharata* epic. Cohen Stuart's prefatory remarks to his edition of Yasadipura's text abound with apologies to his audience for subjecting them to such decadent, confused, and bastardized material. He mercilessly disparages Yasadipura's comprehension of Old Javanese as well as his literary skills in Modern Javanese (A. B. Cohen Stuart, *Bråtå-Joedå: Indisch Javaansch Heldendicht, Verhandelingen van het Bataviaasch Genootschap van Kunsten and Wetenschappen,* vols. 27–28 (Batavia, 1860).

22. For more on the *pujongga,* see the introduction to my *Writing the Past, Inscribing the Future.*

23. See Poerbatjaraka's assessment of Yasadipura's contributions to Javanese literary culture in his historical survey of the literature. A scholar from Surakarta who himself composed a poetic Modern Javanese rendition of another Kawi classic (*Serat Smaradhahana* [composed Surakarta, 1916; inscribed Surakarta, 1923], MS. SP 169 Ca; SMP KS 431), Poerbatjaraka gratefully acknowledges Yasadipura's role in the transmission of the old literary culture that had been in danger of extinction. But, as a Leiden-trained philologist, Poerbatjaraka *also* repeats the negative evaluation initiated by Cohen Stuart of Yasadipura's linguistic (in)competence in the same Old Javanese idiom that he is credited with saving (*Kapustakan Djawi* [Jakarta: Djambatan, 1952], 133–48).

24. For a comprehensive introduction to the *pesantrèn,* see Zamakhsyari Dhofier, *Tradisi Pesantren* (Jakarta: LP3ES, 1982). See also chapter 5 of my *Writing the Past, Inscribing the Future.*

25. The court poets were not the only ones who enjoyed *pesantrèn* educations as part of their preparation for royal service in the late eighteenth and early nineteenth centuries. In his nineteenth-century study of traditional Javanese education, J. F. G. Brumond notes that *pesantrèn* education was considered normal training for other courtiers of the Surakarta Palace as well (*Het Volksonderwijs onder de Javanen* [Batavia: Van Haren Noman and Kolff, 1857], 28). And even Javanological philology apparently got its start in the *pesantrèn,* for another notable *pesantrèn* student was G. F. C. Gericke, the German philologist and Bible translator who founded the colonial Institute of Javanese Language in Surakarta in 1834. In 1829, during the Dipanegara War, Gericke joined with candidate courtiers of the Surakarta Palace

for a six-month course of study at the famous Tegalsari *pesantrèn* in Panaraga, East Java. Anthony Day has noted that both there and later in Surakarta his "vision consistently filtered out possible Islamic meanings of Islamic learning institutions and texts" in a way that was nothing short of fantastic ("Islam and Literature in South-East Asia," in *Islam in South-East Asia,* ed. M. B. Hooker [Leiden: Brill, 1983], 134).

26. The following sketch of Yasadipura's life and works is based in large part on a (poorly documented) biography that was published in 1939 as part of the bicentennial celebration of the founding of Surakarta (R. Sasrasumarta et al., *Tus Pajang: Pèngetan Lalampahanipun Swargi R.Ng. Yasadipura I, Abdi-dalem Kaliwon Pujongga ing Surakarta Hadiningrat* [Surakarta: Budi Utomo, 1939]).

27. In the twentieth century, the term *santri* has come to mean a pious Moslem, one who strictly adheres to the precepts of his or her faith. In nineteenth-century Javanese manuscripts, however, *santri* designates an often itinerant student of Islamic religion and theology; *kaum* (or *kaum keputihan*) was the term conventionally used in these earlier texts to designate a pious Moslem.

28. For a concise synopsis of the text, see R. Poerwa Soewignja and R. Wirawangsa, *Pratélan Kawontenaning Boekoe-boekoe Basa Djawi,* 2 vols. (Batavia: Ruygrok, 1920–21), 1:74–75. On the attribution of authorship to Padmanagara, see (Kyai T. Padmanagara) *Serat Tékawardi* (composed [Kartasura, 1726–45]; inscribed Surakarta, [late nineteenth century], MS. Reksa Pustaka, Istana Mangkunagaran [henceforth RP] A 76; SMP Mangkunagaran [henceforth MN] 305.1), i.

29. On Pakubuwana's flight to Tegalsari, see F. Fokkens "De Priesterschool te Tegalsari," *Tijdschrift voor Taal-, Land-, en Volkenkunde (TBG)* 24 (1878): 318–36. Pakubuwana II is said to have composed a didactic text on Islamic theology and ritual obligations during his stay in Panaraga. That text stresses the importance and power of *sastra* (writing and/or literature), both Javanese and Arabic (I.S.K.S. Pakubuwana II, *Serat Wulang-dalem Sampéyan-dalem Ingkang Sinuhun Kangjeng Susuhunan Ingkang Kaping II* [composed Panaraga, 1742; inscribed Surakarta, (1841) and 1885/6] MS. SP Uncatalogued; SMP KS 337.15, and SP 210 Na–B; SMP KS 367).

30. On Kalijaga, see Clifford Geertz, *Islam Observed* (Chicago: University of Chicago Press, 1973), 25ff. and passim.

31. *Suluk* (from the Arabic *sulûk* 'traversing the Sufi way') designates complex texts that write allusively and often symbolically of matters that concern Islamic mystical practice and belief. Interestingly, Dutch philologists have quite consistently wished to deny or underplay the Arabic/Islamic etymology of the term *suluk* while retaining its usage as a generic marker of "Javanese mystic songs." See, for example, Pigeaud, *Literature of Java,* 1:85; and G. W. J. Drewes, "Wat valt er te verstaan onder het Javaanse Woord *Suluk?*" *BKI* 148, no. 1 (1992): 22–30. Among the *suluk* attributed to Prince Wijil Kadilangu are the spunky, antiauthoritarian *Suluk Besi* and the gravely orthodox *Suluk saking Kitab Candra;* see my *Javanese Literature in Surakarta Manuscripts,* 262.

32. On Yasadipura's role in the founding of the new kingdom, see *Sri Radya Laksana* (Surakarta: Budi Utomo, 1939).

33. Yasadipura's roles in the political and marital intrigues of the early years of Surakarta are documented in *Babad Prayut* and *Babad Pakepung,* both of which he composed or coauthored. Some of those exploits are also outlined in Sasrasumarta's *Tus Pajang.*

34. Pakubuwana III (1732–88) authored several works. In addition to a literary translation of the kakawin *Arujuna Wiwaha,* the king also composed three *suluk* texts: *Suluk Martabat Wahdat Wakidiyat, Suluk Bayan Maot,* and *Suluk Sasmitaning Sanjata Cipta.* See my *Javanese Literature in Surakarta Manuscripts,* 1:234, 260–61, 265.

35. Pakubuwana IV (1768–1820) was himself an accomplished and prolific writer. His didactic *Wulang Rèh* is conventionally acclaimed a masterpiece of Javanese writing. He wrote a number of other Islamic didactic works, as well as several *suluk* (*Suluk Dhudha, Suluk Purwaduksina, Suluk Dumununging Manah, Suluk Dumununging Toya, Suluk Dumununging Siti,* and *Suluk saking Kitab Usul-mubin*); on these *suluk,* see ibid, 261–62, 265–66.

36. *Babad Kartasura Pacina* (composed Surakarta, late eighteenth century; inscribed Surakarta, s.a.), MS. SP 186 Ca–B, SMP KS 43; *Babad Giyanti,* 21 vols. (Batavia: Balai Pustaka, 1937–39); (with R.T. Sastranagara), *Babad Prayut* (composed Surakarta, late eighteenth century, inscribed Surakarta, 1854), MS. RP B32b, SMP MN 212; *Babad Prayut dumugi Pakepung* (composed Surakarta, late eighteenth century– early nineteenth century, inscribed Surakarta, 1885), MS. SP Uncatalogued, SMP KS 59. For an illuminating analysis of excerpts from *Babad Prayut,* see Pemberton, *On the Subject of "Java",* 39–52.

37. R.Ng. Yasadipura I, *Serat Ménak,* 25 vols., 46 pts. (Batavia: Balai Pustaka, 1933–37). On the censorship, see Poerbatjaraka, *Kapustakan Djawi,* 149.

38. Ibid.

39. Personal communication, I.S.K.S. Pakubuwana XII. A talismanic manuscript of the *Tajusalatin* that is associated with Pakubuwana III and Pakubuwana IV is still preserved in the library of the Kraton Surakarta (MS. SP 140 Ca; SMP KS 340.1).

40. See *Serat Suluk Jaman Karaton-dalem ing Surakarta* (compiled Surakarta, 1870; inscribed Surakarta, 1870), MS. SP 244 Na; SMP KS 481, at 190–242, 305–9. On the classification of the *Déwaruci* as a *suluk,* see my *Writing the Past, Inscribing the Future,* 259–61.

41. For an edition and annotated translation into English of Yasadipura's *Cabolèk,* see S. Soebardi, *The Book of Cabolèk* (The Hague: Nijhoff, 1975).

42. Punapa malih rasaning kawi / Bima Suci kalawan Wiwaha / pan sami kèh sasmitané / ngenting rasaning ngèlmu / yèn patitis kang mardikani / kadyangga kawi Rama / punika tesawup (*Cabolèk* VIII:6; Soebardi, 114). The translation is my own.

43. In the *Cabolèk,* for example, see VIII:6–7 and IX:4,6 (Soebardi, 114, 134).

44. Mas Ronggasasmita, *Suluk Acih* (compiled Aceh, 1815; inscribed Surakarta, 1867), MS. SP 15 Ca; SMP KS 502, at 56.

45. It is, and especially was, normal for Javanese to change names repeatedly. A new name would be taken upon passage of each of life's milestones, that is, upon recovery from a serious illness, upon marriage, upon a new job, upon career promotions, and so on. The elder Yasadipura also had a series of names (and nicknames), among them: Bagus Banjar, Jaka Subuh, Kudapangawé, Ky. Ng. Posliyun, and Tus Pajang.

46. Around 1745, Pakubuwana II (r. 1726–49) established the Tegalsari *pesantrèn,* which he endowed by royal foundation, in gratitude to Kyai Kasan Besari [I] for the succour the holy man had provided him in 1742. Kyai Iman Besari II (the second son of Kyai Iman Besari I) became the *kyai* of the *pesantrèn* in about 1800 (F. Fokkens, "De Priesterschool te Tegalsari," 318–22). This Iman Besari II (1762–1862) had been a *pesantrèn* classmate (*sadhérèk satunggal puruhita*) of Yasadipura II (Komite Ronggawarsitan, *Serat Babad Cariyos Lalampahanipun Suwargi Radèn Ngabéhi Ronggawarsita Pujongga Ageng ing Nagari Surakarta Hadiningrat* [henceforth *Babad Ronggawarsitan*] [Surakarta: Marsch, 1931], 1:6). Presumably their teacher was Iman Besari I, or possibly Kyai Yahya (the first Iman Besari's eldest son and immediate successor). In 1805, Iman Besari II was married to a widowed niece of the Yasadipura's royal patron, Pakubuwana IV. The son of that union was to become the *Bupati* of Panaraga, R.M.T. Cakranagara (R.Ng. Wirapratana and [Ki Padmasusastra], *Sejarah Ageng ing Karaton Surakarta* [compiled Surakarta, ca. 1900–1940; typed s.l., s.a.], MS. RP B77; SMP MN 690, at 91–92; and *Kagungan-dalem Serat Babat Sengkala: Kawit Pulo Jawi Dipun isèni Tiyang nuliku Taun ongka 1 dumugi Taun 1854* [MS. SP 220 Ca–A; SMP KS 1A], at 69).

47. *Serat Lokapala Sekar Ageng* (composed Surakarta, 1807; inscribed Surakarta, 1807), MS. RP D 31, SMP MN 483; *Serat Lokapala* (composed Surakarta, 1819, inscribed Surakarta, early to mid-nineteenth century), MS. RP D 28, SMP MN 482.

48. For a genealogy and discussion of this translation, see my *Writing the Past, Inscribing the Future,* 258–59.

49. Yasadipura II's best-known Kawi-Javanese lexicon was his *Serat Dasanama Jarwa* (Surakarta: Albert Rusche, 1916). His commentary on the past is found in an interpretive reading of Rongga Janur's eighteenth-century *Serat Pralambang Uran-uran Semut Ireng* (SMP RP A 44a; SMP MN 406).

50. See R.T. Sastranagara (R.Ng. Yasadipura II), *Wicara Keras* (composed Surakarta, 1817), MS. RP 58 A; SMP MN 381.2.

51. R.T. Sastranagara (R. Ng. Yasadipura II), *Babad Pakepung* (composed Surakarta early nineteenth century; inscribed Surakarta, 1885/86), MS. SP 70 Ca; SMP KS 60.

52. R.T. Sastranagara (R.Ng. Yasadipura II), *Serat Ambiya,* 2 vols. (composed Surakarta, ca. 1820–23; inscribed Surakarta [late nineteenth century]), MS. RP O 22 and A 48, SMP MN 295–96; *Serat Nabi Musa* (composed Surakarta, 1810–12; inscribed Surakarta, 1810–12), MS. SP 67 Na, SMP KS 530.

53. Among these works are his *Serat Brata Sunu,* his *Serat Sasana Sunu,* and a version of the *Serat Séwaka.*

54. For the text of this *suluk* and an interpretation of it by Yasadipura II's younger brother, R.Ng. Hawikrama (a.k.a. Yasadipura III), see *Serat Suluk Jaman Karaton-dalem ing Surakarta,* 264–88.

55. A complete edition of the *Centhini* was recently published by Karkono K. Partokusumo (*Serat Centhini: Suluk Tambangraras,* 12 vols. [Yogyakarta: Yayasan Centhini, 1985–91]). For a convenient synopsis of the text (in Javanese and Indonesian), see Sumahatmaka's *Ringkasan Centini [Suluk Tambangraras]* (Jakarta: Balai Pustaka, 1981).

56. Benedict Anderson has a provocative take on the encyclopedic and potentially contestatory nature of this text in his "Professional Dreams: Reflections on Two Javanese Classics," in *Language and Power: Exploring Political Cultures in Indonesia* (Ithaca: Cornell University Press, 1990), 271–89.

See also S. Soebardi's valuable study of the orthodox elements of *pesantrèn* Islam as depicted in the *Centhini* ("Santri Religious Elements as Reflected in the Book of Tjentini," [*BKI* 127 [1971]: 331–49). In this piece Soebardi counters the mainstream philological assessment of the *Centhini,* an assessment that has tended to downplay the vital Islamic nature of the poem in favor of its "encyclopaedic Javanism."

57. Nahuys to the Kommissaris Generaal, Sourakarta den 19 April 1828, missive no. 41 geheim LaM, Ministerie van Kolonien no. 4133 in the Algemen Rijksarchief, The Hague.

58. See Anjar Any, *Raden Ngabehi Ronggowarsito: Apa Yang Terjadi?* (Semarang: Aneka, 1980), 42.

59. In his enormously influential *Javaansche Zamenspraken,* Winter attributed to the elder Ronggawarsita a recension of *Panji Semawung* (C. F. Winter, *Javaansche Zamenspraken,* vol. 1 [Amsterdam: Johannes Muller, 1882 (orig. 1848)], 189). No manuscript witness of that work or any other work signed by this Ronggawarsita remains in the major Surakarta repositories. Nor were any of his writings ever published—unless, of course, anonymously or under another's name.

60. Mas Ronggasasmita, *Suluk Acih,* 2, 52–55.

61. Ronggasasmita, *Serat Walisana* (composed Surakarta, early nineteenth century; inscribed Surakarta, 1899), MS. SP 11 Ca; SMP KS 28.

62. *Babad Sengkala kang kaurut saking Kagungan-dalem serat Babad* (composed and inscribed Surakarta, ca. 1830–38), MS. SP 6 Ta; SMP KS 1C.7, at 2:127.

63. Among his names were: Bagus Burham, Mas Ng. Pajangswara, and Mas Ng. Sarataka.

64. *Babad Ronggawarsitan,* 1:6.

65. Ibid., 1:105–7.

66. Ibid., 2:13–62.

67. Ronggawarsita was Cohen Stuart's assistant when he was preparing his edition and translation of Yasadipura I's *Serat Bratayuda.* See Cohen Stuart's disparaging remarks on Ronggawarsita's talents in his preface to this translation (*Bråtå-Joedå,* 1:8, 25–26).

68. The paper was the *Bramartani;* it began publication in 1855.

69. For a listing of works attributed to Ronggawarsita, see Simuh, *Mistik Islam Kejawen Raden Ngabehi Ranggawarsita* (Jakarta: University of Indonesia Press, 1988), 51–52; and Anjar Any, *Raden Ngabehi Ronggowarsito: Apa Yang Terjadi?,* 114–16.

70. See *Serat Bratayuda Kawi mawi Jarwa sarwi Pikajengipun* (composed Kediri, 1157, and Surakarta, mid-nineteenth century; inscribed Surakarta [by Ronggawarsita?], mid-nineteenth century), MS. RP D 6; SMP MN 472.

71. For a good introduction to Ronggawarsita's *Pustaka Raja,* see Laurie Sears, *Shadows of Empire: Colonial Discourse and Javanese Tales* (Durham: Duke University Press, 1996), chap. 3.

72. Notable among these compositions are his *macapat* histories *Serat Witaradya* (which he coauthored with "Pris Winter" [F. L. Winter?] and *Serat Cemporèt.* For a sensitive reading of *Serat Cemporèt,* see A. Day, "Ranggawarsita's Prophecy of Mystery," in *Moral Order and the Question of Change: Essays on Southeast Asian Thought,* ed. David K. Wyatt and Alexander Woodside (New Haven: Yale University, Southeast Asia Studies, 1982), 194–217.

73. *Serat Tapel Adam* (composed and inscribed Surakarta, 1864/65), MS. SP 115 Na, SMP KS 9.1; *Serat Kaol saking Kitab Musarar* (composed and inscribed Surakarta, [1864/65]), MS. SP 115 Na, SMP KS 9.2.

74. Among these, *Suluk Saloka Jiwa* and *Suluk Suksmalelana.*

75. That is, the *Wirit Hidayat Jati.* For text, Indonesian translation, and analysis, see Simuh, *Mistik Islam Kejawen R. Ng. Ranggawarsita.*

76. *Serat Cakrawarti* (composed and inscribed Surakarta, 1843/44), MS. RP I 9 and I 10; SMP MN 2–3.

77. Al Qur'ân (inscribed Surakarta [by R.Ng. Ronggawarsita?], mid to late nineteenth century), MS. RP A1a; SMP MN 300. The handwriting of the manuscript, a translation into Javanese prose of the Qur'ân, is very similar to that of the *pujongga* Ronggawarsita.

78. For text and translation of the *Serat Kalatidha,* see J. Joseph Errington, "To Know Oneself the Troubled Times: Ronggawarsita's *Serat Kala Tidha,*" in *Writing on the Tongue,* ed. A. L. Becker (Ann Arbor: University of Michigan, Center for South and Southeast Asian Studies, 1989), 85–138. For a note on its intertextual composition, see the introduction to my *Writing the Past, Inscribing the Future.*

79. See, for example, R.Ng. Ronggawarsita, *Serat Pustaka Raja Madya: Jayabaya* (composed Surakarta, mid–nineteenth century; inscribed Surakarta, mid to late nineteenth century), MS. RP D 128; SMP MN 15, at 456 verso–475 verso. See also R.Ng. Ronggawarsita's draft autograph manuscript, *Serat Jangka Jayabaya tuwin Lambanging Nagari akaliyan Lambanging Para Ratu* (composed Surakarta, mid–nineteenth century; inscribed Surakarta, s.a.), MS. Museum Radyapustaka [henceforth Rp], Uncatalogued; SMP Rp 370.

80. For the *Centhini*'s Jayabaya prophecy, see *Serat Centhini: Suluk Tambangraras,* ed. Karkono K. Partokusumo, 3:342–46; 4:1–6; see also 4:125–28. The *Centhini*

version is itself adapted from earlier prophecies of Java's past and future, notably the early eighteenth-century *Pralambang* text edited, translated, and analysed by J. Brandes in his "Iets over een Ouderen Dipanegara in Verband met een Prototype van de Voorspellingen van Jayabaya," *Tijdschrift voor Nederlandsch-Indie* 32 (1889): 368–430.

81. Snouck Hurgronje, *Adviesen van Snouck Hurgronje 1889–1936,* ed. E. Gobee and C. Adriaanse (The Hague: Nijhoff, 1959), 2:1222–23.

82. See note 21.

REFERENCES

Anderson, Benedict. "Professional Dreams: Reflections on Two Javanese Classics." In id., *Language and Power: Exploring Political Cultures in Indonesia.* Ithaca: Cornell University Press, 1990.

——, ed. and trans. "The *Suluk Gatoloco:* Parts One and Two," *Indonesia* 32 (October 1981): 109–50; 33 (April 1982): 31–88.

Anjar Any. *Raden Ngabehi Ronggowarsito: Apa Yang Terjadi?* Semarang: Aneka, 1980.

Babad Sengkala kang Kaurut saking Kagungan-dalem Serat Babad. (Composed and inscribed Surakarta, ca. 1830–38). MS. Sasana Pustaka, Karaton Surakarta (henceforth SP) 6 Ta; Surakarta Manuscript Project (henceforth SMP) Karaton Surakarta (henceforth KS) 1C.7.

Benda, H. J. "Christian Snouck Hurgronje and the Foundations of Dutch Islamic Policy in Indonesia," *Journal of Modern History* 30, no. 4 (1958): 338–47.

Brandes, J. "Iets over een Ouderen Dipanegara in Verband met een Prototype van de Voorspellingen van Jayabaya," *Tijdschrift voor Nederlandsch-Indie* 32 (1889): 368–430.

Brumond, J. F. G. *Het Volksonderwijs onder de Javanen.* Batavia: Van Haren Noman and Kolff, 1857.

Cohen Stuart, A. B. *Bråtå-Joedå, Indisch Javaansch Heldendicht, Verhandelingen van het Bataviaasch Genootschap van Kunsten and Wetenschappen.* Vols. 27–28. Batavia, 1860.

Couperus, Louis. *The Hidden Force,* trans. Alexander Teixeira de Mattos, rev. and ed. E. M. Beekman. Amherst: University of Massachusetts Press, 1985.

Day, A. "Islam and Literature in South-East Asia." In *Islam in South-East Asia,* ed. M. B. Hooker. Leiden: Brill, 1983.

——. "Ranggawarsita's Prophecy of Mystery." In *Moral Order and the Question of Change: Essays on Southeast Asian Thought,* ed. David K. Wyatt and Alexander Woodside. New Haven: Yale University, Southeast Asia Studies, 1982.

Dhofier, Zamakhsyari. *Tradisi Pesantren.* Jakarta: LP3ES, 1982.

Drewes, G. W. J. "The Struggle between Javanism and Islam as Illustrated by the *Serat Dĕrmogandul*," *Bijdragen tot de Taal-, Land- en Volkenkunde* (henceforth *BKI*) 122, no. 3 (1966): 309–65.

———. "Wat valt er te verstaan onder het Javaanse Woord *Suluk?*" *BKI* 148, no. 1 (1992): 22–30.

Earle, Arthur. "A Month in Java in 1889." Typescript.

Errington, J. Joseph. "To Know Oneself the Troubled Times: Ronggawarsita's *Serat Kala Tidha*." In *Writing on the Tongue,* ed. A. L. Becker. Ann Arbor: University of Michigan, Center for South and Southeast Asian Studies, 1989.

Fasseur, C. "The French Scare: Taco Roorda and the Origins of Javanese Studies in the Netherlands." In *Looking in Odd Mirrors: the Java Sea,* ed. V. J. H. Houben et al. Leiden: Vakgroep Talen en Culturen van Zuidoost-Azië en Oceanië Rijksuniversiteit te Leiden, 1992.

Florida, Nancy. *Javanese Literature in Surakarta Manuscripts.* Vol. 1: *Introduction and Manuscripts of the Karaton Surakarta.* Ithaca: Cornell University Southeast Asia Program, 1993.

———. *Writing the Past, Inscribing the Future: History as Prophecy in Colonial Java.* Durham: Duke University Press, 1995.

Fokkens, F. "De Priesterschool te Tegalsari." *Tijdschrift voor Taal-, Land-, en Volkenkunde* 24 (1878): 318–36.

Geertz, Clifford. *Islam Observed.* Chicago: University of Chicago Press, 1973.

———. *The Religion of Java.* Glencoe: Free Press, 1960.

Houben, V. J. H. "Afstand van Gebied met Behoud van Aanzien." M.A. Thesis, Leiden University, 1976.

Kagungan-dalem Serat Babat Sengkala: Kawit Pulo Jawi Dipun-isèni Tiyang nalika Taun ongka 1 dumugi Taun 1854. Composed Surakarta, s.a.; inscribed Surakarta, [ca. 1924]. MS. SP 220 Ca–A; SMP KS 1A.

Karkono K. Partokusumo. *Serat Centhini: Suluk Tambangraras.* 12 vols. Yogyakarta: Yayasan Centhini, 1985–91.

Kern, R. A. "De Javaan als Moslim." In *Onder Palmen en Waringins: Geest en godsdienst van Insulinde,* ed. J. Poortenaar and W. Ch. Coolhaas. Naarden, n.p. [1945].

Komite Ronggawarsitan. *Serat Babad Cariyos Lalampahanipun Suwargi Radèn Ngabéhi Ronggawarsita Pujongga Ageng ing Nagari Surakarta Hadiningrat.* Surakarta: Marsch, 1931.

Kumar, Ann. *The Diary of a Javanese Muslim: Religion, Politics, and the Pesantren, 1883–1886.* Canberra: Australian National University Press, 1985.

[Padmanagara, Kyai T.]. *Serat Tékawardi.* Composed [Kartasura, 1726–45]; inscribed Surakarta, [late nineteenth century]. MS. Reksa Pustaka, Istana Mangkunagaran [henceforth RP] A 76; SMP Mangkunagaran [henceforth MN] 305.1.

[Padmasusastra, Ki,] and R.Ng. Wirapratana. *Sejarah Ageng ing Karaton Surakarta.* Compiled Surakarta, [ca. 1900–40]; typed s.l., s.a. MS. RP B77; SMP MN 690.

Pakubuwana II, I.S.K.S. *Serat Wulang-dalem Sampéyan-dalem Ingkang Sinuhun Kang-jeng Susuhunan ingkang kaping II.* Composed [Panaraga, 1742]; inscribed Surakarta [1841 and 1885/6]. MSS. SP Uncatalogued; SMP KS 337.15 and SP 210 Na–B; SMP KS 367.

Pakubuwana IX, I.S.K.S. *Wulang Putra* [composed 1876]. In *Serat Wira Iswara.* Jakarta: Balai Pustaka, 1979.

Pemberton, John. *On the Subject of "Java".* Ithaca: Cornell University Press, 1994.

Pigeaud, Theodore G. Th. *Literature of Java.* 4 vols. The Hague: Nijhoff, 1967–80.

Poensen, C. *Brieven over den Islâm.* Leiden: Brill, 1886.

Poerbatjaraka, R.M.Ng. *Kapustakan Djawi.* Jakarta: Djambatan, 1952.

———. *Serat Smaradhahana.* Composed Surakarta, 1916; inscribed Surakarta, 1923. MS. SP 169 Ca; SMP KS 431.

al Qur'ân. Inscribed Surakarta [by R.Ng. Ronggawarsita?, mid to late nineteenth century]. MS. RP A1a; SMP MN 300.

Raffles, Sir Thomas Stamford. *The History of Java.* 2 vols. London: Black, Parbury and Allen, 1817. (Reprint, London: Oxford University Press, 1965.)

Ricklefs, M. C. *A History of Modern Indonesia.* London and Basingstoke: Macmillan, 1981.

Ronggasasmita, Mas. *Serat Walisana.* Composed Surakarta, early nineteenth century; inscribed Surakarta, 1899. MS. SP 11 Ca; SMP KS 28.

———. *Suluk Acih.* Composed Aceh, 1815; inscribed Surakarta, 1867. MS. SP 15 Ca; SMP KS 502.

Ronggawarsita, R.Ng. *Serat Cakrawarti.* Composed and inscribed Surakarta, 1843/44. MS. RP I 9 and I 10; SMP MN 2–3.

———. *Serat Jangka Jayabaya tuwin Lambanging Nagari akaliyan Lambanging Para Ratu.* Composed Surakarta, mid–nineteenth century; inscribed Surakarta by R. Ng. Ronggawarsita, s.a. MS. Rp [Museum Radyapustaka] Uncatalogued; SMP RP [Radyapustaka] 370.

———. *Serat Kaol saking Kitab Musarar.* Composed and inscribed Surakarta, [1864/65]. MS. SP 115 Na; SMP KS 9.2.

———. *Serat Pustaka Raja Madya: Jayabaya.* Composed Surakarta, mid–nineteenth century; inscribed Surakarta, mid to late nineteenth century. MS. RP D 128; SMP MN 15.

———. *Serat Tapel Adam.* Composed and inscribed Surakarta, 1864/65. MS. SP 115 Na; SMP KS 9.1.

Sartono Kartodirdjo. *The Peasants' Revolt of Banten in 1888.* The Hague: Martinus Nijhoff, 1966.

———. *Protest Movements in Rural Java.* Kuala Lumpur: Oxford University Press, 1973.

Sasrasumarta, R., et al. *Tus Pajang: Pèngetan Lalampahanipun Swargi R.Ng. Yasadipura I, Abdi-dalem Kaliwon Pujongga ing Surakarta Hadiningrat.* Surakarta: Budi Utomo, 1939.

Sears, Laurie. *Shadows of Empire: Colonial Discourse and Javanese Tales.* Durham: Duke University Press, 1996.

Sedhah, Empu, and R.Ng. Ronggawarsita. *Serat Bratayuda Kawi mawi Jarwa sarwi Pikajengipun.* Composed Kediri 1157 and Surakarta, mid–nineteenth century; inscribed Surakarta [by Ronggawarsita?], mid–nineteenth century. MS. RP D 6; SMP MN 472.

Serat Centhini: Suluk Tambangraras, ed. Karkono K. Partokusumo. 12 vols. Yogyakarta: Yayasan Centhini, 1985–91.

Serat Darmagandhul. Composed [Kedhiri, late nineteenth century]; inscribed Surakarta, 1921. MS. SP 132 Ca; SMP KS 517.

Serat Suluk Jaman Karaton-dalem ing Surakarta. Compiled Surakarta, 1870; inscribed Surakarta, 1870. MS. SP 244 Na; SMP KS 481.

Simuh. *Mistik Islam Kejawen Raden Ngabehi Ranggawarsita.* Jakarta: University of Indonesia Press, 1988.

Snouck Hurgronje, C. *The Achehnese.* Vol. 2. Leiden: Brill, 1906.

———. *Adviesen van Snouck Hurgronje, 1889–1936,* ed. E. Gobee and C. Adriaanse. Vol. 2. The Hague: Nijhoff, 1959.

Soebardi, S. *The Book of Cabolèk.* The Hague: Nijhoff, 1975.

———. "Santri Religious Elements as Reflected in the Book of Tjentini." *BKI* 127 (1971): 331–49.

Soewignja, R. Poerwa, and R. Wirawangsa. *Pratélan Kawontenaning Boekoe-boekoe Basa Djawi.* 2 vols. Batavia: Ruygrok, 1920–21.

Sri Radya Laksana. Surakarta: Budi Utomo, 1939.

Sumahatmaka, R.M.Ng. *Ringkasan Centini (Suluk Tambangraras).* Jakarta: Balai Pustaka, 1981.

Tsuchiya, Kenji. "Javanology and the Age of Ranggawarsita: An Introduction to Nineteenth-Century Javanese Culture." In *Reading Southeast Asia.* Ithaca: Cornell University, Southeast Asia Program, 1990.

Winter, C. F. *Javaansche Zamenspraken.* Vol. 1. Amsterdam: Johannes Muller, 1882. Originally published in 1848.

Yasadipura I, R. Ng. *Babad Giyanti.* 21 vols. Batavia: Balai Pustaka, 1937–39.

Occidentalism and Orientalism: Perspectives on Legal Pluralism

Lloyd I. Rudolph and Susanne Hoeber Rudolph

In our 1965 article "Barristers and Brahmans" we led off with British pride in the fact that they had "given India justice such as the East has never known before."[1] We told a different story. The British raj, we argued,

> sometimes by design but more often by inadvertence, advanced the written, more uniform, and professionally interpreted law of the twice-born castes (*dharmasastra*) at the expense of the parochial, diverse, and orally transmitted customary law of villagers even as Anglicization began to supersede Indian legal conceptions and social arrangements.[2]

Our exploration of the relationship between "traditional" and "modern" law was embedded in a larger project, a book called *The Modernity of Tradition*. Written between 1962 and 1965, incubated from 1956 when we first visited India, and published in 1967, it critiqued then dominant modernization theories. Guided by an Enlightenment unilinear historical vision, 1960s modernization theories recognized

> nothing of value in the past and saw the hope of mankind in the future. . . . [B]uilding on such assumptions, theorists of social change in new nations have found a dichotomy between tradition and modernity. Useless and valueless, tradition has been relegated to an historical trashheap. Modernity will be realized when tradition has been destroyed and superseded.[3]

We argued that social change was more often based on the continuities of adaptation than on the discontinuities of rupture. The past, we thought, often informed the present and shaped the future. "Tradition" and "modernity" were at best useful abstractions. As reifications they obliterated or totalized

differences. Contestations based on internal differences among ideas and practices were lost from view. Here is how we put the argument thirty years ago:

> If tradition and modernity are seen as continuous rather than separated by an
> abyss, if they are dialectically rather than dichotomously related, and if
> internal variations are attended to and taken seriously, then those sectors of
> traditional society that contain or express potentialities of change from
> dominant norms and structures become critical for understanding the nature
> and processes of modernization. . . . [R]ecessive themes in ["traditional"]
> cultural patterns and psychological makeup that can be mobilized by some-
> what changed historical circumstances become grist for the mill of social
> change.[4]

This view informed our analysis in "Barristers and Brahmans: Legal Cultures and Social Change." The British, until 1858 in the form of the East India
Company, encountered a society with a wide variety of possibilities. We noted,
for example, that parochial customary law (as we then called it) embodied
features that were often quite different from the "overarching pattern of sacred
law that was cultivated and interpreted by Brahmans." We argued that as
British rule began to reshape Indian practice and ideas, a perceived "need for
more uniform law . . . [led raj jurists and administrators to] strengthen the
second [Brahmanic law] at the expense of the first [parochial customary
law]. . . . [I]ndigenous high-culture law aided in establishing a national legal
framework."[5]

We now recognize how much our study of legal cultures in the context of
British rule was embedded in the intellectual currents of the 1950s and 1960s.
Let's start by putting inverted commas around the "tradition" and "modernity"
we used in the title of our book, *The Modernity of Tradition.* The inverted
commas signify for us the contingency with which postmodern skepticism
surrounds the essentialisms of modern epistemology and teleology. Putting
"tradition" and "modernity" in inverted commas can help us to shed the reified
binary baggage that clouded our earlier analysis.

Our essay on legal cultures and the book on the modernity of tradition in
which it figures were written in the shadow of the Parsonian wave that swept
American academic social science in the 1950s and 1960s. Parsons was a,
perhaps *the,* master totalizer. His 1949 magnum opus was called *The Social
System;* one size, it seemed, fit all, regardless of time, place, or circumstance.
Using his pattern variables, he and modernization theorists whom he influenced wrote universalized, teleological accounts of social change.[6] He told the

Faculty Committee on Behavioralism at Harvard in 1954: "A long-term program of scholarly activity which aims at no less than a unification of theory in all fields of the behavioral sciences is now envisaged."[7] He was also a master dichotomizer; his pattern variables bifurcated past and present into five systematically connected binaries, suggesting a progressive, enlightenment future that would supersede an obsolete, retrograde past.[8] The marks of tradition, ascription, affectivity, collectivity, particularity, and diffuseness, were destined to be replaced by modern orientations, achievement, affective neutrality, self-orientation, universalism, and functional specificity. His theoretical realism needed no inverted commas.

Weber, whom Parsons purported to expound, had insisted that ideal types should be treated as models *of* reality, not models *for* reality or *as* reality.[9] Parsons and modernization theorists who followed him missed or ignored this crucial epistemological injunction. Their studies located the movement from tradition to modernity via the pattern variables in specific times and places, that is, they used the pattern variables as models *for* reality and then *as* reality.[10]

We not only tried to get beyond the binarisms of modernization theory; we also were present at the founding of a postcolonial critique when, in the introduction to *The Modernity of Tradition,* we spoke about an "imperialism of categories and historical possibilities." "The myths and realities of Western experience," we warned, can "set limits to Western social scientific imagination, and modernity becomes what we imagine ourself to be."[11] Western social science and history had, we argued, often created categories of analysis out of its own historical experience and then treated them as universal.

Despite our concern about an "imperialism of categories," we see what we wrote thirty years ago as not going far enough, in part because we were awkwardly positioned between inner and outer critiques, one foot uncomfortably located in the box of modernization assumptions, the other unstably located outside. We were trying to get outside the box, but our exit was hindered by the shackles of "modernity" and "tradition." We were constrained, too, by the pervasive functionalism of modernization theory. Thus we spoke of "the need for more uniform law that followed the introduction of the British raj" implying that "need" and/or "structure" independent of history as process, that is independent of practice and "events,"[12] conjunctures and disjunctures,[13] voice and agency, explained why and how legal cultures changed. Now, thirty years later, we would take a more "constructivist" approach to explaining why and how Warren Hastings, with the aid of Sir William Jones and other pioneering Orientalists of the Asiatic Society, could turn to high-culture Brahmanic and Islamic law texts to administer justice in Bengal[14] and beyond.

De-Occidentalizing the Imperial Other: Oriental Knowledge
in the Making

When we published "Barristers and Brahmans" in 1965,[15] the large body of postcolonial scholarship published in the 1980s was yet to be written—no Gramscian hegemony or counterhegemony, no Foucauldian/Saidian knowledge as power. Subaltern studies had not yet reoriented much of Indian historical scholarship, let alone spread beyond "Indian" history to the pages of the *American Historical Review*.[16] Scholarship on law in the former colony and, more broadly, on its history was inspired either by modernization theory or by imperial viewpoints. Often they coincided in hegemonic intent, for example, giving India "justice such as the East has never known." We had read and written about Gandhi but had not adequately "heard" the message in *Hind Swaraj,* his 1909 critique of "modern civilization." Writing on the eve of inventing *satyagraha* in South Africa, he showed in *Hind Swaraj* his awareness of how imperial categories and practice had become hegemonic, not least through the legal system of the empire and the lawyers it spawned.[17]

We take Edward Said's *Orientalism* (1978)[18] as a kind of watershed for how scholars of India identified, read, and interpreted evidence. Recognizing what Ashis Nandy (in 1983) called the "intimate enemy,"[19] they sought to de-orientalize (in Saidian terms) or decolonize (in Nandy's formulation) scholarly representations of knowledge, to get out of the box of imperial and modernization categories, to launch liberating inner and outer critiques that could open the way to alternative ways of seeing and representing, knowing and explaining.

Much of the new writing on India has been done in the shadow of a Saidian critique of orientalism, a critique refurbished and extended to India in Ronald Inden's 1990 book, *Imagining India.*[20] Orientalist knowledge, Said argued, provided civilizational and historical justifications for Britain's imperial project. Said-inspired postcolonial scholarship, which soon overlapped with postmodern scholarship, attempted to show how imperial and modernization formulations depended on the successful construction and reproduction of cultural hegemony, for example, of a world of cooperative, *comprador,* or loyal "brown sahibs" with mentalities occupied by an "intimate enemy."

The postcolonial and postmodern critique of "orientalism" was liberating; it delegitimized and disempowered colonial knowledge at a historical time when direct political hegemony was waning, revealing societies and discourses hidden by imperial historiography and literary products. The critique was also delusive. By dehistoricizing the imperial other, the critique stereotyped and essentialized. Who they were, what they knew, their motives, and intentions were reduced, reified, and abstracted into an undifferentiated hegemonic project. Power and/or class interests became the dominant, even the exclusive, source of knowledge and legitimacy.[21]

The obverse of orientalism is occidentalism.[22] We would like to address the occidentalist construction by investigating the voice and agency of the imperial other.

We are not alone in making efforts to "de-occidentalize" the hegemonic West that Edward Said constructed in 1978 when he launched "Orientalism" as an epistemology. Others who have taken up the task include Raymond Schwab (*The Oriental Renaissance: Europe's Rediscovery of India and the East, 1680–1880,*[23] published in France in 1950 but available in English); Martin Bernal (*Black Athena: The Afroasiatic Roots of Classical Civlization,* 1987); Wilhelm Halbfass (*India and Europe: An Essay in Understanding,* 1988); O. P. Kejariwal (*The Asiatic Society of Bengal and the Discovery of India's Past,* 1988), and Rosane Rocher. In "British Orientalism in the Eighteenth Century" she finds that Edward Said "does to orientalist scholarship what it accuses orientalist scholarship of having done to the countries east of Europe; it creates a single discourse, undifferentiated in space and time and across political, social, and intellectual identities."[24]

These commentators have characterized what we, in this essay, call "Occidentalism," stereotyping knowledge generated by the "colonial" or "imperial" European other. European, including British, modes of knowing and the knowledge they produced were not uniform or uncontested. Events, persons and narratives have been seen and explained by the requirements of power and the practise of hegemony in the colony, hardly at all by variations and contestations in the metropole and its intellectual surroundings in Europe. Here we examine in a particular context how an "orientalist" epistemology can homogenize, decontextualize, and totalize an "imperialist West" in ways that deprive its history of multiple narratives.

If we were to rewrite our 1965 account of "legal cultures and social change" in the light of the intervening Saidian turn to "orientalism" we would challenge the claim that always and necessarily power dominates knowledge and knowledge serves domination. We would follow Marx in arguing that agency can be relatively autonomous of structure, indeed that agency expressed in discursive formations and practices can shape structure.[25]

We may have written about what "the British"—even particular persons such as Hastings—thought and did, that is, up to a point we attended to agency, process, and context, but we, too, stererotyped and totalized. We didn't adequately attend to why "they," the British, the imperialist other, thought what they thought and did what they did. We did not adequately examine their worldviews, intentions, and motives. We focused more on function and its consequences than on meaning and its relation to action.

William Jones and the Recognition of Civilization beyond Europe

Sir[26] William Jones and Warren Hastings provide our exemplars for illustrating what we mean by de-occidentalizing the imperial other. They were leading figures for our analysis in 1965 of "legal cultures and social change." Why did Warren Hastings, who became the East India Company's first Governor-General, and the stellar scholars, also servants of the Company, who comprised the founding generations of the Asiatic Society of Bengal, adopt a policy of legal pluralism that applied "the laws of the Koran with respect to Mohammedans and that of the Shaster with respect to Hindus?" Why did Jones construct a world composed of Hindus and Muslims? A postcolonial perspective leads to reading nineteenth- and twentieth-century categories and outcomes into the mentalities and intentions of eighteenth-century actors. The motive becomes imperial power, the tactic religious division. Power becomes as unnuanced a determinant of thought as control of the means of production.

The colonial experience was characterized by a particular sequencing in the forms and content of knowledge related to European intellectual currents. By placing the civilizational viewpoint early on and the ethnographic viewpoint later, this sequencing seems to have influenced the construction of a dual [Hindu and Muslim] civilization in India.

Hindu and Muslim were not natural categories, neither self-evident nor transparent. We know that contemporaneously and in immediately preceding centuries other nonexclusive ethnic, community, and territorial identities "marked" social categories—for example, Turcs, Iranis, Turanis, Afghans, Rajputs; among "Muslims," Sunnis, Shias, Sufis; among "Hindus," *sampradaya*s such as Vaishnavites, Shivites,[27] Kabirpanthis, Dadupanthis, and other *bhakti* communities; and a myriad of territorially dispersed lineage and caste communities. Such categories had provided mental maps not only for actors within a subcontinent that, in the late nineteenth century, became "India,"[28] but also for "outsiders," travelers and intruders from Greece, China, central Asia, and Europe.

The Frenchman, François Bernier, in his *Travels in the Mugul Empire, A.D. 1656–1668,* tells us that Aurangzeb's court "is a medly of *Usbecs, Persians,*

Arabs, and *Turks*" and that Mughal armies are "composed of either natives, such as *Ragipous* [Rajputs] and *Patans,* or genuine *Mogols.*" No mention is made in this context of "Mohammedans" or "Hindus."[29] During the fourteenth to the sixteenth centuries, when "Hindu" and "Muslim" rulers jostled each other in the Deccan, categories of self and social identification were as often ethnic as they were religious.[30] And Sheldon Pollock tells us that in the "ethnically coded representations of difference" found in Sanskrit texts written after "the coming of the Central Asians . . . the *religious* identity of the Central Asians is not once thematized."[31]

We read the ideas and actions of Hastings and his Asiatic Society colleagues, including their construction of Hindu and Mohammedan, as shaped by two concerns: the sources and meaning of "civilization" conceived of within the framework of world history; and, for Hastings in particular, but not exclusively, a powerful sense of being *local* rulers. It led them to do what they thought local rulers did, rely on the laws of the peoples to administer justice. Hastings', Jones' and their Asiatic Society colleagues' "civilizational eye" saw the legal pluralism of the peoples under their authority as large, coherent cultural wholes defined by great languages and their classic texts. Later, as we argued in "Barristers and Brahmans," the ethnographic eye of subsequent generations of Company administrators led many of them to see legal pluralism differently, as diverse local laws and customs defined by oral traditions.[32]

William Jones, the most creative of the late-eighteenth-century British Orientalists, powerfully shaped the civilizational eye of late-eighteenth-century legal pluralism. Appointed to a judgeship in Bengal in 1782,[33] Jones arrived in Calcutta in September 1783. Thirty-seven years old, he was already a distinguished orientalist and legal scholar. Dead at forty-eight (1794), he had in the intervening eleven years revolutionized the ways civilization, the history of Europe, and universal history were perceived and understood. On the way to doing so, he also helped to establish and legitimize East India Company authority in Bengal. Should we read the transformation of knowledge he wrought as a consequence of being a servant of British conquest, power, and rule? Or should we read his creation of Oriental knowledge as arising from his early involvement with Oriental learning and from his career as legal scholar and judge? Was the Asiatic Society that he founded in 1784 and led for a decade only a handmaiden of British imperial hegemony?

These large questions about discursive formations, epistemic communities, and the sociology of knowledge can be approached by more particular, contextual questions about motives and consequences. As a first-year student at University College, Oxford, in 1764, Jones took up the study of Arabic by employing a Syrian named Mirza, whom he maintained in Oxford at his own expense. Seeing the affinity between Arabic and Persian, the young Jones also started learning Persian. By 1768 he had translated the history of Nadir Shah, the *Tarikh-i-Nadiri,* into French (for King Christian VII of Denmark) and, in 1770, into English, a translation that brought him "great fame but little money." An Orientalist in the making, no doubt, but it seems unlikely that he acquired his knowledge with a view to ruling India.

Jones had mastered Greek, Latin, and French, and was proficient in a variety of other European languages. In 1770 he published a pathbreaking *Grammar of the Persian Language.* Language and literature is what he did well, but it didn't pay. He turned to the bar as a better prospect for earning a livelihood than being a linguist and Orientalist. Again, he distinguished himself as a scholar, this time of the law. His *Essay on the Law of Bailments* (published in 1781) was regarded as a classic. U.S. Supreme Court Justice Joseph Story, who coined the phrase, "the reign of King Mob" to characterize Andrew Jackson's presidency, tells us that even if Jones had not written anything else, "he would have left a name unrivaled in the common law for philosophical accuracy, elegant learning, and finished analysis".[34]

In an era when service in Bengal with the East India Company was perceived as a way, perhaps the best way, to make one's fortune, Jones sought "a vacancy on the India Bench." After a tortuous four-year delay, and only after the personal intervention of King George III, he was offered the appointment in 1782. It provided a way, as he saw it, to combine his pursuit of Oriental knowledge with his legal calling.

What did he think about as he began his career in India? He appears to have thought about the satisfactions of pursuing his interest in law and about the charms of discovering great civilizations, projects that were closely related because the law provided access to civilization. During the five-month voyage to India on the frigate *Crocodile* to become a puisne judge in the Supreme Court at Calcutta, Jones, considering what he would like to study during his stay in India, noted down a list of sixteen topics.[35] The first two were "The laws of the Hindus and Mohammedans" and "The History of the ancient world." The topics implicate him with respect to both his impending obligations as a judge for the East India Company and his goal of pursuing Oriental knowledge. He would use the knowledge he expected to acquire about Hindu and Mohammedan law to govern more effectively and legitimately, and, as the founder and leader of the Asiatic Society of Bengal, he would generate Oriental knowledge about India and contribute to the meaning and sources of civilization and world history.

He reports his thoughts soon after his arrival:

When I was at sea last August, I found one evening, on inspecting the observations of the day, that India lay before us, and Persia on the left, whilst a breeze from Arabia blew nearly on our stern. It gave me inexpressible pleasure to find myself in the midst of so noble an amphitheatre, almost encircled by the vast regions of Asia, which has ever been esteemed the nurse of sciences, the inventoress of delightful useful arts, the scene of glorious actions, fertile in the productions of human genius, abounding in natural wonders, and infinitely diversified in the form of religion and government, in the laws, manners, customs, and languages, as well as in the feature and complections of men. I could not help remarking how important and extensive a field was yet unexplored, and how many solid advantages unimproved.[36]

Romantic, extravagant, yes. But "Power?"

Power was part of the project but not the whole of it. Why, for example, in 1785 did Jones learn Sanskrit—and what consequences followed from his doing so? The decision arose in part from a realization that "he would not be able to do justice to his judicial work if he did not learn the language of the Hindu law books."[37] And why did he think so? Jones agreed, as we have seen, with the Governor-General, Warren Hastings, that "the inhabitants of the land . . . [should] be governed according to their own laws." He had learned that indigenous advisers were not always to be trusted. English judges would have to consult the texts. They "could not," Jones felt, "be expected to learn two languages, Sanskrit and Persian, in which the laws of the Hindus and the Mohammedans were framed."[38] These were circumstances that led him to conclude that he "would not be able to do justice to his judicial work if he did not learn the language of the Hindu law books."

Soon he had translated what he took to be India's leading legal text, the "Ordinances of Manu,"[39] and begun work on the posthumously published four-volume *Digest of Hindu Laws.*

But these practical and legal preoccupations did not exhaust his reasons for learning Sanskrit. His interest in Sanskrit was a sequel to his earlier linguistic interests, first in Greek and Latin, then in Arabic and Persian. Languages provided access to civilizational texts and to the search for civilization that animated a current of the eighteenth century's literary imagination and intellectual life.

It is possible to argue that 1785, the year Jones began to learn Sanskrit, and his subsequent mastery of Sanskrit texts, led to a Copernican-like revolution[40] in Europe's—and India's—view of civilization and world history. Certainly his and his colleagues' knowledge of Sanskrit texts helped reconstitute the way civilization was understood in eighteenth-century Europe. By February 1786, when he delivered an address "On the Hindus," the third of his ten annual discourses to the Royal Asiatic Society, Jones was in a position to make the oft-quoted remarks about Sanskrit that were to begin the study of comparative philology and mythology and through them shape new understandings of civilization and human history:

> Sanskrit language, whatever be its antiquity, is of a wonderful structure; more perfect than the Greek, more copious than the Latin, and more exquisitely refined than either, yet bearing to both of them a stronger affinity, both in the roots of the verbs and in the forms of grammar, than could possibly have been produced by accident; so strong, indeed, that no philologer could examine them all three, without believing them to have sprung from some common source, which, perhaps, no longer exists.[41]

His remarks led to a transformation in the way Europeans conceived of themselves and others. Before Jones, knowledge about the Orient was acquired and presented in ways that addressed European agendas. Despite the retreat of Europe's Christian worldview before the forces of modern philosophy, science, and politics in the seventeenth and eighteenth centuries,[42] discourses remained Eurocentric until Jones and other Asiatic Society scholars wrought their revolution in understanding civilization and world history. Montesquieu's canvas for his *Esprit des Lois* included the Orient; Voltaire had turned first to China, then India, in his efforts to construct a rational ground for religious discourse.[43] But both were primarily concerned to critique and reconstruct *European* thought about civilization, history, and politics.[44] Until the Asiatic Society's Orientalists created an autonomous knowledge base for "Indology,"[45] European scholars and intellectuals wrote about the alien peoples and civilizations of newly discovered lands with European projects in mind.[46]

The "tradition of exploring Indian thought in its original sources and contexts of understanding," Halbfass argues,

> was first achieved towards the end of the Age of Enlightenment, through the scholarly works and programmatic activities of the British 'Orientalists' in Bengal, above all W. Jones [1746–1794], Ch. Wilkins [1749–1836], and H. Th. Colebrooke [1765–1837]. As these scholars turned to the original Sanskrit texts, the use of Persian and other intermediary languages became

obsolete. No longer isolated achievements, their effort led to the establishment and institutionalization of a research tradition—the tradition of modern Indology.[47]

The term "Orientalist" has been transformed by the Saidian epistemological turn from a term of honor to a term of dishonor, from approbation to opprobrium. This "occidentalization" of the imperial other is no less an impoverishment and totalizing of intellectual history than its obverse, the "orientalization" of the colonial other. Sir William Jones deserves a more nuanced reading.

What has this construction of Jones to do with the law, and with the policy choices made by Hastings and those who served him in the East India Company? The epistemological eye of the eighteenth century was civilizational, not ethnographic. It saw history and society as huge constructs, defined by classical language and by powerful texts. Gibbon's publication in 1776 of the first volume of his *Decline and Fall of the Roman Empire* gave a powerful impetus to a civilizational idea already well developed in the mind of an era. For Jones, the Sanskrit language and the texts that defined Hinduism marked such a civilization. His knowledge of Arabic and Persian made it readily apparent that the Hindu law found in the Shastras did not exhaust the legal practices found in Bengal. Muslims who "followed" the "law of the Koran" qualified as another civilization. The Sanskrit-based civilization of the "Hindus" challenged the idea that Europe was *the* world civilization. It seems plausible then to view a civilizational trope rather than a communal dichotomy as the source of Jones' construction of Indian law in terms of Hindu and Mohammedan classical texts.

Warren Hastings as an "Indian" Ruler

Warren Hastings, like Sir William Jones, was an early Orientalist who used his knowledge of India to govern in Bengal. If Jones' choices with respect to the law were influenced by a civilizational trope, Hastings' image of himself as a ruler was shaped by Mughal history. As the canonical Messrs. Thompson and Garrett put it: "Hastings' place is not with the proconsuls of our orderly period, but with such men as Akbar."[48]

"If [Hastings] had a model for Bengal," John Keay, a historiographically acute historian of the East India Company, writes, "it was inspired not by dreams of British empire but what he took to be the traditions of Moghul empire. Outlining his proposed reforms to the Chairman of the Company he stressed that they included 'not one which the original constitution of the

Mogul Empire hath not before established . . . and rendered familiar to the people.' He would 'found the authority of the British government in Bengal on its [Bengal's] ancient laws.' " India was " 'a great nation . . . '; its people were 'not in a savage state' and they had little to gain from the imposition of a 'superior wisdom from outside.' India should be administered by Indians and in accordance with Indian custom. . . . No other governor-general or viceroy," Keay continues, "would last anything like as long as Hastings and no other would approach his profound understanding of India."[49]

Although Hastings is sometimes claimed by British and nationalist historians as a progenitor of the British empire in India, the claim obscures the profound differences between British activities in the eighteenth and the nineteenth centuries. A great deal of postcolonial critique and discourse operates within the boundaries of an anachronistic nation-state epistemology and narrative.[50] Actors' identities and motives are taken to be determined by their membership in an imperialist British nation-state whose agenda of power and domination through hegemony they are taken to embrace.

If it is doubtful that individual or collective motivations are exhausted by a single or dominant motive such as the pursuit of national power (or commercial gain),[51] "national" power becomes an even more doubtful master determinant when we recognize that eighteenth-century historical actors, especially in Asia, but also in Europe, do not "yet" operate within the boundaries of nation-state epistemes. Nation-states are said to strive for congruence between the markers of "ethnicity"—language, culture, history—and political territoriality. In the nineteenth and twentieth centuries, that congruence, that putative subordination of identities and motives to nation-state goals and purposes, were portrayed as controlling domestic political discourse and action and as justifying states' claims to monopoly sovereignty at home and in the anarchic space of "international relations."

As we read the histories and biographies, actors on the Indian subcontinent in and before the eighteenth century lacked a nation-state conception and vocabulary. Nor did they make a sharp distinction between indigenous and foreign persons or make claims to an overriding, territorially based national loyalty. Afghans and Iranis and Turks and other earlier central Asian peoples— Shakas, Kushans—had entered the subcontinent to pluck the alleged riches of "Hindustan." Some remained to found dynasties and become an element in the complex ethnic mix that characterized regions North and South. Before the territorial nation-state was naturalized and universalized, there were no transparent or self-evident criteria to mark the British as more foreign than the

Lodis, the Surs, and the Timurids—or the Portuguese, the Dutch, the French—
or to lead British merchants to think of themselves as different from other
traders.

In a land where the fluidity of elites was such that many rulers did not share
the ethnic identity of their subjects, the English too could think of themselves
as indigenous, that is, as no more or less foreign than other rulers. Like other
resourceful captains and military entrepreneurs, eighteenth-century English-
men adapted to and often adopted the ways of the country. When Company
servants assumed the Diwani of Bengal, they understood themselves to be, and
were understood as, equivalent to the *nawab bahadur.* Before the nation-state
froze both territoriality and identity, Company servants were like earlier and
contemporary adventurers who flowed across lands without frontiers. It is in
this context that we speak of Hastings imagining himself as a "native" ruler.

Outside Bengal, Hastings' image of the Company's presence on the subcontinent was "to exert, from behind its ring fence[52] of subordinate states, a
stabilizing and responsible influence as one among several of the subcontinent's powers."[53] Indeed Hastings' identification with Bengal, his local support and popularity, his sense of being an autonomous ruler, and the reliability
and loyalty of his allies on the subcontinent may have led him to contemplate
independence. "If there was ever a moment when the Company in India might
have withheld its allegiance to the Directorate," Keay argues, "it must surely
have been in 1784–85."[54] Political extinction in the shape of Dundas', Fox's,
and finally Pitt's bills stared it in the face. The defiant example of the American
colonies was fresh to the mind and indeed largely responsible for focusing so
much parliamentary attention on India. Moreover, in Hastings India had a
Governor-General who, "provoked beyond reason, just might have fancied his
chances. . . . [W]hether a unilateral declaration of independence was ever
seriously entertained we shall never know."[55] George Smith, a member of the
Bengal Council, wrote to Henry Dundas: "He [Hastings] might have attempted, and successfully, a dismemberment of this country from the British
empire." He didn't, so it seems, out of commitment to the Company. In Hastings' words, "no man ever served them [the Company] with a zeal superior to
my own, or perhaps equal to it."[56]

Appointed Governor of Bengal in 1772,[57] he interpreted his instructions to
"stand forth as *diwan*" and to effect "the complete transformation" of Company affairs as "a carte blanche . . . to return the government to its 'first
principles.'" Among those principles was that "any goverment in India should
enjoy the approbation of the people." Inter alia he also engaged in a "flurry of

legal reforms" that featured taking over and reforming the Nawab's system of civil and criminal courts in conjunction with the study and codification of Hindu and Muslim law.[58]

Hastings and those who served with him did not understand themselves as agents of empire or as alien rulers. They shared a view common to indigenous rulers, that they were enjoined to recognize and respect the customs and laws of those they ruled.[59]

The king's task was to uphold the laws and customs of the various communities that lived in his realm, not to create law. "The king" says *Manusmriti*, a major *dharmasastras* translated by William Jones, was "created as the protector of the classes and the stages of life, that are appointed each to its own particular duty, in proper order."[60] Law attached to communities rather than to territory; it was particular rather than universal. When Henry Thomas Colebrooke, founder in 1823 of the Royal Asiatic Society, published his compilation of "Hindu Law," he featured an injunction from Bhrigu, a mythical lawgiver, that each category of person should litigate controversies according to their own law: "The frequenters of forests should cause their differences to be determined by one of their own order; members of a society, by persons belonging to that society; people appertaining to an army, by such as belong to the army;" or "husbandmen, mechanics, artists, men of a low tribe, dancers, persons wearing the token [of a religious order], and robbers or irregular soldiers, should adjust their controversies according to their own particular laws."[61]

Hastings and his circle "heard" the idea that indigenous kings were expected to base their rule on the laws and customs of corporate groups, including castes, religions, tribes, and craft and territorial communities.[62] Hastings specifically opposed "importing English laws and customs" and took special pains to ensure that "in all suits regarding inheritance, marriage, caste and other religious usages and institutions, the laws of the *Koran* with respect to the Mahomedans and those of the *shaster* with respect to the *Gentoos* shall be invariably adhered to; on all such occasions the *Moulvies* or *Brahmins* shall respectively attend to expound the law, and they shall sign the report and assist in passing the decree."[63] When Hastings learned that the *Moulvies* and *Brahmins* sometimes took advantage of their exclusive knowledge to mislead the English judge for monetary considerations, he concluded that English judges would have to know the laws of the land at first hand.

Beginning in about 1776, four years after Hastings assumed the governorship of Bengal, "a definitive change came about in [its] intellectual climate, the prime factor in the change being the personality of Warren Hastings."[64] The year 1776 was remarkable for the publication of watershed "civilizational" texts, including a text commissioned by Hastings, Nathaniel Halhed's *A Code of Gentoo Laws.*[65] What we seem to be witnessing in the evolution of Hastings' sensibilities is a convergence of practical appreciation of local law as "useful to the state"[66] with a growing appreciation of what William Jones, a decade later, would characterize as civilizational texts.

The "uses of the state" clearly do not exhaust the reasons that led Hastings to the texts of Indian civilization. They do not explain, for example, why he (and William Jones) characterized Charles Wilkins' 1785 English translation of the *Bhagavad Gita,* a text they thought would displace all previous understanding of the religion and literature of the Hindus, as a "gain of humanity" and as evidence that the ancient writings of India would "survive when the British dominion in India shall have long ceased to exist. . . ."[67] That characterization suggests that the civilizational eye saw features that went beyond utility.

Legal Pluralism as Multiculturalism: A Uniform Civil Code vs. Minority Rights

We turn in the concluding section of our reconsideration of "legal cultures and social change" to contemporary aspects of the topic. We didn't pay much attention in 1965 to how processes making for uniformity and pluralism affected contemporary discourse or politics. Writing in 1995, we want to relate such processes to legal questions convulsing Indian public life toward the end of the twentieth century.[68]

Legal pluralism is not simply a question of values. It is also a question of power, of who gets what, when, and where. "Universality" in the law is not only valued by enlightenment liberals and socialists; it is also the strategy of centralizing modern states. Pluralism in the law is both a norm and the strategy of those who favor dividing and sharing sovereignty with culturally diverse communities.[69]

The Indian Supreme Court's 1985 decision in the *Shah Bano* case revived and restructured the debate between proponents of legal uniformity and proponents of legal pluralism. The court held that a divorced Muslim woman was entitled to support from her husband, contrary to orthodox Muslim opinion that support was the responsibility of her blood relatives or a religious body. Many Muslims believed that the decision deprived them of control over their personal law.

Proponents of legal uniformity support a uniform civil code (UCC), and proponents of legal pluralism argue for minority rights in the form of diverse personal laws. The debate turned on what to do about Article 44 of the constitution, a "directive principle" of state policy that calls on the Indian state "to secure for the citizens a Uniform Civil Code throughout the territory of India." Such principles are non–judiciable, but they express widely supported aspirations. The constitutional call for a uniform civil code became the object of national debate after a Rajiv Gandhi Congress government in 1986 "reversed" the *Shah Bano* decision by passing a Muslim Women (Protection of Rights) Act,[70] a legislative act that contributed to the anger of Hindu nationalists, who destroyed the Babri Masjid (mosque) on December 6, 1992, precipitating a crisis in Hindu-Muslim relations.

These events raise the question: how did Indian public discourse about difference move from the civilizational and ethnographic to the multicultural? We have seen how the Orientalists of Warren Hastings' generation tried to apply the law of the Shastras to Hindus and of the Koran to Mohammedans. They did so, we have argued, for civilizational rather than for what would have been at the time anachronistic "communal" reasons. In "Barristers and Brahmans" we showed how processes of "Brahmanization" and "Anglicization" tended to make legal doctrine and practice more uniform. Until the revolt of 1857, well-placed utilitarians and evangelicals sought to make the law more uniform by eliminating uncivilized, "barbaric" practices such as *sati* (1829) and not allowing Hindu widows (often adolescents) to remarry (1856).

A new discourse began after the 1857 revolt. The event had destroyed British confidence. The sensation of loss of control, not only military but also cultural, was unexpected and sudden. "Henceforth, the British in India would always walk in fear. . . . [They] stepped back permanently into their neat little compound, fenced and right-angled, of facts and rules."[71]

Queen Victoria's 1858 proclamation pledged not to intervene in India's "religious" practices. Nonintervention was thought to be an appropriate remedy for the causes that led to the 1857 revolt, utilitarian and evangelically inspired "reforms" and "annexations" under the doctrine of "lapse."[72] From the times of Lords Bentinck and Ellenborough (1835–1844), a newly zealous reforming attitude had gained ground. For the post-Orientalist utilitarian-cum-evangelical generation (ca. 1835–57), "India wasn't just a commercial matter . . . India had become a Sacred Trust. The British had . . . turned into Empire builders and Christian zealots."[73]

Victoria's 1858 noninterference proclamation was, of course, a doctrine, not a practice. Gordon Johnson argues that Henry Maine's cautious, conservative approach to legal reform can be taken to epitomize the way post-1858 British rule in India managed change while pursuing a doctrine of nonintervention. "As Law Member [1862–69], Maine passed no striking laws. . . . Although . . . [he was] responsible for over two hundred separate Acts, his colleagues are remarkably unanimous in their welcome of his low key approach. Sir Richard Strachey found that Maine's virtue lay in that 'he limited itself to the actual requirements of his time' while Courtney Ilbert . . . praised Maine for abstaining 'from passing a great many measures of doubtful utility'. Here was no adventurous law-giver as Macaulay had been thirty years before."[74]

Nevertheless, even Henry Maine's Acts "gave legislative form to civil usages and religious practices of particular groups of Indians, and here, while there were some notable exceptions as regards marriage, the overall tendency was to put into statute form customary laws and to do so in ways which were prevalent at the time. This gave a specious authenticity to particular versions of Hindu law."[75] This kind of rationalization tended to move legal pluralism outward and upward from the diversely constituted periphery toward a more uniform national level, setting the stage for the struggle in the 1990s between minority rights based on the legal pluralist law and the various perceived requirements of the Directive Principle's Article 44: "to secure a uniform civil code for the citizens" of India.

The story of rationalization and codification between Maine's time and 1990 illustrates how, between the ends of the nineteenth and twentieth centuries, the legal pluralism perceived by the ethnographic eye was transformed from local cultural diversity to something that shared a family resemblance with the national civilizational diversity that Hastings' and Jones' generation had constructed toward the end of the eighteenth century. By the 1990s, civilizational differences were presented in the contemporary language of multiculturalism[76] rather than, as in Jones, Colebrooke, and others, through the now lost from view[77] civilizational texts. Illustrative of rationalization processes that moved legal pluralism toward differentiated uniformity is the much cited and disputed Shariat Act of 1937. Contrary to much public discourse on the subject, it didn't codify Muslim law. Rather, in the face of widely varying practice, including, for example, adherence by some Muslim groups to Hindu laws of succession, it tried to rationalize it by declaring that all Muslim personal matters will be governed by the Shariat.[78]

By the 1990s, the Hindu nationalist BJP's (Bharatiya Janata Party's) post-*Shah Bano* advocacy of a UCC had placed the contest between legal uniformity and legal pluralism at the center of Indian political debate.[79] The contest pitted the fundamental rights of *individuals* against the rights of minority *groups*. Article 14 of the constitution, which provides for equality before the law and equal protection of the laws, is not easily or always compatible with Article 29, which protects the rights of linguistic and cultural minorities.[80] The relationship of Articles 14 and 29 became critical when, after *Shah Bano,* this conflict began to pit the legal pluralism of community personal laws against efforts, in the name of majority democracy and parliamentary government, to implement Article 44's injunction to implement a Uniform Civil Code.

As we write in December 1995, many voices and forms of collective action continue to move the country toward the kind of polarization that marked the destruction of the Babri Masjid on December 6, 1992.[81] But other voices and forms of collective action are creating forums and practices that can establish a middle ground between legal pluralism and legal uniformity and between minority rights and individual rights.

Representative of a new discourse that makes a UCC compatible with the continuing existence and integrity of personal law is S. P. Sathe's argument that "the Constitution doubtless visualizes the emergence of a uniform civil code but does it mean a single law for all?. . . Within one nation there can exist a number of legal systems. In fact federal government," he continues, "means the coexistence of such multiple laws. . . . This means that Maharashtra may have its own family law different from that of Karnataka. In the U.S. each state has its own matrimonial law."

A uniform law, Sathe argues, "does not necessarily mean a common law but different personal laws based on uniform principles of equality of sexes and liberty for the individual. . . . Revision of the personal laws," he concludes paradoxically, "will ultimately take us towards a uniform civil code. Such a uniformity can sustain the diversity of laws."[82]

Thirty years after its publication we leave our "reconsideration" of "Legal Cultures and Social Change" with this account of one of its principal themes, the struggle between legal uniformity and legal pluralism. We see the contestation as an open-ended story about balancing the uniformity of a civil code that protects individual rights with the diversity of personal laws protected by minority rights. Hopefully it will be the story of an unstable yet viable equilibrium that combines the legal equality of human rights with a postcivilizational, postethnographic "multiculturalism."

NOTES

1. Secretary of State for India, Sir Samuel Hoare, cited in Penderel Moon, *Strangers in India* (London: Faber, 1944), 48.

2. *The Modernity of Tradition: Political Development in India* (Chicago: University of Chicago Press, 1967), 254. First published by the University of Chicago Press in 1967; Midway paperback 1984; New Delhi and Hyderabad: Orient Longman, 1969; paperback, 1987.

3. Ibid., 3.

4. Ibid., 10–11.

5. Ibid., 12.

6. See Robert Nisbet, *Social Change and History: Aspects of the Western Theory of Development* (London, Oxford, New York: Oxford University Press, 1969), particularly chapter 8, "Reflections on a Metaphor."

7. Report by the Faculty Committee, *The Behavioral Sciences at Harvard* (Cambridge: Harvard University Press, June, 1954), 114.

8. These binaries are: ascription/achievement; affectivity/affective neutrality; collectivity orientation/self-orientation; particularism/universalism; and diffuseness/specificity (Talcott Parsons and Edward Shils, *Toward A General Theory of Action* [Cambridge: Harvard University Press, 1951], 77).

9. We develop this view of Weber's methodology in "Authority and Power in Bureaucratic and Patrimonial Administration: A Revisionist Interpretation of Weber on Bureaucracy," *World Politics,* 31, no. 2 (January 1979).

10. Again, see Robert Nisbet's *Social Change and History,* where, in a section of chapter 8, "The Abuses of Metaphor," he reviews the work of then leading practitioners of Parsonian modernization theory, Walt Rostow, Marion Levy, and Neil Smelser, as well as Parsons himself (251–67).

11. *The Modernity of Tradition,* 7.

12. See William H. Sewell, Jr., "Political Events as Cultural Transformations: Insecurity, Collective Effervescence, and Collective Creativity in the Summer of 1789," typescript, August 1994; and Veena Das, *Critical Events: An Anthropological Perspective on Contemporary India* (Delhi: Oxford University Press, 1995), where Das, like Sewell, shows how critical events such as the *Shah Bano* case (to be discussed below) or the storming of the Bastille can transform or reconstitute mentalities and practices.

13. We have in mind particularly Michel Foucault's critique of efforts to write "total history" in the face of "ruptures." "In place of the continuous chronology of reason, which was invariably traced back to some inaccessible origin, there have appeared scales that are sometimes very brief, distinct from one another, irreducible to a single law" (*The Archeology of Knowledge and the Discourse on Language* [New York: Pantheon, 1972], 9).

14. Administering justice beyond English persons and East India Company (EIC)

factory territories became more pressing after 1772 when the "dual system" was replaced by more direct EIC responsibility as diwan of the Mughal emperor.

15. "Barristers and Brahmans in India: Legal Cultures and Social Change," *Comparative Studies in Society and History* 8, no. 1 (1965).

16. *AHR* 99, no. 5 (December, 1994), where a section of the *Review* was devoted to "Subaltern History" with articles on India (Gyan Prakash, "Subaltern Studies as Postcolonial Criticism"), Africa, and Latin America.

17. For a comprehensive interpretation of Gandhi's critique of "modern civilization" and his special, perhaps unique, capacity to mount a counter–hegemonic formation to "modernity," see Ashis Nandy, "From Outside the Imperium: Gandhi's Cultural Critique of the West," in *Traditions, Tyranny and Utopias: Essays in Political Awareness* (Delhi: Oxford University Press, 1987).

Gandhi wrote *Hind Swaraj, or Indian Home Rule,* his critique of modern civilization, in 1909 aboard ship on the way back from London to a "South Africa" whose formation (in 1910) was under discussion in London, the "metropole of modern civilization."

18. Orientalism, Said argued, was "the corporate institution for dealing with the Orient—dealing with it by making statements about it, authorising views of it, describing it, by teaching it, settling it, ruling it: in short, Orientalism as a Western style for dominating, restructuring, and having authority over the Orient" (*Orientalism* [New York: Pantheon, 1978], 3).

A bit further on he makes the further claim that "*all academic knowledge* about India and Egypt is somehow tinged and impressed with, violated by, the gross political fact" of their being British colonies (*Orientalism,* 11; our emphasis).

Aijaz Ahmad, in a critical review ("Between Orientalism and Historicism: Anthropological Knowledge of India," *Studies in History* [n.s.], 7, no, 1 [1991]) of Edward Said's *Orientalism* and of Ronald Inden's *Imagining India* (of which more below), finds three incompatible as well as indefensible meanings of "Orientalism" in *Orientalism:* (1) "Anyone who teaches, writes about, or researches the Orient . . . is an Orientalist, and what he or she does is Orientalism"; (2) "Orientalism is a style of thought based upon an ontological and epistemological distinction between 'the Orient' and . . . 'the Occident'. . . . *This* Orientalism can accommodate Aeschylus, say, and Victor Hugo, Dante and Karl Marx"; and (3) "Taking the late eighteenth century as a very roughly defined starting point Orientalism can be discussed and analyzed as the corporate institution for dealing with the Orient. . . . [I]n short, Orientalism is a Western style for dominating, restructuring, and having authority over the 'Orient'" (141–42).

19. Ashis Nandy, *The Intimate Enemy: Loss and Recovery of Self under Colonialism* (Delhi: Oxford University Press, 1983).

20. Said's *Orientalism* was published in 1978. We count Ronald Inden's *Imagining India* (Oxford: Basil Blackwell, 1990) as a continuation and updating of Said's orientalism epistemology via a problematic version of Gramscian discourse on hegemony. "The bold message of Said's *Orientalism,*" Inden tells us, is to "directly confront the central

question of knowledge and its multiple relations to power in orientalist representations of Asians." Those relations have "privileged . . . the knowledge of the orientalist . . . in relation to that of the Orientals, and it *invariably* places itself in a relation of intellectual dominance over that of the Easterners. It has appropriated the power to represent the Oriental, to translate and explain his [and her] thoughts and acts. . . . [I]t authorizes the area studies specialist and his colleagues in government and business to aid and advise, develop and modernize, arm and stabilize the countries of the so-called third world. In many respects the intellectual activities of the orientalist have even produced in India the very Orient which it constructed in its discourse . . . [as exemplified in] Gandhi's concept of non-violence . . . [which was] singled out long ago as a defining trait of the Hindu character" (38; our emphasis).

Aijaz Ahmad (in "Between Orientalism and Historicism") is surprised that Inden, unlike Said, who avoids identifying an archive or a voice that might tell us what being Muslim or Arab involves, has the temerity to discuss an authentic India. It can be found in India's sacred geography (what Ahmad unkindly calls the *"Ganga jal* view") and in thirteenth-century kingship, the "constitutive element" of Indian civilization. In counting kingship as Indian civilization's constitutive element Ahmad finds that Inden not only commits the epistemological sin of essentialism but also celebrates a form of patriarchy that justifies "the monarch's absolutist right . . . to the bodies of women [and] to the labour of the direct producers" (155–63; quote at 162).

Inden creates his Orientalist master narrative by targeting the mother of all hegemonic texts—the one that he argues controls all the others—James Mill's scurrilous *History of India* (1817), written to counter William Jones's Indology. For different voices on the Mills that recognize agency and historical change, see Uday Mehta, *British Liberalism in Nineteenth Century India* (forthcoming); and Lynn Zastoupil, *John Stuart Mill and India* (Stanford: Stanford University Press, 1994). Mehta analyses the dilemmas of British liberalism that flow from colonial rule; Zastoupil shows why and how the later John Stuart Mill repudiated the views and policies of his father with respect to India and Indian reform.

21. They have done so by adopting formulae (largely from Foucault and from the pre–*Culture and Imperialism* Edward Said of *Orientalism*) that hold that power determines knowledge and knowledge serves power. From the subaltern perspective, counter-hegemonic voices and the class interests of the ruled are able to constitute more valid forms of knowledge and more legitimate forms of power than the knowledge and power produced by ruling or hegemonic elites.

For a reading of these ways of seeing and explaining, see Edward Said, "Foreword," in Ranajit Guha and Gayatri Chakravorty Spivak, eds., *Selected Subaltern Studies* (New York: Oxford University Press, 1988), particularly v–vii.

22. As will become evident, we use the term *occidentalism* in a different sense from Sudipta Kaviraj's recent use of the term in his essay "The Reversal of Orientalism: Bhudev Mukhopadhyay and the Project of Indigenist Social Theory," in Vasudha Dalmia and Heinrich von Stietencron, eds., *Representing Hinduism: The Construction*

of Religious Traditions and National Identity (New Delhi, Thousand Oaks, London: Sage Publications, 1995). In that essay Kaviraj speaks of "The Theory of the Other: Occidentalism" (266–67). As is clear from the title of his essay he tells how an *Indian,* the late-nineteenth-century "traditional" Bengali intellectual, Bhudev Mukhopadhyay, from an Indian civilizational perspective ("indigenist social theory"), occidentalized, that is, simplified and homogenized, the British imperial other. In our account, we show how scholars in and of the West, Edward Said, Ronald Inden and others, occidentalized (stereotyped and totalized) Western scholars of the Orient, including the eighteenth-century British Orientalists (e.g., William Jones and his Asiatic Society colleagues).

The pervasiveness and persistence of Said's totalizing Occidentalism is evident in two recent books that, inter alia, give accounts of Sir William Jones, whom we treat below. Thomas Metcalf's *Ideologies of the Raj* (Cambridge: Cambridge University Press, 1995), takes the view that Jones and his fellow scholars were "attracted by the 'glories' of ancient India's civilization" and "sought to convince their fellow countrymen of what they perceived as the 'fertile and inventive genius' of the Hindus" and of the "wonderful structure, more perfect than the Greek" of the Sanskrit language, whose literature was "more copious than the Latin." "*Yet,*" Metcalf continues, "the Orientalist project . . . was clearly fitted to the needs of Europe. Classification *always* carried with it a presumption of hierarchy"—and of rule (14). A similar recognition then repudiation of Jones' appreciation for Indian civilization is found epitomized in Kate Teltcher's statement that "this desire to recover ancient Indian traditions underlies much of Jones's work, *but,* as Bernard Cohn and Javed Majeed have pointed out, Jones's pursuit of authentic law was motivated by his conviction that the Hindu and Muslim court advisers were uniformly untrustworthy" (*India Inscribed: European and British Writing on India 1600–1800* [Delhi: Oxford University Press, 1995], 196, our emphasis).

23. First published in 1950 as *La Renaissance orientale* (Paris: Editions Payot), it was translated from French into English by Gene Patterson-Black and Victor Reinking and published by the Columbia University Press in 1984.

Edward Said's foreword, a slightly revised version of his "Raymond Schwab and the Romance of Ideas" (*Daedalus* [issue "In Praise of Books"] 105, no. 1 [Winter 1976]), appeared two years before his *Orientalism.* Curiously, it shows no signs of the impending assault on Orientalists and the knowledge they produced. He says in his 1976 essay that Schwab's *Oriental Renaissance* "is of great importance for understanding the transformation of culture and learning that took place at the end of the eighteenth century and the beginning of the nineteenth. . . . Schwab is uncompromising and more unstinting [than Foucault] with information supporting the case for the Orient-as-cause. . . . Schwab [shows] the active changes that take place in knowledge of the Orient. . . . India acquired a whole figurative dimension in Western literature . . . [from the work of] the Lake poets to Emerson, Whitman, the Transcendentalists . . . Schelling . . . Heine, Goethe . . . Friedrich Schlegel," Nietzsche, and Schopenhauer (xvi–xvii and passim).

24. See Rosane Rocher, "British Orientalism . . ." (in Carol A. Breckenridge and

Peter van der Veer, eds., *Orientalism and the Postcolonial Predicament* [Philadelphia: University of Pennsylvania Press, 1993]), 215.

David Ludden's "Orientalist Empiricism: Transformations of Colonial Knowledge" and Nicholas Dirks's "Colonial Histories and Native Informants: Biography of an Archive," in the same volume, show how local voices and narratives recovered by colonial administrators were "lost" in the maw of imperial indifference and bureaucracy, leaving the way open for colonial "orientalist" knowledge to become Indian nationalist knowledge of the colonial subject.

While he didn't use the term *occidentalism,* Aijaz Ahmad, in "Between Orientalism and Historicism," shows how Said totalized the "West" by arguing that it knew itself from the "beginning," i.e., from Aeschylus to Marx and beyond, through constructing an inferior, degraded, Oriental other.

James G. Carrier's preface to *Occidentalism; Images of the West* [Oxford: Clarendon, 1995] frames the essays that follow by outlining three versions of occidentalism: (1) the "often unspoken . . . assumptions about Western societies" that Western anthropologists use oppositionally "to interpret the non-Western societies they study"; (2) the West that emerges oppositionally from "bits shipped out to the colonies" as "people outside the West" create distinctive identities; and (3) "the ways that Westerners represent the West to themselves" (viii–ix).

25. The reference is to Marx's well-known observation in "The Eighteenth Brumaire of Napoleon Bonaparte" that "Men make their own history but they do not make it just as they please."

For a recent account of the relationship between agency and structure, see Alexander Wendt, "The Agent-Structure Problem in International Relations Theory," *International Organization* 41, no. 3 (1987): 335–70.

26. We use the "Sir" in identifying William Jones to recognize the somewhat "miraculous" moment in his life, on the eve of his departure for India to take up a judgeship in Bengal, when he acquired the title. He would serve the East India Company under the Bengal presidency governor, Warren Hastings, soon (1784) to become the Company's first Governor-General in India. After impatiently and anxiously waiting for three years, King George III, thought by some to be mad, personally intervened on his behalf to secure his appointment.

"The main stumbling block in the way of his appointment was the Lord Chancellor, Lord Thurlow, who gave way only when the King himself intervened. King George III's letter to Thurlow saying that he would take Jones's appointment in Bengal as a personal compliment was dated 1 March 1782; on 4 March the appointment was publicly announced; on 20 March Jones was knighted, married on 8 April and 12 April set sail for India" (Kejariwal, *Asiatic Society,* 33).

The King's intervention on Jones's behalf is altogether curious when one considers that Thurlow's reluctance to support the appointment seems to have been based in part on Jones' opposition to the war against the American colonies, whose cause he defended against the King's first minister, Lord North. "There is but one remedy," Jones said, "abandon for ever all idea of American dependence; declare them independent States, and open a general treaty of pacification" (Jones to Viscount Althorp, 1 March 1782, in Garland Cannon, ed., *Letters of Sir William Jones,* 2 vols. [London: Oxford University Press, 1970], vol. II, 515–17, as quoted in Kejariwal, *Asiatic Society,* 32–33).

27. Our knowledge of *sampradaya* has been enhanced by conversations with Catherine Clementine-Ojha, who is working on a study of the reasons and consequences of Jaipur Maharaja Ram Singh's transfer in the mid-1860s of court patronage from a Vaishnava to a Shaiva *sampradaya.*

28. See Sudipta Kaviraj, "The Imaginary Institution of India," in Partha Chatterjee and Gyanendra Pandey, eds., *Subaltern Studies VII: Writings on South Asian History and Society* (Delhi: Oxford University Press, 1992), 1–39.

29. François Bernier, *Travels in the Mogul Empire, A.D. 1656–1668* (London: Humphrey Milford, Oxford University Press, 1934), translated and annotated by Archibald Constable; 2d ed., revised by Vincent Smith, 209.

30. See Cynthia Talbott, "From Mleccha to Asvapati: Representations of Muslims in Medieval Andhra," and Phillip Waggoner, "Understanding Islam at Vijayanagara," papers presented at the forty-sixth Annual Meeting of the Association for Asian Studies, Boston, March 24–27, 1994.

31. Sheldon Pollock, "Ramayana and Political Imagination in India," *Journal of Asian Studies* 52, no. 2 (May 1993): 285–86.

In a similar vein, Muzzaffar Alam's "Assimilation from a Distance: Confrontation and a Sufi Accommodation in Awadh Society" (revised version [1994?] of a paper presented at a Seminar on "Regional Varieties of Islam in Medieval India," University of Heidelberg, July 1989) argues that it is misguided to view the relationship between religion and medieval Indian society as "determined by the religious affiliations of the participants" (1). He concludes that "in the period under consideration . . . the society was not always divided strictly on community lines even in times of conflict. Muslim rulers lavishly favored one section of the Rajput Hindus in the midst of their fierce fights against another. . . . [T]he Rajputs too saw as their enemies only those Muslim gentry who they believed to be the Muslim ruler's agents and appropriators of their ancient rights and privileges. . . . As there was no homogeneous Hindu community, the followers of Islam too entertained diverse notions of [its] piety and spirituality. . . . [Similarly] *Sharia* and *tariqa,* and for that matter Islam, acquired . . . a variety of forms and meanings (37).

32. It was British provincial administrators such as Thomas Munro in Madras and Mountstuart Elphinstone in Bombay who wanted to create official tribunals that would be responsive to local custom and precedent. Such tribunals, they believed, would be in touch with local practice. Munro, by statute, gave new life to village *panchayats;* both he and Elphinstone encouraged *panchayat*-like proceedings for cases intermediate between village and district (Rudolph and Rudolph, "Barristers and Brahmans," 264).

33. See note 26 for some of the circumstances surrounding the appointment.

34. Kejariwal, *Asiatic Society,* 31.

35. The sixteen topics were: (1) The laws of the Hindus and the Mahomedans; (2) The history of the ancient world; (3) Proofs and illustrations of Scripture (Jones was always careful to mask his "Deism"); (4) Traditions concerning the deluge, etc.; (5) Modern politics and geography of Hindustan (Jones took care to show that his search for civilizational knowledge would appear useful to the Company); (6) Best mode of governing Bengal (see [5] comment); (7) Arithmetic and geometry and mixed sciences of the Asiatics; (8) Medicine, chemistry, surgery, and anatomy of the Indians (he did a major translation that dealt with these topics); (9) Natural products of India; (10) Poetry, rhetoric, and morality of Asia (his translation of *Sakuntala* profoundly affected European thought and sensibility, including, particularly, Goethe's); (11) Music of the eastern nations (again, a major translation); (12) The She-king or 300 Chinese odes; (13) The best accounts of Tibet and Kashmir; (14) Trade, manufactures, agriculture, and commerce of India; (15) Mughal administration; and (16) Maharatta constitution (Kejariwal, *Asiatic Society,* 29).

36. William Jones, "A Discourse on the Institution of a Society for Enquiring into the History, Civil and Natural, the Antiquities, Arts, Sciences, and Literature of Asia," *Asiatic Researches,* vol. 1, ix–x, as quoted in Kejariwal, *Asiatic Society,* 27–28.

37. Kejariwal, *Asiatic Society,* 47. Until 1785, Jones thought he could depend on Wilkins, who had acquired a reputation for his knowledge of Sanskrit. He had written to Wilkins that: "All my hopes . . . of being acquainted with the poetry, philosophy, and arts of the Hindus, are grounded on the expectations of living to see the fruits of your learned labours" (47).

38. Kejariwal, *Asiatic Society,* 64.

39. Ibid.

40. Taking the phrase from Spengler, Kejariwal used this trope to characterize Jones's effect on historical understanding: "Sir William Jones . . . may be called the Copernicus of history" (*Asiatic Society,* 28).

Hegel, who read the Asiatic Society Orientalists but fairly early got over his admiration for Indian civilization, characterized the effect of Jones' linkage of Sanskrit with Greek and Latin and invention of a common Indo-Aryan civilizational past as resembling that of Columbus' discovery of the New World (Kejariwal, *Asiatic Society,* 72, quoting from J. Beveridge, "On the Study of Indian History," *Calcutta Review* 87 [1888]: 43).

Use of the "Columbus' Discovery of the New World" trope does not relieve Hegel from being an—perhaps *the*—arch villain in the construction of Saidian-style "Orientalist" knowledge. Kejariwal charges him with "illegitimately" relegating Sanskritic civilization to an "archaic past" that has been superseded by absorbtion within a developmental scheme and with "pushing to the margins those seen as radically different." Only James Mill, author of the *History of India* (1817), rivals Hegel in denigrating India. For an insightful critique of Hegel on India in the context of contemporary pluralist epistemologies see Joseph Prabhu, "Hegel, India, and Contemporary

Pluralism," paper given at the 91st Annual Meeting of the American Philosophic Association, Eastern Division, Boston, December 29, 1994, 25.

41. *Asiatic Researches* (Calcutta) vol 1: 422–23, as quoted in Kejariwal, *Asiatic Society,* 47, and R. Schwab, *Oriental Renaissance,* 41.

The argument about how big and important Jones' contribution was has overtones of the differences between Thomas Kuhn and Stephen Toulmin over the term *scientific revolution,* with Kuhn emphasizing disjuncture from anomalies and Toulmin innovations. Franklin Edgerton, one of America's leading Sanskritists, evaluates Jones' contribution this way:

> That languages often resemble each other is obvious enough. Even the specific fact that Sanskrit resembles Greek and Latin had been seen before. But no one before Jones had drawn the inference that these resemblances must be explained by the assumption of common descent from a hypothetical earlier language "which perhaps no longer exists." At this moment modern comparative grammar was born.

42. The rise of the modern worldview and the story of modernity's three hundred-year career is brilliantly told in Stephen Toulmin's *Cosmopolis: The Hidden Agenda of Modernity* (Chicago: University of Chicago Press, 1990). Toulmin locates the rise of modern philosophy (e.g., Descartes), modern science (e.g., Newton preceded by Copernicus and Galileo), and the politics of the modern state (e.g., Hobbes) in the search for certainty and order generated by scepticism and the violence associated with conflicts over religious truth.

43. For this reading of Voltaire, see Halbfass, *India and Europe,* 57–58.

44. See Melvin Richter's introduction, particularly section 6, "The Spirit of the Laws (1748)," in *Montesquieu: Selected Writings* (Indianapolis and Cambridge: Hackett, 1990), for a critical appreciation of Montesquieu's approach and "methodology." Richter makes a strong case for Montesquieu as a comparativist and the originator of a Weberian-like "ideal type" hermeneutics. But Montesquieu's central concern with despotism and liberty arise from a European orientation and agenda. He would, we think, agree with Weber when he said: "A product of modern European civilization, studying any problem of universal history, is bound to ask himself to what combination of circumstances the fact should be attributed that in Western civilization, and in Western civilization only, cultural phenomena have appeared which [as we like to think] lie in a line of development having *universal* significance and value" (*The Protestant Ethic and the Spirit of Capitalism* [New York: Scribner's, 1958], 13).

45. Kejariwal, *Asiatic Society,* 26. Halbfass writes that although "a basic willingness to see religious, philosophical and cultural traditions, including the European tradition itself, no longer solely 'through one's own domestic eyes' was often postulated in the eighteenth century . . . . [and] there was a whole literary genre of works following the scheme of Montesquieu's *Lettres persanes* ['Persian Letters,' 1721] and pretending to present foreign exotic views of Europe . . . this program of seeing oneself and others

with 'foreign eyes' remained usually quite abstract and stereotypical in practice, specifically with regard to India, or it was simply a stylistic device" (*India and Europe,* 62).

The complex story of the timing and relative influence of British vs. French Orientalists, including an evaluation of Anquetil Duperron's contribution, can be followed in Schwab, *Oriental Renaissance,* and Halbfass, *India and Europe.*

46. Carl Becker, in his *The Heavenly City of the Eighteenth Century Philosophers* (New Haven: Yale University Press, 1964), strongly argues this view.

47. Halbfass, *India and Europe,* 62.

48. Quoted in Keay, *Company,* at page 401, from E. Thompson and G. T. Garrett, *Rise and Fulfilment of British Rule in India* (1934).

49. John Keay, *The Honourable Company: A History of the English East India Company* (New York: Macmillan, 1991), 395, 394.

50. Sudipta Kaviraj problematizes master narratives and essentialist constructions of "nation" and—by implication—state in "The Imaginary Institution of India." They were, he argues, "narrowly committed to a telling of a particular kind: an account which separated out the great chaos of varying ideological events into a single thread [2]. . . . The recipient of narrative cannot be just anybody: it is only some people belonging to particular categories who are privileged by the narrative" (33).

51. For an account of imperial conquest and rule that features cultural and psychological motives, see Joseph Schumpeter's *Imperialism and Social Classes* (New York: Meridian, 1955). Schumpeter was arguing more against structural explanations that entailed materialist motives (e.g., Hobson and Lenin) than against motives arising from the pursuit of national power and state competition.

52. K. M. Pannikar characterized the concept of the "ringed fence," in traditional geopolitical terms, as "the defence of your neighbor's territories, of course at his expense, in order to protect your own territories." This is what Hastings, who set great store on securing Oudh as part of a "ring fence" to keep out the Marathas and any other restless warlords capable of threatening Bengal's tranquillity, did in relation to his ally, the Nawab of Oudh. See Keay, *Company,* 400.

53. The quote is from Keay, *Company,* 415. He is summarizing Hastings' objectives in the treaty of Salbai, a treaty that concluded a war with the Marathas, the Company's principal rival on the subcontinent. "The keystones of Salbai," Keay writes, "were . . . a provision whereby both signatories undertook to oblige their allies to observe the peace indefinitely and, following from that, a provision whereby the Marathas were to force Hyder Ali, their erstwhile ally, to withdraw from the Carnatic and likewise observe peace thereafter. Here was the basis for a comprehensive and lasting settlement" (415).

54. The attack on the Company's independence was accompanied by attacks on Hastings. In May 1784, the House of Commons passed a vote of censure against his conduct; it did not lead, however, to his quitting his post as Governor-General. In May 1786, the House decided to impeach him for "high crimes and misdemeanours" on 22 articles covering the entire gamut of his administration. The trial opened in 1788 and stretched on for seven years, when he was acquitted on all counts. Twenty years later,

when he appeared at the bar of the House to tender evidence on Company rule, he was greeted with a standing ovation.

55. "History is constructed," Keay observes, "from what men did and what they wrote. What they thought and said in private—especially if of a treasonable nature—is seldom apparent. One can only conjecture" (*Company,* 419).

Still there was some reason to suppose that independence was contemplated and not out of reach. "Cornwallis, who would succeed [Hastings] two years later, conceded that he was 'beloved by the people' and even Macaulay, his fiercist critic, would credit him with 'a popularity such as . . . no other governor has been able to attain.' His ability was unquestioned. The loyalty of the Nawabs of Oudh and the Carnatic was founded on his personal friendship. The Nizam and Scindia were firmly attached to the British interest. Only Tipu Sultan remained to give trouble, and Tipu could have been tamed with a renegotiated Mangalore" (419).

Hastings, it seems, would have had a lot of support in Bengal. He was not the only one to feel bitter. George Smith, a member of the Bengal Council, refers in a letter to Dundas to a "a furore of petitioning" against Pitt's bill in both Calcutta and Madras. "Disaffection was rife among the King's officers . . . among the Company's officers . . . and among the Company's civilians. . . . But Smith's advice to Dundas was to make no concessions. It was concessions that had encouraged the American colonists to fight. Better just stand firm against the chimerical idea of Independence. . . . '[O]ur [Indian] condition is very different from that of the Irish and Americans'" (419–20).

56. Quoted in Keay, *Company,* 420.

57. Hastings had entered Company service in 1750 as a £5 per annum "writer."

58. Keay, *Company,* 398, 396, 397.

59. For a fuller development of this view, see our "The Subcontinental Empire and the Regional Kingdom in Indian State Formation," in Paul Wallace, ed., *Region and Nation in India* (New Delhi: Oxford University Press and IBH Publishing Co., 1985).

60. Wendy Doniger, trans., with Bryan K. Smith, *The Laws of Manu* (New Delhi and London: Penguin, 1991), 131.

61. Henry Thomas Colebrooke, "On Hindu Courts of Justice," *Transactions of the Royal Asiatic Society of Great Britain and Ireland,* vol. 2 (London: Parbury, Allen, 1830), 174, 177.

62. Amrita Shodan shows how, in the course of the 1820s, Mountstuart Elphinstone's law collectors moved from looking for a variety of legal sources—court cases, Shastris, heads of castes, common people, others knowledgeable about the law—to concentrating mainly on castes as the units of legal practices. The form of inquiry in turn intensified the propensity for courts to treat caste as *the* form of community that generated law ("Legal Representation of Khojas and Pushtimarga Vaishnavas," Ph.D. diss., Department of South Asian Languages and Civilizations, University of Chicago, 1995, 15). Her account also provides an interesting microcosm of how the compilation of local practice was then converted into firm rules by the courts, freezing as definitive

practices that were often highly contested and under other circumstances might well have "evolved."

63. From *Proceedings of the Committee of Circuit at Kasimbazar,* 15 August 1772, quoted in Bharatiya Vidya Bhavan, *History and Culture of the Indian People,* 8:361.

64. Kejariwal, *Asiatic Society,* 43.

65. It was the year inter alia of Jefferson's Declaration of Independence, Adam Smith's *The Wealth of Nations,* and Edward Gibbon's *The Decline and Fall of the Roman Empire.* For a recent account of the intellectual currents that engulfed Gibbon and probably affected Jefferson and Smith as well as Hastings and Halhed, see David Womersley's introduction to his new edition of *Decline and Fall,* vol. 1 (London: Allen Lane, Penguin, 1994), xi–cvi.

66. The phrase "useful to the state" occurs in a 1784 Hastings letter to the chairman of the East India Company, Nathaniel Smith. This context should be kept in mind when Hastings is pictured as an early examplar of "Orientalism." Kejariwal quotes a paragraph from this letter (at page 24 of *Asiatic Society*) and reports that the full text of the letter can be found in P. J. Marshall, *The British Discovery of Hindustan in the Eighteenth Century,* (Cambridge: Cambridge University Press, 1970), 184–91.

67. Kejariwal, *Asiatic Society,* 24, 21.

68. For the current discourse on legal pluralism see Vikash N. Pandy and Akhileshwar Pathak's "Sociology of Law in India: Postscripts and Prospects," *Economic and Political Weekly,* August 5–12, 1995, 1974–77, where they discuss "Legal Pluralism/ Legal Anthropology" and its current "critical legal studies" version in "Law as Discourse." Inter alia they review work and scholarship on "legal sociology" by us, Derrett, Marc Galanter, Upendra Baxi, and Rajeev Dhawan.

For an innovative conceptionalization of "legal sociology," see Veena Das' accounts in *Critical Events* (1995) of the *Shah Bano* case, the Roop Kanwar *sati,* violence against the Sikhs after Indira Gandhi's assassination, and the Bhopal gas explosion, where she implicates and analyses legal discourse and practice in her analysis of *victim* and *suffering.* Das shows how inter alia legal discourse and practices have shaped thought and action about the state, community, gender, and the construction and use of memory.

69. This is the argument that Partha Chatterjee advances and problematizes in "Secularism and Toleration," *Economic and Political Weekly,* July 9, 1994, 1768–77. Many of the issues he raises there were examined in the context of legal decisions by John C. Mansfield ("The Personal Laws or a Uniform Civil Code?" in Robert D. Baird, ed., *Religion and Law in Independent India* [Delhi: Manohar, 1993], 139–77) and are further examined in the next section, "Legal Pluralism as Multiculturalism: A Uniform Civil Code vs. Minority Rights."

Conflicts among multiculturalism framed as minority rights; popular sovereignty framed as democratic majoritarianism; and equal citizenship framed as individual rights and legal equality, were featured in papers prepared for the Second International Liechtenstein Research Program on Self-Determination held at the Woodrow Wilson

School of Public and International Affairs, Princeton University, June 10, 1995. See particularly Daniel A. Bell, "Comments on MinXin Pei's . . . A Strategy for Improving Minority Rights in China" (where he argues that "*a priori* there is no reason to believe that representatives of majority interests will respect the rights of minorities" and cites the murder by the Chinese government of one-fifth of the Buddhist population of Tibet as an example); and Michele Lamont, "Cultural Dynamics of Exclusion of Community in France, the United States, and Quebec." The conference papers are to appear in Wolfgang Danspeckgruber and John Waterbury, eds., *Self-Determination in Our World* (New York: Oxford University Press).

70. For a condensed account of the *Shah Bano* case, the controversy it engendered, and the Muslim Women Act that followed, see the section on "Confessional Politics" in our *In Pursuit of Lakshmi: The Political Economy of the Indian State* (Chicago: University of Chicago Press, 1987), 36–47.

71. Marian Fowler, *Below the Peacock Fan: First Ladies of the Raj*, Harmondsworth: Penguin, 1988), p. 150. Fowler contrasts the easy familiarity with and admiration for India and things Indian of Emily Eden (sister of George Eden, Governor-General 1836–42) with the alienation and fear of Charlotte Canning (wife of Lord Canning, Governor-General before and during the 1857 revolt and Viceroy from 1858 until 1862). Emily Eden "had played chess with Dost Mahomed and taught English to Pertab Singh. . . . The Eden sisters [Fanny as well as Emily] had caught glimpses of Mughal magic and magnificence, of Peacock Thrones ablaze with light, enough to fire their imaginations, enough to see by. . . ." After 1857, such "easy conviviality between Indian ruler and English was . . . gone forever. . . . They sensed that the Indians hated them; and so they ruled with an iron hand, but one which trembled a little" (150).

72. The classic text for "reform" is the late Eric Stokes' *The English Utilitarians in India* (Oxford: Clarendon Press, 1959). Part 3, "Law and Government," particularly sections 3 and 4 on "Macaulay as Law Member" and "The Penal Code," is specially relevant to our theme of "legal cultures and social change."

"Lapse" was a doctrine practised particularly by Governor-General Dalhousie (1848–56), barring succession in princely states of adopted heirs. It rationalized even if it did not legitimize an East India Company policy of "annexation," which made expansion possible without resort to war. Narratives of the 1857 rebellion feature the consequences of "annexations" at Jhansi and Oudh.

73. Fowler, *Peacock Fan,* 121.

74. Gordon Johnson, "India and Henry Maine," in Mushirul Hasan and Narauani Gupta, eds., *India's Colonial Encounter: Essays in Memory of Eric Stokes* (Delhi: Manohar, 1993), 31.

Johnson makes clear that "Maine's contemporaries recognized that his influence spread far beyond the making of laws. His serious writing—particularly *Ancient Law* and *Village Communities East and West*—had a profound effect on how Indian society was observed and understood." Among other things, Maine saw India with an ethnographic eye, arguing "strongly against there being any uniform or clearly stated set of

Indian law: rather the whole was a mess of shifting customs which varied from place to place and over time" (33, 34).

75. Johnson, "India and Henry Maine," 32.

76. See Amy Gutman, ed., *Multiculturalism; Examining the Politics of Recognition* (Princeton: Princeton University Press, 1994). The book contains Charles Taylor's essay "The Politics of Recognition" (with comments by Susan Wolf, Steven Rockefeller, and Michael Walzer) and Jurgen Habermas' "Struggles for Recognition in the Democratic Constitutional State," essays that address themes and problematics relevant to our discussions of legal pluralism, minority rights, and majoritarian democracy.

In the context of contemporary multiculturalism, Dipankar Gupta, in his essay "Secularisation and Minoritisation: Limits of Heroic Thought" (*Economic and Political Weekly,* September 2, 1995), argues that anybody, anytime, can become a minority, a phenomenon that can radically problematize legal thought and practice with respect to minority (group) and individual rights.

"Otherizing," Gupta argues, can happen suddenly with little or no warning; thus Tamils, who were usually English speakers, were made into an endangered minority in Bombay with the rise in the early 1960s of the Shiv Sena under Bal Thackery. Similarly the Sikhs, who had thought of themselves for marriage purposes and in other ways as a version of the "Hindu" community, became an endangered and alienated minority after operation Blue Star attacked the Golden Temple in Amritsar and Sikhs were attacked and killed in Delhi and elsewhere in north India after Mrs. Gandhi's assassination. In the United States, one can point to the emergence of gays and lesbians as a constructed minority in need of group as well as individual rights.

77. We say lost-from-view civilizational texts because, after the trauma of 1857 and the subsequent establishment of English-language learning in universities, the "Sanskrit literary tradition" was separated and marginalized. The result, in G. N. Devy's view, was to render "the links between modern Indian literature and Sanskrit literary traditions . . . tenuous. . . . The modern Indian critic [and, we might add, the modern legal scholar and practitioner]" Devy continues, "can say that India *had* a glorious [Sanskritic] tradition . . . a thousand years ago . . . but he is unable to use this tradition as a living tradition which shares a frame of reference within which his normal intellectual activity takes place" (*After Amnesia: Tradition and Change in Indian Literary Criticism* [Bombay: Orient Longman, 1992], 27–28).

Our story about British Orientalist learning dates this disjunction not one thousand years ago but in the post-1857 era. Some of the ground for the 1857 disjunction was prepared by the influence and interventions of evangelicals and utilitarians, particularly as expressed in Macaulay's 1835 minute on education and its implementation in school and higher education.

Mukhand Lath's current work on Sanskrit literary forms and criticism will show that they remained viable but enclaved in the nineteenth century (personal communication).

78. See inter alia Katherine Ewing, "Introduction: Ambiguity and *Sharia't*—A Perspective on the Problem of Moral Principles in Tension"; and David Gilmartin,

"Customary Law and the Shari'at in British Punjab," both in Katherine P. Ewing, ed., Shari'at *and Ambiguity in South Asian Islam* (Berkeley: University of California Press, 1988), 1–24, 43–62. See also Gregory C. Kozlowski, "Muslim Personal Law and Political Identity in Independent India," in Robert D. Baird, ed., *Religion and Law in Independent India* (Delhi: Manohar, 1993), particularly "Creating Muslim Personal Law" (79–82).

The story of the preindependence rationalization of Hindu law is best told in Harold Lewis Levy, "Indian Modernization by Legislation: The Hindu Code Bill," Ph.D. diss., in Political Science, University of Chicago, 1973. An account of the passage of the Hindu code bills in 1955 and 1956 over the resistance of the then President of India, Rajendra Prasad, can be found in Gene D. Overstreet, "The Hindu Code Bill," in Lucian Pye, ed., *Cases in Comparative Politics: Asia* (Boston: Little, Brown, 1970). Ronojoy Sen covers substantial portions of the literature on rationalization of Hindu and Muslim law in "The Uniform Civil Code Issue in Indian Politics; The Decline of Congress Secularism," M.A. thesis, in Political Science, University of Chicago, 1995. Special mention should be made of the essays in Asghar Ali Engineer, ed., *The Shah Bano Controversy* (Bombay: Orient Longman, 1987); and of Tahir Mahmood's study, *An Indian Civil Code and Islamic Law* (Bombay: N. M. Tripathi, 1976).

79. By late 1995, with the eleventh Parliamentary election just three or four months away, strains began to appear within the BJP over its commitment to a UCC. Not only were some in the party reluctant to drive away Muslim votes so vital for success in the crucial northern state of Uttar Pradesh, but also moderate and fundamentalist Hindus were having second thoughts about a UCC. It had dawned on some that a UCC was not the same thing as "their" Hindu Code and that its effects might not be confined to preventing Muslims from having several wives and divorcing them at will. A UCC could jeopardize the Hindu undivided joint family, a legal fiction that can reduce tax liabilities and make it possible to discriminate against female members of the family by inter alia depriving them of equal property rights.

80. Article 29, what might be called the multicultural clause, provides that: "Any section of the citizens of India . . . having a distinct language, script [read Gurmukhi for Sikhs and Urdu for many Muslims] or culture [the identity and way of life, the "ethnicity," inter alia of Muslims, Sikhs, and Christians] shall have the right to conserve the same." According to Durga Das Basu, Article 29 protects "the cultural, linguistic and similar rights of any section of the community who might constitute a 'minority' from . . . the democratic machine . . . being used as an engine of oppression by the numerical majority" (*Introduction to the Constitution of India,* 16th ed. [New Delhi: Prentice-Hall of India, 1994], 367). Articles 25 guarantees individual citizens the right to "profess, practise and propagate" their religious beliefs. John Mansfield, after an extended discussion, concludes that "the Constitution neither requires that the system of personal laws be abolished nor that they be retained" ("Personal Law v. Uniform Civil Code," 148–157, quoted at 157).

The 1950 Indian Constitution's protection of minority rights in Article 29 predates the amendment of the U.N.'s Universal Declaration of Human Rights (Art. 27) protecting minority rights: "In those States in which ethnic, religious or linguistic minorities exist, persons belonging to such minorities shall not be denied the right, in community with the other members of their group, to enjoy their own culture, to profess and practise their own religion, or to use their own language."

81. For an insightful account of the causes and consequences of the confrontation, see Ashis Nandy, Shikha Trivedy, Shail Mayaram, and Achyut Yagnik, *Creating A Nationality: The Ramajanmabhumi Movement and the Fear of the Self* (New Delhi: Oxford University Press, 1995). S. Gopal, ed., *Anatomy of a Confrontation: The Babri Masjid-Ramjanmabhumi Dispute* (Delhi: Viking, 1991), provides "secularist" readings by prominent academic intellectuals of the dispute's discourses and politics.

82. S. P. Sathe, "Uniform Civil Code: Implications of Supreme Court Intervention," *Economic and Political Weekly,* September 2, 1995. Imtiaz Ahmad's "Personal Laws: Promoting Reform from Within" (*Economic and Political Weekly,* November 11, 1995), makes a similar argument. Ahmad has played a role in bringing together Muslim intellectuals and *ulema.* So has Mushirul Hasan, whose "Muslim Intellectuals, Institutions, and the Post-Colonial Predicament" (*Economic and Political Weekly,* November 25, 1995), provides a learned and persuasive case for introducing laws and practices commensurate with "Indian Islam." Saabeeha Bano, in "Muslim Women's Voices: Expanding Gender Justice under Muslim Law" (*Economic and Political Weekly,* November 25, 1995), argues on the basis of results of an opinion survey among Muslim women in Delhi that the gender justice objectives that a UCC might realize can be achieved by a process of reform of personal laws.

John C. Mansfield concludes his article "The Personal Laws or a Uniform Civil Code?" (in Baird, *Religion and Law in Independent India*) with the observation that a Uniform Civil Code should not entirely eliminate diverse personal law because of the importance of preserving the identity "of . . . ethnic or religious group[s] within a territorial state [and their] being able to maintain [their] distinctive identity and through this . . . members' sense of existing and having meaning" (175–76).

For versions of the debate about and politics of the battle over a uniform code, see "Uniform Civil Code: Striking Down a Right," *India Today,* June 15, 1995; Abida Samiuddin, "Status of Hindu and Muslim Women: A Comparative Study," *Mainstream,* July 8, 1995; and "Uniform Civil Code; A Calculated Gambit," *India Today,* July 31, 1995.

Our "Modern Hate: How ancient animosities get invented" (*New Republic,* March 22, 1993) dealt inter alia with the tension in India between multiculturalism and Hindu nationalism.

The Origins and Impact of the Renaissance Sense of History: Notes on the Humanist as an Intellectual Type

Anthony Grafton

I.   Let Us Now Praise Obscure Men: The Renaissance Humanist as a New Social Type

The first great satire on the modern academic world appeared in 1515, under the appropriate title *Epistolae obscurorum virorum—Letters of Obscure Men.*[1] This great work of epistolary fiction represented itself as the correspondence of a whole series of Dominican friars, professors and others. These men opposed the introduction of Hebrew studies into the curriculum and wished to suppress Jewish scholarship and burn the Talmud and other central texts of the Jewish tradition. Many letters reveal their authors or protagonists in the classic roles of later medieval satire: as lustful clerics unable to refrain from the sins of the flesh. Ortwin Gratius warns his friend Master Mammotrectus, for example, to stay away from one Margaret: he should eat consecrated salt on Sundays, sprinkle himself with holy water, and bear in mind the principle that "Ars Margarethae est mirabile rete"—"Margaret's *ars* is a great snare" (1.34). But their chief errors are intellectual ones. Obsessed with the gothic detail of late scholastic theology and burning with hatred of the Jews, they bury themselves in theological minutiae with the zest of anti-Semitic pigs hunting particularly rich truffles. Master John Pellifex raises the question of whether saluting a Jew by accident constitutes a mortal sin (1.2); Leopoldus Federfusius discusses the "very subtle" theological and physical problem of whether the foreskin of a Jewish man who converts to Christianity will regenerate itself (1.37). A gallery of grotesques, the obscure men reveal themselves to be as foolish and ignorant as they are undisciplined.

This satire reached and amused a wide public: gossip had it that the book made Erasmus, who had treated the theological faculties just as roughly in his time, laugh so hard that an abscess on his face burst. But, like Erasmus's own *Praise of Folly,* the *Letters of Obscure Men* was more than a squib. Its authors, Crotus Rubeanus and Ulrich von Hutten, used wit to attack what they saw as serious intellectual problems. Their work, moreover, represented only one maneuver in an ongoing battle. From the middle of the fifteenth century, humanist scholars applied the new tools of classical philology to the New and Old Testaments as well as to classical texts. They argued that the scholastic theologians, who used the Vulgate or Latin text of the Bible only, often misunderstood what the text had to say and sometimes repeated its errors. These misunderstandings and errors, in turn, could be corrected only by consulting the original texts from which St. Jerome had translated the Bible into Latin: the Hebrew text of the Old Testament and the Greek text of the New. And only the humanist scholars who had mastered the three languages of Scripture, who knew how to identify and remedy textual errors, and who tried to read their text as its author had meant it to be read could justly claim intellectual authority over the interpretation of the Bible.[2]

Johannes Reuchlin, the German lawyer whose stays in Medicean Florence inspired him to learn Greek and Hebrew, argued forcefully that Christian scholars must apprentice themselves to rabbis if they hoped to understand the Old Testament. He produced a Hebrew grammar and a much more elaborate treatment of Cabalistic methods for interpreting the Scriptures, which he saw, as Pico had, as the core of the Jewish tradition.[3] These ideas would have been radical enough at any point in the later Middle Ages. But in the years around 1500 they were incendiary. Traditional theologians already fiercely resented the humanists' efforts to "use their sickle to harvest another man's crops"—to extend their professional jurisdiction into theological, as well as philological, territory. Throughout Germany, moreover, Jews and Christians were coming into sharper and sharper conflict—a conflict not softened at all by the fact that the Christians, who normally began the fights, were so much more powerful than their opponents. Events normally followed what soon became a fixed pattern. A purported discovery of bones in Jewish houses led to the accusation that one or more Jews had committed ritual murder of children, in order to obtain the Christian blood they needed for magical and liturgical purposes. Torture dragged confessions from suspects and persuaded them to implicate others. Crude, vivid woodcuts on broadsides carried the image of the murderous Jew from marketplace to marketplace throughout imperial territory: more elegant illustrations conveyed the same message to readers of expensive books like the *Nuremberg Chronicle.* City administrations used the opportunity to attack the Jewish communities, who had previously enjoyed imperial protection.[4] In this context, intellectual debates about the use of Hebrew became murderously sharp. A convert from Judaism named Pfefferkorn rallied political and religious authorities to confiscate and burn Jewish books. His own pamphlets offered informative accounts of Jewish customs—for example, the rituals of confession practiced on Yom Kippur—in order to reveal the perfidy of their practitioners. Reuchlin defended the Jews, as both lawyer and theologian. An array of attacks and counterattacks, *Judenspiegel* versus *Augenspiegel,* appeared. Among other defensive moves, Reuchlin published as a testimonial in his own defense a volume of *Clarorum virorum epistolae*— letters of famous men, humanists who praised his learning. This, in turn, set the imaginations of the two younger humanists, Hutten and Crotus Rubeanus, to spinning out the brilliant polemical fantasies of the *Letters of Obscure Men.*[5]

From our point of view, the most salient aspect of this text lies not in its tales of clerical misconduct but in its insistence that the obscure men and their allies represented radically different social and intellectual types. Over and over again, as the obscure men defend their conduct or attack that of others, they misinterpret their texts in a systematic way. Like good scholastics, they quote their authorities without reference to the original contexts of their utterances: "Because Ezekiel 11 says, 'Rejoice, young man, be glad in your youth,' I am of cheerful heart. And you must know that my love affairs have gone well. Does Ezekiel not say: 'Now he shall fornicate in his fornication'? Why, then, may I not sometimes purge my reins? I am no angel, but a man, and to err is human" (1.9). Again and again, the humanists offer a sardonic counterpoint, either reading their texts correctly or exposing their opponents' errors by silent sarcasm. A doctor named Antonius describes how he had proved, in humanist company, that Caesar could not have written his *Commentaries.* His proof took the standard form of a syllogism: "One who is busy with arms and continual labors cannot learn Latin. But it is so that Caesar was always in wars and great labors: therefore he could not be learned or learn Latin." Erasmus, who had been listening, merely smiled—because, so Antonius said, he recognized that he could not answer this brilliant demonstration (1.42). In fact, of course, the great humanist smiled contemptuously at the scholastic's characteristic lapse into anachronism: his failure to see that a Roman general might not have to work as hard as a fifteenth-century Landsknecht to write good Latin. The contrast between these two enterprises is clear. The intellectual of the older type—the scholastic theologian—assembles authoritative quotations not as a beaver builds a dam but as a magpie makes a nest. He takes no interest in the larger context from which they came. More generally, he fails to realize that their authors had lived in a world different from his own—one in which Latin, for example, was not a learned but a living language. The intellectual of the new type knows these methodological points so well that he need not even state them. The authors of the satire and their reader smile disdainfully in shared philological correctness, as their enemies refute themselves out of their own mouths. The collision between two kinds of learning could not have been portrayed more sharply by any direct form of description than it was by the two young humanists' slapstick satire.

II. Humanism and the Classical Past

Modern accounts of Renaissance humanism diverge on many points. Some historians, above all Paul Oskar Kristeller, believe that it primarily represented the revival of a set of disciplines and concerns that had been connected in antiquity. The humanists, they argue, reasserted the value and interest of the rhetorical tradition, with its associated disciplines of grammar, moral philosophy, and history. Their opposition to scholasticism, which gained headway in the Italian universities just as humanism was establishing itself in courts and cities, amounted less to an effort at intellectual subversion than to a new chapter in the quarrel between rhetoric and philosophy that had begun almost two thousand years before in Athens.[6] Others, like Eugenio Garin and Hans Baron, have argued that humanism represented a radically new intellectual movement. The humanists, who insisted on the supreme value of an active, civic life, were the first modern intellectuals. The principled advocates of action against contemplation, republics against monarchies, and modernity against the stultifying authority of tradition, they developed an intellectual program that used classical ingredients in strikingly new ways. Their battles with the scholastics were not one more set of sparks produced by the rubbing together of rival disciplines but the explosion naturally caused by the clash of two radically divergent worldviews: two ways of using the past to shape the present so different that nothing and no one could reconcile them fundamentally.[7]

These debates have lasted two generations and more, inspiring monographic work of high value on both the Italian and the Northern Renaissance but leaving many issues in dispute. It is obviously impossible to survey the entire field in a single essay, much less to assess them in the light of a wide range of primary sources. My much more modest aim is to inquire into one side of the humanist program, one on which representatives of both schools have laid great emphasis: the development of a new, historical method of reading and interpreting texts—texts that included not only the so-called Greek and Latin classics but also an increasingly wide range of sources in Hebrew and other languages.

Though many scholars have attempted to describe this phenomenon, no one has offered a more brilliant or a more influential formulation than Erwin Panofsky. In a series of brilliant essays, the fullest of which he wrote in collaboration with Fritz Saxl, he set out to define the difference between the several renascences of classical texts and forms that took place during the Middle Ages and the full-scale Renaissance, which he localized in fifteenth-century Italy.[8] Medieval artists and scholars, Panofsky explained, studied individual classical texts or imitated individual classical forms. But they did not see classical forms and their original content—or motifs and themes—as organically connected, as joint, though different, expressions of a single civilization. Only in the late fourteenth and early fifteenth centuries did humanists come to see the ancient world as a whole, a coherent culture that stood at a fixed difference from their own. When they did so, the shock of recognition was immense, and the intellectual change involved revolutionary. It was, in fact, every bit as radical as the contemporary transformation of the visual arts by the formulation of a strict system of one-point perspective. Panofsky, characteristically, speculated over and over again on what he saw as these contemporary and analogous changes of cultural focus. The end of the medieval "principle of disjunction" and the creation of a modern system of perspective became, for him, the double expression of a single phenomenon: the rise of a naturalistic art, for whose practitioners the way to nature lay through the antique (eventually, of course, the classical form of realism would be overcome and supplanted, in its turn, by other forms).

Both those who see the humanists as the inheritors of classical rhetoric and those who emphasize their modernity agree with Panofsky on the sharpness of their historical sense. The humanists, so most accounts agree, replaced the anachronistic methods of reading characteristic of the Middle Ages with contextual ones. They emphasized the need to interpret every text in the light of the known details and reconstructed background of its author's life. They insisted that everything—from texts to language itself—evolved in the course of time. Scholars who hoped to make sense of a given piece of Latin prose must begin by amassing solid knowledge of the development of the Latin language over the centuries: only then could they verify or falsify the ascription of a text to an author, correct scribal errors that had crept in over the centuries, and assess its worth as a stylistic model and a source of moral and pragmatic precepts. By insisting on the need to embed a text in a historical apparatus before trying to interpret it or apply its lessons in one's own writing and action, the humanists created modern philology. At the same time—so those who emphasize the radical novelty of humanism would generally say—they undermined scholasticism. As the text we began from suggests, they showed that the scholastics who had long dominated theology faculties in the universities of northern Europe and were beginning to establish themselves in the Italian ones did not know how to read the texts on which their social and intellectual authority rested. The texts that an Aquinas had cited as impersonal, atemporal "authorities," like the works of Aristotle, were in fact the historically conditioned products of fallible humans: the elaborate structures of inference that they assembled from their quotations were houses of cards, which a simple historical argument could demolish. The historical method of the humanists—like their new deftness at using the printing press to win an audience and establish their own reputations—formed an essential part of their new intellectual style, their new model of intellectual life.[9]

In the course of the sixteenth century, to be sure, the humanists' ideals and methods continued to evolve. They began to study Hebrew and Arabic as eagerly, if not as successfully, as Latin and Greek; to collect information about the histories, religions, and languages of ancient Egypt, Mesopotamia, and Persia as well as those of Greece and Rome; to imply, as Jean Bodin did in his *Methodus ad facilem historiarum cognitionem,* that historical examples from Turkish or Arabic sources might have as much to teach westerners in search of an appropriate model for the perfect constitution for their country as those handily collected in Latin by Valerius Maximus; or to state outright, as Joseph Scaliger did in his *Opus novum de emendatione temporum,* that the ancient Gauls and Mesopotamians had far outdone the Greeks and Romans in some forms of intellectual creativity. But the new, encyclopedic orientation of later humanistic scholarship is usually taken as a natural expansion of, not a diversion from, the historicist enterprise at the core of earlier humanism.

My plan is simple. I will use two case studies to raise some questions about the humanists' model of historical sensibility. What were its sources? What fissures and tensions does it reveal under examination? What is its relation, if any, to other models of textual scholarship that the humanists knew and studied? I seek not to refute Panofsky—or anyone else—but to stand back from the generalities and look, a little more directly than I and others have done before, into the scholarly and polemical alembics in which the new sensibility took shape.

III. Lorenzo Valla: New Historicist?

No one has been invoked more often as a case in point of the novelty of humanism than the Roman scholar Lorenzo Valla, whose brilliant career as a translator, commentator on, and imitator of the ancients stretched across the first half of the fifteenth century. A peerless historical critic, Valla did not hesitate to reduce any authority to its true, historical dimensions. Early in his career he infuriated the lawyers at the University of Pavia by a sharp attack on the most prestigious jurist of the fourteenth century, Bartolus of Sassoferrato, whose theories about colors he shredded. Later he argued that the theological texts long ascribed to Dionysius the Areopagite, which provided the neo-Platonic scaffolding for many doctrines and practices of the medieval church, could not have been written by their purported author, a Greek converted by St. Paul himself. He dismissed the *Donation of Constantine*—the brilliant text that described how the Emperor Constantine, miraculously cured of leprosy by the intervention of Pope Sylvester, gave the popes the western Empire to rule and decamped to Constantinople—as a forgery designed to support the doctrine of papal supremacy in the west. He even dared to correct the Vulgate text of the New Testament against the Greek from which it came. Valla's *Collatio Novi Testamenti,* though less widely read in his own day than his attack on the *Donation,* was published by Erasmus in 1505. It provided the main model for the Dutch humanist's more systematic effort to base theological studies on a philological approach to the original texts of the Bible. Valla thus undermined the whole edifice of scholastic theology, which rested on the assumption that the Vulgate represented what the Bible said, word for word and verse for verse.[10]

Valla carried out this work of demolition with machinery he himself had devised and constructed. He compiled the first modern empirical guide to classical Latin usage and syntax, the six books of *Elegancies of the Latin Language,* which would be the humanist's and philologist's pillow book for a century and more. Only the knowledge of classical usage that this task had given him made possible his demonstration that supposed classics were not genuine. Valla and his students agreed that this body of work was preeminently original, that he treated his predecessors not as posts on which to lean but as rugs on which to trample. As he asked in one famous letter, why write at all if not to correct the errors of some earlier writer? This fearless critic of all texts and sources seems to owe little or nothing to tradition.

In fact, both Valla's historical study of the Latin language and some of his wider historical theses drew freely on classical and late antique precedents. Consider, first of all, his meticulous study of the history of Latin. Any reader of Valla's learned the primary humanist lesson that language has a history—one organically connected with that of the wider culture it served and embodied. In his history of Ferdinand of Aragon, for example, he devoted a wonderfully edgy passage to the question of place names:

> When the Romans took over Gaul, they divided it into two provinces, Citerior and Ulterior. Each had its own regions, defined by fixed boundaries and names; almost all of these are now different. Hence I, who am writing for men of the present and the future, must use not the original names, but those that are now and have long been used, if I want all my readers to understand me.[11]

Valla used the resources he assembled so lavishly with dexterity and wit. He produced masterly Latin prose. He demolished the "kitchen–Latin" of his opponents, like Poggio (in one wonderful text he portrays another humanist's kitchen–boy dissecting Poggio's Latin howler by howler). And he used the same set of tools, applying them not to composition but to exegesis, to dismantle the Latin of the *Donation of Constantine*. This text used nonclassical terms like *satrap* and conflated words always distinguished in classical Latin, like *seu* and *et*. Hence, Valla argued, it could not come from the period it claimed as its own: the fourth century A.D.[12]

Valla derived the content of his book from massive and direct study of the original sources. But he derived its method in large part not from his mother wit but from another set of ancient, or at least late antique, texts—the grammatical works of Priscian and Donatus and the vast commentary on Virgil of Servius. The late Roman teachers who produced these books spoke and wrote a Latin quite different from that of the classical texts they explicated. Their pupils came to Virgilian hexameters as ours might to Shakespeare: barely able to construe, and quite unable to reproduce or imitate, the canonical classic of their culture and the core text of their curriculum. Accordingly, the grammarians compiled a vast treasury of observations about the meanings of words, their metaphorical extensions, and parallel passages in other texts. They dissected the delicate tissues of classical Latin and laid bare their underlying structure and matter much as Valla would, and centuries earlier. And they warned their students, endlessly, that the Latin of their own day differed in numerous respects from that of their canonical but irregular classics—and that reason, as embodied in the grammatical tradition, had often changed inherited custom. Here, for example, is Servius on a line in Virgil's *Aeneid:*

> *Insomnia terrent.* Both *terret* and *terrent* are found. But if we read *terret, insomnia* will mean a vigil. For the older writers wished to make this distinction between vigils and what we see in dreams: that *insomnia* as a feminine singular noun would mean a vigil, and *insomnia* as a neuter plural noun would mean what we see through a dream. . . . You should therefore note that if we say *terret,* the form of speech will be antique. (4.9)

Servius did not have a sharp intelligence to rival Valla's. But he did have a similarly penetrating eye for possible confusions and a similar detective's gift for discovering the fault lines of historical change in what previous grammarians had seen as the seamless fabric of the Latin tradition.[13]

There was a difference, to be sure. Servius corrected the usages of Virgil as often as he explained them. He found many far-fetched extended uses of terms and many simple solecisms in the *Aeneid.* He needed, moreover, as Robert Kaster has shown, to establish that his own authority as the guardian of a cultural canon took precedence even over that of the authors in the canon. Servius dealt with Virgil's literary sins and his own social ambitions by the same simple maneuver. He argued, over and over again, that Virgil had failed to distinguish between words with different senses—or had spoken in ways that had subsequently, and rightly, been defined as improper. The critic ruled the poet.

Valla, by contrast, insistently treated the canonical authors, not the post-canonical commentators, as the standard of correctness in Latin. By doing so he made a social and professional move that imitated Servius'; he established his own authority as the consummate grammarian. But he also made a more profound intellectual move, which subverted his fourth-century model: he established his authority by asserting (and proving) his command of a specific, chronologically defined kind of Latin, that of the Golden Age.

Valla realized that all languages, including Latin, change over time. Accordingly, he accepted that new Latin words could still properly be coined for new inventions like the clock and the cannon. But he refused to let these justifiable innovations interfere with his sharply argued, meticulously documented version of what Latin had been at its classic best. Insofar as Valla insisted on the virtues of one kind of Latin, moreover, his method was not consistently historical. He exalted one stratum in the history of the language as what he called a "sacrament," an outward sign of inward cultural grace.[14] The body of Golden

Latin texts was thus transformed from the historical work of human agents to a perfect standard against which any medieval or modern text or author could be tested and found wanting. Valla evoked not a real landscape studied and documented with photographic intensity, its highlights and shadows meticulously recorded, but an imaginary ideal as flat as it was idealized. For Valla, Golden Latin glowed behind all later forms of writing like the painted backdrop of a Pacific Island paradise in a Hollywood movie, ever out of reach behind the photographed foregrounds with their three dimensions and their natural human flaws. He charged one sector of the classical heritage with a timeless, supernatural power—and to that extent he treated his texts less historically than his late antique forerunners had. The great historicist made his texts not only the bearers of eternal verities but the models of eternally valid forms.

Yet Valla himself also made clear in the course of the polemics provoked by his history of Ferdinand and his criticism of other humanists in Naples that he knew that he could not simply establish a canon of perfect Latin and rely on it. As we have seen, Valla explicitly pointed out that he could not consistently use classical place-names in his Latin, since some had changed and others had come into being, and he wrote for a modern, not an ancient, world and public. Language, he argued, rested on nothing more or less than custom, and custom changed with time. The ancients, moreover, had already realized this point and put it into effect in their own writing: "I see that this was the general practice of the ancients. For these and other places came repeatedly to be called by different names, and the old language is simply an old custom of speaking."[15] Similarly, Valla called mounted scouts *caballerii* or *equerii,* rather than *equites.* Seeking out a classical term for things that had not existed in the ancient world could lead only to error and confusion: "Anyone can see that new names must be fitted to new things. This was the custom of the ancients, from whom we have our rules and derive our examples."[16] Valla digressed at such length on this point that he eventually excised the passage in question from his history and passed it on to his friend Giovanni Tortelli, who in turn published it as an article in his own massive reference work on the Latin language, the *De orthographia.*[17]

Like Leon Battista Alberti—who called on the precedent of Cicero to defend his own decision to write in Italian, the language of his contemporaries—Valla used a classical precedent to defend his apparent departures from a strictly classical vocabulary. Salvatore Camporeale and Vincenzo de Caprio have identified his source. Quintilian, in his *Institutio oratoria,* had highlighted the role that *consuetudo,* 'custom' should play in forming a good orator's choice of words. The speaker of real Latin, Quintilian argued, must sometimes follow modern, oral usage rather than the practice of older writers: "What is the old language, but an old custom of speaking?"[18]

Valla characteristically put his own twist on his ancient source, turning Quintilian's question into a statement. Nonetheless, Valla saw his historical method as classical. And he defended it against his literary enemy Bartolomeo Facio, as Mariangela Regoliosi has shown, by invoking still another ancient authority. Facio criticized Valla sharply for introducing such lexical problems into his history of Ferdinand. Valla replied by arguing that this apparent departure from the classical precepts for historians writing works of pragmatic content and rhetorical appeal in fact rested on the best of ancient authorities.[19] As his predecedent for discussing problems of language in a historical work, however, Valla cited not a grammarian or a rhetorician, but a historian: Thucydides. The historian of the Peloponnesian wars, whose work Valla translated, for the first time, into Latin, had devoted even more space than Valla to subjects that Facio would have condemned as irrelevant to history. He had anticipated Valla's exploration of the mutability of culture and language in the *Archaeology*, where he discussed the cultural development of Greece between Homer's time and his own.[20] His example proved that a historian must be ready to discuss linguistic problems, at least when they reflected substantial changes in the order of society—like the rise of the name "Hellas" for all the Greeks.[21] Valla's model of style, of how to write history while thinking historically, in short, came from Servius, Quintilian, and Thucydides—as well as from his own remarkable mother wit.

It should by now be clear that Valla's version of humanism and his attitude toward the past were anything but simple. His attitudes ranged from the sharply critical to the simply admiring: he read Latin with both a uniquely sharp eye for meaningful detail and a worshipper's sensitivity to the beauty of the language—that beauty which other humanists had compared, revealingly, to the beauty of the Latin Mass. He built on classical precedents and used the best ancient ingredients in his concoctions: but he combined these in ways that would have startled their creators, making the political historian Thucydides as well as the Roman rhetorician Quintilian into the models for a form of scholarship that neither of them would have recognized as theirs. Valla's model of scholarly work is simultaneously historical and unhistorical, ancient and modern: a thing more complex, and often more contradictory, than the *Letters of Obscure Men* would suggest.

IV.   Humanist Hebrew Studies, Christian and Jewish:
Philologues sans frontières?

From the beginning of the fifteenth century the scholarship of the humanists began to stretch, to embrace not only the Greek and Latin languages and traditions but also a wide range of others. The Egyptian tradition, as represented in the distorting mirror of the neo-Platonic manual on hieroglyphs by Horus Apollo, came to light early in the fifteenth century. Over time, this late antique text inspired a Europe-wide vogue for obelisks, pyramids, and inscriptions written in spurious hieroglyphs, which became a central element in imperial and royal pageantry.[22] It also prepared the way for a second, even more complicated representation of Egyptian thought and ritual: the dialogues ascribed to the sage Hermes Trismegistus, which were written in the second and third centuries A.D. Translated into Latin by Marsilio Ficino, these seductive texts carried the notion that philosophy had begun not in Greece but among the barbarians from Prague to Paris and beyond. They were accompanied by other Near Eastern revelations written in Greek, which proved almost as attractive: the Persian, as represented even less accurately by Greek texts attributed to Zoroaster; the Chaldean, as represented by oracles in Greek verse collected and interpreted in late Antiquity; and the Orphic.[23] By the end of the fifteenth century, in short, humanists were accustomed to the idea that traditions not originally written in Greek and Latin were as ancient as, or more ancient than, the classics of Greece and Rome. The past of mankind turned into a carnival hall of mirrors: humanists gazed with hypnotic intensity at Greeks and Persians, Brahmins and Orphics, all of whom resembled one another almost perfectly—but always showed distortions and differences that fascinated and troubled the critical onlooker.

As Europe expanded, moreover, intellectuals came into contact not only with traditions of classical texts, but also with traditions of post–classical textual scholarship: with the efforts of designated groups to preserve and transmit the central teachings of a canonical text or texts. They used methods as diverse as oral recitation—in the case of the Meso-American scholars whose ability to recall their past so fascinated and irritated European missionaries— and the precise collation of variants and compilation of commentaries—in the case of the Chinese literati whose customs and costumes Jesuits like Matteo Ricci worked hard to imitate.[24] How far did the encounter with non-western forms of scholarship affect the humanists' methods? How far did contact with the humanists reshape the ways in which non-western scholars dealt with their own classics?

As we have already seen, no outside tradition of scholarship fascinated humanists more or proved more controversial than the Jewish. This offered richer rewards, at least potentially, than any of the others. Hebrew was, after all, the language not of pagan texts but of what had become a fundamental Christian one: the Old Testament. Many Christian scholars believed, with Johannes Reuchlin, who wrote a series of pioneering guides to the Hebrew language and its literal and higher meanings, that the Hebrew language was the original one, the language of power in which God had spoken to men and angels and with which He had brought the world itself into being. Others, like Guillaume Postel, identified it with the language of Adam, in which names corresponded to the natures of the things they designated.[25] The mysteries of Hebrew numerology might offer insight into the most secret messages of the Bible. Jewish scholars able to explicate their methods of commentary, moreover, could be found throughout continental Europe. Even the harassed Jewish communities of the Holy Roman Empire—where Reuchlin found it hard to buy the books he wanted, and some rabbis refused to help outsiders—provided Reuchlin with his first lessons. In Italy, the expulsion of Jews from the Hispanic world and the consequent closing of the great Sicilian yeshivas brought texts and teachers into close proximity with Christian scholars who demanded their services. Some, like Pico's translator Flavius Guillelmus Ramundus Mithridates, converted to Christianity and told their eager, gullible customers that the Talmud and the Cabala contained the Christian doctrine of the Trinity. Others, like Johannan Alemanno, insisted on a more equal form of intellectual exchange, swapping Cabalistic mysteries for neo-Platonic ones and maintaining what they took to be intellectual independence even as their exposure to the philosophy of Plotinus and Porphyry gradually altered their hermeneutics and metaphysics.[26] In both cases, humanist and Jewish styles of textual analysis came into close and potentially explosive contact. What sort of effects did exposure to Jewish learning have on the humanists, and exposure to the humanist historical method on the Jews?

Humanist attitudes toward their Jewish informants varied radically. Joseph Scaliger expressed one widely held view when he described the lessons in Talmudic reading he had had with a convert from Poland whom he had installed at his own university in Leiden: "We read a great deal of the Talmud together with equal pleasure and profit. He had learned the Talmud by memory from his boyhood, following the custom of the Jews, without any grammatical instruction. Therefore I often corrected him on points of grammar, and he was willing to have me show him these things. But his skill as a Talmudist was extraordinary, and such as only a Jew who has been trained by childhood can attain."[27] Only a Christian, Scaliger continued, who had access to a native informant like his, could hope to identify the unmarked proverbs, allusions, and quotations with which the Talmudic text swarmed. But only a Christian grammarian like Scaliger could reduce the language to the scientific principles that the poor native had never imagined could apply. The native supplies orally transmitted knowledge, while the humanist expert subjects it to rational analysis: this schema naturally inspires discomfort in the twentieth-century reader. But it was not the only one. Johann Buxtorf the elder, the most important Hebraist of the generation after Scaliger's, consorted eagerly with practising Jews. He spoke with pride, as Reuchlin had, of the years he had spent in their synagogues and study houses, and treated his direct contact with Jewish scholarly circles in Cracow and Prague as the guarantee of his scholarly authority.[28] As in many other cases of cultural contact—one thinks of the Jesuits in China—a spectrum of power relations and intellectual possibilities governed relations between Jews and Christians.

No field of scholarly enterprise that engaged both Jews and Christians was more delicate or more contentious than the establishment of the text of the Hebrew Bible. Christian attitudes toward the Hebrew text were often charged with suspicion. Medieval polemicists had accused the Jews of deliberately corrupting their text, perhaps as early as the time of Constantine the Great, in order to discredit the versions of it used by Christians. The points that indicate the vocalization of the consonantal text of the Hebrew Bible, for example, were often dismissed by Christian scholars as a late addition, or at least as of low importance, and sometimes condemned as a Jewish effort to disguise the true meaning of the text. Even Cardinal Ximenes, whose great *Complutensian Polyglot Bible* presented the text in columns, the Vulgate flanked by the Hebrew and Greek, revealed his true feelings when he remarked that the central position of the Vulgate resembled that of Christ, crucified between two thieves. Yet it was a Christian printer, Daniel Bomberg, who set out to create an orderly printed rabbinic Bible, with the help of Jewish scholars, and Christian humanist theologians as well as pious Jews waited eagerly for the results. Methodological collisions were inevitable.

The nature of the Hebrew text made the editorial problems even more severe than normal ones. The consonantal text of the Hebrew Bible appeared in medieval manuscripts in a variety of forms, all of them of bewildering visual complexity. Vowel points and accents gave guidance to the pronunciation of the text. An apparatus of notes in the margins and at the ends of books instructed the reader on all sorts of details of spelling and pronunciation and apparently cited variant readings. These notes varied from recension to recension and were often corrupt to boot. Jacob ben Chayim ibn Adoniyah, who edited the *Rabbinic Bible* of 1524–25, complained that he had found the Masoretic books "in the utmost disorder and confusion" and that many of the textual comments in the Masora "are written in a contracted form and with ornaments, so much so that they cannot at all be deciphered." He also knew that a great medieval scholar, David Kimhi, had argued that the Masora did contain genuine variant readings. When Ezra and the men of the Great Synagogue set out to reassemble the Bible after the Babylonian exile, Kimhi argued, they had found different readings in different texts. Their apparatus recorded their findings.[29] Jacob ben Chayim rejected this opinion decisively, arguing that Ezra and his scribes had derived their entire marginal apparatus from existing, authoritative manuscripts. His own work was intended to present readers with the text of the Bible as it had been, not only in the time of the Great Synagogue but in that of the first Temple. Nonetheless, the spectrum of opinions that he had to describe in order to refute them indicated that the biblical text he edited might rest in part on weak or late foundations: that it might, indeed, be impossible to recover the primitive scriptures as they had been before the Exile.[30]

A second Jewish scholar, Elias Levita, set out to analyse the constitution of the text of the Bible still more systematically.[31] He argued that the apparent variants in the Masora had indeed been added by the men of the Great Synagogue. They had not, however, done so because the Biblical text was in confusion in their time. Rather, they had recorded explanations for peculiar, apparently problematic word forms that went back, like the forms themselves, to Moses, and had been passed down orally until the time of Ezra. He thus managed to synthesize Kimhi's acute historical analysis of the transmitted biblical text with Jacob ben Chayim's desire to preserve its antiquity and authority.[32] But after collecting all the evidence, Elias came to a second conclusion more radical than Kimhi's. The very vowel points and accents found in the body of the Hebrew text, he argued, did not go back to the original or even to the time of Ezra and the Great Synagogue. They had in fact been added to the text, in the last centuries of the first millennium A.D., by Jewish scholars in Tiberias and elsewhere—a conclusion that subsequent scholarship has thoroughly confirmed.[33]

The nature of the arguments with which Elias tried "to do battle against those who say that [the vowel points] were given on Sinai" is especially revealing.[34] He collected opinions of earlier scholars on the subject and discussed them fully. But he then pointed out that if the vowel points really had been given by Moses on Sinai or devised by Ezra in Jerusalem, historical evidence would exist to prove the point. So radical a change would have left a deposit in the record. But a survey of it found none:

> First, in all the writings of our Rabbins of blessed memory, whether the Talmud, or the Hagadah, or the Midrash, there is not to be found any mention whatever of, or any allusion to, the vowel points or accents. Is this possible?

Second and third, examples from the Talmud showed that its authors had read a biblical text without vowels, and assumed that actors in later books of the Bible had read an unvocalized Torah. Fourth, and decisively:

> Almost all of the names of both the vowel points and the accents are not Hebrew but Aramaic and Babylonian. . . . Now, if it were true that they were given on Sinai, what is the meaning of Aramaic names at Mount Sinai? Were not all the commandments given on Sinai in Hebrew?[35]

The nature of this demonstration is clear. Elias imagined what would have happened if the vowel points had formed part of the biblical text in ancient times. They would have had Hebrew names, not the Aramaic ones that re-flected their real origin in postexilic Judaism. They would have been men-tioned in the Talmud. A particular historical situation would have given rise to a particular set of testimonies. But these were not to be found.

    This argument lies outside the norms of traditional Jewish scholarship. The Masoretes had compiled systematic lists of the various textual inconsistencies on which their apparatus provided guidance for the reader. Individual Jewish scholars like ibn Ezra and Kimhi had noticed inconsistencies in the biblical text and devised hypotheses to account for their origin. And Pico della Mirandola credited Jewish acquaintances with at least one remarkable piece of historical detection that resembles Elias' work in striking ways. Most Jews and Christians believed, in the Renaissance, that the *Yosippon,* the medieval He-brew reworking of Josephus's *Jewish War,* was in fact the original text of that work. No one had a keener appetite than Pico for mysterious Jewish books. But his friends explained that the Hebrew *Yosippon* was a late reworking, not the original source, of the real Greek writings of Josephus. Only that fact—they clearly saw—could explain the text's numerous references to medieval French place names. This example of Jewish criticism, not that of Christian humanist scholarship, seems to have inspired Pico when he questioned the authenticity of the *Testimonium Flavianum,* a passage about Jesus supposedly preserved by (but actually interpolated into) Josephus.[36]

But the argument that Elias Levita advanced about the biblical text seems to attack widespread attitudes about the nature and authority of the biblical text—in particular, those of the Jewish Cabalists, some of whom held that the vocalized Masoretic text was exactly what Moses had received on Sinai.[37] Structurally Elias' work resembles Valla's *Declamation on the Donation of Constantine.* Valla had argued there that the historical evidence proved that Constantine had never given his western empire to the Church. After all, he pointed out, a political and religious earthquake on that scale would have precipitated tremors throughout the Christian world—tremors that would, in turn, certainly have been recorded by the sensitive seismographs of contemporary historians and polemicists. But they either remained silent or attested, uniformly, that Constantine had been a Christian from boyhood and that he never relinquished the empire in the west. If the popes had ruled the west, they must have had a coinage of their own: but no coins with the names of the popes attested to their overlordship. An event of this transcendent importance would have been recorded in the ancient world in monuments, and would have been mentioned in texts that could be cited. But no such witnesses spoke when the record was examined.[38] Like Elias Levita, in short, Valla imagined what the historical record would have to include if the hypothesis contrary to his own held. He thought his way into the historical situation in question and showed that it could not have given rise to the textual tradition that in fact existed. Only one conclusion was possible: the tradition lied or had become corrupt, and must be set aside if one hoped to understand the historical facts underneath.

Neither Valla nor Elias Levita succeeded in rejecting all unfounded traditions: Valla cited forged texts as well as genuine ones, and Elias argued as strenuously for the correctness of the vowel points, for their fidelity to the oral teaching of Moses, as he did for the late dating that called their historicity into question. But the fundamental similarity of intellectual style seems clear. For all the differences of institutional and social context, for all the ethnic and religious prejudices that separated them, they worked at a common enterprise, employing the same basic tools to the same basic effect. Valla's model of humanism might have been composite and revealed fissures and fractures under stress. It still proved powerful enough to reshape the Jewish as well as the Christian approach to tradition, by providing Elias with the Archimedean point that enabled him to shift a mass of traditional data into a new relation and position.

Like all collisions, however, the interaction of Hebrew and Christian scholarly traditions included reactions as well as actions. Naturally, the Christians who studied Cabalistic ideas in Europe did not accept and develop what they found in Jewish mystical texts simply because they liked what they read. Pico and his successors followed an ancient model—that of such Fathers of the Church as Eusebius—when they argued that a monotheistic, essentially Christian tradition in theology had existed long before Christ himself appeared.[39] They believed that ancient sages like Hermes Trismegistus and Zoroaster—whom they regarded as the sources of the almost Christian philosophy of Plato—had handed down a primeval revelation over the centuries. And they were therefore predisposed to accept the validity and quality of Cabalistic tradition, which also presented itself as a primeval wisdom handed down in secret over the centuries by wise teachers. Pico, for example, saw the Cabala simply as one case of the larger phenomenon of oral transmission of an originary revelation:

> To reveal the most secret mysteries and sublime *arcana* of divinity—those which lie hidden beneath the bark of the law and the rough dress of its words—to the ordinary people would be to give the sacrament to dogs and sprinkle pearls before swine. Therefore it was not the work of human prudence, but of divine command, to keep these things secret, to be communicated only to the perfect—among whom alone, says Paul, he speaks wisely. The ancient philosophers religiously observed this custom. . . . The sphinxes sculpted on Egyptian temples warned that mystic teachings should be kept inviolate from the profane crowd by the difficulties of enigmas. . . . This is confirmed, above all, by Dionysius the Areopagite, who says that the most secret mysteries were passed on by the founders of our religion from mind to mind, without letters, without writing, by the intermediary of the word. In exactly the same way, when by God's order the true interpretation of the law was divinely revealed to Moses, it was called Cabala, which is the Hebrew word for what we call "receptio": that is, because each received that doctrine not through written texts, but in successive revelations, each from the other, as though by the law of inheritance.[40]

Postel, similarly, compared the Cabalistic tradition with such well-known pagan counterparts as the oral teachings of Brahmans and the Druids.[41]

Moreover, as Wirszubski and Idel have shown, both Jewish informants and Christian recipients altered the fabric of Cabalistic tradition to suit their needs. Sixteenth-century Christian Cabalists were no philo-Semites. Pico confidently insisted that the Cabala provided verification for central Christian doctrines. Reuchlin and Postel presented themselves as wrenching hidden treasures from the unclean hands of their Jewish possessors in order to put them, at long last, to Christian use.[42] They suppressed the anti-Christian overtones and undertones of some Cabalistic doctrines. They paid little attention to the distinctions, glaringly visible in the light of recent research, between Spanish and Italian traditions in the Cabala, and laid far more weight than was philologically justified on the magical side of Cabalistic practice.[43]

Nonetheless, Christian exegetes found their practices reshaped in fundamental ways by the Jewish texts they mishandled. Reuchlin, for example, treated the Cabala not as a parallel to but as the source of the *prisca philosophia* of Pythagoras. In doing so, as Idel has shown, Reuchlin adopted a thesis previously advanced by a fifteenth-century Italian rabbi, Eliahu Hayyim ben Benyamin.[44] Reuchlin went so far as to argue that the Cabalistic texts preserved Pythagoras' philosophy better than any Greek ones did and must serve as the source for any reconstruction of it.[45] In doing so he implied that the serious student of ancient Greek philosophy and mathematics must follow his subject into Hebrew as well as Greek sources—a suggestion that Isaac Newton, among others, still found plausible more than a century later.[46]

More generally, the Cabalistic texts that did become available in translations and summaries offered a view of language that fascinated and provoked Christian theologians and philosophers for centuries to come. Many who had only a garbled notion of central Cabalistic theories about cosmology understood clearly that Hebrew was a language of power: that the enlightened student might hope to be vouchsafed a vision of the true alphabet of being itself, a cosmic text written in letters of gold or fire, and that the Hebrew Bible offered the closest counterpart to this experience of direct perception of realities accessible in human time or space.[47] Hermeneutics, given these possibilities, required not study of historical and philological parallels but ingenious manipulation of a textual combinatorics that could resolve any phrase in the Hebrew bible into history, prophecy or philology.[48] Cabala enabled a way of reading irreconcilable with Valla's—one that rested on a view of language and human creativity radically different from his—to establish itself within the humanistic tradition.

By the early seventeenth century, those who accepted such ways of reading certainly outnumbered their opponents. Joseph Scaliger—who occupies, as we have already seen, a high place in modern histories of the humanist tradition—denied the antiquity of the Hebrew vowel points—and that of a central Cabalistic text, the *Zohar,* which seemed to support it.[49] But Johann Buxtorf, to whom he made these arguments, opposed to them the common opinions of the Jews—who held that the vowel points went back to deepest antiquity and the Masoretic apparatus of the Bible at least to Ezra.[50] Early Protestant scholars had tended, on the whole, to deny the antiquity of the vowel points (after all, they considered the Greek New Testament to be the core of the Bible anyway). Late ones, by contrast, insisted that the Old Testament was as literally inspired as the new—and cited the *Zohar* and a raft of later Hebrew commentaries in support of their view. The methods and assumptions of Jewish scholarship flourished, torn from their original context but still recognizably alive, in the centers of Calvinist orthodoxy, and they would not succumb to a philological critique until deep in the eighteenth century.[51]

Humanist and informant, master and slave, historicism and ahistoricism: these simple dichotomies simply do not fit the complex movements briefly discussed here. The historiography of western scholarship badly needs more monographic studies; even starker, however, is the need for new analytical models that can do something more like justice to these Laocoön-like struggles of texts and readers.

NOTES

1. I use the bilingual edition by F. G. Stokes (London, 1909); translations are mine.

2. See in general J. Bentley, *Humanists and Holy Writ* (Princeton, 1983).

3. On Reuchlin, see in general *Contemporaries of Erasmus,* s.n. Reuchlin, and W. Schwarz, *Principles and Problems of Biblical Translation* (Cambridge, 1955).

4. R. Po-chia Hsia, *The Myth of Ritual Murder* (New Haven and London, 1988).

5. The most elaborate recent interpretation of the debate over Reuchlin holds that Hutten interpreted it in a way that skewed its interpretation for centuries; see J. H. Overfield, *Humanism and Scholasticism in Late Medieval Germany* (Princeton, 1984), chap. 7; for a more traditional interpretation see E. Rummel, *The Humanist-Scholastic Debate in the Renaissance and Reformation* (Cambridge, Mass., 1995). In any event, the interpretation of the *Epistolae obscurorum virorum* as a manifesto about humanism is not in doubt.

6. See especially Kristeller's collected essays on *Renaissance Thought and Its Sources,* ed. M. Mooney (New York, 1979).

7. See especially E. Garin, *L'umanesimo italiano* (Bari, 1958); and H. Baron, *In Search of Florentine Civic Humanism* (Princeton, 1988).

8. E. Panofsky and F. Saxl, "Classical Mythology in Mediaeval Art," *Metropolitan Museum Studies* 4 (1933): 228–80. See also Panofsky's brilliant short statement in *Kenyon Review* 6 (1944): 201–36; and the fullest formulation of it in *Renaissance and Renascences in Western Art* (Stockholm, 1960).

9. Some of the more formidable arguments to this effect are found in J. H. Franklin, *Jean Bodin and the Sixteenth-Century Revolution in the Methodology of Law and History* (New York, 1963); G. Huppert, *The Idea of Perfect History* (Urbana, 1970); and D. R. Kelley, *Foundations of Modern Historical Scholarship* (New York, 1970). Critiques—by no means in agreement with one another on all points—include E. Hassinger, *Empirisch-rationaler Historismus* (Bern and Munich, 1978); U. Muhlack, *Geschichtswissenchaft im Humanismus und in der Aufklärung* (Munich, 1991); and Z. Schiffman, *On the Threshold of Modernity* (Baltimore, 1991).

10. See in general Kelley, *Foundations,* chap. 1.

11. L. Valla, *Gesta Ferdinandi regis Aragonum,* ed. O. Besomi (Padua, 1973), 10–11 (1.2.1).

12. For the text and context of Valla's work, see W. Setz, *Lorenzo Vallas Schrift gegen die Kostantinische Schenkung* (Tübingen, 1975); on its reception, see G. Antonazzi, *Lorenzo Valla e la polemica sulla la Donazione di Costantino* (Rome, 1985). The recent French translation by J.-B. Giard (Paris, 1993) has useful notes and an important introductory essay by C. Ginzburg.

13. R. Kaster, *Guardians of Language* (Berkeley, Los Angeles, and London, 1988).

14. L. Valla, "In libros Elegantiarum praefatio," in *Prosatori latini del Quattrocento,* ed. E. Garin (Milan and Naples, 1952).

15. Valla, *Gesta,* ed. Besomi, 10–13 at 11 (1.2.1): "ut necesse habeam, cum presentibus futurisque hominibus scribam, non priscis nominibus uti, sed nostro seculo et iam longa etate usitatis, si ab omnibus legentibus intelligi velim, ut veteres quoque ipsos video factitasse; nam et hec et cetera loca fere diversis subinde vocibus appellata sunt, et vetus sermo nihil aliud est quam vetus loquendi consuetudo."

16. Ibid., 1.14.7, 62–63 at 63: "Quare quis non videt rebus novis esse accommodanda nova nomina, ut veteres, a quibus praecepta habemus et exempla sumimus, factitarunt?"

17. Ibid., 194–204; see the more detailed treatment, also by Besomi, in *Italia Medioevale e Umanistica* 9 (1966): 75–121.

18. Quintilian, *Institutio oratoria,* 1.6.43: "Et sane quid est aliud vetus sermo quam vetus loquendi consuetudo?" See V. de Caprio, *La tradizione e la trauma* (Manziana, 1991), 152–62.

19. L. Valla, *Antidotum in Facium,* ed. M. Regoliosi (Padua, 1981), "Introduzione," liii–lxvii.

20. Ibid., 3.1.6, 211.

21. Ibid., 3.4.8, 235: "neque hec disputatio est neque longa, sed perbrevis narratio, neque tam de novo verbo quam de nova re, sicut Thucydides de vocabulo 'Grecie,' idest Ἑλλάδος, fecit."

22. See generally A. Grafton, Foreword to *The Hieroglyphs of Horapollo,* trans. G. Boas (new ed.; Princeton, 1993), with bibliography.

23. See F. A. Yates, *Giordano Bruno and the Hermetic Tradition* (Chicago and London, 1964); and D. P. Walker, *The Ancient Theology* (London, 1972).

24. For the encounter of western with Meso-American cultures of scholarship, see the paper by W. Mignolo in this volume; and J. Cañizares-Esguerra, "Historical Criticism and the 'Dispute of the New World': The Reconstruction of the Amerindian Past in Europe and Mexico, 1750–1800," Ph.D. diss., University of Wisconsin, 1995. The historical and philological methods of the Chinese scholars encountered by Ricci and his colleagues are described in B. Elman, *From Philosophy to Philology* (Cambridge, Mass., 1984).

25. J. Reuchlin, *Briefwechsel* (Tübingen, 1875), 105, 123; G. Postel, *Sefer Jezirah,* ed. W. P. Klein (Stuttgart-Bad Canstatt, 1994), 141.

26. C. Wirszubski, *Pico della Mirandola's Encounter with Jewish Mysticism* (Cambridge, Mass., and London, 1989); M. Idel, "The Magical and Neoplatonic Interpretations of the Kabbalah in the Renaissance," in *Essential Papers on Jewish Culture in Renaissance and Baroque Italy,* ed. D. B. Ruderman (New York and London, 1992).

27. J. J. Scaliger, *Epistolae omnes quae reperiri potuerunt,* ed. D. Heinsius (Leiden, 1627), 594.

28. See Buxtorf's letter to Scaliger of March 17, 1607, in *Sylloges epistolarum a viris illustribus scriptarum tomus I [–V],* ed. P. Burman (Leiden, 1727), 2:362–64; cf. E. Horowitz, "The Eve of the Circumcision: A Chapter in the History of Jewish Nightlife," *Essential Papers on Jewish Culture in Renaissance and Baroque Italy,* ed. D. B. Ruderman (New York and London, 1992).

29. See F. E. Talmage, *David Kimhi: The Man and the Commentaries* (Cambridge, Mass., and London, 1975), 86–94.

30. Jacob ben Chayim ibn Adoniyah, *Introduction to the Rabbinic Bible, Hebrew and English, with explanatory notes by Christian D. Ginzburg, LL.D., and the Massoreth Ha-Massoreth of Elias Levita,* 2d. ed., repr. ed. N. N. Snaith (New York, n.d.).

31. See in general G. E. Weil, *Elie Lévita, humaniste et massorète* (Leiden, 1963).

32. *Massoreth Ha-Massoreth,* ed. Ginzburg, 110–11.

33. For a recent summary, see E. Tov, *Textual Criticism of the Hebrew Bible* (Assen/ Maastricht and Minneapolis, 1992).

34. *Massoreth Ha-Massoreth,* ed. Ginzburg, 121.

35. Ibid., 127–29.

36. G. Pico della Mirandola, *Opera* (Basel, 1572), 385: "Quod petis de Iosepho, scias iustum Iosephum apud Hebraeos non reperiri, sed Iosephi epitoma, id est, breviarium quoddam, in quo et multa sunt commentitia, et quae de decem tribubus ibi leguntur, quae post babylonicam captivitatem postliminio non redierunt, ea esse notha et adulterina ex Hebraeis mihi plures confessi sunt, quapropter illorum Iosepho nulla omnino fides adhibenda. In Iosepho Graeco scio esse quaedam quae de Christo et fidem [fidelem?] et honorificam faciant mentionem, sed eadem esse penitus cum his quae in Latinis codicibus leguntur, non assererem nisi exemplar Graecum, cuius hic mihi nulla est copia, recens legerem."

37. On this point—and on the larger context of Elias' work—see the fundamental

essay of J. Penkower, "A Renewed Inquiry into the *Massoret Ha-Massoret* of Elijah Levita: Lateness of Vocalization and Criticism of the Zohar," *Italia* 8 (1989): 7–73.

38. L. Valla, *Treatise on the Donation of Constantine,* ed. and trans. C. B. Coleman (New Haven, 1922; repr. New York, 1971), 66–83.

39. See Walker, *The Ancient Theology.*

40. Pico, *Oratio,* in *Oeuvres philosophiques,* ed. O. Boulnois and G. Tognon (Paris, 1993), 62–64.

41. Cf. Klein, introduction to Postel, *Sefer Jezirah,* 25–27; and Postel's commentary, 80–82.

42. Postel, *Sefer Jezirah,* ed. Klein, 60–62.

43. See M. Idel, introduction to J. Reuchlin, *On the Art of the Kabbalah,* trans. M. Goodman and S. Goodman (Lincoln, 1993), v–xxix.

44. Ibid., xiii–xiv.

45. Ibid., 38: "Eruenda igitur inde fuerant fere omnia."

46. B. P. Copenhaver, "Jewish Theologies of Space in the Scientific Revolution: Henry More, Joseph Raphson, Isaac Newton, and Their Predecessors," *Annals of Science* 37 (1980): 489–548.

47. Postel, *Sefer Jezirah,* ed. Klein, 112–15.

48. See, most accessibly, the examples in Reuchlin, *On the Art of the Kabbalah,* trans. Goodman and Goodman.

49. Scaliger to Buxtorf, June 1, 1606, *Epistolae,* 523–24.

50. J. Buxtorf, *Tiberias sive commentarius masorethicus* (Basel, 1620). Cf., in general, D. C. Allen, *The Legend of Noah* (Urbana, 1949; repr. 1963).

51. See A. Grafton, *Defenders of the Text* (Cambridge, Mass., 1991), chap. 9.

History and Law in Sixteenth-Century Peru: The Impact of European Scholarly Traditions

Sabine G. MacCormack

1. Introduction

Modern definitions of scholarship do not mesh well with those current in sixteenth-century Spain and Peru. The very term *scholarship* does not translate readily into sixteenth-century Spanish. Scholarship in its several aspects of *ciencia, erudición,* and even *sabiduría*[1] was of course practised in the universities. Hence, scholars in Spanish society were the graduates—the bachelors, *licenciados,* and doctors—of one of over sixty Spanish universities,[2] or they might have studied abroad, and they were qualified in liberal arts, canon law, law, theology, or medicine. But although graduation gave these scholars a recognizable social identity along with career prospects, it did not foster or produce the same mental characteristics in everyone. This, at any rate, was what in the later sixteenth century the physician Huarte de San Juan thought: good Latinists, by virtue of having learnt the language by recourse to memory, were likely to lack speculative intelligence, while theologians had a high degree of such intelligence but were usually forgetful, and lawyers tended to be endowed with a middling sort of intellect.[3]

Moreover, not everyone who might lay claim to scholarship had darkened the doors of a university. The poet Garcilaso de la Vega, who addressed an elegant Horatian ode in Latin to the learned Aristotelian Juan Ginés de Sepúlveda,[4] bore as his device "con la espada y con la pluma."[5] His verses, pervaded as they were with Platonist ideas, had by the end of the century become the object of much learned exegesis by professional scholars with degrees, but Garcilaso himself died as a warrior serving his king in 1536. Garcilaso's kinsman, the historian Garcilaso de la Vega the Inca, was born in Cuzco in 1540 and adopted the poet's armorial device as his own. The Inca likewise enjoyed little formal education, but he amassed a scholarly library and in his old age was a valued member of a circle of *eruditi* in Cordoba. His *Royal Commentaries of the Incas* are, inter alia, a work of very great learning. Equally, it would be hard to deny a scholarly dimension in the historical work of the soldier Pedro Cieza de León, or in that of the *conquistador* Juan de Betanzos, who also lacked formal education but became a much respected translator of Quechua.

In thinking of the impact of European or Spanish scholarly traditions in the land of the Incas, and of the ways in which these traditions helped or hindered an understanding of Inca culture and politics, we must accordingly begin with some distinctions. Betanzos, Cieza, Garcilaso, and the several other *conquistadores* and soldiers who wrote about the Incas during the early years after the invasion were not in any technical sense scholars. They nonetheless perpetuated a tradition of secular learning and historical writing in the vernacular that went back to the historical compilations of Alfonso X in the thirteenth century.[6] As a result, they shared certain ideas and methods of enquiry, thanks to which they transformed the *terra incognita* of the Inca past into a series of narratives in Spanish.

On occasion historians in Spanish Peru contributed opinions bearing on current political and administrative issues,[7] but they rarely stood in the political mainstream. Lawyers, on the other hand, acted as negotiators between the warring factions of invading Spaniards, and once peace had been established they filled influential positions as administrators and royal officials. These were men who had enjoyed a formal education which, moreover, equipped them with a shared language and the ability to direct shared administrative and judicial procedures. Their interests, unlike those of historians, were overwhelmingly practical. Thus, where a historian might be led by the exigencies of a given subject to write an excursus or aside, lawyers, whose responsibility it was to ensure the smooth running of the Peruvian Viceroyalty, were more likely to stick to the issue at hand, leaving the interpretation of Inca and Andean culture to others.

The European learned traditions that found a voice in the Andes were thus far from uniform. Indeed, exponents of the different strands of these traditions, the historical, the legal, and, in the missionary field, the theological, which I have discussed elsewhere,[8] did not often agree with each other. In addition, the Inca empire was no monolith, but a polity that encompassed a vast range of linguistic, political, cultural, and ecological variety. It was, however, one of the paradoxes of the workings of colonial culture and politics in Peru that this variety was increasingly homogenized, at least in a superficial sense. When the

Spanish arrived in 1532, for example, the people of almost every valley spoke their own language, with "the general language of the Inca, known as Quechua"[9] serving as a sort of *lingua franca*. By 1700, however, these regional languages along with many other expressions of cultural diversity had almost completely disappeared.[10] While describing some aspects of the distinct European discourses, whether historical or legal, as they affected Andean rationality,[11] I will thus be offering an explanation of why and how that reality became so much more homogeneous in the process.

2. "Cuzco, another Rome"[12]

The earliest accounts of the Incas share a certain hesitancy: a recognition, on the one hand, that here was a remarkable polity, the likes of which had not been seen before; and, on the other hand, a search for appropriate vocabulary accompanied by cursory and clumsy comparisons between Inca comportment and the comportment, for example, of "Moors and Turks," between Andean sacred buildings and the "mezquitas" of the recently conquered kingdom of Granada.[13] Before long, however, a stable theme crept into these comparisons. This was that, in some sense, the Incas resembled the Romans. The Roman aqueduct of Segovia was compared to Inca monumental constructions,[14] and Inca roads reminded Spaniards of Roman counterparts.[15] Rome thus provided sixteenth-century students of Inca history, culture, and politics with an explanatory context. The "new things" that were being learned about Peru were indeed new, but not to such an extent that they could not be integrated into older cognitive structures.

There existed, however, a further dimension to these reflections about Incas and Romans, a dimension that was rarely if ever stated explicitly, even though it helped to determine what Spaniards observed about the Incas and how they described it. The Romans, as everyone knew, had acquired their power by conquest, and among the regions thus conquered had been the Iberian Peninsula. Sixteenth-century interpretations of this reality diverged widely. Some historians, perpetuating the ideas expressed in the *Primera Crónica general de España* of Alfonso X, viewed Spanish cultural and national identity as going back to the beginnings of human history in the peninsula. The Romans had indeed ruled in Spain, but they had done so by virtue of their capacity for equity and moderation and had, for the most part, allowed the freedom-loving Iberians to act less as subjects than as partners and "friends."[16] Other historians, such as Ambrosio Morales and Antonio Agustín, as well as the linguistic scholar Bernardo Aldrete, who subjected ancient sources to a more critical scrutiny, viewed Roman government in the peninsula in less rosy terms. According to them, the Roman presence in Spain had been characterized by periods of bitter warfare, by the exaction of tribute, and by the imposition of the Latin language, thanks to which only remote traces of earlier Iberian languages survived in contemporary Spanish.

At the same time, there was one issue on which exponents of these divergent interpretations of Roman governance not only in Spain but also throughout Europe did agree: they all accepted as valid the Roman claim to sovereignty about which they read in Roman imperial literature and legislation.[17] The extensive ancient literature of Roman self-criticism and of resistance to Roman rule, on the other hand, found little or no resonance in early modern Spain and Europe. Underlying these attitudes was a recognition of empire as a distinct and legitimate form of government, a form of government that differed from national monarchies, aristocracies, or republics. A similar recognition also speaks in several early modern histories of the Incas, and indeed was present in writings about the Incas from the very beginning. Miguél de Estete, who was among the followers of Francisco Pizarro at Cajamarca, where in 1532 the Inca ruler Atahuallpa was captured and then killed, noticed a contrast between the polities on and beyond the frontiers of the Inca empire and that empire itself. Describing how Pizarro's company had reached the Inca settlement of Tumbez in northern Peru, Estete observed:

> From this settlement begins the peaceful dominion of the lords of Cuzco and the good land. For although the lords further back and the lord of Tumbala, which was large, were subject to the Inca, it was not as peacefully as from here onward. For these lords only recognized the Incas and offered a certain tribute, but no more; from here onward, however, they were all very obedient vassals.[18]

Elsewhere, Estete observed that in every settlement throughout Peru there were "governors and judicial officials who had been installed by that great lord [Atahuallpa]."[19] State storehouses, which Estete saw in large numbers in various parts of Peru, were indications of the effective functioning of Inca government and of that government's ability to collect tribute.[20] A further token of the activity of the Inca state was its roads. Estete was impressed by their excellence and commented on the Inca postal runners who conveyed information between Cuzco and the ends of the empire:

> This city of Cuzco was the head of all these kingdoms, where the rulers normally resided. Four roads converged there and joined in a cross, coming

from four subject kingdoms, or provinces, of considerable size, which were Chinchasuyo, Collasuyo, Andisuyo, and Condesuyo. These [provinces] paid tribute to their rulers, and here [in Cuzco] was established the imperial seat.[21]

The tacit model here is Rome, which also was an "imperial seat," *silla imperial.*

Some twenty years after Estete wrote his account of Peru, Pedro Cieza de León, a great connoisseur of the Incas and the Andes, who had studied some of the classical historians, produced a description of Peru and a history of the Incas. The imperial scale of Inca governance that had impressed Estete was now investigated and described in much greater detail and on the basis of information that Cieza had collected from Inca nobles in Cuzco. A handful of incidental, although explicit, comparisons between Inca and Roman buildings and institutions are scattered throughout Cieza's text,[22] but here also the most crucial comparisons with Rome are tacit and concern not so much this or that particular of Inca dominion, but rather the principles on which this dominion was built.

Cieza was deeply impressed by the sheer extent of the Inca empire and interested himself in how this vast territory could have been gained. From his informants in Cuzco and elsewhere, he learned that the Incas had proceeded by means of a combination of alliance–building and military pressure, but whenever possible had avoided open warfare. This was why the Alfonsine model of Roman diplomacy and warfare in Spain, inspired as these had been by the Romans' perceived capacity for love and friendship, *amor y amistad,* resonated in Cieza's conception of how the Incas had acquired and managed to retain their empire. In general, he thought, the Incas approached prospective subjects in friendship, bestowing on them benefits such as inculcating a civilized lifestyle and teaching agriculture and textile production; here, according to Cieza, was the reason why, frequently, people were willing to obey the Incas without the need for military intervention.[23] When, however, a war did have to be fought, the Incas, who rarely lost a battle, were ready to grant generous terms, and their demand for tribute was moderate.[24] On the other hand, their vengeance in response to rebellion could be ferocious, and their judicial system was harsh. The Inca state storehouses, for example, were always filled with all manner of supplies for war and peace:

When thus the Inca was lodged in his dwelling and the men of war had been accommodated, there was never lacking so much as one single item, however large or small, with which to supply them all. But if thanks to theft or a breach of the peace anything at all was missing [from the storehouses] . . . the [offenders] were punished with great severity. In this matter, the Inca lords adhered so closely to justice that they would not have omitted exacting punishment, even if it had to be upon their own sons.[25]

The cultivated sixteenth-century reader might here remember a variety of *exempla* in early Roman history when fathers punished their sons for rebellion or disobedience. In addition, Vergil's memorable precept, that Rome's task was "to spare the conquered and subject the proud" exactly described the methods of Inca warfare as understood by Cieza. And finally, Cieza, like Estete, thought of Cuzco as the "head of the empire of the Incas and their royal seat." The four royal roads, leading to the four parts of the empire, started out from Cuzco's central square; "in this way," added Cieza, "just as in Spain the ancient [Romans] divided the entire country into provinces, so these Indians took stock of the provinces of this vast land by means of their roads."[26]

Even Juan de Betanzos, who had married a sister of the Inca Atahuallpa and was deeply steeped in the historical memories of her kinsmen, on occasion turned to Roman antecedents. He thus compared the religious institutions of the Inca Pachacuti to those of the Romans, and when reporting on this Inca's legislation regarding the education of the young, he wrote:

[Pachacuti] decreed that the young girls likewise attend to their appointed tasks and for this purpose he selected certain [ladies] described as *Cozcoynacacuna,* as we would say certain Roman matrons, and he decreed that from that time their sons and daughters should be instructed and taught.[27]

Roman poets and historians who recounted the foundation story of Rome usually included in their accounts of these legendary events some form of divine assistance, so that Rome's very origins declared its glorious future and constituted a mandate for worldwide sovereignty. In poetry, such themes, anchored as they were in myth, could be accommodated more readily than in historical writing. This was why the historian Livy, who recounted the legendary origins of Rome, periodically commented on the unreliability of the traditions at his disposal and on the contradictions that they enshrined. Little certainty could be expected in matters so ancient, but at the same time the nature of Livy's theme prevented him from simply omitting the troublesome ancient materials. Historians of the Incas were faced with a very similar problem. Cieza, who was the first European to endeavor to sort legend from historical fact regarding the foundation of Cuzco and the origins of the Inca empire, found that different versions of the story could not be reconciled very readily and therefore chose to follow the account given him by the Inca nobles of Cuzco.

Three brothers and their three sisters had set out from openings in a rock at Pacaritambo, the "inn of the dawn." After a variety of supernatural occurrences, Manco Capac, who was one of the brothers, had, with his sister consort, founded the city. Their simple abode was later to be transformed into the temple of the Sun known as Coricancha, the "enclosure of gold." However much Cieza respected the Inca nobles of Cuzco, this story of their origins did not satisfy him because of the many obviously mythological episodes that it contained. He therefore interpreted the story historically by rationalizing it. The three brothers from Pacaritambo likely as not had been

> three brave and valiant men of lofty outlook who originated from some village near Cuzco or arrived from some other part of the highlands of the Andes and, after due preparation, conquered and gained their empire.[28]

Similar rationalizations of myths of origin were also current in classical antiquity, and Cieza perhaps derived his method of interpretation from Diodorus Siculus, whose work he mentioned.

There was, however, one component of the foundation myth of Cuzco that Cieza, rationalizations notwithstanding, also accepted at face value. The Inca rulers claimed that they, like their first progenitor, Manco Capac, were sons of the Sun, and that it was at the Sun's behest that they pursued their imperial mission. In accord with this claim, Cieza divided Andean history into a period before and a period after the advent of the Incas. Before the Incas, Andean people lived separated from each other in scattered hilltop settlements and forts, embroiled in perennial warfare and speaking "strange languages." Government, beyond the episodic dominion of some warrior chief, was unknown. It was the Incas who created nucleated villages and towns at lower altitudes, as well as introducing agriculture and the other arts of civilization. The imperial mission of the Incas was thus part and parcel of the story of their origins. Indeed, the story of origins ratified that mission. The same position obtains with respect to the story of the origins of Rome as told by Livy and others. While questioning the accuracy of the traditions he reported, as was inevitable, Livy at the same time integrated these traditions into his account of the unfolding of Roman history, thereby validating Roman expansion as a process that was not simply the product of aggressive warfare.

The resulting historiographical dilemma was noticed by Garcilaso de la Vega, who had read the early books of Livy with care.[29] There was no avoiding the fact, Garcilaso thought, that the stories of Inca origins were legendary. But it was equally obvious that the Incas themselves had in some sense believed these stories and had referred to them by way of explaining and validating their conduct, just as Livy's Romans had done with regard to their myths of origin. However, seventy years after the Spanish invaders had destroyed the Inca empire, it was not enough to say on the one hand that the ancient stories were legendary and on the other that they articulated an imperial mission. For, by the time Garcilaso began to write, a number of lawyers and theologians had claimed that the Incas had been tyrants and their story of origins a simple falsification.[30]

In the face of such assertions, Garcilaso coined a new term, which he perhaps derived from Livy, to describe the traditional stories of Inca beginnings: they were *fabulas historiales,* historical fables,[31] distinct from pure fiction but not the same as history. In his childhood, Garcilaso had listened to his Inca kinsmen recounting the historical fables of their forebears, and when he grew older they instructed him in

> their laws and government; comparing the new government of the Spanish with that of the Incas, distinguishing different crimes and punishments and their severity; they told me how their kings acted in peace and war, how they treated their vassals, and how they were served by them. Beyond that, they told me as being their own son all their idolatry, their rites, ceremonies, and sacrifices, their greater and lesser festivals and how they celebrated them. . . . In sum, they told me everything that they had in their republic.[32]

There was thus a crucial difference between ancient histories, as told to the young, and a practical, fact-based understanding of Inca government, law, and religion, such as was appropriate for adults. Nonetheless, the two were inseparable. Having described the foundation of Cuzco by the first Inca Manco Capac as a *fabula historial,* Garcilaso noted that the doings of this first Inca were emulated by all his descendants, "so that, having spoken of his achievements, we will have spoken of those of all the others." Cieza had already observed that there existed considerable overlap in what was told about different Inca rulers, all of whom in some fashion resembled Manco Capac. This was because the ancient stories that were told to the young and to each ruler at his accession laid down precedents, rules of conduct, and ethical and political principles that the Incas liked to see exemplified by each of their kings.[33] Cieza adjusted the shape of his history to this reality in that, having recounted the foundation of Cuzco and the doings of Manco Capac, he interrupted his chronological narrative in order to treat diverse aspects of Inca government thematically. In this way, he pointed out, he was able to avoid repeating the same or similar material for each reign. In short, both Cieza and Garcilaso recognized that the character of Inca governance was defined by Inca origins and by the way these origins were remembered. The position in ancient Rome had been very similar. In a grief-stricken poem about the Roman civil wars, Horace recalled how, when founding Rome, Romulus had killed his brother Remus:

It is thus: a harsh fate drives the Romans,
the crime of fratricide:
for the blood of innocent Remus was spilt on the earth,
a curse on all his descendants.[34]

Garcilaso viewed Inca origins in a more positive light, but he also recognized that the present was conditioned by the past, even if that past was legendary. "We will carefully tell those events," he wrote,

which are more historical, leaving aside many others as irrelevant or too detailed; and although some of what has been said, and of what will be said hereafter, may appear legendary, I thought it best not to omit these matters in order to avoid removing the foundations upon which the Indians draw when recounting what was greatest and best in their empire.[35]

3. "Their songs, ballads, carols, and remembrancers"[36]

Spanish historians of the Incas, as we have seen, thought about the Andean past by way of returning, again and again, to the explanatory context of the Roman empire and classical antiquity in general. But this European context could serve no useful purpose without trustworthy Andean informants, without individuals whose understanding of the historical past could be viewed as being in some sense comparable to a European understanding. From quite early on, Spaniards had observed that Inca celebrations were accompanied by the recitation of *cantares,* of "songs" praising past rulers by way of instructing and exhorting the ruler of the present. Miguél de Estete described such an occasion, when, in 1534, Atahuallpa's brother Manco Inca was celebrating a recent victory in Cuzco and

in their songs they told what each one of those rulers had conquered and the grace and valor of his person. They also gave thanks to the Sun for allowing them to see that day, and a priest rose up and admonished the Inca in the name of the Sun, and as being the son of the Sun, [saying] that [the Inca] ought to look to what his forebears had achieved and to imitate them.[37]

Cieza mentioned this same occasion as a memorable one, and at the same time investigated the broader context. From his most trusted informants, who were the Inca nobles of Cuzco, he learned that when an Inca ruler died his deeds and character were evaluated and a formal record was composed of these matters, which was so reliable that "today they tell among each other what happened five hundred years ago as though it had been ten."[38] This record was in due course recited before the newly inaugurated Inca ruler. "Oh Inca, great and powerful," a wise old man would intone,

"may the Sun, the Moon, the earth, the mountains, the trees and rocks, and your fathers preserve you from misfortune and make you prosperous, blessed, and fortunate above all others who have been born. Know that the things that befell your predecessor are these." And then, saying this, with eyes lowered to the ground and hands held down, they gave account and reason of all that they knew, which they were able to do very well because there are many among them who have a long memory, a subtle mind, and lively judgment, able to give a full account, as we who are here today and hear them can testify."[39]

While Inca governance, and the Incas' ideas about their origins reminded Spanish historians of imperial Rome, the recitations about the Inca past that Spaniards heard in Cuzco had analogs closer to home. Like others who described such recitations, Cieza often referred to them as *cantares,* 'songs'. This term had a very specific meaning. A variety of epic poems described as *cantares* circulated in sixteenth-century Castile in both print and manuscript, among the most famous being the story of Rodrigo Diaz de Vivar known as the Cid.[40] As early as the thirteenth century the compilers of Alfonso X, recognizing the historical content of this and several other *cantares,* integrated parts of them into the *Primera Crónica General de España,* which circulated in a published version in Cieza's day.[41] Elsewhere, Cieza described recitations about the Inca rulers of the past as *romances y villancicos,* 'ballads and carols'. These likewise had been widely practised genres of legendary and historical poetic narration in medieval Castile, and examples of such poems figured in sixteenth-century printed collections.[42] Thus, when Spaniards in Peru listened to "old men" and "wise men" reciting Inca traditions, the experience was not altogether alien. Perhaps this was why some of these Spaniards, in particular Cieza, were able to discern in the poems they heard a "rhetorical and abundant phrasing," and a "well-ordered" quality of narrative even though they had not acquired a complete mastery of Quechua.[43] Furthermore, to describe the recitations of the "old men" and "wise men" of Cuzco and the provinces of the Inca empire as *cantares, villancicos,* and *romances,* amounted to attributing to these texts the explicit status of a historical narrative that could be and was incorporated into Spanish histories of the Incas.

But difficulties of translation, both verbal and cultural, were numerous. Although Cieza himself appears to have learned some Quechua, he collected much of his information with the help of translators.[44] However, even the most skilled of translations conveyed the original meanings only selectively, as will become apparent if we consider some items from among a handful of Quechua terms and phrases that survive within the Spanish narratives that were written in the sixteenth century.

According to Juan de Betanzos, who lived in Cuzco and whose knowledge of Quechua was excellent, the Inca Pachacuti, as we have seen, decreed that Inca girls were to be supervised by women known as "*Cozcoynacacuna,* as we would say, . . . Roman matrons."[45] This paraphrase brings to mind socially respected married women of the Roman republican period, such as figured in medieval catalogs of distinguished women.[46] But in effect the Quechua term contains meanings that have no real European equivalents. *Ynaca* is a cloth worn over the head by women; at the same time, the term indicates that the cloth in question was a finely woven one, with designs, while *ynacca nusta* was a noble lady of Inca lineage.[47] Different kinds of patterns and qualities of cloth denoted an individual's regional origin, social status, and age group, given that the ritual of initiation for both men and women entailed several changes of clothing, all differently woven.[48] Certain kinds of cloth were produced in the home, but the most precious varieties, such as the *ynaca* mentioned here, which were woven by specialists who worked under state supervision and patronage, could only be obtained as a gift from the Inca.[49] The term *cozcoinacacuna* thus provides a glimpse into the functioning of Inca society that is hinted at by the Roman analogy. But this analogy achieves little by way of alerting the reader to the complexities of Inca society and cultural politics.[50]

A very different and more complex set of issues is raised by the triumphal song that Inca Pachacuti instructed the noble ladies of Cuzco to sing in celebration of his triumph over the Soras. Betanzos recorded both a Spanish translation and the original text, which, however, is not in Quechua but in a composite idiom containing Quechua, Aymara, and pan-Andean terms, along with elements of Puquina grammar, this being one of the many Andean languages that ceased being spoken before the eighteenth century.[51] In the song, the Inca is described as "Inca Yupanqui, son of the Sun," a standard way of referring to the Inca ruler that was recorded in Quechua by many different historians. Jan Szemiński, who has analysed this text, suggests that the language is the frequently mentioned "secret language of the Incas," the language that the Inca nobility of Cuzco spoke among themselves which was no longer current when Garcilaso, who was born in Cuzco in 1540, was growing up in that city.[52]

Many Spaniards were profoundly impressed by the pan-Andean character of the Inca empire, by the fact that wherever they went, they encountered the same urban planning and the same system of administering justice and managing economic resources. It was this universality of the various forms of public life throughout the Andes that reminded the invaders of the Roman empire and gave meaning to Garcilaso's idea that Cuzco was indeed "another Rome." This aspect of the Inca empire, however, which was readily intelligible to Europeans of the sixteenth century, went hand in hand with other aspects, which were not.

The "private language of the Incas," which no Spaniard appears to have learned, highlights one aspect of this difficulty. Bruce Mannheim's recent work on colonial Quechua poetry comments on the coded, multivalent quality of much of this poetry, the manner in which meaning is concealed by poetic forms and conventions. Quechua poems of the colonial period and the present, expressions, as Mannheim describes it, of a "nation surrounded," conceal meaning with the deliberate intention of communicating only selectively, communicating, that is, only to those capable of internalizing and thereby decoding a given poem's content. Put differently, such poems exclude one potential public in the very act of including another. The same was obviously the case with regard to the "private language of the Incas."

Inca historical traditions as expressed in the *cantares, villancicos,* and *romances* that Cieza heard were likewise exclusive communications. Repeatedly, Cieza refers to the controlled, edited quality of these recitations. When an Inca ruler died,

> the old men of the people discussed the quality of the life and customs of their dead king and in what way he had benefited the republic and what battles he had won. . . . These matters being settled among them, along with others that we do not fully understand, they decided whether the dead king had been such that a glorious reputation should remain of him, so that by virtue of his valor and good government he should remain among them forever. The [old men] then called upon the principal remembrancers . . .[53]

who were able to give an account of what had happened in the kingdom, so
that they might evaluate [the record of the reign] among themselves.[54]

Elsewhere, Cieza pointed out that an Inca's shameful or ignoble deeds and
characteristics were deleted from the official record, this being the reason, he
thought, why some reigns were so poorly documented.[55] The version of Inca
history that was recited at festivals in Cuzco, and that Spanish inquirers studied, was thus a history that had been reviewed by the elite. Furthermore, these
versions of the Inca past were in some sense the property of the ruling Inca in
that, as Cieza noted, "these *cantares* could not be published or recited except in
the presence of the ruler,"[56] in whose service the "principal remembrancers"
mentioned by Cieza did their work of remembering.[57] This edited and controlled quality of Inca historical narratives helps us to understand a factor that
both Cieza[58] and Garcilaso highlighted, namely, that "having told the life of
[the first Inca ruler Manco Capac] we will have told that of all these rulers."[59]

The Incas recognized remembering as a formal skill or calling, which is
why remembrancers were included as a distinct group in a list of specialized
Andean occupations compiled by a Spanish historian.[60] The Quechua term
describing them is *quipucamayoc*. A *quipu* is a bundle of knotted cords of
different colors that encoded narrative or numerical information, and *camayoc*
refers to a person possessing a specialized skill or task.[61] Spaniards regularly
described the *quipus* as a form of writing, or as books, and they were profoundly impressed by the accuracy and scope of Inca administrative *quipus*.
They also understood the importance of *quipus* as a vehicle for preserving
historical information, the *cantares, romances,* and *villancicos* that Cieza and
others heard. However, no Spaniards appear to have learned how to make or
read a *quipu,* a fact that is fundamental in evaluating the impact of European
scholarly traditions in the Andes.

The preservation of accounts of the Inca past was in the hands of the Inca
ruler and, after his death, of his lineage, whose task it was to maintain the cult
of his mummified body and to administer his property. Meanwhile, a new
historical record was created on behalf of the succeeding ruler, which would
likewise in due course be preserved by his lineage; the different Inca lineages,
in turn, were assisted in their task of maintaining the memory of their ancestors' deeds by their *quipucamayocs*. The Spanish invasion destroyed the very
raison d'être of these historical traditions, which articulated and justified Inca
governance as exercised both by the Inca ruler himself and by the lineages of
past rulers. Second, the nature of the record that was preserved by the
quipucamayocs presented a problem of recognition. Given that the *quipus,* as

Spaniards understood them, constituted some equivalent to writing, the skill of reading them did not turn out to be communicable to the new ruling class. Even the much admired administrative *quipus* of the Incas were immediately translated into writing and into Spanish,[62] and as a result their Andean and Inca keepers were displaced by Spanish notaries and scribes. With regard to historical *quipus,* this process of displacement was accelerated by the fact that, as we have seen, the preservation of the Inca past was in the hands, and in the interests, of the very people who were most severely affected by invasion and conquest, that is, the Inca elite.

The Inca past contained many components that were not intelligible or recognizable in the light of either the European past or Castilian learned traditions. This, and the rapid disappearance of the *quipucamayocs* as a group of experts who possessed a skill of daily political and cultural importance, led to the speedy transformation of Inca historical traditions into a unitary, chronologically ordered narrative analogous to European precedents. Spaniards such as Juan de Betanzos, Pedro Cieza de León, and Pedro Sarmiento de Gamboa, who conversed at length with *quipucamayocs* and other individuals who had lived under and served the last Inca rulers, all expected to find in the Andes a past that responded to European concepts of historical order. That is, they looked for successions of rulers, such as the emperors of ancient Rome, or dynasties, such as ruled the kingdoms of early modern Europe. A dynasty of Inca rulers, son succeeding father, was therefore what they found in the Andes. Once this dynasty was in place, as early as 1551, it was next to impossible to discover how the Incas had actually succeeded one another and how, therefore, they had actually projected their entitlement to rule to their many subjects and allies.[63]

Inca historical traditions were composed and preserved on behalf of the Inca elite, whereas European works of history were composed for publication. A monarch might indeed wish to control the content of history, but success was inevitably partial because, as the poet Horace had already understood very well,[64] once a book had left the author's study it could never be recalled. The irreversibility of publication was greatly heightened in Europe after the invention of printing. Even in the Andes, the survival of oral traditions hostile to the Incas long after the Incas had gone demonstrates that Inca control of historical narrative also was only partially successful. Nonetheless, once Spanish historians appropriated Inca history, this history changed in both content and purpose, precisely because it was composed according to criteria that aimed at inclusiveness and objectivity, and not at a selection of data that expressed an imperial mission and the ideas and ideals of a ruling class. In addition Spanish historians, who wrote, in the last resort, for publication, addressed a public that was defined by its access to literacy and printed books and not so much by reference to its relationship with the Inca or any other ruling elite. In this way, an exclusive, focused, and purposeful communication by the Inca elite was transformed into a much more inclusive and general communication that addressed a European reading public interested in "the things of Peru." The resulting process of displacement, whereby Inca reality was modified and transformed by the new governmental practices of the Spanish, by their learned traditions, and by their methods of propagating these learned traditions as well as information in general, can be further illustrated by examining early colonial concepts of Inca law.

4. The "Ordinances" of Inca Pachacuti

The Roman imperial past equipped Spanish historians of the Incas with a set of concepts that enabled them to locate the Inca empire on a map of diverse political structures that ranged from village communities to city republics, monarchies, and empires. Similarly, medieval historical narratives from Castile rendered the recitations of "wise men" in Cuzco accessible to Spaniards with an interest in the Inca past. At the same time, as we have seen, the very recognizability of the Inca past veiled those aspects of it for which Europe offered no parallels. This was also the case in matters relating to Inca law. At the same time, questions regarding the nature of Inca law and the content of Inca legislation raised practical issues of a kind that affected the recording of Inca history only marginally. For history was a matter of describing the past, whereas questions of Inca law and the resulting issue of relating Inca with Spanish law conditioned governmental practice in Spanish Peru. This practical dimension in the study of law gained an ever-increasing importance as lawyers and other governmental officials endeavored to create a coherent and practicable administrative system in the Andes.

That the Incas had a legal system of some kind was apparent even to the first Spaniards in Peru. Miguél de Estete, one of the "men of Cajamarca," observed that "this nation [of the Incas] of Cuzco lived scattered throughout all the provinces [of Peru and was engaged] in administering justice,"[65] and soon cases brought before the Audiencia in Lima forced Spanish lawyers to interest themselves in the nature of the claims that were being made by Andean litigants. Nonetheless, thanks to the breakdown of all order in the Andes that followed the Spanish invasion and wars of conquest, the very existence of Inca law came to be questioned during the early colonial period.[66] It was under these circumstances that in about 1550 the surviving kinsmen of Atahuallpa, wishing to point out that in the past Peru had been an ordered polity, informed Juan de Betanzos that their ancestor the Inca Pachacuti had issued a set of twenty-seven laws or "ordinances" dealing with Cuzco and the provinces of the Inca empire. Following the historiographical fortunes of these ordinances provides further insight into the impact of European scholarly traditions—this time legal ones—in Peru, while also supplying a context for considering conflicts of law in the practical and political sphere.

Some of the Inca Pachacuti's laws, as they were described to Betanzos, dealt with matters arising in Cuzco, while others concerned the governance of the provinces of the empire. Laws addressed to Cuzco include regulations for the distribution of goods from Inca storehouses and for punishing theft from these storehouses and elsewhere. There are also laws of marriage, laws covering false testimony, and laws regulating the use of fine cloth. Similar laws are repeated in more general terms elsewhere, and a number of them rest on common sense. This is also true of most of the laws affecting the provinces, which regulate the maintenance of roads, bridges, and *tambos*,[67] and the conduct of soldiers and of local administration. A handful of laws affecting Cuzco, however, has no parallel of any kind, and would thus appear to record the authentic legal practice of the Inca capital. One such law points to the high risk of fire in Cuzco, where all houses were roofed with thatch, and decrees that if a house caught fire the neighbors could in the absence of the owner take his possessions, while also being obliged to help quench the fire. If subsequently it emerged that the fire was not caused by owner's neglect, the neighbors were to restore his possessions and help rebuild the house. Another law that gives a vivid insight into the life of the city regulated the raising of children born out of wedlock and related matters:

> [The Inca] ordered and commanded that lest young men while still unmarried go after married women and *mamaconas*,[68] there should be established a certain house where a number of women from among those who were taken in the wars were to live, so that the young men could have converse with them. . . . If one of these women became pregnant, the child was to be raised elsewhere and be called *capci Churi*, which is to say child of the community.

Here, Betanzos intervened to explain that the Incas believed that a child born after a woman had had intercourse with two or three men in close succession was thought to be the child of all three men. He continued:

So that babies thus born be raised, [the Inca] ordered that there be a house with women from the provinces and villages whose children had died, who were to raise these babies. Likewise, he ordered that the lords designated to supervise the affairs of the people should command straw to be laid beneath the bridges of the brook and river that passed through the city, at the edge of the water, and that the babies to whom *mamaconas* or nobly born ladies had given birth secretly and in hiding should not be killed but should, once they had been born, be placed by night beneath these bridges [and that no one observing a baby being thus deposited should inquire after its origin] and that these guardians should every morning look beneath the bridges to see whether there was a baby, and should take the babies thus found to be raised by the above-mentioned women.[69]

Some fifty years after Betanzos collected his information in Cuzco, the missionary Martín de Murúa produced a list of the ordinances of Inca Pachacuti, and shortly thereafter the Andean historian Guaman Poma de Ayala wrote down a set of somewhat similar ordinances, which he attributed to Pachacuti's successor Tupa Yupanqui.[70] By this time, a body of literature had come into existence that praised the strict laws of the Incas as exemplary and contrasted the harmony and affluence of the Inca empire with the social chaos and perennial shortages of colonial Peru. The ordinances of Murúa and Guaman Poma reflect these circumstances, in that they invite the conclusion that the Inca empire was a strictly regulated, ordered, and affluent society, the very opposite of conditions at the end of the century.

Furthermore, the ordinances of Murúa and Guaman Poma reflect the ideas and ideals of a European and Christian legislator, so that these ordinances reproduce a variety of generalized Andean regulations, a number of laws that could only be derived from Judeo-Christian precepts, and a tiny residue of legal practice that can be attributed to the Incas. As regards the European layer in these texts, both Guaman Poma and Murúa thought, for example, that the Incas prohibited menstruating women from offering sacrifice, a rule that is more likely to have been derived from *Leviticus* than from Inca or Andean practice.[71] According to Murúa, the Incas had the custom of bestowing honorable burial on those of their enemies who had fallen in battle—but according to the much more reliable evidence of Betanzos, the opposite was the case.[72] Both Murúa and Guaman Poma thought that women and the poor could not give evidence in Inca litigation, the former because of their "levity" and the latter because they were likely to succumb to bribes;[73] but a law of this kind presupposes Spanish judicial procedure and was perhaps invented as a commentary on it. Laws in Murúa and Guaman Poma that proclaim Cuzco as the "court and capital" of "these kingdoms" evoke Spanish formulations regarding Madrid as the seat of the royal court,[74] and Guaman Poma's idea that Inca law was to be "observed and obeyed" likewise depends on Spanish precedent.[75] Finally, where Betanzos had distinguished laws affecting Cuzco from those affecting the provinces of the empire, Murúa replaced this distinction with one separating law regulating civilian life from the law of war, because in Europe the latter constituted a distinct juridical category. Legal rules distinguishing conduct in the capital city from conduct in the rest of a country, on the other hand, were unknown in sixteenth-century Europe.[76] Murúa thus introduced his Inca laws about warfare with the remark that "for the conduct of war, the Inca made the following ordinances" and proceeded to describe a legitimate *casus belli* as viewed by his Incas in terms reminiscent of the declaration of war that, according to Livy, Tullus Hostilius had issued against Alba Longa.[77]

In such a context, the specifics of Inca legal practice that speak in Betanzos' rules about fires in Cuzco and the care of illegitimate babies were inevitably lost to view, wiped away by exponents of European legal thinking who approached problems with different juridical principles in mind. Their preconceptions were reinforced by individuals born and raised in the Andes, such as Guaman Poma, who were eager to prove to the invaders that the conquered world of the Incas had possessed its own order and integrity; and indeed a number of Spaniards were eager to prove the same thing. But, in the last resort, the proof could only be conducted by appealing to the juridical categories and learned traditions of the now dominant culture.

This same dilemma is spelled out in the manner in which Spanish Peru was governed during the sixteenth century. The lawyers who sat as judges and pleaded cases in the Audiencias of Lima and Charcas had been educated in Spain, and their norms of professional conduct were likewise Spanish. But, before long, Andean cases were brought before these experts that defied the legal system in which they had been trained. Most troublesome was litigation involving tribute payments, and thus land, because Inca and Andean ideas about rights of access to land did not correspond to Spanish ones. In the face of conflicting claims, the Spanish tended to try imposing one simple rule, namely, that ownership of land should be adjudicated to the party who had enjoyed it under the Incas, and that tribute payments should match whatever had been collected by the Incas. While these principles raised a host of unforeseen difficulties, they also reinforced some significant misconceptions about the Andean and Inca past.

The Incas were fond of claiming that theirs had been the first and indeed the only ordered polity in the Andes, and that before their own advent Andean people had lived in social chaos and without the arts of civilization such as agriculture, weaving, and architecture.[78] From the beginning, the Spanish were inclined to accept this claim, despite much evidence, such as the still functioning Chimu capital in northern Peru,[79] because this theory of political development had important European analogs. Cieza's Manco Capac, for example, who called together people from the vicinity of Cuzco "with love and kind words"[80] resonated not only with the story of the Romans who had governed in Spain "with love and friendship" but also with Cicero's orator, a "great and wise man," who gathered people living scattered in fields and forest retreats into ordered settlements and taught them civilization.[81] In the work of subsequent historians of the Incas, this Ciceronian image of Manco Capac became ever more elaborate,[82] not merely because the lure of classical antiquity was strong but also because such a model of the progress of civilization was reinforced by the manner in which Spanish officials and lawyers formulated their questions and thus organized information about the Andes.

In 1553, the Spanish crown issued one of a very large number of questionnaires about tribute payments, which was in due course answered by Hernando de Santillán, lawyer and *oidor* of the Audiencia of Lima. The lawyer Juan Polo de Ondegardo also responded to this questionnaire, and very similar questions were asked in regional inspections conducted on behalf of the Spanish crown in order to assess tribute payments.[83] All these questionnaires inquired about the quantity of tribute payments in Spanish Peru, the manner in which they should be collected, and what they were to consist of, whether cash or kind, while at the same time accepting Inca practice as the crucial point of departure. But this was more easily said than done, as is revealed by the very form of the responses that lawyers in Peru sent back to Madrid. At issue were not merely various practical problems, such as the transition to a monetary economy and the huge drop in the population of Peru that followed invasion and conquest, but also the very concept of what constituted society and sovereignty.

Before entering on his task, accordingly, Santillán outlined the history of the Incas and their system of government,[84] pointing out that the first question he was to answer "deals with the lords who governed the Indians of these provinces." But all the question had asked was "what tributes [they had] paid in the time of their infidelity . . . ," the issue of who had governed being incidental to this primary concern of the crown. However, Santillán, and similarly Polo de Ondegardo, were seeking to establish a context in which they could explain the existence and functioning of the threefold division of lands that the Incas had made, one part being for the state religion, one for the Inca, and the third for the people, pointing out that this had to be understood before one could discuss tribute. In addition, the division of land was relevant in turn to how one could think about sovereignty in Peru, which also bore on the question of tribute.

These complications were aggravated by a problem resulting from the presence of the Spanish in Peru, which was discussed at length by Polo de Ondegardo. The Incas being gone, Spaniards considered themselves entitled to claim as their own lands that had formerly been assigned to the Inca and the state religion, while at the same time collecting tribute from the remainder. But, as Polo pointed out, this resulted in a double payment of tribute because the Incas had never taken anything from this last category of land. Rather, by way of serving the Inca ruler, people had worked the lands assigned to him and to the state religion, reserving crops harvested from lands that had been assigned to themselves for their own exclusive use.[85] Other forms of serving the Inca, such as weaving and construction, had likewise left this category of land untouched. Spanish demands for what amounted to double tribute payments, Polo argued, were the direct outcome of failing to understand how the Incas had governed.[86] This difficulty, as viewed by Polo, was compounded by a further one, which concerned the status of the individual within the Inca state, or, more precisely, the absence of such status. According to Polo, the concept of personal freedom was unknown to the Incas because, throughout, the Incas had dealt with communities, not with individuals. The Inca ruler had assigned work to be performed in his service not to individuals but to communities, and in each community the *curacas,*[87] whose authority and position the Inca had ratified, supervised the distribution of this work. Hence, Polo observed, litigation about land between Andean individuals was practically unheard of in early colonial Peru. Rather, the cases that were heard in the Audiencias were almost invariably disputes between communities.[88]

Polo thought that the Spanish ought to continue governing and taxing Andean people as communities, not as individuals, thereby curtailing their freedom but at the same time preserving some semblance of the order established by the Incas, while simultaneously avoiding the expense and effort of creating annual census records of *tributarios.*[89] Practical considerations thus went hand in hand with more theoretical ones. The ordering of political society by reference to groups and to hierarchies of authority, Polo thought, was both universal and beneficial, and he quoted Aristotle to prove his point:

The entire government of our republic consists of the ordained subjection which we maintain in relation to one another, and the restraint imposed on anyone running wild. Examples are readily to hand: children are subject to parents, wives to husbands, servants to their masters; friars to their superiors, and clerics to the bishop. In sum, there is no one without a superior whom he fears, and if anyone strays the force of the law bears on his punishment and judges attend to the law's execution, thanks to which republics have perpetuated themselves and continue to do so until this day.[90]

However, Aristotle notwithstanding, Polo was not interested in imposing a European political order in the Andes. For, while recognizing how much irreversible change the Spaniards had effected in Peru,[91] he believed that as much as possible of the government of the Incas should be salvaged and that no new measures should be introduced without understanding "[Andean] customs and laws."[92] Santillán was one among many to share this view. "Before the Incas began to rule," he wrote,

> there existed no government or public order. Rather, in each valley or province there was a *curaca,* or principal lord, . . . and each of these valleys was at war with its neighbor, and for this reason there existed no commerce or communication among them. And in each valley a language was spoken different from the next. . . . In general, no one achieved power or reduced the land to a kingdom and empire until the Incas began to rule, and their sovereignty and government extended further and was more civilized and ordered than any other that is remembered in that land. And even outside it, . . . [the Incas] ruled so well that they ought to be praised and even imitated.[93]

Similarly, Polo wrote that before the Incas people in the Andes lived like "animals," without any discernible political authority,[94] and that the admirable legal and social order that the Spanish found had been created by the Incas. Polo recognized that the beginning of Inca imperial expansion predated his own time only by some three hundred years,[95] but, Polo thought, no one in the Andes remembered any other major state, so that, in effect, the Incas had ruled from time immemorial.

5. Conclusion

The image that sixteenth-century historians painted of the Incas was to some extent shaped by the shadow of Rome, by the idea that in some sense the Roman and Inca empires resembled each other, that Rome provided an explanatory context in which the Incas could be understood. Lawyers thought about the Incas in more practical terms because they were occupied, day by day, with the government of Peru. The specifics of Inca landholding, taxation, and related issues thus occupied their attention much more than did the process of Inca imperial expansion and the deeds of individual Incas.[96] Polo de Ondegardo discovered the mummified body of Inca Pachacuti, along with the "*quipus* and accounts" of his deeds; but, Polo wrote, there was no time on that occasion to inquire as to what exactly these *quipus* said; and with this he continued his discussion of practical matters.[97] Lawyers did not need the Roman empire as an explanatory context to understand the Incas, and altogether referred surprisingly little to European models or antecedents for what they found in the Andes. But that did not mean that they were not also agents of a Spanish scholarly tradition in the Andes, and agents of profound change.

The Incas had brought to the Andes an administrative uniformity that did not exist before, and with it had gone a certain degree of cultural and religious uniformity. But it was in Spanish Peru that Quechua supplanted the many regional languages of the Andes, while Christianity eliminated the many forms of religious and cultural diversity that had been accommodated within the Inca state religion. Yet the lawyers who were instrumental in implementing this profound transformation were, as we have seen, conservatives in many respects, even though their very conservatism entailed its own mode of innovation. The three features that we have noted in their ideas and activities: a tendency to foster uniformity, along with a desire to preserve some part of the Inca order, and a tendency, in spite of this conservatism, to help implement radical change, are reflected in a document from Laraos of the year 1597. Laraos is situated in the Andes southeast of Lima, and originated as a resettlement community organized in 1569 by the local governor Dávila Brizeño. Twenty-eight years later, in 1597, this community produced a document in Quechua and Spanish describing the boundaries of its land, with an accompanying map. According to the Quechua text, the boundaries between Laraos and its neighbors had been established by the Inca Tupa Yupanqui, who had personally walked along the boundary line. On August 8, 1597, the *curaca* of Laraos with seven old men again walked this boundary line, inspecting the landmarks and boundary stones that defined it by way of reestablishing the community's claims to the land. The document was signed by the seven old men, the *curaca,* and the Andean notary who wrote it down. On the same page appears the Spanish text, which mentions the same witnesses, along with representatives of neighboring communities. The map displays the boundary markers and landmarks that are also mentioned in the text, but the way in

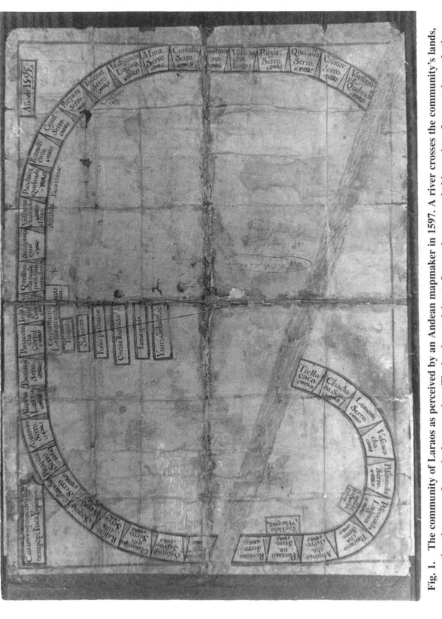

Fig. 1. The community of Laraos as perceived by an Andean mapmaker in 1597. A river crosses the community's lands, separating the upper from the lower moiety. The land pertaining to Laraos is surrounded by a ring of mountains and other natural features which set it aside from the land of neighbouring communities. (Lima, Archivo Nacional, Tit. Com. 3,41C.)

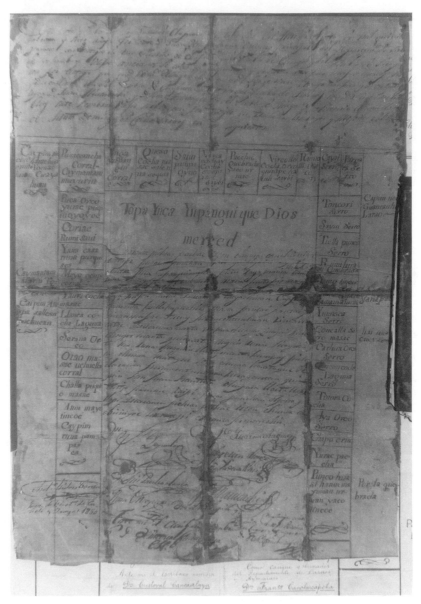

Fig. 2. Declaration claiming, in Quechua, that the lands of Laraos had been assigned to this community by the Inca Tupa Yupanqui, and that in 1597 the *curaca* with seven old men walked along the boundaries. Their signatures with that of the notary appear at the bottom of the page. The declaration is surrounded by the same place names as appear on the map in figure 1, but here, they are arranged as a doorway. Possibly, the design seeks to evoke a myth of origins, such as that of the Incas (see p. 283), claiming that the people of Laraos emerged from a rock or other feature of the landscape. (Lima, Archivo Nacional, Tit. Com. 3,41C.)

which this map is conceptualized has little to do with European maps. Rather, what it shows is the river dividing Laraos into its upper and lower moieties, each of which is ringed by its own boundary on which the landmarks form a continuous band (see figs. 1 and 2).[98]

This document is a testimony of the old and the new in the Andes at the end of the century, a testimony of continuity along with headlong innovation such as also describes the impact of European scholarly traditions in the Andes. The people of Laraos looked back to the Inca Tupa Yupanqui to explain the existence of their community, even though that community had been created by the Spanish. At the same time, the Inca's claim to rule was expressed anachronistically in Christian terms, for he appears in the document as "Tupa Inca Yupanqui by the Mercy of God." Behind this anachronism, and behind the claim that Laraos was the creation of Tupa Inca Yupanqui, lurks a profound paradox, which characterized the culture of early colonial Peru. On the one hand, the Spanish had supplanted the Incas, but, on the other, the Incas constituted the precondition of Spanish existence in Peru. Viewed from the Andean vantage point that speaks through our document from Laraos, however, what the Spanish were doing had to remain quite simply unintelligible unless it could be formulated by reference to the Incas. In its own day, Inca dominion had been much contested and resisted. But, in retrospect, the Incas legitimated and explained the political existence of Andean people in the present, which was precisely what, from their different vantage point, Spanish historians and lawyers also thought.

NOTES

1. See Sebastián de Covarrubias, *Tesoro de la Lengua Española o Castellana* (Madrid, 1611; rpt. Madrid, 1984), s.v. conocimiento ciencia; Real Academia Española, *Diccionario de Autoridades* (Madrid, 1726; rpt. Madrid, 1984), s.v. ciencia, erudición, sabiduría.

2. See Francisco Martín Hernandez, *La formacion clerical en los colegios universitarios españoles (1371–1563)* (Vitoria, 1961); Richard L. Kagan, *Students and Society in Early Modern Spain* (Baltimore, 1974); Jean-Marc Pelorson, *Les Letrados. Juristes castillans sous Philippe III. Récherches sur leur place dans la société, la culture et l'état* (Poitiers, 1980).

3. Huarte de San Juan, *Examen de ingenios para las ciencias* (Baeza, 1575; rev. ed. Baeza, 1595; ed. Esteban Torre [Madrid, 1976]; this latter is the edition I cite), chap. 1, 72ff., Huarte's observation on his classmates; chap. 5, 127, on the incompatibility of memory and understanding (*entendimiento*) in the same person. Huarte's ideas were

controversial, and this last passage was one of many to be deleted from the edition of 1575 by the censors.

4. Garcilaso de la Vega, *Obras completas,* ed. Elias L. Rivers (Madrid, 1968), ode 3, p. 197.

5. "With the sword and with the pen."

6. See S. MacCormack, "History, Memory, and Time in Golden Age Spain," *History and Memory* 4, no. 2 (1992): 38–68; Robert B. Tate, *Ensayos sobre la historiografía peninsular del siglo XV* (Madrid, 1970).

7. The most notable example is Pedro Sarmiento de Gamboa, who wrote his *Historia Indica* by way of substantiating and confirming the enquiries of the Viceroy Toledo, which had the purpose of minimizing the impact of the Inca past and Inca adminstrative practice on Spanish Peru so as to impose peninsular institutions. See the introductory study by G. Lohmann Villena in *Francisco de Toledo: Disposiciones gubernativas para el Virreinato del Perú, 1569–1574,* ed. Maria Justina Sarabia Viejo, 2 vols. (Seville, 1986–89).

8. "Ubi Ecclesia? Perceptions of Medieval Europe in Spanish America," *Speculum* 69 (1994): 74–99.

9. This is how the great Jesuit lexicographer and grammarian described the language of the Inca in the title of his grammar, *Gramatica y arte nueva de la lengua general de todo el Perú llamada lengua Qquichua o lengua del Inca* (Lima, 1607, rpt. n.p., 1842).

10. This point was made by Bruce Mannheim in *The Language of the Inka since the European Invasion* (Austin, 1991). Jerónimo de Vivar, *Crónica de los reinos de Chile,* ed. Angel Barral Gomez (Madrid, 1988; completed in 1558) repeatedly comments on the distinct languages of neighboring valleys, observing that Quechua was widely understood and used by the Spanish as a language in which to negotiate.

11. I take the phrase from Jurgen Golte's *La racionalidad de la organización andina,* 2d. ed. (Lima, 1980), a study that explains Andean social organization, property rights, and methods of agricultural and pastoral production as responses to the Andean environment; these responses contain, Golte argues, their own autonomous logic and rationality. The work was inspired by J. V. Murra's *Formaciones económicas y politicas andinas* (Lima, 1975).

12. For "Cozco, que fue otra Roma en aquel Imperio" see Garcilaso de la Vega the Inca, *Primera Parte de los Comentarios reales de los Incas,* ed. Carmelo Saenz de Santa Maria, *Biblioteca de autores españoles,* vol. 133 [Madrid, 1963; hereafter *Primera Parte*], proemio al lector.

13. Cf. S. MacCormack, "The Fall of the Incas. A Historiographical Dilemma," *History of European Ideas* 6 (1985): 421–45 at 422f.

14. Pedro Sancho, *An Account of the Conquest of Peru,* trans. P. A. Means (New York, 1917), chap. 17, 156, writes as follows about the fortress of Sacsayhaman, which overlooks Cuzco: "The Spaniards who see [the stones of Sacsayhaman] say that neither the bridge of Segovia nor any of the other edifices which Hercules or the Romans made

is so worthy of being seen as this. The city of Tarragona has some works in its walls made in this style . . ."

15. The comparison lay to hand because at this very time the Roman settlements and roads of Spain (many of the roads were still in use) were being studied by antiquarians. See Ambrosio Morales, *Las antiguedades de las ciudades de Espana que van nombradas en la Corónica* . . . (Madrid, 1792: vol. 10 of Morales' collected works).

16. Charles Fraker, "Scipio and the Origins of Culture: The Question of Alfonso's Sources," *Dispositio* 10, no. 27 (1987): 15–27.

17. Juan Luis de la Cerda, *P. Virgilii Maronis Aeneidos Libri sex priores. Argumentis, Explicationibus, et Notis illustrata* (Madrid, 1612), (commentary on *Aeneid* 6), 847–53 assembles some of the approving verdicts on Roman imperialism from ancient literature.

18. Miguél de Estete, *Noticia del Perú. (Colección de libros y documentos referentes a la historia del Perú* [hereafter *CLDRHP*], second ser., vol. 8, Lima, 1924), 20.

19. Estete, *Noticia,* 21.

20. Estete, *Noticia,* 51.

21. Estete, *Noticia,* 48 (see also 22), 48ff. (roads), 51 (runners).

22. Pedro Cieza de León, *Primera parte de la Crónica del Perú,* ed. F. Pease (Lima, 1986; hereafter *Primera parte*), chap. 1, 37 (Inca roads and road of Hannibal across the Alps, chap. 38 (Vestal Virgins), chap. 89, 253 (bridges of Cordoba and Alcantara). See also *Segunda parte,* chap. 27, 80 (Coricancha, Torre de Calahora, and Hospital Tavera in Toledo).

23. Pedro Cieza de León, *Segunda parte de la Crónica del Perú,* ed. F. Cantú (Lima, 1986; hereafter *Segunda parte*), chap. 17, 47; *Primera parte,* chap. 100 (Inca Viracocha's amistad and favor for Cari of Chucuito), but contrast chapter 47, 156 concerning Paltas, where this policy of amistad did not work out in the end.

24. Cieza, *Segunda parte,* chap. 17, 47; chap. 18, on tribute; cf. chap. 20, on reverence for the Inca ruler.

25. Cieza, *Primera parte,* chap. 44, 144.

26. Cieza, *Primera parte,* chap. 92, 258.

27. Juan de Betanzos, *Suma y narración de los Incas* (Madrid, 1987), book 1, chap. 20, 99a; book 1, chap. 21, 109a: "y para que ansi mesmo las muchachas viesen y examinasen en lo ya dicho mando que fuesen senaladas ciertas Cozcoynacacuna que dice como decimos ciertas matronas romanas y mando que sus mismos hijos y hijas desde aquella hora fuesen ansi impuestos y doctrinados." On Cozcoynacacuna, cf. Maria Rostworowski, "Estratificación social y el Hatun Curaca en el mundo andino," in her *Ensayos de historia andina. Élites, Etnias, Recursos* (Lima, 1993), 41–88, at 50f.

28. Cieza, *Segunda parte,* chap. 6 (end).

29. See Claire Pailler and Jean-Marie Pailler, "Une Amérique vraiment latine: pour une lecture 'Dumézilienne' de l'Inca Garcilaso de la Vega," *Annales ESC* 47, no. 1 (1992): 207–35.

30. José de Acosta, *Historia natural y moral de las Indias* (Mexico, 1962), book 6,

chap. 11. Acosta, a Jesuit missionary, derived most of his material on the Incas from the lawyer Juan Polo de Ondegardo. Another writer who worked under the influence of lawyers, and used a legal methodology, that is, the questionnaire, was Pedro Sarmiento de Gamboa (cf. above, note 7). Among the most trenchant statements about Inca tyranny is that in Juan de Matienzo, *Gobierno del Perú,* ed. Guillermo Lohmann Villena (Lima, 1967), book 1, chap. 1.

31. Livy had used the term *fabula* to describe uncertain historical traditions; see 5, 21, 8 inseritur huic loco fabula . . . ; Garcilaso, *Primera parte,* book 1, chap. 18, esp. 31a: "digo las fábulas historiales que en mis niñezes oí . . ."

32. Garcilaso, *Primera parte,* book 1, chap. 19, 31a, 31b.

33. See Cieza, *Segunda parte,* chap. 11, on what the "remembrancers" did and did not say. I translate the Quechua term *quipucamayo* (custodian of the knotted cords, *quipus,* that served the Incas as memory aids for numerical and narrative information) as "remembrancers." For an important new contribution to research on *quipus,* see Gary Urton, "A New Twist in an Old Yarn: Variation in Knot Directionality in the Inka Khipus," *Baessler-Archiv,* Neue Folge, Band 42 (1994): 271–305.

34. Horace, *Epode* 7, 17–20.

35. Garcilaso, *Primera parte,* book 1, chap. 19, 32a.

36. "Romances y villancicos," Cieza, *Segunda parte,* chap. 11, 27; "cantares o romances," and "cantares honrados," 28. In *Segunda parte,* chap. 12, Cieza continues the discussion of cantares and explains *quipus,* the chapter being entitled: "de como tenian coronistas para saber sus hechos por ellos. . . ." See also Martín de Murúa, *Historia del origen y genealogia real de los Reyes Incas del Perú* (1590; ed. C. Bayle, Madrid, 1946), book 3, chap. 25, 223ff., on narrative and numerical *quipus.* For villancicos, see Covarrubias, *Tesoro,* and the *Diccionario de Autoridades,* (above n. 1) explaining this as a rustic form of poetry, which was imitated and refined in a courtly context.

37. Miguél de Estete, *Noticia,* 55: "en los cantares trataban de lo que cada uno de aquellos señores habia conquistado y de las gracias y valor de su persona, dando gracias al Sol que les abía dejado ver aquel dia, y levantandose un sacredote amonestaba de parte del Sol al Inga como a su hijo que mirase lo que sus pasados habian hecho y que así lo hiciese el . . ."

38. Cieza, *Segunda parte,* chap. 11, 28.

39. Cieza, *Segunda parte,* chap. 12, 30.

40. For collections of *romances* with historical themes, see *El Romancero viejo,* ed. Mercedes Diaz Roig (Madrid, 1994); and the *Romancero* edited by Paloma Diaz-Mas, with an introduction by Samuel G. Armistead (Barcelona, 1994). Cf. F. J. Norton, *A Descriptive Catalogue of Printing in Spain and Portugal, 1501–1520* (Cambridge, 1978), nos. 1005 and 261, for printed versions of the *crónica* of the Cid.

41. The edition (Zamora, 1541) was the work of the royal chronicler Florián de Ocampo.

42. On early printed collections of *romances,* see Diaz Roig, *El Romancero viejo,*

10–16; and Diaz-Mas, *Romancero,* 42–48, with further bibliography. The historiography of the invasion and conquest of Peru was itself constructed in large part from oral traditions with poetic components. For an example, see Francisco López de Gómara, *Historia general de las Indias* (Caragoca, 1555; facsimile of the Inca Garcilaso de la Vega's copy, with his marginal notes, Lima, 1993), chap. 181, fol. 81 verso, recording Francisco de Carabajal's couplet:

Estos mis cabellicos madre
dos a dos se los lleva el aire.

The verses express Carvajal's dismay when an important group of supporters desert the cause of Gonzalo Pizarro. Garcilaso de la Vega also cited these verses and attributed them to Carvajal, but in a different context (see id., *Segunda parte,* book 5, chap. 35.

43. Cieza, *Segunda parte,* chap. 11, 27. While Cieza evidently thought that Quechua historical and narrative poetry was in some respects comparable to such poetry in Spanish, some missionaries looked for similar equivalencies in the spiritual and theological realm. The Franciscan missionary Luis Jerónimo de Oré thus composed Quechua hymns, in what he described as Sapphic verse, to match equivalents in the Roman Breviary. See his *Symbolo Catolico Indiano* (Lima 1598; facsimile, Lima, 1992), chap. 17, fol. 63 recto and verso.

44. See Cieza, *Segunda parte,* chap. 4, with Francesca Cantú's introduction, xxix ff.

45. Above, at n. 27.

46. See Maria Rosa Lida de Malkiel, *La Idea de la Fama en la Edad Media Castellana* (Mexico, 1952), 251ff.

47. See Diego Gonzalez Holguín, *Vocabulario de la lengua general de todo el Perú llamada Qquichua o del Inca* (Lima, 1608; Lima, 1952), 368: "Inaca, la mantellina de la cabeza. Incaca inacalla pachallicuni, o palla pallalla, Vestirse galanamente la mujer muy pintada. . . . Inaca acsu o ynacalliclla, Vestido de mujer galan pintado de lavores . . . Ynacca nusta, La senora de ayllu de Incas o noble . . ."

48. Sabine MacCormack, *Religion in the Andes. Vision and Imagination in Early Colonial Peru* (Princeton, 1991), 115f.; John V. Murra, "Cloth and Its Functions in the Inca State," *American Anthropologist* 64 (1962): 710–28.

49. See the list of professions, mentioning different kinds of weavers, in Murúa, *Historia* (above n. 36) book 3, chap. 67, 332f. Cf. the similar list, by Francisco Falcón, in *Representación hecha por le licenciado Falcón en el concilio provincial . . . ,* in *CLDRHP* 12:149 (Lima, 1918).

50. A different question about the relationship between Inca and Spanish culture in the early years after the Spanish invasion is posed by Inca Pachacuti's last song. It is given only in Spanish by Betanzos (*Suma,* pt. 1, chap. 32, 149a) and Sarmiento (*Historia Indica,* ed. C. Saenz de Santa Maria, *Biblioteca de autores españoles,* vol. 135 [Madrid, 1965], chap. 47, 252b). Cf. Garcí Sanchez de Badajoz 63.XXV, licion quinta,

homo natus de muliere, *The Life and Works of Garcí Sanchez de Badajoz,* ed. Patrick Gallagher (London, 1968), 148.

> *Betanzos:*
> Desde que florecia como la flor del huerto
> hasta aqui he dado orden y razon en esta vida y mundo
> hasta que mis fuerzas bastaron y ya soy tornado tierra.
> *Sarmiento:*
> Nací como lirio en el jardin y ansí fui criado,
> y como vino mi edad, envejecí, y como habia de morir,
> así me sequé y morí.
> *Garcí Sanchez de Badajoz:*
> De muchas tristezas lleno,
> assi como flor salí
> y me sequé.

Sarmiento and Betanzos are not dependent on each other, so the Inca tradition about Pachacuti's song would seem to be authentic. But perhaps the two authors selected this song because of the resonance of its sentiment with a Castilian poem.

51. Jan Szemiñski, "Un texto en el idioma olvidado de los Incas," *Histórica* 14, no. 2 (Lima, 1990): 379–89.

52. Garcilaso stated (*Primera parte,* book 7, chap. 1, 246b) that "los Incas tuvieron otra lengua particular que hablaban entre ellos, que no la entendian los demas indios, ni les era licito aprenderla, como lenguaje divino. Esta me escriben del Peru que se ha perdido totalmente, porque como perecio la republica particular de los Incas, perecio tambien el lenguaje de ellos." For Inca titulature, see Betanzos, *Suma,* pt. 1, chap. 20, 100a: "Capac capaapoyndichori, que dice rey solo senor hijo del sol." For a further piece of Quechua in Betanzos, see *Suma,* pt. 1, chap. 20, 101b, but here we have an early example of Christian acculturation, perhaps to be juxtaposed with the short address in Domingo de Santo Tomás, *Gramatica o Arte de la Lengua general de los indios de los Reynos del Perú* (Valladolid, 1560; Madrid, 1994), 87ff.

53. The original term is *quipucamayos* (cf. n. 33).

54. Cieza, *Segunda parte,* chap. 11, 27.

55. Cieza, *Segunda parte,* chap. 11, 28: "se callava sin contar los cantares de otros que los buenos y valientes." Cf. chap. 33, 101, regarding Mayta Capac, about whom Cieza was able to learn only little: "Deste Inga no quentan los orejones mas de que Mayta Capac reyno algunos anos en el Cuzco." A trace of the Inca convention mentioned by Cieza is perhaps preserved in the narrative convention of Garcilaso, who regularly passes over matters distasteful to him by saying that he will omit such matters "for being odious."

56. Cieza, *Segunda parte,* chap. 12, 30: "que estos cantares no pudiesen ser publicados ni dichos fuera de la presencia del senor."

57. Collapiña, Supno y otros Quipucamayos, *Relación de la descendencia, gobierno y conquista de los Incas,* ed. J. J. Vega (Lima, 1974), 20: "de nuevo habian de comenzar nuevo mundo de Ticcicapac Inga," in this case Atahuallpa, who gives this as his reason for executing *quipucamayos* and destroying *quipus* that recorded information he found undesirable.

58. See n. 33.

59. Garcilaso, *Primera parte,* chap. 19, 32a: "asi los reyes como los no reyes se preciaron de imitar en todo y por todo la condicion, obras y costumbres de este primer principe Manco Capac; y dichas sus cosas, habremos dicho la de todos ellos."

60. Murúa, *Historia,* (above n. 36), book 3, chap. 67, 333. Note that, apart from *quipucamayos,* Murúa mentions several other professions that involved record keeping.

61. On *camay* and related terms, see Gonzalez Holguín, *Vocabulario,* (above n. 47) 46f.

62. See John V. Murra, "Las etno-categorias de un *khipu* estatal," in id., *Formaciones económicas y politicas del mundo andino* (Lima, 1975), 243–54; and Maria Rostworowski, "La visita de Urcos de 1572, un kipu pueblerino," in her *Ensayos de historia andina,* (above n. 27), 363–83.

63. S. MacCormack, "'En los tiempos muy antiguos . . .' Como se recordaba el pasado en el Perú de la colonia temprana," *Procesos. Revista Ecuadoriana de Historia* 7, no. 1 (Quito, 1995), 3–33.

64. Horace, *Epistles,* 1, 20.

65. Estete, *Noticia,* 50.

66. The lawyer Hernando de Santillán expressed the opinion that the Incas had no laws, while at the same time he himself described Inca legal practice on a variety of matters: possibly he was thinking that the Incas lacked a fixed and codified legal system. See Hernando de Santillán, *"Relación del orígen y gobierno de los Incas,"* in *Crónicas de interés indigena,* ed. E. Barba, *Biblioteca de autores espanoles,* vol. 209 (Madrid, 1968), sec. 12, 107.

67. *Tambos:* Inca postal stations.

68. *Mamaconas:* women chosen for the service of the Sun or the Inca.

69. Law about fires: Betanzos, *Suma,* pt. 1, chap. 21, 104a; babies etc.: ibid., 107–8, (passage in brackets heavily abridged in translation).

70. Murúa, *Historia,* (above n. 36), book 3, chap. 73, 352–55, very similar to the later version in Martín de Murúa, *Historia general del Perú, origen y descendencia de los Incas,* ed. M. Ballesteros Gaibrois (Madrid, 1962), book 2, chap. 22, 88; Guaman Poma, *Nueva Crónica y buen gobierno,* ed. J. V. Murra, Rolena Adorno, and J. Urioste (Madrid, 1987; hereafter *Nueva Crónica*), 182ff.

71. Guaman Poma, *Nueva Crónica,* 188; Murúa, *Historia general,* book 2, chap. 22, 90; *Leviticus* 12:2.

72. Murúa, *Historia general,* book 2, chap. 22, 89, line 25; Betanzos, *Suma,* book 1, chap. 20, 101b.

73. Guaman Poma, *Nueva Crónica,* 185–86; Murúa, *Historia general,* book 2,

chap. 22, 89, l. 15. Cf. Juan Polo de Ondegardo, "Informe . . . al licenciado Briviesca de Muñatones," in *Revista Historica,* vol. 13 (Lima, 1940), 129: "para determinar sus causas ni era menester juramento ni testigos sino tan solamente la presencia de las partes."

74. Guaman Poma, *Nueva Crónica,* 183: "hordeno y mando en esta gran ciudad, cavesa destos rreynos, ayga un pontifize"; Murúa, *Historia general,* book 2, chap. 22, 89, line 12: "mandó que la corte y cabeça de sus reinos fuese la ciudad del Cuzco, a quien llamaban Tupa Cuzco, y en ella asistiesen los de su consejo."

75. Guaman Poma, *Nueva Crónica,* 182: "Hordenamos y mandamos en estos rreynos y señoríos que se guarde y que se cumpla." See for a Spanish antecedent of the formula "guardar . . . cumplir," *Recopilación de leyes de los reynos de las Indias mandadas imprimir . . . por Don Carlos II* (Madrid, 1681; Madrid, 1973), book 2, title 1, law 1, fol. 126 recto: "las leyes . . . sean guardadas, cumplidas y executadas." When, on the other hand, both Murúa (*Historia general,* book 2, chap. 22, 90, line 16) and Guaman Poma (*Nueva Crónica,* 186) observe that the Incas punished those who buried their dead in their own houses, a genuine Andean practice is described; see, for burial of the dead within the house, Jeronimo de Vivar, *Crónica de los reynos de Chile,* ed. Angel Barral Gomez (Madrid, 1988), chap. 8, 63; and Cieza, *Primera parte,* chap. 19, 73.

76. However, such rules were not unknown in another premodern society, the Roman empire; see, for laws regulating appropriate attire in the city of Rome, *Theodosiani Libri XVI,* ed. P. Krueger and T. Mommsen (Berlin, 1905), book 14, title 10.

77. Murúa, *Historia general,* book 2, chap. 22, 90, line 25: "Para la guerra hizo las hordenansas siguintes: que primero que se empesase la guerra por alguna ocasion que ubiese, por embajadores se demandase la cosa robada, satisfacion de la ynjuria y si los enemigos no quisiesen hazer justicia, ni bolber lo que abian llebado, entonces mobiesen la guerra," with Livy, *Ab urbe condita,* book 1, chap. 22.

78. Expressed in Andean terms, the Incas viewed themselves as bringing about a Pachacuti, a turning around of time and the world; see S. MacCormack, "Pachacuti: Miracles, Punishments, and Last Judgement. Visionary Past and Prophetic Future in Early Colonial Peru," *American Historical Review* 93 (1988): 960–1006; see also note 57, above, for Inca Atahuallpa's reign as a new beginning.

79. For example, Cieza, *Primera parte,* chap. 68, 206: "Los que son naturales deste valle (de Pacasmayo) antes que fuessen senoreados por los Ingas, eran poderosos y muy estimados de sus comarcanos."

80. "Con amor y buenas palabras": Cieza, *Segunda parte,* chap. 8, 22.

81. Cicero *De inventione* 1.1, 2. For Roman "love and friendship" for the proud inhabitants of Spain, see note 16.

82. The culmination of Ciceronian imagery and terminology, carefully interspersed with Andean material, is reached by Garcilaso de la Vega, *Primera parte,* book 1, chaps. 16–17.

83. Santillán, *Relación,* (above n. 66), reproducing the questionnaire at pp. 100–102; Polo de Ondegarde, "Informe" (above n. 73), after some introductory statements,

reproduces the questions one by one and gives his responses. See also Inigo Ortiz de Zúñiga, *Visita de la provincia de León de Huánuco en 1562,* vol. 1 (Huanuco, 1967), 16–19 (questionnaire signed in Ghent, 1559), 12–16 (questionnaire for this inspection, dated Lima, 1661). Polo de Ondegardo, *Notables daños de no guardar a los indios sus fueros* (ed. L. Gonzalez and A. Alonso, *Polo de Ondegardo: El Mundo de los Incas,* Madrid, 1990), 37, mentions the questionnaire of 1553, although in the treatise he does not repeat the questions.

84. Santillán began his account of the Incas with the story of their origin from Pacaritambo. He regarded this story as historical; note his reason in *Relación,* 103b: "los primeros ingas fueron naturales de dicho Pacaritambo . . . parece esto ser cierto, porque la lengua que los Ingas hablan y la que ellos hicieron general y comun en toda la tierra que conquistaron es la lengua quichoa, la cual es particular y natural de dicho Pacaritambo, do dicen ser su principio." This simple model of linguistic diffusion, while it does not correspond to the actual process of the spread of Quechua in the Andes (cf. Bruce Mannheim, *The Language of the Inca since the European Invasion* [Austin, 1991], 31 ff.), does express a theory of cultural development that was current in the sixteenth century; see Lidio Nieto Jimenez, *Bernardo José de Aldrete, Del origen y principio de la lengua Castellana ò Romance que oi se usa en España. Ideas linguisticas de Aldrete* (Madrid, 1975), 61 ff. (this is volume 2 of Nieto Jimenez' edition of Aldrete's *Origen*). On the myth of Pacaritambo, see the illuminating study by Gary Urton, *The History of a Myth. Pacariqtambo and the Origin of the Incas* (Austin, 1990).

85. Polo returned to this issue several times, aware as he was that Spaniards found the issues hard to grasp; see J. V. Murra, *The Economic Organization of the Inca State* (Greenwich, 1980), 29 ff.

86. Polo de Ondegardo, *Notables daños,* chap. 4, 50: "si ahora en nuestro tiempo se tasa de otra manera porque así pareció conveniente, claro está que serán dos tributos: el uno quitarles las tierras y el otro el que ahora les mandan dar."

87. *Curaca:* "local lord."

88. Polo de Ondegardo, *Notables daños,* chap. 6, 60–61; chap. 8, 65 ff.; cf. his "Informe," (above n. 73), 150, 164.

89. Polo de Ondegardo, *Notables daños,* chap. 9, 73 ff.

90. Polo de Ondegardo, "Informe," 175, (slightly condensed translation); for the authority of parents over children, husbands over wives, and so on, see Aristotle *Politics* 1.2, 1253b, 1254b. The repercussions of Aristotle's ideas on the state and nature of slaves were extensively discussed in sixteenth-century Spain; see A. Pagden, *The Fall of Natural Man. The American Indian and the Origins of Comparative Ethnology* (Cambridge, 1982).

91. On the undesirability of change, see Polo de Ondegardo, "Informe," 159; see also his *Notables daños,* 37–38. On the negative impact of change brought by Spanish interference in Andean institutions, and the irreversible character of such change, see *Notables daños,* 69: "no tiene rremedio."

92. Polo de Ondegardo (*Notables daños,* 76) regarded the administration of the

Viceroy Antonio de Mendoza as exemplary because he insisted that Mexico and Peru could not be ruled without visiting the land, understanding the "capacity" of the Indians, and "saber sus costumbres y fueros."

93. Santillán, *Relación,* (above n. 66), 104.

94. Polo de Ondegardo, *Notables daños,* 39: "antes que estos indios fuesen sujetos al Inca, cuando eran bestias"; 42: "cada provincia defendia su tierra sin ayudarle otro ninguno como eran behetrias."

95. Polo de Ondegardo, *Notables daños,* chap. 1, 40.

96. Note Polo's observation that it would be easy to establish how long the Incas had ruled in the various parts of Peru, but he is too busy with the task in hand to do so (*Notables daños,* chap. 1, 42).

97. Polo de Ondegardo, "Informe," 154.

98. Archivo Nacional, Lima, Titulos de Comunidades 3, 41C.

Gnosis, Colonialism, and Cultures of Scholarship

Walter D. Mignolo

1. Introduction

The process of Western colonial expansino toward the end of the fifteenth century was part and parcel of the enlargement of human interactions through alphabetic literacy and the commercial implementation of the printing press. Initially, alphabetic literacy began to be constructed as a Greek invention and connected, implicitly, with other Greek inventions such as philosophy and history, two of the longest lasting disciplines in the history of Western scholarship. Literacy, history, and philosophy have been, since the early colonial periods, three basic models used by early Western men of letters and later, by scholars and intellectuals, to evaluate and locate in a planetary hierarchy of other forms of writing, of keeping records of the past, building genealogy, and interpreting the world. One of the results of this process toward the end of the nineteenth century was the rearticulation of the order of knowledge and the insertion of history and philosophy between the social and the human sciences (Foucault). By then, Western cultures of scholarship had been so entrenched with literacy and colonialism that they began to be assumed as a universal form of knowledge even by scholars and intellectuals educated and working in locations governed by colonial legacies. Spreading literacy meant spreading education from elementary to higher education in the colonial domains or creating the conditions for members of the indigenous elite to be educated in the metropolitan centers of the empire. This article explores some aspects of these processes during the early colonial pcriod and in the context of Spanish imperial expansion.

2. Writing Grammars of Amerindian Languages

Writing grammars was one important set of actions and strategies employed by Spaniards to "(re)organize" and "(re)arrange" the languages of native communities. The significance of the process is still perhaps little understood, although the facts are quite well known.[1] For what is at stake when language systems in which the distance between the oral and the written is considerably larger than the one existing in languages with alphabetic or syllabic writing systems, began to be organized according to the rules that have been made explicit for languages with a long alphabetic/written tradition? In grammar after grammar of Amerindian languages written during the sixteenth and seventeenth centuries, authors took it for granted that Latin was a universal linguistic system that could be used to supply the explicit structure of those languages whose grammar had not yet been written. Such a conviction was so strong that Domingo de Santo Tomas (1499–1570), for instance, wrote in the prologue to his grammar of Quechua that this language "is so in agreement with Latin and Castilian in its structure that it looks almost like a premonition [prediction] that the Spaniards will possess it" ("tan conforme a la latina y española y en el arte y artificio della, que no parece sino que fue un pronostico que los españoles la habian de poseer").[2] Thus, it is clear that the significance of writing grammars of primordially spoken languages is that by "colonization of language" we should not only understand "(re)arrangement" but also "possession." Such an observation does not deny the good intentions and the outstanding contributions of grammarians such as Domingo de Santo Tomas in Peru and Alonso de Molina (d. 1585) and Horacio Carochi (d. 1662) in Mexico.[3] It merely points toward the philosophy of language that justifies the colonization of Amerindian languages. When Carochi noted, for instance, that Náhuatl lacked seven letters (chap. 1), he was acting under the conviction that there is a universal alphabet to represent linguistic sounds and it so happened that the Mexican language did not have all the sounds that can be represented by the universal (Roman) alphabet.

The possession I am referring to is of a particular kind, and it differs from what is also, in fact, colonization and possession of languages in the expansion of Amerindian cultures before the Spanish invasion. Acosta, among many others, reported that:

> Como iban los señores de México y de Cuzco conquistando Tierras, iban también introduciendo su lengua, porque aunque hubo y hay gran diversidad de lenguas particulares y propias, pero la lengua cortesana del Cuzco

corrio y corre hoy dia mas de mil leguas y la de Mexico debe correr poco menos.[4]

Acosta was certainly not interested in exploring the implications of the colonization of language but, rather, in looking for shortcuts and advantages for the process of conversion. His observation is useful, nevertheless, because it helps in understanding—by comparison—the imposition of languages during territorial expansion in pre-Columbian times, and the imposition of Castilian and the possession of Amerindian languages during territorial expansion in the context of the "modern world system." In the second case, both alphabetical writing and printing not only allowed for the possession of Amerindian languages by writing their grammars and having them reproduced and distributed in printed form, but were also instrumental in the imposition of the Roman alphabet and in the suppression of the Amerindians' own writing systems.[5]

Let's take a step back in order to contextualize the action of writing grammars of Amerindian languages. Writing grammars was connected with the Spanish colonization of Amerindian cultures in the well-known anecdote in which Queen Isabella received the first Castilian grammar from Elio Antonio de Nebrija. Furthermore, the fact that Queen Isabella was born the same year in which printing was invented, and that Elio Antonio de Nebrija published one of the first grammars of any modern European language the same year that Columbus made Europeans aware that there were people and lands on this earth unknown to them, adds to the anecdotes surrounding the colonization of Amerindian languages. The way in which Nebrija (or rather the Bishop of Avila) told the Queen that grammars were necessary for the consolidation of kingdoms has often been mentioned and celebrated:

Now, Your Majesty, let me come to the last advantage that you shall gain from my grammar. For the purpose, recall the time when I presented you with a draft of this book earlier this year in Salamanca. At this time, you asked me what end such a grammar could possibly serve. Upon this, the Bishop of Avila interrupted to answer in my stead. What he said was this: "Soon Your Majesty will have placed her yoke upon many barbarians who speak outlandish tongues. By this, your victory, these people shall stand in a new need: the need for the laws the victor owes to the vanquished, and the need for the language we shall bring with us." My grammar shall serve to impart them the Castilian tongue, as we have used grammar to teach Latin to our young.[6]

The concise and powerful argument advanced in the introductory notes to his *Gramática* is well known, and it is not necessary to go into detail here.[7] It is worthwhile to remember, however, that one of the remarkable features of Nebrija's argument was his claim for a pact between "armas y letras" at the precise moment when the kingdom of Castile was becoming a modern state ruled by men of letters. The flourishing of the arts, especially the art of languages, or *grammatica,* was rhetorically emphasized by Nebrija, constructing the image of a new beginning atop the ruins left by the enemies of the Christian faith:

> Now that the Church has been purified, and we are thus reconciled to God, now that the enemies of the Faith have been subdued by our arms, now that just laws are being enforced, enabling us all to live as equals, what else remains but the flowering of the peaceful arts? And among the arts, foremost are those of language, which sets us apart from the wild animals; language, which is the unique distinction of man, the means for the kind of understanding that can be surpassed only by contemplation.

It comes as no surprise that Queen Isabella was striving to understand what use a grammar of a vernacular language could possibly have. Although she was aware of the prestige that would be brought to the tongue by having a grammar, which until then had been restricted to the language of the Scriptures (Hebrew, Greek, and Latin), she was not yet making the connection between language and power via colonization. To think about such issues was the task of the humanist (*litteratus*) and man of letters (*jurisperitus*) rather than of women and men of arms. Nebrija was very familiar with Lorenza Valla's reevaluation of "letters" in order to save the Roman Empire from total ruin.[8] He is credited with the introduction of humanist ideas in Spain, and as a humanist he knew that the power of a unified language, via its grammar, lay in teaching it to barbarians, as well as controlling barbarian languages by writing their grammars. Nebrija was able to persuade Queen Isabella that her destiny was not only to conquer but also to civilize. The expression "to civilize," rather than "to colonize," serves to represent the program and motivations of sixteenth-century men of letters.

Within a contemporary context of thought and the needs for decolonization, it is easy to understand that what for Nebrija was to "civilize" for (some of) us (humanists and social scientists of the "postmodern" era) could be translated as to "colonize." The past, as well as any other possible world, cannot be changed; it can only be understood. Understanding, which is a way of speaking the present, can be used either to maintain or to change the images of the past. Actual worlds can, indeed, be changed. The thin line between understanding the past and speaking the present runs parallel to the line between understanding the "other" and speaking among "ourselves." For, in the final analysis, understanding the "past" as well as the "other" does not interfere with the ways the present is understood; rather, the reverse is true: it seems that there are actual needs that push us (humanists and social scientists) to know/understand the past and to speak the present. Speaking (or, better, saying) the present, implies engaging in a discursive domain of interactions in which both the "knowing" (or epistemological) and the "understanding" (or cultural/ hermeneutical) subjects invest in a given field of (academic, scientific) knowledge as well as in their political positions. Such investment in the "acquisition" and transmission of knowledge and understanding of the past or of the other seems to be, at the same time, an investment whose dividends are collected not always and exclusively in the account of "truth" but also in the account of "power." In the analysis, knowing and understanding means knowing and understanding in certain "ways." Thus, the semantic change from *civilize* to *colonize* reveals not only a change in understanding the past but also a change in the ways "they" (*letrados* in the sixteenth century) spoke their present and "we" (humanists and social scientists in the twentieth century) speak ours. Change at this second level may not take place, and as a result speaking the present also means a continuity with the past.

To understand how Nebrija was speaking his present, it is necessary to understand that his argument rested on a philosophy of language whose roots could be traced back, on the one hand, to Saint Augustine and the merging of Platonic and Christian tradition in order to solve the problem of a unified language, needed to counteract the plurality of existing tongues; and, on the other hand, to Valla's (1406–57) *Linguae Latinae elegantiarum libri sex,* written to save Christian Rome from linguistic and cultural illiteracy (*barbarus*).

In Spain, and some forty years after Nebrija composed his Grammar, Luis Vives (familiar with Saint Augustine's work and responsible for the critical edition of his works orchestrated by Desiderio Erasmus), was delineating "la questione de la lingua" in terms of the contrast between the primordial language spoken by Adam and the Tower of Babel as the event that initiated linguistic diversity.[9] Saint Augustine's strong belief in one original language came from the evidence of the Scriptures and also from his Platonic theoretical framework. As a neo-Platonist and Christian Saint Augustine, in reading the Holy Book, assumed the metaphysical principles of an original unity from which the plurality and multiplicity of things could be derived. The original and unified language, according to Saint Augustine, need not and could not be named because it was not necessary to distinguish it from other human languages. It could be called human language or human locution (*De civitate Dei* 16.11, 1). However, the human language was not enough to keep human beings happy and away from transgressing the law, as expressed in the project of building a tower to reach heaven. The division of languages that caused the division of people and communities reached the number seventy-two and each of them was identified with a particular name. It was at this point that it became necessary to find a name for the primordial language in order to distinguish it from the rest. Saint Augustine had good reasons to believe that the original (primordial) language was Hebrew.

While Vives was acquainted with Saint Augustine and was developing a philosophy of language that would be used, directly or indirectly, by the missionaries colonizing native languages,[10] Nebrija was somehow rewriting Valla's program outlined in the preface to his *Linguae latinae elegantiarum* (Valla 1952). Valla realized that rebuilding an empire was not a goal that could be reached by means of arms. He intended, instead, to achieve it by the expedient of letters. By contrasting the Latin used by his ancestors with the expansion of the Roman Empire, and by underlining the strength of the language as a unifying force over the geographical conquests, Valla foresaw Rome's recovery of its lost power and, as a consequence, predicted the central role that Italy was assigned to play in the future. Certainly it was difficult for Nebrija, in 1492, to anticipate much about the future colonization of the New World. It should have been clear to him, however, that Castile had an opportunity to take the place of the Roman Empire. If the preface to his *Gramática Castellana* was indeed a rewriting of Valla's preface, the historical conditions had changed: while Valla was attempting to save an already established empire in decadence, Nebrija was predicting the construction of a new one.

There are other issues that deserve to be compared. Valla's fight against the barbarians, his belief that the history of civilization is the history of language (in anticipation of Vico), and the strong connections he perceived between language and empire, are issues that are repeated by Nebrija. There are, however, some significant differences. Nebrija visualized the center of the empire in Castile instead of Italy, and Castilian as the language of the empire instead of Latin. It naturally follows that grammars of native Amerindian languages were written mainly in Castilian, using Nebrija's Latin (not Castilian) grammar as a model.[11] It is interesting to note also that histories of the New World were mainly written in Castilian. From these differences follows tension between Latin as the language of learning and Castilian as the language of politics and conversion. Consequently, the time had arrived to move from writing grammars of native languages to writing histories of natives' memories.

3. Writing Histories of Amerindian Memories

The first histories of Amerindian cultures known in Europe were written by members of the culture that introduced Western literacy to the natives.[12] In the process, the native forms of recording the past and transmitting it to future generations suffered the consequences of literacy both in the form of learning a new form of writing and reading and of being narrated (perhaps without knowing it) by those who were introducing the alphabet.[13] Spanish historiographers acted in the belief that the alphabet was a necessary condition of historiographical writing. They recognized that Amerindians had means of recording the past (either by oral narratives or in picto-ideographic writing), although the Spaniards did not acknowledge that it was the Amerindian equivalent of historiographical writing. Once they concluded that the Amerindians did not have historiography they appointed themselves to write and put in a coherent form the narratives that, according to the Spanish historiographers, the Amerindians narrated in a thoroughly incoherent manner.[14] When a situation such as this arises, in which the act of writing the history of a community means, at the same time, both suppressing the possibility that the community may be heard and not trusting the voice of the "other," we are witnessing a good example of the colonization of discursive genres (or types). The case seems to be similar to that of writing grammars. While, in the former case, grammars take the place of the implicit native organization of languages, writing histories takes the place of explicit native organization of past oral expression and nonalphabetic forms of writing. In the first case, an implicit knowledge is ignored; in the second, an explicit knowledge is being rewritten. Let's approach these issues from two different perspectives, one devoted to the alphabet and the idea of the book and the other to writing history.

3.1. The Alphabet and the Colonization of Amerindian Memories

Writing histories of non-Western human communities was one of the ways in which Western men of letters colonized the genres (or discursive types) in which men with similar functions within native cultures (the *tlamatinime,* for instance, among the Aztecs) preserved their collective memories. Not much attention was paid by Spanish historians and missionaries to the discursive types or genres of Amerindian cultures. One of the explanations for their lack of interest may be related to the Spaniards' own renaissance theories of writing and to the fact that genre theories in the Renaissance were based on the experience of alphabetic writing and on Greco-Roman traditions. We need to consider changing perspectives in cognitive theories and in philosophies of language,[15] as well as empirical evidence about genre classifications in Meso-america.[16] Before exploring these issues in more detail, I would like to consider two interrelated aspects: the colonization of writing (alphabetization), on the one hand, and the colonization of sign-carriers. The "book" in sixteenth-century Europe, both as an object and a system of representation, was taken for granted and used as a reference point to interpret other sign-carriers and systems of representations as well as to collect and organize the information gathered from members of a culture with different sign-carriers and systems of representation attached to them. For instance, the ideological systems in which *book, amoxtli,* and *vuh* were imbedded in each respective culture, Spanish, Aztec, and Maya-Quiche-Cachickel, were suppressed by the men of letters who had the book as the normal sign-carrier for a normal sign-system, which was the one constituted by the letter of the alphabet. Notice that *book, vuh,* and *amoxtli* are all terms derived from names that, in Maya, Náhuatl, and Latin, referred to the bark of different kinds of trees from which a solid surface for writing purposes was prepared.[17]

Diego de Landa in the Yucatan Peninsula and Diego Valadés in Mexico are two examples helpful in understanding the relevance of the alphabet in the colonization of Amerindian languages, and the philosophy of writing (*escritura, écriture*) and the concept of the book that underscored the missionaries' beliefs and justified their actions.[18] Two of the best-known performances of Diego de Landa in the Yucatan Peninsula were burning the Maya's written records (called *vuh* in Maya-Quiche and translated as "books" in Castilian) and his attempt to translate Mayan hieroglyphs into the letters of the Roman alphabet. While book-burning was not something that only happened in the colonization of the New World, translating hieroglyphs into alphabetic units was one of the first efforts I know of to use the letters of the alphabet as a means of conquest and colonization. Landa's assumption that hieroglyphs were a form of alphabetic writing was certainly amazing. I am not trying to discredit Landa's perception of signs, which in the Maya system represented classes of sounds, but rather the presuppositions underlying his conception of the history of writing. The very act of looking for correspondences between signs representing ideas and signs standing for classes of sound seems to indicate not only a conception of writing that is clearly evolutionary and hierarchic but also that the unquestioned assumption that (the best form of) writing should necessarily represent speech. Landa's implicit beliefs are often expressed today as explicit assumptions: any system of graphic signs that could be used as an alternative to oral discourse would be considered "true" writing.

The second example, also very well known, is an early version of the mnemonic technique for learning the alphabet assembled by Diego Valadés (1579). In the chapter devoted to different forms of exercising memory (a common strategy among rhetoricians), Valadés developed a "theory" of Roman letters based on the sounds and their arbitrarily projected graphic images. In the first mode, the images of the letters were formed by the sounds of the voice and were illustrated with proper names: *A* from Antonio, *B* from Bartolome, and so on. This is most interesting because the obvious graphic nature of every letter was the image of the letter according to the figure it was supposed to resemble. Teaching the alphabet to persons whose culture was different from the Italian tradition and alien to the Roman alphabet requires a stretch of the imagination. Valadés developed a "translation" into figures common to the Aztec world of the graphic images of the letters he found in a treatise by Ludovico Dolce[19] about methods of increasing mnemonic capacities.

I am not in a position to measure the consequences of such a strategy when it is imposed on a person who has to exchange his oral mnemonic devices for graphic ones. I am concerned with the consequences of the colonization of writing (at least in the first two generations), when members of the colonized culture had to rearrange their flow of sound in speech and accommodate them to the "word" and some twenty graphic signs. Granted, once the change had been produced, the effects after the first two generations would scarcely be perceived by the members of subsequent generations, who would be educated within the new system.[20] However, the colonization of writing consists precisely in an alternative perception and organization of the world by means of written signs, which conflict with or replace the ones already in place. The outcome of this complex process would be the adaptation of the new writing systems by members of the colonized cultures (i.e., Garcilaso de la Vega in Peru and Fernando de Alva Ixtlilxochitl in Mexico); the use of alphabetic writing transgressing or ignoring the orthographic rules and subordinated to the more familiar way of picture-writing (e.g., the exceptional case of Guaman Poma de Ayala in Peru); and, finally, those texts that we cannot talk about either because they were not written or because we do not yet know about them. Writing is more likely to be successfully colonized than is speech. While all forms of traditional Amerindian writings have completely disappeared and have been replaced with alphabetic writing, the colonization of speech was not equally successful. Even today, hundreds of communities in Latin America are living according to the worldview inherited from their pre-Columbian ancestors. And the millions of people who still speak Amerindian languages bear witness to the fact that the colonization of graphic languages, which are an extension of the hands, was more successful than the colonization of verbal languages, which are inscribed in the body.

3.2.   Writing (Scratching on Solid Surfaces) and the Idea of the Book

It was not by chance that the alphabet was so naturally linked to the idea of the book that they were both part of a larger ideological system in which the possibility of writing in something that was not a manuscript codex or a printed book (e.g., writing on clay tablets, deer skins, or scrolls) was not considered at all or was viewed as an activity of the remote past. It was the ideology of writing and of the book that explains part of the dialogue between the first twelve Franciscan friars arriving in Mexico and the representatives of the Aztec nobility. Mendieta offered a brief summary of this dialogue in which, according to the author, after the friars informed the Aztec representatives about their goals and explained the Christian doctrine to them, the *"principales"* readily accepted what the friars told them. When we read the *Coloquios y Doctrina Christiana* (1524) in Sahagún's version, we may conclude that Mendieta gave an accurate report of what happened. However, when the text is read in the Náhuatl version or in recent translations offered in Spanish or English, a totally different picture emerges. And a great deal of the difference is related to the idea of writing and to the authority attributed to the book by the Franciscan friars.[21] Let's take a closer look at this dialogue.

The dialogue, whose written pieces Sahagún collected and wrote in 1565, took place in 1524, perhaps over a period of several days or even weeks. The temporal aspect of the scene of speaking is not clear in the written version. Roughly, the situation is reported as follows. After hearing the explanation of the Christian doctrine, the Aztec "principales" asked the Franciscan friars whether they had to abandon their own gods and traditions. To the affirmative reply of the friars, the Aztecs asked for a reason. The friars answered that everything they needed to know was written in the Divine Book. This simple answer is indicative of the extent to which the Franciscan friars were prisoners of the tyranny of the alphabet and the idea of the book, that they had already forgotten the oral tradition of what they trusted as the Divine Book. Neither could they make sense of the answer provided by the Aztec "principales" about their own gods and semiotic authorities equivalent to the Christian Divine Book.

Let me disclose some of the facts I have in mind at this point. Ernst Robert Curtius[22] called our attention, over forty years ago, to the amount and the significance of the images that different cultures had constructed to represent their ideas about writing and about the book. He began his survey with the Greeks, noting that they did not have any "idea of the sacredness of the book, as there is no privileged priestly caste of scribes." The well-known disparagement of writing in Plato's dialogue is a complementary example, showing that attitudes toward writing and the book in ancient Greece were not exactly as renaissance men of letters thought they were. It is also well known, in fact, that in the last part of Plato's *Phaedrus* Socrates attempts to convince Phaedrus that writing is not an aid to memory and learning. On the contrary, Socrates argues, writing can only "awaken reminiscences" without replacing the true discourse lying in the psyche of the wise man, which must be transmitted through oral interaction. It should be underlined that Socrates was mainly concerned with "writing" in its relationship to knowledge and its transmission rather than with the "book." When writing was still an activity performed on papyrus, which did not have the shape of what later on (second century of the Christian era) would take the shape of the medieval codex, it would have been impossible to build around a roll of papyrus scratched without punctuation the same idea built by medieval and renaissance intellectuals around an object made of bound paper, illuminated, and with increasing conventions and instructions to position the graphic signs on a page. It is hard today, and it was already hard for a lettered person in the sixteenth century, to imagine that in Greece it was impossible to imagine knowledge or information organized in a single volume instead of several rolls made of skin or Egyptian papyrus. Whether or not the later distinctions of a narrative (or book) into chapters (or books) were a derivation of a set of rolls conforming to a thematic unit, or roll, it would be outside of our purpose to pursue here. However, if one thinks of the rich vocabulary associated with graphic semiotic interactions inherited from the Greeks, and if one also remembers that the idea of the sacred book was alien to them, for they were more concerned with writing than with books, it could be concluded that *roll* or *biblos* cannot be translated as "book" and be made part of the history of the book without imposing the current meaning of *book* upon *biblos,* or making *biblos* a forerunner of the "book," without understanding the meaning (or the idea) that was associated with the object in ancient Greece. The ideas that in ancient Greece were associated with *biblos* were perhaps close to the ideas the Aztecs associated with *amoxtli.* Spaniards disregarded this difference, and translated both as "book." Nevertheless, while they were proud of placing themselves in the Greco-Roman tradition, they at the same time destroyed Mesoamerican "amoxtli" and "vuh," which they considered books written by the devil.[23]

Certainly, the destruction of Mesoamerican "books" because they were dictated by the Devil, and the use of the written "Holy Book" as a proof that Amerindians were wrong in their beliefs, were just two of the ways in which we can relate writing, the Roman alphabet, and the book to the colonization of languages. Between the act of writing and the object called a book as sign-carrier and container of knowledge, lay a third phenomenon: genres or discursive types. Historical narratives are neither the sign nor the book, as writing is not just the act of inscribing graphic marks on solid surfaces or speech the production of sound waves. Speaking and writing imply producing sound waves and graphic marks according to a set of rules and cognitive frames. The first have been called "grammars" and the second "genres." Spaniards not only wrote grammars for native Amerindian languages, but also used their own discursive genres to write down Amerindian memories, and their own books to replace Amerindian "amoxtli" and "vuh."

3.3.   Letters, Barbarians, and the Writing of History

Landa reported, in 1566, the events that took place at the beginning of the conquest of the Yucatan Peninsula, between 1533 and 1550 approximately. Valadés' book, published in 1579, is one of the best examples of the Franciscan education in Mexico: a blend of Greco-Roman and Amerindian traditions. Let's go back to the very beginning of the literacy campaign, in Mexico, a few years after the arrival of the twelve Franciscan friars whose dialogue with the Aztec "principales" was mentioned previously. Pedro de Gante, one of the key figures who participated in the education of the Amerindians, reported, in a letter addressed to Philip II and dated in 1529, the actions taken and the efforts made by the Franciscan friars when they arrived in Mexico with the mission of converting the barbarians to Christianity. De Gante underscored the friars' efforts in learning the native languages and commented on the difficulties involved in the task, since the natives were "people without writing, without letters, without written characters and without any kind of enlightenment." Values, we know, support actions and orient strategies. Pedro de Gante also reported in detail how they proceeded in order to transmit the "letter" to those who did not possess it:

All that time approximately one thousand children were gathered together, and we kept them locked up day and night in our house, and they were forbidden any conversation with their fathers and even less with their mothers, with the only exception of those who served them and brought them food; and the reason for this was so that they might neglect their excessive idolatries and their excessive sacrifices, from which the devil had secured countless souls.[24]

The paragraph shows that the letter was not instilled without violence. The violence, however, was not located in the act of assembling and incarcerating the youngsters day and night, but rather in the act of forbidding the children conversations with their parents, particularly with their mothers. In a primarily oral society, in which virtually all knowledge is transmitted by means of conversation, the preservation of oral contact was contradictory to the effort to teach Amerindians how to read and write. Thus, forbidding conversations between the children and their mothers meant, basically, depriving them of the living culture embedded in their language and preserved and transmitted in speech. The colonization of language took place at several levels. At one level was the introduction of the letter: not only the skill of reading and writing, but of reading and writing the text written by those who were teaching those skills. The philosophy of language underlying the missionaries' belief was prompted by the connections they perceived between lack of letters and lack of enlightenment. Consequently, in the "chain of writing" Renaissance men of letters fabricated for themselves, alphabetical writing was, on the one hand, the most perfect, and superior to Chinese and Mesoamerican writing systems; and, on the other, it was related to the construction of the other as "barbarian." In this picture, lack of "letters" was a sufficient condition to equate the illiterate with the uncivilized or barbarian.

Where does the question of writing history fit into the previous scenario? The Renaissance philosophy of language was not just concerned with writing. It was concerned with speech (when the condition was the origin of language and the diversity of languages); with the syntactic and logic structure of the sentence (when the issues were matters of grammar and logic); and with the structure of discourse (when the question was the disciplines of the trivium and, later, the inclusion of poetica and historica in the realm of grammar, rhetorica, and dialectica, or logic). Writing began to be an issue with the Renaissance celebration of the letter[25] and with the encounter between cultures with different writing sytems. Thus, when the Jesuit José de Acosta (working in Peru toward the end of the sixteenth century) wrote a letter and asked his colleague Antonio Tovar, in Mexico, how was it possible that the Indians could have history if they did not have writing (he meant alphabetic writing), and how was it possible that they could speak with such admirable figures of speech if they did not have rhetoric, Acosta was not implying that lack of letters meant lack of intelligence (for Acosta was not a Franciscan and was not on the side of de Gante). He believed, however, in the chain of writing systems in a hierarchy of human cultures according to their written achievements. Between the early years of the sixteenth century, in which de Gante equated lack of letters with lack of enlightenment, and the final years of the same century, when Acosta did not deny the Amerindians' intelligence (although he still did not regard them as equals), the connections between lack of letters and barbarity was articulated in the mid–sixteenth century by the Dominican Bartolomé de las Casas in his *Apologetica historia sumaria.*[26] According to las Casas, the term 'barbarus' referred to three different cultural types. The first alluded to human beings who lost control of themselves, whose minds had been overwhelmed by their passion. The second type was described in terms of language. The third type was the "barbarian" *sensu literalis,* and they were so because of the regions they inhabited, because they were not governed by laws, and because they did not have justice. I am obviously interested in the second type of "barbarians," in which Adam's primordial language and Babel's confusion of tongues were used, this time not in order to explain the origin of language or to justify the most perfect (Valla's Latin and Nebrija's Castilian) but to distinguish the barbarians from the civilized. Let's pause to ponder both de Gante's dictum and Acosta's question in relation to Las Casas' definition.

It is not surprising that language was, on the one hand, equated with speech or tongues (in Romance languages *lingua, lengua, linguaggio, lenguaje, langue, langage*) and, on the other, was recognized as one (if not the) specific feature that distinguished human beings from animals, instrumental in developing and organizing social life. Such beliefs were understandable, not necessarily because the influence of Platonic philosophy of language discredited writing, but because Platonic philosophy of language was based on the experience of a civilization whose oral means of learning were being threatened by the introduction of writing.[27] It is common sense to understand that, while speech was linked to the differences between human beings and animals and is fundamental to the construction of the idea of "humanes," writing was so recent to Plato (and is so recent in the history of human civilizations) that it was only natural that the idea of language was associated with speech, and with a system of writing (the alphabetic) in which the distance between the sound and the graphic sign was so small as to seem almost nonexistent. The shift from spoken to written language in the transmission of learning was one of the crucial steps in constructing the difference between barbarians and the civilized. In las Casas's world all knowledge (*scientia*) was text-dependent. It was therefore understandable that there existed a distinction between the knowledgeless barbarians and the lettered civilized, as if knowledge and the letters of the alphabet were one and the same. For las Casas, as well as for his sixteenth-century fellows, they indeed were. They also established the meaning of *letrados* (the lettered ones) as a social role attached to and representing learning. The ability to create a system of writing, and the access to power and knowledge that such a system conferred, were the ultimate token of the superiority of the "civilized" man over the "barbarian."[28]

The preceding discussion should contribute to our understanding of why historians of the Indies of the first century showed a strong concern for the ways in which the Amerindians preserved their memories. This concern was not, of course, neutral. It was formulated by those who in the act of framing the question "How can the Amerindians have history if they do not have writing?" were describing the very idea of the activity they were performing: to write history as a linear narrative in which the chain of words (a concept difficult to imagine in nonalphabetic writing systems) was one and the same as the chain of events. This idea of history would have been very difficult to understand for people who were not acquainted with alphabetic writing and did not know exactly how a flow of sounds could be broken up into words, and even less how to relate sequences of words with sequences of events. The Tlamatinime, for instance, who were used to reading from bottom to top and in a "boustrophedon" pattern, may have had some difficulties in "translating" the relationships between words and events, departing from their own experience of telling stories by looking at the paintings of their pictographic written codices. I understand that inverting the process would have been equally difficult. However, it was the Spanish Renaissance men of letters who were asking the question and not the Aztecs. "Humanism" and "renaissance" were concepts literally from a different "history." That is why Spaniards either complained about the lack of coherence in Amerindian oral narratives or simply ignored the patterns in which the Amerindians cast their own narratives. The philosophy of language with which missionaries and men of letters were armed extended itself from grammar to complex genres, and allowed them to conclude that if Amerindians did not have similar kinds of writing and a similar philosophy of language they would not be able to produce clear accounts of their own past: history was the way to do it, and history was a matter of alphabetic written narratives. This conclusion was a sufficient condition for the missionaries and men of letters to become the self-appointed chroniclers the Amerindians apparently did not have.[29]

Let me offer some specific examples to illustrate and support the previous statement. In book 1, chapter 1, of his *Historia general y natural de las Indias* (1535), Oviedo emphasized that from the moment of his arrival in the Indies he was concerned with finding out how the Indians recalled their origins and the "things" (*las cosas*) of their ancestors. He observed that on the island of Santo Domingo their songs, called Areytos, constituted their books or memoriales. Almost a century later Garcilaso de la Vega the Inca—whose work reflects the tension between the organization and transmission of the culture of his ancestors and the ideas of writing and of the book of the European Renaissance— asked his uncle about his knowledge about the origin of the Inca kings (*Comentarios reales de los Incas,* 1609: 1:xv). Garcilaso asked, specifically, how the Incas could remember past events if they did not have writing. Garcilaso further specified his own question by telling his uncle that in Castile, as well as in other nearby nations, there were divine as well as human histories and, consequently, Castilians knew how many years had passed since God had created Heaven and Hell; they knew everything about the transformations of one empire into another, and they knew everything about their own kingdoms. If they knew all this, concluded Garcilaso, it was because they had books. The question was finally formulated more or less as follows: "Since you [the Incas] do not have books, what memories do you have of your past?" A beautiful example, indeed, of "diatopical hermeneutics" in which the narrative first person avoids identifying itself with either "they" or "you." The identification occurs, however, not in the prenominal form but in the "natural" complicity between the object (the book) and the actions (recording the past).

A few decades before Garcilaso, Acosta stepped forward to take a position in the debate about whether the Amerindian lacked intelligence. With persuasive arguments, he supported the idea that Amerindians were intelligent human beings. He supported his arguments with examples of what Amerindians had and what they had achieved. One of his main examples was the Mexican calendar and their complex and sophisticated ways of keeping time records. However, in book 6 of his *Historia natural y moral de las Indias* (1590), Acosta changed direction and, instead of talking about what the Amerindians had or had achieved, he began to talk about what the Mexicans did not have. It is not surprising that the first thing he mentioned was the fact that nobody had discovered that "the Indians make use of letters." From chapter 6 to chapter 11 (book 6), Acosta developed a theory of writing based on a philosophy of language whose debt to Aristotle he freely admitted.

Acosta believed that letters were invented to signify the words we pronounce and that words are immediate signals of the concepts and thoughts of man (he was, of course, referring to human beings). Both letters and voice were created in order to understand things: voice for those who could communicate directly in the same space, letters for both those who could not be present and those who, in the future, would be able to read what had been written. Acosta emphasized that signals or signs that were produced to signify something other than words could not truly be called letters even though they could be written: a painted image of the sun is not a cluster of written letters depicting the sun, but a painting. Based on this assumption, Acosta made two inferences: (1) man (human beings) has three different ways of recording memories, by letters and writing (whose primary examples are the Greeks, Latins and Hebrews), by painting (whose primary examples Acosta found in almost every known civilization), and by ciphers and characters; (2) none of the civilizations of the Indies used letters, but they did employ both images and figures. It was only natural that Acosta was surprised by Tovar's report about the ways the Aztecs kept memories of their past and their elegant ways of speaking. This is the context in which Acosta's question to Tovar ran parallel to Garcilaso's question to his uncle: how could the Indians—asked Acosta—preserve their memories of so many varied things for such a long time without writing (by which he meant alphabetic writing)? How could they—insisted Acosta—have such wonderful speeches ("arenga y oraciones") if they did not have rhetoric (by which he meant the set of written norms that governed oral discourses)? Tovar, who was in Mexico and familiar with the "art of memory" practised by the Aztecs, attempted an explanation of how both remembering the past and remembering long sentences could have worked without the help of letters. He agreed, however, with Acosta's concerns about the Aztecs' lack of writing. "You should know," said Tovar in his letter to Acosta, "that even if they had different types of figures and characters, which they used to 'write things' [escribir las cosas], their figures and characters are not as sufficient as our writing." Tovar went on to say that Mexicans had figures and hieroglyphs by means of which they painted things. And for those things they could not paint, because they did not have an image, they combined different characters to convey as much as they could or wished. From what we know today about Náhuatl writing, Tovar seems to refer to "pictographic representations" (of things, persons, gods, etc.) and "ideographical glyphs" (representing metaphysical concepts such as movement, day, night, and so on). But of course this was not enough to be called writing.[30]

The Renaissance theory of writing held by Spanish men of letters should become clear from these examples. Its application to Amerindian culture elicited Acosta's typology of writing and the complicity between writing and history. According to the marriage between history and alphabetical writing, it was concluded that anybody can keep records of the past but history can only be written with letters. What was the foundation for this conception of writing history? What was the philosophy of history that made such a connection with writing? It is common knowledge that within the legacy of Imperial Rome works such as the *Ad Herennium, De Oratore,* and *Institutione Oratoria* were the basic rhetorical treatises for any humanistic education. They imposed and transmitted the idea that history is narration and narration is the central part of constructing a text, *dispositio.* It is also a well-known fact that Quintilian in the *Institutione Oratoria* (book 2, chap. 5) distinguished three kinds of narrations: *fabula,* which was the furthest removed from truth and applied to tragedy and epic; *argumentum,* a feigned narrative, which applied to comedy; and, finally, *historia,* which was considered the true narration of past events. The complicity between history and alphabetic writing comes from a culture whose learned members were able to write sophisticated treatises (rhetoric) about oral discourses (oratory). They laid the groundwork for conceiving the writing of history in terms of the fundamentals of oratorial discourse, all of which was a by-product of the imposition and growing relevance of alphabetic writing as the main learning device. Later, as basic treatises of humanistic education, the works of Cicero and Quintilian shaped the minds of those who would write histories of the New World.[31]

A turning point takes place when the same treatises were also employed in the New World to educate the native elites. The history of education in the New World shows the paths the colonization of language followed at the level of cultural literacy.

1. By writing the history of the Amerindians' past the missionaries as well as men of letters translated oral narratives and picto-ideographic writings into alphabetic writing in historic form. By doing so, they integrated both the Amerindians' past and their patterns of time reckoning and storytelling into a providential conception of history that ran parallel to the evolutionary and progressive history of writing.

2. The few Amerindians educated in the New World and in Spanish colleges (e.g., Santa Cruz de Tlatelolco) "integrated" the Renaissance philosophy of writing and historiographical conceptions into their writing of Amerindian history (e.g., Ixtlilxochitl, Tezozómoc, and Muñón Chimal-

paín) and had to negotiate the conflict between the forces of their own traditions (both in the content of their memories and in the way of remembering and transmitting them) with the rhetorical (i.e., the trivium) education they received in Castilian institutions. This created tension between the past, which the Amerindian historians needed to remember, fix, and transmit, and the models of writing and writing history of a tradition that was not their own. The spectrum in which these tensions were manifested goes from historical writing in native languages (Chimalpaín or Tezozómoc writing in Náhuatl), to Ixtlilchochitl writing in Spanish but in Mexico, Garcilaso de la Vega writing in Spanish but in Spain, and Poma de Ayala writing in a broken Spanish and using drawings more than alphabetic writing.[32]

Beyond these wide spectrums in which colonization of language begins to generate resistance to it, we find extreme cases of an unwritten history that begin to come to the fore.

4. The Decolonization of Languages and Memories

The colonization of Amerindian languages and memories required the introduction of a tool (alphabetic writing) and of discursive frames (the Renaissance system of genres), which were adapted and used by the Amerindians in order to sustain their own cultural traditions. These alternative "histories," either collective enterprises, such as the *Popol Vuh* and the *Books of Chilam Balam* (both written down around the mid–sixteenth century) in the Mayan Peninsula, or texts by individuals, such as Muñón Chimalpaín or Ixtlilxochitl in Mexico (both written in the first decades of the seventeenth century), punctuate, on the one hand, the plurilingual and multicultural character of colonial situations and, on the other, illustrate how such written practices collided with the Renaissance philosophy of language and writing held by missionaries and men of letters.

Open resistance, or resistance through adaptation, was the counterpart of the colonization of language. Not every step taken toward the alphabetization of the natives resulted in the desired effects. Three examples of resistance and decolonization illustrate the unexpected (from the missionaries' perspective) consequences of literacy. The first has been reported by Mendieta (*Historia eclesiástica indiana,* 1597) and happened in Mexico; the second was noted by Fray Francisco Ximenez and happened in Yucatan; the third came from colonial Peru, and is seen by comparing Garcilaso de la Vega with Guaman Poma de Ayala.

The children who, according to Pedro de Gante's letter to Philip II, were said to have been locked up in the monasteries, were not entirely from noble families. As is natural, the Aztec noble families had no reason to trust the friars' intentions and motives. Thus, instead of sending their own children, they sent the children of their vassals. Mendieta made a point of reporting that those who were dishonest with the friars suffered consequences, for since the vassals learned how to read and write they ended up overruling their own superiors: ("aquellos hijos de gente plebeya siendo alli doctrinado en la ley de Dios y en saber leer y escribir, salieron hombres habiles, y vinieron despues a ser alcades y gobernadores, y mandar a sus senores" (book 3, chap. 15).

It is within the context of unexpected consequences that native "books" from the Yucatan Peninsula, such as the several *Books of Chilam Balam* or the *Popol Vuh* from the highlands of Guatemala, among others, can be explained.[33] There is enough evidence to believe that the former (which were written in Yucatec language and in European script), were transcriptions into alphabetic writing of the old hieroglyphic (or "painted") codices. Historians of the Yucatan Peninsula[34] had reactions to native writing systems and "books" similar to those of the historians of the Aztec civilization. They reported, for instance, that the natives would read the book in their assembly, that some of them were read to the rhythm of the drums, that others were sung, and still others were enacted. There is also evidence that these "books," as we know them today, were compiled not before the seventeenth or the eighteenth centuries. Consequently, what today is considered an "encyclopedia" or mixture of genres presumably existed, before they were compiled in a single unit, as a diversity of genres common to pictographic writing (book-keeping, time-reckoning) without parallel in oral genres. The colonization of genres in this case was not successful. As time went on, the European script that the friars were so eager to transmit in order to be more effective in the Christianization of the natives was used by the latter to stabilize their past, to adapt themselves to the present, to transmit their own traditions to future generations and, in summary, to resist the colonization of language.[35]

Rigoberta Menchú's recent narrative of the life and deeds of a Quiche community is a clear example of the unwritten history of resistance, as Rigoberta's very act of narration is a clear example of continuing resistance. Rigoberta reports, for example, that there are several moments, in raising a child, in which the adults talk to him or her about the importance of their tradition. Here is Menchú's report of the day the child turns ten years old:

They [the elders] tell them [the children] that they [the children] will be young men and women and that one day they will be fathers and mothers. This is actually when they tell the child that he must never abuse his dignity, just as his ancestors never abused their dignity. It's also when they remind them that our ancestors were dishonored by the White Man, by colonization. But they don't tell them the way that it is written down in books, because the majority of Indians can't read or write, and don't even know that they have their own texts. No, they learn it through oral recommendations, the way it has been handed down through the generations. They are told the Spaniards dishonored our ancestors' finest sons, and the most humble of them. And it is to honor these humble people that we must keep our secrets. And no one except we Indians must know.[36]

In colonial Peru, Garcilaso de la Vega was the perfect example of the adaptation (in order to criticize it) to Western literacy, while Guaman Poma epitomizes the use of alphabetic writing in order to resist the literacy of the colonizer.[37] In fact, while Garcilaso was able to write as a Castilian native speaker, to learn and apply European conceptualizations of writing history, and to adjust himself to the social role (i.e., *letrado*) corresponding to writing activities, Guaman Poma resisted every single instance of integration or adaptation. One of the results was that Garcilaso quickly became the representative voice of the Incas while Guaman Poma was forgotten or registered in the history of historiography as a moment of shame for the Castilian language and culture. In his *"coronica"* to King Philip III, Guaman Poma expressed his acute dissatisfaction through a counter-proposal for the administration and government of Peru, using alphabetical writing together with pictorial representation. He was able to intermingle the literacy of his own ancestors with Western literacy, to make himself understood by his "others" without losing his own identity. While Guaman Poma's writing illustrates resistance to colonization, his exclusion from the history of Latin American culture for at least four and a half centuries is a clear example of the colonization of writing and genres. Perhaps the "chronicles of the impossible"[38] are, at the same time, narratives of resistance.

When compared with the *Popol Vuh* and the *Books of Chilam Balam,* Garcilaso and Guaman serve to illuminate several aspects of literacy in a colonial situation. They both preserved the authorial identity already linked to Western literacy; they used Castilian instead of their own native language to convey their message to a Castilian audience (in spite of the obvious differences); and they wrote for an audience that was detached from the act of writing and would not need to crouch down and look at the pictures while listening to the authors' narrations. On the contrary, the "books" from the Yucatan Peninsula were anonymous and collective, written in the native languages and, consequently, addressed to a native audience, which preferred "listening" to an oral performance to "reading" the pages of a "book."

Conclusion

Today, successive colonial legacies are still entrenched in the cultures of scholarship, even in those cases in which scholars are critical of colonialism. This double bind should not discourage us, since it can hardly be otherwise: to engage in scholarly practices implies the need to work, at least partially, within the scholarly legacies of colonialism. The situation is complex, but allow me to simplify it somewhat. Because of Western expansion, cultures of scholarship are mainly practised in the major colonial languages (and the colonial languages of the second wave of colonial expansion—English, French, and German). However, before the very recent and short history of the modern colonial languages (Italian, Spanish, and Portuguese), there were millenarian languages in which knowledge was produced, transformed, stored, and transmitted, although this process may not have had the same administrative organization as cultures of scholarship in the West, including the post-Renaissance reframing of Greek gnoseological legacies. Chinese, Hindi, Arabic, Hebrew, and Japanese are languages in which categories of thought were forged, expanded, transformed, and used for the organization of culture and society for centuries before the short and recent history of cultures of scholarship under Western colonial domination.

Certainly, neither the introduction of Western technology nor the cultures of scholarship in non-Western countries or regions implies that a duplication of sixteenth-century Spain was automatically introduced into Mexico, or that a duplication of the United States will be automatically introduced in South Asia. There is no question that Spain in the sixteenth century became what it was because of its colonialism in the Indies and Mexico/Tenochtitlan. However, mutual changes today are more accelerated than in the sixteenth century. Cultures of scholarship are expanding their spectrum from close complicity with the state, in the late nineteenth and early twentieth centuries, to a more critical perspective on structures of domination, both in the previous metropolitan center and urban peripheries of colonial structures and in the more and more ubiquitous locations of economic and scholarly practices in this current stage of globalization. Of course, today colonial structures of domination have not yet vanished but they have been displaced and rearticulated.

There is one last question I would like to address, although I do not have time to develop it: the question of categories of thought and of languages of scholarship. Some of my examples (e.g., the notions of the "book" and of "history") show that *thinking from* colonial legacies can no longer be a practice grounded in the Greek classical legacy invented in the West after the European Renaissance. If we take the case of the legacies of Spanish colonialism, the crucial role played by Arabic in the formation of cultures of scholarship in the Iberian Peninsula can hardly be forgotten. On the other hand, we cannot forget the remaining conflictive zones of languages and thoughts in the Americas between categories inherited from Amerindian and from European fragments in the colonial world shall be kept in mind. The "beginning" of thinking and the foundation of cultures of scholarship in and about the Americas should be located at the intersection and transformation of conflictive ethnic categories, those of worlds in expansion and those moving from worlds that have been forced to radical transformations.

NOTES

1. The politics of language in Mexico has been studied by Shirley Brice-Heat (*La política del lenguaje en México: de la colonia a la nación* [Mexico, 1972]); and by Gonzolo Aguirre Beltrán (*Lenguas vernáculas: Su uso y desuso en la enseñanza: la experiencia de México.* [Mexico, 1983]). Ascensión León-Portilla has traced the history of the grammars of the Náhuatl language written in Mexico (*Tepuztlahcuilolli. Impresos en Náhuatl. Historia y bibliografía* [Mexico, 1988]).

2. *Grammatica o Arte de la lengua general de los Indios de los reynos del Perú* (Quito, 1947).

3. Alonso de Molina, *Arte de la lengua Mexicana y Castellana* (Mexico, 1571); Horacio Carochi, *Arte de la lengua mexicana con la declaración de los adverbios della* (Mexico, 1640).

4. José de Acosta, *Historia natural y moral de las Indias* (1590; Mexico, 1962), book 6, chap. 20.

5. The processes of transformation and ultimate obliteration of Amerindian writing systems have been studied by Birgit Scharlau and Mark Munzel, *Quelqay. Mundliche Kultur und Schrifttradition bei Indianern Lateinamerikas* (Frankfurt, 1986), 97–155, 171–220; and by Serge Gruzinski, *La colonization de l'imaginaire. Sociétés indigènes et occidentalisation dans le Mexique espagnol, XVe–XVIIIe siecle* (Paris, 1988).

6. *Gramática de la lengua castellana* (Salamanca, 1492; ed. I. Gonzalez-Llubera, London, 1926), prologue.

7. Eugenio Ascensio, "La lengua compañera del imperio: historia de una idea de Nebrija en España y Portugal," *Revista de filología española* 43 (1960): 399–413;

Francisco Rico, *Nebrija contra los bárbaros. El cánon de gramáticos nefastos en las polémicas del humanismo* (Salamanca, 1978); Victor García de la Concha, ed., *Nebrija y la introducción del renacimiento en España* (Salamanca, 1981).

8. Lorenzo Valla, "In sex libros Elegantiarum praefatio," in *Prosatori latini del Quattrocento,* E. Garin, ed. (Milan, 1952); Ottavio Besomi e Mariagneli Regoliosi, *Lorenzo Valla e l'umanesimo italiano.* Atti del convegno internazionale di studi umanistici (Padova, 1986): Franco Gaeta, *Lorenzo Valla: filogia e storia nell'umanesimo italiano* (Naples, 1955).

9. Luis Vives, *De tradendis disciplinis* (1533? London, 1964), 4:299–300.

10. See, for instance, Vázquez de Espinosa's narrative (1620) in which he "naturally" harmonized the history of Amerindian languages with the confusion of tongues after Babel and the migration of the ten tribes of Israel to the New World (*Compendio y descripción de las Indias Occidentales* [Washington, D.C., 1969] 3:14).

11. It has been taken for granted among Náhuatl specialists that Nebrija's Castilian grammar was the model followed in writing the grammars of Amerindian languages. See, for instance, Frances Karttunen, "Nahuatl Literacy," in *The Inca and Aztec States, 1400–1800,* G. A. Collier, R. Rosaldo, and J. D. Wirth, eds. (New York, 1982), 396; and Ascensión León-Portilla, *Tepuztlahcuilolli. Impresos en Náhuatl. Historia y bibliografía* (Mexico, 1988), 6. The same beliefs have been expressed by Vicente Rafael, as regards the Tagalog language, in the Philippines (*Contracting Colonialism. Translation and Christian Conversion in Tagalog Society under Early Spanish Rule* [Ithaca, 1984], 23–54). I have argued elsewhere (Walter D. Mignolo, "Nebrija in the New World: The Question of the Letter, the Discontinuity of the Classical Tradition and the Colonization of Native Languages," *L'Homme* 122–124 (1992): 187–209, that it was the Latin grammar rather than the Castilian that served as a model. More importantly, the two ideological programs articulated by Nebrija in each grammar should be taken into account when dealing with the colonization of native languages.

12. Walter D. Mignolo, "Cartas, crónicas y relaciones del descubrimiento y de la conquista," in *Historia de la literatura hispanoamericana. Epoca colonial,* Luis Iñigo Madrigal, coordinator (Madrid, 1982), 57–125; Walter D. Mignolo, "El metatexo historiográfico y la historiografía indiana," *Modern Language Notes* 96 (1981): 358–402.

13. Birgit Scharlau and Mark Munzel, *Quelqay. Mundliche Kultur und Schrifttradition bei Indianern Lateinamerikas* (Frankfurt, 1986); Walter D. Mignolo, "Literacy and Colonization: The New World Experience," *Hispanic Issues* 4 (1989): 51–96.

14. Although this statement could be nuanced, there is a long tradition from Juan Ramón Pané (1493) to Fray Juan de Torquemada (1615), via José de Acosta (1590), in which this belief is clearly expressed. See Walter D. Mignolo "Zur Frage der Schriftlichkeit in der Legitimation der Conquista," in *Der eroberte Kontinent. Historische Realität, Rechtfertigung und literarische Darstellung der Colonisation Americas,* Karl Kohut, ed. (Frankfurt am Main: Vervuert, 1991), 86–102.

15. Jerome S. Bruner, "Going Beyond the Information Given," in Bruner, *Beyond the Information Given* (New York, 1973), 218–39; Eleanor Rosch, "Principles of

Categorization," in *Cognition and Categorization,* E. Rosch and B. Lloyd, eds. (New York, 1978), 28–49; M. M. Bakhtin, "The Problem of Speech Genres," in Bakhtin, *Speech Genres and Other Late Essays,* Vern W. McGee, trans. (Austin, 1986), 60–102; W. D. Mignolo, "Semiosis, Coherence, and Universes of Meaning," in *Text and Discourse Connectedness,* M. E. Conte, J. S. Petrofi and E. Sozer, eds. (Philadelphia, 1989), 483–505.

16. Munro S. Edmonson and Patricia Andrews, *Literatures. Supplement to the Handbook of Middle American Indians,* vol. 3 (Austin, 1985); Miguel León-Portilla, *Toltecayotl. Aspectos de la cultura Náhuatl* (Mexico, 1982), 72–100.

17. Ramón Arzápalo Marín, "The Indian Book in Colonial Yucatán," and Walter D. Mignolo, "Signs and Their Transmission: The Question of the Book in the New World," in *Writing without words: Alternative Literacies in Mesoamerica and the Andes,* Elizabeth H. Boone and Walter D. Mignolo, eds. (Durham: Duke University Press, 1995), 220–70.

18. Diego de Landa, *Relación de las cosas de Yucatán* (1566) trans. by A. M. Tozzer, (Cambridge, 1941) and by Williams Gate, *Yucatan Before and After the Conquest.* New York: Dover, 1978; Diego Valadés, *Rethorica Christiana* (1579; Spanish trans. Mexico, 1989).

19. *Dialogo nel qual si ragiona del modo de accrescere e conservar memoria* (Venice, 1562).

20. For this process of transformation, see Serge Gruzinski, "Peinture et écriture," in *La colonization de l'imaginaire. Sociétés indigènes et occidentalisation dans le Mexique espagnol, XVIe–XVIIe siècle* (Paris, 1988), 15–100.

21. Fray Gerónimo de Mendieta, *Historia eclesiástica indiana* (1595; Mexico, 1971); Bernardino de Sahagún, *Coloquios y Doctrina Christiana (The Coloquios of 1524),* (1565; Miguel León-Portilla, ed. and trans. Mexico, 1986); Jorge Klor de Alva, trans., "The Aztec-Spanish Dialogues, 1524," *Alcheringa* 4, no. 2 (1980): 5–192.

22. *European Literature and the Latin Middle Ages,* W. R. Trask, trans. (1948; rpt. Princeton, 1973).

23. *Bíblos* was the name used in Greece to designate the inner bark of a reed; Greeks called the reed *pápyros.*

24. Joaquín García Icazbalceta, *Nueva colección de documentos para la historia de México. Códice Franciscano. Siglo XVI* (Mexico, 1941), 204.

25. See Antonio de Nebrija, *Introductiones latinae* (Salamanca, 1481); *Grámatica de la lengua castellana* (Salamanca, 1482); and *Reglas de orthografía en la lengua castellana* (Alcalá de Henares, 1517). See also Walter D. Mignolo, "Nebrija in the New World: The Questions of the Letter, the Discontinuity of the Classical Tradition, and the Colonization of the Native Languages," *L'Homme* 122–124 (1992): 187–209.

26. Acosta's letter and Tovar's answer have been reprinted by Joaquín García Icazbalceta in *Don Fray Juan de Zumárraga, Primer Obispo y Arzobispo de México* (Mexico, 1881), 2:263–67. The fourth kind of "barbarians" were defined by Las Casas

in the epilogue of his *Apologética historia sumaria* (1555?; ed. Edmundo O'Gorman, Mexico, 1967).

27. Eric Havelock, *Preface to Plato* (Boston, 1963); Eric Havelock, *The Literate Revolution in Greece and Its Cultural Consequences* (Princeton, 1982). Jacques Derrida's grammatological reflections (*De la grammatologie* [Paris, 1967]), which are difficult to ignore without alarming the érudites in critical theory, did not take into account the tension and conflict between the oral and the written in Plato's philosophy of language or the inversion of Platonic philosophy by the Renaissance philosophy of language.

28. For the semantic field associated with *litteratus/illiteratus* in the Middle Ages, see Michael T. Clanchy, *From Memory to Written Record: England, 1066–1307* (London, 1979). For the Spanish renaissance, see Luis Gil Fernández, *Panorama Social del Humanismo Español (1500–1800)* (Madrid, 1981); and Aron Gurevich, "Popular Culture and Medieval Latin Literature from Caesarius of Arles to Caesarius of Heisterbach," in *Medieval Popular Culture: Problems of Belief and Perception* (Cambridge, 1988), 1–39.

29. The European concepts of historiographical writing in connection with the history of the Indies were laid out in Walter D. Mignolo, "El metatexto historiográfico y la historiografía Indiana," *Modern Language Notes* 96 (1981): 358–402; for Spanish historiography of the period, see S. Montero Díaz, "La doctrina de la Historia en los tratadistas españoles del siglo de Oro," *Hispania* 4 (1941): 3–39. For Italy, see E. Maffei, *I trattati dell'arte storica dal Rinascimento al secolo XVII* (Naples, 1897); and Giorgio Spini, "I trattatisti dell'arte storica nella Controriforma italiana," in *Contributi alla storia del Concilio di Trento e della Controriforma,* Luigi Russo, ed. (Florence, 1948), 109–36.

30. The question, again, is what should be called writing. And the question, again, is whether "writing" in the past and in non-Western cultures should be called that which resembles what Westerners understand by writing. This would be the opinion, for instance, of Walter Ong (*Orality and Literacy: The Technologizing of the Word* [London, 1982]). We could construe a theoretical definition or description of acceptance for writing any kind of graphic system that establishes some kind of link with speech (Piotr Michalowski, "Early Mesopotamian Communicative Systems: Art, Literature, and Writing," in *Investigating Artistic Environments in the Ancient Near East,* Ann C. Gunter, ed. [Washington, D.C., 1990], 53–69), although such a definition may not tell us much about how people conceived graphic interactions in different times and cultures. The etymology of "writing," in several languages, is related to "carving." In Greek *gráphein* meant "to carve." In Latin *scribere* indicated a physical action of inscribing graphic marks in solid surfaces, and it was metaphorically related to "plowing." In Mesoamerica, however, the words referring to "writing" underlined the colors of the inks used and, therefore, the accent was on "painting": *tlacuilo,* in Náhuatl, referred to the scribe and meant, literally, 'behind the painting' (*tla* = behind and *cuilo* = painting). For a description of Mesoamerican writing systems, see Hans Prem and Berthold Riese,

"Autochthonous American Writing Systems: The Aztec and Maya Examples," in *Writing in Focus,* F. Coulmas and K. Ehlich, eds. (New York, 1983).

31. Ignacio Osorio Romero, *Colegios y profesores Jesuitas que enseñaron Latin en Nueva España (1521–1787)* (Mexico, 1979); *Tópicas sobre Cicerón en México* (Mexico, 1976); *La enseñanza del Latín a los indios* (Mexico, 1990).

32. See the masterful summary by Enrique Florescano in "La reconstrucción histórica elaborada por la nobleza indígena y sus descendientes mestizos," in *La memoria y el olvido. Segundo Simposio de Historia de las Mentalidades* (Mexico, 1985), 11–20. See also Andrés Lira González, "Letrados y analfabetas en los pueblos de Indios de la ciudad de México: la historia como alegato para sobrevivir en la sociedad política," in the same volume (61–74).

33. Mercedes de la Garza, "Prólogo," in *Literatura Maya* (Caracas, 1980); Munro S. Edmonson and Victoria Bricker, "Yucatecan Maya Literature," in *Literatures: Supplement to the Handbook of Middle American Indians* (Austin, 1985), 44–63.

34. Diego de Landa, *Relación de las cosas de Yucatán* (ca. 1566); Sanchez de Aguilar, "Informe contra idolorum cultores del obispado de Yucatán [1639]," *Anales* 1, no. 6 (1892): 13–122; Avendaño y Loyola, "Relación de las dos entradas que hice a la conversión de los gentiles ytzaes y cehaches," manuscript (1696), (Newberry Library, Chicago); Diego López Cogolludo, *Historia de Yucatán* (1688; Campeche, 1954).

35. Alfred Tozzer, *Maya Grammar with Bibliography and Appraisement of the Works Noted* (Cambridge, 1921), vol. 9; Ralph L. Roys, *The Book of Chilam Balam of Chumayel* (Washington, D.C., 1933); Mercedes de la Garza, ed., *Literatura Maya* (Caracas, 1980); Dennis Tedlock, trans., with introduction and commentary, *Popol Vuh: The Definitive Edition of the Mayan Book of the Dawn of Life and the Glories of Gods and Kings* (New York, 1985). Adrian Chavez, trans., *Pop Wuj. Libro del tiempo. Poema mito-historico ki-che* (Buenos Aires, 1987).

36. Rigoberta Menchú and Burgos Debray, *I Rigoberta Menchú . . . an Indian Woman from Guatemala* (London, 1984), 13.

37. Roberto González Echevarria, "The Law of the Letter: Garcilaso's *Comentarios* and the Origin of Latin American Narrative," *The Yale Journal of Criticism* 1, no. 1 (1987): 107–31; Rolena Adorno, *Guaman Poma: Writing and Resistance in Colonial Perú* (Austin, 1986).

38. Frank Salomón, "Chronicles of the Impossible: Notes on Three Peruvian Indigenous Historians," in *From Oral to Written Expression: Native Andean Chronicles of the Early Colonial Period,* R. Adorno, ed. (Syracuse, 1982).

Schooling, Language, and Knowledge in Literate and Nonliterate Societies

F. Niyi Akinnaso

The relationships among schooling, language, and knowledge—especially through the systematic comparison of the organization, form, function, and acquisition of institutionalized knowledge—in literate and nonliterate societies has hardly been examined. This essay attempts such an analysis, focusing on knowledge acquired through the use of language, because language is the major medium for imparting knowledge in schools and for social reproduction in the larger society, because knowledge acquired through the use of language is readily identifiable and testable, and because language is one of the major terms of the present analysis. The proposed elastic concept of schooling views schooling as a cover term for institutionalized learning in any society, literate or nonliterate. It thus questions the analytical adequacy of the received, Euro-American, concept of schooling as a unitary phenomenon based on the dual assumption that the school specializes in the transmission of literate knowledge and that literacy education is coterminous with formal education.

The logical corollary to this literacy-based concept of schooling, an oversimplified view of education in nonliterate societies, denies that schooling and its experience exist in these societies. This view contrasts the formal education of the Euro-American model with the informal education or enculturation in nonliterate cultures (see, for example, Roberts and Akinsanya 1976). Stanley Diamond provides a simplistic summary of the canonical perspective on education in nonliterate societies:

Learning in such societies is embedded in socialization. That is, the learning of skills and attitudes has not been functionally rationalized in segregated institutions; it takes place in a network of personal relations based on the

339

paradigm of kinship. There are no socially discrete and discontinuous, hierarchically structured, impersonally administered learning groups; and there are no subtly engineered examination systems creating and perpetuating an "educational elite." Formal schools in primitive societies would be as strange and as repugnant as jails. (Diamond 1971:301)

This simplistic view gives rise to the major misconception that education in nonliterate societies either does not exist in terms of organized training or the systematic transfer of advanced knowledge or, if it exists, does not promote social differentiation or foster subcultures (Ridout 1971).

Such notions about education in nonliterate societies apparently derive, in part, from a narrow, ethnocentric view of schooling that misconstrues the true nature of education. I shall argue that schooling, by no means an alien practice in these societies, does occur in them, but scholars have hardly acknowledged this because they are unwilling to recognize schooling as a variable cultural practice organized in a variety of ways for a variety of aims. Just as the lexicon and grammar of a language are tailored to suit the needs of its speakers, so, in some sense, schools and school learning strategies are often tailored to suit the social needs of a given society, reinforcing Durkheim's position that education can do no more than reflect society.

I shall refer to knowledge acquired in schools and school-like settings as institutionalized knowledge. This is knowledge whose form and content are relatively standardized and based on values deriving from a group's collective representations rather than the whims and caprices of individuals (see Durkheim 1915). Such knowledge is usually consciously imparted and consciously learned. This essay draws upon cross-cultural comparative data from various nonliterate societies; describes the organization, form, function, and acquisition of institutionalized knowledge; then uses these findings as a grid to reexamine several continua of variations in types of learning and types of knowledge. It provides an extended analysis of data on Yoruba divination against these backgrounds, highlighting the relationships among schooling, language, and knowledge in a nonliterate society. These findings indicate that literacy is not a precondition for the existence of schooling and its experience and that the distinction between formal and informal learning does not depend on, nor is it isomorphic with, the distinction between literacy and nonliteracy. If these findings are taken seriously, then they suggest several implications about the received interpretations of literacy and school learning, in particular, and social theory, in general. Some of these implications are highlighted and discussed, although none exhaustively.

Background

The convergence of interests in the theory and practice of literacy that has blossomed within the past two decades has led to a flood of comparative studies of literate and nonliterate cultures, especially of the differential forms of knowledge associated with the two types of sociocultural organization (see, for example, Goody 1977, 1986, 1987; Scribner and Cole 1973, 1981; Ong 1982; Street 1984; Cook-Gumperz 1986; Olson 1977, 1988; Olson, Torrance, and Hildyard 1985; Finnegan 1988; Schousboe and Larsen 1989). One emerging focus of interest is the relationship between formal and informal learning and the nature of knowledge fostered by each type of learning in both literate and nonliterate societies.

Despite the flood of such studies, it is fair to say that, due largely to several interrelated factors, much less progress has been made in understanding the nature and role of formal education and forms of knowledge in nonliterate societies than in understanding these same phenomena in literate societies. First, literacy, schooling, and even formal learning were thought to be coterminous until recently, when a distinction was drawn between them, especially by Scribner and Cole (1973, 1981). Second, more work on literacy has been devoted to the uses and functions of literacy and literate knowledge than to exploring the resources used in nonliterate societies to perform the functions conventionally associated with literacy. The resulting bias for preserved records fostered by the adoption of writing has entailed the neglect of areas of human experience for which there are no records (see especially Ewald 1988). Third, the ubiquity of Western-type schools, the universalization of mass schooling, and the increasing focus on the educational role of schools in literate societies have led to the diminishing interest in the educational role of comparable institutions in nonliterate societies. Thus, the diploma disease developed and nurtured by the credential society has intensified the diminishing interest in the knowledge structures of noncredential societies. Finally, until very recently, anthropologists ignored the role of schools and schooling in traditional societies, focusing instead on traditional patterns of socialization and enculturation and avoiding direct comparisons between Western and traditional schooling practices. Indeed, early anthropologists, with the possible exception of Melville Herskovits (see below), did not consider schooling a traditional institution; rather, they regarded schooling as a colonial intrusion and its study as an analysis of social and cultural change for which traditional ethnographic and structural-functionalist theories were ill equipped. Those early anthropologists who did venture to examine the role of Western-type schools in traditional

societies limited their investigations essentially to the clash of cultures between Western and traditional education, thus focusing on discontinuities and
ignoring possible similarities (see, for example, essays by Read, Redfield,
Nash, and the Hunts in Middleton 1970).

The adoption of the distinction between oral and literate culture as the given
starting point, leading to a focus on the differences and conflicts between the
two cultural traditions, is perhaps the major reason for the lopsidedness in
literacy research. Against this dichotomous stance, some researchers have set
up polar typologies that reify orality and literacy, putting their faith in the latter
and, therefore, emphasizing its essential elements (for further discussion and
critique of the typologies, see Akinnaso 1981, 1982a, 1985; Street 1984; Finnegan 1988; Ewald 1988; Schousboe and Larsen 1989). Although all researchers agree that literacy involves major changes in forms of communication and the organization of knowledge, they do not agree on the social,
political, economic, and, especially, cognitive consequences of these changes.
There are, however, basically two schools of thought.

One school includes Havelock, McLuhan, Olson, Ong, Stock, and early
Goody. It proposes a deterministic model that projects literacy as a causal agent
and interprets the sociocultural changes associated with it in terms of epistemic
changes. The development of writing is also linked to that of science (Goody
1977:51); of the city (Sjoberg 1960:33); and of a vast range of social, economic, and political structures (Goody 1977, 1986; Ong 1982). These scholars
commonly assume that schooling developed only after writing was adopted.
Hence, the school, regarded as the "central institution of literate culture"
(Goody 1982:204), is thought to be peculiar to literate societies.

Goody's extensive work on literacy (notably, Goody and Watt 1963; Goody
1968, 1977, 1980, 1986, 1987) highlights the causative argument (which, at its
extreme, tends to portray literacy as an autonomous agent in social evolution),
while demonstrating the facilitating argument (literacy as a social construct,
with culture-specific consequences). Thus, although Goody acknowledges in
some places that literacy is a variable resource for storing, augmenting, and
disseminating knowledge (e.g., Goody 1986), he nevertheless presents literacy
in other places as a mode of creating knowledge, arguing, for example, that the
development of science "*followed* the introduction of major changes in the
channels of communication in Babylonia (writing), in ancient Greece (the
alphabet), and in Western Europe (printing)" (1977:51, emphasis added) and
wondering why anthropologists accepted the equation that man equals language but avoided the one that equates civilization with writing (1980:120).

The other school, typified by Scribner, Cole, Graff, Finnegan, Street, and, sometimes, Eisenstein, has been more cautious in interpreting the sociocultural changes associated with literacy. These changes are seen as resulting more in altered social and institutional practices than in the development of unique cognitive operations and social structures. To advocates of this view, then, literacy is a facilitating or enabling agent, promoting the elaboration of preexisting structures and the deployment of preexisting cognitive capacities into specific channels socially and ideologically sanctioned by the user group.

Scribner and Cole are particularly careful in distinguishing between cognitive capacities and cognitive skills, arguing that the former are universal and uniform while the latter are culture-specific and variable (Scribner and Cole 1973; Cole and Scribner 1974). Thus, although literacy facilitates the acquisition of certain cognitive skills and operations, it does not, in itself, engender novel cognitive capacities (see also Akinnaso 1981). The effects of literacy, they argue, are better studied through empirical comparisons of literate and nonliterate subjects than through the analysis of sociohistorical data.

No wonder, then, that Scribner and Cole were among the first to question the lopsidedness in literacy research (Scribner and Cole 1973; Cole and Scribner 1974). Their 1973 study, the first explicit comparison of formal and informal learning in both literate and nonliterate societies, highlights the need to look back to the organization and transmission of knowledge in nonliterate societies in the hope of finding significant contributions to our knowledge of formal learning and literacy education. However, their study fell short of recognizing the existence of schooling as an indigenous institution in nonliterate societies. Moreover, because their main interest was in formal education's cognitive consequences, Scribner and Cole based their comparison on "the differential intellectual consequences of formal learning embodied in the school and the informal learning of practical life" (1973:553), thus emphasizing the discontinuities between formal and informal education.

This leads to an apparently endemic major flaw in the comparative study of oral and literate cultures, namely the comparison of mismatched parameters (see Akinnaso 1982a, 1985; Tannen 1982; Biber 1988). Scribner and Cole recognized that the ideal comparison should have been between formal learning in literate and nonliterate societies and blamed the mismatch on lack of sufficient data concerning the nature and dynamics of formal learning in nonliterate societies (1973:555). But perhaps another reason for limiting such comparisons to formal (school) versus informal (practical) learning was the dual assumption that the institution of schooling does not exist in nonliterate societies and, therefore, that what could be termed formal education in such societies takes place only in noninstitutional settings (1973:555). If these assumptions hold true, then significant discontinuities are not likely to exist between formal and informal learning within nonliterate societies. Does it then follow that nonliterate societies totally lack the functional learning systems fostered by formal learning and associated with schooled literacy? Could Stanley Diamond have been right in his denigrating views about education in such societies?

The wide range of studies now available provides further evidence for extending the initial observations by Scribner and Cole (1973) and reexamining Diamond's (1971) characterization of learning in nonliterate societies. For a start, I will limit discussion to two groups of studies: one on the learning and cognitive demands of navigational skills in Micronesia and medieval Europe and the other on the social organization of learning in secret societies in Western and Eastern Africa.

Previous Studies

Anthropologists and cognitive psychologists are by now very familiar with the studies of navigation in Micronesia and medieval Europe by Gladwin (1970), Lewis (1972), Finney (1976), Frake (1985), and Gell (1985). The earlier studies by Gladwin, Lewis, and Finney provide detailed information on how nonliterate seafarers were trained in the hazardous and cognitively demanding art and science of navigation, while the latter studies by Frake and Gell examine the cognitive and logical basis of navigation. Frake (1985:256) summarizes the importance of these earlier studies:

> The lesson to be drawn from these studies is that the islanders' seafaring exploits do not depend on some uncanny intuitive powers, nor on personality quirks driving people to seek danger, nor on the luck of lost sailors adrift at sea, nor even on rote-learned "local knowledge." Instead these navigational abilities depend on a profound general knowledge of the sea, the sky and the wind; on a superb understanding of the principles of boatbuilding and sailing; and on cognitive devices—all in the head—for recording and processing vast quantities of ever changing information.

We also learn from these studies how novices were taught the complex skills of navigation (see, in particular, Gladwin 1970). Scribner and Cole (1973:555) themselves commented on the instructional strategies as follows:

> He [Gladwin] makes abundantly clear that formal instruction of this kind represents more than apprentice training; it involves didactic teaching and

the deliberate, disciplined mastery of large bodies of information which are embedded in well-developed theoretical frameworks.

Surely we are dealing here with the acquisition of specialized knowledge. Whatever the dynamics of the teaching and learning processes might be, they could not have been haphazard nor simply embedded in informal socialization processes. If they were, everyone in these societies would have been a navigator. The ethnographic fact is clear: only a very few succeeded in learning the art and science of navigation, and even fewer were able to apply the acquired skills.

Alfred Gell's argument that all navigation, from the simplest to the most sophisticated, has a uniform logical basis (1985) supports Frake's submission that preliterate seafarers had the cognitive capacities and skills to learn and practice the complex art of navigation. The complex cognitive devices that they developed for correlating solar with lunar time, and their oral construction of regimes of the moon and tide, provided the basis for written and, more recently, computerized tide and current tables which the modern sailor, like his preliterate predecessor, normally acquires through special schooling.

The second group of studies, by Watkins (1943), Little (1949, 1965, 1966), Gibbs (1965), Fulton (1972), Lancy (1975), and Murphy (1980), focuses on the training of novices in a West African secret society, what and how they learn, the uses of the knowledge, and the relationship between specialized knowledge and social structure. Following an earlier study by Wallis (1904), Watkins (1943) provides perhaps the first detailed account of the educational relevance of *poro* training, a widespread educational scheme among the Mende, Vai, Kpelle, Krima, Gola, and other related groups in West Africa. Focusing on the Mende and Vai practices, the study reveals that "every district or subchiefdom has its own school [for poro training] and special reserved forest for the purpose" (1943:668); that the period of training lasts from two to eight years, depending on the group (1943:669); that "the first instruction involves a series of tests in order to determine individual differences, interests, and ambitions" (1943:670); that the instruction given is wide-ranging, covering "all the arts, crafts, and lore of native life, including a variety of games and sports, . . . all the laws and traditions of the tribe, . . . recognition and use of various medicinal herbs," and "the secrets of wild animals . . . how they live, how to recognize their spoor, and how to attack them" (1943:670–71); and that a final examination is administered prior to graduation: "The boys make a number of demonstrations, covering a day or more. Then there are various examinations administered by the representatives [of the tribal chief and elders who constitute the Board of Examiners]" (1943:672). The richness of the curricula, the formality of the training, the reliance on language for part of the instruction, and the intensity of the "thorough physical, mental, and moral test" (1943:672) administered to the trainees no doubt led Watkins to consider poro training as schooling, hence his description of the training ground as "the 'bush' school."

Lancy (1975) takes Watkins's study a step further by providing a point-by-point comparison of the organization of learning in poro training and in Liberian public schools. In both types of school, learning is formally organized and takes place in prescribed settings and at prescribed times. Teachers (initiators) are officially distinguished from learners (initiates). The same techniques, such as rote memorization and avoidance learning, are employed, and the consequences of learning are similar:

> Like the initiation ceremony, the school confers status, indoctrinates with esoteric and useless information, and changes the pupil's view of himself, his family, and his society. (Lancy 1975:379)

The bush school thus provides a template upon which the characteristics of the public school are built. To those children who migrated between the two types of school, one was, in a sense, an extension of the other (Murphy 1980).

Drawing upon data from the same ethnographic area, Murphy (1980) provides findings that are essentially complementary to those of Watkins and Lancy. Murphy's account provides more data about the duration of training and subject matter in the bush schools. Training averages about four years, and the subjects include history; medicine; poisoning skills; special esoteric language; secrets and skills associated with sex roles; agricultural skills and technical skills for making baskets, mats, hammocks, and so forth. Special emphasis is placed on knowledge of history, medicine, and esoteric language because such knowledge constitutes the special powers of the successful learner. Once initiated, elders make special efforts in sustaining the barriers and boundaries that protect their knowledge from encroachments. An initial step in this direction is the oath of secrecy administered to the initiate before he is taught anything. Although Murphy does not address the issue of formality as such, his analysis of the social organization of poro training sheds further light on how specialized knowledge is acquired and used in nonliterate societies. More significantly, he concurs with Watkins, Lancy, and others that the bush school is an appropriate referent for poro training.

The poro initiation and training apparently underlie most forms of formal training among the Kpelle, who attach a great deal of importance to apprenticeship training (Lancy 1975, 1980). Typically, a skilled Kpelle worker often needs to know more than the skills of his craft or trade. For example, the blacksmith must master all three subroles of "the skilled worker, the big-man and the medicine man" in order to fulfill that role effectively (Lancy 1980:267). Informal and formal training, with emphasis on the latter, enable the worker to fulfill these requirements. Thus, although "observation and imitation as learning techniques are present[,] . . . there is a much greater emphasis on performance, evaluation, and motivation" (Lancy 1980:270).

Jack Goody's comparative study of alternative paths to knowledge in oral and literate cultures provides evidence which corroborates the above findings (Goody 1982, also 1987: chap. 7). Drawing upon his research among the LoDagaa of Northern Ghana, Goody distinguishes three modes of acquiring knowledge in nonliterate societies: the practical, traditional, and spiritual. Among these people, traditional knowledge is specialized knowledge that the natives themselves recognize as such. This type of knowledge "is transmitted in the partially decontextualized situation of the Bagre . . . as well as in the course of other ceremonies" (1982:208). Goody (1982:204) comments further:

One aspect of this knowledge is a certain similarity, in the setting of its transfer, with the way that written knowledge, and knowledge of writing, is transferred in that central institution of literate culture, the school itself. The neophytes are separated off from society by being enclosed within the walls of the long-room, where they are kept cooped up for several hours at a time.

Moreover, we are told that the primary mode of transmission in the *Bagre* ceremony is language (1982:202) and that the long myth recited to neophytes in the course of the ceremony "is partly about the ceremony itself and partly about the origin of culture and the problems of mankind" (1982:203). Thus, the language of the myth is both informative and metacommunicative. There is also evidence of change and incremental growth in the knowledge acquired:

I am concerned to stress that oral cultures are not simply incessant re-duplications of the same thing, the model of perfect reproduction, a pre-literate photo-copier. There is some growth, or at least change of knowledge, sometimes perceived as growth by the actors. (Goody 1982:207)

The West African findings are replicated in East Africa, where the Luba of Zaire practice similar training procedures for initiates into the Bumbudye secret society (Burton 1961; Reefe 1975, 1977; Studstill 1979). A very different picture of formal learning in Luba society emerges from these studies from that which others have led us to expect.

We learn that kinship is not the basis for membership or advancement in the Bumbudye secret society (Reefe 1975:106; Studstill 1979:73). In terms of the social organization of learning, the society offers at least seven main grades of tuition, each lower grade a prerequisite to admission to the next higher grade. Each grade specializes in one or two main areas of knowledge, which include religion, history, geography, and (oral) literature. For example, during the second grade, locally known as *kusubuka,* "the candidate learned the names and significance of many symbols and deities which were carved out of wood in the early days, but which later tended to be simply drawn in the sand or indicated with a stick," while the third stage teaches "in addition to geography . . . a sign language which could be used by the Bumbudye to send messages written on wood or bark. These were used in medical ritual and healing also" (Studstill 1979:73–74). Burton (1961:166) corroborates this with an account of how geography is taught in the seclusion of a hut called the *lukala:*

> [On the walls of the lukala], the whole country from the Lualaba to the Sankuru (approximately 200 miles) is marked, with the chief lakes and rivers, the noted abodes of spirits, and the capitals of the various chiefs. The initiate is questioned as to where each chief resides, and where each river flows, the names of the tutelary spirits of each locality, etc.

The fourth stage, "at which one became an important figure in the hierarchy of authority" (Studstill 1979:74), deals with learning the complex symbolism of the *nkasa* (singular lukasa). "The nkasa were mnemonic devices made of a hand-sized piece of wood encrusted with beads and shells, repositories of a vast amount of oral literature and other information" (1979:74). There are at least three distinct categories of nkasa, each emphasizing a certain kind of knowledge (Reefe 1970:50). For example, one category, called *lukasa lwa nkunda,* "the long hand of the pigeon," bears information on mythical heroes and early rulers and on the mythical migration routes of the Luba. The symbolism of the nkasa is extremely complex, as each bead and shell can be interpreted in a variety of ways at the same time, the interpretation in each case depending on the nature of the enquiry. Thus, in the analysis of one lukasa alone, Studstill was provided with cosmological, mythical, historical, and sociological interpretations of the different cowries, carved markings, and bead patterns (1979:75).

What is of immediate importance here is that the Bumbudye association of the Luba provides a model of formal learning replete with features which are thought to be unique to Western schooling (see Studstill 1979, for details). Studstill, with particular reference to Diamond's views, sums up the similarities between Bumbudye training and modern schooling:

> The system apparently included precisely the "hierarchically structured, impersonally administered learning groups," with "subtly engineered examination systems creating and perpetuating an educated elite," to which Diamond refers in modern schooling systems. (1979:76)

Studstill's remarks have very wide applicability beyond Africa. For example, there is a great deal of evidence that elaborate schooling was also practised in preliterate Polynesia. According to Luomala, "New Zealand and the Society Islands had famous houses of learning, really primitive universities, at which the ancestral lore, genealogies, traditions, religion, magic, navigation, agriculture, literary composition, and all the arts and crafts were taught by learned priests" (cited in Herskovits 1973:45). In New Zealand, in particular, aboriginal schools opened for five months out of the year, teaching the youth from dawn until midnight. There were two main courses of study: the Upper Jaw, which dealt with cosmology and the gods; and the Lower Jaw, which treated earthly matters. Lessons were held in detached settings, and teachers were not necessarily the relatives of the learners. These observations inevitably take us back to Melville Herskovits who, as far back as 1947, maintained against the majority that schooling was part of the educational system of nonliterate societies:

> Education carried on by means of schooling in the hands of specialists cannot be overlooked in considering the training of the young among nonliterate peoples. . . . Africa and Polynesia provide most instances of schooling, properly speaking, in nonliterate cultures. (Herskovits 1973:43)

Types of Learning

The above accounts provide a basis for distinguishing between the two fundamental types of learning, namely, informal and formal learning. The conjunctive behavior of two features, formality and institutionalization, is central to the distinction. Ideally, informal learning lacks both features, whereas formal learning is characterized by the presence of both (for more details on the concept of formality in social analysis, see Irvine 1979). Learning is said to be formal when several aspects of the learning environment and the activities that take place within it, and the content, can be said to be systematically organized in some specifiable ways (for case studies, see Irvine 1979; Akinnaso 1985). Formality and informality, as used here, should be viewed as a continuous dimension of variation, rather than a rigid dichotomy between types of learning and types of knowledge. However, the terms of the following analysis give the impression of a dichotomy only because emphasis is placed on issues on opposite ends of the continuum; but the goal is to draw the essential contrast between two ideal types. As in real life, formal and informal learning overlap considerably, as do distinctions between practical and specialized knowledge.

Informal Learning

Most studies of informal learning have been done in nonliterate societies and by anthropologists as part of more general enquiries into socialization or enculturation processes (see, for example, Mead 1928, 1930, 1943, 1964; Fortes 1970; Raum 1940; Whiting 1941; Cohen 1971). These studies have repeatedly drawn attention to four major characteristics of informal learning: particularism, contextualization, observation, and imitation. Informal learning is said to be particularistic because it occurs in closed social networks, such as the family and the peer group, and because the content of learning is often inseparable from the teacher's identity. In other words, the value of what is learned is closely related to the identity of the teacher, just as the expectations for performance are phrased in terms of the identity of the learner instead of what he has accomplished (Cohen 1971:25), thus reinforcing Cohen's claim that informal learning fuses emotional and intellectual domains.

The second characteristic, contextualization, is the interaction among the learner, teacher, context and activity. In informal learning, optimal contextualization is achieved when all four features are in close interaction. The interaction among these features underlies Fortes's tripartite formula for informal learning, which consists of mimesis, identification, and cooperation (Fortes 1970) and which Margaret Mead endorsed under the terms of imitation, identification, and empathy (Mead 1964). Contextualization entails the third and fourth characteristics of informal learning: observation and imitation. Because informal learning is embedded in ongoing activity, there is little or no need for language to mediate the learning process. Instead, learning is done by watching (observation) and doing (imitation) rather than by decoding words and interpreting rules.

Expressive behavior, including language, tends to be relaxed in informal learning because of the emphasis on contextualization, observation, and imitation and because of the absence of institutional sanctions. Rules and regulations are absent; the dynamic situation takes care of language choice and demeanor. Finally, informal learning is embedded in everyday life, taking place consciously or unconsciously. For such learning to take place, no prescribed setting, schedule, topic, centralized focus, or institutional structures are necessary. Furthermore, fees are not normally charged, just as there is no direct social investment in the learning process.

Formal Learning

With the study of secret societies and highly specialized rituals, anthropologists moved from everyday socialization processes to the processes by which specialized knowledge is transmitted in nonliterate societies. Such studies as those previously reviewed provide us with information about the nature of formal learning in such societies. Similarly, we can infer the salient characteristics of formal learning in literate societies from studies of school learning, especially by cognitive and developmental psychologists as well as school ethnographers.

Formal learning displays certain common characteristics across time and space. First, it is a form of learning organized deliberately to fulfill the specific purpose of transmitting certain values, attitudes, skills and forms of knowledge worthy of special transmission within a given society. The emphasis on what is transmitted in a particular case varies from culture to culture and from program to program within a given culture. For example, among the Yoruba of Southwestern Nigeria, certain didactic rituals, such as *aàpọ̀n* among the Idanre subgroup, emphasize the values and expectations associated with male social maturation; but others, such as initiation and training in the *ifá* cult, involve the transmission of a broad range of values, attitudes, skills, and various forms of specialized knowledge discussed below.

In order for formal learning to be effective, it is usually separated from normal, daily routines; hence its second major characteristic is decontextualization. Ideally, unlike informal learning, formal learning involves minimal or reduced interaction among learner, teacher, context, and action. Typically, the learner is separated from home, placed under a distinct authority and put through standardized activities and systematized procedures. As learning becomes the focus of activity, forms of symbolism, such as rules and words, gain prominence over demonstration as the mechanism of learning. We saw, for example, in the Bumbudye secret society, how language replaced demonstration in the geography lesson and in interpreting the nkasa. This aspect of formal learning is at the heart of studies of school learning by such cognitive psychologists as Jerome Bruner (1966:62):

> the important thing about school as now constituted is that it is removed from the immediate context of socially relevant action. This very disengagement makes learning an act in itself and makes it possible to embed it in a context of language and symbolic activity . . . words are the major invitations to form concepts rather than action.

The shift from demonstration to language as the primary mode of transmission leads to linguistic discontinuities and the development of register peculiarities, especially phonological elaboration and esoteric lexicon (Akinnaso 1982b, 1985). Thus the language of formal education takes on special characteristics of its own, attracting special labels, such as ritual or literate or written language and elaborated code. In extreme cases, as in the lower Congo, initiates must avoid speaking their natural language and instead may only use a special language (Van Gennep 1960:81), just as Latin was used as the language of learning in Renaissance Europe (Ong 1959, 1971). Ong's use of ritual metaphors in discussing the role of Latin during this period is very suggestive: learning Latin was seen as "a renaissance puberty rite" (1959:103) and "the first step toward initiation into the closed world" (1971:121). Drawing upon Ames' work, Goody (1986:26) provides a comparative case from South Asia: in Sri Lankan monastic education, "much of the learning utilizes a dead language, Pali, preserved for religious purposes in a manner that resembles the use of Latin in medieval Europe."

The third important characteristic of formal or school learning, institutionalization, is the degree to which the social group or, more usually, a professional group, takes responsibility for the mode, form, and content of learning. The institutionalization of schooling (Ramirez and Boli 1987) and of certain ritual practices (Lancy 1975; Murphy 1980; Akinnaso 1982b) is part of the attempt by nation-states or social groups to perform the more usual functions of indoctrination and social role selection while also controlling access to specialized knowledge and power.

Institutionalization leads to several consequences. One is that the place of learning becomes a school, leading to a shift from one or two learners drawn from the demonstrator's closed network (a notable characteristic of informal learning) to a group of learners drawn from an open network much larger than the teacher's. For example, " 'Bush schools' [for poro training] are often large, sometimes containing several hundred initiates at a time" (Murphy 1980:196).

Although learners are drawn from disparate backgrounds, they often must fulfill an additional requirement of sharing certain verifiable qualifications, such as age, sex, ethnicity, certain skills or abilities, or membership in a religious group or social circle. Moreover, the group or class status of the learners is often marked by special uniforms, costumes, bodily marks, or, as in some initiation rituals, no clothing at all.

Another consequence is that teachers, often clearly designated as such, although the terms vary from society to society, replace the familiar figures (parents and peers) who characterized informal learning. Whatever the terms used, the designation is both real and symbolic: teachers are usually older, sometimes dress specially (or at least differently), and have titles. They are usually strangers to the novices or learners and are associated with special knowledge and power.

A third feature of institutionalization, the establishment of rules, regulations, and conventions, governs the appearance, language use, and behavior of both learners and their teachers. These rules, regulations, and conventions typically derive from values sanctioned by the affected professional groups— ritual performers in nonliterate societies and literate professionals in literate societies. The specialization of language learned in school (to which we shall return later) results from such rules, regulations, and conventions. Although their primary goal is to regulate the conduct of school activities and the behavior of teachers and learners, these rules, regulations, and conventions often function as a boundary between formal and informal learning, on the one hand, and between the school and the rest of society, on the other. As Barth (1990:643) observed in his study of the *guru-dama* relationship in Bhutan, the regulated language of formal learning thrives on

> strategies of mystifying, complicating and interposing an elaborate ceremonial language of honorific or technical terms . . . [which] serve primarily to lengthen and enhance the relationship between Guru and pupil, and to exclude outsiders from the circle of disciples.

A fourth consequence of institutionalization, the investment of huge amounts of capital in the learning enterprise, occurs usually through the heavy taxation of individual learners or through the diversion of the group's or nation's accumulated resources to educational investment. In nonliterate societies, "there seems to be no activity . . . which soaks up more of the group's resources than initiation" (Lancy 1975:376). Among the Ojibway of North America, an initiate reckoned he paid up to $10,000 for initiation (Goody

1982:206). Among the Luba, "initiation fees were paid in the form of beads and shell money, copper crosses, which were also used as currency by the Luba, chickens and goats" (Studstill 1979:73). Similarly high initiation fees have been documented for apprenticeship to Yoruba cults of divination (Bascom 1969, 1980; Abimbola 1976). Furthermore, communal contributions of money, labor, equipment toward the construction of shrines and the performance of communal rituals are quite common in nonliterate societies as are contributions of "food, goods, and money extracted from the parents of children in the 'bush schools' " (Murphy 1980:200). These high initiation fees and communal contributions parallel expensive tuition (especially in professional schools) and the huge budgetary allocation for education in literate societies. Perhaps one dominant characteristic of formal learning that emerges from the above description is the incorporation of an elaborate ritual and symbolic order that sets apart the province of meaning from the paramount reality of everyday life (Kapferer 1981:261). In a sense, most other characteristics of formal learning derive from its ritual nature (see Akinnaso 1985, for details).

Types of Knowledge

The qualitative differences between informal and formal learning lead to differences in types of knowledge. The basic distinction here is between practical and specialized knowledge. Practical knowledge is normally acquired through informal learning, that is, in interaction, largely within the home and the peer group; through participation in the events themselves; and through experience. Consequently, practical knowledge is not a secret form of knowledge but, rather, one that members of a given society normally share equally. It provides not only the basis for cultural membership in a group but the basic information required to function as an ordinary member of that society. Specialized knowledge, on the other hand, is normally transmitted in institutions through formal learning. Different cultures envision specialized knowledge in different ways: as power, wealth, property, a prerequisite for membership in a group, or as a technical requirement for performing certain acts or functions (Murphy 1980; Barth 1990). This may well explain why specialized knowledge is often protected (sometimes hoarded) by particular individuals, professional groups, or institutions and why certain minimum qualifications and expensive tuition are often required for access to such knowledge.

Although specialized knowledge is not necessarily regarded as a secret form in contemporary literate societies, there are numerous subtle, and even legal, ways of guarding such knowledge, especially through the activities of professional associations and, sometimes, government bureaucracies. Despite the professed public nature of information in literate societies, access to specialized knowledge is often constrained by social, structural, and hidden factors; and knowledge and the uses of writing, though no longer limited by law as they used to be (see Gelb 1952), remain limited in practice and, especially, in degree and quality.

Not all forms of specialized knowledge are transmitted in institutions, although prior institutional learning is apparently necessary to gain full comprehension of that knowledge. For example, certain kinds of specialized knowledge are acquired in the course of ceremonies and discussion with elders (see Goody 1982). This, however, represents a leakage of secret or professional knowledge of the sort that results from watching a specialized television network news program, such as NBC's "Meet the Press," in which professionals are engaged in serious discussion.

Spiritual knowledge is a form that is not mediated by humans but comes directly from those supernatural powers, spiritual forces, and other agencies believed to control the ability to reveal the secrets of the universe to man (see, e.g., Goody 1982). The acquisition of spiritual knowledge is often linked with some form of dissociation or inspiration: a detached setting, such as the shrine, the woods, or the bedroom; unusual times, such as the dead of night; or some kind of psychophysical transformation, such as visions, trances, and dreams. I will not be concerned with this or any noninstitutional form of knowledge.

Initiation and Schooling in a Nonliterate Society

Against the above backgrounds, the remainder of this essay provides a description of one type of institutionalized knowledge, namely, divination, among Yoruba in southwestern Nigeria and shows how that form of knowledge is transmitted in the school in the sense in which the term is used here. What type of knowledge is divination? What is its structure? How is it acquired? What is the nature of the linguistic form in which this knowledge is encoded? To what extent can the learning of divination be regarded as formal learning? I shall attempt to answer some of these questions below. However, two preliminaries are necessary. First, it is necessary to distinguish between initiation and schooling. The former is used henceforth in a restricted sense to refer to the rites, ceremonies, or instructions with which one is made a member of a cult, sect, society, or some special group or certified as having completed a set of instructions or satisfied certain prescribed standards; but the latter refers to formal, institutional learning and instructional practices of a more enduring character.

In general, initiation is often shrouded in secrecy and mystery because it is based on the idea that "the value of knowledge is enhanced by veiling it and sharing it with as few as possible" (Barth 1990:641). Moreover, initiation performances are largely nonverbal and symbolic; and, as Barth (1990:643) has observed, "The novices are supposed to be transformed by the rite itself, not by what has been transmitted to them of the knowledge it contains."

In Yoruba divination, as we shall see, initiation occurs at major points of transition to accept the prospective trainee formally into the appropriate cult; to mark major transitions from one grade to another during training; and to accept the trainee formally into professional practice (see Bascom 1969). This should be distinguished from the more rigorous training sessions of schooling, which may last several years. Initiation may be an integral component of schooling or can occur by itself, outside of schooling, as in some initiation ceremonies, such as *aàpón* (the Idanre dialectal term for a male maturation ritual). Unlike initiation rituals, schooling's major goal is to impart knowledge and skills to accredited learners rather than hide them. If this distinction between initiation and schooling is applied to formal training in the Kpelle and Luba secret societies discussed earlier, then it becomes clear that the initiation training generally described in the literature is indeed more complex and consists of both initiation and schooling as defined here.

Second, rather than describing learning as it actually occurred in a particular setting, I will be positing an idealized version of how the knowledge of divination is acquired, thus emphasizing the general properties of Yoruba divination. In doing this, however, I shall draw upon published work on Yoruba divination and my own ethnographic work and experience in Yoruba culture, my primary culture. There is an implicit comparison with the social organization of learning in Western-type schools, a comparison I shall draw more explicitly later.

The Process of Divination

Divination is a specialized ritual which uses extraordinary powers of communication to reveal occult realities. These revelations serve to reassure members of a society as to their precise standing in relation to one another, to the society as a whole, and to the cosmological order that includes, at one end, the plants and beings of the wild and, at the other end, the ancestors and the gods. The success and persistence of divination rituals, like other specialized rituals, depend largely on this reassurance (see Leach 1968; Werbner 1989).

The Yoruba are known to practice as many as five or six methods of divination (Bascom 1969). However, the most important and reliable methods are those based on the manipulation of palm nuts, cowry shells, or a divining chain and the recitation of specific oral texts associated with particular configurations of these objects. Only two types of divination are text–based in this sense, namely, *ifá* and *ẹ̀ẹ̀rìndínlógún* (also referred to as the "sixteen-cowry" divination or simply "sixteen cowries"; see Bascom 1980). The striking similarities between the two types (see below) make it possible to regard them as variations of the same system of divination. At the same time, however, each has unique characteristics (also discussed below), which qualify it for separate treatment. For example, each type of text-based divination is practised within a distinctive cult. These cults are widespread, with practitioners in Nigeria, Benin Republic (old Dahomey), Porto Novo, Brazil, and Cuba (see especially Bascom 1952, 1969). Although *ifá* is by far the most popular and the most respected form of divination among the Yoruba, the focus here is on *ẹ̀ẹ̀rìndínlógún* because I have been studying this system for quite some time and because (as Bascom rightly observed) it has received much less attention than it deserves. However, while focusing on *ẹ̀ẹ̀rìndínlógún,* corroborative or supplementary data will be provided for *ifá,* as appropriate.

Like *ifá* (see Bascom 1969; Abimbola 1976, 1977, for details), *ẹ̀ẹ̀rìndínlógún* divination is both a body of knowledge and a system of social, emotional, and pathological control, employing relevant historical and mythological precedents contained in the special divination corpus to be recited, chanted, or sung (as appropriate) by the diviner. Although a simpler system than *ifá,* both in its textual repertoire and in its range of applications, it is, nevertheless, very similar (indeed, identical in some respects) to *ifá* because it is a mythological, historical, and structural derivative of *ifá* (Bascom 1980:18–21; Akinnaso 1982b). To a great extent the *ifá* and *ẹ̀ẹ̀rìndínlógún* texts share similar myths, stories, and themes and employ similar methods of acquisition and performance.

The basic differences between the two texts are in the size of the corpus to be memorized and recited by the diviner and the instruments and methods used in invoking the text to be recited in a given case. Whereas *ifá* makes use of 256 (16 times 16) configurations (of the divining instrument), of which 16 are basic, *ẹ̀ẹ̀rìnínlógún* makes use of 17 configurations, which parallel the 16 basic *ifá* configurations (see Bascom 1980). Furthermore, while *ifá* makes use of *ìkín* sacred palm nuts as the instrument for invoking the appropriate text, *ẹ̀ẹ̀rìndínlógún* employs *owó ẹ̀rọ̀ mẹ́ẹ̀rìndínlógún,* the "sixteen sacred cowry shells" that gave the system its name. Interestingly, the number of palm nuts used in *ifá* is also sixteen, the same number of basic *odù* in both systems. *Ifá* also makes use of the *ọ̀pẹ̀lẹ̀* (the divining chain), whereas *ẹ̀ẹ̀rìndínlógún* does not appear to have an alternative instrument. Moreover, *ifá* makes use of a divining bag (which is flattened out so that the *òpèlè* can be cast on it) and a sacred divining tray, a specially carved wood board, symbolically decorated at the edges. The inner surface of this board is covered with *ìyè* (sacred powder obtained specially from wood dust).

In *ifá*, appropriate graphic signs are made on the powdered tray, depending on the configurations of the *ikín* or *òpèlè* cast on the flattened divining bag (for details, see Bascom 1969; chap. 4; Abimbola 1976:26–32). In *èèrìndínlógún*, on the other hand, the sacred cowry shells are cast on a basketry tray woven in rectangular or circular fashion. Because wood dust is not used, there is no way of making signs on the tray as in *ifá*. Instead, the sixteen cowries are cast on the tray in such a manner that the cowries themselves function as the signs. When the sixteen cowries are cast, one of seventeen possible configurations (from zero to sixteen) appears, depending on how many cowries fall with their eyes up and how many fall with their eyes down. The emergent pattern corresponds to an *odù*, a body of text, consisting of hundreds of *ese* (narratives). For example, when there are eight cowries facing eye up and eight down, the configuration is an *odù* known as *Èjì Ogbè*, with which certain specified *ese* are associated. Once the *odù* has been determined by the first toss of the cowries, the diviner begins to recite the narratives associated with it until stopped by the client, who ordinarily selects the narrative relevant to that specific case. Basically, each *ese* contains a complete narrative account of a known historical or unknown mythological consultation, consisting of a named diviner, a named client, a specified problem, the diviner's recommendations, including a list of sacrificial items, the client's reactions, and their consequences. Thus, each complete narrative has a fixed structure and is marked off from other narratives by a complete story of a given mythological or historical consultation sandwiched between a formulaic prologue and epilogue. The epilogue commonly contains moral exhortations (for further details, see Bascom 1980; Akinnaso 1982b).

Usually, more specific information can be obtained through a process known as *ibò dídì*. It involves additional casts of the cowries and choice between specific alternatives on the basis of the rank order of the seventeen *odù* (see table 1). Choice is restricted to two alternatives, between left hand and right hand. The choice among more than two alternatives is made only by asking them in sequence and receiving yes or no answers to specific questions. In general, predictions are of two categories: *ire* (blessing) and *ibi* (evil). Each category is a composite, and its members are ranked in order. Further inquiries can be made about the specific nature and recipient of the blessing or evil and

TABLE 1.   The Rank Order of the Odù[a]

First rank[b]		Second rank		Third rank	
eji ogbe	(8)	owonrin	(11)	ika	(13)
ofun	(10)	osa	(9)	oturupon	(14)
irosun	(4)	odi	(7)	ofun kanran	(15)
ogunda	(3)	obara	(6)	irete	(16)
eji oko	(2)	ose	(5)	opira	(0)
okanran	(1)				
ejila sebora	(12)				

[a]Figures indicate the number of cowries lying with their eyes up.
[b]The ordering within each rank follows the pattern suggested by one diviner (see Bascom 1980:7).

what should be done to realize or avert the prediction. *Ìbò* is an interesting process symbolizing the quest-for-knowledge motif that characterizes the entire divinatory process. Etymologically, the word *ìbò,* a nominal derivative of the verb *bò* (to cover), means hidden object. It is used in this nominal form mainly as part of the esoteric lexicon of divination. *Ìbò* is represented by two small objects, namely, the breastbone of a small tortoise (which designates a positive response) and a small pebble (which designates a negative response). *Ìbò dídì* is the process of hiding (but also of uncovering) the objects.

The client holds one of these objects in each hand and asks the god of divination to indicate which hand is selected by the configuration of the sixteen cowries. For example, a client who consults a diviner specifically to find out what is in store for him in the new year may stop the diviner after the latter has recited an *ęsę* that predicts ire to find out which of the five major folk categories of blessings are predicted. These are: *ire àìkú* (long life); (2) *ire ajé* (money); (3) *ire obìnrin* (women, i.e., wives); (4) *ire ọmọ* (children); and (5) *ire ibùjóòkó* (a new abode). At this juncture, the client is presented with the objects of the *ìbò,* which the client holds in both hands, whispers into them one of the five categories of ire about which specific information is required, separates the objects by keeping one within each closed fist, and then, with fists still tightly closed, the client stretches her or his arms toward the divining paraphernalia in a gesture of readiness. Then the diviner throws the cowries and interprets the resulting configuration according to the guide provided in table 2.

The right hand is indicated with a single cast if any of the seven first-ranked *odù* appears in the ensuing configuration. However, if any of the second-ranked *odù* appears, a second cast of the cowries is required. If one of the second-ranked *odù* appears on this second cast, then the right hand is selected; but if a first-ranked *odù* appears on the second cast, then the left hand is chosen. If,

TABLE 2. Procedure for *Ìbò* Selection

Cast	*Odù*	Choice
First	first-ranked	right hand
	second-ranked	second cast required
	third-ranked	start all over again
Second	first-ranked	left hand
	second-ranked	right hand
	third-ranked	start all over again

during the first or the second cast of the cowries, any of the third-ranked *odù* appears, then it is concluded that there is no answer. The entire process may then be repeated until there is an answer, be it positive or negative. A positive answer is produced when the object in the chosen hand is the tortoise's breast-bone; the answer is negative if the object is the small pebble. If, for example, a positive answer is produced at the end of the exercise, the client may want to have more specific information, for example, about the specific recipient of the promised blessing: Will it be the client, a relative, a close friend? There is no theoretical limit to the number of fine tunings nor to the *ìbò* that can be performed at a given divination session.

Once the client is satisfied with the answers provided through the process of *ìbò,* the next stage is to work out, again through *ìbò,* the details of the sacrifice prescribed in the relevant *ẹsẹ* which triggered the fine tuning done so far through *ìbò.* Sacrifice, an obligatory feature of every divination session, is offered either to ensure the promised blessing (if the prediction is positive) or to avert evil (if the prediction is negative). Sacrifices may be offered in the privacy of the client's home, in the village shrine, or at the diviner's shrine, although the diviner's shrine is often preferred, perhaps to ensure proper procedure and the efficacy of the sacrifice. Recipients of the sacrifice may vary from ritually significant trees (such as the *ìrókò* tree) to ancestors and recognized divinities; also, further information can be obtained about the ingredients of the sacrifice, as well as where, when, and how it is to be offered. All these choices are settled through the process of *ìbò.* In all cases, however, the latitude of the diviner's recommendations is constrained by the historical or mythological precedent contained in the relevant *ẹsẹ* which motivated the present predictions. The *ìbò* procedure recalls interesting aspects of spider divination practised by the Mambila who live on either side of the Nigeria and Cameroon border (Zeitlyn 1990). In both cases, the client asks the questions through the diviner, who employs some mysterious procedure; and the god of divination provides the answers in binary alternatives.

Initiation

Among the Yoruba, the initiation and training of professional diviners offers a clear example of institutionalized learning reminiscent of the ancient guru-dama relationship in India and contemporary teacher-pupil relationship in Western-type educational institutions. The trainee is separated from home, placed under distinct authority and put through a systematic program of instruction. In Yoruba, the training begins with initiation into the relevant cult. For example, before learning ẹẹrìndínlógún from the cult of Òrìṣàńlá, the trainee is first initiated into this cult. Historically, most practitioners of ẹẹrìndínlógún belonged to this cult. Trainees are usually initiated early, from age ten or even earlier, although there is no upper age limit. The cost of initiation, paid in the form of cash, goods, and services, is very high (Bascom 1969:81–82, 1980:10). Being normally young and so unable to afford the expenses, initiates must have a sponsor who must provide all necessary funds and sacrificial items, including fish, tortoise, hen, pigeon, snail, rat, and the flesh from the elephant.

The initiation proper, which lasts seven days, is a combination of physical, spiritual, and symbolic experiences. Typically, the initiation takes place at the shrine of Òrìṣàńlá. The initiate's hair is completely shaved and a series of seven small cuts known as gbéré is made in the scalp, but the hair near the cut is saved and pounded along with bits and pieces from all the sacrificial items in the above list. This concoction becomes a sacred medicine fashioned into a small lump and applied to the gbéré in the initiate's scalp. The medicine must not fall off as it must be worn for seven days. The initiate's sponsor can take it off and keep it when the initiate goes to sleep, but the sponsor must remember to put it back the next day after the initiate has taken a shower. These physical acts of shaving the initiate's hair and making gbéré in the initiate's scalp are symbolic of the initiate's separation from home and the laity and recall the symbolic acts of dissociation which characterize initiation rituals (Turner 1969).

The next stage in the initiation is drinking the blood of the sacrificial animal specifically chosen through a special divination completed earlier. After the blood-drinking, Orisanla mounts the initiate, takes possession of the initiate in a trance and speaks through that person, usually in a special voice. This act recalls how secret knowledge was acquired in preliterate Scandinavia, as told in an old Norse story:

> One old Norse story, represented on stones at Manx and Iona, relates how Sigurd killed a huge dragon, and toasted its heart over a fire. In doing this he

touched the hot dragon's heart, and, burning his finger, put it in his mouth, with the result that he immediately became possessed of "all the knowledge of the two worlds." (Goody 1982:211)

Similarly, in order to "get his special capacity for speech and communication" with the nonhuman world, the Northern Tswapong diviner in southern Africa eats a given animal's cooked diaphragm stuffed with that animal's various parts and covered by hot embers (Werbner 1989:33).

The symbolism of food (or drink) in these experiences should not be taken literally because it provides an important metaphor for the acquisition of specialized or deep knowledge. Among the Yoruba, certain forms of knowledge come largely from supernatural sources. In order to acquire such knowledge, initiates are often required to eat certain things but to avoid others. Indeed, among the Yoruba, the symbolism of food is used not only as a metaphor for the acquisition of deep knowledge but also for the acquisition of important roles. For example, the acquisition of chieftaincy is often cast in food metaphors through the use of verbs of eating. Thus, *Ó jẹ oyè* (literally translated as he ate chieftaincy, means he became a chief) or *Ó jẹ Ọba* (literally, he ate the king, meaning he became king). These complex metaphors developed historically from the literal act of a new king eating the heart of his deceased predecessor as part of the succession ritual.

The symbolism of food or drink, as used in this initiation, takes on an additional significance as the blood-drinking experience transforms the initiate in the preparation for important ritual roles and other-world experiences. An important aspect of this transformation is the ability to understand a different language, which is very crucial because the other worlds are characterized by other modes of communication. Although the transformation may enable the initiate to understand such modes in general, special training is often necessary in order to acquire productive competence in a specific or a new one.

At the end of the blood-drinking ceremony, the initiate is given a symbol of *Òrìṣàńlá*, a white piece of bone or ivory treated with the blood from the cut in the initiate's scalp, to take home. This symbol must be preserved throughout the initiate's life. At this time also, the initiate may purchase sixteen sacred cowries for a personal shrine but does not need to learn how to divine with them. Most *ẹẹrìndínlógún* initiates, in fact, remain only at the level of devoted worshippers of *Òrìṣàńlá*, and do not become diviners. However, if and when the initiate decides or is chosen to become a diviner, the initiate may return to the initiator, usually referred to as *babalórìṣà* (father of Orisa worshippers) or *awolórìṣà* (diviner for Orisa worshippers), if that person can also perform divination. If the initiator is not a practising diviner, the initiate must look elsewhere for a teacher.

Schooling

Although learning how to divine (especially to memorize the text) continues virtually throughout a diviner's lifetime, several years of continuous training are required before an apprentice is graduated and allowed to divine by himself professionally. The diviners estimate that the length of time required to complete the systematic training of the apprenticeship varies from a minimum of ten to fifteen years, with some very smart learners completing it in much less, to a never-ending process. As in *ifá* (Abimbola 1976:18),

> there are usually many drop-outs during the training with only a small percentage of those who start the training completing it successfully. This is due to several factors of which the most important are firstly the mental rigour and secondly the extremely hard conditions of living involved in the training.

Although each trainee's progress depends largely on memory skills, intelligence, communicative ability, and perseverance, four distinct but overlapping stages of training can be recognized (see table 3). Stage II, in particular, overlaps considerably with the others.

Training begins with Stage I and consists mainly of teaching the apprentice how to use the sixteen sacred cowries: how to preserve them; how to hold and toss them on the divining tray; and, most important, how to recognize their various configurations and relate each configuration to a specific *odù,* the deity affiliation of each *odù,* and the range of sacrificial items associated with it.

The most cognitively demanding part of the training by far is Stage II, in which the apprentice memorizes the form and content of the various *odù* and their constituent *ęsę*. First, the apprentice learns the names of the seventeen *odù* and their defining characteristics. Then he concentrates on one *odù* at a time, usually beginning with *Èjì Ogbè,* which has the half-and-half configuration. Although the major operative unit in each *odù* is the *ęsę,* memorization of the text, as discussed below, is done line by line (although, as is quite evident in the text, the line is an analytical, rather than a native, category; see Akinnaso 1985, for a discussion of the criteria for lineal segmentation).

In the next phase, the trainee learns the appropriate rhetorical method of presenting the memorized text through conscious training and through observ-

TABLE 3. Training Scheme

Stage	Program	Years
I	Learning how to use the sacred cowries	2–3
II	Memorizing the basic text	3–4
III	Learning the preservation and uses of leaves and herbs	3–4
IV	Specialization and memorization of more texts	2–4
	Total number of years	10–15

ing the trainer's performance of divination for clients. The trainee can also improve his or her competence by attending the regular assemblies of professional diviners in which knowledge of the text is freely shared. Learning the appropriate manner of rhetorical presentation is as important as memorizing the text because knowledge of the text alone does not make a diviner; the trainee must know how to recite the text in the proper manner (see Akinnaso 1982b, 1985). Another essential part of the training in Stage II is learning the sacrifice that accompanies each *odù* in general and each *ẹsẹ* in particular. In most cases, the sacrificial list forms part of the *ẹsẹ;* the trainee must learn both the items of sacrifice prescribed in each *ẹsẹ* as well as the formulaic structures in which the items occur (see Akinnaso 1985). In addition, trainees are required to memorize special esoteric chants that must be recited when certain types of sacrifice are offered.

Stage III of the training, particularly important for diviners who wish to practice as herbalists or local "doctors," instructs the trainee in the nature and uses of medicinal herbs, where and how to obtain them, and how to make them into concoctions of varying degrees of potency. However, the lessons at this stage are not totally divorced from those learned in the earlier stages, as there is a great deal of overlap. In a few cases, formal training may terminate at Stage III; and the trainee can be formally initiated into the local professional group of diviners after passing the appropriate tests. In a majority of cases, however, the trainee usually opts for more specialized training (Stage IV), such as healing, childbearing, or forecasting the future of newly born babies. If the trainee's intended specialization is outside the competence of the current trainer, then that trainee may have to travel farther away to another part of Yorubaland in search of an appropriate specialist. Such specialist training lasts from two to four years and focuses on learning the uses of new herbs and memorizing additional specialized texts. Again, Abimbola (1976:25) provides corroborative evidence from *ifá:*

Among the most important areas in which the priest of *Ifá* may specialize, the most important are healing, chanting of *Ifá* texts, and knowledge of rare texts in the literary corpus.

Specialization in a particular field sometimes takes the priest of *Ifá* to distant places. It may happen, for example, that the only *Ifá* priest who is a renowned specialist in healing is, at a certain time, in a particular part of Yorubaland. In such a case, all *Ifá* priests who want to specialize in healing will have to go to that particular specialist for training. In this way, all successful *Ifá* priests usually travel a great deal throughout Yorubaland acquiring more knowledge and broadening their outlook on life.

Learning Strategies

The learning and practice of Yoruba divination are essentially formal activities. Contrary to the traditional view that learning in nonliterate societies is exclusively bound by context (Fortes 1970; Bruner 1966), a great deal of the training in learning how to divine is done out of context and employs strategies used in schools for learning, such as repetition, rote learning, question-and-answer sessions, use of special language and decontextualized discussions about Yoruba history, mythology, medicinal practices, and so forth. In this section, I will select and discuss some of the characteristics of learning how to divine and show how the combination of these features and the frequency of their occurrence bring about a learning practice that can properly be described as schooling.

I begin with the teachers, learners, class size, and method of student recruitment. Teachers are normally elderly, practising diviners and members of the professional group of diviners that meets regularly and in moments of social crisis to share experiences and exchange ideas. In literate terms, these meetings function like professional conferences and seminars:

> In most communities *Ifá* priests also meet regularly once every month and once every year. The yearly meeting is observed as a festival which is known as *Mole*. . . . Perhaps the most interesting aspect of the annual *Mole* festival and the other congregational assemblies of *Ifá* priests is the chanting of *Ifá* texts which is referred to as *iyere*. (Abimbola 1976:15)

Ẹ̀rìndínlógún diviners hold similar meetings, emphasis being placed on the annual meetings.

Diviners are distinguished from their apprentices and the rest of the people by their professional title, appearance, conduct, and the special knowledge they possess. *Ẹ̀rìndínlógún* diviners are known as *awolórìṣà,* that is, *awo ilé Òrìṣà,* literally, secret-house-Orisa (deity), meaning keeper of Orisa's secrets, while *ifá* diviners are known as *babaláwo,* that is, *bàbá (tí ó) ni awo,* literally, father-(who-he-) have-secret, meaning father (who has or keeps secrets). In both systems, diviners are often physically distinguished by what they wear and how they make their hair. One of the physical marks of distinction is the beaded bracelet worn on the left wrist. *Ẹ̀rìndínlógún* diviners are further distinguished by their plaited hair, adopted in recognition of the female origin of *ẹ̀rìndínlógún.* Although *ifá* diviners do not plait their hair like women, they nevertheless adopt a variety of styles, ranging from partial to complete shaving, depending on their rank (Bascom 1969).

In both *ifá* and *ẹ̀rìndínlógún* cults, there is a strong professional association in which members are hierarchically ordered and guided by strict codes of conduct with established mechanisms for enforcement. However, the much more developed *ifá* professional association is characterized by a more elaborate hierarchical structure that, in many respects, parallels the larger political organization (Bascom 1969; Abimbola 1976).

Apprentices are often younger people, although adult learners are not uncommon. Although regular apprentices undergo the normal curriculum, a functional curriculum exists for adult learners. As Bascom (1969:85) reports for *ifá,* "Individuals who learn *ifá* as adults may pay a diviner to teach them rather than serving as apprentices; there are no fixed rates for this, but in 1937 one man was giving his teacher food and palm wine, plus a penny a day to teach him for as long a period each day as he wanted." Although some of the learners may come from home during training, the majority of them are boarded in the compound of the teacher, paying their tuition in cash and in kind. Moreover, even when formal training has been completed and the new graduate begins to divine on his own, "he must give his teacher part of whatever he receives as payment (*eru*) through divining, and this obligation continues as long as the teacher lives" (Bascom 1969:86). Finally, practising diviners can attend refresher courses "by paying other diviners to teach them specific verses or medicines" (Bascom 1969:86).

Learners and their teachers need not be related, although an apprentice may learn from his father. Typically, "[a] father often prefers to have his son learn . . . from another diviner, so that he will not be treated too leniently but will be given sufficient discipline to learn well" (Bascom 1969:84). Membership in the same ethnolinguistic group (apparently to facilitate communication between teacher and pupil), rather than kinship or lineage ties, is the major criterion for admission to initiation and apprenticeship. Although few apprentices go much beyond their immediate localities for basic training, most often do for advanced training.

Although many candidates may be in line for initiation, each one is initiated in turn. Similarly, each apprentice has a specific program of training, although many apprentices may be enrolled simultaneously with the same master. There is no prescribed class size. The number of apprentices with a given diviner is determined largely by the latter's fame and track record. Before religious conversion, colonization, and literacy, divination was very popular and widespread in Yorubaland. During this booming period, a diviner could have as many as fifteen apprentices or more, about a third of whom might successfully complete the training. However, with the institutionalization of mass Western schooling and, especially, the inauguration of free primary education in Yorubaland in the 1950s, enrollment for training in divination declined sharply—so sharply that by 1951 Salako, the knowledgeable *ẹẹrìndínlógún* diviner from Igana, had no student in his school (Bascom 1980:11–12). About the same time, the late Chief Lemikan Akinlaye, a very popular *ifá* diviner from Idanre, had only two apprentices on roll. He, however, recounted a period when his father had over ten apprentices, although he himself never had more than five at a time.

The classroom is a variable setting, ranging from the diviner's shrine through the shrine of *èṣù*, the devil, to the *orîta*, the mythical T-junction, in which some spirits are believed to reside, and the forest, the home of most supernatural forces and important leaves and herbs. Moreover, because the apprentice lives with his master, learning could take place virtually anywhere, as the need arises. Typically, however, most learning takes place at the shrine. The divination text is usually memorized there, as each learning session is often preceded by the chanting of an esoteric text to alert and invoke the god of divination. The invocation wakes up the divining paraphernalia, thus facilitating the transmission of the text.

The basic curriculum of both *ifá* and *ẹẹrìndínlógún* training consists mainly of learning the configurations of the appropriate divining instrument; memorizing the text associated with each configuration; learning the names of sacrificial items associated with each *ẹsẹ;* and knowing the names of medicinal herbs and how to make necessary concoctions from them. The learner is also taught important aspects of Yoruba history, mythology, philosophy, medicine, and religious practices. In addition to the transmission of esoteric knowledge, the curriculum includes the deliberate transmission of values and attitudes consonant with ethical practice in Yoruba culture and professional practice in divination. More important for his practice, the learner acquires appropriate sociolinguistic and rhetorical skills. Finally, as in most formal training programs, the learner undergoes various tests during this training.

True, the apprentice learns certain aspects of divination by direct observation, but a great deal of learning is by specific instruction (Bascom 1969:85). Decontextualization is thus a necessary feature of the instructional strategy. For example, in order to learn the various configurations of the divining instrument and the names of the associated *odù* in *ifá,* the learner does not begin with the real divining paraphernalia nor in an actual divination session. Rather, the teacher prepares a surrogate divining chain, "usually of pieces of calabash joined by a simple cord, with which the pupil practices identifying the sixteen paired figures, followed by the combinations" (Bascom 1969:85). This recalls the training procedures in the Bumbudye secret society, in which the names and significance of many symbols and deities are learned through their drawings in the sand.

Similarly, the text is deliberately taught and memorized rather than merely acquired by observation and imitation. The master diviner recites one complete line at a time, and the trainee repeats the words after him several times until the whole line is retained in memory. This is done for each line until the whole *ẹsẹ* has been fully memorized. After memorizing the basic *ẹsẹ* in a given *odù,* the apprentice proceeds to another *odù.* It must be emphasized that the volume of text to be memorized for each *odù* is very large indeed. Each *odù* is said to contain hundreds of *ẹsẹ* or narratives, each average *ẹsẹ* being as long as nearly two pages of print (see, e.g., Bascom 1969, 1980). Consequently, no single diviner can know all the *ẹsẹ* in each *odù,* which is why diviners go on learning more and more throughout their lives. It would appear, however, that most diviners often know more *ẹsẹ* in *Èjì Ogbè* than in any other *odù.* For example, Salako's repertoire consists of as many as forty-nine *ẹsẹ* in *Èjì Ogbè* in *ẹẹrìn-dínlógún* (Bascom 1980:54–185). This may well be due to the importance attached to *Èjì Ogbè* (partly, perhaps, because of its half-and-half configuration and partly because of the variety of blessings contained in the *odù*) and the precedence accorded *Èjì Ogbè* in the learning process: Most diviners begin their teaching of the text with *Èjì Ogbè.*

The importance attached to the correct memorization of the text reinforces the formality of its acquisition:

The *ẹsẹ* is memorized with such a great reverence that not a single word is missed. It is considered extremely sacrilegious for anybody to add or subtract anything from the corpus. The *ẹsẹ* must always be learnt in the very form in which it has been preserved and disseminated from ancient times. It is believed that in this way the texts in the *ifá* literary corpus have been kept free from errors. The corpus, therefore, remains till today one of the most reliable genres of Yoruba oral literature. (Abimbola 1976:20)

Thus, as in literate religions—Judaism, Christianity, and Islam—Yoruba divination is a text-based system of knowledge, although its text is entirely oral. Its orality notwithstanding, the divination text is also characterized by the relative fixity of literate religious texts (cf. Sherzer 1983). To be sure, there are interesting differences and similarities of detail between oral and written religious texts. For one thing, literate religious texts, such as the Qur'an, are indisputably graphically fixed, while it can be argued that oral religious texts, such as the *ifá* text, are not indisputably the same as previous recountings. It is, however, true that both oral and literate religious texts are susceptible to variable interpretations and that both are replicated from generation to generation because of their immense value for cultural continuity. It is in the attempt to replicate the original oral text of *ifá* and *ẹẹ̀rìndínlógún* that rote learning is employed in the training, as in traditional Qur'anic pedagogy (see Wagner and Lofti 1983).

Given the emphasis on rote learning, Yoruba divination pedagogy, like Qur'anic pedagogy, is expected to facilitate memory skills (Scribner and Cole 1981; Wagner and Lofti 1983). Rote learning, to be sure, has been criticized for emphasizing memory skills at the expense of logical and creative thinking. Memorization is, however, only one of the several techniques employed in traditional apprenticeship training (Lave 1977).

Moreover, rote and creativity are not necessarily incompatible in Yoruba divination. Although emphasis is on exact memorization during training, a certain amount of improvisation is allowed in the narrative portions of the text during performance, so long as the main plot, theme, and rhetorical structure of the narrative are preserved (see Akinnaso 1982b). In the course of actual divination sessions, diviners exploit such improvisatory possibilities in an attempt to accommodate change into their memorized text. For example, after the introduction of Islam to Old Oyo, the following lines were incorporated into an *ifá* narrative by an Oyo diviner in an attempt to mimic Muslim converts as they chanted their prayers in Arabic (Abimbola 1969:96):

Wutuwutu yaaki
Wutuwutu yambele

Ka sure patapira
Ka fewu alaari fonkun amodi
Lekeleke eye imole

These lines begin with vocables mimicking Arabic sounds, in the opening grammatical parallelism. It lacks semantic content, thus symbolically criticizing Muslim converts for reciting Qur'anic texts whose meaning they do not know. However, beyond the initial play on words or sounds, a very sharp criticism is leveled, in the condensed metaphor of the fourth line, against Muslims who are accused of using *alaari* (highly expensive traditional clothing) to rub a nose (*fonkun*) filled with filthy mucus. The implication of this metaphor for the diviner's conception of the Islamic religion is very clear. In a witty, diplomatic closure, however, the text ends with the color metaphor associating the whiteness of the pigeon (*lekeleke*) with the white robe of the Muslim preacher (*imole*).

Although improvisation is often downplayed (even sometimes denied) by practising diviners, diviners in everyday practice attempt to increase their clientele by outstripping one another in their ability to contextualize the memorized texts through improvisation. In such situations, not only the memorized text is important but also the diviner's sociolinguistic and rhetorical skills and his or her ability to manipulate lexical substitutions, syntactic parallelisms, wordplay, and so forth, in such a way as to fit the canonical structure of the established narrative, while contextualizing the message and meaning of the text. By contextualizing portions of the text, diviners reflect ongoing social change by admitting new material into an otherwise fixed text.

Another important learning strategy involves the employment of mnemonics such as repetition, recurrent units, and formulaic structures in memorizing and recalling the text. For example, the apprentice soon learns that each *ese* contains certain units which recur with regularity, although the content varies from *ese* to *ese*. Thus, in order to assist the learners, the teacher may explain the logic of each *ese,* so that the learner will know how to organize his knowledge of the narratives. An Idanre diviner explains that it is important for the trainee to know that each *ese* begins with *ijúbà* (acknowledgment and prologue); that each names a diviner and a client; that each mentions *irúbo* (a prescription for sacrifice) and a list of sacrificial items. As in the famous Homeric poems and the Yugoslav epics, the structural arrangement of the text provides an important mnemonic for memorization and recall.

An important aspect of the training in Yoruba divination is the examination system. Various tests are given in the course of training. In *ifá,* for example, the learner's mastery of the configurations and the associated text is frequently assessed: "Frequent tests are given by marking a figure on the divining tray or forming it with the divining chain, and asking the boy to give its name and to recite its verses" (Bascom 1969:85). At the end of the training, two major tests are given. First, a mock final is administered to the novice by his seniors (Bascom 1969:85):

> They give him a divining tray, powder, and palm nuts and tell him to divine. He marks the figures on the tray, names them, and recites the verses [i.e., ẹsẹ], but one verse for each figure [i.e., odù] is sufficient for him to pass.

If the trainee is successful at this stage, then he can present himself for the final initiation, which involves both the final examinations and the graduation ceremony:

> Initiation forms the climax of many years of hard work, and it is usually celebrated with the pomp and dignity that it deserves. The would-be priest is taken into the forest where high-ranking Ifá priests examine him on different fields in which he has received instructions. They also caution him to adhere strictly to the ethics and secrets of his profession. (Abimbola 1977:13)

An interesting aspect of the examination system is the question-and-answer method employed in testing knowledge of such specific aspects embodied in the texts as Yoruba history, mythology, philosophy, and geography. Because the answer to a specific question may be scattered over several narratives, the learner must search his repertoire of narratives and extract the relevant portions in answering the question. This implies that the learner is not just a passive memorizer of texts, but, rather, must internalize and analyse the texts in order to use his knowledge in specific circumstances.

When one compares learning how to divine with learning how to weave among the Yoruba, one notices a striking difference. Although the latter is done largely by watching and doing, the former combines these with two additional attributes: language is used as the predominant mode of transmitting and acquiring the texts, and much of the teaching and learning occurs out of context, thus recalling the characteristics of school learning that Bruner emphasized (1966). As in typical classroom learning, the trainee is asked to memorize and learn material that has no natural context; he also asks and answers questions and engages in several noninstrumental communicative tasks. In this learning situation, the trainee is no longer using words for the purpose of manipulating people or things but is manipulating words as words.

The nature of the language used in divination has been studied in some detail (see for example, Werbner 1973, 1989; B. Tedlock 1978, 1982; Akinnaso 1985; Zeitlyn 1990). The findings reveal striking similarities between the properties of divination language and those of formal, written language. Typically, both kinds of language are institutionalized, authoritarian, stylized, detached, formal, and relatively inaccessible; are characterized by register peculiarities, archaisms, esoteric lexicon, elaborated grammatical structures, and semantic density; and, consequently, are discontinuous with everyday, conversational language (see Akinnaso 1985, for further details). One of the major reasons suggested for these similarities is that both kinds of language are acquired in school or school-like settings regulating the form and structure of language (Werbner 1973; B. Tedlock 1978; Sherzer 1983; Akinnaso 1985).

There are also historical reasons for the shared characteristics between divination and written language. Diviners were among the first group of professionals in nonliterate societies to develop a professional language (Loewe and Blacker 1981; Akinnaso 1982b, 1985). A major consequence of this development is that the language of the divination ritual became more and more removed from everyday conversational language. The history of writing manifests a similar process of linguistic differentiation (Gelb 1952; Gleason 1961). Like the restriction of divination skills to a few, literacy was initially restricted to priests and professional groups; and written language was subjected to conscious refinements in the attempt to separate it from everyday language (Gleason 1961).

Indeed, the training of *ifá* diviners shares various traits with the training of Catholic priests in those special schools called seminaries, as described in Peter Burke's account of the uses of literacy in early modern Italy (Burke 1987:31):

> The systematic, separate, professional education of the clergy in seminaries was another part of this movement [i.e., the "Catholic Reformation" or "Counter-Reformation"]. Seminaries were founded in Italy from the 1560s onwards. . . . As a result, priests became better educated, and also more remote from ordinary people.

Although seminaries and divination schools serve quite different purposes, they both arose from the need to train professionals who would explain to novices and the laity the meaning of sacred texts which had become completely divorced from their original authors. During the course of their training, these professionals develop special exegetical abilities and become speakers of the appropriate language of authority. These attributes and the specialized knowledge they have acquired become the chief source of their power in society.

Implications

The above analysis shows very clearly that the type of knowledge upon which Yoruba divination is based—its value system, its problems and techniques, its language, the teaching and learning strategies—reflect the general properties of specialized knowledge and formal learning, which are relatively discontinuous with those of everyday, practical knowledge and informal learning. If this opposition is taken seriously, then certain implications follow for language and communication, social structure, educational practices, and the relationship between knowledge and power. To start with, it is clear from the foregoing analysis that divination is based on secret knowledge that only few members of Yoruba society can acquire through special schooling. This limitation on access to divinatory practice implies that mass schooling of the Western type could not be expected. Besides, there are practical limitations on the number of pupils that a diviner-teacher could have at a time. Another implication of the secrecy of divinatory knowledge and its institutionalization is its dependence on a special language with its own register peculiarities (Akinnaso 1982b, 1985; Werbner 1989). This immediately leads to linguistic discontinuities within the Yoruba society as within other societies (literate and nonliterate) in which certain forms of knowledge are institutionalized (see, especially, Bloomfield 1927; Ferguson 1959; Havelock 1963; Newman 1964; Browning 1982; Sherzer 1983; Akinnaso 1985; Werbner 1989; Barth 1990).

Havelock, for one, sees the distinction as one between the "poetic" language used for "preserved communication" and the "prosaic" language used for "the casual and ephemeral converse of daily transaction" (Havelock 1963:134–35). Browning (1982:49) concurs with Havelock, stressing the primordial existence of Greek diglossia:

> The use of different forms of the language in different situations is characteristic of the earliest stages of the Greek language. . . . The Homeric poems are composed in a form of Greek which was no one's mother tongue and which is the result of a very long development, possibly stretching back to Mycenean times. All subsequent epic poetry, and indeed all hexameter verse, was normally composed in the Homeric Kunstsprache, whatever the native dialect of the poet himself or the everyday language of the community in which or for which he worked.

It must be admitted, of course, that although the language of specialized, institutionalized knowledge is substantially different from that of everyday life at virtually every level of linguistic analysis, the emphasis varies from level to level according to the type of knowledge and society. Register peculiarities are known to foster boundaries between types of knowledge, even within the same cultural tradition. Thus, for example, divination chants are readily distinguishable from funeral dirges, just as a medical prescription is distinguishable from a recipe. In terms of variations in sociocultural organization, differences are manifested more in lexical and grammatical choices in literate societies (Halliday 1967; Biber 1988) and more in phonological and lexical choices, as well as in semantic ambiguities, in nonliterate societies (Parkin 1979; Hymes 1981; D. Tedlock 1972, 1983; Sherzer 1983; McDowell 1983; Akinnaso 1985; Werbner 1989). At the phonological level, for example, recitation, chanting, and singing are among the preferred ways of speaking in divination and similar oral, ritual performances, just as esoteric lexicon, tropes, and multiple interpretations abound at the lexical and semantic levels where "paradoxes, ambiguities, and suspended meanings" become the essential features of communication (Werbner 1989:38). On the other hand, the emphasis in standard written communication (notably, academic writing), where the functional load shifts from the phonological to the lexical and grammatical levels, is on explicitness (Olson 1977; Biber 1988). Some of these differences result partly from variations in modality between speech and writing (Akinnaso 1982a).

For comparative purposes, two observations follow from the foregoing: linguistic discontinuities are not peculiar to literate societies and the elevated or elaborated variety in both types of society must share certain similarities of form and function, in addition to manifesting similar consequences for their users. Consequently, Vygotsky's observation that schooling inculcates specialized uses of language (Vygotsky 1978, 1987; see also Lucy 1988) applies to schooling in both literate and nonliterate societies, although Vygotsky had only the former in mind. Indeed, recent research has demonstrated that the effects of schooling on language derive not from literacy, per se, but from specific training in certain skills, such as the memorization of specially organized text, the use of decontextualized language, and the use of two-dimensional representations (see, for example, Scribner and Cole 1973; Rogoff 1981). Which aspect of language will be affected by schooling and to what degree varies modally from culture to culture according to variations in schooling practices, especially instructional strategies, classroom interaction patterns, and the goals of schooling. The available medium (spoken or written) in which language is transmitted is also a factor, although the import of this factor has been called into question by recent research on the relationship between spoken and written language (Akinnaso 1985, 1988; Biber 1988). These variables notwithstanding, the effects of schooling on language in both literate and nonliterate societies can be expected to be similar, differing mainly in degrees of more or less, rather than of all or nothing.

It is also clear from the foregoing analysis that differential access to knowledge of divination and its language has implications for social structure. Clearly, in Yoruba society, not everyone can divine; and those who can are not ordinary people but, rather, "the physicians, psychiatrists, historians, and philosophers of the communities to which they belonged" (Abimbola 1977:11). Thus, like the traditional Southeast Asian guru (see Barth 1990), the Yoruba diviner's role is not limited to ritual and instructional contexts. Moreover, Yoruba diviners possess a wealth of proverbs, aphorisms, and etiological knowledge which abound in the memorized divination text. This knowledge is further supplemented by the worldly experience that the diviner acquires as he travels about different parts of Yorubaland and even beyond in search of leaves and herbs, more text to add to his corpus, or even in search of clients. This wealth of knowledge, often judiciously displayed in the solution of social problems, such as the arbitration of disputes (Akinnaso 1985:337), thus recalls the tendency to use oral ritual texts in validating ongoing social action (Gumperz 1964; Leach 1965).

The variety of roles, the rich store of knowledge, and the enviable communicative abilities endow diviners with considerable power in society. Even when they do not hold political offices, diviners exert considerable influence over politicians (traditional chiefs and modern, professional politicians alike) who consult them for advice. Indeed, in traditional Yoruba society, most kings maintain an advisory group of diviners, a group that is most elaborate in its organization in Ile-Ife, the ritual headquarters of the Yoruba kingdom (Bascom 1969: chap. 10). In performing their multiple roles as healers, intellectuals, philosophers, political advisers, and arbitrators, Yoruba diviners, like the Brahmins of Hindu civilization, have unparalleled access to knowledge of ideas, events, and problems in their society and are, therefore, in a position to control the relations of people to those ideas, events, and problems. Although they may not necessarily be wealthy individuals (of course, some are), diviners often accumulate a great deal of symbolic capital which, in the absence of economic accumulation, is used as a means for controlling people (see Bourdieu 1977).

This analysis of the social organization of schooling and formal learning and its consequences in a given nonliterate society suggests that it is not necessary to look further to explain the difficulties that schooling and formal learning may present to learners. Apart from demonstrating that, even in non-literate schools, there are those who fail to learn, it also provides an important reason why schools produce failures: Many learners fail to successfully complete their training not because of cognitive deficiencies or some specific incapacities but because many of the various demands of schooling and formal learning are discontinuous with those of everyday life and practical learning. These discontinuities are compounded when the school system is based on cultural and linguistic practices that are markedly different from those of the learners. Yet this is exactly the situation in many developing countries and in many poor and minority neighborhoods in so-called postindustrial societies like the United States.

Scribner and Cole (1973) suggested a twofold solution: move the practical realities of everyday life into the school and introduce the techniques of the school to the context of practical learning in everyday life. In the developing countries, in particular, where schooled literacy is a relatively recent experience, it is important to integrate the techniques of informal and formal learning in the oral cultures with the new culture of schooled literacy. I would further add the need to demystify formal school learning by making explicit to learners those assumptions which underlie such learning and which are often embedded in the curriculum, the texts, the teaching models, and the social organization of learning.

I concur with Scribner and Cole (1973:558) that "a complete theory of formal education requires analysis of phenomena at several levels of social organization, as well as their interactions." However, I would stress that the phenomena to be analysed must be sought in both literate and nonliterate societies. Comparative data from both types of society are necessary in the construction of a valid theory of formal school learning because they can direct attention to essential features of formal learning that are now neglected or misconceived. Furthermore, comparative studies of types of knowledge and types of learning can help to illuminate certain important issues in psychological and social theories. For example, a comparative study of formal and informal learning in both literate and nonliterate societies is a prerequisite for resolving the ongoing arguments among psychologists about the cognitive consequences of formal and informal learning and among anthropologists about the social determination of knowledge and about the distinction between egalitarian and nonegalitarian societies.

Scribner and Cole (1973) posed the psychological question and followed it up in their groundbreaking study, *The Psychology of Literacy* (1981). The present study reinforces their observation that schooling entails formal learning, but formal learning in turn entails specific learning strategies and cognitive tasks. However, this study goes further in demonstrating that schooling is not a unique characteristic of Western literacy and that the distinction between formal and informal learning does not depend on, nor is it isomorphic with, the distinction between literate and nonliterate.

Although the anthropological debate about the social determination of knowledge has not been fully laid to rest (see, for example, Howe 1981 versus Bloch 1977), there seems to be general agreement that knowledge is, indeed, socially determined. The disagreement is over which type of knowledge is socially determined and the consequences of the social determination of knowledge for cultural reproduction and social change. The above analysis indicates that a thorough study of the social organization of knowledge, its distribution, and how it is acquired is a necessary precondition for its classification. When the same parameters are used to compare the same type of knowledge across societies, the findings often reveal striking similarities, as this study has demonstrated. Beneath these apparent similarities, however, are subtle variations in the shared characteristics. For example, this study shows that with regard to one type of knowledge, institutionalized knowledge, there are shared patterns (such as formality, rote learning) and patterned variations (such as class size, learning environment) across societies. These patterned variations, I would argue, are the proper indices of the social determination of knowledge. The very distinction between literate and nonliterate culture is an extension of such variations: the one prototypically transmits by pen and paper, and the other by word of mouth. Although this essay reveals how the variations are manifested in a single case, the focus has been on the shared patterns which underlie these variations across literate and nonliterate societies.

In his 1989 Huxley Memorial Lecture, Fredrik Barth (1990) touched on these and other issues, emphasizing in particular the differential "transactions over knowledge" of different cultural groups. For example, in comparing the Melanesian initiator and the guru of the ancient Asian tradition, Barth observed that "the Guru realizes himself by reproducing knowledge [through teaching and exemplification], the initiator by hedging it [that is, by guarding treasured secrets until the climactic day when he must create a performance for novices]" (1990:642). Barth further argued that the principal contrast between the forms and regional patterns of distribution of knowledge in Southeast Asia and Melanesia is "generated by the contrastive distribution of these two roles, and is a historical reflection of their effects over time" (1990:652). The pressures on the transmitters of specialized knowledge and the reward for their efforts are quite different in both cases. The differences in the form and content of knowledge in both types of society should, therefore, occasion no surprise.

Bhutan's guru-dama relationship, as described by Barth (1990), recalls several aspects of the relationship between the Yoruba diviner and his novices. Both are involved in a web of social relations and transactions governed by the transmission of institutionalized knowledge. Both relationships are characterized by textual interpretation and exegesis as well as the more general processes of schooling and formal learning. There are, however, important differences of detail. In Yoruba divination, knowledge is transmitted largely by memorized oral texts and oral learning, whereas a combination of sacred written texts and oral learning is employed in the guru mode of transmission. Furthermore, although the Southeast Asian guru is clearly distinguishable from the Melanesian initiator, the Yoruba diviner typically combines the roles of the Melanesian initiator, the Southeast Asian guru, and many others. A comprehensive knowledge of the Yoruba diviner requires a thorough knowledge of all of these roles. However, a thorough study of the Yoruba diviner alone cannot in itself go beyond mere "butterfly collecting" (à la Leach); fine-grained crosscultural comparisons are necessary for the assessment of the social determination of knowledge and its consequences.

The present analysis also has implications for another controversial distinction often made in anthropology between egalitarian and nonegalitarian societies: that the basis for distinction should be generally by differences either in the structure of power relations or in the relations of production. Thus, the presumed autonomy of individuals in so-called egalitarian societies, in which "adults do not exercise authority over one another" (Buenaventura-Passon and Brown 1980:111), is contrasted with the hierarchical power structure in nonegalitarian societies. Working from the perspective of the relations of production, Woodburn (1978, 1982) sees the distinction between egalitarian and nonegalitarian societies as one between two types of economic systems. Egalitarian societies, he argues, have economies based on an immediate return on labor, but social inequalities which characterize nonegalitarian societies are generated by delayed-return economies. However, an important yet often neglected factor in this distinction is the nature of knowledge and skills and how they are transmitted in both types of society. Brunton (1989), who examines this issue in several egalitarian societies, pitches his findings against those of Woodburn (1982), who concluded that the locus of the transmission of knowledge and skills in egalitarian societies is the peer group. Brunton submits,

I have no difficulty in accepting his statement in regard to *technical* skills. The environment imposes its own regimen. There are, for instance, only a limited number of ways to use a bow-and-arrow or a spear effectively. Expertise can be the outcome of casual demonstration, observation and continual self-monitoring, or simple trial and error. . . . But the kind of knowledge incorporated into world views, rituals and even healing practices is far more variable, far less subject to the disciplines of reality. . . . Unless there are at least some individuals who are recognised as having the right to evaluate the correctness of these kinds of cultural practices when they are passed on to others—i.e., individuals with authority—their persistence is fortuitous. (1989:679)

We are thus back to the basic distinction between practical and specialized knowledge and the types of learning fostered by the two types of knowledge. I would agree with Brunton that a thoroughgoing egalitarianism exists when a society lacks individuals with authority who control access to specialized knowledge. Schools and school learning, as described above, would be absent in such a society; and if there are no schools, then a key agent in social and cultural reproduction is lost. If such a society does in fact exist, then it would be difficult for it to maintain cultural continuity. Although Flanagan (1989) did not give close attention to the question of the unequal distribution of knowledge in his otherwise wide-ranging review of the literature on egalitarian societies, he nevertheless came to a negative verdict: "There are no egalitarian societies. Nor . . . are there simple societies. However, there are egalitarian contexts, or scenes, or situations" (Flanagan 1989:262).

It may well be that Diamond's notion of the social organization of learning in nonliterate societies derives from his knowledge of so-called egalitarian societies, which, as Ingold (1983:554) has observed, are "so few, and their existence so hedged around by special circumstances, that doubts must inevitably arise as to the significance of [these societies] as constituting the supposed baseline of social evolution." But Diamond's observations are useful, if only in providing yet another instance of the "usefulness of the useless" (Owusu 1978). By denying nonliterate societies the experience of schooling and formal learning, Diamond sensitizes us to the evolutionary question about the origin of schooling and institutionalized knowledge. On the basis of the evidence provided here, it would appear that writing is not a precondition for the development of schooling and its experience. Rather, the baseline of the social evolution of Western-type schools is to be found in a mixture of features from traditional apprenticeship training, initiation, and schooling in nonliterate societies.

Without doubt, this essay has stimulated more questions than it has been able to answer. Some of the questions include whether or not textualized knowledge evokes different responses in oral and literate cultures; whether or not restricted schooling (where there are severe limitations on admission) or mass schooling of the Western type (where admission is apparently open to all members of the society) involves differences in the way that knowledge is presented; whether or not the purveyance of knowledge in the urban American, British, or Japanese schools has the same import for learners as in the relatively secluded divination schools.

These are valid and interesting questions requiring analysis of scalar differences in the social organization of schools and the effects and consequences of schooling for individuals and societies in both literate and nonliterate societies. Although such an analysis is beyond the scope of the present essay, it is not too much to speculate that the findings are likely to reflect gradations of more or less rather than of all or nothing. More comparative research is needed to confirm or disconfirm this speculation.

NOTE

This essay developed out of an earlier one of the same title prepared for an international symposium on the cognitive consequences of literacy, organized by Pierre Darsen in 1986. As more and more data were collected and analysed, the emergent findings and ideas were presented to various audiences at the University of Wisconsin at Parkside (1987); New York University (1988); Vassar College (1988); and Temple University (1989). I am grateful to Lillian Trager, Gerald Greenfield, Bambi Schiefflin, Connie Sutton, Charles Briggs, Jim Collins, and Jonathan Friedlaender for making the presentations possible in the various institutions and thus providing valuable opportunities for discussion and criticism of my ideas. For their comments and suggestions for improvement, I must also thank the reviewers and editors of *CSSH*. Finally, I am grateful to the following agencies, which provided various forms of support for various parts of the study, and/or the writing up: Council for International Exchange of Scholars (Fulbright grant #87-10252); the Spencer Foundation; the Wenner-Gren Foundation; the Center for Writing and Literacy, which is funded by the Graduate Research Initiative of the State University of New York at Albany; and, finally, the Computer Center of the Polytechnic of North London, Ladbroke House, which provided facilities for the final draft. The constructive critics of the presentations and earlier versions of the paper should be credited, rather than blamed, for whatever its quality has turned out to be.

REFERENCES

Abimbola, W. 1976. *IFÁ: An Exposition of Ifá Literary Corpus.* Ibadan: Oxford University Press.

———. 1977. *Ifá Divination Poetry.* New York: NOK Publishers.

Akinnaso, F. N. 1981. "The Consequences of Literacy in Pragmatic and Theoretical Perspectives." *Anthropology and Education Quarterly,* 12:163–200.

———. 1982a. "On the Differences between Spoken and Written Language." *Language and Speech,* 25:97–125.

———. 1982b. "The Literate Writes and the Nonliterate Chants: Written Language and Ritual Communication in Sociolinguistic Perspective," in *Linguistics and Literacy,* William Frawley, ed., 7–36. New York: Plenum Press.

———. 1985. "On the Similarities between Spoken and Written Language." *Language and Speech,* 28:323–59.

———. 1988. "The Sociolinguistics of Communication in Speech and Writing," in *Communication and the Evolution of Civilization,* W. Leeds-Hurwitz, ed., 175–89. Needham Heights: Ginn Press.

Barth, F. 1990. "The Guru and the Conjurer: Transactions in Knowledge and the Shaping of Culture in Southeast Asia and Melanesia." *Man* (N.S.), 25:640–53.

Bascom, W. 1952. "Two Forms of Afro-Cuban Divination," in *Acculturation in the Americas,* vol. 2 in *Proceedings of the 29th International Congress of Americanists,* S. Tax, ed., 169–79. Chicago: University of Chicago Press.

———. 1969. *Ifá Divination: Communication between Gods and Men in West Africa.* Bloomington: Indiana University Press.

———. 1980. *Sixteen Cowries: Yoruba Divination from Africa to the New World.* Bloomington: Indiana University Press.

Biber, D. 1988. *Variation across Speech and Writing.* Cambridge: Cambridge University Press.

Bloch, M. 1977. "The Past and the Present in the Present." *Man* (N.S.), 12:278–92.

Bloomfield, L. 1927. "Literate and Illiterate Speech." *American Speech,* 2:432–39.

Bourdieu, P. 1977. "The Economics of Linguistic Exchanges." *Social Science Information,* 16:645–68.

Browning, R. 1982. "Greek Diglossia Yesterday and Today." *International Journal of the Sociology of Language,* 35:49–68.

Bruner, J. S. 1966. "On Cognitive Growth," in *Studies in Cognitive Growth,* J. S. Bruner, R. R. Oliver, and P. M. Greenfield, eds. New York: Wiley.

Brunton, R. 1989. "The Cultural Instability of Egalitarian Societies." *Man* (N.S.), 24:673–81.

Buenaventura-Passon, E.; and S. E. Brown. 1980. "Forced Transition from Egalitarianism to Male Dominance: The Bari of Columbia," in *Women and Colonization,* M. Etienne and E. Leacock, eds., 109–33. New York: Praeger.

Burke, P. 1987. "The Uses of Literacy in Early Modern Italy," in *The Social History of Language,* P. Burke and R. Porter, eds., 21–42. Cambridge: Cambridge University Press.

Burton, W. F. P. 1961 [1939]. *Luba Religion and Magic in Custom and Belief.* Tervuren: Musée Royal de l'Afrique Centrale, *Annales des Sciences Humaines,* 35.

Cohen, Y. A. 1971. "The Shaping of Men's Minds: Adaptations to Imperatives of Culture," in *Anthropological Perspectives on Education,* M. L. Wax, S. Diamond, and F. O. Gearing, eds., 19–50. New York: Basic Books.

Cole, M.; and S. Scribner. 1974. *Culture and Thought.* New York: Wiley.

Cook-Gumperz, J., ed. 1986. *The Social Construction of Literacy.* Cambridge: Cambridge University Press.

Diamond, S. 1971. "Epilogue," in *Anthropological Perspectives on Education,* M. L. Wax, S. Diamond, and F. O. Gearing, eds., 300–306. New York: Basic Books.

Durkheim, E. 1915 [1912]. *The Elementary Forms of the Religious Life.* London: Macmillan.

Ewald, J. 1988. "Speaking, Writing, and Authority: Explorations in and from the Kingdom of Taqali." *Comparative Studies in Society and History,* 30:2, 199–224.

Ferguson, C. A. 1959. "Diglossia." *Word,* 15:325–40.

Finnegan, R. 1988. *Literacy and Orality: Studies in the Technology of Communication.* Oxford: Basil Blackwell.

Finney, B., ed. 1976. *Pacific Navigation and Voyaging.* Wellington: The Polynesian Society.

Flanagan, J. G. 1989. "Hierarchy in Simple 'Egalitarian' Societies." *Annual Review of Anthropology,* 18:245–66.

Fortes, M. 1970 [1938]. "Social and Psychological Aspects of Education in Taleland," in *From Child to Adult: Studies in the Anthropology of Education,* J. Middleton, ed., 14–74. New York: The Natural History Press.

Frake, C. O. 1985. "Cognitive Maps of Time and Tide among Medieval Seafarers." *Man* (N.S.), 20:254–70.

Fulton, R. M. 1972. "The Political Structures and Functions of Poro in Kpelle Society." *American Anthropologist,* 74:1218–33.

Gelb, I. J. 1952. *A Study of Writing.* Chicago: University of Chicago Press.

Gell, A. 1985. "How to Read a Map: Remarks on the Practical Logic of Navigation." *Man* (N.S.), 20:271–86.

Gibbs, J. L., Jr. 1965. "The Kpelle of Liberia," in *Peoples of Africa,* J. L. Gibbs, Jr., ed. New York: Holt, Rinehart and Winston.

Gladwin, T. 1970. *East Is a Big Bird: Navigation and Logic on Pulawat Atoll.* Cambridge, MA: Harvard University Press.

Gleason, H. A., Jr. 1961. *An Introduction to Descriptive Linguistics.* New York: Holt, Rinehart and Winston.

Goody, J. 1977. *The Domestication of the Savage Mind.* Cambridge: Cambridge University Press.

————. 1980. "Thought and Writing," in *Soviet and Western Anthropology*, E. Gellner, ed., 119–33. London: Duckworth.

————. 1982. "Alternative Paths to Knowledge in Oral and Literate Cultures," in *Spoken and Written Language: Exploring Orality and Literacy*, D. Tannen, ed., 201–15. Norwood, NJ: Ablex.

————. 1986. *The Logic of Writing and the Organization of Society*. Cambridge: Cambridge University Press.

————. 1987. *The Interface between the Written and the Oral*. Cambridge: Cambridge University Press.

————, ed. 1968. *Literacy in Traditional Societies*. Cambridge: Cambridge University Press.

————; and I. Watt. 1963. "The Consequences of Literacy." *Comparative Studies in Society and History*, 5:3, 304–45.

Gumperz, J. J. 1964. "Religion and Social Communication in Village North India." *Journal of Asian Studies*, 23:89–97.

Halliday, M. A. K. 1967. *Grammar, Society, and the Noun*. London: University of London.

Havelock, E. A. 1963. *Preface to Plato*. Cambridge, MA: Harvard University Press.

Herskovits, M. J. 1973 [1947]. "Education and the Sanctions of Custom," in *Cultural Relevance and Educational Issues: Readings in Anthropology and Education*, A. J. Ianni and E. Storey, eds., 29–48. Boston: Little, Brown.

Howe, L. E. A. 1981. "The Social Determination of Knowledge: Maurice Bloch and Balinese Time." *Man* (N.S.), 16:220–34.

Hymes, D. 1981. *"In Vain I Tried to Tell You": Essays in Native American Ethnopoetics*. Philadelphia: University of Pennsylvania Press.

Irvine, J. T. 1979. "Formality and Informality in Communicative Events." *American Anthropologist*, 81:773–90.

Kapferer, J. 1981. "Socialization and the Symbolic Order of the School." *Anthropology and Education Quarterly*, 12:258–74.

Lancy, D. F. 1975. "The Social Organization of Learning: Initiation Rituals and Public Schools." *Human Organization*, 34:457–68.

————. 1980. "Becoming a Blacksmith in Gbarngasuakwelle." *Anthropology and Education Quarterly*, 11:266–74.

Lave, J. 1977. "Cognitive Consequences of Traditional Apprenticeship Training in West Africa." *Anthropology and Education Quarterly*, 8:177–80.

Leach, E. R. 1965 [1954]. *Political Systems of Highland Burma*. Boston: Beacon Press.

————. 1968. "Ritual," in *International Encyclopedia of the Social Sciences*, D. L. Sills, ed., 520–26. New York: Macmillan.

Lewis, D. 1972. *We the Navigators*. Honolulu: University of Hawaii Press.

Little, K. L. 1949. "The Role of the Secret Society in Cultural Specialization." *American Anthropologist*, 51:199–212.

————. 1965. "The Political Function of the Poro (Part I)." *Africa*, 35:349–65.

————. 1966. "The Political Function of the Poro (Part II)." *Africa,* 36:62–71.

Loewe, M.; and C. Blacker, eds. 1981. *Divination and Oracles.* London: George Allen and Unwin.

Lucy, J. 1988. "The Role of Language in the Development of Representation: A Comparison of the Views of Piaget and Vygotsky." *The Quarterly Newsletter of the Laboratory of Comparative and Human Cognition,* 10:99–103.

McDowell, J. H. 1983. "The Semiotic Constitution of Kamsa Ritual Language." *Language in Society,* 12:23–46.

Mead, M. 1928. *Coming of Age in Samoa.* New York: Morrow.

————. 1930. *Growing Up in New Guinea.* New York: Morrow.

————. 1943. "Our Education Emphases in Primitive Perspective." *American Journal of Sociology,* 48:633–39.

————. 1964. *Continuities in Cultural Evolution.* New Haven: Yale University Press.

Middleton, J., ed. 1970. *From Child to Adult: Studies in the Anthropology of Education.* New York: The Natural History Press.

Murphy, W. P. 1980. "Secret Knowledge as Property and Power in Kpelle Society: Elders versus Youth." *Africa,* 50:193–207.

Newman, S. 1964. "Vocabulary Levels: Zuni Sacred and Slang Usage," in *Language in Culture and Society,* D. Hymes, ed. 397–406. New York: Harper and Row.

Olson, D. R. 1977. "From Utterance to Text: The Bias of Language in Speech and Writing." *Harvard Educational Review,* 47:257–81.

————. 1988. "Mind and Media: The Epistemic Functions of Literacy." *Journal of Communication,* 38:27–36.

Olson, D. R.; N. Torrance; and A. Hildyard, eds. 1985. *Literacy, Language, and Learning: The Nature and Consequences of Reading and Writing.* Cambridge: Cambridge University Press.

Ong, W. 1959. "Latin Language as a Renaissance Puberty Rite." *Studies in Philology,* 56:103–24.

————. 1971. *Rhetoric, Romance, and Technology: Studies in the Interaction of Expression and Culture.* Ithaca, NY: Cornell University Press.

————. 1982. *Orality and Literacy: The Technologizing of the Word.* London: Methuen.

Owusu, M. 1978. "Ethnography of Africa: The Usefulness of the Useless." *American Anthropologist,* 80:310–34.

Parkin, D. 1979. "Straightening the Paths from Wilderness: The Case of Divinatory Speech." *Journal of the Anthropological Society of Oxford* (JASO), 10:147–60.

Ramirez, F. O.; and J. Boli. 1987. "The Political Construction of Mass Schooling: European Origins and Worldwide Institutionalization." *Sociology of Education,* 60:2–17.

Raum, O. F. 1940. *Chaga Childhood.* London: Oxford University Press.

Reefe, T. Q. 1975. "A History of the Luba Empire to c. 1885." Berkeley: University of California. Ph.D. disser.

————. 1977. "Lukasa: A Luba Memory Device." *African Arts,* 10:49–50.

Ridout, W. M., Jr. 1971. "Education and Elites: The Making of the New Elites and the Formal Education System in the Congo." Stanford: Stanford University. Ph.D. disser.

Roberts, J. I.; and S. K. Akinsanya, eds. 1976. *Educational Patterns and Cultural Configurations.* New York: David McKay Co.

Rogoff, B. 1981. "Schooling and the Development of Cognitive Skills," in *Handbook of Crosscultural Psychology,* H. Triandis and A. Heron, eds., vol. 4, 233–94. Rockleigh, NJ: Allyn and Bacon.

Schousboe, K.; and M. T. Larsen, eds. 1989. *Literacy and Society.* Copenhagen: Akademisk Forlag and Center for Research in the Humanities.

Scribner, S.; and M. Cole. 1973. "Cognitive Consequences of Formal and Informal Education." *Science,* 182:553–59.

————. 1981. *The Psychology of Literacy.* Cambridge, MA: Harvard University Press.

Sherzer, J. 1983. *Kuna Ways of Speaking: An Ethnographic Perspective.* Austin: University of Texas Press.

Sjoberg, G. 1960. *The Preindustrial City: Past and Present.* New York: Wiley.

Street, B. V. 1984. *Literacy in Theory and Practice.* Cambridge: Cambridge University Press.

Studstill, J. D. 1979. "Education in a Luba Secret Society." *Anthropology and Education Quarterly,* 10:67–79.

Tedlock, B. 1978. "Quiche Maya Divination: A Theory of Practice." Albany: State University of New York. Ph.D. disser.

————. 1982. "Sound Texture and Metaphor in Quiche Maya Ritual Language." *Current Anthropology,* 23:269–72.

Tedlock, D. 1972. *Finding the Center: Narrative Poetry of the Zuni Indians.* New York: Dial.

————. 1983. *The Spoken Word and the Work of Interpretation.* Philadelphia: University of Pennsylvania Press.

Turner, V. 1969. *The Ritual Process: Structure and Anti-Structure.* Chicago: Aldine.

Van Gennep, A. 1960 [1909]. *The Rites of Passage,* M. B. Vizedom and G. L. Caffee, trans. London: Routledge and Kegan Paul.

Vygotsky, L. 1978 [1930]. *Mind in Society: The Development of Higher Psychological Processes.* Cambridge, MA: Harvard University Press.

————. 1987 [1934]. *Thought and Language.* Cambridge, MA: M.I.T. Press.

Wagner, D. A.; and A. Lofti. 1983. "Learning to Read by 'Rote'." *International Journal of the Sociology of Language,* 42:111–21.

Watkins, M. H. 1943. "The West African 'Bush' School." *American Journal of Sociology,* 48:666–75.

Werbner, R. P. 1973. "The Superabundance of Understanding: Kalanga Rhetoric and Domestic Divination." *American Anthropologist,* 75:1414–40.

————. 1989. *Ritual Passage, Sacred Journey: The Process and Organization of Re-*

ligious Movement, chap. 1. Washington, DC: Smithsonian Institution and University of Manchester Press.

Whiting, J. M. W. 1941. *Becoming a Kwoma.* New Haven: Yale University Press.

Woodburn, J. 1979. "Minimal Politics: The Political Organization of the Hadza of North Tanzania," in *Politics in Leadership: A Comparative Perspective,* W. A. Shack and P. S. Cohen, eds., 244–64. Oxford: Clarendon Press.

———. 1982. "Egalitarian Societies." *Man* (N.S.), 17:431–51.

Zeitlyn, D. 1990. "Professor Garfinkel Visits the Soothsayers: Ethnomethodology and Mambila Divination." *Man* (N.S.), 25:654–66.

Genealogies of Reading and the Scholarly Cultures of Islam

Brinkley Messick

Any renaissance begins by going back to the heritage, any thought capable of change proceeds from a contemporary reading of the past.

—Muslim Students Association
(Cairo, 1975)[1]

Behind the ever-present textual symbol of the clenched and upraised Quran, an important subtheme of late-twentieth-century Islamist movements is the reappropriation of selected medieval treatises by leading thinkers and by a new reading public. Perhaps the most significant instance of this phenomenon in the Sunni world involves the writings of the noted jurist Ibn Taymiyya (1268–1328). One particularly influential modern reading of his work is by Sayyid Qutb, the mid-twentieth-century Egyptian literary critic turned Muslim Brother theoretician. Sayyid Qutb's own works, which comprise key passages drawing on legal-political arguments elaborated by Ibn Taymiyya, have had an enormous impact in Egypt and in many other Sunni Muslim settings from Morocco to Central and Southeast Asia. As used by Sayyid Qutb and other contemporary thinkers, and read by thousands more in widely available popular printed editions, Ibn Taymiyya may fit the characterization of him as the "father of the Islamic Revolution" (Sivan 1983; cf. Sivan 1985:94–107).

Generationally distinct from comparable turn-of-the-twentieth-century developments in the Arab literary renaissance and from the Islamic reform movement of the early nationalist era (Hourani 1962), contemporary rereadings have occurred in changed contexts that include not only the very different social and political predicaments of postcolonial nation-states, but also such specific institutional developments as the availablity of mass circulation printed editions (and other media) and long established state systems of universal education (Eickelman 1992). In examining a particular local instance of contemporary readings of classical texts, I attend in passing to the texts in question, which illustrate a broader (or alternative) range of interests than those represented by the Ibn Taymiyya phenomenon, but my main analytic interest is to elucidate the distinctive forms of reading involved.

In the process, I rethink my own understandings of Islamic discursive modernity. In a previous work (Messick 1993), I examined the case of the transformation of the scholarly culture of late-nineteenth and twentieth-century highland (North) Yemen. In that analysis, I placed emphasis on a series of ruptures and other more gradual shifts which, together, seemed to describe the decisive end of the old system of instruction, along with its patterns of knowledge transmission, notions of textual authority, and forms of writing. Here, in part II, I consider some instructional developments from the 1980s, and especially the 1990s, that pose challenges to my earlier account of a discursive discontinuity.

I begin, however, in part I, with an interrogation of comparative research on Islamic scholarship, specifically concerning the general problem of the "oral" in this literate culture, and including the centrality of a recitational form of "reading" and instruction known as *qara'a*. My analysis of recent reading developments in Yemen depends on an understanding of a number of specific features and relations of the classical and transitionally modern Islamic scholarly practices of the early twentieth century.

I Comparison

In the West, Muslim scholarship generally is held in high esteem both for its transmissions and elaborations of earlier knowledges, notably significant parts of the Greek corpus,[2] and for its own unique creations in numerous other fields, including the "queen" of the old Muslim academic disciplines, Islamic law. Although complex, diverse, and thoroughly literate, this scholarly tradition nevertheless has posed a comparative problem. This centers on the characterization of some distinctive features of Islamic textuality and the associated modes of instruction. Conventionally phrased, the features in question involve the interrelation of oral and written modalities, specifically, the place of the oral in the sphere of the written (or, perhaps, the reverse, the place of the written in that of the oral).

In recent comparative research, the techniques of this venerable scholarly culture have typically been classified as mixtures. For example, in his pioneering ethnographic and historical inquiry into traditional Islamic education, focused on the scholarly world of the Yusufiyya *madrasa* (institution of higher learning) in Marrakesh in the 1930s, anthropologist Dale Eickelman (1978:487; see also 1985) describes the pedagogical style as

> intermediate between oral and written systems of transmission of knowledge. Its key texts existed in written form but were conveyed orally, to be written down and memorized by students.

Similarly, in his recent synthetic overview of Islamic scholarship, historian Aziz al-Azmeh (1986:155) describes the instructional system as "composite." Other observers, such as Jeanette Wakin (1972:4) addressing the evidential status of written notarial texts, have found specific related aspects of this scholarly culture to be "ambiguous."

Although neutral in intent, such classifications and evaluations implicitly invoke polar standards: either a fully "written" system for knowledge transmission as opposed to a completely "oral" one, or, at least, a system identifiable as principally one thing or the other. As opposed to some type of sui generis analysis (which would activate the reverse problem of noncomparability), the Muslim system has been inscribed, in terms such as "intermediate," "composite," or "ambiguous," in implicit dichotomies at once too ideal and also perilously close to the worn, unilineal continuum stretching outward, and backward, from "us" to "them."

This last danger is realized in the comparative work of Jack Goody (1968, 1977, 1986, 1987) in which such phenomena as formal instructional emphases on recitation and memorization are classified as elements of "guru"-type educational systems, and thus of situations of "restricted literacy." Although revised in Goody's most recent work, his original measure for "restricted" was provided by the purported early Greek model of "widespread literacy," and behind this conception was the assumed unique significance of the West. Its distinctive features overridden, the Islamic case is lumped together with subcontinent and East Asian systems into the generic category of complex, but non-western and premodern, "traditional" literacies. Such comparison, with a tilt to a western yardstick and evolutionary conceptions, is perhaps best illustrated by the position taken, in passing, on the Islamic case by Walter Ong (1982:26). In Ong's view, Muslim cultures "never fully interiorized writing."

Such comparative conclusions misunderstand Muslim literate culture. That such a venerable textual and instructional system could pose problems of characterization has less to do with the features of the case than with the limitations of our means of comparison. At the same time, recent interdisciplinary and cross-cultural work on textual cultures (e.g., J. Boyarin 1993a) has begun to unsettle our assumptions about the nature of modern textual communities in the West, which had provided implicit models for "fully written" systems of knowledge transmission. As opposed, for example, to standard (ideological) conceptions of a distinctively modern "reading" as a silent and solitary phenomenon, new attention is being given both to listening for sounds and "voices" in written texts and also to the social aspects of reading (Long 1993).

Scholarly Culture

Franz Rosenthal, perhaps best known as the principal English translator of Ibn Khaldun (Rosenthal 1958), published a short but seminal account of *The Technique and Approach of Muslim Scholarship* (1947) together with monumental studies of Islamic historiography (1968) and of the central Muslim concept of "knowledge" (*'ilm:* 1970). All are outwardly framed in terms of Rosenthal's interests in civilizational comparisons, primarily the relations between Islamic phenomena and the West, from Greek antiquity to the modern era of print, although he concludes his work on *'ilm* with some comparative suggestions about Indian and Chinese notions of knowledge and patterns of scholarship. In the first of these works, Rosenthal (1947:2–5) opens with a review of a number of discrepant western understandings, from Hegel down to nineteenth- and early-twentieth-century Orientalists, about the nature of Muslim intellectual activity. Citing a number of standard misconceptions— concerning fatalism, incapacity for change, a history of intellectual decay, tendency toward fanaticism, and so on—Rosenthal comments on their "inherent contradictions" and, generally, on the "unfounded feeling of superiority" in "western opinions concerning Muslim scholarship" (4). Inside his comparative frames, analyses turn to Arabic manuscript sources, which in various ways are "permitted to speak for themselves" (4).

The first section (6–40) of the 1947 work is entitled "The Written Word as the Basis of Knowledge." Here Rosenthal takes up the theme of orality, mainly represented by memorization, and again frames his analysis comparatively and critically. "Modern scholars," he writes (6), "living in a world where memorized knowledge no longer plays a significant role, have been fond of devoting their attention to the great number of reports about the remarkable powers of memory possessed by Muslim scholars." Rather than this emphasis on difference, however, Rosenthal takes the position that "in spite of all the real and affected reverence paid to memorized knowledge, Muslim civilization, as much as any higher civilization, was a civilization of the written word" (7). At the same time, he acknowledges, as "noteworthy facts," not only the "memorizing of the Quran and of vast quantities of traditions as well as poems and stories," but also the "marked preference for oral instruction as compared to knowledge acquired from books."

To make his point about the highly elaborated and culturally specific understandings of the written word in the Muslim "manuscript age," Rosenthal turns to a treatise that provides a "systematic treatment" of this topic. The selected theoretical text, one of many in the *Adab al-'alim wa-l-muta'allim* ("Culture of the teacher and the learner") genre,[3] is "permitted to speak" at length (8–18) on such detailed matters as the care of books, lending and borrowing, copying, collation of copies with originals, corrections and marginal notes, handwriting issues, variant readings, erasures, punctuation, abbreviation, marking quotations, "footnotes," and tables of contents and "indexes."

Where Rosenthal's works contribute importantly to our understanding of the classification structures of Islamic concepts of "knowledge," the specific achievements of the discipline of history, and the detailed dimensions of classical textual culture, they do so in an eclectic manner, drawing on sources spanning many periods and settings. More focused in design is George Makdisi's fundamental study of the Muslim madrasa, the institution of higher learning, which principally concerns eleventh-century Baghdad. As his title, *The Rise of Colleges: Institutions of Learning in Islam and the West* (1981), indicates, however, the book also has important comparative concerns. The thrust of the work is in its detailed institutional histories, typologies, and descriptions, and the main comparative point in this regard is to distinguish the university, as a western organizational form, from the Muslim "college," the madrasa, based on the individually created charitable endowment. Otherwise, there are numerous parallels "in the institutions, in the methods of instruction, in the posts, as well as in the more general phenomena, such as the prominence and pervasiveness of legal studies, the resulting decline and subordination of the literary arts, and the crowning achievement of the Middle Ages: the scholastic method in law and theology, with their *quaestiones disputatae* and *reportationes*" (224).

For Makdisi, the "most basic technical term" of classical Islamic education is the verb *qara'a,* which now means "to read" in standard Arabic, but which then meant "to read out, read aloud, recite" (1981:141, 241–43, 271).[4] Condensed in Makdisi's definition, both in his modifiers and in his inclusion of "recite" within the set of meanings, is the key issue of oralization within reading, as compared with the assumption of silence in the modern English verb "to read." Makdisi notes that the meaning of *qara'a* "goes back" to that of the Quran, which means "recitation." He also finds *qara'a* comparable in semantic range to the twelfth-century Christian term *legere,* as explicated by his sources, Hugh of St. Victor and John of Salisbury. He also sees an equivalence between the derived terms *qira'a* (recitation) and *lectio* (lecture).

In the instructional context, *qara'a* means "to teach," that is, to teach a text, which is either read aloud by the teacher or recited directly from memory, and either "heard," an authoritative form of reception in itself, or taken down as dictation by a lesson circle of students. Here the social and public, as opposed to the modern individual and private dimensions of "reading" are salient. Beyond the postures of listening or taking dictation, and beyond the give-and-take of questions and answers or disputation in the lesson circle, the student's decisive, active relation to a teacher was conveyed by a compound, the verb *qara'a* plus the preposition *'ala* ("to"). If the "reading aloud" by the teacher initiated an authoritative textual transmission, the eventual "reading aloud," by the student, from his own transcription of the text, "to" the listening teacher, finalized it. Makdisi remarks, however, that whereas an Oxford or Cambridge student still "reads" a subject, that is, studies under a teacher, this sense of the verb "has disappeared from the modern Arabic scene."

An important recent contribution to this line of research on Islamic education is Jonathan Berkey's *The Transmission of Knowledge in Medieval Cairo* (1992), where the comparative concern is intracivilizational. Berkey (14) opposes a "tendency to treat developments in different Islamic societies as fundamentally comparable and interchangeable" and offers instead a richly "circumstantial" account of phenomena in Mamluk Egypt, 1250–1517. In addition to *adab* works, biographical histories, and intellectual genealogies, this study is based on *waqfiyya*s, the deeds of endowment for the various institutions of learning—a source not available to Makdisi. Stressing the "social context" of knowledge transmission, Berkey includes innovative chapters on informal connections between the world of scholarship and the military elite (the Mamluks), on women and education, and on instructional relations in the urban social setting.

In his pivotal chapter on instruction, Berkey (1992:21–43) underscores the well-known Islamic emphasis on the "personal connection" in the student-teacher interchange, on authority conferral by *personae* rather than by institutional *loci.* In his treatment of the oral and written relations at the center of this personalized transmission process, Berkey (24) also notes the oral "bias" in his sources regarding the nature of the "system." Where practices of silent (and thus private) reading in the Europe of the early Middle Ages may have been impeded by technical deficiencies in the available writing system, in the medieval Islamic case, despite the "lack" (from the western perspective) of written vowels, there was no such blockage. Instead,

> the system clearly *preferred* reading aloud and the oral transmission of texts, and thereby sought the exact and undeviating replication of the knowledge transmitted through any given book. (28; emphasis in original)

Both Makdisi and Berkey cite the characteristic assertions that define the oral transmission complex. Verses attributed to Ibn al-Najjar (d. 1245) compare knowledge retained in and recitable from memory to knowledge contained in books (Makdisi 1981:101–2):

> If retentive memory's not what you possess,
> Your collecting of books is quite useless!
> Would you dare, in company, nonsense say,
> When your learning at home is stored away?

An *adab* work (Berkey 1992:26) compares knowledge gained in personalized (oral) instruction with instruction obtained from reading books:

> One should not study with another who himself studied only from books, without having read [them] to a learned *shaykh* [teacher]. Taking knowledge from books [alone] leads to spelling errors and mistakes and mispronunciation. Whoever does not take his learning [*'ilm*] from the mouths of men is like he who learns courage without ever facing battle.

Berkey concludes, however (1992:26), that "the overall attitude toward writing and the physical, written book as a means of transmitting knowledge remained ambivalent." But perhaps this finding of ambivalence represents an external view, whereas internally the situation was one of contestation, based on disciplinary and other differences. Perhaps the "system" was not a unitary phenomenon but rather there existed competing, or divergent, viewpoints on the standards of knowledge and the criteria for instruction. As opposed to the situation that obtained in the law-centered instruction program studied by both Makdisi and Berkey, for example, Rosenthal (1947:7) noted that

> the historian and theologian entirely relies upon written material. Memorized knowledge has no longer any place in his work.

Modernity

In research on Muslim instruction and textual relations in the twentieth century a different set of comparative problems emerges.[5] Although the focus of Dale

Eickelman's *Knowledge and Power in Morocco: The Education of a Twentieth-Century Notable* (1985) is on the formation of a young rural scholar in the Yusufiyya madrasa in Marrakesh, the significant context is French colonial rule. Prior to the colonial period, Islamic education in Morocco, with its unusually developed emphasis on memorization, was neither static nor in decline. Eickelman (1978:487) was cited above for his characterization of the associated instructional style as "intermediate," in oral/written terms, since the "key texts existed in written form but were conveyed orally, to be written down and memorized by students." A key contribution of this analysis, however, is the identification through ethnography and oral history of informal instructional processes that pass without notice in such sources as the biographical histories and the adab literature on instruction. In such written sources, it is the dyadic chains of teacher-student transmission and the formal lesson circle (*halqa*) that structure accounts, whereas Eickelman argues that it was "peer learning" and informal reading circles among students that were the principal sites for the understanding of the memorized texts.

Colonial rule led to several dramatic changes in this world of instruction. These included, within the old madrasas themselves, first, the appearance of reformist shaykhs and some new subject matter in the 1920s, and then reorganization and government control imposed by the French in the 1930s. Outside these old institutions, the French established a competing, and eventually dominant, system of western-style government schools, while less successful "Free Schools" with alternative instruction in Arabic were organized early on by Moroccans. In this context, the effective "collapse" of the old system of Islamic education occurred in the 1930s. By independence in 1956,

> higher religious learning was an empty shell of its former self. Men of learning retained widespread popular respect but their numbers were no longer being reproduced. (Eickelman 1985:161)

After independence, the national secondary school system (in which I taught in the early 1970s), consisting of baccalaureat-level training and a continental-style reliance on memorization in some subjects, was expanded and extended, as was the equivalently structured university system. In the 1980s, however, the French language and the European cast of the curriculum were phased out in a process of "Arabization." At the newly demarcated "preschool" level, reorganized, government-supervised Quranic schools specializing in rote acquisition of the sacred text were joined by various types of modern-style preschool and their comprehension-oriented readings in the Arabic equivalents of "Dick and Jane" books (Wagner, Messick, and Spratt 1986; Wagner 1994; cf. Messick 1993:75–84 on the Yemeni equivalent).

Despite the institutional "collapse" (Eickelman 1985:164), the Moroccan madrasa-based "paradigm of valued knowledge as fixed and memorizable" persisted. The current version of the old system, now referred to as "original" education, is located institutionally in government-organized "Islamic institutes" (ma'ahid al-islamiyya), developed in the 1960s, and in branches of the Qarawiyyin University in Fes. "Memorization still occurs" in "original" education, but

> it is on the basis of mass production to a standard curriculum, complete with examinations, as opposed to the style of earlier institutions. It also systematically introduces students to the reading and writing of secular texts, something that traditional Quranic schools did not do. (Eickelman 1985:171)

The basic "shift" identified by Eickelman (1985:168) is from a body of knowledge designed for and maintained in memory to (a different) one "consulted" in written texts. As one consequence, "the older generation of men of learning consider their younger replacements as essentially ignorant, knowing little of Islamic law beyond the bilingual French and Arabic handbooks prepared by the Ministry of Justice" (168).

Adjusted for important differences in history and setting, particularly the absence of a western colonial period, my account (Messick 1993, chaps. 4–6) of an Islamic instructional system and its demise in highland Yemen is comparable in many respects. Although less predominant than in Morocco, memorization was important, starting with at least part of the Quran in Quranic school and then proceeding to short manuals of law and grammar at the beginning of higher instruction in the madrasa. Memorization was one of three basic modalities of textual acquisition in what I refer to as the "recitational complex." Most advanced texts, including many longer works of law, were studied in the second, "reading aloud to" (qara'a 'ala) method discussed by Makdisi, based on an initial dictation or recitation, teacher to student, and a final verification, "reading aloud," student "to" teacher. In a third modality, also discussed by Makdisi (1981:141, 243), certain types of text, most of them collections of hadith (sayings and doings of the Prophet), were transmitted through the authoritative "hearing," without dictation-taking, of a text recited or read aloud to a group of listeners. Although essential in practice, the roles of written texts, techniques of writing and such activities as "peer learning" were backgrounded in the representations (in biographical works and in adab treatises) of all three modes of this recitational complex in favor of an ideological emphasis on the oral-aural transmission links between teacher and student. One of my comparative interventions was to characterize this as a culturally specific logocentrism (after Derrida 1974), a privileging of the medium of human "presence" and of the spoken word together with a distrust of the human absence associated with the "dangerous supplement," writing.

There are two further general features of this recitational complex with respect to its centrality in the scholarly and political system of textual authority. One is that this "textual habitus" involved a whole series of equivalent concerns, overt privilegings of the oral channel accompanied by quiet reliances on the written, not only in instruction but also in such areas as adjudication and in such specific doctrines as that of evidence, all of which lent a coherence across the diverse domains of authoritative discursive activity. A second feature, however, is that this recitational complex was at the same time limited in scope; its concerns were confined, in instruction for example, to the authoritative core of the academic disciplines, whereas, as Rosenthal noted, such fields as historiography, or the so-called "foreign (i.e., Greek) sciences," exhibit only small traces, if any, of such concerns. Even within the core disciplines—law, hadith, grammar, etc.—the recitational orientation was operative only with respect to fundamental texts, known as the *mutun* (sing. *matn*), which were memorized and recited (with the Quran as paradigm), but not to the expansive and never memorized commentary literatures (*sharh,* pl. *shuruh*). Beyond the core subjects and their basic texts, beyond the theory of the judge's presence and his word, beyond the doctrine that excluded documentary evidence, more conventional (from a western perspective) techniques of reading and writing replaced the interrelated forms of memorization, recitation, dictation, reading aloud, and hearing. And beyond all this was a surround of general literate life and ordinary textual usages, including a routine notion of "reading" (*mutala'a*) understood to be silent and private.

An initial group of western-style, Lancaster-descended, "new method" schools—new in both subjects of study and organizational form—was instituted by the Ottomans in district towns in the then Province of Yemen well before the turn of the twentieth century, but the madrasa of the mosque lesson circle persisted, with some important hybridized modifications, as the principal educational institution until the northern Yemeni Republican Revolution of 1962 and the founding of the new nation-state's government school system. As opposed to the restricted intellectual genealogies associated with shari'a and other branches of knowledge, the contemporary state schools inculcate the specialized knowledges of the nation and the citizen to a student body universal in design. The particularized transmission license (*ijaza*) of the old teacher-student relation has given way to the standardized state diploma.

An interconnected aspect of this broad discursive rupture was associated with the introduction of print technology (again by the Ottomans). Received in a culturally specific way,[6] print not only made the first newspapers possible but also altered the old manuscript-era discourse of such key scholarly productions as history writing (Messick 1993:123–31). At the same time, the relation of the spoken and the written was transformed with the advent of new forms and ordered institutions of authoritative knowledge. Less encumbered by logo-centric concerns about its unreliability, writing now could be backed by state registration, while the older "spiral" spatial style of handwritten letters and documents gave way to the ruled frames of "straightened" texts (Messick 1993:231–50).

II 1990s Readings

By the final decade of the twentieth century highland Yemeni towns such as Ibb,[7] a provincial capital of about 5,000 before the Revolution that had grown to about 50,000, had several Kuwaiti-built elementary schools, separate inter-mediate schools for boys and girls, and one or more secondary schools. As opposed to the pre-Revolutionary, Quranic school to mosque-madrasa se-quence, with its central focus on the Quran and then the law and supporting subjects, the national school system teaches (at the elementary level), in addi-tion to "Islamic instruction," Arabic language, mathematics, social studies, sciences and health, and art.

In the early 1980s, however, a competing school system of "Religious Institutes" (*ma'ahid al-diniyyah* or *al-'ilmiyyah*) had emerged, partly in reac-tion to the perceived secularism of the national schools with their highly politicized expatriate teachers (from Egypt, Syria, and Jordan). These institutes initially had endowment (*waqf*)[8] funding similar to that supporting the old mosque-madrasas, but later there were plans to incorporate them into the budget of the Ministry of Education. Unlike the "original" educational institu-tions of the same name in Morocco, the Yemeni institutes offer an array of subjects similar to those of the regular national schools but with the intent of providing stronger formation in Islamic subjects.

The first national university (San'a' University) was founded in 1971, and by the early 1990s branches of its four Colleges (Shari'a and Law, Literature, Sciences, and Commerce and Economics) were being instituted in selected provincial capitals. Shari'a law, the former "queen" of the madrasa disciplines, had been displaced from centrality in advanced instruction, and from its place as the shared knowledge of all scholars. Now it is taught only in the diluted form of "Islamic civilization" in high schools, while focused study occurs in one of four tracks in university education. There it is taught comparatively, as composed of several possible "schools" (*madhahib,* sing. *madhhab*) of thought, rather than, as previously, either as the school of the region or as that of the state. Postgraduate training in law, mainly for the formation of a modern judiciary, takes place at the High Judicial Institute.

Muhammad Aziz, a native of Ibb town, briefly attended one of the remaining Quranic schools in his neighborhood but stopped at the legally mandated age to enroll in the town's elementary-level Revolution School. He proceeded through the grades and from school to school in Ibb until he graduated with a diploma from the secondary school, after which he spent his year of compulsory service in the army. Following this military service, his father, a town merchant, supported him for a year in England so that he could study English at language institutes in Kent and London. During this time he took the TOEFL exam for the first time. Returning to Yemen in 1981, he worked briefly for Yemenia Airways and then enrolled at San'a' University in the College of Literature, where he joined the Department of English, majoring in English literature and minoring in Arabic. He received his B.A. in 1986 and then taught English for a year at the intermediate school level, under Ministry of Education auspices, as his required national service. Then, under appointment by the Ministry of Civil Service, he worked briefly as a translator in the Ministry of Public Works, but the pay was low and there was little work to do. He went back to the Ministry of Education, but found no teaching positions available, and so he accepted a post as a translator in the Ministry's Cultural Relations Department. Again, there was not much work to do. So, while retaining his Ministry position, he returned to the university to begin an M.A. program, taking courses with American, British, Egyptian, Sudanese, and Yemeni professors in American literature ("Modern Southern Authors"), the English novel, English drama, linguistics (including translation from English to Arabic) and neoclassical and Romantic poetry. But he could not complete the degree, due to family circumstances, and he returned to Ibb and took a position as a teacher of elementary English at the local Religious Institute.

Thus a modern Yemeni student's career in higher education, typical in many respects but unusual in the family's ability to finance a year of study abroad and, for Yemenis who did not grow up in Aden, the choice of English as a major. However, there is another side to this career, which began to surface during the years of Muhammad's undergraduate training at San'a' University.

This aspect of his training and instructional life raises questions about the persistence of older bodies of knowledge and older modes of transmission.

In a sketch of this other side of his career, written as part of an application for further study abroad, Muhammad describes, in English,[9] how the student side of it began:

> During my studies at the university, particularly at the end of the second year, through the holiday which was three months, I found a shaykh in my town Ibb teaching Arabic, focusing on syntax. His name is 'Abd Allah Yahya Al-'Ansi. I took his permission to join the group which he was teaching in a mosque called Al-Asadiyya [built in the thirteenth century as a madrasa] during the time of the afternoon prayers. So, I learnt syntax from a book called *Al-Kawakib al-durriyyah* [by al-Ahdal]. After finishing that book, we turned to another field which was a book known as *Sharh Matn al-Rahabiah*—which is about dividing inheritance among heirs. This was in the holiday of the fourth year.

A first observation to be made is simply that the shaykh and lesson circle format of instruction, in one of the classic subjects, grammar, continues to a limited extent on an informal basis. The location is a neighborhood mosque rather than the Great Mosque, which was the town's former formal madrasa. Inheritance, a key branch of Islamic jurisprudence, is also a traditional subject (see Messick 1993:285, n27).

Later, after completing his B.A. degree and returning to his home town and taking the position as an English instructor, he pursued more instruction in this pattern.

> I joined another shaykh called 'Ali bin 'Ali to study Quran reciting (*tajwid*)—one should utter each letter of the Quran correctly in a phonetical way. Also, I learnt some aspects of Islamic jurisprudence (*fiqh*).

"Some aspects": Muhammad does not write further about his efforts to study the law, the former centerpiece of advanced instruction, but he told me what happened. He approached 'Ali bin 'Ali, the last of the elderly teachers of the former madrasa at the Great Mosque, who now lives in a new apartment built for him on top of the empty old residence of the town's former students and poor teachers. 'Ali bin 'Ali told him to begin on his own by memorizing the introductory law text in verse form known as the "Cream" (*Zubad*), by Ibn Raslan (d. 1440),[10] and then to return to him for instruction proper. This pattern—acquisition of one or more concise basic texts through memorization and without a direct relation with a teacher—was the standard opening procedure in the old system. It was a step preparatory to regular lesson circle instruction in which the text would be recited or dictated by the teacher together with his commentaries and, if necessary, further explanations. Although the text in question is very short, twenty pages in one lithograph edition, and is in the mnemonically accessible form of a poem, Muhammad "did not see the point" of memorizing it and, although he tried, was unable to do so. Thus, a second observation: memorization, formerly essential, is no longer so readily practicable.

Muhammad continues, referring to other books he was reading on his own,

> when I found ambiguities in books concerning Islamic culture I was reading at home, I would would ask my shaykh and other scholars about the issues to be clarified.

This recalls what went on previously in the Ibb madrasa: "for the most part," a scholarly old judge told me in the mid-1970s, "the method of study rested upon independent student efforts prior to formal instruction, with consultation with the teacher only in cases of intractable issues" (Messick 1993:88–89). It also recalls a nineteenth century poem eulogizing an Ibb teacher as "our scholar and the interpreter of our era / Who clarified the ambiguous and the obscure" (45).

Muhammad had begun to accumulate a personal library, including a number of works on law, hadith, and history. A third observation: the market availablity of printed editions structured his purchases and thus, in part, his studies. Ever-increasing numbers of Yemeni classics and also treatises from nonindigenous schools of thought not previously in circulation in Yemen, or in circulation only in a limited fashion in expensive manuscript copies, were now widely available. He also had acquired a few old manuscript works, including one that had been a local student's collection of study texts, a handwritten artifact of "recitational" study (cf. Chartier 1992:55–56). This manuscript comprised texts in grammar and several other subjects, including the already mentioned basic law text, the *Zubad* of Ibn Raslan.[11]

A further significant moment in this informal parallel career concerned Muhammad's study of works of history, a subject not taught in the old madrasa. The technique, however, was a modified form of *qara'a 'ala*, the practice of reading aloud or reciting a text to the teacher. The important modification here is that there was no initial instruction from the teacher to the student.

I used to read a history of Yemen through my own book, which was called *Muluk al-tijan,*[12] while my instructor [shaykh] was listening and looking at his own copy and correcting mistakes, if any. Then, in the same way, I read a book called *Al-Suluk fi tabaqat al-'ulama' wa-l-muluk* [edited] by [a former Ibb resident and teacher, Muhammad] Al-Akwa'. After that, I read another book called *Tarikh al-Yaman al-musamma bi tarikh San'a' wa Zabid* by Imarah al-Yamani.

Observation four is that this key old method of qara'a 'ala continues to exhibit vitality, although, as in this instance, it is both modified and applied to new subject matter. Formerly, this method was the predominant form of teacher-student instruction, in the old shaykh and lesson circle format, in such core topics as law, hadith, and grammar. Books such as the *Zubad* and others utilized in the old curriculum were discursively designed for this type of recitational instruction, and they absolutely required the teacher's supporting commentary to flesh out their bare bones presentations. Recently, however, in these key old subject areas local authors have written new works with very different discursive constitutions. Two such books, in jurisprudence and in the theory of hadith, were presented to me with the identical remark: "This is a book that doesn't need a teacher, the teacher is the text."[13]

Later, initiating a significant turn toward giving rather than receiving instruction, Muhammad got a request from some young men he regularly sat with chewing *qat* in the afternoons. In this manner he became a debutant "shaykh" and began a new phase in his alternative career.

These fellows asked me to teach them some basic principles of Islam. I started to read [to them] a book called *Tazkiat al-nufus* by three writers, al-Ghazzali, Ibn Rajab Al-Hanbali, and Ibn al-Qayyim. The fellows were listening with admiration while I read and explained some ideas, particularly the Sufi notions concerning human behaviors toward God.

Observation five is to note the existence of an adult men's "reading" group. Prior to the Revolution in Ibb and other Yemeni towns there were study groups of leading, politically active scholars in which newly available, imported printed works such as Jurgi Zaydan's books on Islamic history and Ibn Khaldun's *Muqaddimah* were read aloud by individuals taking turns in the sitting room. Muhammad's activity is different. His fellows are not scholars, but they are literate and able to understand classical Arabic, and he alone is the reader and commentator. One clear thread of continuity here is the perceived sufficiency of the act of audition, of hearing a text read aloud. How differently the analytic problems of reception must be conceived here as compared with our theories emphasizing the dialectics of authors and readers. Here the key relation is between the "reader-interpreter" and his auditors, all based on a different culture and technology of communication.

Sufi, or Islamic mystical thought, was not taught in the mosque-madrasa, where "shari'a-minded" scholars, as Hodgson (1974:403) refers to them, actively rejected Sufi approaches as estatic deviations. Of course, Sufis, including those in Ibb around the turn of the century (see Messick 1993:274–77), had their own circles, but these are better known for ritual than for instruction. Sufi activity in Ibb and elsewhere in the Sunni region of Lower Yemen was suppressed, along with practices of saint veneration, under Shi'i-Zaydi rule by the imams of Upper Yemen from the demise of the Ottoman Empire in 1918 until the Revolution of 1962. A sixth observation, then, is to underscore the mystical content of some of these rereadings, especially since the Sufi tradition is anathema to legalists of the Ibn Taymiyya school, medieval and modern.[14] Is this type of "reading group" a descendant, in some respect, of earlier local Sufi instruction?

Muhammad next "taught" his group one of the most famous works of Islamic thought, which, among other features, is known for its integration of legal materials with Sufi thought.

> Then I pursued reading and explaining another book called *Ihya' 'ulum al-din* ["Revival of the Religious Sciences"] by Hugat al-Islam al-Ghazzali [d. 1111] in four volumes. This book was comprehensive and useful for listeners to come up with a complete idea about Islam in general and the method of approaching God in particular, i.e., knowing about some thoughts of Sufi scholars. The admiration for this book was astonishing, and I was asked to reread it for the group, since it covers the most important ideas needed about the Muslim life in general. I hesitated at the beginning and then agreed to their request.

Makdisi (1981:217–18; cf. Rosenthal 1970:95) states that in the premodern period this text was considered appropriate for "reciting that would be understood by the common people, and the consequences of which would not be harmful." According to Makdisi, this was the work of one type of "popular preacher" (the *qari' al-kursi*) of the era, who characteristically worked sitting down and inside, and always reading aloud from a book rather than reciting from memory—this as opposed to a second type, who delivered his text from memory, while standing and outside in the street.

A seventh observation concerns Muhammad's status as "reader" to his fellows. While clearly not a "preacher," he also is not a shaykh in the old sense of one who transmits a specific text on the authority of his reception of it, through instruction, from his own shaykh. He is more like the more advanced student who is sought out informally for "readings" in a situation of peer learning (Eickelman 1985:100–101). In the old madrasa, however, the identities of teacher and student were relative. Thus, a premodern Ibb historian (al-Burayhi 1983:99) describes an individual, perhaps like Muhammad, "studying with those more learned than he and teaching those less so." Added to all this in Muhammad's case, however, is the question of a perceived crossover of instructional authority from his university training.

Muhammad's second reading of al-Ghazzali's book was interrupted as he had to go to the capital city to retake the TOEFL exam, for which he had been preparing.

> I was unsatisfied [with the TOEFL score], for I didn't prepare well with guidebooks on how to score good results. And this was attained by personal efforts, without any assistance, neither from teachers, who didn't exist in the town, nor from books, which weren't available.

His study for the English test was a solitary process, at least away from the university community, where there are study groups. The interruption (in his account) of the TOEFL exam in his second "reading" of al-Ghazzali prompts an eighth observation: Muhammad integrates in his life two very different sets of cultural practices (and associated genealogies) of reading and writing.

The conclusion to Muhammad's statement provides a quick listing of a number of other works he "read" and commented on, and an indication of at least one text the "fellows" actively rejected.

> After coming back from San'a', I began to read a book called *Al-Tawhid al-a'zam* by Shaykh Ahmad bin 'Alwan [a Sufi from Lower Yemen]. The book was another contribution toward understanding more about how to approach God in terms of knowledge. After that, I brought another book, *Iqaz al-himam fi sharh al-hikam,* the Hikam by Ibn 'Ata Allah al-Sakandary and the Sharh [commentary] by Ibn 'Ajibah [a Moroccan Sufi]. The book was fascinating, especially with respect to the psychology of revelations. It was esteemed as another contribution to reviving spiritual values. I also presented a new book called *Tafsir al-Khazin* [on Quran exegesis], by M. al-Khazin. I read the interpretation of the first Quranic *sura,* "al-Baqarah,"

which covers the most frequent litigations and some other aspects of family relations and the Islamic doctrine of *tawhid* [unity]. Other works by al-Ghazzali were also introduced to be taught, such as *Bidayat al-Hidayah, Minhaj al-'Abidin, al-Arba'in fi Usul al-Din, al-Munkidh min al-Dalal, al-Iqtisad fi al-I'tiqad,* and some treatises such as "Minhaj al-'Arifin," "Risalat al-Ta'ir," and, finally, "Risalat al-Wa'adh." I also recited and read some poems from a book called *al-Futuh,* by Shaykh Ahmad bin Alwan [Yemeni Sufi].

I went on, introducing a book called *Fajr al-Islam,* by Ahmad Amin. It was unpreferable to the group, as they were used to spiritual readings. Instead, I brought another book of history called *al-Kamil fi al-Tarikh* by Ibn al-Athir. This book was somehow acceptable. We read the two initial volumes in its series of nine volumes, hoping that we could finish it in the near future.

Conclusion: Two Readings

[A]nthropologists who seek to describe rather than moralize will consider
each tradition in its own terms—even as it has come to be reconstituted by
modern forces—in order to compare and contrast it with others.

—Talal Asad 1993:200

Projects of comparison now must attend to new degrees of discursive diversity within nonwestern traditions. In Islamic cases, while premodern shari'a scholarship may be loosely identifiable as a "tradition," in its many schools of thought and its regional versions, in its debates between literalists and rationalists, and in its dialogue with Sufism, it was far from a simple or stable unity. If early influences from various other traditions, the translation movement (Greek to Arabic), and the subsequent role of the "foreign sciences" also are taken into account, it is clear that the "tradition" was hybridized from the outset. Already the product of centuries of accumulated local scholarly developments, each local version of this "tradition" in the modern era articulated first with specific colonial (western or indigenous Ottoman) ideas and institutions and later with the modernizing concepts and innovations of a specific nation-state.

My brief analysis of materials on some forms of reading in Yemen in the 1990s relies neither on psychological assumptions about civilizational orality (and associated reasoning deficiencies) nor on evolutionary assumptions concerning anticipated courses of change, both of which marked mid-twentieth-century western conceptions of the nature of (modern) Muslim textuality.[15] For modernization theorists of the 1950s, the expectation, given forward development, was an outcome ever more like the West. To the extent that societies, in some senses, *have* become more like the West, this is due to history and hegemony rather than to evolution. Such theorizing also was sharply disconnected from such coexistent realities as, to take early postcolonial Egypt as an example, Sayyid Qutb studying the works of Ibn Taymiyya, Nobel Prize winner Naguib Mahfouz producing his early novels, and a century-old newspaper tradition. A key feature of Orientalist discourse may be recalled in this connection. Inquiry of this type operated with a characteristic "textual attitude" (Said 1979:92), one "dogma" of which was that "abstractions about the Orient, particularly those based on texts representing a "classical" Oriental civilization, are always preferable to direct evidence drawn from modern Oriental realities" (300).

The historical argument I have outlined here is genealogical, in part. Understanding the identified aspects of Yemeni reading in the 1990s requires a conception of prior techniques and conceptions of reading and writing utilized in the sphere of the old madrasa and beyond in the larger literate surround. Although an understanding of this indigenous textual background is necessary to an analysis of these present day practices, it is at the same time insufficient. The further tasks of characterization are to integrate evidences of discursive dislocations, the thrust of my previous study (1993), with a new example being books that "do not need a teacher," and of wholly new phenomena, represented here, for example, by Yemeni university training in English. How do an indigenous tradition (as transformed) and a nonindigenous tradition (as received) interact? Is it in the manner of a simple mixture, with the separate ingredients remaining more or less identifiable—a university career and an "alternative" career—or as a more complex compound, a new synthesis? Or is it in many different ways at once? In relation to recent work on "hybridities" in particular colonial settings[16] my account represents some fragments of a specific history of past, and ongoing, hybridization.

I have not managed to make sustained comparisons with the "West," although I have mentioned in passing trips to England and the transmission of elements of the western tradition by American, English, Egyptian, Sudanese, and Yemeni teachers at the university. More research is required on all such matters and, for example, on the circuitous receptions of the "southern novel." Here my main comparative concerns have been intracivilizational, and have included a sampling of work on historical forms of recitation, reading aloud, and writing in Islamic scholarly milieus; a somewhat more extended juxtaposition of two modern cases, Morocco and Yemen; and the above-mentioned genealogical approach to the local Yemeni "tradition." More focused inter-civilizational comparisons might consider the relationship of contemporary Islamic lesson circles and other reading groups to related phenomena past and present, from reading among Natalie Davis' sixteenth-century French peasants (1975) to Elizabeth Long's women's reading clubs in present day Houston (1993), or Jonathan Boyarin's yeshiva study circle on the Lower East Side of New York (1993b). While research on such forms of reading in the United States endeavors to recover voiced materialities and social relations, that in the Islamic world must attend to related characteristics, which have not disappeared in plural forms of "reading."

My emphasis on rereadings has left many unanswered questions. Whether or not the Islamist movements, in Yemen (Dresch and Haykel 1995) or elsewhere, are a "failure" (Roy 1994), the Ibn Taymiyyah phenomenon clearly is part of a much larger and more diverse rethinking and reappropriation. What is the cultural specificity and significance of such rereadings in late modernity? What kind(s) of textual authority is associated with the persistence of forms of personalized scholarship in an age of mechanical, and electronic, reproduction? What sorts of interpretive communities are these? Such questions will require further work on texts such as those Muhammad "read," on the framings provided in the commentaries provided, and on such gatherings of "fellows," about whom I know, in this case, little more than that they originally extended an invitation and that they once rejected a proposed book.

NOTES

1. *Nazarat Mu'asira fi Turathina* ("Contemporary Reflections on Our Heritage"), University of Cairo, 1975, 1–2 (quoted in Sivan 1985:69).

2. See Goitein 1968 on the selectivity of transmission of the Greek corpus. For Aristotelian thought in Islam, see Peters 1968.

3. There are many variations in the titles in the *adab* genre concerned with instruction. Rosenthal (1947, 1970) provides further references, as does Berkey (1992:4n, 22n, 23n, 26n, and 38n on the adab of "dictation" in instruction). The twelfth- or thirteenth-century treatise by Burhan al-Din al-Zarnuji, *Ta'lim al-muta'allim, tariq al-ta'allum* (Cairo, 1977) has been translated by G. E. von Grunebaum and Theodora M. Abel in *Instruction of the Student: The Method of Learning* (1947). I have relied on the thirteenth-century treatise by al-Nawawi, which appears in the opening sections of his legal commentary, *al-Majmu'*, 1:46–67 (see also 28–46).

For recent work on adab, see the important volume edited by Metcalf (1984). Adab works are treatises about various institutions; the example cited here is concerned with instruction. Other examples include the well-known *adab al-qadi* genre, on the judgeship, and, less known, the *adab al-mufti* literature, on the muftiship (see Masud 1984; Masud, Messick, and Powers, 1996; an example is found in the previously cited commentary by al-Nawawi, immediately following his section on instruction).

4. Compare the treatment of the related Hebrew verb *qr'* by Daniel Boyarin (1993).

5. I discuss only examples of research on Sunni institutions. Work on comparable twentieth-century Shi'i systems includes Fischer (1980), who comparatively discusses three types of "scriptural school," the yeshiva, studium, and madrasa; and Mottahedeh (1985), who provides a detailed discussion of the formation of a mullah while also attending to the emergence of the Iranian national school system. On the works and methods of a single scholar in the medieval period, see Kohlberg 1992.

6. See Messick n.d.b.

7. I have worked in Ibb since the mid 1970s (see Messick 1978).

8. See Messick 1993:95–98; and, generally, Makdisi 1981:35–74.

9. Muhammad wrote this draft in late 1993 in preparation for his application statement seeking funding for further education in the United States. I encouraged him to include a description of his informal study and teaching with his account of his formal academic career in public school and the university. I use it with his permission, quoting it as he wrote it, changing only some spellings and transliterations.

10. This text, which I should have cited in Messick 1993, was also a standard manual for Shafi'is.

11. In the bookshops Muhammad could find a new edition of a legal commentary (embedding the commented-upon *Zubad* within) by a nineteenth-century resident of Ibb (al-Mufti 1988).

12. More precisely, this is the *al-Tijan fi Muluk Himyar,* by a historian, 'Abd al-Malik Ibn Hisham, who died in A.D. 834.

13. The *fiqh* book, on personal status law, was given to me by a former imamic era judge, later the presiding judge of the Ta'izz Province Court, and now member of the Consultative Assembly, Muhammad Yahya Mutahar (Mutahar 1985, 1989). The hadith work (al-Ghurbani 1980) remains unpublished and is by my friend Muhammad 'Ali al-Ghurbani, who died in 1991. Al-Ghurbani's book embodies "modern methods"—simplified expression, clear presentation, and careful organization—and is intended for contemporary Yemeni secondary school, Religious Institute, and university students. It is designed also for a new style of self-instruction, as it provides not only summaries of key ideas at the ends of chapters but also concluding questions.

14. For the Shafi'is of Lower Yemen a somewhat more comfortable relation existed with the Sufi tradition. The *Zubad* legal manual has an unusual final chapter devoted to Sufism, and its author was known as a Sufi. For background on the local Sufi tradition, see Messick 1993:49–50, 273–77.

15. Such conceptions were the contorted products of narrow disciplinary vantage points and their period-specific positivisms. The theorizing in question occurred in two versions. Among literature specialists and historians, the scholars most familiar with the

enormous and diverse corpus of Arab writings, past and present, there were assumptions about the "oral" qualities of the Arabic language and its relation to Arab psychology (see Shoubi 1951; Issawi 1951; and Hadeed 1952) and an essentialized "Arab mind" (see Patai 1976, chap. 4, "Under the Spell of Language"). Work on the Arab novel, modern history writing, and political discourse also coexisted with such incompatible conceptions. H. A. R. Gibb (1947:5), for example, observed that "upon the Arab mind the impact of artistic speech is immediate; the words, passing through no filter or logic or reflection, which might weaken or deaden their effect, go straight to the head." Bernard Lewis (1960 [1950]:132) deployed a similarly simplistic psychology in portraying Arabic as having a "vivid, concrete and pictorial vocabulary with each term having deep roots in a purely Arab past and tradition," which "allowed of the direct and uncushioned impact of ideas on the mind through concrete and familiar words and of unrestricted penetration to and from the deeper layers of consciousness."

A second version of this disconnection between the features of textuality everywhere in evidence and theoretical accounts is specific to social scientists of the period. By midcentury disciplinary training and disposition, social scientists tended to be ahistorical and less acquainted—often virtually unacquainted—with the literary heritage of the Middle Eastern cultures they studied. For such scholars, the equivalent psychological approach placed emphasis on the "oral" in terms reminiscent of the "enchanted" or the "savage." Morroe Berger (1964:139), for example, makes an explicit reference to the "now" of contemporary society:

> The Arab's virtual obsession with oral functions can hardly escape notice; it strikes the observer in Arab reverence for language and oral arts as well in the Arab attitude toward food. The richness of Arabic has had an almost bewitching effect upon those for whom it is the native language. . . . The spoken word has entranced Arab society before and after Islam, in poetry (which is chiefly oral rather than written), in sermons, in song, and now even in political speeches.

16. See, for example, Bhabha 1985; Prakash, forthcoming; and criticism by Asad (1993:251, 263) and Chatterjee n.d.

REFERENCES

Arabic
al-Ahdal, Muhammad bin Ahmad bin 'Abd al-Bari. 1884. *al-Kawakib al-Durriyyah.* Cairo (supercommentary on *al-Ajurrumiyyah*).
Amin, Ahmad. 1961. *Fajr al-Islam.* Cairo: Maktabat al-Nadah al-Misriyyah.
al-Burayhi, 'Abd al-Wahhab ibn 'Abd al-Rahman. 1983. *Tabaqat al-sulaha'* (Ta'rikh al-Burayhi), ed. 'Abd Allah al-Hibshi. San'a': Markaz.
al-Buqri. n.d. *Sharh matn al-rahabiyyah.* N.p.

al-Ghazzali. 1934. *al-Munqidh min al-dalal.* Damascus: Matba'at Ibn Zayrun.

al-Ghazzali. 1964. *Kitab al-Arba'in fi usul al-din.* N.p.

al-Ghazzali. 1972. *Minhaj al-'abidin.* (includes *Bidayat al-hidayah*). Cairo: Maktabat al-Jundi.

al-Ghazzali. 1982. *Ihya' 'ulum al-din.* N.p.

al-Ghazzali. 1988. *al-Iqtisad fi al-i'tiqad.* Cairo: n.p.

al-Ghurbani, Muhammad b. 'Ali. 1980. *'Ilm usul al-hadith.* ms.

Ibn 'Ajibah, Ahmad ibn Muhammad. 1961. *Iqaz al-himam fi sharh al-Hikam.* Cairo: Mustafa al-Babi al-Halabi.

Ibn 'Alwan, Ahmad. 1990. *al-Tawhid al-A'zam.* San'a': Markaz al-Dirasat wa-l-Buhuth al-Yamani.

Ibn 'Alwan, Ahmad. n.d. *al-Futuh.* N.p.

Ibn Athir, 'Izz al-Din. 1929–30. *al-Kamil fi al-tarikh.* Cairo: Idarat al-Tiba'ah al-Muniriyyah.

Ibn Hisham, 'Abd al-Malik. 1928/9. *al-Tijan fi muluk Himyar.* Haydrabad: n.p.

Ibn Rajab, 'Abd al-Rahman ibn Ahmad, and Ibn al-Qayyim and al-Ghazzali, 1985. *Tazkiyat al-nufus.* Beirut: Dar al-Qalam.

Ibn Raslan, Ahmad b. Husayn (al-Ramli). 1953. *Matn al-Zubad.* Cairo: n.p.

Imarah al-Yamani. n.d. *Tarikh al-Yaman al-Musama' bi Tarikh San'a' wa Zabid.* N.p.

al-Janadi, Muhammad ibn Ya'qub. 1983. *al-Suluk fi tabaqat al-'ulama' wa-l-muluk,* ed. M. al-Akwa'. Yemen: Ministry of Information and Culture.

Khazin al-Baghdadi, 'Ali ibn Muhammad. 197–. *Tafsir al-Quran al-Jalil.* 4 Vols. Beirut: Dar al-Ma'arifah.

Mutahhar, Muhammad Yahya. 1985. *Ahkam al-Ahwal al-Shakhsiyyah.* Vol.1. Cairo: Dar al-Kitab al-Masriyyah; 1989. Vol. 2. San'a': Dar al-Fikr.

al-Mufti al-Hubayshi al-Ibbi, Muhammad b. 'Ali b. Muhsin. 1988. *Fath al-Mannan,* ed. 'Abd Allah al-Hibshi. San'a': Maktabat al-Jayl al-Jadid.

Nawawi, Abu Zakariyya Muhyi al-Din. n.d. *al-Majmu'.* Cairo: n.p.

Zarnuji, Burhan al-Din. 1977. *Ta'lim al-muta'allim, tariq al-ta'allum,* trans. G. E. von Grunebaum and T. M. Abel. *Instruction of the Student: The Method of Learning.* (New York, 1947).

Western languages

Abou Hadeed. 1952. "Psychology and the Arabic Language," *Middle East Journal* (Winter), 112–14.

Asad, Talal. 1993. *Genealogies of Religion.* Baltimore: Johns Hopkins University Press.

al-Azmeh, Aziz. 1986. *Arabic Thought and Islamic Societies.* London: Croom Helm.

Berger, Morroe. 1964. *The Arab World Today.* Garden City, N.Y.: Anchor Books.

Berkey, Jonathan. 1992. *The Transmission of Knowledge in Medieval Cairo.* Princeton: Princeton University Press.

Bhabha, Homi. 1985. "Signs Taken for Wonders: Questions of Ambivalence and Authority under a Tree outside Delhi, May 1817," *Critical Inquiry,* vol. 12, 144–165.

Boyarin, Daniel. 1993. "Placing Reading: Ancient Israel and Medieval Europe," in *The*

Ethnography of Reading, ed. J. Boyarin, pp. 10–37. Berkeley: University of California Press.

Boyarin, Jonathan. ed. 1993a. *The Ethnography of Reading.* Berkeley: University of California Press.

Boyarin, Jonathan. 1993b. "Voices around the Text: The Ethnography of Reading at Mesivta Tifereth Jerusalem," *The Ethnography of Reading,* ed. J. Boyarin, pp. 212–37. Berkeley: University of California Press.

Chartier, Roger. 1992. *The Order of the Book.* Stanford: Stanford University Press.

Chatterjee, Partha. n.d. "The Disciplines in Colonial Bengal," paper presented at CSST, University of Michigan, January 27, 1995.

Davis, Natalie Zemon. 1975. "Printing and the People," in Davis, *Society and Culture in Early Modern France,* pp. 189–226. Stanford: Stanford University Press.

Derrida, Jacques. 1974. *Of Grammatology.* Baltimore: Johns Hopkins University Press.

Dresch, Paul and Bernard Haykel. 1995. "Stereotypes and Political Styles: Islamists and Tribesfolk in Yemen," *International Journal of Middle East Studies,* 27:4, 405–431.

Eickelman, Dale F. 1978. "The Art of Memory: Islamic Education and Its Social Reproduction," *Comparative Studies in Society and History,* 20:4, 485–516.

Eickelman, Dale F. 1985. *Knowledge and Power in Morocco.* Princeton: Princeton University Press.

Eickelman, Dale F. 1992. "Mass Higher Education and the Religious Imagination in Contemporary Arab Societies," *American Ethnologist,* 19:4, 643–55.

Fischer, Michael M. J. 1980. *Iran: From Religious Dispute to Revolution.* Cambridge, Mass.: Harvard University Press.

Gibb, H. A. R. 1947. *Modern Trends in Islam.* Chicago: University of Chicago Press.

Goitein, S. D. 1968. "The Intermediate Civilization," in id., *Studies in Islamic History and Institutions,* pp. 54–70. Leiden: Brill.

Goody, Jack. 1977. *The Domestication of the Savage Mind.* Cambridge: Cambridge University Press.

Goody, Jack. 1986. *The Logic of Writing and the Organization of Society.* Cambridge: Cambridge University Press.

Goody, Jack. 1987. *The Interface Between the Written and the Oral.* Cambridge: Cambridge University Press.

Goody, Jack, ed. 1968. *Literacy in Traditional Societies.* Cambridge: Cambridge University Press.

Hitti, Philip K. 1943. *The Arabs: A Short History.* Princeton: Princeton University Press.

Hodgson, Marshall. 1974. *The Venture of Islam.* 3 Vols. Chicago: University of Chicago Press.

Hourani, Albert. 1962. *Arabic Thought in the Liberal Age, 1798–1939.* Oxford: Oxford University Press.

Issawi, Charles. 1951. "The Arabic Language and Arab Psychology," *Middle East Journal* (Autumn), 525–26.

Kohlberg, Etan. 1992. *A Medieval Muslim Scholar at Work: Ibn Tawus and his Library.* Leiden: Brill.

Lewis, Bernard. 1960. *The Arabs in History* (revised ed. 1958; first published 1950). New York: Harper and Row.

Long, Elizabeth. 1993. "Textual Interpretation as Collective Action," in J. Boyarin 1993a, pp. 180–211.

Makdisi, George. 1981. *The Rise of the Colleges.* Edinburgh: Edinburgh University Press.

Masud, K., B. Messick and D.S. Powers, eds. 1996. *Islamic Legal Interpretation: Muftis and Their Fatwas.* Cambridge, Mass.: Harvard University Press.

Messick, Brinkley. 1978. "Transactions in Ibb: Economy and Society in a Yemeni Highland Town." Ph.D. diss., Anthropology, Princeton University.

Messick, Brinkley. 1993. *The Calligraphic State.* Berkeley: University of California Press.

Messick, Brinkley. n.d.a. "Written Culture," paper presented at a CSST Conference on Culture, University of Michigan, 1993.

Messick, Brinkley. n.d.b. "On the Question of Lithography." *Culture and History.*

Metcalf, Barbara Daly, ed. 1984. *Moral Conduct and Authority: The Place of* Adab *in South Asian Islam.* Berkeley: University of California Press.

Mottahedeh, Roy. 1985. *The Mantle of the Prophet.* New York: Simon and Shuster.

Ong, Walter J. 1982. *Orality and Literacy.* London: Methuen.

Prakash, Gyan. Forthcoming. "Authorizing Science as Modernity in Colonial India," in *Subaltern Studies* IX, Shahid Amin and Dipesh Chakrabarty, eds. Delhi: Oxford University Press.

Rosenthal, Franz. 1947. *The Technique and Approach of Muslim Scholarship.* Rome: Pontificium Institutum Biblicum.

Rosenthal, Franz. 1968. *A History of Muslim Historiography.* Leiden: Brill.

Rosenthal, Franz. 1970. *Knowledge Triumphant.* Leiden: Brill.

Roy, Olivier. 1994. *The Failure of Political Islam.* Cambridge: Harvard University Press.

Said, Edward. 1978. *Orientalism.* New York: Vintage.

Shoubi, Eli. 1951. "The Influences of the Arabic Language on the Psychology of the Arabs," *Middle East Journal* (Summer), 284–302, and replies by Issawi (1951) and Abou Hadeed (1952).

Sivan, Emmanuel. 1983. "Ibn Taymiyya, Father of the Islamic Revolution," *Encounter* 60 (May), 41–50.

Sivan, Emmanuel. 1985. *Radical Islam: Medieval Theology and Modern Politics.* New Haven: Yale University Press.

Wagner, Daniel A. 1994. *Literacy, Culture and Development: Becoming Literate in Morocco.* Cambridge: Cambridge University Press.

Wagner, D., B. Messick, and J. Spratt. 1986. "Studying Literacy in Morocco," in *The Acquisition of Literacy: Ethnographic Perspectives,* B. B. Schieffelin and P. Gilmore, eds., pp. 233–60. Norwood, N.J.: Ablex.

Wakin, Jeanette. 1972. *The Function of Documents in Islamic Law.* Albany: SUNY Press.

Contributors

F. Niyi Akinnaso is Professor of Anthropology at Temple University.

Nancy Florida is Associate Professor of Asian Languages and Cultures at the University of Michigan, Ann Arbor.

Anthony Grafton is Professor of History at Princeton University.

Sally Humphreys is Professor of History, Anthropology, and Greek at the University of Michigan, Ann Arbor.

Uli Linke is Associate Professor of Anthropology at Rutgers University.

Sabine G. MacCormack is Professor of History and Classical Studies at the University of Michigan, Ann Arbor.

Brinkley Messick is Associate Professor of Anthropology at the University of Michigan, Ann Arbor.

Walter D. Mignolo is Professor and Chair in the Department of Romance Studies, and Professor in the Program of Literature and Cultural Anthropology at Duke University.

Lloyd I. Rudolph and Susanne Hoeber Rudolph are Professors of Political Science at the University of Chicago.

Helen F. Siu is Professor of Anthropology at Yale University.

Stefan Tanaka is Associate Professor of History at the University of California, San Diego.

Patrick Wolfe is an Australian Research Council Postdoctoral Research Fellow in the History Department at the University of Melbourne.

Index